The Self in Social Interaction

VOLUME I: *Classic and Contemporary Perspectives*

VOLUME II: *A Socio-Cognitive Approach*

The Self in
Social Interaction

Edited by

CHAD GORDON *and* KENNETH J. GERGEN

VOLUME I: *Classic and Contemporary Perspectives*

John Wiley & Sons, Inc.

NEW YORK   LONDON   SYDNEY   TORONTO

10 9 8 7 6 5 4 3 2

Library of Congress Catalog Card Number: 68-18629

SBN 471 31675 X

Printed in the United States of America

Preface

At many points in the history of science, particular institutions have had marked influence in shaping theoretical development. Often this has occurred where institutional arrangements bring together and encourage the cooperation of investigators with diverse perspectives who share an interest in a substantive area that lies at the common border of their particular disciplines. Such is the role played by Harvard University's Department of Social Relations in the development of this book and its companion volume to be published subsequently.

The two authors were trained in widely separated locales, and in different disciplines—sociology and psychology. On joining the faculty of the Social Relations Department, we found that in spite of divergent backgrounds our thoughts were developing toward similar ends. Respective interests in understanding aspirations toward major goals in life and in strategies of self-definition led us to conclude independently that the self was a concept of crucial importance in making sense of these substantive areas. Mutual discussions at this point were both challenging and enlightening. Each was able to offer conceptual perspectives, suggest important contributions from the past, and expand the scope of the other's research methods.

From these discussions it was but a short step to deciding how we might integrate on a theoretical level the research that each had been carrying out independently. The possibility of developing a comprehensive theory from the rich history of the topic of self, as found in the separate disciplines and from our own work, seemed highly compelling. A further advantage was to be found in the fact that we could make use of data collected under vastly differing circumstances by a wide variety of methods.

At this stage in our planning we envisioned a single volume that would contain the results of our research and joint theorizing. As matters progressed and each attempted to influence the other by suggesting the classic writings on the self as viewed from his own perspective, it became clear that the idea of a single volume was shortsighted. We had found the cross-fertilization of theory from the two disciplines truly an engaging experience, and nowhere did there seem to be a volume that conveniently offered such an experience to others. The need for a companion volume containing classic work on the self seemed urgent for additional reasons. The literature on the self is a truly vast one and has demanded the attention of investigators from all branches of the behavioral sciences. In spite of this fact, no volume existed which systematically set forth basic issues or major themes persisting across this range of investigation. We felt that the development of such a volume would do much to clarify such issues and might serve to stimulate and enlighten anyone concerned with the individual and social process, whether his approach be that of psychologist, sociologist, philosopher, therapist, educator, theologian, guidance counsellor, or the like. For the formal investigator it was hoped that not only would significant departures on a systematic or theoretical level be fostered, but that he would be encouraged to seek out the empirical consequences of much of the untested thinking contained in the volume. Teachers from wide-ranging disciplines and their students have also figured importantly in our thinking about the book, most especially those involved with programs of study for graduate students and advanced undergraduates.

The decision to put together a preliminary volume was many steps removed from the subsequent problems of determining what constituted "the core." To be sure, there were certain authors whose work clearly deserved to be represented. However, the fact that each of us had been able to suggest readings unknown to the other indicated that there might be important contributions unknown to either of us. The possibility set off an extensive survey of the literature, which revealed that our initial fears had been well founded. The available literature on the self within the behavioral sciences far exceeded our most liberal calculations. In the process of searching the literature, a bibliography was begun which now contains over 2500 references.

The task of selecting from this vast literature a single set of outstanding contributions was an onerous one. In order to carry it out several guidelines were employed. Although we wished to include many of the classical and widely recognized writings in the field, we also wished to introduce the readers to some of the fresh and envigorating ideas of lesser known persons. Thus, for example, while it was clear that George Herbert Mead, Charles Horton Cooley, and William James must be included, we also wanted to re-introduce writers such as Alfred Schutz and James Mark Baldwin. To us their work was challenging and yet seemed largely overlooked in current times. It also seemed important to illustrate through various selections the complementary role played by work emanating from both psychology and sociology. On the one hand this was an attempt to point up important convergences, and on the other it was an attempt to invite the traditionalist to consider novel departures. A third intention was to demonstrate the utility of the concept of self in theoretical as well as empirical practice. Not only was it important to show how a series of seminal thinkers had utilized aspects of self-conception to explain and understand social behavior, but solid empirical studies based on hypotheses involving self-conception were also at a premium.

Such guidelines, however, failed to yield a completely satisfying group of contributions. Somehow a volume that included only works already published elsewhere seemed limited in scope. Second, many of the pieces that we wished to include were written many years ago by persons whose thoughts might have evolved considerably since the initial work appeared. The possibility of having the benefit of hindsight from such persons seemed very attractive. In addition, we were aware of a number of persons who were carrying out important work involving self-conception, but who had not yet published pieces in a form suitable for the volume. For these reasons it was decided to commission a number of articles specifically designed for the present volume. Over one quarter of the contributions appearing here are of this variety. In addition, several authors either wrote addenda to reprinted works or took an active hand in editing their work for the present publication.

During the preparation of this volume we have had reason to be grateful to a large number of persons. First in this regard, of course, are the authors who contributed original papers or who permitted us to edit and reprint their existing work. Second are the publishers who extended their permissions for reprinting from the original sources.

We are also much indebted to our colleagues in the Social Relations Department. We benefitted greatly at the very outset from the wise counsel of Gordon Allport, Erik Erikson, David Riesman, and Talcott Parsons. Thomas Cottle and Edward Tiryakian were kind enough to provide thoughtful criticism and suggestions at auspicious moments. Erving Goffman of Berkeley gave us good advice at an early point, and many of the orienting concerns on which the collection is based have been derived from Ralph Turner and Harold Garfinkel of U.C.L.A.

The services of Jane Bullock, Mary Gebhart, Georgia Grant, Christine Gresser, Margie Nichols, David Richards, Janet Scott, and Judith Tipton have been invaluable in carrying out the seemingly endless nettlesome tasks associated with assembling a collection of this kind. We are especially grateful to the publisher and to our editor, William Gum, for providing a wide latitude within which to work. Finally, we wish to express great appreciation to our wives, Joanne and Eleanor, whose encouragement, supportiveness, and patience were continuously valuable assets.

C.G.
K.J.G.

Cambridge, Mass.
March 1968

Contents

The Self in Social Interaction

Part *I* Introduction

"Know thyself" and "Unto thine own self be true" are exhortations that distill important aspects of the Western World's cultural wisdom. They have the ring of unquestionable ethical validity and are felicitous injunctions for uncles or commencement speakers to intone for the enlightenment of those about to enter the corrosive world. Yet, despite the certitude of uncles and commencement speakers, the nature of the self to which attention and allegiance are to be directed remains highly problematic.

Difficulties are fostered in part by the tenuous and constantly changing aspects of human experience. What characteristics of experience are universally recognized as being either "self" or "not self"? Further difficulties are semantic in nature. In the behavioral sciences alone, the concept of self has been used to refer to at least a dozen different aspects of personality. Not only is a different referent implied by each usage, but the actual existence of the referents is also questionable. The problems in the behavioral sciences are compounded by the inherent necessity of basing knowledge of internal process and structure on external behavior or on the vagaries of introspection. Both the inferential leap necessitated by the external-behavior approach and the method of observation involved with introspection are fraught with potential error. And yet, in spite of this network of entanglements, students of human behavior have long considered "the self" to be the explanatory construct *sine qua non.*

This attention to the concept of self has been particularly marked since the inception of the behavioral sciences. The young disciplines of psychology and sociology alone have accounted for over 2000 publications concerning the self. These have ranged from discussions of the basic nature and properties of self to exacting studies linking specific dimensions of self with limited aspects of behavior. The self has figured prominently in theory and research on social control, economic behavior, social deviance, personal aspirations, psychological development, interpersonal attraction, social influence, psychopathology, and psychotherapy, to name but a few. In the face of the obstacles mentioned, the vitality and utility of the concept of self seem well documented.

It is against this backdrop that a need for this book seemed apparent. First, investigators in many of the areas just cited are typically unaware of major contributions in related fields. This fact may be traced in part to the tendency toward increased specialization in the behavioral sciences, but more directly to disciplinary boundaries, which often determine the range of issues and information a researcher deals with from day to day. The divisions between sociology, social psychology, and clinical psychology are noteworthy for their pernicious effects on

1

the cross-fertilization of ideas. It is hoped that this volume may help to break down these separatist tendencies.

The emphasis placed on the self in sociology and psychology has also been subject to the vagaries of ideological fashion. In sociology, it has only been within the past decade that significant attention has been directed toward the early writings of George Herbert Mead and Charles Horton Cooley. Perhaps this resurgence depended on the firm entrenchment of sociology within the behavioral sciences; the security of a stable academic identity may have finally allowed excursions into the reaches of mind. Within the discipline of psychology, the concept of self was also popular during the early decades, only to be squelched by the rise of behaviorism in the 1930s. When this period of self-conscious scientism had run its course, a new flowering of interest in self took place. This book is thus an attempt to draw together the more outstanding contributions deriving from the sociological and psychological traditions, and to provide an impetus for integration of the thinking and research that form the basic foundations in the field. In these ways the book may be of utility to the neophyte as well as the seasoned investigator. Finally, it is hoped that this volume may serve to stimulate further investigation of significant theoretical and empirical problems.

ORIENTING ISSUES

Long and diverse scholarly traditions have helped us to understand something of the nature of consciousness in general and, to a more limited degree, some of the special features of reflexive- or *self*-consciousness. Such traditions have contributed much to shaping current thinking and research on the self. However, from this heritage emerge a number of key issues or dilemmas that recur in varying forms throughout this book as well as in the vast body of related literature. This recurrence is partially indicative of the unresolved state of these questions. However, inasmuch as many departures in the area can be framed in terms of their stance with regard to these issues, it seems of considerable value to outline a number of them at the very outset.

The Self as Fact versus Construct

Within the many pages of this volume there will be a persistent tendency to talk of self as an existing entity or actuality. Investigators will speak of self as if it were an individual's material possession, perhaps in the same class as his wordly goods. Self-esteem will be discussed as if it had substantive properties locatable in time and space. For many, such ways of speaking are only abbreviated forms of discussing the individual's "concept" of self. However, even here, the *concept* is spoken of as if it had real-world properties. This mode of thinking has created serious problems within the behavioral sciences in general and in thinking about self-conception in particular.

One of the major outcomes resulting from the impact of the philosophy of science on the behavioral sciences has been an appreciation for observable fact. Events that can be witnessed reliably by a group of dispassionate observers are thus held to be better candidates for scientific investigation than those that do not yield to direct observation. Indeed, many investigators would rule out any theoretical construct that could not be tied to data available for reliable observation. From this point of view the notion of self would be a poor candidate for scientific scrutiny. There are simply no facts available for common observation to which a person's "conception of self" may be directly tied. From this orientation, the self might be considered an artifact, fostered by the misleading Cartesian distinction between mind and body in combination with the fallacious tendency to assume that all words refer to actual entities.

In view of this type of criticism, several metatheoretical stances have emerged. The most positivistic approach has been to consider the self synonymous with certain aspects of the individual's overt behavior. For example, in the selection by Bandura and Walters (Chapter 17), the term "self-control" could easily be replaced by "behavioral control." For these authors self-control refers essentially to patterns of action which are initially learned from the social milieu but may emerge later in rather autonomous forms.

For the most part, investigators in the field have not adopted this approach. Equating self with overt behavior generates problems in distinguishing "self-behavior" from behavior that is "not self." If self is synonymous with all external behavior, the concept would be both undifferentiating and superfluous. In addition, one of the more compelling reasons for studying the self has been the common surmise that behavior is guided and modulated by internal process. In effect, psychological process is commonly felt to precede behavioral output. The more moderate and most widely adopted position has thus been to view the self as an explanatory concept with hypothetical properties. That is, in order to explain the impact of certain environmental events on the person's behavior, it has been useful to theorize in terms of self-conception. For example, if we observe that parents continuously attempt to convince a child that he is weak and ineffective, and later find that the child will take few risks or attempt to achieve very little, the construct of self may play an important role in explaining the relationship between the two observations. Thus we may say that the child has learned a certain conception of self from his parents, and this conception of himself as an inferior person causes him to feel that he cannot succeed.

The major rationale for this position is that the concept of self has utility for understanding and predicting conduct. The yardstick of validity in this case is not whether or not there actually exists a mental entity or process. Rather, if the construct allows one to make better predictions, understand more thoroughly the relationship among variables, or in any way increase one's comprehension of social behavior, the construct is acceptable.

If it is found that certain behavioral patterns are predicted incorrectly by use of the construct, the hypothetical claims related to the construct can be modified. For example, for most investigators it can be said that self-conception refers roughly to the person's subjective cognitions and evaluations of himself. It is often further assumed that the person will behave in a way that is consistent with his self-conceptions. Where this is not found to be the case, we may simply modify or restrain our assumptions, and we can explore those factors related to consistent behavior as opposed to behavior that is inconsistent with self-conception. The majority of the work represented in this volume either implicitly or explicitly adopts this mode of thinking about self. It forms the basic logic underlying research in psychology and is fully implicit in the symbolic interactionist position.

Yet a good number of investigators have remained discontent with an orientation that holds self-conception to be purely hypothetical in nature. They have been struck by the reality of subjective life and the fact that people commonly give voice to internal feelings and thoughts about themselves. From a scientific point of view, the problem with subjective data is that they do not meet the criticism of interobserver reliability—a psychological "fact" is available only to the single individual experiencing it. Even for this individual, the "fact" may not be entirely apparent or the individual may be unable to view it in an unbiased fashion. Scientifically valid facts, however, are normally considered to be those about which a collection of independent and neutral investigators may agree. It was largely because of this assumption that for a time introspection was ruled out as a valid source of data in psychology.

The matter does not end, however, with the reasonable objections to introspection. A common methodological approach in research on self-conception involves directly eliciting from an individual certain verbal statements or assessments of himself. These communications are overt and subject to the criteria of interobserver reliability in coding or scoring. In addition, these various procedures often yield data of extreme value in predicting or explaining the individual's subsequent conduct; they thus satisfy the criterion of utility. Finally, it is possible to establish partial links between these overt behavioral events and internal events or processes, if one maintains the position that such terms as "experience," "awareness," "feeling," and "conception" are all hypothetical in nature. Thus, although one may be convinced privately that such events are real, it is not good science to assume their actuality or that what one is measuring is an adequate index of underlying reality. In essence, the prime importance of the "reality" of subjective experience may lie in its capacity to motivate investigation, investigation carried out with conviction and optimism with regard to its ultimate outcome.

The Self as Subject versus Object

One of the major distinctions made in the literature on the self is an outgrowth of the philosophic soil in which academic psychology was initially nurtured. This is the distinction, stated most cogently by William James in the 1890s, between pure experience and the contents of experience. We commonly recognize both the existence of conscious activity and the objects of that consciousness. Although such a distinction seems clear enough on the surface, it creates particularly difficult conceptual problems.

The first of these concerns the referent of the concept of self. From one standpoint it seems perfectly reasonable to view the self as the "I" or the experiencing subject. After all, it is probably this capacity for experiencing that the individual recognizes as most basic to being a self. The Cartesian dictum *"cogito ergo sum"* is not only intellectually compelling, but also has pronounced emotional overtones. Individuals generally feel an emotional commitment to their existence as selves over and above their commitment to the various objects to which consciousness may be directed. Chapters 3 to 7 in this volume essentially reflect this point of view as well as do those that extensively utilize the concept of ego.

On the other hand, the equation of self with experience is not entirely satisfactory. If this were done, there would be no way of separating self-psychology from the total psychology of personal experience. The latter would include all processes of thinking, perceiving, remembering, feeling, and the like. Virtually any psychological process that involved conscious experience would be implicated, and the result would be that the concept of "self" would be virtually nondiscriminating and empty of substantive meaning.

Yet many investigators have been unhappy with the continuation of what they consider an unnecessary duality. For them, the radical split between the *I* and the *Me* (to use James's terms) is a superfluous and artificial one. After all, it is difficult to conceive of consciousness in any pure or abstract form, without a content; moreover, conscious content cannot be said to exist in the absence of consciousness. In a sense, our language may be misleading in this instance. To say "I am thinking of *X*," "I perceive *Y*," or "I am conscious of *Z*" linguistically implies the separate existence of a conscious "I" and some other entity *X, Y,* or *Z*. However, as James pointed out, we need not allow our language to trick us into dividing experience into two separate things. Instead, we can speak of *the process* of experience and recognize that the duality only represents separate modes of approach or emphasizes separate aspects of the same process.

In accepting the singularity of the process of experience, we may still disengage a self-psychology from an all-inclusive psychology of experience. One may be conscious of features in the outside world or, on the other hand, conscious of attributes, properties, and processes that pertain to himself. It is these latter instances that would fall under the purview of a psychology of self. It is the way in which these experiences are linked to the social milieu that forms the major focus of this volume. At the same time, this viewpoint suggests that ultimately a thoroughgoing understanding of self will have to be linked to both an understanding of other psychological processes (e.g., perception, learning, emotion, etc.) as well as to patterns and processes of social interaction.

The Self as Structure versus Process

In addition to the previously mentioned proclivity for the self to be spoken of as an object, there is an equally prevalent tendency for the self to be considered structural in character. Psychologists have long used a structural model of man to good advantage. The metaphor here is typically mechanical in nature. The psychological system is viewed as a series of mechanical or structural parts, each perhaps acting in some reciprocal way with other parts. Single elements may affect other elements in the system, but psychological process is viewed as an outcome of the interaction of components. The elements constituting the system are largely considered stable and unchanging. When alterations do occur, they are usually seen as the result of long-term influences, and the modification of one part does not necessarily affect all other components.

Such a view is particularly advantageous when dealing with the stability of the individual over time and across circumstances. It is equally helpful when looking at the slowly accumulating effects of the environment on the individual's conception of self. This view would also be consistent with instances in which an investigator has focused on the continuities in a person's behavior from one situation to another, the effects of self-esteem level on various behaviors, the effects of role training on self, or the function of self in determining perception.

While one may view self as primarily structural in nature, a less popular but equally challenging viewpoint emphasizes process over structure. This approach is similar to concentrating on the process of thinking rather than on the thoughts themselves, or the process of perceiving rather than on individual perceptions. There has been little emphasis on "self-process" per se; investigators have concentrated on more general cognitive processes from which notions of self can be derived. As we may deduce from the preceding discussion, one of the foremost proponents of this approach was William James (Chapter 3), who focused on the stream of consciousness, from which he was able to derive self-experience. Such an approach deemphasizes long-term continuities and trans-situational stability. Rather, it suggests a constantly changing internal world where self-relevant experiences are often transient.

As can be seen, these two orientations tend to be related to our discussion of self as subject versus object. If one views self primarily as the object of experience, and finds that assessment devices yield self-descriptions that are at all reliable or organized, a structural model is implied. If, on the other hand, one views the self as the process of experience, with its evanescent and fleeting images and feelings, the structural model is not particularly appropriate. Ultimately it will be necessary to account for both these orientations within the same theory. As we shall see in the pages that follow, stability and organization do tend to characterize one's evaluation of self to some degree, and yet the experience of self may be subject to a host of situational influences and pressures. We shall return to this issue in Volume II.

The Self as Single versus Multiple

This book contains numerous instances in which the self is spoken of in the singular. *"The* self-concept," "a person's identity," "one's self picture," and so on, are all common expressions. In keeping with this tendency is a strong commitment to view the self as a single entity, concept, gestalt, or collage of perceptions. The writings of Mead (Chapter 4), Backman and Secord (Chapter 28), Lecky (Chapter 29), Fromm (Chapter 32), and Rogers (Chapter 44) are all quite suggestive of this viewpoint. Such a view lends itself to the structural orientation discussed above inasmuch as stability is likely to be an important counterpart of singularity. Any research orientation involving the prediction of behavior on the basis of single measures of self would also be quite compatible with this viewpoint. Such approaches assume that the person has a baseline manner of viewing himself, and that this basic view will influence his behavior over time and across situations.

In contrast to this position is one suggesting that self be viewed as multiple in character. This view is fostered in part by the observation that an individual's behavior is not only highly variable from one situation to another but also often inconsistent. Variations in conduct, then, may cause one to infer variation on a psychological level. The individual's experience over time also tends to corroborate this position, since the person may have varying feelings about himself and varying perceptions of himself as he moves from one social setting to another. Yet strict phenomenological analysis does not clinch the issue either. Theorists such as Allport (Chapter 2) and Erikson (Chapter 18) also point out that the person does recognize a continuing identity over time. The chapters by James (Chapter 3), Baldwin (Chapter 14), Gordon (Chapter 11), Gergen (Chapter 30), Goffman (Chapter 31), Sullivan (Chapter 15), and Jourard (Chapter 43) all tend to emphasize multiplicity, and they form a challenging contrast to the singularity position.

This issue will also be treated further in Volume II. Suffice it to say at this point that although empirical results would do much to clarify matters, the problem is not totally soluble on empirical grounds. A broader observation base, particularly with regard to the effects of situations on behavior and to processes of experience, may point the way to a solution. However, as in the case of the structure versus process issue, solution is to some extent a matter of theoretical preference. That is, to the extent that one deals in hypothetical constructs, the choice of constructs or their nature is not altogether a matter of factual dispute. Criteria such as parsimony, heuristic utility, and system logic play an especially important role in determining theoretical preference.

There are, of course, other broad distinctions that may be applied to the various contributions contained in this volume. For example, many of the pieces are highly theoretical in nature, whereas others emphasize systematic empirical work. The chapter by Crowne and Stephens (Chapter 13) is devoted entirely to methodology. Many of the contributions center on the relationship of self to the broader social system; others are highly psychological in nature. The chapters by Maslow (Chapter 26) and Hilgard (Chapter 36) are almost completely nonsocial. In addition, there are distinctions between normal and abnormal self-conceptions, reactive versus proactive aspects of self, and so on. Such distinctions, however, do not reflect a state of unresolve as much as they reflect separate emphases. In each case the separate emphases may serve to complement one another, and as a result, contributions have been carefully selected for this volume specifically to demonstrate the range of valid concerns in the area.

ORGANIZATION OF VOLUME I

Volume I is organized into six topical Parts and an Epilogue. Each Part contains papers that approach the major topic from divergent viewpoints. Many of the orienting issues already discussed served as guides to balancing the various perspectives and approaches existing in the literature. While the materials within any Part cohere with respect to central concerns, there are also themes that recur throughout the volume. Emphases on interpersonal communication, self-esteem, alienation, psychoanalytic theory, autonomy, and control, for example, are common across Parts. The introductions to the various sections are intended partially to call attention to these recurrent themes. In addition, the introductions provide a brief overview of each Part's contents, the interrelationship among the contributions, and rationale for inclusion of specific chapters.

A word is in order concerning the particular selections of topic areas. Part II contains only two chapters, the first by Talcott Parsons and the second by Gordon Allport. These chapters are primarily intended to illuminate the place of the concept of self in the two major traditions represented in this book: the sociological and the psychological. Whereas Parsons centers on the place of self-conception within the general theory of action, Allport views a number of important trends in the history of psychology.

Part III follows with a group of papers that illustrate and develop a series of major conceptual distinctions. Classic papers by William James and George Herbert Mead are central to this Part. While these offerings develop the subject-object distinction, they also establish lines of approach that permeate the remainder of the volume. Particularly important are James' focus on the stream of consciousness and Mead's presentation of symbolic interactionism. Three remaining subsections complete this unit. In the first, the accent is on the experiential aspects of the self, and the influence of the philosophical heritage is most noticeable. The second subunit presents a number of important attempts to distinguish among various aspects of self as experienced.

These range from Cooley's seminal treatment of the various meanings of "I" and Schilder's classic discussion of body image to the more contemporary treatments of Turner and Gordon. The final subunit bears on a crucial aspect of self-experience: feelings of personal esteem or worth. Although this section contains only two contributions, this topic receives continuing attention throughout the volume.

The remaining Parts of Volume I are designed to explore in greater detail a number of substantive areas emerging from the initial or orienting papers. Part IV is devoted to the development of self-conception. From the abundant literature in this area four distinct and yet complementary approaches deal with the topic of child development. An integrated array of Erikson's important contributions on identity and identity diffusion carries the discussion through the realm of adolescence. Whereas the early contributions in the volume are heavily oriented toward psychological development, the chapters on adult socialization (by Brim, Preiss, and Lynd) bring into focus again the broad social milieu. The topic of self-development is carried into old age by Back and Gergen, and the significance of death in self-conception is treated in a compelling fashion by Lifton. The vast majority of the papers within this Part deal with normal development; thus an additional subunit was felt necessary to cover somewhat unique or rarefied circumstances. Thus, in addition to including one of Maslow's long revered discussions of self-actualization, chapters on minority group membership (Kardiner and Ovesey) and total institutions (Goffman) were also felt to be essential.

While Part IV deals primarily with "inputs" to self-conception, Part V is primarily concerned with "outputs," or the ways in which self-conception is related to behavior. Three subunits are included. The first of these subunits deals with the function of self-conception in motivating and directing social behavior; the second illustrates a variety of ways in which self-conception influences the person's evaluations and judgments of the world around him; in the final subunit self-conception is shown to figure prominently in processes of adaptation and social control.

Although this volume thus far represents major traditions within both the psychological and sociological domains, it does not do full justice to the important place of self-conception in thinking about problems of adjustment and mental illness. Part VI is intended to compensate for this. Marx's classic discussion of the pathology of capitalism introduces a theme that prevails throughout much of the Part—alienation. The papers by Horney and Keniston both deal specifically with the topic, and Laing's discussion of schizophrenia is closely related. The two final contributions, those of Jourard and Rogers, are slightly more optimistic in their concentration on the relevance of psychotherapy to self-conception.

The theme of determinism prevails throughout the contributions to this volume. Self-conceptions are largely viewed as passive products, crystallized, and ultimately determining patterns of conduct. Whereas this emphasis is of sound merit within the scientific framework, man often feels a profound commitment to autonomy and independent action. The contribution by David Riesman, appearing here as an epilogue, was included as a way of giving voice to this commitment, and to form a significant challenge for expanding the horizons of future inquiry into self-conception.

Part *II* *Theoretical Contexts*

The two initial contributions to this volume are intended to set the stage for all that follows. Basic to each of these chapters is the author's keen appreciation of the history of thought within his discipline. In each case, dominant themes within the tradition have been focused so that they illuminate both the richness and importance of the concept of self in understanding the social behavior of individuals.

In Chapter 1, Talcott Parsons initially centers on the succession of threats to Western man's feelings of free will and autonomy posed by the Copernican revolution, the Darwinian theory of evolution, Marxian materialistic determinism, and Freudian theory. In combination with the number and size of current social institutions, the increased differentiation of role-involvements, and the present emphasis on achievement, not only does alienation become a significant issue, but the individual is increasingly concerned and doubtful about who and what he is. It is against this background that Parsons proceeds to analyze the psychological, social, and cultural factors involved in deriving a scientifically legitimate concept of identity and alienation.

Primary in Parsons' analysis is the view of the human personality as a system faced with the same function problems as cultural, societal, or biological systems. These four system problems (adaptation, goal attainment, integration, and pattern–maintenance) are, of course, essential to Parsons' more general theory of action. Over the course of the socialization process, four corresponding aspects of personality become differentiated. *Id* energy is seen as differentiated with respect to the adaptive interchanges of capacities and pleasures with the individual's organism. The *ego* becomes differentiated with respect to its function in attaining goals for the individual. In particular, differentiation occurs as the ego becomes involved in organized role relations in order to mediate the individual's energies and capacities. The *superego* represents the personal values of the individual and is articulated with the normative aspects of the social system. It thus serves an integrative function. *Identity* functions in the domain of pattern–maintenance and represents the progressively differentiated meanings of self provided through social encounter.

Parsons suggests that these meanings are most likely to reflect the person's major cultural commitments and group memberships. They serve to locate the person with respect to such socially important dimensions as sex and age, citizenship, ethnicity, lineage, marriage, parenthood, and occupation. Typically, the relevant dimensions are highly *generalized* and shared with many other persons. However, the individual's *particular* position on these dimensions are derived "precipitates of interaction," and their exact combination is unique to each individual.

By derivation from action theory's principle of cybernetic hierarchy of control among the four subsystems, Parsons proposes that identity (once firmly established through socialization) is the most stable subsystem of personality. It can function to control the individual's cultural expression, social interaction, and use of organismic capacities.

In the final section of the paper Parsons returns to the issue of alienation, and he suggests that each new perception of a threat to autonomy simultaneously engenders an increased capacity to *utilize* knowledge of determining factors in the interest of promoting *greater* autonomy of action *within* the new framework. Thus, even with an increase in role pluralism, for example, the individual is provided with an opportunity to achieve an identity embodying a new richness and previously unattainable degree of autonomy and freedom from fixed categorical constraint. The reader will want to contrast this discussion of alienation with those appearing in Part VI of this volume.

Whereas Parsons moves from a concern with broad social processes to matters of personal identity, in Chapter 2 Gordon Allport's initial concentration is on the internal or psychological process. Allport proposes eight aspects of the proprium: *bodily sense* (sensations from within the organism and an awareness of its boundaries); *self-identity* (sense of a continuous separate existence); *ego-enhancement* (tendencies toward self-assertion, self-love); *ego-extension* (all identification with objects, persons, or collectivities called "mine"); *rational process* (synthesis of inner needs and outer reality through planning, problem solving, coping with situations, etc.); *self-image* (phenomenal awareness of present attributes and future aspirations, whether reasonable or illusory); *propriate striving* (the tension maintaining and future-directed motivations, making for unification of personality and action); and, finally, *the knower* (the "monitor" before which the other aspects appear as contents). It is this eighth aspect of the proprium, the knower, which Allport selected for reconceptualization in his appended note. He clearly contrasts the self-as-experiencer with the seven varieties of content.

Within this chapter Allport has set forth a conceptual framework that may challenge researchers for many decades to come. The themes suggested by the seven aspects of self, or proprium, are essentially those about which most of this volume is concerned. The state of knowledge concerning each of these areas varies widely; facts concerning the relationship among the aspects are virtually nonexistent. Clearly, the horizons of exploration are very broad. On the other hand, we are unable at this point to relegate, as Allport has done, the study of the self-as-knower to the domain of philosophy. Part III of Volume I is devoted to this area of concern, and it shall again be discussed in Volume II.

Chapter 1 The Position of Identity in the General Theory of Action

TALCOTT PARSONS

Identity has become a fashionable term that generally includes the technical psychology of personality, but the term also very broadly concerns the intellectual community, particularly in the United States. The spread of such terms—the closely related "alienation" also comes to mind—is generally symptomatic of the strains created by changes in the structure of the society and in the cultural "definition of the situation." In this case I may merely suggest that on the social side it is in part a consequence of the increasingly elaborate structural differentiation of the society, which produces increasing pluralization of the role-involvements of the typical individual. This means both an often bewildering range of possible choices and complex cross-pressures once commitments have been made. On the cultural side it seems to me primarily a matter of coming to terms with our developing knowledge of the nature of the social and psychological world in which we live.

Perhaps this theme may serve to introduce our main argument. Since the emergence of sophisticated intellectual understanding of the human condition, there has been severe ambivalence over what has been formulated in modern philosophy as the question of free will and determinism. Speaking from a motivational rather than a philosophical point of view, the conspicuous phenomenon has been the tendency for an advance in intellectual understanding to produce a reaction of despair at the apparent limitation of freedom or, closely related, an alleged derogation of human dignity that the new understanding of determinants seemed to imply.

Without carrying the series back beyond the origins of the "modern" world view, the reader will be aware of the furor produced in the Western world by the "Copernican Revolu-

tion," which resulted in the reduction of the status of the planet earth from the one central focus of the Divine Creation to merely a unit in a vast deterministic system that seemed to operate by its own "laws" independent of either Divine or human will. A second case in which the problem of "special creation," and hence in some sense "election" was at stake, was the advent of Darwinism, with its implication of the integral place of man in the whole terrestrial organic world on a basis that seemed to preclude the older conception of special creation "in the image of God." Man was held to be "only an animal," allegedly like any other, and the great religious traditions therefore seemed to have been definitively refuted. Of course in these two cases it was God's freedom more than man's which seemed to be drastically limited. Man, however, was held to be a participant in Divine freedom by virtue of his special status on Earth and in the organic world. Hence his freedom as well as his dignity was felt to be impaired.

In due course, however, men have become reconciled to the new perspectives. Indeed, modern astronomy has produced a new sense of awe and wonder at the vastness and complexity of the world of what, significantly, are called "celestial" bodies and at the immense variety and sweep of the organic world, the subtle refinements of adaptive mechanisms, and the directedness of the processes of organic evolution.

For a little over a century we have been seriously involved in another phase of the incursion of new determinisms into the received conceptions of the human condition. These are "closer to home" in that they concern the nexus of social relationships in which men are involved and the personality of the human individual himself, so far as both of these are accessible to understanding by the methods of empirical science. The first context was perhaps dramatically brought into the sphere of deter-

SOURCE. This paper was prepared originally for this volume.

minism initially by the Marxian theory. To my mind a highly significant second phase, which basically supersedes Marx, has come with the modern sociological movement, intimately connected with the names Sigmund Freud, Emile Durkheim, and Max Weber.

In the structure of its thought and in the attendant attitudes, Marxism is a kind of "latter-day Calvinism." In the social sphere it selects for emphasis the components that are least deeply involved in the personality of the individual and its moral grounding in the culture and the institutions of society—the economic components. It elevates this set of "factors" into the supreme determinant of human social life, like the "sinful flesh" in Calvinism. Determinism is not, however, conceived to be ultimate and unalterable but is held to be subject to specific, "historical" conditions. These conditions are subject to change by a supreme effort of collective will, the organized effort of the "elect," the party leaders of the "proletariat." Then a totally new condition of freedom can be brought into being, in which the older determinisms will completely lose their force.

The Marxian "dialectic" thus after a fashion "synthesizes" the new deterministic insights of economics with a ringing assertion of the reality of freedom and autonomy, *if* the *right things* are done by people rightly placed in the system. In less dramatic form, the whole theory of "culture" has asserted that Darwinian determinism need not reduce man to the level of "pure" animality, because by culture he can learn to control and use his animal traits as well as the physical environment.

Since the beginning of this century the developments of sociology and the psychology of personality have been closely interlinked and have drawn the deterministic circle a long step closer and tighter. These developments pose the problem even more acutely than before: How can man feel autonomous and free? Western intellectuals remain deeply fascinated by Marxism, yet it can be said that these classic problems have entered into a new phase since Marx. We can speak of an extension into the new definition of the situation: the Marxian theme of alienation. Essentially this is the formula for the alleged meaning to the individual "worker" of the deterministic nature of the "system" in which he is embedded, which denies to him what are postulated to be the essential controls over the conditions of his labor and the disposal of its products. To-

day, however, the sense of alienation is not confined to economic determinisms but is extended in one direction to political determinisms (the individual being conceived as subjected to an "alien" power system) and in another to "psychological" determinism. In the latter case people become very unsure of the quality of their own motives or of their origins. The suspicion then spreads that modern man, despite his ostensibly "voluntary" and subjective life, is being actuated by forces of which he is unaware and which he would very likely disapprove were he aware of them.

At the personality level, we have the factors that came into the intellectual community through Freudian sources. They are intricately complicated by additional insights derived from "culture and personality" studies and from the newer sociology: that the very structure of the society itself is involved in the same deterministic system, that the determinism is more than just economic, that it involves considerations of values and the legitimation of normative structures as well as the "external" conditions of action, and that in this connection the line between what is social and what is "psychological" (in the sense of being constitutive of the individual personality) is very difficult to draw. These developments are most intimately associated with the antinomy of determinism and freedom.

All this has been the cultural accompaniment—by no means simply the "product"—of a process of immense complication of the social structure. The system of primary role-involvements of individuals has become greatly differentiated, but at the same time the social systems which are an essential focus of "concern" have been enormously extended, to the point that now virtually the whole world is involved from the point of view of *any* single sophisticated individual. Hence the individual is enormously more aware of and concerned with what and who he is in the whole universe of identities of kinds of people in the terrestrial world.

These processes seem to me to be the sources from which the problem of identity (as related to but distinguished from that of alienation) has emerged into its present prominence in Western culture, particularly in the United States. It is of course understandable that identity problems should be particularly acute in the sensitive sectors of the younger generation, since these individuals are in fact entering into an interactive system that is much more complex and ramified than that faced by their elders at a comparable stage of the life cycle.

The themes of alienation and identity seem to refer to two closely related but distinct aspects of the situation of the individual in modern society and culture. One is the awareness of aspects of the system in which one is placed that are beyond the range of control felt to be "normal" and that operate in ways which may be interpreted as hostile or even meaningless. The other is the problem of "locating" oneself in the system, which is particularly difficult because location in this sense is not merely a matter of cognitive recognition of fact and its interpretation but of commitment to alternatives within a broad range of choice. The cognitive and the "conative" aspects of the problem are of course intricately interrelated.

In the face of such "fashionable" concepts of the intellectual world as alienation and identity, it is the task of the social scientist to attempt to clarify their possible scientifically legitimate meanings by presenting the best analysis he can of the features of the psychological, social, and cultural situations that are involved. The remainder of this chapter is devoted to this task, with special reference to the problem of identity.

I have referred to drawing the circle within which the problem of determinism is raised "closer" to the core of individual personality. To understand what is meant by this and some of its implications, it is necessary to discuss the nature of the problem of social *interaction* as this concept is being worked out in contemporary social psychology.

The importance of Marxism is partly attributable to the fact that Marx carried the interactive implications of the interdependence of participants in a market system farther than did his predecessors in English classical economics. The situation for the action of any one participant was determined by the past and prospective actions of all the other participants. Furthermore, under the assumptions of economically rational behavior—pursuit of "self-interest"—which Marx shared with the classical economists and other utilitarians, the prospective action was predictable as long as the "capitalistic" system remained intact.

One of the most critical of these assumptions was that of the "givenness" of the consumption wants of individuals. These were partially determined by biological needs, such as the need for food, but in the higher cultures it was the citadel of the individual's freedom to seek whatever might, in the utilitarian phrase, "give him pleasure." Deterministic uniformities were then confined to the level of interactive *means* individuals adopted in pursuit of the satisfaction of their wants.

The modern analysis of social interaction since Marx has basically questioned this assumption. Perhaps the most important version of the newer view is that developed by Durkheim. Directly criticizing the utilitarian view, which is also the Marxian view, he showed that such order as existed within a market system could not be accounted for without the assumption of the involvement of a normative system of institutions, including property and contract. In the conditions of its operation, contract is analytically independent of the *interests* (in precisely the utilitarian-Marxist sense) of the participants, whether these be the exploiting or the exploited elements or both.[1]

Durkheim's search for the basis of this independent influence led him to the conception that their regulatory operation, which "constrained" the individuals in the market, must rest in important part on their *moral* authority. Moral authority in turn could not be effective unless individual participants in the system were *committed* to act in accord with these norms and/or the values underlying them. Looked at in terms of the psychology of personality, commitment in this sense meant that these normative components of the structure of the society and culture had become *internalized*. The values and norms of the society thereby become *constitutive parts* of the personalities of its members; they are no longer only aspects of the situation external to the individual.

What I have called the normative component does not stand alone in any of the three primary subsystems of action: the individual personality, the social system, and the cultural system. Its relations to other components in all three cases and in their interrelations with each other are complex and cannot be discussed briefly or without technical analysis. What is important here is the fundamental insight that the traditional disjunction (which had run so deep in Western thought) between

[1] See Durkheim, Emile, *The Division of Labor in Society,* tr. George Simpson (Glencoe, Ill.: The Free Press, 1960) Book I, Chapter VII, and "The Determination of Moral Facts," *Sociology and Philosophy,* tr. D. R. Pocock (Glencoe, Ill.: The Free Press, 1953), pp. 35–67.

the organism, the personality of the individual, and the structure of his society and culture is untenable. Durkheim's version of this insight did not stand alone; it converged most impressively with those of Freud and the American social psychologists who are usually called "symbolic interactionists," notably George Herbert Mead.

There are perhaps two crucial general points. The first is that in *any* system of human cultural-level social interaction, *every* individual, as a unit in such a system, must always be treated *both* as an *actor* who is "motivated" (has wants, goals, value-commitments and of course affects or "feelings") *and* as an *object of orientation,* not only for the other actors in the system but also for himself. What I have called the theory of action is most fundamentally built on the interrelations between these two essential perspectives.

The second critical point is that every individual is involved in *multiple* interactive systems, so that the part of his motivational system which is "engaged" will vary from one interaction context to another, just as his significance as object will also vary. These many interactive involvements of the same individual personality do not constitute a random aggregate but a system, a system which like all other living systems is subject to the types of malintegration we call "pathological" but which is definitely structured. It is built up by an evolutionary process which sociologists usually call "socialization," starting with the simplest possible structure and differentiating from this core initial reference point, which seems to be what Freud called oral identification.

These two points both have implications for our conception of the identity of the individual. First, to function adequately in the psychological and the sociological contexts and in their continual interplay with each other, the personality of the individual must be definable as a sufficiently clearly established and focused *object,* both to the individual himself as answers to the questions of who and what he is and to the others with whom he interacts. Here it must be remembered that the personality as object is the product of a social process within a cultural framework; identity is not biologically given. Second, the fact of increasingly prominent role-pluralism means that individuals are subject to centrifugal pressures in that each context of role-involvement has its own distinctive expectations, rewards, and obligations. It becomes an imperative of personality

functioning to achieve a sufficient level of integration of these components. The internalized conception of what the individual is is the natural reference point for this integration. Here again it is essential to remember that individualization is a product of the process of differentiation we have in mind. Hence fitting into specific institutionalized categories becomes decreasingly sufficient as a focus of personality-definition. If, for example, we use occupational categories, (e.g., physician), the further question beyond this identification, however important that is, is what special kind of physician within the medical rubric, and, when this is followed to sufficiently detailed levels, what kind of person in his non-professional capacities.

It seems to be useful and correct to use the term *identity* in a technical sense to designate the *core system of meanings of an individual personality* in the mode of *object* in the interaction system of which he is part. Considerable elucidation of this statement will be necessary.

IDENTITY AND SOCIALIZATION

The term identity, as used here, designates a structural aspect of the personality of the individual, conceived as a system. The biologizing tendencies of psychological theory are so strong that the following statement will not be widely accepted. I should, however, like to assert first that at the level of what I call the theory of action, it is *essential* to distinguish analytically between the personality as a system and the behavioral organism as well as between both of these and the social and cultural systems. All four are primary subsystems of the more generalized and comprehensive system of action. It is of course organism and personality which are inherently most directly linked with the status of what we call the *individual.*

"Action" I define as a system of the behavior of living organisms which is organized—and hence controlled—in relation to systems of cultural meaning at the symbolic level.[2] This in turn implies generalized *codes* in terms of which particular symbols and their combinations, which embody and communicate *information,* have meanings, since it is essential to the concept of a symbol that its meaning is not directly derivable from its

---

[2] This statement is redundant to the extent that the concepts cultural and symbolic imply each other—neither exists without the other.

intrinsic properties as an object—thus the meaning of a "word" is not deducible from the acoustic properties of its phonetic make-up.

The analytical line of distinction between organism and personality then lies in the fact that the *structure* of the personality as a system is composed of "objects" which have been *learned* in the course of life experience, that experience having been "codified" in terms of culturally given codes, however important the individuals' idiosyncratic modifications of those codes and of the object meanings "formulated" in them.[3] The analysis of the process of socialization, to which Freud made by far the greatest contribution, enables us to give a broad outline of the development of this aspect of personality in the individual case.

The fundamental reference point is Freud's basic insight that the focal "reality" (i.e., his famous reality principle) is the reality of the environment of social relationships of the child; hence "object relations" are *social* relations, not relations to physical objects. The personality of the individual is built up through the *internalization* of social objects. It is particularly important that precisely in the terms used by Freud in the later phases of his theoretical development, this process centers in the *ego* and not in the first instance in the superego; it is the ego which is governed by the reality principle.[4]

Freud himself, however, was not fully clear that the internalization of social objects requires a *dual* level of organization. To use sociological terminology, which Freud did not, what is internalized is *both* a role-relation and a collectivity as object. Freud does state clearly that the development of a role on the part of a child must include internalization of the reciprocal role of the parent.[5] Hence the

learning of one role was at least complicated by the necessity to understand and within limits be able to "perform" at least one complementary role in the same system. The collectivity aspect then can be said to be a matter of the basis on which the two or more roles are in fact complementary, that is, are "integrated" with each other. This above all involves the internalization of certain *normative* components which define, in the normative sense, the relations between the complementary roles. The "I-We-You" triad of ordinary language provides a critical reference point. In role terms, what *I* do and, normatively as well as predictively, am expected to do do not "make sense" without reference to mutual expectations involving *you*. The relation between them, however, implies a third term, the collective *we*. Some of the normative components are differentiated—you and I are not expected to act in the same way. But other components are common, both actors being members of the same collectivity, and there are problems of the collectivity which are our *common* concern.

Socialization in this reference proceeds by differentiation (and of course the complementary processes of integration) starting with the simplest possible diadic structure, that of mother and infant. The first identification—in Freud's own usage—may be conceived as the collectivity formed by this association, in which the autonomy of the infantile "personality" is minimal. It proceeds, however, to the internalization of a much more actively autonomous mother-child love relationship in the pre-oedipal stage, then to the oedipal stage and beyond.

The details of this process cannot be discussed here. However, it is essential that the socializing agencies are progressively more highly differentiated social systems—for the oedipal period the nuclear family as a whole, then (in modern societies) family plus school class, and so on, eventually to the point of full adult status. Each step involves the addition to the previous role-repertoire of at least one new role, in a more complex and higher-level collectivity system. Thus primary school is more complex than the intrafamilial world of the pre-oedipal child, and the adolescent world of secondary school is more complex than that of primary school.

From one critical point of view this is a process of *upgrading*. The child is expected to learn, and allowed to perform, a *new* role in a collectivity from which he was previously excluded, membership in which both carries

---

[3] There is an area of behavioral phenomena for which the controlling codes are genetically given; this has traditionally been called the field of instinct. Many of these phenomena underlie the action level of human beings' behavior. But there seems no doubt whatever that when we speak of symbolic or cultural levels of behavior, the control system is located in learned codes. In any case, whatever the empirical balance, our *theoretical* concern is with this level.

[4] Cf. Talcott Parsons, "Social Structure and the Development of Personality," Chapter 4 in *Social Structure and Personality* (Glencoe, Ill.: The Free Press, 1964).

[5] Cf. Sigmund Freud, "On the Internalization of Sex Role: The Feminine Case," in *Theories of Society,* ed. by Parsons, Shils, Naegele, and Pitts (Glencoe, Ill.: The Free Press, 1961), Vol. II, pp. 852 ff.

higher prestige and entails more serious responsibilities than did the previous one.

It is in the complex consequences of this differentiating and upgrading process that the most crucial problems of the relation between the personality of the individual and the social and cultural systems are to be found. A personality system is the *organization* at a symbolic level of the behavior of a *particular* living organism. Its history as a personality begins in the simple intrafamilial relations involved in its birth and early childhood. It must extend and differentiate *from there,* and can in one sense never escape its origin. Both its principal characteristics as organism and its early characteristics as personality are inseparable from this influence. These reference points constitute an indelible component of the identity of any adult person.[6]

In any society, however, "growing up" must involve attenuating these "primordial" reference points in favor of the increasing importance of roles and collectivity internalizations, which are independent of them. Thus level of school performance is not ascribed to family membership, nor, in turn, is adolescent peer-group membership a simple function of either family background or primary school performance—though of course there are positive correlations.

Because of this factor of independence, however, these upgraded memberships stand in a problematical relation to the object-relations of the earlier phases of socialization. In Freud's still paradigmatic account we may distinguish two components of "strain," the biosocial "maturational" component and the "structurally variable" component. Even given the psychological possibilities of regression, no adult human being in any society can remain realistically an infant or even a pre-oedipal child and at the same time participate fully in the adult interaction system. The most dramatic case of this imperative of growing up is the incest taboo. Freud established that the relations between pre-oedipal children and parents are definitely *erotic.* Possibly because of the "guilt by association" of siblings of opposite sex, this can be extended to the view that the

nuclear family is, in one primary aspect, an "erotic association." The central meaning of the incest taboo in this context is the normative assertion that the matured child must renounce his erotic attachments to members of his nuclear family of orientation in order to free himself for participations outside it.

In Freud's terms, the nuclear family of orientation becomes the prototype of the central category of the *lost object.* It is of course clear that an adult male, and indeed female, cannot treat the relation to his mother as the equivalent of the pre-oedipal situation. At the very least, his immensely increased involvements with extrafamilial concerns imply renunciation in this field. The incest taboo is the most conspicuous institutionalization of this renunciation—generalized to include all members of the nuclear family of orientation, not only the mother. It is an "order" on the part of the society, to break away from childhood affiliations, in favor of those opening up in sectors of the wider society beyond the nuclear family.

Though the concrete object relation is necessarily changed, and the concrete object in the old sense is "lost," the internalized object system remains permanently part of the personality system. The erotic love object may thus be lost and the need for it repressed, but by a remarkable transformation this older internalized object-system becomes the primary basis of the need for adult genital erotic relationships, thereby perpetuating from generation to generation the affective economy of personalities in relation to the family system. With all the cross cultural variability of kinship system it can still be said that this process is basically one of biosocial maturation.

The process by which individuals, especially boys, in an "industrial" type of society are sifted through the educational system and choose or are allocated to occupational roles is a primary example of what has been called the structurally variable process, which produces other and on the whole different kinds of "strain." For these societies there is no early childhood role component closely cognate with the adult role type, and as a collectivity the nuclear family is in certain respects the antithesis of the collective organization of occupational functions. To some extent a boy's father can serve as a "role model," but especially in the higher occupations the extent is quite limited. Hence there is much less possibility of relatively direct "transformation"

---

[6] "Denial" of this component of identity, such as a light-skinned Negro "passing," is still a recognition of it, since this origin becomes a "secret" which has to be carefully guarded. One's biological and social parentage is, if known, an ineluctable exigency that *must* somehow be "coped with"; it cannot simply be "wished away."

between childhood object systems and those of adulthood than in the case of familial roles.

These two cases illustrate two principal types of developmental sequence in the course of which essential components of identity are laid down. The first involves the central problem of origin and the continuity between membership in family of orientation and family of procreation, within the universalistic framework of generation and sex roles. Answers to the question "Who and what am I?" always include sex, generation, and the child of what parents, whose spouse and the parent of what children. Furthermore, it is a rare adult male in our type of society who would omit from his answer to such a question any reference to his occupation. Here, however, the possible complications are enormous and hence the problem of the level of specification of the answer is most important. This author, for example is a "university professor." But this does not say at what university, in which faculty— arts and sciences, law, medicine, and so forth— in what discipline in what department, and many other possible specifications. Nevertheless, the label "professor" can scarcely be omitted from any designation of identity, not only by others but by the individual himself.

What is often called role-pluralism is a salient characteristic of modern society. The adult individual is the focus of a complex role-set or system, hence the answer to the question "Who is he?" may be relative to the context of relevance—a student, for example, is seldom interested in knowing about the parents of his teacher. If these plural role involvements, which become more complex as a function of both his own status-level and the complexity of the society, are to be feasibly carried out by the same individual, they need to be integrated with each other. There is by now ample evidence that exposure to excessive role conflict is one of the most important factors in generating psychopathology, especially, though not exclusively, in childhood.[7]

It was with this problem in mind that I previously defined identity as the *core* system of meanings of the individual personality as object. Somewhat broader than this reference to the object mode is the conception of the *integrity* of a person, his capacity to be not only cognitively consistent but integrated both as actor and as object in all of the principal modalities of his life, in his several roles, and in those references that cannot adequately be analyzed in a sociological context.

IDENTITY AND THE OTHER SUBSYSTEMS OF PERSONALITY

In the preceding brief sketch of some highlights of the socialization process, I focused the discussion on the relation of the personality to the social system. This relationship has often been neglected in two ways. On the one hand, the biologizing tendency, as I have called it, of so much recent and contemporary psychology tends to see the "real" aspects of the personality in the organism in respects abstractable from the nexus of social relationships in which the individual is and has been involved. On the other hand, the "Culture and Personality" school, imbued as it has been with the anthropological emphasis on culture, has stressed cultural patterning. This is far closer to the present point of view than biologism, but it tends to bypass very important considerations. I shall now attempt, very sketchily, to integrate the three references since I think they all bear upon the problem of identity as I have posed it. The framework I shall present is little more than an interpretation and very modest extension, in terms of the theory of action, of Freud's scheme.

A system of action, at the most general level, may be conceived as differentiated into four analytically distinct primary subsystems. Three of these are clear and well known: cultural system, social system, and the individual personality. I have suggested further that the behavioral[8] organism must be carefully distinguished analytically from the personality. Only on this basis can Freud's doctrine that the structure of the personality consists of the "precipitates of lost objects" make any kind of sense, for the structure of the organism is *anatomical,* and neither behavioral nor social.

Each subsystem of action constitutes an environment, or sector of the environment, from

---

[7] *Schizophrenia and the Family,* Theodore Lidz, Stephen Fleck, and Alice R. Cornelison (New York: International Universities Press, 1965).

[8] In analytical terms, it is not the total organism but what I am calling its behavioral component that should be treated as part of the action system. The primary metabolic systems, for example, stand on a different level, which Murray has called the "vegetative." Behavior most generally is that aspect of organic functioning which constitutes "responses" to inputs of information (in the technical sense) from the environment, responses which in turn articulate with the "needs" of the organism.

the point of view of every other. As an open system, each interchanges outputs and inputs with each of the others. The personality clearly is dependent on "his" own organism for a whole set of fundamental facilities: locomotion, manipulation of physical objects, and above all for processing of information through the sensory organs, the central nervous system, and the information-output apparatus, especially the functions of speech.

Freud, more than any other, was the primary discoverer of the fact that at the interface of social organization and early socialization these organic capacities were organized and tied into the social system by the mechanism of erotic pleasure. This is certainly organically rooted and seems to be a specialization and extension of the more generalized pleasure mechanism which functions in much instrumental behavior of the relatively higher organisms,[9] but it is differentiated from this in the direction of being much more definitely social. It is not correct to say that erotic pleasure is communicated between persons and/or organisms in a sense in which meanings linguistically coded are communicated. It is, however, *mutually* stimulated, and the social object of stimulation seems to have functional priority. Indeed Freud's analysis of narcissism makes it clear that only when personality has developed sufficiently so that an individual has become an object to himself is there strong motivation to autoeroticism. In turn, however, this is derivative from the experience of stimulation by others: in the case of most children, this is by the mother. It seems to be nearly as unlikely that the "feral child" will learn a normal erotic complex without social interaction as it is that he will invent a language.

In the primarily affective or motivational (as distinguished from the cognitive) context, it can be said that the erotic complex is the primary integrative bond between organism, personality, and the more "primordial" aspects of the social system, where the nuclear family is characterized by erotic bonds among its members. On this "base" the primary differentiation takes place between two of Freud's three major subsystems of the personality. The newly formed "self"—very much in the sense of Cooley and Mead—is "organized" in control of his own body not only by developing

a capacity for erotic pleasure but also by *focusing its use* in the context of primary social relationships. The primary arena of his *goal*-orientation thus becomes that of his social nexus, his object relations in Freud's sense. Here pleasure becomes the primary *reward* for the fulfillment of expectations of *ego*-oriented action. Thus his principal process of active adaptation to the social environment comes to be through "realistic" behavior controlled by ego mechanisms. By this path the ego comes to be differentiated from the id. Reality-orientation and pleasure-seeking are no longer ascribed to each other, so that maximization of erotic pleasure is no longer the only meaningful goal. This comes very close to the origin of what McClelland calls "achievement motivation," the concern with goal-attainment, which is relatively dissociated from erotic interests.

By this point the personality is no longer to be conceived of primarily as the facility for maximizing the interests, welfare, or "drives" of the organism, including especially its pleasure interests. Rather, the new level of autonomy of the personality in a sense reverses the relation: the organism becomes a *facility* available (with due regard to the conditions of its operation) in the interests of the personality. Here we may conceive the id as the subsystem of personality primarily differentiated with reference to the function of mediating relations with the individual's own organism. The ego, on the other hand, is the subsystem primarily differentiated with reference to managing the individual's social relationships, his role-participations in the social system.

If, however, these two primary functions are to be stabilized and coordinated with each other, there must be a focus of control which in a cybernetic sense is superordinate to both ego and id. This is the functional position to which Freud assigned the superego. His own conceptualization in this area was, however, considerably less clear-cut than in the other two, and he sometimes spoke of an "ego-ideal" as distinct from the ego. It is a possible extension of Freud's analysis in this field that constitutes the main idea I wish to put forward here.

If we differ from the culture and personality emphases in insisting on a distinction between social and cultural systems, and if we adhere to the position previously stated that the ego is the primary point of articulation of the personality with the social system—in the technical analytical sense—articulation with the

---

[9] Cf. James Olds, "Self-Stimulation of the Brain," *Science,* **127** (1960), pp. 315–324.

cultural system has not yet been analytically accounted for in our scheme. I suggest that, in the sense of major intersystem interchanges, this is the appropriate position for the superego as a primary subsystem of the personality, but that this decision implies a further distinction. Put in action theory terms, this would make the supergo the *integrative* subsystem of the personality but leave the question of interpreting the superego's pattern-maintenance function unresolved.

In analyzing social systems we have become accustomed to the importance of a systematic distinction between values and norms. Values are common to the members of a collective system and not differentiated to match differences either in the function or the situation of differentiated parts or subsystems. Norms, on the other hand, are differentiated in these ways. For example, the social values concerning the family should be held in common by husband and wife, but the norms by which their actions are guided should be differentiated as an aspect of the differences in their roles.

Thus the superego is the subsystem of the personality which articulates directly with the *normative* aspect of the cultural system. Its focus, however, does not rest in societal values as such, but in "personal" values, which, in the most highly differentiated form, may be thought of as the *conscience* of the individual. It, like the internalized social object system, is internalized in the course of processes of social interaction—as Freud made quite clear. It seems to undergo its first clear step of differentiation from the ego in the oedipal transition. It is thus in a certain critical sense to be regarded as the "precipitate" of what Freud called the "parental function" as a lost object.[10]

It is important not to confuse the superego as a subsystem of the personality with either the pattern-maintenance or the adaptive subsystem of the *social* system. Where the action system generally is sufficiently highly differentiated, the "moral order" of the society becomes, as Durkheim clearly saw, in the first instance dependent on the commitments of conscience of its individual members. The "value system" of the society "defines the situation" for the operation of conscience of the individual, but it is not the same as the situation. Furthermore, the trend to the "privatiza-

tion" of religion, and hence the shift of its collective aspect to the status of voluntary association, fits in the same context. The cultural system (through the medium of conscience) *legitimates* the individual's value-commitments *not only* in his social roles and collectivity memberships but also in a variety of extrasocial contexts. The superego is the integrative subsystem of the personality not only in that it integrates the plural role-involvements of the same personality with each other, but also in that it integrates role-involvements with other aspects of personal value-commitment. This extension beyond the level of social involvement is particularly important for the problem of identity.

Coming back to the personality of the individual then, we may say that his value-commitments which are involved in the superego are oriented toward their implementation in the processes of action, through mobilization of id energies and ego-direction. The superego, as the integrative subsystem of the personality, is not, however, the main "executive" agent of implementation but rather the coordinator of these various implementive processes. Here it is again above all essential to keep the individual's plural role involvements as well as his nonsocial concerns in mind.

The identity system would then, relative to the superego, be the "ground" on the basis of which these coordinative and implementive processes should gain their meaning for the individual actor. It is the point of coincidence of the "I" who do these things and the "me" which is object both to self and to others. As such the identity system does not "act," but it is the reference ground for interpreting the meaning of his actions of and for the individual himself.

If the genetic origin of the superego lies in the oedipal internalization of parental function, it is important to note that the conception of it put forward here implies that its structure is not to be confined to that level. This is of special importance because parental function is the sociological boundary structure between the nuclear family and the wider society of which it is a part. In the principal subsequent phases of socialization, the child internalizes new role and collectivity structures of progressively wider scope[11] which eventually come to include

---

[10] Cf. Sigmund Freud, "The Ego and the Super-ego," *Theories of Society. op. cit.,* Vol. II, pp. 733 ff.

[11] Cf. Talcott Parsons, "The School Class as a Social System," *Social Structure and Personality, op. cit.,* Chapter 6.

his citizenship role in the national society and beyond that some status in "world society." The individual's order of participation in all of these many subsystems of his society raise moral problems for him which are not readily dealt with by the standards of the parental function as Freud uses that concept.

It is here particularly important that the differentiation of the superego from the ego implies *generalization* at the cultural level. This involves the phenomena brought to attention by Piaget in his famous work on *The Moral Judgment of the Child*.[12] Such capacities mature well beyond the oedipal period and hence the phenomena of conscience as discussed here constitute a restructuring of personal values in the light of continuing experience. It is furthermore important to note that this implies the development of cognitive capacities in the individual which articulate with the levels of cognitive generalization and integration in the cultural system as a whole. These relatively independent cultural standards, both cognitive and evaluative, are a precondition of individual autonomy relative to *any* role and collectivity membership.

It is a cardinal tenet of the theory of action that the subsystems of an action system which are the principal agents of interchange (both with the environments of the system and with each other in the integrative reference) must articulate with a reference base that is to some extent independent of any and all of them. This is what we have been calling the pattern-maintenance subsystem. For living systems generally this is best exemplified by the genetic constitution of the organism. The basic tenet of its insulation from the environment is stated in the generalization of the noninheritance of acquired characteristics. By definition, in the case of action, "symbol replaces gene"—to quote Alfred Emerson.[13] I think it is legitimate to consider the pattern-maintenance systems in action as centering at the level of the *codes* in which particularized and concrete meanings (information) are organized and articulated. For the cultural system itself, which is paramount in action, these codes are classifiable as religious, evaluative (moral), aesthetic (expres-

sive), and empirical-cognitive. For the social system they are basically evaluative, normative in the narrower sense (legal), political, and economic.

It seems to me appropriate to use the term "identity" to designate the pattern-maintenance code-system of the individual personality. First, it should be stated that this is to be treated basically as *learned;* it is a product of the individual's own life-experience, his interaction with his environment. The only genetically given structural components of action systems are the inborn human *capacities* to learn cultural-level behavior and action (for example, manual skills, erotic sensitivities, and speech and cultural organization, etc.) through the central nervous system.

Identity is learned in the process that we concretely call social interaction, but it is not to be conceived as only social in the analytical sense. It is, to use Freud's term, a "precipitate" of interaction processes, which gains a relative independence of its origins, since the crucial objects become "lost objects." As such it can, in the cybernetic sense, "control" the individual's social action as well as his organic behavior and cultural "expression" and production.

Once fully established, however, a system of identity has the highest level of stability of any primary component of the personality. This is for better or worse, because often it interferes with effective "functioning" in the real world, just as the genetic constitution of a species may become maladaptive.[14] Above all, it cannot be changed by the more ordinary environmental rewards and frustrations, as mediated either through the ego or the id, as these were sketched in the foregoing discussion. It is more directly sensitive to superego influence but is still *cybernetically* superordinate to the superego.

If we are correct in conceiving the individual's identity as a code structure, it follows that as such it is not primarily an aggregate or even an integrated system of internalized social objects in Freud's sense of object relations. It is, rather, the reference-frame *within which* personal meanings can be concretely symbolized and thus "expressed," "acted out," "implemented," or what not. In this sense it is not itself a set of concrete meanings but a set of

12 Jean Piaget, *The Moral Judgment of the Child* (Glencoe, Ill.: The Free Press, 1948; First Edition, 1932).

13 Alfred Emerson, "Homeostasis and Comparison of Systems" in *Toward a Theory of Human Behavior,* Roy Grinker, ed. (New York: Basic Books, 1956), pp. 147–163.

14 Erik H. Erikson, "Identity," in *New International Encyclopedia of the Social Sciences* (New York: Macmillan, 1967).

patterns for the organization and canons for the interpretation and articulation of meanings. Above all it is not an aggregate of "motives" in the usual sense, but is "metamotivational."

If "motivation" as the organization of personality with special reference to ego-function is the focus of its psychology, then the line of argument here presented is that motivation becomes "intelligible," or better in the German sense of *verstehbar,* only with the postulation of such as identity-frame. This identity-frame is more derivable from the current input-output balances of the personality with its environments than is the pattern of functioning of an organism derivable from its recent nutritional or respiratory intakes, for example along the mythical line that a man who has eaten a beefsteak becomes thereby "strong as a steer."

It has been said earlier that the identity system of a personality does not itself "act" but in some way serves to "control" processes of action. The relevant kind of control would be that referred to by speaking of a person acting "in character." Most normally integrated people have relatively stable orientation patterns in dealing with situations and people. Many attempts to classify personalities, such as introverted or extroverted, may be said to refer primarily to this level. Similarly, such generalized traits as autonomy or dependency, emotional warmth or aloofness, may be used for illustration. Like other variable features of the personality, identity-control may vary between relative rigidity and restrictiveness and relative looseness, with some kind of optimal flexibility in between. Thus the psychopath or sociopath is generally thought of as a personality type with minimal "internal" control.

An individual's identity as the core of his personality system in these terms would have to be thought of as involving a complex balance of components of generality and individuality. Every individual, it goes without saying, is the "child" of his culture and of his society, and of course of his special experience within both. Being an American living in the mid-twentieth century is *constitutive* of my identity. If, for example I should "defect" to Communist China, I would always remain to myself and others "that American who defected," or "became converted," according to the perspective. I could never have the identity of Chinese Communist without the "American" understratum, unless I had been born and brought up entirely within the Chinese Communist system.

Thus cultural commitments and collectivity memberships that are highly generalized and widely shared are inevitable components of an identity, the more so the more "sophisticated" the individual is. At the same time, the *combination* of components which has been precipitated to constitute an individual identity is variable from case to case and at some level is unique. This, moreover, is increasingly the case the more highly differentiated the social and cultural systems with which that individual has come into close contact. It is thus very clear that from the present perspective there is no probability that individual identities will be flatly uniform in any society, and less so the more advanced in the sense of differentiation the society and culture are.

Individuality, however, is always a function of the generality of some components of the relevant code system. The individuality of an author's style is made possible in part by the general "codification" of the language in which he writes. Mere eccentricity in the use of language is not by itself a canon of individuality of style, and least of all of "originality" in the culturally valued sense.

From this perspective it is possible to return to the problems from which the discussion of this chapter took its departure. It is a central fact that not only personality but the total phenomenon of culturally formed action is structured in terms of codes. Outside a few such special fields as linguistics it is difficult to grasp that systems of this character imply a very special relation between elements of constraint and the conditions of freedom, which is somewhat different from the combination involved with reference to the more familiar technological and even economic conditions of freedom. Seen in the perspective of organic evolution, culturally codified orientation systems are the most potent innovations which have yet emerged in adding "generalized adaptive capacity" to living systems.[15] The essential feature of the systems under discussion here is that the "establishment" of a firm and structured code, and its "learning" at the level of internalization (not merely of informational "knowing"), opens up vast new ranges of flexible possibility in its use. The familiar example of the myriad possible technological applications of new contributions to generalized basic science is only one of many cases in point. The

---

[15] Cf. Talcott Parsons, "Evolutionary Universals in Society," *American Sociological Review,* **29** (June, 1964), pp. 339–357.

more "basic" the scientific advance, the more it is not merely an increment of information in the detailed sense, but rather an innovation in the structure of cognitive codes.

If this basic perspective applies to codes in the specialized areas of culture, it does so as well to the institutional codes that are central to the structure of societies. For example, the level of generalization of the legal code structure of a society is one of the most important criteria of the evolutionary advancedness of that society, and this is a condition of the access of its members to ranges of freedom which are not open in less advanced societies. The modern level of freedom of occupational choice and career line, for example, is not possible in societies that lack a highly generalized legal system in the fields of property, contract, monetary transactions, and conditions of employment. The alternative to such institutional codification is not freedom from constraint but ascription of status.

If the importance of symbolic-cultural codes as a condition of freedom is central to the cultural system itself and to the institutions of societies, it is no less so to the personality of the individual and to its relations to both society and the cultural system. Indeed we have suggested that erotic pleasure itself operates as such a codified system regulating certain crucially important relations between personality and organism. If this is the case in this area, how much more so it is in the others.

It is of course a commonplace that a price of the adaptive potential of living systems is their instability. Death of the individual as the inevitable fate of the higher organisms certainly belongs in this context. So does the exposure to "pathological" disturbances of their organization and functioning. On the broadest grounds, one would expect that with the advancement of precisely the levels of organization which involve cultural codes, susceptibility to this order of disturbances would increase rather than decrease. The guaranteed stability of the solid granite mountain is not for the more "delicate" modes of organization of human action. This point in turn involves the linkage between the potential for instability and that for innovative change, the fundamental evolutionary potential of living systems.

From the point of view of decision–making and commitment of units of action, this factor of instability appears as uncertainty and risk. Above all, creative ventures are inherently risky. Risk-taking can, however, be "reason-able" in taking relatively specific knowable hazards into account and preparing for contingencies. Relative to a standard of such reasonable risk-taking—very difficult to define concretely for particular cases—there tends to be a bifurcation into two types of relatively "irrational" orientation: (1) the "demand" for security, the meaning of which is an attempt to minimize risk by renouncing creative opportunities because of the possibility, sometimes probability, of things "going wrong"; and (2) a "utopian" orientation which minimizes or ignores the constraining conditions of creative success by asserting that, since the goal is inherently desirable, the important thing is to become committed to it and act upon this commitment, regardless of prospects of success (this is what Weber called the orientation of *Wertrationalität*).

The advancement of knowledge, in the ways discussed at the beginning of this chapter, has a double incidence. On the one hand it makes people aware of limiting factors—"determinisms"—of which they were previously not so acutely aware—whether as in the case of the Copernican Revolution they constrained the previously conceived Divine freedom, or as in the case of Marxian economic determinism, which constrained the freedom of man. On the other hand the advancement of knowledge is *itself* an aspect of the development of the cultural system and as such of the creation of new forms and levels of the codification of the culture in the sense meant here. This is increasingly the case for that branch of empirical cognitive culture we call the disciplines dealing with action in our technical sense. Their achievements not only increase our knowledge *about* the action phases of the human condition, but the very existence of this codified knowledge can lead to *changes* in the human condition. This includes of course the personality of the individuals as well as societies and cultures. Just as there could be no "managed economy"—in a sense not confined to socialism—without economics as a science, there could be no type of personality *identified* as a "scientist" before the development of science.

My suggestion is that the negative, constraining aspects of such types of cultural innovations tend to be particularly salient in the earlier phases of their impact on a developing action system, both in its social and its personality subsystems. Seen in this light, we can interpret the ubiquity of the theme of alienation, following the spread of Marxism, at least in one important part as the reaction to a feeling of loss of freedom, of helplessness, in the face of new knowledge or "insights" about the codified order of the modern type of economy. Today there are new phases of the sense of alienation that root in the impact of new insights into the orderliness of the deeper layers of the social system and of the personality, and of their intimate interdependence. The "alienated" want absolute "spontaneity," which dares to assert that man is *not* constrained in the ways in which the new knowledge suggests he must be.

The typical story of a long succession of such innovations, however, is that they have provided the conditions for a new stage of the development of freedoms. Knowledge in the field of physical science has opened up altogether new technological possibilities. The new institutional structures of the modern economy—roughly since the industrial revolution—have opened up a quite new level of standard of living and rate of economic progress, and scientific understanding of these developments has opened up new possibilities of control of the economy. It is my view that the same is true of the new institutionalization in the field of personality and social structure and of the new levels of scientific understanding of them.

In similar terms, it is understandable that personal identity should have become increasingly problematical for sophisticated individuals. As noted, the reference systems within which such identities must be established have in fact been increasing in complexity and in the course of establishment are full of ambiguities. Furthermore, the understanding of this complexity has even more strikingly increased, so that the difficulties of the process become magnified. Beyond this, there is an increasing possibility that an identity involves a significant component of achievement: by the individual himself and/or by his socializing agents, made possible by utilizing the manifold opportunities which have been opening up and knowledge of ways to control the process. However, the possibility of achievement under certain circumstances can increase anxiety about capacity to achieve.

There is no reason to suppose that the considerations of this paper in any way exhaust the factors involved in the prominence of negative diagnostic themes—asserting that this is an age of alienation and of confused identities—among intellectuals of the current sociopsychological scene. There does, however, seem to be a case that they are relevant, and that careful consideration of them in the light of our knowledge of specific situations may help to solve some of the difficulties of orientation that seem to be so distressing to our fellow-intellectuals.

Chapter 2 Is the Concept of Self Necessary?

GORDON W. ALLPORT

Author's Note. The following pages were written some fifteen years ago. In the meantime I have changed my position in only one respect. It seems to me now that the troublesome problem of "the knower" should be more sharply segregated from the other seven propriate functions. Although we are not continuously aware of our body, of our continuity in time, of our self-esteem, of our self-extensions, self-image, coping, and striving, we can be, and at times are, acutely conscious of each of these aspects of selfhood. All of these functions can be, and are, objects of knowledge. In this sense they comprise what James called the "empirical me." Some of them, of course, are relatively passive functions (such as bodily sense, a sense of possessions); some are more energic (propriate striving, coping); but all seven can clearly be objects of our knowledge. But the nature of "the knower"—the process of knowing that we know—is still elusive, and is not iself an object of knowledge.

Hence in my book *Pattern and Growth in Personality* I have separated the problem of the knower (and consigned it to philosophy),[1] leaving only the first seven functions as compromising the proprium.

This shift of position does not affect the exposition here offered. I would still conclude that self, ego, or proprium are vital and central for a science of psychology. And I would also still argue that we need to use these concepts in a carefully discriminated manner to avoid obscurity and homuncular regressions in our thinking. (Cambridge, August 1966)

Does psychological science need the concept of *self?* Philosophy may need it; theology may need it, but it is entirely conceivable that a concept useful to philosophy or theology may turn out to be merely an impediment in the path of psychological progress.

Since the time of Wundt, the central objection of psychology to *self,* and also to *soul,* has been that the concept seems question-begging. It is temptingly easy to assign functions that are not fully understood to a mysterious central agency, and then to declare that "it" performs in such a way as to unify the personality and maintain its integrity. Wundt, aware of this peril, declared boldly for "a psychology without a soul." It was not that he necessarily denied philosophical or theological postulates, but that he felt psychology as science would be handicapped by begging so important a question. For half a century few psychologists other than Thomists have resisted Wundt's reasoning or his example.[2] Indeed we may say that for two generations psychologists have tried every conceivable way of accounting for the integration, organization, and striving of the human person without having recourse to the postulate of a self.

In very recent years the tide has turned. Perhaps without being fully aware of the historical situation, many psychologists have

SOURCE. Gordon W. Allport, *Becoming,* New Haven, Conn.: Yale University Press, 1955, pp. 36-56. Copyright 1955. Reprinted by permission of Yale University Press.

[1] G. W. Allport, *Pattern and Growth in Personality* (New York: Holt, Rinehart, and Winston, 1961), Chapter 6.

[2] Until about 1890 certain American writers, including Dewey, Royce, James, continued to regard self as a necessary concept. They felt that the analytical concepts of the New Psychology lost the manifest unity of mental functioning. But for the ensuing fifty years very few American psychologists made use of it, Mary Whiton Calkins being a distinguished exception; and none employed "soul." *See* G. W. Allport, "The Ego in Contemporary Psychology," *Psychological Review,* **50** (1943), pp. 451–478; reprinted in *The Nature of Personality: Selected Papers* (Cambridge: Addison-Wesley, 1950).

commenced to embrace what two decades ago would have been considered a heresy. They have reintroduced self and ego unashamedly, and, as if to make up for lost time, have employed ancillary concepts such as *self-image, self-actualization, self-affirmation, phenomenal ego, ego-involvement, ego-striving,* and many other hyphenated elaborations which to experimental positivism still have a slight flavor of scientific obscenity.

We should note in passing that Freud played a leading (if unintentional) role in preserving the concept of ego from total obliteration throughout two generations of strenuous positivism. His own use of the term, to be sure, shifted. At first he spoke of assertive and aggressive ego-instincts (in a Nietzschean sense); later for Freud the ego became a rational (though passive) agency, whose duty it was to reconcile as best it could through planning or defense the conflicting pressures of the instincts, of conscience, and of the outer environment. With the core concept thus preserved, even with stringently limited meanings, it was easier for dynamically inclined psychologists, including the neo-Freudians, to enlarge the properties of the ego, making it a far more active and important agent than it was in the hands of Freud.

There still remains, however, the danger that Wundt wished to avoid, namely that the ego may be regarded as a *deus ex machina,* invoked to reassemble the dismembered parts of the throbbing psychic machine after positivism has failed to do so. The situation today seems to be that many pychologists who first fit personality to an external set of co-ordinates are dissatisfied with the result. They therefore reinvent the ego because they find no coherence among the measures yielded by positivistic analysis. But unfortunately positivism and ego-theory do not go well together. Bergson has criticized the use of "ego" in this face-saving way by likening the process to the dilemma of an artist. An artist, he says, may wish to represent Paris—just as a psychologist may wish to represent personality. But all he can do with the limitations of his medium is to draw this and then that angle of the whole. To each sketch he applied the label "Paris," hoping somehow that the sections he has ablated will magically reconstitute the whole.[3]

Similarly in psychology we have a state of affairs where empiricists, finding that they have gone as far as possible with analytic tools and being dissatisfied with the product, resort as did their predecessors to some concept of self in order to represent, however inadequately, the coherence, unity, and purposiveness they know they have lost in their fragmentary representations.

I greatly fear that the lazy tendency to employ self or ego as a factotum to repair the ravages of positivism may do more harm than good. It is, of course, significant that so many contemporary psychologists feel forced to take this step, even though for the most part their work represents no theoretical gain over nineteenth-century usage. Positivism will continue to resent the intrusion, and will, with some justification, accuse today's resurgent self-psychologists of obscurantism.

The problem then becomes how to approach the phenomena that have led to a revival of the self-concept in a manner that will advance rather than retard scientific progress.

A possible clue to the solution, so far as psychology is concerned, lies in a statement made by Alfred Adler. "What is frequently labeled 'the ego,'" he writes, "is nothing more than the style of the individual."[4] Life-style to Adler had a deep and important meaning. He is saying that if psychology could give us a full and complete account of life-style it would automatically include all phenomena now referred somewhat vaguely to a self or an ego. In other words, a wholly adequate psychology of growth would discover all of the activities and all of the interrelations in life, which are now either neglected or consigned to an ego that looks suspiciously like a homunculus.

The first thing an adequate psychology of growth should do is to draw a distinction between what are matters of *importance* to the individual and what are, as Whitehead would say, merely matters of *fact* to him; that is, between what he feels to be vital and central in becoming and what belongs to the periphery of his being.

Many facets of our life-style are not ordinarily felt to have strong personal relevance. Each of us, for example, has innumerable tribal habits that mark our life-style but are

[3] H. Bergson, *Introduction to Metaphysics* (New York: G. Putnam's Sons, 1912), p. 30.

[4] A. Adler, "The Fundamental Views of Individual Psychology," *International Journal of Individual Psychology,* **I** (1935), pp. 5–8.

nothing more than opportunistic modes of adjusting. The same holds true for many of our physiological habits. We keep to the right in traffic, obey the rules of eitquette, and make countless unconscious or semiconscious adjustments, all of which characterize our lifestyle but are not *propriate*, i.e., not really central to our sense of existence. Consider, for example, the English language habits that envelop our thinking and communication. Nothing could be of more pervasive influence in our lives than the store of concepts available to us in our ancestral tongue and the frames of discourse under which our social contacts proceed. And yet the use of English is ordinarily felt to be quite peripheral to the core of our existence. It would not be so if some foreign invader should forbid us to use our native language. At such a time our vocabulary and accent and our freedom to employ them would become very precious and involved with our sense of self. So it is with the myriad of social and physiological habits we have developed that are never, unless interfered with, regarded as essential to our existence as a separate being.

Personality includes these habits and skills, frames of reference, matters of fact and cultural values, that seldom or never seem warm and important. But personality includes what is warm and important also—all the regions of our life that we regard as intimately and essentially ours, and which for the time being I suggest we call the *proprium*. The proprium includes all aspects of personality that make for a sense of inward unity, even though these aspects are at times in conflict. Unity does not necessarily mean harmony.

Psychologists who allow for the proprium use both the term "self" and "ego"—often interchangeably; and both terms are defined with varying degrees of narrowness or of comprehensiveness. Whatever name we use for it, this sense of what is "peculiarly ours" merits close scrutiny. The principal functions and properties of the proprium need to be distinguished.

To this end William James over seventy years ago proposed a simple taxonomic scheme.[5] There are, he maintained, two possible orders of self: an empirical self (the *Me*) and a knowing self (the *I*). Three subsidiary types

comprise the empirical Me: the material self, the social self, and the spiritual self. Within this simple framework he fits his famous and subtle description of the various states of mind that are "peculiarly ours." His scheme, however, viewed in the perspective of modern psychoanalytic and experimental research, seems scarcely adequate. In particular it lacks the full psychodynamic flavor of modern thinking. With some trepidation, therefore, I offer what I hope is an improved outline for analyzing the propriate aspects of personality. Later we shall return to the question, Is the concept of *self* necessary?

THE PROPRIUM

1. Bodily Sense

The first aspect we encounter is the bodily *me*. It seems to be composed of streams of sensations that arise within the organism— from viscera, muscles, tendons, joints, vestibular canals, and other regions of the body. The technical name for the bodily sense is *coenesthesis*. Usually this sensory stream is experienced dimly; often we are totally unaware of it. At times, however, it is well configurated in consciousness in the exhilaration that accompanies physical exercise, or in moments of sensory delight or pain. The infant, apparently, does not know that such experiences are "his." But they surely form a necessary foundation for his emerging sense of self. The baby who at first cries from unlocalized discomfort will, in the course of growth, show progressive ability to identify the distress as his own.

The bodily sense remains a lifelong anchor for our self-awareness, though it never alone accounts for the entire sense of self, probably not even in the young child who has his memories, social cues, and strivings to help in the definition. Psychologists have paid a great deal of attention, however, to this particular component of self-awareness, rather more than to other equally important ingredients. One special line of investigation has been surprisingly popular: the attempt to locate self in relation to specific bodily sensations. When asked, some people will say that they *feel* the self in their right hands, or in the viscera. Most, however, seem to agree with Claparède that a center midway between the eyes, slightly behind them within the head, is the focus. It is from this cyclopean eye that we estimate what lies before and behind ourselves, to the right or left, and above and below. Here, phenomenolog-

[5] *Principles of Psychology* (New York: Henry Holt, 1890), **I**, ch. 10.

ically speaking, is the locus of the ego.[6] Interesting as this type of work may be, it represents little more than the discovery that various sensory elements in the coenesthetic stream or various inferences drawn from sensory experience may for certain people at certain times be especially prominent.

How very intimate (propriate) the bodily sense is can be seen by performing a little experiment in your imagination. Think first of swallowing the saliva in your mouth, or do so. Then imagine expectorating it into a tumbler and drinking it! What seemed natural and "mine" suddenly becomes disgusting and alien. Or picture yourself sucking blood from a prick in your finger; then imagine sucking blood from a bandage around your finger! What I perceive as belonging intimately to my body is warm and welcome; what I perceive as separate from my body becomes, in the twinkling of an eye, cold and foreign.

Certainly organic sensations, their localization and recognition, composing as they do the bodily *me,* are a core of becoming. But it would be a serious mistake to think, as some writers do, that they alone account for our sense of what is "peculiarly ours."

2. Self-Identity (Continuity over Time)

Today I remember some of my thoughts of yesterday; and tomorrow I shall remember some of my thoughts of both yesterday and today; and I am subjectively certain that they are the thoughts of the same person. In this situation, no doubt, the organic continuity of the neuromuscular system is the leading factor. Yet the process involves more than reminiscence made possible by our retentive nerves. The young infant has retentive capacity during the first months of life but in all probability no sense of self-identity. This sense seems to grow gradually, partly as a result of being clothed and named, and otherwise marked off from the surrounding environment. Social in-

teraction is an important factor. It is the actions of the other to which he differentially adjusts that force upon the child the realization that he is not the other, but a being in his own right. The difficulty of developing self-identity in childhood is shown by the ease with which a child depersonalizes himself in play and in speech.[7] Until the age of four or five we have good reason to believe that as perceived by the child personal identity is unstable. Beginning at about this age, however, it becomes the surest test a human being has of his own existence.

3. Ego-Enhancement

We come now to the most notorious property of the proprium, to its unabashed self-seeking.[8] Scores of writers have featured this clamorous trait in human personality. It is tied to the need for survival, for it is easy to see that we are endowed by nature with the impulses of self-assertion and with the emotions of self-satisfaction and pride. Our language is laden with evidence. The commonest compound of self is *selfish,* and of ego *egoism.* Pride, humiliation, self-esteem, narcissism are such prominent factors that when we speak of ego or self we often have in mind only this aspect of personality. And yet, self-love may be prominent in our natures without necessarily being sovereign. The proprium, as we shall see, has other facets and functions.

4. Ego-Extension

The three facets we have discussed—coenesthesis, self-identity, ego-enhancement—are relatively early developments in personality, characterizing the whole of the child's proprium. Their solicitations have a heavily biological quality and seem to be contained within the organism itself. But soon the process of learning brings with it a high regard for possessions, for loved objects, and later, for ideal causes and loyalties. We are speaking here of whatever objects a person calls "mine." They must at the same time be objects of

---

[6] E. Claparède, "Note sur la localisation du moi," *Archives de psychologie,* **19** (1924), pp. 172–182.

Another school of thought has placed considerable stress upon the total body-image. Its variations are said to mark changes in the course of development. Schilder, for example, points out that in experience of hate the body-image itself contracts; in experience of love it expands, and even seems phenomenally to include other beings. See P. Schilder, *The Image and Appearance of the Human Body,* Psyche Monograph (London: K. Paul, Trench, Trubner Co., 1935), p. 353.

[7] Cf. G. W. Allport, *Personality. A Psychological Interpretation* (New York: Henry Holt, 1937), pp. 159–165.

[8] The term "proprium" was a favorite of Emanuel Swedenborg. He used it, however, in the narrow sense of selfishness and pride, a meaning that corresponds here fairly closely to "ego-enhancement." See his *Proprium,* with an introduction by John Bigelow, New York, New Church Board of Publication, 1907. I am grateful to Professor Howard D. Spoerl for his clarification of this matter.

importance, for sometimes our sense of "having" has no affective tone and hence no place in the proprium. A child, however, who identifies with his parent is definitely extending his sense of self, as he does likewise through his love for pets, dolls, or other possessions, animate or inanimate.

As we grow older we identify with groups, neighborhood, and nation as well as with possessions, clothes, home. They become matters of importance to us in a sense that other people's families, nations, or possessions are not. Later in life the process of extension may go to great lengths, through the development of loyalties and of interests focused on abstractions and on moral and religious values. Indeed, a mark of maturity seems to be the range and extent of one's feeling of self-involvement in abstract ideals.

5. Rational Process

The ego, according to Freud, has the task of keeping the organism as a whole in touch with reality, of intermediating between unconscious impulses and the outer world. Often the rational ego can do little else than invent and employ defenses to forestall or diminish anxiety. These protective devices shape the development of personality to an extent unrealized sixty years ago. It is thanks to Freud that we understand the strategies of denial, repression, displacement, reaction formation, rationalization, and the like better than did our ancestors.

We have become so convinced of the validity of these defense mechanisms, and so impressed with their frequency of operation, that we are inclined to forget that the rational functioning of the proprium is capable also of yielding true solutions, appropriate adjustments, accurate planning, and a relatively faultless solving of the equations of life.

Many philosophers, dating as far back as Boethius in the sixth century, have seen the rational nature of personality as its most distinctive property. (*Persona est substantia individua rationalis naturae.*) It may seem odd to credit Freud, the supreme irrationalist of our age, with helping the Thomists preserve for psychology the emphasis upon the ego as the rational agent in personality, but such is the case. For whether the ego reasons or merely rationalizes, it has the property of synthesizing inner needs and outer reality. Freud and the Thomists have not let us forget this fact, and have thus made it easier for modern cognitive theories to deal with this central function of the proprium.

6. Self-Image

A propriate function of special interest today is the self-image, or as some writers call it, the phenomenal self. Present-day therapy is chiefly devoted to leading the patient to examine, correct, or expand this self-image. The image has two aspects: the way the patient regards his present abilities, status, and roles; and what he would like to become, his *aspirations* for himself. The latter aspect, related to what Karen Horney calls the "idealized self-image,"[9] is of especial importance in therapy. On the one hand it may be compulsive, compensatory, and unrealistic, blinding its possessor to his true situation in life. On the other hand, it may be an insightful cognitive map, closely geared to reality and defining a wholesome ambition. The ideal self-image is the imaginative aspect of the proprium, and whether accurate or distorted, attainable or unattainable, it plots a course by which much propriate movement is guided and therapeutic progress achieved.

There are, of course, many forms of becoming that require no self-image, including automatic cultural learning and our whole repertoire of opportunistic adjustments to our environment. Yet there is also much growth that takes place only with the aid of, and because of, a self-image. This image helps us bring our view of the present into line with our view of the future. It includes, of course, our conception of what other people think of us. Fortunately the dynamic importance of the self-image is more widely recognized in psychology today than formerly.

7. Propriate Striving

We come now to the nature of motivation. Unfortunately we often fail to distinguish between propriate and peripheral motives. The reason is that at the rudimentary levels of becoming, which up to now have been the chief levels investigated, it *is* the impulses and drives, the immediate satisfaction and tension reduction, that are the determinants of conduct. Hence a psychology of opportunistic adjustment seems basic and adequate, especially to psychologists accustomed to working with animals. At low levels of behavior the familiar formula of drives and their condi-

---

[9] Karen Horney, *Neurosis and Human Growth: The Struggle toward Self-Realization* (New York: Norton, 1950).

tioning appears to suffice. But as soon as the personality enters the stage of ego-extension, and develops a self-image with visions of self-perfection, we are, I think, forced to postulate motives of a different order, motives that reflect propriate striving. Within experimental psychology itself there is now plenty of evidence that conduct that is "ego involved" (propriate) differs markedly from behavior that is not.[10]

Many psychologists disregard this evidence. They wish to maintain a single theory of motivation consistent with their presuppositions. Their preferred formula is in terms of drive and conditioned drive. Drive is viewed as a peripherally instigated activity. The resultant response is simply reactive, persisting only until the instigator is removed and the tension, created by the drive, lessened. Seeking always a parsimony of assumptions, this view therefore holds that motivation entails one and only one inherent property of the organism: a disposition to act, by instinct or by learning, in such a way that the organism will as efficiently as possible reduce the discomfort of tension. Motivation is regarded as a state of tenseness that leads us to seek equlibrium, rest, adjustment, satisfaction, or homeostasis. From this point of view personality is nothing more than our habitual modes of reducing tension. This formulation, of course, is wholly consistent with empiricism's initial presupposition that man is by nature a passive being, capable only of receiving impressions from, and responding to, external goads.

The contrary view holds that this formula, while applicable to segmental and opportunistic adjustments, falls short of representing the nature of propriate striving. It points out that the characteristic feature of such striving is its resistance to equilibrium: tension is maintained rather than reduced.

In his autobiography Ronald Amundsen tells how from the age of fifteen he had one dominant passion—to become a polar explorer. The obstacles seemed insurmountable, and all through his life the temptations to reduce the tensions engendered were great. But the propriate striving persisted. While he welcomed each success, it acted to raise his level of aspiration, to maintain an over-all commitment. Having sailed the Northwest Passage,

he embarked upon the painful project that led to the discovery of the South Pole. Having discovered the South Pole, he planned for years, against extreme discouragement, to fly over the North Pole, a task he finally accomplished. But his commitment never wavered until at the end he lost his life in attempting to rescue a less gifted explorer, Nobile, from death in the Arctic. Not only did he maintain one style of life, without ceasing, but this central commitment enabled him to withstand the temptation to reduce the segmental tensions continually engendered by fatigue, hunger, ridicule, and danger.[11]

Here we see the issue squarely. A psychology that regards motivation exclusively in terms of drives and conditioned drives is likely to stammer and grow vague when confronted by those aspects of personality—of every personality—that resemble Amundsen's propriate striving. While most of us are less distinguished than he in our achievement, we too have insatiable interests. Only in a very superficial way can these interests be dealt with in terms of tension reduction. Many writers past and present have recognized this fact and have postulated some principles of an exactly opposite order. One thinks in this connection of Spinoza's concept of *conatus,* or the tendency of an individual to persist, against obstacles, in his own style of being. One thinks of Goldstein's doctrine of *self-actualization,* used also by Maslow and others, or McDougall's *self-regarding* sentiment. And one thinks too of those modern Freudians who feel the need for endowing the ego not only with a rational and rationalizing ability but with a tendency to maintain its own system of productive interests, in spite of the passing solicitations of impulse and environmental instigation. Indeed the fortified ego, as described by neo-Freudians, is able to act contrary to the usual course of opportunistic, tension-reducing adaptation.

Propriate striving distinguishes itself from other forms of motivation in that, however beset by conflicts, it makes for unification of personality. There is evidence that the lives of mental patients are marked by the proliferation of unrelated subsystems, and by the loss of more homogeneous systems of motivation.[12]

[10] Cf. G. W. Allport, "The Ego in Contemporary Psychology," *Psychological Review,* **50** (1943), pp. 451–478.

[11] Ronald Amundsen, *My Life as an Explorer* (Garden City, N.Y.: Doubleday, Doran, 1928).
[12] Cf. L. McQuitty, "A Measure of Personality Integration in Relation to the Concept of the

When the individual is dominated by segmental drives, by compulsions, or by the winds of circumstance, he has lost the integrity that comes only from maintaining major directions of striving. The possession of long-range goals, regarded as central to one's personal existence, distinguishes the human being from the animal, the adult from the child, and in many cases the healthy personality from the sick.

Striving, it is apparent, always has a future reference. As a matter of fact, a great many states of mind are adequately described only in terms of their futurity. Along with *striving,* we may mention *interest, tendency, disposition, expectation, planning, problem solving,* and *intention.* While not all future-directedness is phenomenally propriate, it all requires a type of psychology that transcends the prevalent tendency to explain mental states exclusively in terms of past occurrences. People, it seems, are busy leading their lives into the future, whereas psychology, for the most part, is busy tracing them into the past.

8. The Knower

Now that we have isolated these various propriate functions—all of which we regard as peculiarly ours—the question arises whether we are yet at an end. Do we not have in addition a cognizing self—a knower—that transcends all other functions of the proprium and holds them in view? In a famous passage, William James wrestles with this question, and concludes that we have not. There is, he thinks, no such thing as a substantive self distinguishable from the sum total, or stream, of experiences. Each moment of consciousness, he says, appropriates each previous moment, and the knower is thus somehow embedded in what is known. "The thoughts themselves are the thinker."[13]

Opponents of James argue that no mere series of experiences can possibly turn themselves into an awareness of that series as a unit. Nor can "passing thoughts" possibly regard themselves as important or interesting. To whom is the series important or interesting if not to *me?* I am the ultimate monitor. The self as *knower* emerges as a final and inescapable postulate.

It is interesting to ask why James balked at admitting a knowing self after he had so lavishly admitted to psychology with his full approval material, social, and spiritual selves. The reason may well have been (and the reason would be valid today) that one who laboriously strives to depict the nature of propriate functions on an empirical level, hoping thereby to enrich the science of psychology with a discriminating analysis of self, is not anxious to risk a return to the homunculus theory by introducing a synthesizer, or a self of selves.

To be sure, the danger that abuse might follow the admission of a substantive knower into the science of psychology is no reason to avoid this step if it is logically required. Some philosophers, including Kant, insist that the pure or transcendental ego is separable from the empirical ego (i.e., from any of the propriate states thus far mentioned).[14] Those who hold that the knowing itself is not merely an aspect of the self as known (as James argued), but is "pure" and "transcendental," argue, as Kant does, that the texture of knowledge is quite different in the two cases. Our cognition of our knowing self is always indirect, of the order of a presupposition. On the other hand, all features of the *empirical self* are known directly, through acquaintance, as any object is known which falls into time and space categories.[15]

While their metaphysical positions are directly opposed, both Kant and James agree with their illustrious predecessor, Descartes, that the knowing function is a vital attribute of the self however defined. For our present purpose this is the point to bear in mind.

We not only know *things,* but we know (i.e., are acquainted with) the empirical features of our own proprium. It is I who have bodily sensations, I who recognize my self-identity from day to day; I who note and reflect upon my self-assertion, self-extension,

---

[13] *Principles of Psychology,* **I**, ch. 10.

[14] Kant's position on this matter is summarized in the following pronouncement: "One may therefore say of the thinking I (the soul), which represents itself as substance, simple, numerically identical in all time, and as the correlative of all existence, from which in fact all other existence must be concluded, that it *does not know itself through the categories,* but knows the *categories* only, and through them all objects, in the absolute unity of apperception, *that is through itself.*" *Critique of Pure Reason,* trans. by M. Müller (London: Macmillan, 1881), p. 347.
[15] For a fuller discussion of this matter see F. R. Tennant, *Philosophical Theology* (Cambridge: University Press, 1928), **I**, ch. 5.

my own rationalizations, as well as upon my interests and strivings. When I thus think about my own propriate functions I am likely to perceive their essential togetherness, and feel them intimately bound in some way to the knowing function itself.

Since such knowing is, beyond any shadow of doubt, a state that is peculiarly ours, we admit it as the eighth clear function of the proprium. (In other words, as an eighth valid meaning of "self" or "ego.") But it is surely one of nature's perversities that so central a function should be so little understood by science, and should remain a perpetual bone of contention among philosophers. Many, like Kant, set this function (the "pure ego") aside as something qualitatively apart from other propriate functions (the latter being assigned to the "empirical me"). Others, like James, say that the ego *qua* knower is somehow contained within the ego *qua* known. Still others, personalistically inclined, find it necessary to postulate a single self as knower, thinker, feeler, and doer—all in one blended unit of a sort that guarantees the continuance of all becoming.[16]

We return now to our unanswered question: Is the concept of self necessary in the psychology of personality? Our answer cannot be categorical since all depends upon the particular usage of "self" that is proposed. Certainly all legitimate phenomena that have been, and can be ascribed, to the self or ego must be admitted as data indispensable to a psychology of personal growth. All eight functions of the "proprium" (our temporary neutral term for central interlocking operations of personality) must be admitted and included. In particular, the unifying act of perceiving and knowing (of comprehending propriate states at belonging together and belonging to me) must be fully admitted.

At the same time, the danger we have several times warned against is very real: that a homunculus may creep into our discussions of personality, and be expected to solve all our problems without in reality solving any. Thus, if we ask "What determines our moral conduct?" the answer may be "The self does

it." Or, if we pose the problem of choice, we say "The self chooses." Such question-begging would immeasurably weaken the scientific study of personality by providing an illegitimate regressus. There are, to be sure, ultimate problems of philosophy and of theology that psychology cannot even attempt to solve, and for the solution of such problems "self" in some restricted and technical meaning may be a necessity.

But so far as psychology is concerned our position, in brief, is this: all psychological functions commonly ascribed to a self or ego must be admitted as data in the scientific study of personality. These functions are not, however, coextensive with personality as a whole. They are rather the special aspects of personality that have to do with warmth, with unity, with a sense of personal importance. In this exposition I have called them "propriate" functions. If the reader prefers, he may call them self-functions, and in this sense self may be said to be a necessary psychological concept. What is unnecessary and inadmissible is a self (or soul) that is said to perform acts, to solve problems, to steer conduct, in a transpsychological manner, inaccessible to psychological analysis.

Once again we refer to Adler's contention that an adequate psychology of life-style would in effect dispense with the need for a separate psychology of the ego. I believe Adler's position, though unelaborated, is essentially the same as the one here advocated. An adequate psychology would in effect *be* a psychology of the ego. It would deal fully and fairly with propriate functions. Indeed, everyone would assume that psychology was talking about self-functions, unless it was expressly stated that peripheral, opportunistic, or actuarial events were under discussion. But as matters stand today, with so much of psychology preoccupied (as was Hume) with bits and pieces of experience, or else with generalized mathematical equations, it becomes necessary for the few psychologists who are concerned with propriate functions to specify in their discourse that they are dealing with them. If the horizons of psychology were more spacious than they are I venture to suggest that theories of personality would not need the concept of self or of ego except in certain compound forms, such as *self-knowledge, self-image, ego-enhancement, ego-extension.*

---

[16] P. A. Bertocci, "The Psychological Self, the Ego, and Personality," *Psychological Review,* **52** (1945), pp. 91–99.

Part III *The Nature and Dimensions of the Self*

Thus far we have seen that the concept of self is often used to refer to both the process and the reflexive contents of conscious thinking. Before this peculiar duality can be used in any coherent theoretical manner, a number of its features should be examined more closely. Four clusters of conceptual issues immediately suggest themselves. These concern the fundamental logic and interrelations of self as both subject and object, the special organizing character of the self-as-experiencer, the actual contents and organization of the self-as-experienced, and the more general sense of self-evaluation. The contributions appearing in Part III are chosen with the special intent of illuminating these issues.

THE SELF AS BOTH SUBJECT AND OBJECT

The investigation of consciousness is as old as philosophy, and the identification of thinking or experiencing as the essence of conscious existence did not wait for self-psychology. Yet one of the first investigators to discuss the dual nature of self-consciousness and to specify some of the major contents of that consciousness was William James. In the classic passages from *Psychology* (1890), Chapter 3 of this book, James' concentration on the personal quality of an individual's thought and experiences led him to make a distinction that still influences our understanding: the self as simultaneously *I* and *Me*. James conceived of the *I* as that aspect of the self which is "pure ego," or the *subject* which actively experiences, perceives, feels, imagines, chooses, remembers, or plans. The *Me* constituted an object of experience, known to that consciousness. James thought of the "self-as-known" as being composed of the *Material Me* (e.g., body, clothes, immediate family, home, property, creative products, etc.), the *Social Me* (e.g., reputation, recognition, fame, honor in the eyes of significant audiences, etc.), and the *Spiritual Me* (consciousness of active states of thinking, feeling, and behaving).

The *I* was also said to experience certain feelings in connection with the various *Me's*. On the positive side were the many varieties of self-satisfaction ("pride, conceit, vanity, self-esteem, arrogance and vainglory"); on the other hand, self-dissatisfaction included feelings of "modesty, humility, confusion, diffidence, shame, mortification, contrition, the sense of obloquy, and personal despair." His notion that courses of conduct are often chosen rather than predetermined suggested a number of variables to him; from these he constructed what might well be called James' Law concerning level of self-esteem. As James succinctly put it:

$$\text{Self-Esteem} = \frac{\text{Success}}{\text{Pretensions}}$$

> Such a fraction may be increased as well by diminishing the denominator as by increasing the numerator. To give up pretensions is as blessed a relief as to get them gratified; and where disappointment is incessant and the struggle unending, this is what men will always do. . . . Everything added to the Self is a burden as well as a pride . . . our self-feeling is in our power.[1]

In this way James' formulation pointed to the importance of the person's aspirations and the outcomes of his behavior in determining level of self-esteem. These ingredients will be found quite central in the Cooley (Chapter 12), Crowne and Stephens (Chapter 13), Rosenberg (Chapter 33), and Rogers (Chapter 44) discussions of self-esteem. Indeed, James' formulation of the self was sufficiently rich and comprehensive that his brief chapter develops topics of central concern throughout this book.

George Herbert Mead discussed the issues of self-conception from the perspective of pragmatic philosophy. In his three books,[2] and especially in the 1925 article in part reprinted here as Chapter 4, he established the social act as the unit around which consciousness "cuts out and fashions" objects relevant to various courses of social conduct. These objects include the individual as he becomes an object to himself. Through a process of imaginatively taking the perspective of others with whom he interacts, many of the "attitudes" of significant others are incorporated into one's views of self. More fundamentally, the person only becomes a self at all through this process of role-taking in relation to specific and then more generalized others. Once an individual's self has become objectified in the contexts of particular courses of social conduct, this self serves as one basis of control over that individual's future conduct. Thus at the core of Mead's theory are the propositions that an individual (*a*) will conceive of himself much as he believes significant others conceive of him, and (*b*) will tend to act in accord with expectations he imputes to these significant others concerning the way "people like him" should act. As can be seen, from this departure the self-as-experienced is derived from the engagement of pure ego in social interaction. Although vague about the contents of self-conception, Mead's work is profoundly significant in its emphasis on communicative interaction as the cornerstone of self-conception and social control.

THE SELF AS EXPERIENCER

Although James and Mead set the stage for the dialogue between the subjective and objective aspects of self, others have found it useful and more parsimonious to deal with with active consciousness alone. Alfred Schutz is one of the most important of these figures in that he was among the first to bridge the gap between social science and phenome-

---

[1] William James *Psychology: The Briefer Course* (New York: Henry Holt, 1892), pp. 187–188.
[2] *The Philosophy of the Present* (La Salle, Ill.: Open Court Pub. Co., 1932); *Mind, Self and Society* (Chicago, Ill.: U. of Chicago Press, 1934); *The Philosophy of the Act* (Chicago, Ill.: U. of Chicago Press, 1938).

nological philosophy. Schutz was a devotee of Edmund Husserl and devoted much of his life to injecting into social science Husserl's general method of analyzing the way in which human consciousness singles out certain features from the perceptual field as subjectively meaningful.[3] Particularly important are Schutz' theoretical and methodological analyses of the *natural attitude,* or that perceptual stance with which ordinary people approach the world of daily life.[4] His goal was to elucidate the interpretations that persons placed upon their *projects of action* or goal-directed conduct.

In Chapter 5 Schutz first analyzes the temporal aspect of the natural attitude, distinguishing among inner time or *durée,* outer or cosmic time, and standard or civic time. These distinctions are related to a formulation of the tenses of action involved in planning and reflecting (e.g., imagined completion, the vivid present, and recollection of past accomplishments). Schutz uses the issues of time and tense perspective to draw interesting parallels between his own use of the idea of self and Mead's distinction between the *I* and *Me.* An elaboration of these time and tense considerations appears in Gordon's discussion of self-conceptions (Chapter 11).

For Schutz, the cardinal feature of the social world is its *intersubjectivity.* This view emphasizes the shared-in-common and mutually sanctioned set of expectations and interpretative categories within a culture. This line of thought is of special importance in the context of Part III since the person's subjectively organized knowledge about his world of daily life forms a frame of reference for the interpretation of new information about himself and his actions. Schutz also considers a primary feature of the natural attitude to be an absence of doubt that things might be other than they are given through culturally provided interpretations. This special *epoche,* or suspension of doubt regarding the reality of the culturally given, may be considered a basis for social stability and solidarity.

Following explicitly from Alfred Schutz' accent on the lived world of daily life is Harold Garfinkel's "Aspects of the Problem of Common-Sense Knowledge of Social Structures." Garfinkel centers on the "common culture" that underlies ordinary communication and interaction. These shared understandings are seen as intimately related to the recognition of commonplace events, the arousal of emotions, and bewilderment when others fail to support one's suppositions. Garfinkel's discussion is relevant to self-conception in at least two ways. For one, the person's identity as a member-in-good-standing of a particular group or culture is fostered by his ability to act upon these "seen but unnoticed" background assumptions. In addition, an individual's self-esteem is in large part based on his feelings of competence in behaving within a given framework of understanding. Any disruption of the presupposed features of action dramatically challenges one's senses of competence, morality, or sanity. This latter point is particularly relevant to the situation of cultural strangers and persons in marginal social positions (Kardiner and Ovesey, Chapter 24; Goffman, Chapter 25).

---

[3] Cf. Edmund Husserl, *Ideas* (1913), first translated into English by W. R. Boyce Gibson (New York: Macmillan, 1931).

[4] Now collected in three volumes: *I. The Problem of Social Reality, edited* by Maurice Natanson (The Hague: Martinus Nijhoff, 1962), *II. Studies in Social Theory,* edited by Arvid Broderson (The Hague: Martinus Nijhoff, 1964), and *The Phenomenology of the Social World* (Evanston, Ill.: Northwestern Univ. Press, 1967), trans. by George Walsh and Frederick Lehnert.

Schutz' emphases on time perspective and personal choice and on the vital concept of intersubjectivity are amplified and elaborated upon in the original contribution by Edward Tiryakian (Chapter 7). He expands such emphases in a provocative fashion to deal with the openness of the person to his historical milieu and the succession of social situations in which he develops and grows. The distinction (stemming from Heidegger) between ontic and ontological existence and between the corresponding inauthentic and authentic modes of comportment is a far-reaching one, and it shows one more of the points of articulation between modern philosophy and social science. The reader may find this distinction particularly useful in confronting the various treatments of alienation (cf. Parsons, Chapter 1; Marx, Chapter 39; Horney, Chapter 40; and Keniston, Chapter 41) and the discussions of the chameleon-like character of social identity (cf. Turner, Chapter 9; Gergen, Chapter 30; Goffman, Chapter 31; and Jourard, Chapter 43). The distinction also allows Tiryakian to examine some of the ethical implications of what he terms existential phenomenology and serves as an analytic tool for understanding gestures and masks.

THE SELF AS EXPERIENCED

As discussed in the Introduction to this volume, the concept of self as pure experience plays a secondary role in the present context. The chapters to be described in this subsection introduce the dominant orientation of the volume, that orientation centering on the self as an object of experience. It is quite appropriate that Charles Horton Cooley be given an initial say in the matter. Cooley earned his place among the "founding fathers" of the symbolic interactionist position largely by virtue of his formulation of the nature and development of the *social self*. Two long chapters in his *Human Nature and the Social Order* (1902) are devoted to the importance, in the development of self-conception, of a person's interpretations of the judgments held by others toward him. His book is an early landmark in the campaign to supplant the prevailing instinct theories with the view that culture, social organization, and interpersonal communication are all implicated in the shaping of the individual.

The core sections of these two chapters are reprinted here as Chapters 8 and 12. In the first, Cooley extends James' position (Chapter 3) by suggesting that the *sense of appropriation* is essential to all self-conceptions. Cooley regarded the urge to expand the scope of this appropriation-to-self as an instinct that provided energy for stimulating and unifying the individual's activities. The term "self-feeling" was used to refer to this general and presumably innate faculty, which he saw as partially differentiating during the socialization process into innumerable "self-sentiments." The more specific self-sentiments constitute the affective bonds of attachment with particular contents of self-conception.

In contrast to James or Mead, Cooley provides a much more complete account of the major *objects* of self-feeling as they are typically related to the individual's developing sense of control over physical and social reality. These objects include the material body, opinions, purposes, desires, claims, possessions, products of activity, achievements, plans, ambitions, actions, allegiances, friends, or in short: "any idea or system of ideas, drawn from the communicative life, that the mind cherishes as its own." Cooley's position does, of course, neglect those aspects of a person often felt to be "mine" but that are unlikely to be cherished (e.g., shameful stigmata, handicaps, failures, and sins).

Cooley saw the objects appropriated by self-feeling as inherently social in at least three senses. First, these objects were social in that their meaning to the person was furnished by the common language and culture. Second, conceptions of self and their associated evaluations were very often derived from the individual's imaginative construction of the judgments that significant others hold regarding his actions and attributes. Cooley gave the felicitous label "the looking-glass self" to the result of this self-development process. Third, Cooley suggested an important relationship (analyzed in detail by Erich Fromm in Chapter 32) between appropriations to self and love for others. That which is loved is appropriated into the self and thereafter engenders growth and generosity. Yet, "It is only on the basis of a substantial self that a person is capable of progressive sympathy or love. . . ."[5]

The original paper by Ralph Turner (Chapter 9) provides an enlightening contrast to Cooley in grappling with many of the same issues some sixty years later. Whereas Cooley's thinking is seminal, the increase in sophistication and sharpening of central issues is much evidenced in Turner's chapter. Pivotal is his differentiation between stable self-conceptions and situational self-images. This treatment may be effectively compared with the positions developed by Baldwin (Chapter 14), Gergen (Chapter 30), and Goffman (Chapter 31). Equally important is Turner's formulation of self-conception as containing (among other elements) a highly selective organization of evaluative standards concerning what the person is like at his highest potential, what he is striving toward, and what he potentially could be under most favorable conditions and incentives. Not only does this approach emphasize the multiplicity of self-experiences, but it also incorporates the important consideration of time perspective or temporality. This latter theme has been intimated in the earlier treatments of self as a structure of possibilities (cf. Schutz, Chapter 5; Tiryakian, Chapter 7). However, Turner's analysis more formally sets the stage for later discussions that deal with the temporal context of self-conceptions (cf. Gordon, Chapter 11; Back and Gergen, Chapter 22). Self-conceptions are also held by Turner to provide the reference points for assessments of credit and responsibility. Finally, elation or dejection results as the self-image engendered in current interaction episodes surpasses or falls short of cherished and desired characteristics. Thus Turner gives us a much more socially sensitive reformulation of James' Law of Self-Esteem. In Turner's theory we see one of the few serious attempts at integrating the analysis of self-conception with processes of social interaction.

The treatments given to the self-as-experienced by Cooley and Turner give considerable weight to the social anchor of self-conception. On the other hand, the sections of Paul Schilder's now classic *The Image and Appearance of the Human Body* (1935), reprinted here as Chapter 10, center first on self-awareness and only then expand to consider the social context. Schilder calls attention to such aspects of bodily awareness as (1) the tactile, visceral, and visual sensations of inner and outer bodily conditions; (2) the body boundaries, as illustrated most dramatically in the "phantom limb" illusion; (3) bodily posture and movement in time and space; and (4) the location of stimuli in various regions of the body. Schilder was writing from the perspective of early

---

[5] Charles H. Cooley, *Human Nature and the Social Order* (New York: Charles Scribner's Sons, 1902), p. 156.

psychoanalysis and neuropathology and was interested primarily in disturbances of these various bodily aspects as they may result from brain lesions, amputations, and various forms of mental illness. Yet all these aspects of bodily experience are relevant and perhaps crucial to the subjective life of the normally functioning person.

When Schilder does shift his attention to the social underpinnings of body image, he ranges from the provocative to the mystical. Most challenging is his discussion of the relationship between one's own body and the bodies of others. His contention that knowledge of one's own body is intertwined with knowledge of other's bodies could well be applied to other dimensions of self-conception. In essence, self-definition may be partly dependent on the way in which others are perceived to define themselves. Of additional interest is Schilder's emphasis on physical attractiveness—the importance of this aspect of self in determining self-esteem and adjustment has been all too little explored.[6]

James and Cooley speculated at length about the contents of self-consciousness; Gordon's paper (Chapter 11) presents a categorical system designed to capture the contents of this structure of available reflexive meanings as they are translated by the person into self-representations. The free response technique proposed by Gordon allows investigation of salience, organization, and qualitative differentiation of content. Special attention is given to the use of noun-like categories for social identity as distinguished from the adjectival personal attributes. The schema also takes into account temporal perspective, evaluative connotations, and the importance to the individual of various self-aspects. Data from high school and college groups are used to illustrate the meanings subsumed under the thirty categories of the system. One of the unusual features of Gordon's method is that it translates the four system problems that form the core of Parson's general theory of action (adaptation, goal-attainment, integration, and pattern–maintenance) into four very general senses of self. These four system problems are viewed respectively as generic to the individual's feelings of competence, self-determination, unity, and moral worth.

THE VARIETIES OF SELF-EVALUATION

The preceding five chapters all center on the contents of self-reflexive consciousness; however, special attention needs to be given to the emotional underpinnings of these various contents. A person may consider himself a Catholic, male, or alienated, but the importance of these various self-conceptions to the person is largely determined by how he feels about these characteristics and his position with respect to them. Our attention has thus far been directed to this aspect of the self-as-experienced by Allport's discussion of ego-enhancement (Chapter 2), James' treatment of self-esteem (Chapter 3), Turner's explication of elation-dejection (Chapter 9), and Gordon's exploration of the general senses of self (Chapter 11). The remaining chapters in this Part are intended to amplify this concern with one of the more profound dimensions of self-conception.

The first of these two chapters (Chapter 12) again provides Charles H. Cooley with the platform. Cooley is most effective when he is most evocative. With poetic skill, he distinguishes the subtler shadings of self-feelings in such a way as to call out in the reader much of the

---

[6] One of the few exceptions is Erving Goffman's *Stigma* (Englewood Cliffs, N.J.: Prentice-Hall Spectrum Books, 1963), in which the difficulties of the deformed, the maimed, and the ugly are explicated.

emotional tone of the condition being described. Although attention to the qualitative nature of particular self-feelings was a major aspect of Cooley's work on the social self, his contribution has not been sufficiently recognized. Perhaps this is due to the excessive attention now given to the idea of the looking-glass self, or perhaps it is because Cooley's literary style did not lend itself to fruitfulness in the empirical realm. Yet Cooley gave a strong social account of the sources and consequences of various feelings toward self and related many of them to other attributes of self (e.g., stability, receptivity versus internal concern, scope of conscience, confidence, strength, and self-sufficiency versus dependency).

Within the varieties of self-evaluation, Cooley is able to distinguish among the feelings of pride, self-respect, integrity, honor, self-reverence, self-esteem, self-confidence, and hope. He further suggests that it is conceptually necessary to distinguish among self-abandonment, contrition, repentance, self-abnegation, curtailment of ambition for a future self, resentment, and mortification. Each of these feelings is currently and perhaps mistakenly subsumed under the single rubric self-esteem. Cooley also lays special stress on the relationship between self-esteem and virtue or morality, and his discussion serves as an excellent precursor to Pepitone's experimental investigations (Chapter 34). The view that self-esteem "easily and willingly expands, in most of us, and is liable to sudden, irrational, and grievous collapses" forms an interesting contrast to those who view self-esteem as one of the more stable components of personality (cf. Cohen, Chapter 38; and Rogers, Chapter 44).

The Cooley chapter stands in marked contrast to the contemporary methodological analysis of Crowne and Stephens (Chapter 13). The juxtaposition is an enlightening one, however, inasmuch as it documents the history of a concept: from rich theoretical speculations to attempts at delineation in precise operational terms. The Crowne and Stephens chapter is the only methodological exegesis in the volume; it plays an important role in outlining pitfalls that are not only pertinent to the measurement of self-evaluation but common to the gamut of measures used in self-conception work. In particular, issues of broad significance are raised concerning problems of nonequivalent procedures, unclear conceptualization of variables, nonrepresentative behavior sampling, response set contamination, and the generality of self-evaluations.

Chapter 3 The Self

WILLIAM JAMES

The Me and the I

Whatever I may be thinking of, I am always at the same time more or less aware of *myself*, of my *personal existence*. At the same time it is *I* who am aware; so that the total self of me, being as it were duplex, partly known and partly knower, partly object and partly subject, must have two aspects discriminated in it, of which for shortness we may call one the *Me* and the other the *I*. I call these "discriminated aspects," and not separate things, because the identity of *I* with *me*, even in the very act of their discrimination, is perhaps the most ineradicable dictum of common-sense, and must not be undermined by our terminology here at the outset, whatever we may come to think of its validity at our inquiry's end.

I shall therefore treat successively of (A) the self as known, or the *me*, the 'empirical ego' as it is sometimes called; and of (B) the self as knower, or the *I*, the 'pure ego' of certain authors.

A. THE SELF AS KNOWN

The Empirical Self or Me

Between what a man calls *me* and what he simply calls *mine* the line is difficult to draw. We feel and act about certain things that are ours very much as we feel and act about ourselves. Our fame, our children, the work of our hands, may be as dear to us as our bodies are, and arouse the same feelings and the same acts of reprisal if attacked. And our bodies themselves, are they simply ours, or are they *us?* Certainly men have been ready to disown their very bodies and to regard them as mere vestures, or even as prisons of clay from which they should some day be glad to escape.

We see then that we are dealing with a

SOURCE. William James, *Psychology: The Briefer Course* (New York: Henry Holt and Co., 1910), pp. 177–183, 184–188, 190, 191–192, 195–196, 197, 200–203, 205, and 215–216. Reprinted by permission of Holt, Rinehart and Winston, Inc. Copyright 1892, 1920.

fluctuating material; the same object being sometimes treated as a part of me, at other times as simply mine, and then again as if I had nothing to do with it at all. *In its widest possible sense,* however, *a man's Me is the sum total of all that he can call his,* not only his body, and his psychic powers, but his clothes and his house, his wife and children, his ancestors and friends, his reputation and works, his lands and horses, and yacht and bank-account. All these things give him the same emotions. If they wax and prosper, he feel triumphant; if they dwindle and die away, he feels cast down—not necessarily in the same degree for each thing, but in much the same way for all. Understanding the Me in this widest sense, we may begin by dividing the history of it into three parts, relating respectively to—

a. Its constituents;
b. The feeling and emotions they arouse—*self-appreciation;*
c. The acts to which they prompt—*self-seeking and self-preservation.*

a. The constituents of the Me may be divided into three classes, those which make up respectively—

The material me;
The social me; and
The spiritual me.

The Material Me. The *body* is the innermost part of the material me in each of us; and certain parts of the body seem more intimately ours than the rest. The clothes come next. The old saying that human person is composed of three parts—soul, body, and clothes—is more than a joke. We so appropriate our clothes and identify ourselves with them that there are few of us who, if asked to choose between having a beautiful body clad in raiment perpetually shabby and unclean, and having an ugly and blemished form always spotlessly attired, would not hesitate a moment before making a decisive reply. Next, our immediate family is a part of ourselves. Our father and mother, our wife and babes, are bone of our bone and flesh of our flesh. When they die, a part of our very selves is gone. If they do anything wrong, it is our shame. If they are insulted, our anger flashes forth as readily as if we stood in their place. Our home comes next. Its scenes are part of our life; its aspects awaken the tenderest feelings of affection; and we do not easily forgive the stranger who, in visiting it, finds fault with its arrangement or treats it with contempt. All these different things are the objects of instinctive preferences coupled with the most important practical interests of life. We all have a blind impulse to watch over our body, to deck it with clothing of an ornamental sort, to cherish parents, wife, and babes, and to find for ourselves a house of our own which we may live in and "improve."

An equally instinctive impulse drives us to collect property; and the collections thus made become, with different degrees of intimacy, parts of our empirical selves. The parts of our wealth most intimately ours are those which are saturated with our labor. There are few men who would not feel personally annihilated if a life-long construction of their hands or brains—say an entomological collection or an extensive work in manuscript—were suddenly swept away. The miser feels similarly towards his gold; and although it is true that a part of our depression at the loss of possessions is due to our feeling that we must now go without certain goods that we expected the possessions to bring in their train, yet in every case there remains, over and above this, a sense of the shrinkage of our personality, a partial conversion of ourselves to nothingness, which is a psychological phenomenon by itself. We are all at once assimilated to the tramps and poor devils whom we so despise, and at the same time removed farther than ever away from the happy sons of earth who lord it over land and sea and men in the full-blown lustihood that wealth and power can give, and before whom, stiffen ourselves as we will by appealing to anti-snobbish first principles, we cannot escape emotion, open or sneaking, of respect and dread.

The Social Me. A man's social me is the recognition which he gets from his mates. We are not only gregarious animals, liking to be in sight of our fellows, but we have an innate propensity to get ourselves noticed, and noticed favorably, by our kind. No more fiendish punishment could be devised, were such a thing physically possible, than that one should be turned loose in society and remain absolutely unnoticed by all the members thereof. If no one turned round when we entered, answered when we spoke, or minded what we did, but if every person we met "cut us dead," and acted as if we were non-existing things, a kind of rage and impotent despair would ere long well up in us, from which the cruelest bodily tortures would be a relief; for these would make us feel that, however bad might be our plight, we had not sunk to such a depth as to be unworthy of attention at all.

Properly speaking, *a man has as many social selves as there are individuals who recognize him* and carry an image of him in their mind. To wound any one of these his images is to wound him. But as the individuals who carry the images fall naturally into classes, we may practically say that he has as many different social selves as there are distinct *groups* of persons about whose opinion he cares. He generally shows a different side of himself to each of these different groups. Many a youth who is demure enough before his parents and teachers, swears and swaggers like a pirate among his "tough" young friends. We do not show ourselves to our children as to our club-companions, to our customers as to the laborers we employ, to our own masters and employers as to our intimate friends. From this there results what practically is a division of the man into several selves; and this may be a discordant splitting, as where one is afraid to let one set of his acquaintances know him as he is elsewhere; or it may be a perfectly harmonious division of labor, as where one tender to his children is stern to the soldiers or prisoners under his command.

The most peculiar social self which one is apt to have is in the mind of the person one is in love with. The good or bad fortunes of this self cause the most intense elation and dejection—unreasonable enough as measured by every other standard than that of the organic feeling of the individual. To his own consciousness he *is* not, so long as this particular social self fails to get recognition, and when it is recognized his contentment passes all bounds.

A man's *fame,* good or bad, and his *honor* or dishonor, are names for one of his social selves. The particular social self of a man called his honor is usually the result of one of those splittings of which we have spoken. It is his image in the eyes of his own "set," which exalts or condemns him as he conforms or not to certain requirements that may not be made of one in another walk of life. Thus a layman may abandon a city infected with cholera; but a priest or a doctor would think such an act incompatible with his honor. A soldier's honor requires him to fight or to die under circumstances where another man can apologize or run away with no stain upon his social self. A judge, a statesman, are in like manner debarred by the honor of their cloth from entering into pecuniary relations perfectly honorable to persons in private life. Nothing is commoner than to hear people discriminate between their different selves of this sort: "As a man I pity you, but as an official I must show you no mercy"; "As a politician I regard him as an ally but as a moralist I loathe him"; etc., etc. What may be called "club-opinion" is one of the very strongest forces in life. The thief must not steal from other thieves; the gambler must pay his gambling debts, though he pay no other debts in the world. The code of honor of fashionable society has throughout history been full of permissions as well as of vetoes, the only reason for following either of which is that so we best serve one of our social selves. You must not lie in general, but you may lie as much as you please if asked about your relations with a lady; you must accept a challenge from an equal, but if challenged by an inferior you may laugh him to scorn: these are examples of what is meant.

The Spiritual Me. By the "spiritual me," so far as it belongs to the empirical self, I mean no one of my passing states of consciousness. I mean rather the entire collection of my states of consciousness, my psychic faculties and dispositions taken concretely. This collection can at any moment become an object to my thought at that moment and awaken emotions like those awakened by any of the other portions of the Me. When we *think of ourselves as thinkers,* all the other ingredients of our Me seem relatively external possessions. Even within the spiritual Me some ingredients seem more external than others. Our capacities for sensation, for example, are less intimate possessions, so to speak, than our emotions and desires; our intellectual processes are less intimate than our volitional decisions. The more *active-feeling* states of consciousness are thus the more central portions of the spiritual Me. The very core and nucleus of our self, as we know it, the very sanctuary of our life, is the sense of activity which certain inner states possess. This sense of activity is often held to be a direct revelation of the living substance of our Soul. Whether

this be so or not is an ulterior question. I wish now only to lay down the peculiar *internality* of whatever states possess this quality of seeming to be active. It is as if they *went out to meet* all the other elements of our experience. In thus feeling about them probably all men agree.

b. The feelings and emotions of self come after the constituents.

Self-Appreciation. This is of two sorts, *self-complacency* and *self-dissatisfaction.* "Self-love" more properly belongs under the division C, of *acts,* since what men mean by that name is rather a set of motor tendencies than a kind of feeling properly so called.

Language has synonyms enough for both kinds of self-appreciation. Thus pride, conceit, vanity, self-esteem, arrogance, vainglory, on the one hand; and on the other modesty, humility, confusion, diffidence, shame, mortification, contrition, the sense of obloquy, and personal despair. These two opposite classes of affection seem to be direct and elementary endowments of our nature. Associationists would have it that they are, on the other hand, secondary phenomena arising from a rapid computation of the sensible pleasures or pains to which our prosperous or debased personal predicament is likely to lead, the sum of the represented pleasures forming the self-satisfaction and the sum of the represented pains forming the opposite feeling of shame. No doubt, when we are self-satisfied, we do fondly rehearse all possible rewards for our desert, and when in a fit of self-despair we forebode evil. But the mere expectation of reward *is* not the self-satisfaction, and the more apprehension of the evil *is* not the self-despair; for there is a certain average tone of self-feeling which each one of us carries about with him, and which is independent of the objective reasons we may have for satisfaction or discontent. That is, a very meanly-conditioned man may abound in unfaltering conceit, and one whose success in life is secure, and who is esteemed by all, may remain diffident of his powers to the end.

One may say, however, that the normal *provocative* of self-feeling is one's actual success or failure, and the good or bad actual position one holds in the world. "He put in his thumb and pulled out a plum, and said, 'What a good boy am I!'" A man with a broadly extended empirical Ego, with powers that have uniformly brought him success, with place and wealth and friends and fame, is not likely to be visited by the morbid diffidences and doubts about himself which he had when he was a boy. "Is not this great Babylon, which I have planted?" Whereas he who has made one blunder after another, and still lies in middle life among the failures at the foot of the hill, is liable to grow all sicklied o'er with self-distrust, and to shrink from trials with which his powers can really cope.

* * *

c. Self-seeking and *self-preservation* come next. These words cover a large number of our fundamental instinctive impulses. We have those of *bodily self-seeking,* those of *social self-seeking,* and those of *spiritual self-seeking.*

Bodily Self-Seeking. All the ordinary useful reflex actions and movements of alimentation and defense are acts of bodily self-preservation. Fear and anger prompt to acts that are useful in the same way. Whilst if by self-seeking we mean the providing for the future as distinguished from maintaining the present, we must class both anger and fear, together with the hunting, the acquisitive, the home-constructing and the tool-constructing instincts, as impulses to self-seeking of the bodily kind. Really, however, these latter instincts, with amativeness, parental fondness, curiosity and emulation, seek not only the development of the bodily Me, but that of the material Me in the widest possible sense of the word.

Our *social self-seeking,* in turn, is carried on directly through our amativeness and friendliness, our desire to please and attract notice and admiration, our emulation and jealousy, our love of glory, influence, and power, and indirectly through whichever of the material self-seeking impulses prove serviceable as means to social ends. That the direct social self-seeking impulses are probably pure instincts is easily seen. The noteworthy thing about the desire to be "recognized" by others is that its strength has so little to do with the worth of the recognition computed in sensational or rational terms. We are crazy to get a visiting-list which shall be large, to be able to say when any one is mentioned, "Oh! I know him well," and to be bowed to in the street by half the people we meet. Not only the people but the places and things I know enlarge my Self in a sort of metaphoric social way. *"Ça me connaît,"* as the French workman says of the implement he can use well. So that it comes about that persons for whose *opinion* we care nothing are nevertheless persons whose notice we woo; and that many a man truly great, many a woman truly

fastidious in most respects, will take a deal of trouble to dazzle some insignificant cad whose personality they heartily despise.

Under the head of *spiritual self-seeking* ought to be included every impulse towards psychic progress, whether intellectual, moral, or spiritual in the narrow sense of the term. It must be admitted, however, that much that commonly passes for spiritual self-seeking in this narrow sense is only material and social self-seeking beyond the grave. In the Mohammedan desire for paradise and the Christian aspiration not to be damned in hell, the materiality of the goods sought is indisguised. In the more positive and refined view of heaven, many of its goods, the fellowship of the saints and of our dead ones, and the presence of God, are but social goods of the most exalted kind. It is only the search of the redeemed inward nature, the spotlessness from sin, whether here or hereafter, that can count as spiritual self-seeking pure and undefiled.

But this broad and external review of the facts of the life of the Me will be incomplete without some account of the

Rivalry and Conflict of the Different Me's. With most objects of desire, physical nature restricts our choice to but one of many represented goods, and even so it is here. I am often confronted by the necessity of standing by one of my empirical selves and relinquishing the rest. Not that I would not, if I could, be both handsome and fat and well dressed, and a great athlete, and make a million a year, be a wit, a *bon-vivant,* and a lady-killer, as well as a philosopher; a philanthropist, statesman, warrior, and African explorer, as well as a "tone-poet" and saint. But the thing is simply impossible. The millionaire's work would run counter to the saint's; the *bon-vivant* and the philanthropist would trip each other up; and the philosopher and the lady-killer could not well keep house in the same tenement of clay. Such different characters may conceivably at the outset of life be alike *possible* to a man. But to make any one of them actual, the rest must more or less be suppressed. So the seeker of his truest, strongest, deepest self must review the list carefully, and pick out the one on which to stake his salvation. All other selves thereupon become unreal, but the fortunes of this self are real. Its failures are real failures, its triumphs real triumphs, carrying shame and gladness with them. This is as strong an example as there is of . . . selective industry of the mind. Our thought, incessantly deciding, among many things of a kind, which ones for it shall be realities, here chooses one of many possible selves or characters, and forthwith reckons it no shame to fail in any of those not adopted expressly as its own.

So we have the paradox of a man shamed to death because he is only the second pugilist or the second oarsman in the world. That he is able to beat the whole population of the globe minus one is nothing; he has "pitted" himself to beat that one; and as long as he doesn't do that nothing else counts. He is to his own regard as if he were not, indeed, he *is* not. Yonder puny fellow, however, whom every one can beat, suffers no chagrin about it, for he has long ago abandoned the attempt to "carry that line," as the merchants say, of self at all. With no attempt there can be no failure; with no failure, no humiliation. So our self-feeling in this world depends entirely on what we *back* ourselves to be and do. It is determined by the ratio of our actualities to our supposed potentialities; a fraction of which our pretensions are the denominator and the numerator of our success: thus,

$$\text{Self-Esteem} = \frac{\text{Success}}{\text{Pretensions}}$$

Such a fraction may be increased as well by diminishing the denominator as by increasing the numerator. To give up pretensions is as blessed a relief as to get them gratified; and where disappointment is incessant and the struggle is unending, this is what men will always do. The history of evangelical theology, with its conviction of sin, its self-despair, and its abandonment of salvation by works, is the deepest of possible examples, but we meet others in every walk of life. There is the strangest lightness about the heart when one's nothingness in a particular line is once accepted in good faith. *All* is not bitterness in the lot of the lover sent away by the final inexorable "No." Many Bostonians, *crede experto* (and inhabitants of other cities, too, I fear), would be happier women and men today, if they could once for all abandon the notion of keeping up a Musical Self, and without shame let people hear them call a symphony a nuisance. How pleasant is the day when we say, *those* illusions are gone. Everything added to the Self is a burden as well as a pride. A certain man who lost every penny during our civil war went and actually rolled in the dust, saying he had not felt so free and happy since he was born.

Once more, then, our self-feeling is in our power. As Carlyle says: "Make thy claim of wages a zero, then has thou the world under thy feet. Well did the wisest of our time write, it is only with *renunciation* that life, properly speaking, can be said to begin."

* * *

The Hierarchy of the Me's. A tolerably unanimous opinion ranges the different selves of which a man may be "seized and possessed," and the consequent different orders of his self-regard, in an *hierarchical scale, with the bodily me at the bottom, the spiritual me at the top, and the extra-corporeal material selves and the various social selves between.*

* * *

A certain amount of bodily selfishness is required as a basis for all the other selves. But too much sensuality is despised, or at best condoned, on account of the other qualities of the individual. The wider material selves are regarded as higher than the immediate body. He is esteemed a poor creature who is unable to forego a little meat and drink and warmth and sleep for the sake of getting on in the world. The social self as a whole, again, ranks higher than the material self as a whole. We must care more for our honor, our friends, our human ties, than for a sound skin or wealth. And the spiritual self is so supremely precious that, rather than lose it, a man ought to be willing to give up friends and góod fame, and property, and life itself.

In each kind of Me, material, social, and spiritual, men distinguish between the immediate and actual, and the remote and potential, between the narrower and the wider view, to the detriment of the former and the advantage of the latter. One must forego a present bodily enjoyment for the sake of one's general health; one must abandon the dollar in the hand for the sake of the hundred dollars to come; one must make an enemy of his present interlocutor if thereby one makes friends of a more valued circle; one must go without learning and grace and wit, the better to compass one's soul's salvation.

Of all these wider, more potential selves, *the potential social Me* is the most interesting, by reason of certain apparent paradoxes to which it leads in conduct, and by reason of its connection with our moral and religious life. When for motives of honor and conscience I brave the condemnation of my own family, club, and "set"; when, as a Protestant, I turn

Catholic; as a Catholic, freethinker; as a "regular practitioner," homeopath, or what not, I am always inwardly strengthened in my course and steeled against the loss of my actual social self by the thought of other and better *possible* social judges than those whose verdict goes against me now. The ideal social self which I thus seek in appealing to their decision may be very remote: it may be represented as barely possible. I may not hope for its realization during my lifetime; I may even expect the future generations, which would approve me if they knew me, to know nothing about me when I am dead and gone. Yet still the emotion that beckons me on is indubitably the pursuit of an ideal social self, a self that is at least *worthy* of approving recognition by the highest *possible* judging companion, if such companion there be. This self is the true, the intimate, the ultimate, the permanent me which I seek.

* * *

Summary

The following table may serve for a summary of what has been said thus far. The empirical life of Self is divided into:

seen to be the very embodiment of change. Yet each of us spontaneously considers that by "I," he means something always the same. This has led most philosophers to postulate behind the passing state of consciousness a permanent Substance or Agent whose modification or act it is. This Agent is the thinker; the "state" is only its instrument or means. "Soul," "transcendental Ego," "Spirit," are so many names for this more permanent sort of Thinker. Not discriminating them just yet, let us proceed to define our idea of the passing state of consciousness more clearly.

The Unity of the Passing Thought

Already, in speaking of "sensations," from the point of view of Fechner's idea of measuring them, we saw that there was no ground for calling them compounds. But what is true of sensations cognizing simple qualities is also true of thoughts with complex objects composed of many parts. This proposition unfortunately runs counter to a wide-spread prejudice, and will have to be defended at some length. Common-sense, and psychologists of almost every school, have agreed that when-

	Material	Social	Spiritual
Self-Seeking	Bodily Appetites and instincts Love of Adornment, Foppery, Acquisitiveness, Constructiveness Love of Home, etc.	Desire to Please, be Noticed, Admired, etc. Sociability, Emulation, Envy, Love, Pursuit of Honor, Ambition, etc.	Intellectual, Moral and Religious Aspirations, Conscientiousness.
Self-Estimation	Personal Vanity, Modesty, etc. Pride of Wealth, Fear of Poverty.	Social and Family Pride, Vainglory, Snobbery, Humility, Shame, etc.	Sense of Moral or Mental Superiority, Purity, etc. Sense of inferiority or of Guilt.

B. THE SELF AS KNOWER

The I, or "pure ego," is a very much more difficult subject of inquiry than the Me. It is that which at any given moment *is* conscious, whereas the Me is only one of the things which it is conscious *of*. In other words, it is the *Thinker;* and the question immediately comes up *what* is the thinker? Is it the passing state of consciousness itself, or is it something deeper and less mutable? The passing state we have

ever an object of thought contains many elements, the thought itself must be made up of just as many ideas, one idea for each element, all fused together in appearance, but really separate.

"There can be no difficulty in admitting that association *does* form the ideas of an indefinite number of individuals into one complex idea," says James Mill, "because it is an acknowledged fact. Have we not the idea of an army? And is not that precisely the ideas of an indefinite number of men formed into one idea?"

* * *

Our notion of the abstract numbers eight, four, two, is as truly one feeling of the mind as our notion of simple unity. Our idea of a couple is not a couple of ideas. "But," the reader may say, "is not the taste of lemonade composed of that of lemon *plus* that of sugar?" No! I reply, this is taking the combining of objects for that of feelings. The physical lemonade contains both the lemon and the sugar, but its taste does not contain their tastes; for if there are any two things which are certainly *not* present in the taste of lemonade, those are the pure lemon-sour on the one hand and the pure sugar-sweet on the other. These tastes are absent utterly. A taste somewhat *like* both of them is there, but that is a distinct state of mind altogether.

* * *

The simplest thing, therefore, if we are to assume the existence of a stream of consciousness at all, would be to suppose that things that are known together are known in single pulses of that stream. The things may be many, and may occasion many currents in the brain. But the psychic phenomenon correlative to these many currents is one integral "state," transitive or substantive, to which the many things appear.

The Soul as a Combining Medium

The spiritualists in philosophy have been prompt to see that things which are known together are known by one *something,* but a simple and permanent spiritual being on which many ideas combine their effects. It makes no difference in this connection whether this being called Soul, Ego, or Spirit, in either case its chief function is that of a combining medium. This is a different vehicle of knowledge from that in which we just said that the mystery of knowing things together might be most simply lodged. Which is the real knower, this permanent being, or our passing state? If we had other grounds, not yet considered, for admitting the Soul into our psychology, then getting there on those grounds, she might turn out to be the knower too. But if there be not *other* grounds for admitting the Soul, we had better cling to our passing "states" as the exclusive agents of knowledge; for we have to

assume their existence anyhow in psychology, and the knowing of many things together is just as well accounted for when we call it one of their functions as when we call it a reaction of the Soul. *Explained* it is not by either conception, and has to figure in psychology as a datum that is ultimate.

But there are other alleged grounds for admitting the Soul into psychology, and the chief of them is

The Sense of Personal Identity

I have previously stated that the thoughts which we actually know to exist do not fly about loose, but seem each to belong to some one thinker and not to another. Each thought, out of a multitude of other thoughts of which it may think, is able to distinguish those which belong to it from those which do not. The former have a warmth and intimacy about them of which the latter are completely devoid, and the result is a Me of yesterday, judged to be in some peculiarly subtle sense the *same* with the I who now make the judgment. As a mere subjective phenomenon the judgment presents no special mystery. It belongs to the great class of judgments of sameness; and there is nothing more remarkable in making a judgment of sameness in the first person than in the second or the third. The intellectual operations seem essentially alike, whether I say "I am the same as I was," or whether I say "the pen is the same as it was, yesterday." It is as easy to think this as to think the opposite and say "neither of us is the same." The only question which we have to consider is whether it be a right judgment. *Is the sameness predicated really there?*

Sameness in the Self as Known

If the sentence "I am the same that I was yesterday," we take the "I" broadly, it is evident that in many ways I am *not* the same. As a concrete Me, I am somewhat different from what I was: then hungry, now full; then walking, now at rest; then poorer, now richer; then younger, now older; etc. And yet in other ways I *am* the same, and we may call these the essential ways. My name and profession and relations to the world are identical, my face, my faculties and store of memories, are practically indistinguishable, now and then. Moreover the Me of now and the Me of then are *continuous:* the alterations were gradual and never affected the whole of me at once. So far, then, my personal identity is just like the sameness predicated of any other aggregate thing. It is a conclusion grounded either on the resemblance in essential respects, or on the continuity of the phenomena compared. And it must not be taken to mean more than these grounds warrant, or treated as a sort of metaphysical or absolute Unity in which all differences are overwhelmed. The past and present selves compared are the same just so far as they *are* the same, and no farther. They are the same in *kind*. But this generic sameness coexists with generic differences just as real; and if from the one point of view I am one self, from another I am quite as truly many. Similarly of the attribute of continuity: it gives to the self the unity of mere connectedness, or unbrokenness, a perfectly definite phenomenal thing—but it gives not a jot or tittle more.

Sameness of the Self as Knower

But all this is said only of the Me, of Self as known. In the judgment "I am the same," etc., the "I" was taken broadly as the concrete person. Suppose, however, that we take it narrowly, as the *Thinker*, as *"that to which"* all the concrete determinations of the Me belong and are known: does there not then appear an absolute identity at different times? That something which at every moment goes out and knowingly appropriates the *Me* of the past, and discards the non-me as foreign, is it not a permanent abiding principle of spiritual activity identical with itself wherever found?

That it is such a principle is the reigning doctrine both of philosophy and common-sense, and yet reflection finds it difficult to justify the idea. *If there were no passing states of consciousness,* then indeed we might suppose an abiding principle, absolutely one with itself, to be the ceaseless thinker in each one of us. But if the states of consciousness be accorded as realities, no such "substantial" identity in the thinker need be supposed. Yesterday's and today's states of consciousnesses have no *substantial* identity, for when one is here the other is irrevocably dead and gone. But they have a functional identity for both know the same objects, and so far as the bygone me is one of those objects, they react upon it in an identical way, greeting it and calling it *mine,* and opposing it to all the other things they know. This functional identity seems really the only sort of identity in the thinker which the facts require us to suppose. Successive thinkers, numerically distinct, but

all aware of the same past in the same way, form an adequate vehicle for all the experience of personal unity and sameness which we actually have. And just such a train of successive thinkers is the stream of mental states (each with its complex object cognized and emotional and selective reaction thereupon) which psychology treated as a natural science has to assume.

The logical conclusion seems then to be that *the states of consciousness are all that psychology needs to do her work with. Metaphysics or theology may prove the Soul to exist; but for psychology the hypothesis of such a substantial principle of unity is superfluous.*

* * *

Mutations and Multiplications of the Self

The Me, like every other aggregate, changes as it grows. The passing states of consciousness, which should preserve in their succession an identical knowledge of its past, wander from their duty, letting large portions drop from out of their ken, and representing other portions wrong. The identity which we recognize as we survey the long procession can only be the relative identity of a slow shifting in which there is always some common ingredient retained. The commonest element of all, the most uniform, is the possession of some common memories. However different the man may be from the youth, both look back on the same childhood and call it their own.

Thus the identity found by the *I* in its *Me* is only a loosely construed thing, an identity "on the whole," just like that which any outside observer might find in the same assemblage of facts. We often say of a man "he is so changed one would not know him": and so does a man, less often, speak of himself. These changes in the *Me,* recognized by the I, or by outside observers, may be grave or slight.

* * *

Review and Psychological Conclusion

To sum up this long chapter: The consciousness of Self involves a stream of thought, each part of which as "I" can remember those which went before, know the things they knew, and care paramountly for certain ones among them as *"Me,"* and *appropriate to these* the rest. This Me is an empirical aggregate of things objectively known. The *I* which knows them cannot itself be an aggregate; neither for psychological purposes need it be an unchanging metaphysical entity like the Soul, or a principle like the transcendental Ego, viewed as "out of time." It is a *thought,* at each moment different from that of the last moment, but *appropriative* of the latter, together with all that the latter called its own. All the experiential facts find their place in this description, unencumbered with any hypothesis save that of the existence of passing thoughts or states of mind.

If passing thoughts be the directly verifiable existents which no school has hitherto doubted them to be, then they are the only "Knower" of which Psychology, treated as a natural science, need take any account. The only pathway that I can discover for bringing in a more transcendental Thinker would be to deny that we have any such *direct* knowledge of the existence of our "states of consciousness" as common-sense supposes us to possess. The existence of the "states" in question would then be a mere hypothesis, or one way of asserting that there *must be* a knower correlative to all this known; but the problem *who that knower is* would have become a metaphysical problem. With the question once stated in these terms, the notion either of a Spirit of the world which thinks through us, or that of a set of individual substantial souls, must be considered as *prima facie* on par with our own "psychological" solution, and discussed impartially. I myself believe that room for much future inquiry lies in this direction. The "states of mind" which every psychologist believes in are by no means clearly apprehensible, if distinguished from their objects. But to doubt them lies beyond the scope of our natural-science point of view. And in this book the provisional solution which we have reached must be the final word: the thoughts themselves are the thinkers.

Chapter 4 The Genesis of the Self

GEORGE HERBERT MEAD

The term "behavior" indicates the standpoint of what follows, that of a behavioristic psychology. There is an aspect of this psychology that calls for an emphasis which I think has not been sufficiently given it. It is not simply the objectivity of this psychology which has commended it. All recent psychology, insofar as it lays claim to a scientific approach, considers itself objective. But behavioristic psychology, coming in by the door of the study of animals lower than man, has perforce shifted its interest from psychical states to external conduct. Even when this conduct is followed into the central nervous system, it is not to find the correlate of the neurosis in a psychosis, but to complete the act, however distant this may be in space and time. This doctrine finds itself in sympathetic accord with recent realism and pragmatism, which places the so-called sensa and the significances of things in the object. While psychology has been turning to the act as a process, philosophic thought has been transferring contents that had been the subject-matter of earlier psychology from the field of states of consciousness to the objective world. Prebehavioristic psychology had a foot in two worlds. Its material was found in consciousness and in the world of physiology and physics. As long, however, as psychology was occupied with states of consciousness which constituted objects, there was an inevitable duplication. The whole physiological and physical apparatus could be stated in terms of states of consciousness, and solipsism hovered in the background. A psychology that is called upon to analyze the object into the states of consciousness which it is studying may conceivably be an empirical science, but insofar its world is not the world of the other sciences. A behavioristic psychol-

ogy, on the other hand, that is not responsible for the content of the object, becomes a science that is cognate with physiology and dynamics, and escapes the trail of the epistemological serpent.

I am not concerned with the philosophical justification of this attitude of behavioristic psychology; I merely wish to emphasize its inevitable tendency to deal with processes, that is, with acts, and to find its objects given in the world with which all science deals. From Descartes'[1] time on, it has been a border state, lying between philosophy and the natural sciences, and has suffered the inconveniences which attend buffer states. Descartes' unambiguous and uncompromising division between an extended physical world, and an unextended world of thought, when it reached the pineal gland found itself in ambiguous territory, and only avoided compromise by leaving the relations of mind and body to the infinite power of his *deus ex machina*. The difficulties which have attended psychology's regulation of these relations have been only in part metaphysical. More fundamentally they have been logical. The natural sciences start pragmatically with a world that is there, within which a problem has arisen, and introduce hypothetical reconstructions only insofar as its solution demands them. They always have their feet upon the solid ground of unquestioned objects of observation and experiment, where Samuel Johnson placed his in his summary refutation of Berkeley's idealism.[2] Speculative philosophy, beset with the problem of epistemology, found its problem in the nature and very existence of the world inside which the problems of the natural sciences appeared, and which furnished the test of its hypotheses. Thus psychology as

SOURCE. George Herbert Mead, "The Genesis of the Self and Social Control," from *International Journal of Ethics*, (XXXV, April 1925, No. 3), pp. 251–273. Reprinted by permission of The University of Chicago Press. Copyright 1925 by The University of Chicago Press.

[1] René Descartes (1596–1650), French philosopher and scientist. His works, including the *Discourse on Method* (1637) and the *Meditations* (1641), have earned for him the title "father of modern philosophy."
[2] Samuel Johnson (1709–1784), English author. He "refuted" Berkeley's subjective idealism by kicking a stone.

a philosophic discipline carried the epistemological problem into the experience of the individual, but as a science located the problem in a given world which its epistemological problem could not accept as given. Between the two, its sympathies have always been with the presuppositions and method of the natural sciences. On the one hand, as empirical science it has sought to regard the so-called consciousness of the individual as merely given in the sense of the objects of the natural sciences, but as states of consciousness were still regarded as cognitive, they had inevitably inherited the epistemological diathesis. On the other hand, as experimental science it was forced to place states of consciousness within or without the processes it was studying. Placing them in interactionism within the natural processes ran counter to the presuppositions of its scientific procedure, so that the prevailing attitude has been that of epiphenomenalism, an adaptation of Leibnitz' preestablished harmony and Spinoza's parallel attributes. They ran as harmless conscious shadows beside the physical and physiological processes with which science could come to immediate terms. But this proved but an unstable compromise. The conscious streak that accompanied the neuroses could answer only to sensing and thinking as processes; as qualities and significance of things, states of consciousness became hardly tolerable reduplications of things, except in the case of secondary qualities. The molecular structure of things seemed to remove these from the hypothetical objects of physical science, and consciousness proved a welcome dumping ground for them. This bifurcation of nature proves equally unsatisfactory. The horns and the hoofs go with the hide. States of contact experience have no better right to objective existence than those of distance experience. Psychology, however, has not been interested in these epistemological and metaphysical riddles, it has been simply irritated by them. It has shifted its interest to the processes, where phenomenalism is most harmless, appearing as physiological psychology, as functional psychology, as dynamic psychology, and has ignored the problems for which it had no care. The effect of this has been to give the central nervous system a logical preeminence in the procedure and textbooks of psychology which is utterly unwarranted in the analysis of the experience of the individual. The central nervous system has been unwittingly assimilated to the logical position of consciousness. It occupies only an important stage in the act, but we find ourselves locating the whole environment of the individual in its convolutions. It is small wonder, then, that behaviorism has been welcomed with unmistakable relief, for it has studied the conduct of animals in necessary ignoration of consciousness, and it has been occupied with the act as a whole, not as a nervous arc.

But the relief with which one turns to conduct and away from states of consciousness has not disposed of the problems involved in the ambiguous term "consciousness," even for the psychologist. Bergson's theory of perception[3] was at least a step toward the clarification of this ambiguity. It recognizes that insofar as the content of the percept can be termed consciousness, it indicates a diminution of the reality of the object rather than an addition, and this diminution answers to the active interests of the organism, which are represented in the central nervous system by paths of possible response. These coordinated paths in some sense cut out the object of perception. The percept is relative to the perceiving individual, but relative to his active interest, not relative in the sense that its content is a state of his consciousness. It is at least meaningless to lodge the so-called sensuous characters of things in the cortex. When, however, Bergson suggests that certain of these qualities may be the condensation of vibrations, we seem again to be in the presence of qualities that are states of consciousness. Presumably the condensations, e.g., the actual quality of color, do not exist in the object, but in the condensing mind. However, Bergson's statement at least placed the central nervous system in the world of things, of percepts, on the one hand, and on the other placed the characters of things in pure perception in the things themselves; but the divorce of duration, as psychical, from a static intellectualized spatial world left a dichotomy which was functional only from the standpoint of a Bergsonian metaphysics. Neo-realism undertook to return all the qualities of things to the things, over against a mind which was simply aware of the sensa. This simple, radical procedure left problems of a perception which was still cognitive in its nature, which a Critical Realism

---

[3] Henri Bergson, *Matter and Memory,* translated by N. M. Paul and W. S. Palmer (London and New York: George Allen & Co., Ltd., and The Macmillan Company, 1911), especially pp. 22–35.

sought to solve by retreating to representative perception again. It remained for pragmatism to take the still more radical position that in immediate experience the percept stands over against the individual, not in a relation of awareness, but simply in that of conduct. Cognition is a process of finding out something that is problematical, not of entering into relation with a world that is there.

There is an ambiguity in the word "consciousness." We use it in the sense of "awareness," "consciousness of," and are apt to assume that in this sense it is coextensive with experience, that it covers the relation of the sentient organism to its environment insofar as the environment exists for the organism. We thus predicate of this existence of the environment for the organism the attitude of cognition on the part of the organism. The other use of consciousness to which I refer is in the sense of certain contents, to wit, the sense qualities of things, more epecially the so-called secondary qualities, the affections of the body of the sentient organism, especially those that are pleasurable and painful, the contents of the images of memory and imagination, and of the activities of the organism, so far as they appear in its experience. There is another field, that of self-consciousness, to which I am not as yet referring. There is a common character which in varying degree belongs to all of these contents, that is, that these contents could not appear at all, or exactly as they do appear, in the experience of any other organism. They are in this sense private, though this privacy does not imply necessarily anything more than difference of access or of perspective on the part of the different organisms. If we take the pragmatic attitude, referred to above, consciousness in the first sense, that of awareness, would disappear from immediate experience, while the world that is there for the organism would still be there. A particular organism would become conscious from this standpoint, that is, there would be a world that would exist for the organism, when the organism marked or plotted or, to use Bergson's term, canalized its environment in terms of its future conduct. For Bergson, a percept is an object of possible action for an organism, and it is the active relationship of the organism to the distant object that constitutes it an object. Bergson meets the difficulty that the organism can exercise no physical influence upon the distant object by his assumption that consciousness in this sense is in

reality not an addition to the object, but an abstraction from all in the relation of the organism to the object which does not bear upon this action. There arises, then, a selected series of objects, determined by the active interests of the organism.

An environment thus arises for an organism through the selective power of an attention that is determined by its impulses that are seeking expression. This peculiar environment does not exist in the consciousness of the form as a separate milieu, but the consciousness of the organism consists in the fact that its future conduct outlines and defines its objects. Insofar as the organization of one individual differs from that of others, it will have a private environment, though these differences may be called those of standpoint. They are objective differences. They exist in nature. The most fundamental phase of these differences is found in the determination of what the relativist calls a "consentient set," i.e., the selection of those objects which may all be considered as "here" with reference to the individual. It is this set, which is co-gredient with the individual, that constitutes an environment within which motion may take place. These perspectives of nature exist in nature, not in the consciousness of the organism as a stuff. In this relation of a peculiar environment for an individual, there is no implication of an awareness. All that is implied is that the ongoing activity of the individual form marks and defines is world for the form, which thus exists for it as it does not for any other form. If this is called consciousness, a behavioristic psychology can state it in terms of conduct.

Consciousness in the second sense, that of a peculiar content or contents, implies relativity in another sense, in the sense of emergence, as this has been defined by Alexander, in *Space Time and the Deity*,[4] and accepted by Lloyd Morgan, in *Emergent Evolution*.[5] In evolution not only have new forms appeared, but new qualities or contents in experience. It is the sensitivities of forms that are the occasions for the appearance, in the worlds of these forms, of new characters of things, answering to all the senses, and new meanings answering to their new capacities for conduct. And these

 4 Samuel Alexander, *Space, Time, and Deity* (London: Macmillan and Co., 1920), II, p. 14.
5 C. Lloyd Morgan, *Emergent Evolution* (New York: H. Holt, 1923), p. 9.

new characters and new meanings exist in nature as do the forms of physical objects, though they are relative to the sensitivities and capacities of the individual forms.

* * *

If my friend enters the room, and I catch a glimpse of his face, the imagery of his face fills out the countenance, and I see him with his whole complement of features. The same imagery might have figured in my memory of last meeting him. Or it might have figured in the plan I entertained of calling, on the following evening. It belongs either to the passing present, or to the irrevocable past, or to the contingent future. This imagery is for the percipient as objective as the so-called sense object. It may enter that object and be indistinguishable from it. Where it can be distinguished, however, it is recognized as having this private character; that is, while we assume that the color of the object perceived, even if it vary from eye to eye, is in some respects identical for all eyes insofar as the organs are alike, it is not assumed that the image which one has is there for other eyes, or imaginations. While this sole accessibility of imagery to the individual does not in itself render it less objective, it places it at the disposal of the individual, when he attains to a mind which it can furnish. The same is true of the other class of objects which in his experience is accessible only to him. I refer to the objects which the individual possesses from the inside, so to speak, the parts of his organism, especially as they are painful or pleasurable. In the so-called lower animals, there is no evidence that this private field is organized and used as the possession of a self. The passing present is neither extended into a memory series, nor into an anticipated future.

Imagery is but one phase of the presence of the past in the passing present. In the living form it appears as facility in the response, and in the selection of the stimulus, in selective discrimination, in the stimulus. Imagery emerges, in the sense of Alexander, as the content of the past in the stimulus, and as meaning in the response. Imagery and meaning are there in the objects as contents, before they become material for the mind, before the mind appears in conduct.

I have referred to the doctrine of relativity. More specifically, my reference was to formulation of the doctrine given in Professor Whitehead's three books, *The Principles of Natural Knowledge* (1919), *the Concept of Nature* (1920), and *The Principle of Relativity* (1922). What I have had particularly in mind is Whitehead's recognition, as over against current Einsteinian doctrine, that if motion is to be accepted as an objective fact, we must also accept the existence in nature of so-called consentient sets at rest, determined by their relation to so-called percipient events. The same events in nature appear in different consentient sets, as these events are ordered in different time systems, and this ordering in different time systems is dependent upon their relations to different percipient events. Motion in nature implies rest in nature. Rest in nature implies co-gredience, i.e., a persistent relation of here and there with reference to some individual, and it is this that determines the time system in accordance with which events are ordered. If rest is a fact in nature, we must conceive of it as stratified, to use Whitehead's term, by the different temporal perspectives of different individuals, though a group of individuals may have the same perspective; we must, however, remember that this is a stratification of nature not in a static space, but a nature whose extension is affected with a time dimension.

It is this conception of the existence in nature of consentient sets determined by their relations to percipient events that I wish to generalize so that it will cover the environment in relation to the living form, and the experienced world with reference to the experiencing individual. This is evidently only possible if we conceive life as a process and not a series of static physicochemical situations, and if we regard experience as conduct or behavior, not as a series of conscious states. This I take to be the essence of Bergson's philosophy of change, in accordance with which our perceptual world is determined by the actions that are taking place. Conduct does cut out and fashion the objects upon which action is directed. It is only with reference to life as an ongoing process that the animal determines his habitat. The most convincing illustration can be found in the different presentation of the life of a community, in terms of a social statics, the statistical data of population and occupations and the like, or in terms of the actual lives of the different individuals who make up the community. In the latter case we realize that each individual has a world that differs in some degree from that of any other member of the same community, that he slices the events of the community life that are common to all from a different angle from that of any other individual. In Whitehead's phrase, each individual stratifies the common life in a different manner, and the life of the community is the sum of all these stratifications, and all of these stratifications exist in nature. It is this recognition that takes psychology out of its isolation, as a science that deals with what is found in the mind of an individual, and makes of it the standpoint from which to approach reality as it is going on.

It is evident that a statement of the life of each individual in terms of the results of an analysis of that which is immediately experienced would offer a common plane of events, in which the experience of each would differ from the experiences of others only in their extent, and the completeness or incompleteness of their connections. These differences disappear in the generalized formulations of the social sciences. The experiences of the same individuals, insofar as each faces a world in which objects are plans of action, would implicate in each a different succession of events. In the simplest illustration, two persons approach a passing automobile. To one it is a moving object that he will pass before it reaches the portion of the street that is the meeting place of their two paths. The other sees an object that will pass this meeting point before he reaches it. Each slices the world from the standpoint of a different time system. Objects which in a thousand ways are identical for the two individuals, are yet fundamentally different through their location in one spatiotemporal plane, involving a certain succession of events, or in another. Eliminate the temporal dimension, and bring all events back to an instant that is timeless, and the individuality of these objects which belongs to them in behavior is lost, except insofar as they can represent the results of past conduct. But taking time seriously, we realize that the seemingly timeless character of our spatial world and its permanent objects is due to the consentient set which each one of us selects. We abstract time from this space for the purposes of our conduct. Certain objects cease to be events, cease to pass as they are in reality passing and in their permanence become the conditions of our action, and events take place with reference to them. Because a whole community selects the same consentient set does not make the selection less the attitude of each

one of them. The life-process takes place in individual organisms, so that the psychology which studies that process in its creative determining function becomes a science of the objective world.

Looked at from the standpoint of an evolutionary history, not only have new forms with their different spatiotemporal environments and their objects arisen, but new characters have arisen answering to the sensitivities and capacities for response. In the terms of Alexander, they have become differently qualitied. It is as impossible to transfer these characters of the habitats to the conciousness of the forms as it is to transfer the spatiotemporal structure of the things to such a so-called consciousness. If we introduce a fictitious instantaneousness into a passing universe, things fall to pieces. Things that are spatiotemporally distant from us can be brought into this instant only in terms of our immediate contact experience. They are what they would be if we were there and had our hands upon them. They take on the character of tangible matter. This is the price of their being located at the moment of our bodies' existence. But this instantaneous view has the great advantage of giving to us a picture of what the contact experience will be when we reach the distant object, and of determining conditions under which the distance characters arise. If the world existed at an instant in experience, we should be forced to find some realm such as consciousness into which to transport the distance or so-called secondary qualities of things. If consciousness in evolutionary history, then, has an unambiguous significance, it refers to that stage in the development of life in which the conduct of the individual marks out and defines the future field and objects which make up its environment, and in which emerge characters in the objects and sensitivities in the individuals that answer to each other. There is a relativity of the living individual and its environment, both as to form and content.

What I wish to trace is the fashion in which [the] self and the mind [have] arisen within this conduct.

It is the implication of this undertaking that only selves have minds, that is, that cognition only belongs to selves, even in the simplest expression of awareness. This, of course, does not imply that below the stage of self-consciousness sense characters and sensitivity do not exist. This obtains in our own immediate experience insofar as we are not self-conscious.

It is further implied that this development has taken place only in a social group, for selves exist only in relation to other selves, as the organism as a physical object exists only in its relation to other physical objects. There have been two fields within which social groups have arisen which have determined their environment together with that of their members, and the individuality of its members. These lie in the realm of the invertebrates and in that of the vertebrates. Among the Hymenoptera and termites there are societies whose interests determine for the individuals their stimuli and habitats, and so differentiate the individuals themselves, mainly through the sexual and alimentary processes, that the individual is what he is because of his membership within those societies. In the complex life of the group, the acts of the individuals are completed only through the acts of other individuals, but the mediation of this complex conduct is found in the physiological differentiation of the different members of the society. As Bergson has remarked of the instincts, the implements by which a complex act is carried out are found in the differentiated structure of the form. There is no convincing evidence that an ant or a bee is obliged to anticipate the act of another ant or bee, by tending to respond in the fashion of the other, in order that it may integrate its activity into the common act. And by the same mark there is no evidence of the existence of any language in their societies. Nor do we need to go to the invertebrates to discover this type of social conduct. If one picks up a little child who has fallen, he adapts his arms and attitude to the attitude of the child, and the child adapts himself to the attitude of the other; or in boxing or fencing one responds to stimulus of the other, by acquired physiological adjustment.

* * *

A social act may be defined as one in which the occasion or stimulus which sets free an impulse is found in the character or conduct of a living form that belongs to the proper environment of the living form whose impulse it is. I wish, however, to restrict the social act to the class of acts which involve the cooperation of more than one individual, and whose object as defined by the act, in the sense of Bergson, is a social object. I mean by a social object one that answers to all the parts of the complex act, though these parts are found in the conduct of different individuals. The objective of the act is then found in the life-process of the group, not in those of the separate individuals alone. . . . If the social object is to appear in his experience, it must be that the stimuli which set free the responses of the others involved in the act should be present in his experience, not as stimuli to his response, but as stimuli for the responses of others; and this implies that the social situation which arises after the completion of one phase of the act, which serves as the stimulus for the next participant in the complex procedure, shall in some sense be in the experience of the first actor, tending to call out, not his own response, but that of the succeeding actor. . . .

. . . If the objects that answer to the complex social act can exist spatiotemporally in the experience of the different members of the society, as stimuli that set free not only their own responses, but also as stimuli to the reponses of those who share in the composite act, a principle of coordination might be found which would not depend upon physiological differentiation. And one necessary psychological condition for this would be that the individual should have in some fashion present in his organism the tendencies to respond as the other participants in the act will respond. Much more than this would be involved, but this at least would be a necessary precondition. A social object answering to the responses of different individuals in a society could be conceived of as existing in the experiences of individuals in that society, if the different responses of these individuals in the complex acts could be found in sufficient degree in the natures of separate individuals to render them sensitive to the different values of the object answering to the parts of the act.

The cortex of the vertebrate central nervous system provides at least a part of the mechanism which might make this possible. . . .

But the cortex is not simply a mechanism. It is an organ that exists in fulfilling its function. If these tendencies to action which do not get immediate expression appear and persist, it is because they belong to the act that is going on. If, for example, property is a social object in the experience of men, as distinguished from the nut which the squirrel stores, it is because features of the food that one buys innervate the whole complex of responses by which property is not only acquired, but respected and protected, and this complex so innervated is an essential part of the act by which the man buys and stores his food. The point is not that buying food is a more complicated affair than picking it up from the ground, but that exchange is an act in which a man excites himself to give by making an offer. An offer is what it is because the presentation is a stimulus to give. One cannot exchange otherwise than by putting one's self in the attitude of the other party to the bargain. Property becomes a tangible object, because all essential phases of property appear in the actions of all those involved in exchange, and appear as essential features of the individual's action.

The individual in such an act is a self. If the cortex has become an organ of social conduct, and has made possible the appearance of social objects, it is because the individual has become a self, that is, an individual who organizes his own response by the tendencies on the part of others to respond to his act. He can do this because the mechanism of the vertebrate brain enables the individual to take these different attitudes in the formation of the act. But selves have appeared late in vertebrate evolution. The structure of the central nervous system is too minute to enable us to show the corresponding structural changes in the paths of the brain. It is only in the behavior of the human animal that we can trace this evolution. It has been customary to mark this stage in development by endowing man with a mind, or at least with a certain sort of mind. As long as conciousness is regarded as a sort of spiritual stuff out of which are fashioned sensations and affections and images and ideas or significances, a mind as a locus of these entities is an almost necessary assumption, but when these contents have been returned to things, the necessity of quarters for this furniture has disappeared also.

It lies beyond the bounds of this paper to follow out the implications of this shift for logic and epistemology, but there is one phase of all so-called mental processes which is central to this discussion, and that is self-consciousness. If the suggestions which I have made above should prove tenable, the self that is central to all so-called mental experience has appeared only in the social conduct of human vertebrates. It is just because the individual finds himself taking the attitudes of the others who are involved in his conduct that he becomes an object for himself. It is only by taking the roles of others that we have been able to come back to ourselves. We have seen above that the social object can exist for the individual only if the various parts of the whole social act carried out by other members of the society are in some fashion present in the conduct of the individual. It is further true that the self can exist for the individual only if he assumes the roles of the others. The presence in the conduct of the individual of the tendencies to act as others act may be, then, responsible for the appearance in the experience of the individual of a social object, i.e., an object answering to complex reactions of a number of individuals, and also for the appearance of the self. Indeed, these two appearances are correlative. Property can appear as an object only insofar as the individual stimulates himself to buy by a prospective offer to sell. Buying and selling are involved in each other. Something that can be exchanged can exist in the experience of the individual only insofar as he has in his own makeup the tendency to sell when he has also the tendency to buy. And he becomes a self in his experience only insofar as one attitude on his own part calls out the corresponding attitude in the social undertaking.

This is just what we imply in "self-consciousness." We appear as selves in our conduct insofar as we ourselves take the attitude that others take toward us, in these correlative activities. Perhaps as good an illustration of this as can be found is in a "right." Over against the protection of our lives or property, we assume the attitude of assent of all members in the community. We take the role of what may be called the "generalized other." And in doing this we appear as social objects, as selves. It is interesting to note that in the development of the individual child, there are two stages which present the two essential steps in attaining self-consciousness. The first stage is that of play, and the second that of the game, where these two are distinguished from each other. In play in this sense, the child is continually acting as a parent, a teacher, a preacher, a grocery man, a policeman, a pirate, or an Indian. It is the period of childish existence which Wordsworth has described as that of "endless imitation."[6] It is

---

[6] William Wordsworth (1770–1850), English poet. On Mead's point, see Wordsworth's "Ode: Intimations of Immortality" (1807).

the period of Froebel's kindergarten plays. In it, as Froebel recognized, the child is acquiring the roles of those who belong to his society.[7] This takes place because the child is continually exciting in himself the responses to his own social acts. In his infant dependence upon the responses of others to his own social stimuli, he is peculiarly sensitive to this relation. Having in his own nature the beginning of the parental response, he calls it out by his own appeals. The doll is the universal type of this, but before he plays with a doll, he responds in tone of voice and in attitude as his parents respond to his own cries and chortles. This has been denominated imitation, but the psychologist now recognizes that one imitates only insofar as the so-called imitated act can be called out in the individual by his appropriate stimulation. That is, one calls or tends to call out in himself the same response that he calls out in the other.

The play antedates the game. For in a game there is a regulated procedure, and rules. The child must not only take the role of the other, as he does in the play, but he must assume the various roles of all the participants in the game, and govern his action accordingly. If he plays first base, it is as the one to whom the ball will be thrown from the field or from the catcher. Their organized reactions to him he has embedded in his own playing of the different positions, and this organized reaction becomes what I have called the "generalized other" that accompanies and controls his conduct. And it is this generalized other in his experience which provides him with a self. I can only refer to the bearing of this childish play attitude upon so-called sympathetic magic. Primitive men call out in their own activity some simulacrum of the response which they are seeking from the world about. They are children crying in the night.

The mechanism of this implies that the individual who is stimulating others to response is at the same time arousing in himself the tendencies to the same reactions. Now, that in a complex social act which serves as the stimulus to another individual to his response is not as a rule fitted to call out the tendency to the same response in the individual himself. The hostile demeanor of one animal does not

frighten the animal himself, presumably. Especially in the complex social reactions of the ants or termites or the bees, the part of the act of one form which does call out the appropriate reaction of another can hardly be conceived of as arousing a like reaction in the form in question, for here the complex social act is dependent upon physiological differentiation, such an unlikeness in structure exists that the same stimulus could not call out like responses. For such a mechanism as has been suggested, it is necessary to find first of all some stimulus in the social conduct of the members of an authentic group that can call out in the individual, that is responsible for it, the same response that it calls out in the other; and in the second place, the individuals in the group must be of such like structure that the stimulus will have the same value for one form that it has for the other. Such a type of social stimulus is found in the vocal gesture in a human society. The term "gesture" I am using to refer to that part of the act or attitude of one individual engaged in a social act which serves as the stimulus to another individual to carry out his part of the whole act. Illustrations of gestures, so defined, may be found in the attitudes and movements of others to which we respond in passing them in a crowd, in the turning of the head toward the glance of another's eye, in the hostile attitude assumed over against a threatening gesture, in the thousand and one different attitudes which we assume toward different modulations of the human voice, or in the attitudes and suggestions of movements in boxers or fencers, to which responses are so nicely adjusted. It is to be noted that the attitudes to which I have referred are but stages in the act as they appear to others, and include expressions of countenance, positions of the body, changes in breathing rhythm, outward evidence of circulatory changes, and vocal sounds. In general these so-called gestures belong to the beginning of the overt act, for the adjustments of others to the social process are best made early in the act. Gestures are, then, the early stages in the overt social act to which other forms involved in the same act respond. Our interest is in finding gestures which can affect the individual that is responsible for them in the same manner as that in which they affect other individuals. The vocal gesture is at least one that assails our ears who make it in the same physiological fashion as that in which it affects others. We hear our own vocal gestures as others hear them. We may see or feel move-

_____

[7] F. W. A. Froebel (1782–1852), German educator who instituted the kindergarten system. His *Mutter—und Rose—Lidder* (1844) was translated by Susan Bow as *Mother Play* (1895).

ments of our hands as others see or feel them, and these sights and feels have served in the place of the vocal gestures in the case of those who are congenitally deaf or deaf and blind. But it has been the vocal gesture that has preeminently provided the medium of social organization in human society. It belongs historically to the beginning of the act, for it arises out of the change in breathing rhythm that accompanies the preparation for sudden action, those actions to which other forms must be nicely adjusted.

If, then, a vocal gesture arouses in the individual who makes it a tendency to the same response that it arouses in another, and this beginning of an act of the other in himself enters into his experience, he will find himself tending to act toward himself as the other acts toward him. In our self-conscious experience we understand what he does or says. The possibility of this entering into his experience we have found in the cortex of the human brain. There the coordinations answering to an indefinite number of acts may be excited, and while holding each other in check enter into the neural process of adjustment which leads to the final overt conduct. If one pronounces and hears himself pronounce the word "table," he has aroused in himself the organized attitudes of his response to that object, in the same fashion as that in which he has aroused it in another. We commonly call such an aroused organized attitude an idea, and the ideas of what we are saying accompany all of our significant speech. If we may trust to the statement on one of St. Paul's epistles, some of the saints spoke with tongues which had no significance to them. They made sounds which called out no response in those that made them. The sounds were without meaning. Where a vocal gesture uttered by one individual leads to a certain response in another, we may call it a symbol of that act; where it arouses in the man who makes it the tendency to the same response, we may call it a significant symbol. These organized attitudes which we arouse in ourselves when we talk to others are, then, the ideas which we say are in our minds, and insofar as they arouse the same attitudes in others, they are in their minds, insofar as they are self-conscious in the sense in which I have used that term. But it is not necessary that we should talk to another to have these ideas. We can talk to ourselves, and this we do in the inner forum of what we call thought. We are in possession of selves just insofar as we can and do take the attitudes of others toward ourselves and respond to those attitudes. We approve of ourselves and condemn ourselves. We pat ourselves upon the back and in blind fury attack ourselves. We assume the generalized attitude of the group, in the censor that stands at the door of our imagery and inner conversations, and in the affirmation of the laws and axioms of the universe of discourse. *Quod semper, quod ubique.*[8] Our thinking is an inner conversation in which we may be taking the roles of specific acquaintances over against ourselves, but usually it is with what I have termed the "generalized other" that we converse, and so attain to the levels of abstract thinking, and that impersonality, that so-called objectivity that we cherish. In this fashion, I conceive, have selves arisen in human behavior and with the selves their minds.

---

8 "What always, what everywhere (has been believed)."

Chapter 5 On Multiple Realities

ALFRED SCHUTZ

I. THE REALITY OF THE WORLD OF DAILY LIFE

1. The Natural Attitude of Daily Life and its Pragmatic Motive

We begin with an analysis of the world of daily life which the wide-awake, grown-up man who acts in it and upon it amidst his fellow-men experiences within the natural attitude as a reality.

"World of daily life" shall mean the intersubjective world which existed long before our birth, experienced and interpreted by Others, our predecessors, as an organized world. Now it is given to our experience and interpretation. All interpretation of this world is based upon a stock of previous experiences of it, our own experiences and those handed down to us by our parents and teachers, which in the form of "knowledge at hand" function as a scheme of reference.

To this stock of experiences at hand belongs our knowledge that the world we live in is a world of well circumscribed objects with definite qualities, objects among which we move, which resist us and upon which we may act. To the natural attitude the world is not and never has been a mere aggregate of colored spots, incoherent noises, centers of warmth and cold. Philosophical or psychological analysis of the constitution of our experiences may afterwards, retrospectively, describe how elements of this world affect our senses, how we passively perceive them in an indistinct and confused way, how by active apperception our mind singles out certain features from the perceptual field, conceiving them as well delineated things which stand out over against a more or less unarticulated background or horizon. The natural attitude does not know these problems. To it the world is from the outset not the private world of the single individual but an intersubjective world, common to all of us, in which we have not a theoretical but an eminently practical interest. The world of everyday life is the scene and also the object of our actions and interactions. We have to dominate it and we have to change it in order to realize the purposes which we pursue within it among our fellow-men. We work and operate not only within but upon the world. Our bodily movements—kinaesthetic, locomotive, operative—gear, so to speak, into the world, modifying or changing its objects and their mutual relationships. On the other hand, these objects offer resistance to our acts which we have either to overcome or to which we have to yield. Thus, it may be correctly said that a pragmatic motive governs our natural attitude toward the world of daily life. World, in this sense, is something that we have to modify by our actions or that modifies our actions.

2. The Manifestations of Man's Spontaneous Life in the Outer World and Some of its Forms

But what has to be understood under the term "action" just used? How does man with the natural attitude experience his own "actions" within and upon the world? Obviously, "actions" are manifestations of man's spontaneous life. But neither does he experience all such manifestations as actions nor does he experience all of his actions as bringing about changes in the outer world. Unfortunately the different forms of all these experiences are not clearly distinguished in present philosophical thought and, therefore, no generally accepted terminology exists.

In vain would we look for help to modern behaviorism and its distinction between overt and covert behavior, to which categories a third, that of subovert behavior, has sometimes been added in order to characterize the manifestation of spontaneity in acts of speech. It is not our aim here to criticize the basic fallacy of the behavioristic point of view or to discuss the in-

SOURCE. Alfred Schutz, "On Multiple Realities," from *Philosophy and Phenomenological Research*, 5 (June 1945), pp. 533-551. Copyright 1945. Reprinted by permission of *Philosophy and Phenomenological Research*.

adequacy and inconsistency of the trichotomy just mentioned. For our purpose it suffices to show that the behavioristic interpretation of spontaneity can contribute nothing to the question we are concerned with, namely, how the different forms of spontaneity are experienced by the mind in which they originate. At its best, behaviorism is a scheme of reference useful to the observer of other people's behavior. He, and only he, might be interested in considering the activities of men or animals under a relational scheme of reference such as stimulus-response, or organism-environment, and only from his point of view are these categories accessible at all. Our problem, however, is not what occurs to man as a psychophysiological unit, but the attitude he adopts toward these occurrences—briefly, the subjective meaning man bestows upon certain experiences of his own spontaneous life. What appears to the observer to be objectively the same behavior may have for the behaving subject very different meanings or no meaning at all.

Meaning, as has been shown elsewhere,[1] is not a quality inherent in certain experiences emerging within our stream of consciousness but the result of an interpretation of a past experience looked at from the present Now with a reflective attitude. As long as I live *in* my acts, directed toward the objects of these acts, the acts do not have any meaning. They become meaningful if I grasp them as well-circumscribed experiences of the past and, therefore, in retrospection. Only experiences which can be recollected beyond their actuality and which can be questioned about their constitution are, therefore, subjectively meaningful.

But if this characterization of meaning has been accepted, are there any experiences at all of my spontaneous life which are subjectively not meaningful? We think the answer is in the affirmative. There are the mere physiological reflexes, such as the knee jerk, the contraction of the pupil, blinking, blushing; moreover certain passive reactions provoked by what Leibniz calls the surf of indiscernible and confused small perceptions; furthermore, my gait, my facial expression, my mood, those manifestations of my spontaneous life which result in certain characteristics of my handwriting open to graphological interpretation, etc. All these forms of involuntary spontaneity are experi-

enced while they occur, but without leaving any trace in memory; as experiences they are, to borrow again a term from Leibniz, most suitable for this peculiar problem, perceived but not apperceived. Unstable and undetachable from surrounding experiences as they are, they can neither be delineated nor recollected. They belong to the category of *essentially actual experiences,* that is, they exist merely in the actuality of being experienced and cannot be grasped by a reflective attitude.[2]

Subjectively meaningful experiences emanating from our spontaneous life shall be called *conduct.* (We avoid the term "behavior" because it includes in present use also subjectively non-meaningful manifestations of spontaneity such as reflexes.) The term "conduct"—as used here—refers to all kinds of subjectively meaningful experiences of spontaneity, be they those of inner life or those gearing into the outer world. If it is permitted to use objective terms in a description of subjective experiences—and after the preceding clarification the danger of misunderstanding no longer exists—we may say that conduct can be overt or covert. The former shall be called *mere doing,* the latter *mere thinking.* However, the term "conduct" as used here does not imply any reference to intent. All kinds of so-called automatic activities of inner or outer life—habitual, traditional, affectual ones—fall under this class, called by Leibniz the "class of empirical behavior."

Conduct which is devised in advance, that is, which is based upon a preconceived project, shall be called *action,* regardless of whether it is overt or covert. As to the latter, it has to be distinguished whether or not there supervenes on the project an intention to realize it—to carry it through, to bring about the projected state of affairs. Such an intention transforms the mere forethought into an aim and the project into a purpose. If an intention to realization is lacking, the projected covert action remains a phantasm, such as a day-dream; if it subsists, we may speak of a purposive action or a *performance.* An example of a covert

[1] A. Schutz, *Der sinnhafte Aufbau der sozialen Welt,* 2nd ed., Vienna, 1960, pp. 29–43, 72–93.

[2] As to the "reflective attitude" cf. Marvin Farber, *The Foundation of Phenomenology* (Cambridge, 1943), pp. 523ff.; also pp. 378ff.; cf. furthermore Dorion Cairns: "An Approach to Phenomenology," in *Philosophical Essays in Memory of Edmund Husserl,* ed. by M. Farber (Cambridge, 1940); p. 8f. The concept of "essentially actual experiences," however, cannot be found in Husserl's writings. Husserl's view was that, as a matter of principle, every act can be grasped in reflection.

action which is a performance is the process of projected thinking such as the attempt to solve a scientific problem mentally.

As to the so-called overt actions, that is, actions which gear into the outer world by bodily movements, the distinction between actions without and those with an intention to realization is not necessary. Any overt action is a performance within the meaning of our definition. In order to distinguish the (covert) performances of mere thinking from those (overt) requiring bodily movements we shall call the latter *working*.

Working, then, is action in the outer world, based upon a project and characterized by the intention to bring about the projected state of affairs by bodily movements. Among all the described forms of spontaneity that of working is the most important one for the constitution of the reality of the world of daily life. As will be shown very soon, the wide-awake self integrates in its working and by its working its present, past, and future into a specific dimension of time; it realizes itself as a totality in its working acts; it communicates with Others through working acts; it organizes the different spatial perspectives of the world of daily life through working acts. But before we can turn to these problems we have to explain what the term "wide-awake self," just used, means.

3. The Tensions of Consciousness and the Attention to Life

One of the central points of Bergson's philosophy is his theory that our conscious life shows an indefinite number of different planes, ranging from the plane of action on one extreme to the plane of dream at the other. Each of these planes is characterized by a specific tension of consciousness, the plane of action showing the highest, that of dream the lowest degree of tension. According to Bergson, these different degrees of tension of our consciousness are functions of our varying interest in life, action representing our highest interest in meeting reality and its requirements, dream being complete lack of interest. *Attention à la vie*, attention to life, is, therefore, the basic regulative principle of our conscious life. It defines the realm of our world which is relevant to us; it articulates our continuously flowing stream of thought; it determines the span and function of our memory; it makes us—in our language—either live within our present experiences, directed toward their

objects, or turn back in a reflective attitude to our past experiences and ask for their meaning.[3]

By the term *"wide-awakeness"* we want to denote a plane of consciousness of highest tension originating in an attitude of full attention to life and its requirements. Only the performing and especially the working self is fully interested in life and, hence, wide-awake. It lives within its acts and its attention is exclusively directed to carrying its project into effect, to executing its plan. This attention is an active, not a passive one. Passive attention is the opposite to full awakeness. In passive attention I experience, for instance, the surf of indiscernible small perceptions which are, as stated before, essentially actual experiences and not meaningful manifestations of spontaneity. Meaningful spontaneity may be defined with Leibniz as the effort to arrive at other and always other perceptions. In its lowest form it leads to the delimitation of certain perceptions transforming them into apperception; in its highest form it leads to the performance of working which gears into the outer world and modifies it.

The concept of wide-awakeness reveals the starting point for a legitimate[4] pragmatic inter-

---

[3] The presentation given above does not strictly follow Bergson's terminology but it is hoped that it renders adequately his important thought. Here is a selection of some passages of Bergson's writings significant for our problem: *Essai sur les données immédiates de la conscience* (Paris, 1889), pp. 20ff.; pp. 94–106; *Matière et Mémoire* (Paris, 1897), pp. 189–195; 224–233; "Le rêve" (1901) (in *L'Energie spirituelle,* Paris, 1919, pp. 108–111); "L'effort intellectuel" (1902) (*ibid.,* pp. 164–171); "Introduction à la métaphysique" (1903) (in *La Pensée et le Mouvant,* Paris, 1934, pp. 233–238); "Le souvenir du présent et la fausse reconnaissance" (1908) (*L'Energie spirituelle,* pp. 129–137); "La conscience et la vie" (1911) (*ibid.,* pp. 15–18); "La perception du changement" (1911) (in *La Pensée et le Mouvant,* pp. 171–175; pp. 190–193); "Fantômes de vivants" et "recherche psychique" (1913) (*L'Energie spirituelle,* pp. 80–84); "De la position des problèmes" (1922) (*La Pensée et le Mouvant,* pp. 91ff.).

[4] With very few exceptions, vulgar pragmatism does not consider the problems of the constitution of conscious life involved in the notion of an *ego agens* or *homo faber* from which as a giveness most of the writers start. For the most part, pragmatism is, therefore, just a common-sense description of the attitude of man within the world of working in daily life, but not a philosophy investigating the presuppositions of such a situation.

pretation of our cognitive life. The state of full awakeness of the working self traces out that segment of the world which is pragmatically relevant, and these relevances determine the form and content of our stream of thought: the form, because they regulate the tension of our memory and therewith the scope of our past experiences recollected and of our future experiences anticipated; the content, because all these experiences undergo specific attentional modifications by the preconceived project and its carrying into effect. This leads us immediately into an analysis of the time dimension in which the working self experiences its own acts.

4. The Time Perspectives of the "Ego Agens" and their Unification

We start by making a distinction that refers to actions in general, covert and overt, between action as an ongoing process, as acting in progress (*actio*) on the one hand, and action as performed act, as the thing done (*actum*) on the other hand. Living in my acting-in-progress, I am directed toward the state of affairs to be brought about by this acting. But, then, I do not have in view my experiences of this ongoing process of acting. In order to bring them into view I have to turn back with a reflective attitude to my acting. As Dewey once formulated it, I have to stop and think. If I adopt this reflective attitude, it is, however, not my ongoing acting that I can grasp. What alone I can grasp is rather my performed act (my past acting) or, if my acting still continues while I turn back, the performed initial phases (my present acting). While I lived in my acting in progress it was an element of my vivid present. Now this present has turned into past, and the vivid experience of my acting in progress has given place to my recollection of having acted or to the retention of having been acting. Seen from the actual present in which I adopt the reflective attitude, my past or present perfect acting is conceivable only in terms of acts performed by me.

Thus I may either live in the ongoing process of my acting, directed toward its object, and experience my acting in the Present Tense (*modo presenti*), or I may, so to speak, step out of the ongoing flux and look by a reflective glance at the acts performed in previous processes of acting in the Past Tense or Present Perfect Tense (*modo praeterito*). This does not mean that—according to what was stated in a previous section—merely the performed acts are meaningful but not the ongoing actions.

We have to keep in mind that, by definition, action is always based upon a preconceived project, and it is this reference to the preceding project that makes both the acting and the act meaningful.

But what is the time structure of a projected action? When projecting my action, I am, as Dewey puts it,[5] rehearsing my future action in imagination. This means, I anticipate the outcome of my future action. I look in my imagination at this anticipated action as the thing which *will have been* done, the act which *will have been* performed by me. In projecting, I look at my act in the Future Perfect Tense, I think of it *modo futuri exacti*. But these anticipations are empty and may or may not be fulfilled by the action once performed. The past or present perfect act, however, shows no such empty anticipations. What was empty in the project has or has not been fulfilled. Nothing remains unsettled, nothing undecided. To be sure, I may remember the open anticipations involved in projecting the act and even the protensions accompanying my living in the ongoing process of my acting. But now, in retrospection, I remember them in terms of my *past* anticipations, which have or have not come true. Only the performed act, therefore, and never the acting in progress can turn out as a success or failure.

What has been stated so far holds good for all kinds of actions. But now we have to turn to the peculiar structure of working as bodily performance in the outer world. Bergson's and also Husserl's investigations have emphasized the importance of our bodily movements for the constitution of the outer world and its time perspective. We experience our bodily movements simultaneously on two different planes: inasmuch as they are movements in the outer world we look at them as events happening in space and spatial time, measurable in terms of the path run through; inasmuch as they are experienced together from within as happening changes, as manifestations of our spontaneity pertaining to our stream of consciousness, they partake of our inner time or *durée*. What occurs in the outer world belongs to the same time dimension in which events in inanimate nature occur. It can be registered by appropriate devices and measured by our chronometers. It is the spatialized, homogeneous time which is the

---

5 *Human Nature and Conduct* (New York, 1922), Part III, Section III: "The Nature of Deliberation."

universal form of objective or cosmic time. On the other hand, it is the inner time or *durée* within which our actual experiences are connected with the past by recollections and retentions and with the future by protentions and anticipations. In and by our bodily movements we perform the transition from our *durée* to the spatial or cosmic time, and our working actions partake of both. In simultaneity we experience the working action as a series of events in outer and in inner time, unifying both dimensions into a single flux which shall be called the *vivid present*. The vivid present originates, therefore, in an intersection of *durée* and cosmic time.

Living in the vivid present in its ongoing working acts, directed toward the objects and objectives to be brought about, the working self experiences itself as the originator of the ongoing actions and, thus, as an undivided total self. It experiences its bodily movements from within; it lives in the correlated essentially actual experiences which are inaccessible to recollection and reflection; its world is a world of open anticipations. The working self, and only the working self, experiences all this *modo presenti* and, experiencing itself as the author of this ongoing working, it realizes itself as a unity.

But if the self in a reflective attitude turns back to the working acts performed and looks at them *modo praeterito* this unity goes to pieces. The self which performed the past acts is no longer the undivided total self, but rather a partial self, the performer of this particular act that refers to a system of correlated acts to which it belongs. This partial self is merely the taker of a rôle or—to use with all necessary reserve a rather equivocal term which James and Mead have introduced into the literature— a Me.

We cannot enter here into a thorough discussion of the difficult implications here involved. This would require a presentation and criticism of G. H. Mead's rather incomplete and inconsistent attempt to approach these problems. We restrict ourselves to pointing to the distinction Mead makes between the totality of the acting self, which he calls the "I," and the partial selves of performed acts, the takers of rôles, which he calls the "Me's." So far, the thesis presented in this paper converges with Mead's analysis. And there is, furthermore, agreement with Mead's statement that the "I" gets into experience only after it has carried out the act and thus appears experientially as a part of the

Me, that is, the Me appears in our experience in memory.[6]

For our purpose the mere consideration that the inner experiences of our bodily movements, the essentially actual experiences, and the open anticipations escape the grasping by the reflective attitude shows with sufficient clearness that the past self can never be more than a partial aspect of the total one which realizes itself in the experience of its ongoing working.

One point relating to the distinction between (overt) working and (covert) performing has to be added. In the case of a mere performance, such as the attempt to solve a mathematical problem mentally, I can, if my anticipations are not fulfilled by the outcome and I am dissatisfied with the result, cancel the whole process of mental operations and restart from the beginning. Nothing will have changed in the outer world, no vestige of the annulled process will remain. Mere mental actions are, in this sense, revocable. Working, however, is irrevocable. My work has changed the outer world. At best, I may restore the initial situation by countermoves but I cannot make undone what I have done. That is why— from the moral and legal point of view—I am responsible for my deeds but not for my thoughts. That is also why I have the freedom of choice between several possibilities merely with respect to the mentally projected work, before this work has been carried through in the outer world or, at least, while it is being carried through in vivid present, and, thus, still open to modifications. In terms of the past there is no possibility for choice. Having real-

---

6 Cf. G. H. Mead, *Mind, Self, and Society* (Chicago, 1934), pp. 173–175, 196–198, 203; "The Genesis of the Self," reprinted in *The Philosophy of the Present* (Chicago, 1932), pp. 176–195, esp. pp. 184ff.; "What Social Objects Must Psychology Presuppose?," *Journal of Philosophy*, VIII, (1910), pp. 174–180; "The Social Self," *Journal of Philosophy*, Vol. X, 1913, pp. 374–380. See also Alfred Stafford Clayton's excellent book on G. H. Mead: *Emergent Mind and Education* (New York, 1943), pp. 136–141, esp. p. 137. It is doubtless Mead's merit to have seen the relations between act, self, memory, time, and reality. The position of the present paper is of course not reconcilable with Mead's theory of the social origin of the self and with his (modified) behaviorism which induces him to interpret all the beforementioned phenomena in terms of stimulus-response. There is much more truth in the famous chapter (X) of James' *Principles of Psychology*, in which not only the distinction between Me and I can be found, but also its reference to bodily movements, memory, and the sense of time.

ized my work or at least portions of it, I chose once for all what has been done and have now to bear the consequences. I cannot choose what I want to have done.

So far our analysis has dealt with the time structure of action—and, as a corollary, with the time structure of the self—within the insulated stream of consciousness of the single individual, as if the wide-awake man within the natural attitude could be thought of as separated from his fellow-men. Such a fictitious abstraction was, of course, merely made for the sake of clearer presentation of the problems involved. We have now to turn to the social structure of the world of working.

5. The Social Structure of the World of Daily Life

We stated before that the world of daily life into which we are born is from the outset an intersubjective world. This implies on the one hand that this world is not my private one but common to all of us; on the other hand that within this world there exist fellow-men with whom I am connected by manifold social relationships. I work not only upon inanimate things but also upon my fellow-men, induced by them to act and inducing them to react. Without entering here into a detailed discussion of the structure and constitution of social relationship, we may mention just as an example of one of its many forms that my performed acts may motivate the Other to react, and vice versa. My questioning the Other, for instance, is undertaken with the intention of provoking his answer, and his answering is motivated by my question. This is one of the many types of "social actions." It is that type in which the "in-order-to motives" of my action become "because motives" of the partner's reaction.

Social actions involve communication, and any communication is necessarily founded upon acts of working. In order to communicate with Others I have to perform overt acts in the outer world which are supposed to be interpreted by the Others as signs of what I mean to convey. Gestures, speech, writing, etc., are based upon bodily movements. So far, the behavioristic interpretation of communication is justified. It goes wrong by identifying the vehicle of communication, namely the working act, with the communicated meaning itself.

Let us examine the mechanism of communication from the point of view of the interpreter. I may find as given to my interpretation either the ready-made outcome of the Other's communicating acts or I may attend in simultaneity the ongoing process of his communicating actions as they proceed. The former is, for instance, the case, if I have to interpret a signpost erected by the Other or an implement produced by him. The latter relation prevails, if I am listening to my partner's talk. (There are many variations of these basic types, such as the reading of the Other's letter in a kind of quasi-simultaneity with the ongoing communicating process.) He builds up the thought he wants to convey to me step by step, adding word to word, sentence to sentence, paragraph to paragraph. While he does so, my interpreting actions follow his communicating ones in the same rhythm. We both, I and the Other, experience the ongoing process of communication in a vivid present. Articulating his thought, while speaking, in phases, the communicator does not merely experience what he actually utters; a complicated mechanism of retentions and anticipations connects within his stream of consciousness one element of his speech with what preceded and what will follow to the unity of the thought he wants to convey. All these experiences belong to his inner time. And there are, on the other hand, the occurrences of his speaking, brought about by him in the spatialized time of the outer world. Briefly, the communicator experiences the ongoing process of communicating as a working in his vivid present.

And I, the listener, experience for my part my interpreting actions also as happening in my vivid present, although this interpreting is not a working, but merely a performing within the meaning of our definitions. On the one hand, I experience the occurrences of the Other's speaking in outer time; on the other hand, I experience the occurrences of the of retentions and anticipations happening in my inner time interconnected by my aim to understand the Other's thought as a unit.

Now let us consider that the occurrence in the outer world—the communicator's speech—is, while it goes on, an element common to his and my vivid present, both of which are, therefore, simultaneous. My participating in simultaneity in the ongoing process of the Other's communicating establishes therefore a new dimension of time. He and I, *we* share, while the process lasts, a common vivid present, *our* vivid present, which enables him and me to say: "*We* experienced this occurrence together." By the We-relation, thus established, we both—he, addressing himself to me, and I, listening to him—are living in our mutual vivid present, directed toward the thought to be realized in and by the communicating process. *We grow older together.*

So far our analysis of communication in the vivid present of the We-relation has been restricted to the time perspective involved. We have now to consider the specific functions of the Other's bodily movements as an expressional field open to interpretation as signs of the Other's thought. It is clear that the extension of this field, even if communication occurs in vivid present, may vary considerably. It will reach its maximum if there exists between the partners community not only of time but also of space, that is, in the case of what sociologists call a face-to-face relation.

To make this clearer let us keep to our example of the speaker and the listener and analyze the interpretable elements included in such a situation. There are first the words uttered in the meaning they have according to dictionary and grammar in the language used plus the additional fringes they receive from the context of the speech and the supervening connotations originating in the particular circumstances of the speaker. There is, furthermore, the inflection of the speaker's voice, his facial expression, the gestures which accompany his talking. Under normal circumstances merely the conveyance of the thought by appropriately selected words has been projected by the speaker and constitutes, therefore, "working" according to our definition. The other elements within the interpretable field are from the speaker's point of view not planned and, therefore, at best mere conduct (mere doing) or even mere reflexes and, then, essentially actual experiences without subjective meaning. Nevertheless, they, too, are integral elements of the listener's interpretation of the Other's state of mind. The community of space permits the partner to apprehend the Other's bodily expressions not merely as events in the outer world, but as factors of the communicating process itself, although they do not originate in working acts of the communicator.

Not only does each partner in the face-to-face relationship share the other in a vivid present; each of them with all manifestations of his spontaneous life is also an element of the other's surroundings; both participate in a set of common experiences of the outer world into which either's working acts may gear. And, finally, in the face-to-face relationship (and

only in it) can the partner look at the self of his fellow-man as an unbroken totality in a vivid present. This is of special importance because, as shown before, I can look at my own self only *modo praeterito* and then grasp merely a partial aspect of this my past self, myself as a performer of a rôle, as a Me.

All the other manifold social relationships are derived from the originary experiencing of the totality of the Other's self in the community of time and space. Any theoretical analysis of the notion of "environment"—one of the least clarified terms used in present social sciences—would have to start from the face-to-face relation as a basic structure of the world of daily life.

We cannot enter here into the details of the framework of these derived relationships. For our problem it is important that in none of them does the self of the Other become accessible to the partner as a unity. The Other appears merely as a partial self, as originator of these and those acts, which I do not share in a vivid present. The shared vivid present of the We-relation presupposes co-presence of the partners. To each type of derived social relationship belongs a particular type of time perspective which is derived from the vivid present. There is a particular quasi-present in which I interpret the mere outcome of the Other's communicating—the written letter, the printed book—without having participated in the ongoing process of communicating acts. There are other time dimensions in which I am connected with contemporaries I never met, or with predecessors or with successors; historical time, in which I experience the actual present as the outcome of past events; and many more. All of these time perspectives can be referred to a vivid present: my own actual or former one, or the actual or former vivid present of my fellow-man with whom, in turn, I am connected in an originary or derived vivid present. All this occurs in the different modes of potentiality or quasi-actuality, each type having its own forms of temporal diminution and augmentation and its appurtenant style of skipping in a direct move or "knight's move." There are furthermore the different forms of overlapping and interpenetrating of these different perspectives, their being put into and out of operation by a shift from one to the other and a transformation of one into the other, and the different types of synthesizing and combining or isolating and disentangling them. Manifold as these different time perspectives and their mutual relations are, they all originate in an intersection of *durée* and cosmic time.

In and by our social life within the natural attitude they are apprehended as integrated into a single supposedly homogeneous dimension of time which embraces not only all the individual time perspectives of each of us during his wide-awake life but which is common to all of us. We shall call it the civic or *standard time*. It, too, is an intersection of cosmic time and inner time, though, as to the latter, merely of a peculiar aspect of inner time—that aspect in which the wide-awake man experiences his working acts as events within his stream of consciousness. Because standard time partakes of cosmic time, it is measurable by our clocks and calendars. Because it coincides with our inner sense of time in which we experience our working acts, if—and only if—we are wide-awake, it governs the system of our plans under which we subsume our projects, such as plans for life, for work and leisure. Because it is common to all of us, standard time makes an intersubjective coordination of the different individual plan systems possible. Thus, to the natural attitude, the civic or standard time is in the same sense the universal temporal structure of the intersubjective world of everyday life within the natural attitude, in which the earth is its universal spatial structure that embraces the spatial environments of each of us.

6. The Strata of Reality in the Everyday World of Working

The wide-awake man within the natural attitude is primarily interested in that sector of the world of his everyday life which is within his scope and which is centered in space and time around himself. The place which my body occupies within the world, my actual Here, is the starting point from which I take my bearing in space. It is, so to speak, the center O of my system of coordinates. Relatively to my body I group the elements of my surroundings under the categories of right and left, before and behind, above and below, near and far, and so on. And in a similar way my actual Now is the origin of all the time perspectives under which I organize the events within the world such as the categories of fore and aft, past and future, simultaneity and succession, etc.

Within this basic scheme of orientation, however, the world of working is structurized in various strata of reality. It is the great merit of Mead[7] to have analyzed the structurization of the reality at least of the physical thing in its relationship to human action, especially to the actual manipulation of objects with the hands. It is what he calls the "manipulatory area" which constitutes the core of reality. This area includes those objects which are both seen and handled, in contradistinction to the distant objects which cannot be experienced by contact but still lie in the visual field. Only experiences of physical things within the manipulatory area permit the basic test of all reality, namely resistance, only they define what Mead calls the "standard sizes" of things which appear outside the manipulatory area in the distortions of optical perspectives.

This theory of the predominance of the manipulatory area certainly converges with the thesis suggested by this paper, namely that the world of our working, of bodily movements, of manipulating objects and handling things and men constitutes the specific reality of everyday life. For our purpose, however, the otherwise most important distinction between objects experienced by contact and distant objects is not of primary importance. It could easily be shown that this dichotomy originates in Mead's basic behavioristic position and his uncritical use of the stimulus-response scheme. We, on the other hand, are concerned with the natural attitude of the wide-awake, grown-up man in daily life. He always disposes of a stock of previous experiences, among them the notion of distance as such and of the possibility of overcoming distance by acts of working, namely locomotions. In the natural attitude the visual perception of the distant object implies, therefore, the anticipation that the distant object can be brought into contact by locomotion, in which case the distorted perspective of the objects will disappear and their "standard sizes" reestablished. This anticipation like any other may or may not stand the test of the supervening actual experience. Its refutation by experience would mean that the distant object under consideration does not pertain to the world of my working. A child may request to touch the stars. To the grown-up within the natural attitude they are shining points outside the sphere of his working, and this holds true even if he uses their position as a means for finding his bearings.

---

[7] *The Philosophy of the Present* (Chicago, 1932), pp. 124ff.; *The Philosophy of the Act* (Chicago, 1938), pp. 103–106, 121ff., 151ff., 190–192, 196–197, 282–284.

For our purposes, therefore, we suggest calling the stratum of the world of working which the individual experiences as the kernel of his reality the *world within his reach*. This world of his includes not only Mead's manipulatory area but also things within the scope of his view and the range of his hearing, moreover not only the realm of the world open to his actual but also the adjacent ones of his potential working. Of course, these realms have no rigid frontiers, they have their halos and open horizons and these are subject to modifications of interests and attentional attitudes. It is clear that this whole system of "world within my reach" undergoes changes by any of my locomotions; by displacing my body I shift the center *O* of my system of coordinates, and this alone changes all the numbers (coordinates) pertaining to this system.

We may say that the world within my actual reach belongs essentially to the present tense. The world within my potential reach, however, shows a more complicated time structure. At least two zones of potentiality have to be distinguished. To the first, which refers to the past, belongs what was formerly within my actual reach and what, so I assume, can be brought back into my actual reach again (*world within restorable reach*).

* * *

The second zone of potentiality refers anticipatorily to future states of my mind. It is not connected with my past experiences, except by the fact that its anticipations (as all anticipations) originate in and have to be compatible with the stock of my past experiences actually at hand. These experiences enable me to weigh the likelihood of carrying out my plans and to estimate my powers. It is clear that this second zone is not at all homogeneous but subdivided into sectors of different chances of attainment. These chances diminish in proportion with the increasing spatial, temporal, and social distance of the respective sector from the actual center of my world of working. The greater the distance the more uncertain are my anticipations of the attainable actuality, until they become entirely empty and unrealizable.

7. The World of Working as Paramount Reality; The Fundamental Anxiety; The Epoché of the Natural Attitude

The world of working as a whole stands out as paramount over against the many other subuniverses of reality. It is the world of physical things, including my body; it is the realm of my locomotions and bodily operations; it offers resistances which require effort to overcome; it places tasks before me, permits me to carry through my plans, and enables me to succeed or to fail in my attempt to attain my purposes. By my working acts I gear into the outer world, I change it; and these changes, although provoked by my working, can be experienced and tested both by myself and others, as occurrences within this world independently of my working acts in which they originated. I share this world and its objects with Others; I have ends and means in common; I work with them in manifold social acts and relationships, checking the Others and checked by them. And the world of working is the reality within which communication and the interplay of mutual motivation becomes effective. It can, therefore, be experienced under both schemes of reference, the causality of motives as well as the teleology of purposes.

As we stated before, this world is to our natural attitude in the first place not an object of our thought but a field of domination. We have an eminently practical interest in it, caused by the necessity of complying with the basic requirements of our life. But we are not *equally* interested in all the strata of the world of working. The selective function of our interest organizes the world in both respects— as to space and time—in strata of major or minor relevance. From the world within my actual or potential reach those objects are selected as primarily important which actually are or will become in the future possible ends or means for the realization of my projects, or which are or will become dangerous or enjoyable or otherwise relevant to me. I am constantly anticipating the future repercussions I may expect from these objects and the future changes my projected working will bring about with respect to them.

Let us make clearer what is meant by "relevance" in this context. I am, for instance, with the natural attitude, passionately interested in the results of my action and especially in the question whether my anticipations will stand the practical test. As we have seen before, all anticipations and plans refer to previous experiences now at hand, which enable me to weigh my chances. But that is only half the story. *What* I am anticipating is one thing, the other, *why* I anticipate certain occurrences at all. What may happen under certain conditions and circumstances is one thing, the other, why I am interested in these happenings and why I should passionately await the outcome of my prophesies. It is only the first part of these dichotomies which is answered by reference to the stock of experiences at hand as the sediment of previous experiences. It is the second part of these dichotomies which refers to the system of relevances by which man within his natural attitude in daily life is guided.

We cannot unfold here all the implications of the problem of relevance, upon one aspect of which we have just touched. But in a word, we want to state that the whole system of relevances which governs us within the natural attitude is founded upon the basic experience of each of us: I know that I shall die and I fear to die. This basic experience we suggest calling the *fundamental anxiety*. It is the primordial anticipation from which all the others originate. From the fundamental anxiety spring the many interrelated systems of hopes and fears, of wants and satisfactions, of chances and risks which incite man within the natural attitude to attempt the mastery of the world, to overcome obstacles, to draft projects, and to realize them.

But the fundamental anxiety itself is merely a correlate of our existence as human beings within the paramount reality of daily life and, therefore, the hopes and fears and their correlated satisfactions and disappointments are grounded upon and only possible within the world of working. They are essential elements of its reality but they do not refer to our belief in it. On the contrary, it is characteristic of the natural attitude that it takes the world and its objects for granted until counterproof imposes itself. As long as the once established scheme of reference, the system of our and other people's warranted experiences works, as long as the actions and operations performed under its guidance yield the desired results, we trust these experiences. We are not interested in finding out whether this world really does exist or whether it is merely a coherent system of consistent appearances. We have no reason to cast any doubt upon our warranted experiences which, so we believe, give us things as they really are. It needs a special motivation, such as the irruption of a "strange" experience not subsumable under the stock of knowledge at hand or inconsistent with it, to make us revise our former beliefs.

Phenomenology has taught us the concept of phenomenological *epoché,* the suspension of our belief in the reality of the world as a device to overcome the natural attitude by radicalizing the Cartesian method of philosophical doubt.[8] The suggestion may be ventured that man within the natural attitude also uses a specific *epoché,* of course quite another one than the phenomenologist. He does not suspend belief in the outer world and its objects, but on the contrary, he suspends doubt in its existence. What he puts in brackets is the doubt that the world and its objects might be otherwise than it appears to him. We propose to call this *epoché* the *epoché of the natural attitude.*[9]

---

[8] Cf. Farber, *loc. cit.,* p. 526f.

[9] Although the point of view of the present paper differs in many respects from his, I should like to call attention to Herbert Spiegelberg's very interesting paper "The Reality-Phenomenon and Reality" in *Philosophical Essays in Memory of Edmund Husserl* (*op. cit.*) pp. 84–105, which attempts an analysis of dubitability and dubiousness with respect to reality. According to Spiegelberg, reality-criteria are the phenomena of readiness, persistence, perceptual periphery, boundaries in concrete objects, independence, resistance, and agreement.

Chapter 6 Aspects of the Problem of Common-Sense Knowledge of Social Structures[*]

HAROLD GARFINKEL

Editors' Note. Garfinkel has provided a much more extensive treatment of this phenomenon in his "Studies of the Routine Grounds of Everyday Activities," *Social Problems,* No. 2 (Winter 1964), pp. 225–250. An outline of the kind of social phenomenology practiced by Garfinkel and his associates may be found in his "Remarks on Ethnomethodology" circulated to members of the methodology section of the American Sociological Association before the 1965 meetings in Montreal or in his book, *Studies in Ethnomethodology,* Englewood Cliffs, N.J.: Prentice-Hall, Inc., 1967.

Sociologically speaking, "common culture" refers to the socially sanctioned grounds of inference and action that people use in their

SOURCE. International Sociological Association, *Transactions of the Fourth World Congress of Sociology, Vol. IV: The Sociology of Knowledge,* Louvain, Belgium: International Sociological Association, 1959, pp. 51-55. Copyright 1959, Fourth World Congress of Sociology. Reprinted by permission of the International Sociological Association.

* This paper is heavily abridged from an 80-page mimeographed version prepared for and distributed at the session on the Sociology of Knowledge, Fourth World Congress of Sociology, Stresa, Italy, September 12, 1959. Because of space limitations it was necessary to omit materials dealing with the general set "corpus of knowledge" and the procedures for constituting it and its several subsets among which is the corpus of common-sense knowledge; descriptions of the work of the documentary method and a report of an experiment that permitted these workings to be explored; Schutz's descriptions of the attitude of everyday life; the problem of whether the documentary method is a necessary feature of sociological inquiry; the consequences for stable features of social structures of several types of transformations of the presuppositions of the corpus of common-sense knowledge. These materials are treated at appropriate length in the author's book in preparation, "Common-Sense Actions as Topic and Feature of Sociological Inquiry."

This investigation was supported by a Senior Research Fellowship, SF-81 from the Public Health Service. I wish to thank Dr. Eleanor Bernert Sheldon, Egon Bittner, and Aaron V. Cicourel, for many conversations about these materials.

Readers who are acquainted with the magnificent writings of the late Alfred Schutz will recognize the debt that anyone writing on this topic owes to him. The paper is respectfully dedicated to him as an esteemed teacher and sociologist.

everyday affairs[1] and which they assume that other members of the group use in the same way. Socially-sanctioned-facts-of-life-in-society-that - any - bona - fide - member - of - the - society - knows depict such matters as conduct of family life; market organization; distributions of honour, competence, responsibility, goodwill, income, and motives among persons; frequency, causes of, and remedies for trouble; and the presence of good and evil purposes behind the apparent workings of things. Such socially sanctioned facts of social life consist of descriptions of the society from the point of view of the collectivity member's[2] interests in the management of his practical affairs. For the moment, call such knowledge of the organization and operations of the society "common-sense knowledge of social structures."

[1] The concept "everyday affairs" is intended in strict accord with Schutz's usage in his articles, "On Multiple Realities," *Philosophy and Phenomenological Research,* 4 (June 1945), pp. 533–575; and "Common Sense and Scientific Interpretation of Human Action," *Philosophy and Phenomenological Research,* 14 (September 1953), pp. 1–37.

[2] The concepts "collectivity" and "membership" are intended in strict accord with Talcott Parson's usage in *The Social System,* Glencoe, Ill.: The Free Press, 1951, and in Part II, General Introduction, *Reader in Sociological Theory,* dittoed mss. by Talcott Parsons, 1959.

The discovery of common culture consists of the discovery *from within the society* by social scientists of the existence of common-sense knowledge of social structures, and the treatment by social scientists of this knowledge, and of the procedures for its assembly, test, management, transmission, etc., by members of the society as objects of mere theoretical sociological interest.

This paper is concerned with common-sense knowledge of social structures as an object of theoretical sociological interest. Its subject matter is the descriptions of a society which its members, sociologists included, as a condition of their rights to manage and communicate decisions of meaning, fact, method, and causal texture without interference, use and treat as known in common with others, and with others take for granted.

Several aspects of this topic will be sketched: (1) the constituent meanings of the feature "known in common with others" that for a member is "attached" to his descriptions of his society; (2) features of common-sense situations of choice within which the factual status of descriptions of society is decided; (3) Mannheim's "documentary method of interpretation" as an approximation of a method whereby factual status of common-sense descriptions is decided and managed in the face of challenges to adequacy of meaning and evidence; and (4) some logical properties of the corpus of common-sense knowledge of social structures.

I. THE DEFINITIVE FEATURES OF PROPOSITIONS WHICH COMPOSE A COMMON-SENSE DESCRIPTION

A common-sense description is defined by the feature "known in common with any bonafide member of the collectivity" which is attached to all the propositions which compose it. The late Alfred Schutz, in his work on the constitutive phenomenology of situations of everyday life,[3] analyzed the compound charac-

ter of the feature "known in common" into its constituent meanings. *Whatever a proposition specifically proposes*—whether it proposes something about the motives of persons, their histories, the distribution of income in the population, the conditions of advancement on the job, kinship obligations, the organization of an industry, the layout of a city, what ghosts do when night falls, the thoughts that God thinks—*if for the user the proposition has the following additional features, it is called a common-sense proposition.*[4]

1. The sense assigned to the description is, from the member's point of view, an assignment that he is required to make; he requires the other person to make the same assignment of sense; and just as he requires the same assignment to hold for the other person, he assumes that the other person requires the same of him.

2. From the user's point of view, a relationship of undoubted correspondence is the sanctioned relationship between the-depicted-appearance of-the-intended-object and the-intended-object-that-appears-in-this-depicted-fashion.

3. From the user's point of view, the matter that is known, in the manner that it is known, can actually and potentially affect the knower's actions and circumstances, and can be affected by his actions and circumstances.

4. From the user's point of view, the meanings of the descriptions are the products of a standardized process of naming, reification, and idealization of the user's stream of experiences, i.e., the products of the same language.

5. From the user's point of view, the present sense of whatever the description describes is a sense intended on previous occasions that can be intended again in an identical way on an indefinite number of future occasions.

6. From the user's point of view, the intended sense is retained as the temporally identical sense throughout the stream of experience.

7. From the user's point of view, the description has as it contents of interpretation:

(a) a commonly entertained scheme of communication consisting of a standardized system of signals and coding rules, and

[3] Schutz, Alfred, *Der sinnhafte Aufbau der sozialen Welt,* Julius Springer, Wien, 1932; "The Problem of Rationality in the Social World," *Economica,* **10** (May 1943), pp. 130–149; "Some Leading Concepts in Phenomenology," *Social Research,* **12** (February 1945), pp. 77–97; "On Multiple Realities," *loc. cit.,* "Concept and Theory Formation in the Social Sciences," *Journal of Philosophy,* **51** (April 29, 1954), pp. 257–274; "Symbol, Reality, and Society," *Symbols and Society, Fourteenth Symposium of the Conference on Science, Philosophy, and Religion,* edited by

Lyman Bryson and others, New York: Harper and Brothers, 1955, pp. 135–202.
[4] The material in the *following two pages* is based almost entirely upon Schutz's writings. See n. 3.

(b) "What Anyone Knows," i.e., a pre-established corpus of socially warranted descriptions.

8. From the user's point of view, the actual sense that the description has for him is the potential sense that it would have for the other person were they to exchange their positions.

9. From the user's point of view, to each description there corresponds its meanings that originate in the user's and in the other person's particular biography. From the user's point of view, such meanings are irrelevant for the purposes at hand of either: for the user, both he and the other person have selected and interpreted the actual and potential sense of the proposition in an empirically identical manner that is sufficient for their practical purposes.

10. From the user's point of view there is a characteristic disparity between the publicly acknowledged sense and the personal, withheld sense of the description, and this private sense is held in reserve. From the user's point of view, the description means for the user and the other person more than the user can say.

11. From the user's point of view, alterations of this characteristic disparity remain within the user's autonomous control.

These features have the following properties that make them particularly interesting to the sociological researcher:

1. From the standpoint of the collectivity member, these features are "scenic" features of his behavioural environment of objects. By "scenic" I mean that if, for example, we say with respect to the expected correspondence of appearance and object that the member doubts the correspondence, we must assign to the correspondence its feature of a doubted one. Another example. If we say that the member expects that what is known can affect and be affected by his actions, we must assign to what is known, as an object in the member's behavioural environment, its integral feature that it can potentially affect and be affected by his actions. To each of the expectancies that comprise what Schutz called the "attitude of daily life"[5] there is the corresponding expected feature of the object.

2. These constitutive features are "seen but unnoticed." If the researcher questions the member about them, the member is able to tell the researcher about them only by transforming the descriptions known from the perspective and in the manner of his practical ongoing treatment of them into an object of theoretical reflection. Otherwise the member "tells the researcher about them by the conditions under which severe" incongruity can be induced. A reflective concern for their problematic character, as well as an interest in them as objects of theoretical contemplation, characteristically occurs as an abiding preoccupation in the experiences of cultural "strangers."

3. They are used by the collectivity member as a scheme of interpretation in terms of which he decides the correspondence between actual appearances and the objects intended through their successive actual appearances.

4. These expected features are invariant to the contents of actual descriptions to which they may be attached.

5. The sense of described social structures as unified ensembles of possible appearances is supplied by their constituent feature, "known in common."

6. The withdrawal of this feature by alter from ego's descriptions modifies the logical mode of ego's description for alter in a radical way by transforming fact into fiction, conjecture, personal opinion, and the like. Insofar as alter, while retaining this feature for his own accounts, withdraws the feature from ego's descriptions, he removes the enforceable character of ego's claim to competence.

7. Modifications of these constituent meanings of "known in common" transform environments of intended objects to produce the descriptions of social structures of games, of scientific sociological theorizing, of art, of high ceremony, of the theatre play, of official histories, of dreaming, and the like. Dramatic modifications occur in brain injuries, mental deficiency, acute sensory deprivation, hallucinatory drug states. Such modifications are accompanied by corresponding modifications of the social structures produced by actions directed to cultural environments altered in this fashion.

Contrary to prevailing opinion, the common-sense character of knowledge of social structures does not consist in the ironic comparison of such knowledge with "scientific descriptions." Instead, it consists entirely and exclusively in the possibility that (a) the sensible character of what these descriptions describe about the society, and/or (b) their warranted character as grounds for further inference and action, is decided and guaranteed by enforce-

---

[5] Cf. Schutz, "On Multiple Realities," *loc. cit.*

ment of the attitude of daily life as ethical and moral maxims of conduct in theorizing and inquiry. We must suppose that the attidue of daily life operates in the sociological inquiries not only of the members of a society but of professional sociologists as well. Just as sociological inquiries are not confined to professional sociologists, neither is the attitude of daily life confined to "the man in the street."

* * *

The foregoing properties may be summarized by saying the propositions of the common-sense corpus do not have a sense that is independent of the socially structured occasions on which they are used.

Further properties of the set of such propositions may be mentioned briefly.

(a) The propositions that comprise common-sense accounts typically are unwritten, uncodified, and are passed on from one person to a successor through a system of apprenticeship in their use. (b) Various social-psychological researches have demonstrated the sense of a propositon to be a function of the place of the proposition in a serial order; of the expressive character of the terms that comprise it; of the socially acknowledged importance of the events that are depicted; of the relevance to the need dispositions of the user, of what is being referred to—to mention a few. (c) Their sense is structurally equivocal, being dependent upon the developing course of the occasions of their use. Like a conversation, their sense is built up step by step over the actual course of references to them. (d) As of any present state of affairs, the sense of what a proposition now proposes includes the anticipated, though sketchily known, future further references that will have accrued to it. Its present sense for a user is informed by the user's willingness to continue in the progressive realization of its sense by further elaboration and transformation. This feature is commonly referred to as the "spirit" of the proposition.

CONCLUSION

All scientific disciplines have their great prevailing problems to which the methods of the particular discipline represent solutions. In sociology, in the social sciences generally, as well as in the inquiries of everyday life, a prominent problem is that of achieving a unified conception of events that have as their specific formal property that their present character will have been decided by a future possible outcome. Motivated actions, for example, have precisely this troublesome property. It is a matter of great theoretical and methodological import that Max Weber should have defined sociology as the study of human activities insofar as they are governed in their course by the subjective meanings attached to them. In this programmatic statement, Weber provided for this troublesome feature as an essential property of sociology's fundamental occurrences.

The documentary method consists essentially in the retrospective-prospective reading of a present occurrence so as to maintain the constancy of the object as a sensible thing through temporal and circumstantial alterations in its actual appearances. Thereby it shows its particular usefulness as a method that is capable of handling events having this particular time structure. The documentary method occurs as a feature of situations of incomplete information in which effective actions nevertheless must be taken, matters of fact decided, and interpretations made. The method would seem to be an intimate part of a social process wherein a body of knowledge must be assembled and made available for legitimate use despite the fact that the situations it purports to describe (1) are, in the calculable sense of the term, unknown; (2) are in their actual and intended logical structures essentially vague; and (3) are modified, elaborated, extended, if not indeed created, by the fact and manner of being addressed.

Chapter 7 The Existential Self and the Person

EDWARD A. TIRYAKIAN

INTRODUCTION

A specter is haunting the academic halls of the "Lockean Establishment" in psychology—the specter of "Leibnizian insurgency."[1] In this chapter I shall try to elucidate major aspects of the perspective on the person entertained by one group of the insurgents, the existential-phenomenological phalanx.

Within the Lockean Establishment I would situate all the theories of personality that give residual significance to consciousness, which are therefore object-oriented, and all the theories that presuppose that the human person can be "explained" in naturalistic terms by a hedonistic desire to achieve a homeostatic equilibrium with his environment. Broadly speaking, an object-approach is grounded in a stimulus-response model, whether the biophysical stimulus is taken to be external or internal (as in the Freudian model). Once the stimulus (equivalent to the notion of force or cause in Newtonian physics) makes itself felt, the self is taken to respond mechanically, that is, without reflection or cogitation, in a uniform and ultimately predictable manner. Consciousness, if it is recognized in the S-R camp, is a tool of or molded by biophysical drives; its role is therefore assumed to be passive or perhaps, as the classical psychoanalytic formulation, consciousness is reduced to an entity (ego) which plays the hapless buffer role and, like all buffer states, is continually threatened by an adjacent force of aggression. Finally, the object-approach to the person implicitly assumes that the person is an entity detached from other entities except insofar as others provide him with gratification. The image of the person thus is that of a nomadic monad.

Among the radicals seeking to restore psychology to its roots in the descriptive study of consciousness are such figures as Binswanger, May, Rogers, Maslow, Minkowski, Frankl, Boss, and Gordon Allport. Their orientation to psychology has, as common denominators worthy of note, (*a*) a primary subject-concern, which means that the standpoint of the person as an active agent receives immediate rather than residual notice, (*b*) the subject is seen as an immanent development, as a striving to become a totality in a purposeful direction, which development has its "inner logic," (*c*) a shelving of causal analysis and an avoidance of biophysical reductionism. We shall add to these later.

The object-orientation of the general S-R school draws its fundamental model of reality from a philosophical perspective of empiricism, naturalism, and materialism, which crystallized in nineteenth-century "positivism" as a general *Weltanschauung*. For several of the insurgents an important philosophical source of inspiration is existential thought which has important links with both pragmatism (via William James) and phenomenology (via Heidegger, Merleau-Ponty, and others). Existential "analysis" is primarily a philosophizing endeavor that aims at describing the concrete reality of the human subject, of existing man as a totality; there is an implicit rejection of explaining human action in terms of abstract categories (e.g., "neurotic," "manic," etc.) which, in effect, reduce the vital whole to a lifeless part. Since existential philosophy is in part a philosophical anthropology (in the European sense), its insights and analyses of the orientation of the person to reality have had significant appeal among psychologists seeking an alternative philosophical grounding to the one that underlies the Lockean/S-R general model.

Perhaps what is involved in the awakening interest about existential thought is more than an academic matter; it is also a reflection of the historical period. In our postwar world, characterized by significant changes and upheavals in social structure both at home and abroad, a philosophy which seriously addresses

SOURCE. This paper was prepared originally for this volume.
[1] See Gordon W. Allport's lucid exposition of the two psychological traditions in his *Becoming,* New Haven, Conn.: Yale University Press, 1954.

itself to the predicament of the human subject in a world no longer typified by the stability of institutions and the permanence of things around us is in consonance with the reality felt by many. In place of the S-R/psychoanalytical image of the self as an isolated, bleak, negative, lifeless, past-determined, choiceless creature, the existential image of the subject offers a challenging contrast: the human agent is seen as a volitional being who seeks to find meaning in his transactions with reality, to which he is intrinsically related by the nature of his existence; he is a being who fundamentally seeks meaning and a sense to life which cannot be reduced to biological gratification, a being who is animated by a whole gamut of moods and feelings as much as one guided by the intellect. This does not mean that the existential self is depicted as a sweet, syrupy creature; however, what emerges is the whole of human being given in experience.

To give a comprehensive treatment of the existential model of man and his relation to society would, as might be expected, require a volume in itself. What we shall present in this chapter is a sketch of a general existential perspective, which hopefully will suggest to the social scientist still unfamiliar with existential philosophy some of the salient features of this perspective that have a bearing on the personality aspect of social relations. The discussion following, it should be borne in mind, is intended to have a high level of generality rather than being directly testable in controlled experiments, that is, the function of this model is heuristic. Hopefully, the frame of reference will have value in (a) codifying various types of psychological data and (b) suggesting new avenues of research in the interpersonal field. Also, it might be noted that this perspective on personality is part of a more general theory of social existence which is taken to be a *psychosocial* phenomenon; the endeavor of this theory is twofold: first, to describe and elucidate the forms and manifestations of *intersubjective consciousness* as the fundamental human reality; and second, to provide thereby an integrative theoretical scheme for psychology, sociology, and anthropology. Existential phenomenology seems to be an appropriate philosophical grounding for such an interdisciplinary frame of reference. It is essentially a philosophy of the structures and modes of consciousness which opens the world to the human subject; moreover, it stresses the *relationality* of the person: my being or my

concrete existence (*Dasein*) is a being-in-the-world which means it is in part a being-with-others (*Mitsein*). The subject is related to the world directly by the phenomenon of the *intentionality* of consciousness, that is, every psychological act of consciousness intends or is directed toward an object. Thus existential phenomenology has a vital interest in the primary human phenomenon of *perception,* which is a basic activity of the subject, and perception is a psychosocial phenomenon.

I would further like to suggest that an existential and/or phenomenological perspective is not a brand new way of viewing psychological phenomena, or even sociological ones, for that matter. In particular, a phenomenological orientation is at the heart of Gestalt psychology and its offspring (e.g., Lewin's "group dynamics" school), of the "transaction" school brilliantly pioneered by Ames, and of sociometry with its offshoot in "relational analysis."[2] Concerning sociology, I have suggested elsewhere[3] that a reinterpretation of the central theoretical tradition of *subjective realism* (in which we find convergence in the writings of Durkheim, Weber, W. I. Thomas, Scheler, Sorokin, and Parsons) lends itself to an existential-phenomenological philosophical orientation to the nature of reality. The subjective realist viewpoint, *inter alia,* takes society to be not an entity in the sense of a physical object or "thing" occupying a fixed location but rather a psychosocial reality constituted by the intersubjective consciousness of active agents, a reality having recognizable qualities and structures.

The major points we shall cover represent an existential perspective on the human subject. We shall first introduce a cardinal dualism

---

[2] See Hadley Cantril, ed., *The Morning Notes of Adelbert Ames, Jr.,* New Brunswick, N.J.: Rutgers University Press, 1960; Jerome Bruner and Renato Tagiuri, "The Perception of People," in Gardner Lindzey, ed., *Handbook of Social Psychology,* Vol. II, Reading, Mass.: Addison-Wesley, 1954; Renato Tagiuri and Luigi Petrullo, eds., *Person Perception and Interpersonal Behavior,* Stanford, Cal.: Stanford University Press, 1958, reprinted 1965. In the Tagiuri and Petrullo volume, the following should be noted: F. Heider, "Social Perception and Phenomenal Causality," F. Heider, "Perceiving the Other Person," and Robert B. MacLeod, "The Phenomenological Approach to Social Psychology."

[3] Edward A. Tiryakian, "Existential Phenomenology and the Sociological Tradition," *American Sociological Review,* **30** (October 1965), pp. 674–688.

of human existence, the differentiation between ontological and ontic existence; second, we shall draw attention to the significance of the openness of the self; third, the distinction between the *person* and the *existential self* will be exposed, and finally we shall discuss the concept of the *situation* as the key linkage of the self to social reality.

ONTIC AND ONTOLOGICAL EXISTENCE: AUTHENTICITY/INAUTHENTICITY

Aside from radical empiricism, which holds that reality is wholly given by what our sense impressions convey to us, a basic reflection of human thought is that what we find before us is not uniform in significance, that some aspects are more basic than others, and that usually it is the less obvious which is the more important. This qualitative differentiation of reality into what is "more real" and "less real" is given directly in experience when we are aware that some of the things we do or say do not represent the "really me." At the same time, we do not feel that the "not-really-me" is illusory or nonexistent, but rather that it is in some way peripheral or epiphenomenal; yet, and paradoxically, it is the "not-really-me" that we know and are familiar with much more than the "really me."

These preliminary remarks should serve to introduce the reader to a gateway of existential thought: the distinction between two levels of existence, the *ontic* and the *ontological,* with corresponding modes of comportment, the *inauthentic* and the *authentic. Ontic* refers to discrete bodies, to things and objects in the universe given by the senses—to whatever is finite "stuff" capable of being located in space and having recognizable properties (mass, color, weight, height, etc.). *Ontological* refers not to entities but to their ground from which they emerge; ontological signifies the transcendental foundation of empirical entities. For illustrative purpose, we may speak of "the sky," "the horizon," and "the landscape" as the ontological grounding of physical entities. The ontological is the source of unity and identity of phenomenal manifestations or appearances. Applied to the human subject its ontological basis is the *existential self,* which corresponds to the "really me." The being of the existential self is a total structure, *being-in-the-world,* a dynamic unity whose virtual tendency is to actualize its integral possibilities.

Authenticity will be taken to designate comportment of the self carried out with an awareness of the ontological basis of others and in keeping with its own ontological structure (epitomized by Polonius' "Unto thine own self be true"). It is an avoidance of manipulating other persons as one manipulates inanimate objects; authentic comportment eschews identification of the self (and others) as an entity contained in the universe, one having determined properties. It is viewing the self as *being*—a subject—rather than as *having,* that is, a determined object. This further implies that authenticity is genuine action, or "depth behavior" which is reflectively carried out in response to the totality of the person: authenticity implies reflection enriched with commitment, or personal engagement (the engagement of the total self, which includes the body and the soul).

By *inauthentic* is meant comportment which mistakingly identifies the self (either the subject's own self or that of others) as an entity contained in the universe similar to other (nonhuman) things. It involves an implicit denial of the transcendence of the human subject, including in transcendence the temporality of the subject's existence, that is, that our being is structured by an ec-stasy (to use Heidegger's term) of the past and the future in the lived present. Inauthentic behavior is a type of interpersonal relationship which Buber has popularized as the "I-it" relation. Treating and perceiving persons as if they were objects ("it") may be called *objectification,* which refers to both a process and a state; it is reducing the subject to an object, that which grounds to that which is grounded. Objectification in interpersonal behavior has as a further implication that if I treat others as objects, as objects-for-me in particular, then unwittingly I also objectify myself; hence all "I-it" relationships tend to become "it-it" relations.

This may be illustrated in the role relationship between a male and a female prostitute. The prostitute is for the male an *object* of gratification who happens to be a female. For the male, the prostitute is reduced to the dimension of sexual enjoyment. However, there is also an element of dupery in her relationship to him, for the customer is for her an "it," an object not of sexual gratification but of pecuniary gratification. What seems to be a qualitative relationship is really a quantitative one: what counts for him is how much erotic gratification he receives, for her, how much money. This suggests that there is an interchangeability of personnel, for she would exchange partners in favor of one who pays more, he in favor of one who gives greater sexual gratification.

Interpersonal relations which are inauthentically structured into "I-it" relations are not thereby psychologically "unreal" or not meaningful. They can offer pleasure and gratification to the self in the near term and in fact constitute a typical existential defensive mechanism that protects the self from having to face up to itself or to others as *subjects*. The I-it is a psychological object-relation marked by relating to the other in terms of and only in terms of functional specificity (since an object-for-me is determined by specific properties which are instrumental for my ends). Objectification also involves interpreting others as if their activities were determined by single attributes. Thus, to account for the total activity of someone by saying this stems from his "bourgeois background" or his "anal-compulsive" character is to objectify that being. Objectification is thus, upon closer examination, an important instance of *reification* (of solidifying the person, we may say) and of the fallacy of misplaced concreteness.

Parenthetically, we would like to suggest that *neuroses* may be seen as special cases of this type of existential defensive mechanism. The neurotic may be viewed as one who objectifies his fundamental subjectivity (including his becomingness) and that of his significant others; consequently, at the heart of neurosis we suggest there is a refusal to accept responsibility for the neurotic's own being-in-the-world. The I-it neurotic relation as an interobjective relation implies that the neurotic denies his autonomy and the autonomy of the other; to view the self as an object is to view it as determined and without volitional efficacy.

All the well-known Freudian defensive mechanisms (projection, rationalization, etc.) are instances of attempts to stay at the ontic level of existence—the level of complacency, "bad faith," and avoidance of personal responsibility. These shield the subject from being sincere with himself and others, hence from having to act on "good faith." Freud erroneously saw in their presence attempts to ward off sexual anxiety, but from an existential perspective this is reducing an ontological condition to an ontic one, since the being of the subject is irreducible to its sexual quality.

The problem of why the subject seeks to avoid bringing forth his true self to others and, conversely, why he avoids confronting others at the ontological level is an extremely complex problem that mainly lies outside the scope of this paper. However, it may be suggested that objectification has the double function of not getting "hurt" by the other and of not getting "entangled" with the other. There is a substratum of ambivalence attached to intersubjective action: on the one hand, there is a strong attraction to confide in the other, to "let down our hair," to open up and expose our inner sentiments, but on the other hand, the other is also a source of anxiety since he can possess us by our words. Thus a critical condition for intersubjective action is reciprocal *trust,* a condition that cannot be presupposed in every encounter we have of the other.

By keeping interaction at the "objective" level of ontic reality one avoids the more intense and trying intersubjective level of reality. Psychosocial distance in object-relation is very great, even if the object, as in the case of the neurotic, is the subject's own self. On the other hand, such distance in subject-relation, which is grounded in *trust* and probably *respect* as well, is minimal. Objectification thus is a general psychological process of keeping interpersonal and intrapersonal relations at a distance, that is, "objective" or "impersonal." The neurotic has carried this out further than the nonincapacitated individual; at the kernel of the neurosis, we would venture in terms of our general model, is a muted refusal to accept responsibility of one's own ontological structure (including a refusal to become an adult and all that this entails), and along with this the neurotic denies himself and the significant others as subjects worthy of respect and esteem.

Returning to the ontological level of existence, the *existential self is a manifold unity which manifests itself temporally.* Manifestation is a primary existential movement, a coming-into-the-light of perception. Alternatively, existence is actualization, e-mergence, becomingness, realization. The unity of the self encompasses several notions, and these need to be elucidated. The German term *"Dasein,"* used to refer to the human existent, suggests a concrete being who is grounded in a spatial-temporal position (*Da-sein*—a being *there,* and thus not an abstraction). The existential self is an integral whole of corporality and spirituality (or body and psyche) incarnated in human history (the self without psyche or soul would be just "stuff," an entity like other entities; the soul or the psyche without a body would be just an abstraction).

The ontological structure of the self is also a temporal unity: the self that I am fundamentally is a lived present, which is also a present-to-come (future) and a present-that-was (past). The self, following Heidegger's analysis, is a set of possibilities that become realized in time, and their actualization is, at least in part, a function of the subject's volition and acts of choice. Choosing is the possibility of possibilities which is continuously be-before the subject. This immediately implies that no analysis or comprehension of the self can be adequate if it ignores the temporality, corporality, or spirituality of the subject. At the same time, the formulation of the self as a manifold dynamic unity also implies a functional integration so that the body (and its gestures), for example, dis-closes the self and is therefore not just a possession or implement of the self. This may indicate why modern existential thought places a heavy stress on proposing that the subject *is* a body as much as *has* a body.

Of course, to view the body as a utensil, as a possession, in brief, as an object-for-the-self, is a very common phenomenon, particularly in a period when public life (the sector of "*das Man*") makes conspicuous displays of eroticism. This, indeed, is one of the major aspects of objectification in secularized society which can take extreme pathological forms. The body may be reduced to erotic qualities, or it may be reduced to its economic value as a commodity (to be used for fertilizer, for making soap, for its gold content, etc.).

To view the body as an object is to introduce a scissure in the primary, incarnate ontological unity of the self. It leads to what Laing has aptly termed the "schizoid" state,[4] which is a crucial separation of psyche from body at the level of subjective experience. Conversely, to view the other's body as an object is to introduce a fundamental obstacle, an existential hiatus, in interpersonal perception and comportment—the existential subjectivity of the other is then collapsed to his (or her) body, which is phenomenologically transformed into an object-for-me. The body as an object-for-me becomes a material obstacle to be conquered or possessed while at the same time there is a denial that the other's existence transcends his or her body.

On the contrary, the transcendental aspects of the self are immediately presented if we replace an ontic perspective with an ontological one, because the self's subjectivity means that the environment does not invariably determine the course of events followed by the subject (i.e., what lies outside consciousness is transformed immediately by the meaningful interpretations consciousness makes of it), and, moreover, the temporality or historicity of the subject means that the self is not physically contained or exhausted at a given point. The existential self is a temporalizing phenomenon: self-expression and self-unfolding form part of an integral process Jung has termed *individuation*. This indicates that the self is not a permanently determined physical *entity;* nor is it reducible or equivalent to a biological *organism* which has genetically determined stages of biological growth and decay within limits of the nonhuman environment.

The temporal structure of the existential self differs qualitatively from objective, abstract time inasmuch as psychological (and psychosocial) time is multiple and discontinuous. An important aspect here is the reversibility of psychic time structure, so that phenomenologically the existential self may go back on itself (the phenomenon of *regression* is a pathological aspect of this general tendency). However, this can serve the self in a positive as well as in a negative sense: going back in psychological (and psychosocial) time is a return to a more fundamental, de-differentiated (or "primitive") state which enables the existential self to grasp its essential structure more firmly and thereby allows it to return to the present with greater energy at its disposal.

In our existential model of the self, then, there is a supposition that the ontological tendency, the primary movement, is a forward-striving, future-oriented unfolding (remembering that existential being *is* a becoming). Becoming is not random or due to chance factors solely but the resultant of (*a*) the self's possibilities (the "real me" is not tangible but neither is it nonexistent—it is a set of potentialities) and (*b*) objective environmental circumstances. The ultimate meaning of the self's becoming, of what a given individual existence signifies, cannot be determined until the self has exhausted all its possibilities. In existential thought this is often taken to be death—death is viewed as the possibility that ends all possibilities since with death no further becoming in this world is possible.

---

[4] R. D. Laing, *The Divided Self,* Chicago, Ill.: Quadrangle Books, 1960.

If the ontological virtual tendency of the existing self is a nonrandom becomingness—a fulfillment of the self's potentialities in the social world—then the process may be arrested. The progressive actualization of the self may collapse to the ontic level so that the existential self is lost sight of. When the self is identified as an entity (we have previously referred to this as the general inauthentic mode of *objectification*), its temporalization is forgotten, that is, its past and its future are reduced to a "just-here" (an inauthentic present). The human agent is reduced to an *atemporal* entity for whom the daily routine is the only way of life or for whom the enjoyments of the present are all-engrossing but yet self-defeating. We refer to these as manifestations of either *stagnation* or being "in a rut." They manifest the inability and/or unwillingness of the agent to assume the totality of his existence, which in its temporal modality is not just a present but also a past and a future.

THE SELF AS OPEN TO THE WORLD

Inherent in the existential model of self as being-in-the-world is the essential *openness* of personality structure.[5] A prerequisite of subjectivity, it may be suggested, is openness as a mode of human being. Openness is a very complex condition involved in our experiencing the world, and it is worth attempting to explicate some aspects of this condition.

In its ontic appearance as a body, the openness of the self is grounded in its orifices. Inasmuch as the body has symbolic significance for the totality of the self, the holes of the body have a meaning as "doors" and "windows" to the external reality.[6] In this context, we may draw attention to the familiar image of the three monkeys who see no evil, hear no evil, and speak no evil: this symbolizes the self seeking to ward off existential harm (evil spirits) by plugging up its orifices. In

many initiation rites an integral aspect of the ritual (often symbolizing the death of the child and the rebirth of the person as adult) involves plugging up the ears, mouth, and nostrils at a crucial moment so that no evil power can enter into the body.

Another aspect of the openness of the self lies in its historical grounding: being-in-the-world means to participate in social time and thus in history. I am today what I am in part because of my historical past and in part because of what I anticipate to be my historical future. I am also historical in a collective or social sense, that is, I am open to and take as mine the history of my people, and this leads me to realize that I am not contained in my finite and solid appearance but that my being goes out spatially and temporally.

The self then transcends its finiteness as a physical body through its historical consciousness and the consciousness of its intersubjectivity. That is, subjectivity as consciousness is much more ontologically than an individual consciousness (an "I" consciousness): it is a consciousness of temporality and a collective consciousness (the self in integrally also a "we," a "being-together"). Moreover, the historical consciousness of the self is also a historical *conscience:* human historicity is not just cognitively perceived but also morally interpreted and evaluated. Self-awareness, in its fullest sense, then, is not just cognitive awareness of one's finiteness but also awareness of one's historical transcendence, which includes solidarity with one's fellows.

The openness of the self to the world is further grounded in the social (or intersubjective) dimension of existence. Besides the body, which extends the self to others (the self pro-jects itself to others in its bodily gestures, particularly facial ones), thereby mediating the subjective and the environment, a cardinal facet of sociation is language. In this context, language is a primary relational dimension of the existential self. In this sense it may be asserted that subjectivity is also manifested in one's words: *I am what I say.* With language I can ex-press myself, that is, I give of my inner self in an externalizing, objectifying manner. It may be pointed out here that because speaking or uttering words is a dis-closure of the self, of the inner self or "real me," there is a prereflective caution or even anxiety in talking. Much of our communication with others involves indirect commu-

---

[5] Subsequent to writing this article I have come across G. W. Allport's "The Open System in Personality Theory," *Journal of Abnormal and Social Psychology,* LXI (1960), pp. 301–310. I am delighted to note how much the existential model of the openness of the person to the world is in accord with Allport's perspective, especially his remarks on p. 306 f.

[6] Cf. Jean-Paul Sartre, *Existentialism and Human Emotions,* New York: Philosophical Library, 1957, pp. 84–90. See also Ludwig Binswanger, "The Case of Ellen West," in Rollo May *et al.,* eds., *Existence,* New York: Basic Books, 1958, pp. 237–364.

nication (metaphors, innuendos, allusions, ironies, parables), and collective secrets, which represent the essentials of an organzation or a society, may often be divulged only to the initiated by means of a secret (i.e., nonpublic) language. The self's disclosure in language means that it is a giving—and perhaps the fundamental gift and giving as a human activity is words. It may also become a give-away which results in the objectification of the subject; this underlies the symbolic significance of "nailing down" what somebody says or asking him to "put it in writing." By words I may become an object-for-others instead of manifesting my subjectivity.[7]

Language is also a primary mode of taking in the world; discourse is the complementary process of manifesting subjectivity. Naming things and talking about things is a constituent part of perceiving them. This two-way linguistic interchange is, of course, *intercourse*, which in terms of an existential model has its authentic as well as inauthentic mode. If intercourse is object-oriented, it is impersonal, addressed to the others as objects; inauthenticity in discourse implies that I am more motivated to hear myself talk and to have others hear me talk than I am interested in sharing intercourse with others. In inauthenticity, discourse is one-sided; what the other says to me is something that I *hear* in passing but I do not *listen* to ("in one ear, out the other" expresses this attitude). On the other hand, subject-oriented discourse is communion: it is meant for and it expresses the self's real consciousness of the other as subject. As in all aspects of the authenticity/inauthenticity polarity, most of our everyday conversations fall somewhere in between. Without going further into the phenomenological aspects of discourse, let us reiterate that language is a primary feature of existential openness, of being-in-the-world, and moreover that the Being of the world dis-closes itself in words (as in maxims, proverbs, and poetic language). But language is one aspect, not the sole one, of self-expression since the existential self as an integral whole of body and psyche also manifests itself in nonverbal gestures.

Finally, the openness of the ontological structure of the existential self is expressed in encounters of the subject with the realm of the sacred. These are dramatically shown in phenomena of religious possession, wherein the self is suddenly engulfed by the presence of spirits without this being in any way intended. There is, of course, a whole range of "enthusiasm" phenomena ranging from "inspiration," which most people feel at some time or another, to the much more intense and extreme forms of schizophrenic possession, where the individual consciousness feels displaced in its totality by spirits alien to it. Encounters with the sacred are by nature extra-ordinary since they put into relief the ontological basis of the self. Confronted with the sacred (be it the divine or the demonic), the experience of the subject is that this is a qualitatively different interaction from that typical of contacts with others. One cannot hide one's subjectivity from the divine, whereas concealment is always possible in interactions involving the everyday self.

The contacts between the existential self and the realm of the sacred is not reducible to a physical experience such as the contact between objects or solids. An encounter of the subject with ontological reality can also be a very quiet "internal affair," as in the instance of prayer or even in the experience of hearing the call of conscience.[8] When the call of conscience is not only heard but answered, consciousness of self merges into conscience of self, that is, moral cognition (etymologically, consciousness = conscience). In a related vein, it may be suggested that social interaction as intersubjective consciousness is grounded in the openness of the self to the other. Thus interaction is predicated on the ability of the subject to *respond* to the other; a *response* in terms of the ontological self and manifesting a positive awareness of accepting the obligations inherent in the interaction is an act of *responsibility*. The becomingness of the existential self, which is inherent in the existential model, is constituted in part by the voluntary acceptance of responsibility. The notion of *adult* has as much a social significance as a

---

[7] Hegel first traced out the phenomenological process of the alienation of consciousness in his *Phenomenology of the Spirit*.

[8] Even the finite, biophysical image of man contained in psychoanalysis unwittingly acknowledges the transcendental aspect of the self in the terminology of "super-ego," a translation of *"über-ich,"* that which is over or transcends the finite ego. The term "id" means, of course, "it" in German, and the ego-id relationship is an "I-it" one. For various reasons, Freud failed to recognize that the suger-ego (=conscience) is the ontological foundation of the person's being-in-the-world.

biophysical one, and we would suggest a re-interpretation of *maturation* as the process parallelling *socialization:* it is the learning and internalization (or voluntary acceptance[9]) of the responsibilities involved in one's sphere of social interaction.

THE PERSON

Important to the general model under discussion is the notion of *person,* which provides the existential self with a concrete grounding in social space and social time, just as the body (the basis of the *individual*) provides it with a grounding in the physical environment. The person is intersubjective; it is the social self, that is, the self as perceiving others, being perceived by others, and above all interacting with others. Although the person gives the self its social facticity, it does not have a physical referent; that is, the person is not an entity or an object but a *presence*—the presence of the self in the social world.

This social constitution of the person is, of course, indicated by the etymological derivation of the person from the Latin *persona,* meaning mask.[10] This consideration leads to a familiar model of the person as an *actor* whose actions are a function of his roles vis-à-vis others; society taken as the network of social interactions is seen in the image of the stage, as the vehicle of countless social dramas. Insofar as this dramaturgic model is a relational model of social reality which implicitly rejects a subject-object cleavage, this model has existential and phenomenological aspects. The self-as-person exists in a social milieu, is aware of this milieu, and is constituted by a pattern of social activity which is not random but structured by extra-individual, interpersonal norms and expectations.

It is no wonder that one of the best known of contemporary social psychologists/sociologists, Erving Goffman, is, *malgré lui,* first and foremost a phenomenological describer of everyday "typical" social action. At the same time, Goffman and some other "role theorists" tend to fall prey to viewing social reality as just composed of delusions and illusions as characteristics of the social game. In this extremist view of the person as stage actor, the person becomes equated with a stereotyped, fixed mask who plays his socialized role so well that he forgets who he is or what he looks like when the staged performance is over.[11] Absent from this model is the emphasis on *action* as an activity that engages the person as a moral agent, thereby differentiating him from the passivity of nonreflective organisms (which behave as a function of the environment but do not act—or "proact," to use Henry Murray's term). The person seen as victim and/or exploiter of his social setting appears as a *pretence* rather than as a *presence.* In the Goffman perspective, the person is not really a person but more an other-directed chameleon, or worse, a Brownian particle batted back and forth across the social net; the person qua mask-wearer is a "phony" whose surrounding stage props (institutional social settings) are equally "phony." The task of the social scientist who adheres to this model becomes one essentially of "unmasking" the falsehoods hidden by the public mask, and at this point there is an interesting convergence to be noted between Goffman's approach and that of such seemingly different figures as Marx, Freud, and Sartre, since the paramount concern of each of these is the "unmasking" of social appearances. Common to all these writers is a denigration of the person's acts as manifestations of the self's volition, as exercises of the self's ontological autonomy. Goffman no less than Sartre begins with a phenomenological view of the person as a social participant, but each then radicalizes this to a form of social behaviorism from which no depth analysis of the person can emerge.

Some of the difficulty involves viewing the social mask as a mere facade behind which there is nothing. The mask is primarily a regulating screen, a sort of censory (and sensory) apparatus. The social mask protects the existential self from the gaze of the others (of the "they") until such time as the others are identi-

9 This underlies the *voluntaristic* frame of social action, as contained in the views of Durkheim, Weber, Thomas, and, more recently, Talcott Parsons.

10 See the brilliant discussion of the psychosocial dimensions of the mask by Alessandro Pizzorno, "Le Masque," in *Cahiers Renaud-Barrault*, **31** (November 1960), pp. 143–169. For a more available source, see Jean-Louis Bédouin, *Les Masques,* Paris: Presses Universitaires de France (Edition "Que Sais-je?"), 1961.

11 Characteristic of this perspective is Goffman's statement: "I have suggested two extremes: an individual may be taken in by his own act or be cynical about it," *The Presentation of Self in Everyday Life,* Edinburgh: University of Edinburgh Social Sciences Research Centre, 1958, p.11.

fied as being of the same *communitas* as the self (of the "we"). Frequently, the mask of the person is the opposite of what he feels ("laughing on the outside, crying on the inside"). It is in this sense the vehicle of a dialectical transformation of personality.[12]

The mask, by blending in with the rest of the social landscape, is man's natural camouflage since man's proper habitat is the social world. From this psychological consideration, the significance of the mask is that it presents a stereotyped personality, a single seemingly immutable appearance which enables the person to become or remain socially invisible. Its protective function is to hide the true feelings of the self, for the true feelings of the self are what animates the person, what sustains and propels him in the fundamental existential process of becoming. Since such feelings, being at the core of the existential self, can only be expressed in intimacy and privacy, the mask enables the person to circulate freely in public life, particularly though not wholly in situations where the subject experiences a status of subordination vis-à-vis the other.

The very impersonality of the mask gives it its familiarity. Everyone can recognize the mask and what it stands for as a social character. The mask is universal, objective, typical, impersonal.[13] This can provide the mask with an important pedagogic function. In "primitive" societies, it is the mask that instructs the young and reinforces the structure of the moral order that frames the social world. The mask is the public medium of expressing and teaching what is most inherently sacred to the collectivity. The mask mediates the visible and the invisible; it relays one to the other.

We need to trace further the etymology of *person,* which derives not only from *persona* but also more primitively from the Greek *prosopon,* meaning a person as *face.* The face is much more than a composite physical object; it is an existential expression of the self, an appearance and form of the self. In our immediate perception of the other our prereflective response is to his physiognomy, to the face he is; the face is the region of the body which provides immediate attraction (or repulsion) to the other's personality.[14] Stated somewhat differently, the self as person is presented to others in the face.

The wink, the smile, the frown, are direct emanations of the sentient self—indeed, facial gestures (what may be called the "language of the face") are of major importance in regulating the psychological distance between persons. Thus turning your back on someone or looking the other way symbolizes your wish not to face him, that is, your wish not to interact with him; the physical act of not facing someone thus implies a denial of intersubjective consciousness. The same is produced by "making a face" at someone, and the gesture of sticking out the tongue may be interpreted phenomenologically as a radical denial of having anything to say to the other. More broadly, the face as a weapon of the person has various facets such as the well-known powers of the "evil eye," and even more bizarre uses of the face have been noted.[15] The very quality of social interaction, a gauge of intimacy, is indicated by the term "face-to-face contacts." This is another expression of the personal, for face-to-face contacts are requisites for interpersonal relations.

In brief, the face is the appearance of the person as an authentic being; it is a radiation and a glow of the inner, basic self. The mask is very much related to the face, but whereas the face is an unfolding expression of the person, hence an outward appearance of the actualization of the self, the mask is a frozen facial gesture which is impersonal. The person as mask-wearer is existentially inert (a being rather than a becoming), whereas the person as face is animated.

We can also say that the person is the "outer self," the externalization or appearance of the existential self. The outer self is grounded in the body and in society. The body—that which locates the self by giving it facticity in time and space—has two interrelated aspects. There is the body as a physical entity, and there is also the body as a social entity. A person is

---

12 We exclude from present discussion the direct transformation of the personality arising from the wearer being *possessed* by the mask, a phenomenon which may frequently be seen in initiation rites, although it is by no means confined to this.
13 The mask thus has a similar social function to that of the uniform—indeed the two are complementary in a sense for the mask may be viewed as the social cloak of the face and the uniform as a social cloak of the body.

14 Paul F. Secord, "Facial Features and Inference Processes in Interpersonal Perception," in Tagiuri and Petrullo, *op. cit.,* pp. 300–315.
15 Mary Kingsley reported the practice in a region of West Africa of killing a foe by the subject throwing his face at his enemy! See her *West African Studies,* London: Macmillan, 1899, pp. 165 ff.

some-body, and a person who is a nullity in the social order is a no-body. The correlations between the two are subject to historical change (including the whims of fashions), but the relations between the physical state of the body and the social activity of the self are ever-present.[16] The outer self is also grounded in society, which we treat as primarily an inter-subjective reality of consciousness: individual consciousness is structured and constituted by social consciousness.

To summarize, the person is not matter and the person is not spirit (or psyche) but rather the complex interaction of the two, which interaction only unfolds in social life. The person is the *embodiment* of the existential self and partakes of its sacredness; without this ontological foundation, the idea of the person having "rights," including the right to privacy, would be a sheer absurdity or at best a social fiction.

THE SITUATION: ACTUALIZING OF THE SELF

A last component in this brief exposition of an existential model of the person is the notion of the *situation*. What concretizes the self, what transforms the *individual* (as a species-typical member) into a person is its situation. The notion of situation has a phenomenological status that differentiates it from the physicalistic notion of the environment; stated in other terms, the *situation* transcends the physical *site*. A person is situated and situated himself in the world. His interaction with others occurs in situations that are psychologically defined by the person. That is, the site is a physical locale of potentiality, but the situation is an actualization of the locale as a result of the meaning the person finds in it. The situation thus is always to an important extent personal—it is *my* situation, *your* situation, *his* situation; a situation does not exist abstractly as an absolute location. In an authentic engagement, the totality of the person is committed to his situation; a situation makes personal demands upon the self (i.e., demands which call for more than conventional responses), and it is in the attempted response to his situation that a person reveals himself. Of course, the person may avoid committing his existential self to the

situation and phenomenologically remain detached (one symbolic expression of this is to say "his heart is not in it").

Undoubtedly, the most dramatic actions of persons are found to occur in "extreme situations," a term in social psychology that bears affinity with Karl Jaspers' notion of "*Grenz-situation*" or "boundary-situation." What is implied by the notion of "extreme situation" is the breakdown of conventional institutional props, of the customary, of the routine. In a sense, it is a social situation in which the human subjects are totally involved (and not just in a fragmented role aspect, which typifies ordinary social settings). The extreme situation is characterized by destructuration of conventional behavior patterns, radical estrangement from the security and comforts of everyday life, and near-absolute ambiguity and unpredictability.

Extreme situations range in variety from the situation of dying (so well depicted in Tolstoi's *The Death of Ivan Ilyitch*) to collective situations such as the concentration camp[17] and disasters.[18] They could also be said to include no less intense and equally demanding situations as the encounter with the transcendental sacred (as in mystic and other religious experience of the divine or the demonic). The common denominator in all cases would be the dramatic, intense, and extraordinary intersubjective encounter marked by the "nakedness" of the person before the other or others. That is, whereas ordinarily, in the everyday social setting, the existential self manifests itself only indirectly in its comportment, it stands directly revealed in the nakedness of the extreme situation, or perhaps we should say that the extreme situation is highly instrumental to the self-realization and actualization of the existential self.

The extreme situation is par excellence the qualitative social setting wherein the radical fracture of what is normally taken as a given obliges the person to assume personal responsibility in confronting the other. It is in the

---

[16] Cf. Mauss's seminal "Les Techniques du Corps," his *Sociologie et Anthropologie,* Paris: Presses Universitaires de France, 1960, pp. 363–386; also, Pitirim A. Sorokin's complementary *Social Mobility,* New York: Harper, 1927, pp. 319–322.

[17] Of particular interest to an existential perspective which views the extreme situation as one that may lead to self-realization is Viktor E. Frankl's *From Death-Camp to Existentialism,* Boston, Mass.: Beacon Press, 1959; in this vein see also Ernest Gordon, *Through the Valley of the Kwai,* New York: Harper, 1962.

[18] Edward A. Tiryakian, "Aftermath of a Thermonuclear Attack on the United States: Some Sociological Considerations," *Social Problems,* VI (Spring 1959), pp. 291–303.

extreme situation that aspects of psychological depths emerge into the open, whereas in routine social settings they remain latent and invisible; it is in the extreme situation that we can see what sort of a person the subject really is because by the very nature of its destructuration and acute ambiguity, the extreme situation explodes the enigma of the social mask. Both the heights of aristocratic grandeur, of self-abnegation, of heroism, as well as the depths of sordidness, egoism, and cowardice are likely to be found in extreme situations such as disasters or revolutions. In response to the destructuration of the familiar social world, the person will manifest from the deepest confines of the existential self actions that are profoundly religious, demonic or divine (hence extraordinary). This does not mean that a given person will exhibit all ranges of extreme behavior, but we may assert that extreme situations tend to polarize social behavior among members of a collectivity. The extreme situation *personalizes* rather than *individualizes,* for the polarization of behavior has a centripetal aspect as well as a centrifugal one. That is, it may draw persons more firmly together who are able to see each other directly in a way impossible in the everyday routine society; thus the extreme situation is one functional to the genesis of a "we" community feeling just

as paradoxically it is functional to the breakdown of existing communities which have become objectified and no longer lived.[19]

CONCLUSION

We have sought in this chapter to suggest the outlines of an existential model of the self and the person. Although interdependent and interrelated, the two are not identical. The person is the human agent who manifests himself in social space and social time; the existential self is an ontological structure which is potentiality and potency and in which the person is grounded. The person may be viewed as the realization of the self in history; personality is thereby the integration of possibilities that have become realized or manifest with those that have yet to become actualized. The becoming of a person is always a social becoming: I become a person as I progress through social situations (this is the existential basis of the notion of socialization). Yet the end of the existential becoming may not be a finite or empirical one but an extratemporal one, which underlies notions of a personal "calling," "mission," "destiny," and "vocation." If the person becomes enmeshed in the encounter with entities, he becomes depersonalized or objectified—the person is then reduced to being a character, a type, a mask, a thing. Objectification is, in a sense, a *denaturing* of the person, a turning of the person against its authentic, ontological nature. If objectification is a social phenomenon, it should also be kept in mind that the encounter with others is also vital in achieving authentic selfhood, for it is in social participation that one achieves consciousness of the self as a person.

---

[19] As Robert Wilson puts it in interpreting Camus' *The Plague,* "the challenge of extremity may stimulate both a firmer communal bondage and a more ample individual capacity to deal with the environment." Robert N. Wilson, "Albert Camus: Personality as a Creative Struggle," in Robert W. White, ed., *The Study of Lives, Essays on Personality in Honor of Henry A. Murray,* New York: Atherton Press, 1963, p. 361.

BIBLIOGRAPHY

Berdyaev, Nicolas, *Solitude and Society,* London: Geoffrey Bles, 1947.
Durkheim, Emile, "The Dualism of Human Nature and its Social Conditions."
    in Kurt H. Wolff, ed., *Emile Durkheim 1858–1917* Columbus, O.:
    Ohio State University Press, 1960, pp. 325–340.
Jung, C. G., Collected Works, Vol. 9, Part II. *Aion: Contributions
    to the Symbolism of the Self,* New York: Bollingen
    Series, Pantheon Books.
Mauss, Marcel, *Sociologie et Anthropologie,* Paris: Presses Universitaires
    de France, 1960. Part V, "Une Catégorie de l'Esprit Humain:
    La Notion de Personne, Celle de 'Moi'," pp. 331–362.
Merleau-Ponty, Maurice, *Phenomenology of Perception,* London:
    Routledge and Kegan Paul, 1962.

Mounier, Emmanuel, *Manifeste au service du Personnalisme,*
     Paris: Montaigne, 1936.
——, *Le Personnalisme,* Paris: Presses Universitaires de France, 1962.
Pfuetze, Paul E., *The Social Self,* New York: Bookman Associates,
     1954.
Van Ames, Meters, "Mead and Husserl on the Self," *Philosophy and
     Phenomenological Research,* XV (1955), pp. 320–331.

Chapter 8 The Social Self: On the Meanings of "I"

CHARLES HORTON COOLEY

It is well to say at the outset that by the word "self" in this discussion is meant simply that which is designated in common speech by the pronouns of the first person singular, "I," "me," "my," "mine," and "myself." "Self" and "ego" are used by metaphysicians and moralists in many other senses, more or less remote from the "I" of daily speech and thought, and with these I wish to have as little to do as possible. What is here discussed is what psychologists call the empirical self, the self that can be apprehended or verified by ordinary observation. I qualify it by the word social not as implying the existence of a self that is not social—for I think that the "I" of common language always has more or less distinct reference to other people as well as the speaker—but because I wish to emphasize and dwell upon the social aspect of it.

* * *

The distinctive thing in the idea for which the pronouns of the first person are names is apparently a characteristic kind of feeling which may be called the my-feeling or sense of appropriation. Almost any sort of ideas may be associated with this feeling, and so come to be named "I" or "mine," but the feeling, and that alone it would seem, is the determining factor in the matter. As Professor James says in his admirable discussion of the self, the words "me" and "self" designate "all the things which have the power to produce in a stream of consciousness excitement of a certain peculiar sort."

* * *

I do not mean that the feeling aspect of the self is necessarily more important than any

SOURCE. Charles Horton Cooley, *Human Nature and the Social Order,* New York: Charles Scribner's Sons, 1902, pp. 136–141, 144–153, and 155–157. Copyright 1902. Reprinted by permission of Charles Scribner's Sons, Inc.

other, but that it is the immediate and decisive sign and proof of what "I" is; there is no appeal from it; if we go behind it it must be to study its history and conditions, not to question its authority. But, of course, this study of history and conditions may be quite as profitable as the direct contemplation of self-feeling. What I would wish to do is to present each aspect in its proper light.

The emotion or feeling of self may be regarded as an instinct, doubtless evolved in connection with its important function in stimulating and unifying the special activities of individuals. . . .

. . . Meantime the feeling itself does not remain unaltered, but undergoes differentiation and refinement just as does any other sort of crude innate feeling. Thus, while retaining under every phase its characteristic tone or flavor, it breaks up into innumerable self-sentiments. And concrete self-feeling, as it exists in mature persons, is a whole made up of these various sentiments, along with a good deal of primitive emotion not thus broken up. It partakes fully of the general development of the mind, but never loses that peculiar gusto of appropriation that causes us to name a thought with a first-personal pronoun.

* * *

Since "I" is known to our experience primarily as a feeling, or as a feeling-ingredient in our ideas, it cannot be described or defined without suggesting that feeling. We are sometimes likely to fall into a formal and empty way of talking regarding questions of emotion, by attempting to define that which is in its nature primary and indefinable. A formal definition of self-feeling, or indeed of any sort of feeling, must be as hollow as a formal definition of the taste of salt, or the color red; we can expect to know what it is only by experiencing it. There can be no final test of the self except the way we feel; it is that toward which we have the "my" attitude. But as this feeling is quite as familiar to us and as easy to recall as the taste of salt or the color red, there should be no difficulty in understanding what is meant by it. One need only imagine some attack on his "me," say ridicule of his dress or an attempt to take away his property or his child, or his good name by slander, and self-feeling immediately appears. Indeed, he need only pronounce, with strong emphasis, one of the self-words, like "I" or "my," and self-feeling will be recalled by association.

*   *   *

As many people have the impression that the verifiable self, the object that we name with "I," is usually the material body, it may be well to say that this impression is an illusion, easily dispelled by anyone who will undertake a simple examination of facts. It is true that when we philosophize a little about "I" and look around for a tangible object to which to attach it, we soon fix upon the material body as the most available locus; but when we use the word naively, as in ordinary speech, it is not very common to think of the body in connection with it; not nearly so common as it is to think of other things. There is no difficulty in testing this statement, since the word "I" is one of the commonest in conversation and literature, so that nothing is more practicable than to study its meaning at any length that may be desired. One need only listen to ordinary speech until the word has occurred, say, a hundred times, noting its connections, or observe its use in a similar number of cases by the characters in a novel. Ordinarily it will be found that in not more than ten cases in a hundred does "I" have reference to the body of the person speaking. It refers chiefly to opinions, purposes, desires, claims, and the like, concerning matters that involve no thought of the body. *I* think or feel so and so; *I* wish or intend so and so; *I* want this or that; are typical uses, the self-feeling being associated with the view, purpose, or object mentioned. It should also be remembered that "my" and "mine" are as much the names of the self as "I" and these, of course, commonly refer to miscellaneous possessions.

*   *   *

As already suggested, instinctive self-feeling is doubtless connected in evolution with its important function in stimulating and unifying the special activities of individuals. It appears to be associated chiefly with ideas of the exercise of power, of being a cause, ideas that emphasize the antithesis between the mind and the rest of the world. The first definite thoughts that a child associates with self-feeling are probably those of his earliest endeavors to control visible objects—his limbs, his playthings, his bottle, and the like. Then he attempts to control the actions of the persons about him, and so his circle of power and self-feeling widens without interruption to the most complex objects of mature ambition. Although he does not say "I" or "my" during the first year or two, yet he expresses so clearly by his actions the feeling that adults associate with these words that we cannot deny him a self even in the first weeks.

The correlation of self-feeling with purposeful activity is easily seen by observing the course of any productive enterprise. If a boy sets about making a boat, and has any success, his interest in the matter waxes, he gloats over it, the keel and stem are dear to his heart, and its ribs are more to him than those of his own frame. He is eager to call in his friends and acquaintances, saying to them, "See what I am doing! Is it not remarkable?," feeling elated when it is praised, and resentful or humiliated when fault is found with it. But so soon as he finishes it and turns to something else, his self-feeling begins to fade away from it, and in a few weeks at most he will have become comparatively indifferent. We all know that much the same course of feeling accompanies the achievements of adults. It is impossible to produce a picture, a poem, an essay, a difficult bit of masonry, or any other work of art or craft, without having self-feeling regarding it, amounting usually to considerable excitement and desire for some sort of appreciation; but this rapidly diminishes with the activity itself, and often lapses into indifference after it ceases.

It may perhaps be objected that the sense of self, instead of being limited to times of activity and definite purpose, is often most conspicuous when the mind is unoccupied or undecided, and that the idle and ineffectual are commonly the most sensitive in their self-esteem. This, however, may be regarded as an instance of the principle that all instincts are likely to assume troublesome forms when denied wholesome expression. The need to exert power, when thwarted in the open fields of life, is the more likely to assert itself in trifles.

The social self is simply any idea, or system of ideas, drawn from the communicative life, that the mind cherishes as its own. Self-feeling has its chief scope *within* the general life, not outside of it, the special endeavor or tendency of which it is the emotional aspect finding its principal field in the mind by a world of personal impressions.

As connected with the thought of other persons it is always a consciousness of the peculiar or differentiated aspect of one's life, because that is the aspect that has to be sustained by purpose and endeavor, and its more aggressive forms tend to attach themselves to whatever one finds to be at once congenial to one's own tendencies and at variance with those of others with whom one is in mental contact. It is here that they are most needed to serve their function of stimulating characteristic activity, of fostering those personal variations which the general plan of life seems to require. Heaven, says Shakespeare, doth divide

The state of man in divers functions,
Setting endeavor in continual motion,

and self-feeling is one of the means by which this diversity is achieved.

Agreeably to this view we find that the aggressive self manifests itself most conspicuously in an appropriativeness of objects to secure his own peculiar development, and to the danger of opposition from others who also need them. And this extends from material objects to lay hold, in the same spirit, of the attentions and affections of other people, of all sorts of plans and ambitions, including the noblest special purposes the mind can entertain, and indeed of any conceivable idea which may come to seem a part of one's life and in need of assertion against someone else.

* * *

That the "I" of common speech has a meaning which includes some sort of reference to other persons is involved in the very fact that the word and the ideas it stands for are phenomena of language and the communicative life. It is doubtful whether it is possible to use language at all without thinking more or less distinctly of someone else, and certainly the things to which we give names and which have a large place in reflective thought are almost always those which are impressed upon us by our contact with other people. Where there is no communication there can be no nomenclature and no developed thought. What we call "me," "mine," or "myself" is, then, not

something separate from the general life, but the most interesting part of it, a part whose interest arises from the very fact that it is both general and individual. That is, we care for it just because it is that phase of the mind that is living and striving in the common life, trying to impress itself upon the minds of others. "I" is a militant social tendency, working to hold and enlarge its place in the general current of tendencies. So far as it can it waxes, as all life does. To think of it as apart from society is a palpable absurdity of which no one could be guilty who really *saw* it as a fact of life.

Der Mensch erkennt sich nur im Menschen, nur
Das Leben lehret jedem was er sei.[1]

If a thing has no relation to others of which one is conscious he is unlikely to think of it at all, and if he does think of it he cannot, it seems to me, regard it as emphatically *his*. The appropriative sense is always the shadow, as it were, of the common life, and when we have it we have a sense of the latter in connection with it. Thus, if we think of a secluded part of the woods as "ours," it is because we think, also, that others do not go there. As regards the body I doubt if we have a vivid my-feeling about any part of it which is not thought of, however vaguely, as having some actual or possible reference to someone else. Intense self-consciousness regarding it arises along with instincts or experiences which connect it with the thought of others. Internal organs, like the liver, are not thought of as peculiarly ours unless we are trying to communicate something regarding them, as, for instance, when they are giving us trouble and we are trying to get sympathy.

"I," then, is not all of the mind, but a peculiarly central, vigorous, and well-knit portion of it, not separate from the rest but gradually merging into it, and yet having a certain practical distinctness, so that a man generally shows clearly enough by his language and behavior what his "I" is as distinguished from thoughts he does not appropriate. It may be thought of, as already suggested, under the analogy of a central colored area on a lighted wall. It might also, and perhaps more justly, be compared to the nucleus of a living cell, not altogether separate from the surrounding

---

[1] "Only in man does man know himself; life alone teaches each one what he is."—Goethe, *Tasso*-. Act 2, Scene 3.

matter, out of which indeed it is formed, but more active and definitely organized.

The reference to other persons involved in the sense of self may be distinct and particular, as when a boy is ashamed to have his mother catch him at something she has forbidden, or it may be vague and general, as when one is ashamed to do something which only his conscience, expressing his sense of social responsibility, detects and disapproves; but it is always there. There is no sense of "I," as in pride or shame, without its correlative sense of you, or he, or they.

'   *   *   *

In a very large and interesting class of cases the social reference takes the form of a somewhat definite imagination of how one's self— that is any idea he appropriates—appears in a particular mind, and the kind of self-feeling one has is determined by the attitude toward this attributed to that other mind. A social self of this sort might be called the reflected or looking-glass self:

Each to each a looking-glass
Reflects the other that doth pass.

As we see our face, figure, and dress in the glass, and are interested in them because they are ours, and pleased or otherwise with them according as they do or do not answer to what we should like them to be; so in imagination we perceive in another's mind some thought of our appearance, manners, aims, deeds, character, friends, and so on, and are variously affected by it.

A self-idea of this sort seems to have three principal elements: the imagination of our appearance to the other person; the imagination of his judgment of that appearance; and some sort of self-feeling, such as pride or mortification. The comparison with a looking-glass hardly suggests the second element, the imagined judgment, which is quite essential. The thing that moves us to pride or shame is not the mere mechanical reflection of ourselves, but an imputed sentiment, the imagined effect of this reflection upon another's mind. This is evident from the fact that the character and weight of that other, in whose mind we see ourselves, makes all the difference with our feeling. We are ashamed to seem evasive in the presence of a straightforward man, cowardly in the presence of a brave one, gross in the eyes of a refined one, and so on. We always imagine, and in imagining share, the judgments

of the other mind. A man will boast to one person of an action—say some sharp transaction in trade—which he would be ashamed to own to another.

It should be evident that the ideas that are associated with self-feeling and form the intellectual content of the self cannot be covered by any simple description, as by saying that the body has such a part in it, friends such a part, plans so much, etc., but will vary indefinitely with particular temperaments and environments. The tendency of the self, like every aspect of personality, is expressive of far-reaching hereditary and social factors, and is not to be understood or predicted except in connection with the general life. Although special, it is in no way separate—speciality and separateness are not only different but contradictory, since the former implies connection with a whole. The object of self-feeling is affected by the general course of history, by the particular development of nations, classes, and professions, and other conditions of this sort.

*   *   *

Habit and familiarity are not of themselves sufficient to cause an idea to be appropriated into the self. Many habits and familiar objects that have been forced upon us by circumstances rather than chosen for their congeniality remain external and possibly repulsive to the self; and, on the other hand, a novel but very congenial element in experience, like the idea of a new toy, or, if you please, Romeo's idea of Juliet, is often appropriated almost immediately, and becomes, for the time at least, the very heart of the self. Habit has the same fixing and consolidating action in the growth of the self that it has elsewhere, but is not its distinctive characteristic.

As suggested [above], self-feeling may be regarded as in a sense the antithesis, or better perhaps, the complement, of that disinterested and contemplative love that tends to obliterate the sense of divergent individuality. Love of this sort has no sense of bounds, but is what we feel when we are expanding and assimilating new and indeterminate experience, while self-feeling accompanies the appropriating, delimiting, and defending of certain part of experience; the one impels us to receive life, the other to individuate it. The self, from this point of view, might be regarded as a sort of citadel of the mind, fortified without and containing selected treasures within, while love is an undivided share in the rest of the universe. In a healthy mind each contributes to the growth of the other: what we love intensely or for a long time we are likely to bring within the citadel, and to assert as part of ourself. On the other hand, it is only on the basis of a substantial self that a person is capable of progressive sympathy or love.

The sickness of either is to lack the support of the other. There is no health in a mind except as it keeps expanding, taking in fresh life, feeling love and enthusiasm; and so long as it does this its self-feeling is likely to be modest and generous; since these sentiments accompany that sense of the large and the superior which love implies. But if love closes, the self contracts and hardens: the mind having nothing else to occupy its attention and give it that change and renewal it requires, busies itself more and more with self-feeling, which takes on narrow and disgusting forms, like avarice, arrogance, and fatuity. It is necessary that we should have self-feeling about a matter during its conception and execution; but when it is accomplished or has failed the self ought to break loose and escape, renewing its skin like the snake, as Thoreau says. No matter what a man does, he is not fully sane or human unless there is a spirit of freedom in him, a soul unconfined by purpose and larger than the practicable world. And this is really what those mean who inculcate the suppression of the self; they mean that its rigidity must be broken up by growth and renewal, that it must be more or less decisively "born again." A healthy self must be both vigorous and plastic, a nucleus of solid, well-knit private purpose and feeling, guided and nourished by sympathy.

Chapter 9 The Self-Conception in Social Interaction

RALPH H. TURNER

The *self* has traditionally been assigned an important place in formulations regarding the social nature of the individual and the character of social interaction. But referents for the concept *self* have not been fully consistent. Confusion results, for example, when attempts are made to translate G. H. Mead's concept of self-as-process into the more common usage of self-as-object.[1] As names for the alternating phases of an act, the "I" and "me" cannot be made to correspond to such familiar object concepts as "self-conception"[2] or "identity." Furthermore, self-as-object has varied meanings, the most important distinction being between an object thought to be "real" and "enduring" and an object treated as managed and ephemeral. Literature dealing with the *self-conception* and with *identity* includes both types of object.

The treatment of self-as-object often differs from folk usage. When a person expresses the wish that he could "be himself," or observes that a friend was "not really himself today," or projects a search "to find myself," the reference is to an object marked by stability and a quality of genuineness which sets it apart from much of the individual's behavior. Sociologists, however, have often taken Cooley's "looking-glass self" as their model, with the self-conception modified according to each change of mirror.[3] The situational character of self-as-object is argued by Sorokin, who flatly asserts that an individual has no general self but a separate self corresponding to each group in which he participates.[4] Strauss borrows Cooley's "mirrors" and Park's "masks"[5] to supply a descriptive title for his analysis of socialization and the self.[6] Goffman's highly imaginative and influential work has popularized the idea of self as an image the individual "manages" in order to serve his purposes.[7]

There is also, however, a tradition of attention to the self-conception as a more enduring and unifying object. Even Cooley speaks of the looking-glass mechanism only as applying "in a large and interesting class of cases. . . ."[8] And Ralph Waldo Emerson, from whom Cooley borrowed the term and the couplet, wrote his verse to distinguish those who forever search for an answer to the question, "Who am I?," by examining the mirrors carried by their peers from the autonomous sort of person who has no need to rely on such reflections.[9] Thomas and Znaniecki spoke of the life organization as bringing unity to the

---

SOURCE. This paper is largely based on the formulation of social interaction in the forthcoming book, *Family Interaction*, to be published by John Wiley and Sons, Inc.

[1] George H. Mead, *Mind, Self and Society*, Chicago, Ill.: University of Chicago Press, 1935.

[2] We are attempting to retain the technical distinction in meaning between "concept" and "conception," a distinction which is obscured by the frequent discussions of "self-concept." By the "concept of self" we mean the technical concept employed by sociologists, psychologists, and others who attempt to analyze human behavior. By "self-conception" we mean the picture that an individual has of himself. A "concept" is a tool in analysis of human behavior; a "conception" is a set of imagery the investigator seeks to describe, explain, and assess.

[3] Charles H. Cooley, *Human Nature and the Social Order*, New York: Scribners, 1922, Revised Edition, pp. 183 ff.

[4] Pitirim A. Sorokin, *Society, Culture, and Personality: Their Structure and Dynamics*, New York: Harper, 1947, pp. 348–349; and the same idea in William James, *Principles of Psychology*, New York: Macmillan, 1890, Vol. I, p. 294.

[5] Robert E. Park, "Behind our Masks," *Survey Graphic*, **61** (May 1926), pp. 135–139.

[6] Anselm L. Strauss, *Mirrors and Masks: The Search for Identity*, Glencoe, Ill.: Free Press, 1959.

[7] Erving Goffman, *The Presentation of Self in Everyday Life*, Edinburgh: University of Edinburgh, 1956.

[8] Cooley, *op. cit.*, p. 183.

[9] Ralph W. Emerson, "Astraea."

individual's perspective;[10] and Park translated life organization into "conception of self," through which the individual gets and maintains control over his impulses.[11] More recently, Manford Kuhn's use of the Twenty Questions (Who am I?) technique has been directed toward identifying a personal and genuine image.[12]

It is the relationship between these two sorts of self-as-object that most needs specification if the theory of the self is to come to grips with the self-conception as social product and social force. In much of the vast empirical literature so comprehensively reviewed by Wylie,[13] authors were content to treat self-conception merely as a measurable product of social interaction—a sort of curiosity or symptom with no particular function of importance in the ongoing social process. It is the search for function and significance in the self-conception that leads us to examine the two sorts of object.

The aim of this paper is to sketch in preliminary form the relationship between the passing images of self arising and changing in every relationship the individual enters and the often more vague but much more vital sense of self as the real and lasting "I-myself." After a brief effort to clarify the distinction, we shall review first the contribution made by passing images to the lasting self-conception, and then the function of the interplay between the two for social interaction.

THE NATURE OF SELF-CONCEPTION AND SELF-IMAGE

For clarity we shall attempt to employ distinct terms for the two types of object. The picture which the individual sees at a given moment, like the photograph that records one's appearance at an instant of time, will be called a *self-image*. The picture that carries with it

the sense of "the real me"—"I-myself as I really am"—will be called the *self-conception*. The self-image may change from moment to moment. There may indeed be multiple self-images simultaneously in effect, when the individual is aware that his behavior at a given moment looks different to his son, his mother, and his wife. Many self-images will be rejected as false, unrepresentative, or unfair. But the self-conception changes more slowly, exhibits a strain toward coherency, and is felt as inescapable fact by the individual.

It would be foolish to insist that either self-conception or self-image is sharp and clear and capable of precise conceptualization by the individual. Both will vary greatly in clarity. The self-image can be merely a hint of the individual's appearance in one situation and an unmistakably drawn portrait in another. To what extent either self-image or self-conception is tapped by the common adjective checklists, "Who am I?" tests, and similar devices is a moot question. Very likely the responses incorporate some mixture of the two. For reasons that should become apparent later, the self-conception may only be identifiable by observing reactions to changing self-images in controlled situations.

Because the point will not be developed in this paper, we must note one underlying assumption: social roles constitute the organizing framework for the self-conception. As Park observed,

The conceptions which men form of themselves seem to depend upon their vocations, and in general upon the role which they seek to play in the communities and social groups in which they live, as well as upon the recognition and status which society accords them in these roles.[14]

FORMATION OF SELF-CONCEPTION THROUGH INTERACTION

The distinguishing content of any individual's self-conception is established during the interplay between the succession of self-images and his goals and values. Values and images are thrown into unique juxtaposition by his distinctive set of interactive experiences. Each person's self-conception is a selective working compromise between his ideals and the images forced upon him by his imperfect behavior in actual situations. In order to understand how the compromise takes the form that it does in

---

10 William I. Thomas and Florian Znaniecki, *The Polish Peasant in Europe and America,* New York: Dover, 1958, Vol. 2, pp. 1843–1907.
11 Robert E. Park, "The Sociological Methods of William Graham Sumner, and of William I. Thomas and Florian Znaniecki," in *Methods in Social Science: A Case Book,* Stewart A. Rice, ed., Chicago, Ill.: University of Chicago Press, 1931, pp. 154–175.
12 Manford H. Kuhn and Thomas S. McPartland, "Empirical Investigation of Self Attitudes," *American Sociological Review,* **19** (Feb. 1954), pp. 68–76.
13 Ruth C. Wylie, *The Self Concept: A Critical Survey of Pertinent Research Literature,* Lincoln, Neb.: University of Nebraska Press, 1961.

---

14 Park, "Human Nature, Attitudes and Mores," in *Social Attitudes,* Kimball Young, ed., New York: Holt, 1931, pp. 17–45.

the individual case, it is necessary to have in mind a general scheme that outlines the nature of the interaction process.

Interaction Process

An interaction episode begins with a gesture made by one party. Gesture is used here in the broad sense of any behavior that can be assigned some meaning by the actor or observer. A gesture is an incomplete act: by itself it is nothing. The hearer or viewer must determine what it stands for before he in turn can act.[15]

In speaking or acting, ego has in mind some interpretation of his gesture. The gesture may be issued after careful attention to its meaning, or impulsively with interpretation wholly implicit. In either instance the gesture's meaning can be compared with the interpretation which alter appears to have placed on the gesture, as inferred from alter's response. The assignment of meaning not only proceeds the gesture but serves as criterion or standard by which ego judges his gesture after he has made it. Frequently, as a person speaks or acts he attends to his own gesture and remakes or modifies it so that it will fit more closely the meaning he initially had in mind.

Based on his interpretation of his own gesture, ego adopts a state of *preparedness* for certain kinds of response from alter. The term "preparedness" is preferable to the common term "expectation," since it implies a less specific anticipation. Occasionally, as when requesting information, there is a fairly precise expectation, but ego is generally prepared for a broad range of responses. A man commenting on the news, expressing a preference, or complaining of an ache is prepared to cope with a variety of relevant responses but usually not for a response which apparently has nothing to do with the meaning he assigns his gesture, or one which affronts his sensitivities.

Alter now receives ego's gesture, places his own interpretation upon it, and responds upon the basis of that interpretation. But there is not ordinarily a sharp separation between the interpretation and the gesture. From studies in the psychology of perception and memory it is clear that the gesture tends to undergo change into greater conformity with the interpretation placed upon it. Consequently, the very "facts" of the communication as each interactor re-

members them serve to justify his reactions more fully than would the "facts" *à la* tape recording and motion picture. The same assimilation of the remembered gesture to interpretation takes place on the part of ego. Finally, alter, in making his response gesture, has in mind an interpretation of his own gesture and is prepared for a certain range of responses on the part of ego.

The foregoing simple sequence of gesture and response we shall call Stage I of the interaction process. During this stage each person is acting without preconceptions derived from the current interaction sequence. At the close of this stage, each has developed preconceptions. Each now anticipates and measures the gesture of the other against this anticipation or preparedness. In practice, Stage I can only exist in degree, since the total absence of preconceptions is unimaginable.

Stage II we shall call the stage of *testing and revision*. As Stage II begins, ego not only receives and interprets alter's gesture but recognizes it as one for which he is prepared or one that falls outside of the anticipated range. But the state of preparedness precedes interpretation, and the gesture as seen and understood is shaped by alter's state of preparedness. The most general tendency is to place on the gesture some interpretation for which one is prepared. If ego is fully prepared for a gesture of sympathy he may miss the faint note of sarcasm in alter's response; if he expects a slight, even a sincere compliment is likely to appear sarcastic.

The subsequent course of interaction depends upon whether alter's response gesture is recognized as falling within the range for which ego is prepared; we shall speak of alter's gesture as *congruent* if this occurs. When the response is congruent, interaction continues in one of its preestablished directions. But if the response is *noncongruent,* ego has no ready response to continue or terminate interaction on the initial basis, and there is an interruption of the smooth flow of gesture and response. In this case ego may abandon his effort to communicate, attempt to "go back" and reassert his original intention, or disregard his original gesture and respond as if alter had initiated the interaction, thus following the latter's lead. One of these responses may come rather naively, or one may follow a reconsideration of the interaction sequence, often with reflection on the nature and circumstances of each gesture and its interpretation.

---

[15] The reader will recognize the dependence of this formulation on G. H. Mead's work. Cf. Mead, *op. cit.*

The continued interaction follows the pattern of Stage II, with increasing complexity, since it is possible to reconsider any in the string of previous gestures whenever a response is noncongruent. Interaction continues until both are satisfied or until one or both prefers to discontinue interaction.

The foregoing scheme cannot be applied until two processes are clarified. First, the determinants of gesture-interpretation must be specified. Second, the source of the action's direction must be indicated. Action is taken in the form of gesture exchange against the background of a world of objects that each person supplies. How physical stimuli are translated into a set of objects, including events, and subordinated to these objects is the first question. What sorts of events and modifications of events each actor will attempt to bring about constitute the second question.

For present purposes we shall not attempt to answer these questions comprehensively or in detail. The efforts of each participant to guide the course of interaction are governed by his values. Certain implications of this statement will be expanded later as a basis for exploring the function of the self-conception in interaction. We need consider only one source of meaning, which is especially important in understanding the development and function of the self-conception.

Person-Conceptions and Gesture Interpretation

Gesture interpretations are normally based in considerable part upon an idea or "picture" of the gesturer. It is difficult to interpret a person's gestures confidently unless one knows something about him. Are his remarks to be taken seriously or as subtle humor? Is his protest a demand for correction or simple expressive behavior? A gesture is only likely to be fully depersonalized in highly formalized legal, commercial, and intellectual exchange. Normally a gesture is perceived as the action of a particular kind of person. The kinds of response gestures and interpretation for which ego is prepared vary according to the kind of person he thinks the potential responder to be.

In keeping with other features of the state of preparedness, our characterization of a person inclines us to see his gestures as consistent with our conception of him. A joke by a person pictured as a sober type is likely to be missed, whereas serious remarks from a reputed humorist will provoke laughter. When alter's gesture is sufficiently unyielding that it cannot readily be interpreted as the action of the kind of person that ego conceives him to be, the result is confusion and interruption of the thread of communication. Here is a major component in the congruence or noncongruence of gestures, setting in motion the elements of testing and revision which characterize this phase of interaction.

The conception of the gesturer is "tested" by the congruence or noncongruence of his gesture, as part of the general testing of gesture interpretation. Every congruent response reinforces the conception of the gesturer. A single noncongruent response may or may not call the conception into question, depending upon the alternatives available for dealing with the noncongruence. But a succession of noncongruent responses makes it increasingly incumbent upon ego to reexamine his conception of alter. The person is the stable point of reference in the series of gesture exchanges and thus a likely explanation for continued noncongruence.

Person-conceptions are more or less tentative, depending upon the rigidity of generalized role conceptions (occupational, racial, religious, sex stereotypes, etc.) and prior reinforcement through interaction with the person in question. When the conception is not altogether tentative, one device to permit issuance of a revised gesture without altering the conception of the person is to detach the image from the conception. The image that can satisfactorily account for alter's gesture expresses a passing mood or an exceptional situation but not the typical individual. While the mood or situation is in effect, ego must adopt a different strategy in dealing with alter, or temporarily discontinue interaction, all the while watching for the "real" person to re-emerge.

We can summarize the consequence of ego's continuing interaction with the same alter. First, his initially tentative conceptions of alter are modified and replaced until a conception is formed which adequately prepares him to cope with most of alter's gestures without constant disruption and revision of attitude in the course of interaction. Second, as this conception becomes firmly entrenched, ego develops an increasing bias toward interpreting any gesture by alter as the natural act of a person characterized as he sees alter. Third, when alter's gestures are noncongruent, ego tends increasingly to make a separation between the image of the person at the moment and the "true" person, as characterized in his conception.

Thus person-conceptions are both determiners and products of interaction. It is important that these two relationships are obverse aspects of the same process. Person-conceptions are necessary to give stability to interaction while reducing the extent of disruptive noncongruence which results from assuming that a given gesture means the same thing to all who employ it. Person-conceptions guide behavior by enabling ego to assign the meaning to alter's gesture which ego requires in order to formulate his next gesture. But because ego acts upon the basis of the construction placed on alter's gesture, and then is confronted by a response from alter which is either congruent or not, his conception of alter is subjected to test. It is because he must act upon his conception of alter that ego must develop and revise that conception as interaction proceeds.

We have examined the development and change of person-conceptions and the tendency to distinguish image from conception during social interaction in this fashion because the self-conception is at base a special case of person-conception. Ego not only interprets alter's gestures: he interprets his own gestures. The construction he places upon his own gestures rests upon the assumption that he, in making the gestures, is a person of a certain kind. The reassessment that occurs in case of noncongruence may turn to a reconsideration of ego's gesture as well as of alter's response. Every congruent response on the other hand reinforces the conception of self underlying ego's gestures. This is perhaps one of the senses in which Cooley spoke of notions of self and other as inseparable.[16] For in a general way, the noncongruent response that undermines ego's conception of alter also threatens the support for ego's self-conception until congruency can be restored. And the congruent response simultaneously provides reassurance for both self- and other-conceptions.

In general, then, the self-conception is subject to recurring empirical test. Any particular conception of self loses its essential attribute of reality unless it can be implemented to produce a supporting self-image on appropriate occasions. When circumstances do not permit a pragmatic test by results, or when the interval between tests or between action and results is too long, confirmation by the mechanism of the "looking-glass self" becomes especially important.

Like person-conceptions in general, the self-conception is a construct which the individual forms in order to render interaction predictable and manageable. It rests ultimately on its suitability as a guide to the interpretation of one's own gestures. But it differs crucially from other person-conceptions in being formed from the point of view of the actor. The actor's point of view precludes acceptance of a simple average of self-images. Compared with other person-conceptions, the self-conception is more extensively shaped by what the person would like to be or is trying to be. It is for this reason that investigators sometimes mistakenly depict self-dynamics as interplay between the passing images and a sort of ideal self. We must, then, clarify the relationship of self-conception to the values and ideals of the actor.

Values and the Self-Conception

The self-conception starts with values and aspirations, and continues to be represented in value and aspiration terms. At first, in the child, there is a naive merging of "self" with valued models. Whatever he accepts as admirable or likable, he is; the personal characteristics of whomever he is attached to become his own. Only after this fusion of self with values has been destroyed can the individual be said to have acquired a self-conception. But a photographic self—an averaging of self-images—does not replace the set of models and values. This set remains the focal source of the self-conception, with the succession of self-images serving to *edit rather than supplant them.*

The preservation of a set of values and models rather than empirical imagery as the basic component of self-conception is made possible by certain circumstances. One of these is the tendency to identify the person by his motives more than by his actions in most contexts. This tendency in turn arises from the crucial importance of predicting behavior. In most interaction the judgment of what a given action signifies for future behavior is more important than its more direct consequence. The basis for prediction is largely the assignment of motives. Hence, because of the time perspective which governs human action, it is more important to take account of alter's motives than of a particular instance of his be-

---

[16] Cooley, *op. cit.,* p. 127.

havior. And what is more important about ego in guiding the approaches and responses of alter is taken as the more "real" ego. Formulation of the self-conception largely about a constellation of motives permits the individual to escape the import of a strictly photographic conception.

Selective response to self-images is also made possible by the tendency to form the self-conception more on the basis of capabilities than on the basis of accomplishment. Again the temporal setting of human action makes capability often more important than performance, for it indicates what may be expected in the future. In a contest, in any crisis, it is often remarked that a person shows his true colors. Furthermore, during childhood and youth there is a pervasive expectation of improvement, and even accomplishments are interesting principally as indications of the capabilities that will express themselves in more perfected accomplishment later.

Thus, typically, my self-conception is a vague but vitally felt idea of what I am like in my best moments, of what I am striving toward and have some encouragement to believe I may achieve, or of what I can do when the situation supplies incentive for unqualified effort. Because my own perspective on myself, and others' perspectives on me, are time-oriented, this conception seems more real than the reflections from my appearance in most situations. Because of the degree to which interaction can proceed in spite of discrepant interpretations, my conception of myself need not be undermined by a small difference from the conception held by others.

What we have said about the nature of the discrepancy between self-conception and self-images requires some qualification, since it varies according to the realm of behavior, the nature of individual experience, and culture. In some instances the principle that the person is identified by capability must be applied in reverse. Thus a man who has lived a peaceful life for half a century "becomes" a murderer on the basis of a single action, in the eyes of many people. In this instance the behavior is looked upon with such dread and the inhibitions against it are so great that "to be capable" of committing the crime is taken as indicative of the real person. Often in this same vein an unwonted loss of temper or expression of unkind or exploitative attitudes is said to reveal the true person. The offender, like Camus'

stranger, may lag behind his audience in the revision of his self-conception; but he can hardly escape sharing some of the questions that others have about him.

In the course of the life cycle the time perspective shifts. There comes a time—different for different kinds of accomplishment—when the futuristic perspective is foreshortened, and the individual has impressed upon him that what he has not yet accomplished will remain forever unachieved. Isolation of the various forms of readjustment in self-conception attendant upon an altered time perspective is an important task in the study of aging.

American culture embodies future-orientation, pegged to the short-term rather than the long-term view. The future-orientation encourages the formation of a self-conception whose content is considerably more favorable than the representative self-image; but the short span makes the conception difficult to maintain without fairly frequent supporting images.

Some discussions and some empirical investigations have proceeded upon the basis of a distinction between an "ideal self" and an empirically based self-image. But a formulation of this sort errs in assuming that the individual divorces his conception of what he "really is" from his ideal, and it also errs in assuming that an ideal self persists as a dynamic anchorage for social behavior, untouched by experiences of what is likely to be attained. No doubt the persistence of childhood confusion between ideal and actuality, so that the ideals solidify into an ideal self which makes it impossible for the individual to come to terms with reality while retaining self respect, is a component of some personality pathologies. But a crucial part of normal development is the fading away of any pure ideal picture of the self, and emergence to focal importance of the reality-edited self-conception. Editing is carried to the point where the self-conception will "work" as a basis for social action.

Development of the Idea of Self

Further clarification of the manner in which the self-conception develops may be gained from considering the basis on which the *idea* of self emerges. Let us recall that the idea of self underlying growth of a self-conception requires at least (*a*) the vital sense of distinction between self, other selves, and not-selves;

(b) the sense of continuity of the self; and (c) the sense of self as distinct from mere behavior and public appearance.

Early treatments of self have generally dwelt more on the first component than on the others. Such students as Baldwin and James drew attention to the infant's discovery of the boundaries of sensation and physical control.[17] The sensation he receives when he bites his own hand teaches him to distinguish between his own hand and that of another child. But these discoveries offer no clue to the socially more important sense of distinction between one's behavior, body, and possessions in general, and their differing degrees of self-relevance.

Cooley observed that the sense of self is initially a sense of possession, that "mine" is the original meaning of "me." The action to which self-words are instrumental is aggressive and assertive and centers about disputes over possession of objects. As the child attempts to take something that another child has, or to regain what another child has taken from him, he shouts "mine" repeatedly.[18]

The importance of Cooley's observations lay in their linking of the sense of self to vital action. The self-sense is not discovered in quiet reflection but in the course of vigorous effort, especially when that effort brings the individual into rivalry with other persons. In more general terms we can contrast the treatment of self-conception as a passive object—implied in many of the contemporary studies of self-conception—with the assumption that the sense of self arises in connection with active striving in the face of obstacles. It is a simple step to the observation by Dewey that behavior becomes self-conscious when it is blocked in some fashion.[19]

However, Cooley's observations still offer us little in the way of clues to the emergence of the idea of a self—a real "me"—which can be distinguished from behavior and appearances. If we ask why the child should accompany his efforts to take or retrieve objects with the word "mine," we may uncover some clues. There seems little inherent reason for the child to use this term. There is little to

distinguish his behavior from that of two dogs struggling for possession of a bone when we consider only what takes place between the two contestants.

The reference "mine" is relevant and instrumental only because there have been outsiders who interfered in such struggles on the basis of an ethic of ownership. Initially, "mine" is simply a word that represents a claim upon support by parents, teachers, older children, or others who might interfere. But it becomes different from a simple demand for help when it evokes a *code* of ownerhip, which is thought to govern the interfering behavior of outsiders. In referring to a code, the term comes to be a claim for the legitimacy of aggressive and possessive efforts. Ultimately, the child may use it on the assumption that his rival also recognizes the code and that the rival's efforts will be affected by belief in the legitimacy of his position.

The feature of the self-sense to which Cooley called our attention is therefore the implementation of a system of social regulation and control. What is mine is not necessarily identical with what I happen to possess. The distinction exists only because the distribution of objects is controlled by a group or society in which the interacting pair is a part. We can now supplement Cooley's observation by noting that the sense of self arises from that interplay between acts of appropriation and societal regulation.

From this line of reasoning we are led to a more comprehensive conclusion about the sense of self. Possession and ownership describe relationships between the person and objects. But when the sense of "I-myself" as distinct from "mine" is at issue, the question is the relationship between the person and his behavior. Perhaps the beginning of the sense of self revolves about the I-myself relationship because it is simpler to see and understand. But the analogy is clear and undoubtedly helps to guide the child toward the more fundamental sense of self. Just as mine refers to ownership, which is important primarily because it can be distinguished from possession, so the "real me" is important just because it can be distinguished from behavior. In the world of childhood, ownership changes less rapidly than possession; so also is the self more inflexible and continuous than behavior.

The key to the more fundamental sense of self seems to be the exercise of social control

[17] James M. Baldwin, *Mental Development in the Child and Race,* New York: Macmillan, 1900, pp. 334–341; James, *op. cit.,* Vol. I, pp. 291–401.
[18] Cooley, *op. cit.,* pp. 191 ff.
[19] John Dewey, *Human Nature and Conduct,* New York: Holt, 1935.

over individuals by the assignment of credit and responsibility. Human behavior and the social consequences of human action are too complicated to be effectively regulated by simple punishment and reward tied to specific behaviors. Actions are not completed in a moment, and their consequences are often not apparent at the time of action. Their significance for future behavior varies, and the ultimate performance often involves the varied actions of several people.

Assignment of credit and responsibility rather than simple reward-punishment supplies flexibility to social control in several ways. First, it is symbolic action which takes the place of immediate reward and punishment, making possible the deferment of these steps. Second, it facilitates differential reward and punishment of the parties to an action, perhaps holding the initiator more responsible than the follower, and giving more credit to the creator of an idea than to the messenger who delivers it. And third, it allows the punishment and reward to be adjusted to the likelihood that the behavior will be repeated and to the fact that punishment and reward will also affect other kinds of behavior by the same individual. For example, a great composer may be held less responsible for misdeeds, lest the severe punishment should hamper his musical creativeness.

In the broadest sense, and perhaps that first comprehended by the child, the individual is held more fully responsible for wrongdoing which is typical of his behavior, and assigned more credit for typical accomplishments, than he is for a-typical behavior of either kind. But this crude distinction is refined in the exercise of social control by distinguishing the intentional from the accidental, the planned from the impulsive, and that which reflects genuine capability from luck. The child learns that he gains little credit among his peers for knocking down the school champion just once, and that he is punished less severely if he hits another child because of poor aim with a ball than if he carefully takes aim to hurt him.

The social self-as-object is *that object which is held responsible and assigned credit*. The idea of self is distinguished from behavior because there is no simple and direct connection between behavior and the assignment of responsibility and credit. The continuity of the self in time is assumed in connection with the deferment of punishment and reward. The content of the self is formulated out of those elements for which credit and responsibility are assigned.[20]

But we must again return to Cooley and to our discussion of interaction. The self-conception does not arise passively but in conjunction with vital activity. The individual does not simply accept credit and responsibility: he pursues credit and seeks to avoid responsibility for unfortunate happenings. He seeks credit especially in those activities he values most highly, and he seeks to escape responsibility for poor performance in activities he values most negatively. As he acquires the idea of person and self he fills in the self with those contents for which he seeks and claims credit and reluctantly takes responsibility for those items from which he cannot escape. The individual's values, goals, and aspirations provide, then, the initial framework for the self-conception, which must be edited through interaction to the point at which the credit and responsibility the individual takes upon himself do not diverge to an unworkable degree from those assigned him by persons with whom he interacts.

SELF-CONCEPTION AND THE COURSE OF INTERACTION

If the self-conception is a product of interaction, subject to slight but continuous revision according to the exigencies of interaction, so is it a determiner of the course of interaction. In order to examine the effects of the interplay between self-conception and self-image we must return to our outline of the nature of the interaction process.

Identity- and Task-Directed Interaction

The most general term available to designate the locus of direction in interaction is *value*. A value is a category of objects toward which an individual reacts in a positive or negative rather than a neutral fashion. In communication one tends to convey meanings that favor and protect his positive values and discredit his negative values, while disregarding neutral objects (except when communication is merely an instrumentality to maintain social contact). To the extent to which the perceived meanings of alter's gestures appear to promote ego's

---

[20] The normative character of the self is suggested in a volume which deserves much more attention than it has received by students of the social self. Cf. William H. Kirkpatrick, *Selfhood and Civilization: A Study of the Self-other Process*, New York: Macmillan, 1941.

favorably valued objects and to deprecate his negative values, a positive reaction occurs and the direction of communication tends to be continued and reinforced. To the extent to which the perceived meaning of alter's communication threatens ego's positive values and fosters his negative values, ego will try to change the course of interaction in favor of his value system.

Value is a more general term than such concepts as need, drive, urge, impulse, etc. These are psychological concepts which might be used to explain why a person valued certain objects or the intensity of his valuation. For our purposes values can be treated as "given," and their sources may be disregarded. If the investigator is limited to inferring values as ex post facto explanations for the course of interaction, the term is reduced to a tautology. But to the extent to which values can be identified prior to a given interaction episode and observed through other forms of behavior than those being predicted, the charge of tautology is unjustified.

In the simplest interaction, which can be labeled *casual,* ego's interpretation of alter's gesture (or of his own) is organized to allow recognition of the gesture's relationship with ego's value system. Like other aspects of interpretation, recognizing the value-relevance of a gesture is not automatic and is affected by preoccupations, by conceptions of alter based upon interaction, by role conceptions, and by other considerations.

Much interaction is not limited to noting the value-relevance of gestures as they are made, but is governed by some purpose or aim which one or both participants hold in mind throughout a succession of gesture exchanges. Gestures are then not simply expressions of feeling and naive communication but are directed by a stable purpose, and interaction does not shift willy-nilly as one value after another comes into play. When interaction is *directed* (rather than casual) the entire process of assigning meanings becomes organized in relation to the goal or purpose. A goal is simply a value elevated to a special guiding position in interaction. Like preoccupation with any value, pursuit of a goal predisposes the actor to interpret all ensuing experience according to its relevance to that goal. The result is that for the duration of the interaction values are placed in a hierarchy, with some values subordinated to the goal as "means" and "conditions."

The self, or identity, is one type of value which gives direction to interaction. Like any value, it is to be fostered and protected. The self-conception supplies the "content" of the self and provides the principal cues by which the relevancy of gestures to the self is assessed. But the self normally forms the apex and matrix of the individual's value system. In the broad sense in which the self is extended to encompass all the objects that a person values, the self is always the prime director of behavior. But insofar as the objects are identified as values, they are abstracted from the self-conception and can be manipulated and viewed without attention to the self-conception as such.

When interaction is *directed,* it makes considerable difference whether the actor is guided by values as such, or whether attention is specifically focused upon the self-conception. When the actor is guided by values, interaction is directed toward a goal that requires the collaboration of two or more people, but the attitudes of participants toward one another are means and conditions rather than ends. Family members work together to prepare a garden, to play a game of tennis, to plan and execute family finances, to discuss a controversial television program. Following Bales, we shall call interaction of this sort *task-directed.*[21] The task in such activities as watching a television program together need not be sharply focused, but it organizes collaboration among the participants.

On other occasions interaction is primarily directed by each member's concern about how others feel toward him. Ego's chief goal is to control the attitudes of alter toward ego. The task, if there is one, becomes secondary. The goal can be to promote friendly attitudes or hostile attitudes, respect or fear or love. Validation of a particular self-conception becomes the guiding consideration. Consequently, we shall call interaction of this sort *identity-directed.*

The distinction does not correspond exactly with Bales' task versus social-emotional behavior. In groups such as the family there is much interpersonal coordination and control behavior which constitutes simply the central tasks of family interaction. Thus not all social-emotional behavior need be regarded as strictly

[21] Robert F. Bales, *Interaction Process Analysis: A Method for the Study of Small Groups,* Cambridge, Mass.: Harvard University Press, 1951.

identity-oriented. Furthermore, in labeling the behavior as we do, we seek to focus attention upon the difference in the object of attention more than on the mode of expression. Although the very sacredness of the self means that it is capable of generating more emotion than other values, the identity may be fostered deliberately by quite unemotional behavior, just as the defense of impersonal values may be highly emotional in character.

In practice, interaction does not separate neatly into task- and identity-directed forms. The more intimate and comprehensive is any relationship, the more difficult it is to divorce task- from identity-orientations. However, there are far-reaching differences in the way that each type of interaction proceeds, such that intense interaction must almost always turn in one direction or the other. There is an inconsistency between the two directing principles such that one emphasis impedes the other so long as they coexist strongly.

Consequences of Identity-Direction: Attention to Self-Image

In task-directed interaction there is relatively little attention to the self-image as such. In popular terminology, one is not self-conscious. In identity-directed action, however, there is overwhelming preoccupation with the self-image. The difference is not necessarily in the specific stimuli to which attention is directed, but in the objects that are constituted from these stimuli. Preoccupation with self-image means that ego interprets his own gestures as representations of the self, as appearances which can be taken as indications of his true identity; and that ego interprets alter's gestures as indications of the image of ego held by alter, an image bearing upon the conception alter has of ego as a person.

If the weaker of two men is attempting to do the heavier lifting in a collaborative task, this observation can be organized in two different ways in order to afford direction to their action. From the point of view of the task, it can be observed that an exchange of positions would improve efficiency. From the point of view of identities, each may observe how the part assigned him makes him appear. The weaker man sees that a change of positions would augment his appearance of weakness; the stronger man notes that his actually greater strength is disguised by the current division of work. Identity-orientation will likely mean that

the weaker man (ego) sees his own overexertion as creating an image of strength and the stronger man's offer to trade positions as expressing an image of weakness applied to ego.

The self-image may be rather directly communicated or inferred in the situation. The gestures of alter can be given a special interpretation: the offer of sympathy can be understood as an imputation of failure and incompetence to ego; the polite expression of interest can be read as the attribution of admirable qualities. The self-image can be inferred on the basis of the imagined role of someone not present, such as the way one would appear to mother, father, or priest. In each instance the self-image is evaluated as favorable or unfavorable, and accordingly serves as the medium for attempting to reinforce or redirect the course of interaction.

For any self-image to be evaluated there must be some standard of comparison. Here is where introduction of the idea of self-conception makes a major difference from simple conformity and social approval models of human behavior. Without a standard of comparison, the self-image would convey chiefly the sentiment of approval or disapproval detected in alter's gestures, or anticipated on the basis of experience with prior alters. The effect of the self-image in directing the course of interaction would be simply to focus more sharply the pressures on the individual to conform to the wishes of others, with social approval as the effective control mechanism. Failure of convergence toward uniformity in any interaction episode would then have to be credited principally to errors in perception. But with the self-conception as the standard or criterion, the dynamics of social behavior hinge less on immediate approval—which must be gained by uniformization—and more on the generation of self-images that confirm the self-conception.

The self-image in most fundamental terms is *an object constituted out of stimuli in such a fashion that it can be directly compared with the self-conception.* Because the function of the self-image is to enable the individual to interpret his experience as supporting or undermining the self-conception, the self-image is highly selective according to self-relevance. As a criterion, self-conception indicates the types of activity which are relevant and the standards for achievement. To one man, knowledgeability regarding classical literature is an aspect of the self-conception, which leads him to incorporate indications of such knowledgeability in his self-image; to another man this is no part of the self-conception, with the result that he neither spontaneously attends to indications of this sort nor is greatly moved by direct expressions of such an image by others. Only to the extent to which alter appears to generalize from this aspect of his image of ego, taking it as a symptom of a larger sphere of inadequacy that infringes on ego's self-conception, is ego likely to be confronted by a bothersome self-image.

Similarly, it is by comparison with the self-conception that the level of achievement is translated into a favorable or unfavorable self-image. To be told that he will never equal the current baseball home-run king or television-quiz wizard may upset a young boy, but it will seldom be taken as an insult by an older boy or man. An occasional evidence of modest athletic prowess or intellectual attainment is enough to create a favorable self-image in most men. The self-conception incorporates a standard for each relevant type of accomplishment or virtue, a standard which is different for each individual. As a consequence, identical performance by different individuals can be translated into quite different self-images.

Consequences of Identity-Direction: Levels of Interpretation

The existence of a conception of alter makes it possible to interpret his gestures at different levels. The least complicated level, and that which is socially required in much interaction, may be called the *face-value* level. Interpretation at this level means acceptance of the meaning that alter is manifestly communicating, without a search for hidden meanings. But the search for hidden meanings is one way of attempting to deal with noncongruency. And it can become a systematic approach when the person conception requires it—as in dealings with a salesman or politician.

Let us imagine an incident in which a boy is hit by a ball during a Little League baseball game, and his solicitous father runs to ask if he is hurt. The father is prepared for some indication of whether he is hurt badly or only slightly. But the son's nonchalant response that he is unhurt, with an effort to get up and walk to his position as if nothing had happened, is noncongruent. The father will then almost certainly interpret the gesture as concealing his true feelings in front of his peers and suspect that he is actually in pain. Interpretation of this sort, in which the gesture is regarded as concealment or faulty representation of alter's actual feeling, can be called interpretation at the *empathic* level. In empathic interpretation ego imputes an attitude or feeling to alter which is at variance with the face-value meaning of his gesture. An interpretation need not be correct to be empathic, and the feeling it imputes to alter may be favorably or unfavorably viewed. It merely imputes a disguised feeling to alter, but a feeling of which alter is assumed to be fully aware.

There is still a third level that interpretation sometimes takes, called *diagnostic*. A diagnostic interpretation is one that infers from the gesture something about the state of alter which is at variance with the face-value meaning of the gesture *and* of which alter is assumed to be unaware. The classic diagnostic type of interpretation is that of the psychiatrist: the patient's gestures are believed to reveal attitudes of which he is completely unaware to the psychiatrist.

Except under special circumstances, interpretations at other than face-value, and especially at the diagnostic level, are regarded as invasions of personal privacy and attacks on personal dignity. In the baseball illustration, the more the father repudiates the son's denial of injury, the more the son is likely to insist. On the other hand, if the father appears to accept the son's gesture at face value but offers another reason for his son's leaving the game for a few minutes, the son is more likely to acquiesce. Both father and son will then be interpreting the other's gestures empathically while maintaining the appearance of face-value interpretation. The privilege of diagnostic interpretation is one explicitly given to the psychiatrist by his client, and it is subject to withdrawal unless the client is socially defined as incompetent. Parents usually claim the privilege of both empathic and diagnostic interpretations of their children's gestures, although the privilege is likely to be contested and the mode of interpretation reciprocated except when the child-role is completely accepted. Relationships of intimacy, on the other hand, carry with them not only license but obligation for a limited amount of mutual empathic interpretation. The wife expects her husband not to accept her assertion that she "feels fine" at face value, but to recognize the signs of her true feelings.

Systematic review of the circumstances under which empathic and diagnostic interpretations are likely to occur and are likely to be socially acceptable would carry us into aspects of interaction process and of the nature of the self which are outside the scope of this paper. However, for present purposes it is important that the balance among levels of interpretation is different under task-directed and identity-directed interaction. In task interaction, interpretation is preponderantly at the face-value level, each participant being primarily interested in what the other is trying to convey rather than in deeper interpretation. The empathic and diagnostic levels of interpretation become of great importance, however, when interaction is identity-directed. Predicting and anticipating the other's next moves becomes more complex and more crucial, so that it is necessary to go beneath the surface. Furthermore, the communication of person-images is always hedged about by intensive normative regulation, in the interests of avoiding embarassment, slight, or disruption to established interpersonal relationships. Consequently, neither favorable nor unfavorable indications of alter's image of ego can be expressed with the easy spontaneity that applies to other matters, and ego must rely extensively on empathic interpretation if he is not to be naively mislead regarding his self-image.

Consequences of Identity-Direction: Gesture as Interpersonal Technique

In task-directed interaction gestures are a form of communication. While they are communication for a purpose, still they are intended to convey to the receiver the same core meaning they carry to the initiator. In identity interaction the gesture is more often employed to gain a certain kind of reaction from the other. Since the reaction cannot be solicited simply out of shared interest in some task, the gesture must be employed with greater calculation. There is likely to be considerably wider discrepancy between the meanings attributed to the gesture by gesturer and receiver, and the gesture serves to communicate only a part of the meaning the gesturer finds in it. Consequently, when interaction shifts from task- to identity-direction, the gesture ceases to be primarily a device for communi-

cation and becomes an *interpersonal technique*. It becomes a device employed to create a desired type of relationship between two persons, through ego's implanting in alter the desired person-image of ego.

On the surface there is nothing different about interpersonal technique. Only in use of the gesture is there difference—in the attitude of the gesturer toward his own gesture. But the relationship between the culturally standard content of the gesture and the course of interaction is altogether different.

Consequences of Identity-Direction: Credit and Blame

Finally, task interaction involves minimal attention to assigning credit and blame for the course of events. In identity-directed interaction, on the other hand, discussions which are manifestly concerned with tasks are manipulated and interpreted as indications of credit and blame. In ostensible consideration of a scheme to improve the effectiveness of public education, identity-direction means that use of the discussion to claim credit for the new program and assign blame for the current unfortunate conditions will take precedence over making a wise task decision. The identity interaction of lovers is largely taken up with exchanging credits, and again task interaction may be "derailed" because of the preoccupation with maintaining the supportive relationship between identities.

We return with this observation to the earlier assertion regarding emergence of the idea of self. Credit and blame are not simply evaluated as "cause." Causal imputation can only be translated into credit and blame by insertion of the person into the equation. The intimate connection between sense of self and orientations toward credit and blame works reciprocally. Since the self is constituted to a crucial degree out of the acceptance of assignments of credit and blame, sensitization to the self leads the individual to organize his experience so he may find and manipulate indications of credit and blame in his own and others' gestures.

Onset of Identity-Direction

Identity interaction often arises out of task-directed interaction, changing its character and direction. In most general terms, ego shifts from task- to identity-direction when he perceives a discrepancy between self-image and self-conception which threatens to call into question his self-conception. We assume that self-consciousness is like a lens that brings the stimuli from the passing social situation into focus, so that they become recognizable as self-imagery. The focus is one of degree. In extreme instances of casual behavior or intense absorption in task behavior the focus is almost completely absent. The individual can then manifest wide discrepancies from his normal self-conception without recognizing them—not, perhaps, until he reflects afterwards, or until someone else points out to him that he was unusually brilliant or made a fool of himself, are the events brought into focus as a well-formed self-image. In the usual instance there is an imperfect focus which makes the major outlines of self-imagery recognizable, but not the subtleties. The backdrop of passing imagery is enough to bring gross discrepancies to the individual's awareness. As long as gross discrepancies do not appear, the actor continues with his task concerns without important awareness of self. But recognition of any gross discrepancies brings the self-image into sharper focus. As the actor now turns his attention toward the self-image, he sees subtler points of agreement and disagreement between self-image and self-conception. It is in this respect that the individual becomes more sensitive, more easily hurt, and more easily buoyed up, once his attention is fastened on the self-image.

Not all perceived discrepancies are threats to the self-conception, however. First, pegging the self-conception to capability more than performance—the better self rather than the average self—provides a margin of security. Second, the situation need not always call out the real self. Third, the person in whose gestures the image is detected need not be an individual with whom alter must work out a viable basis for continuing interaction. In short, all of the considerations that contribute to formation of a self-conception which is not merely the average self-image also permit minor discrepancies to pass without threatening the self, and thus without invoking a full-scale identity-direction.

If the self-conception sets the standard for behavior, positively as well as negatively discrepant images bring about identity direction. The threat of a negative self-image is that the self-conception will have to be revised downward unless interaction can be directed to revise the self-image satisfactorily. The "threat" of a positively discrepant self-image is that the self-conception will be revised upward if the new self-image can be maintained and can gain the support of others; if this occurs, there is a preoccupation with the self-image, intially concerned with testing and perpetuating the high image. In many people a compliment or an unexpected success sets in motion a flow of easily recognized social technique, such as unwonted graciousness and magnanimity. But a self-image significantly above the self-conception also disturbs the ordinary equilibria among means and ends in behavior, between expectation and performance, and between ego's and alter's behavior. A complex network of interdependent behaviors is thus thrown out of balance, and a new equilibrium must be established if the self-conception is to be raised substantially and made the basis for future interaction. Prior experience with such disequilibrium often makes people resist the elevation of self-conception as strongly as they resist its lowering. But whether the effort is to discount the high self-image in order to protect the stable base of interaction provided by the established self-conception or to extend the high self-image in order to support an improved self-conception, the period of readjustment is one of heightened preoccupation with self, and interaction tends to be identity-directed.

SUMMARY

The self-conception consists of a selective organization of values and standards, edited to form a workable anchorage for social interaction. Typically, the self-conception is a vague but vitally felt idea of what I am like in my best moments, of what I am striving toward and have some encouragement to believe I may achieve, or of what I can do when the situation supplies incentive for unqualified effort. The individual function of the self-conception is to supply stable and workable direction to action by providing a criterion for selective attention to the social consequences and reflections of ego's behavior. The social function of the self-conception is to define the object that warrants the assignment of credit and responsibility, as the basis for social control in relation to an extended time perspective.

The dynamic of the self-conception, both in its formation and in its direction of behavior, lies in the interplay between self-conception and a continuous succession of self-images. Much interaction proceeds under a modus vivendi between self and environment such that little attention is paid to self as object. But when the self-image appears to threaten the self-conception, implying that it should be either lowered or raised, the character of interaction is pervasively altered by heightened preoccupation with self-images, increased use of empathic and diagnostic interpretation of gestures, employment of gestures as interpersonal technique rather than as a mode of communication, and constant efforts to assign credit and responsibility.

Chapter 10 The Image and Appearance of the Human Body

PAUL SCHILDER

The image of the human body means the picture of our own body which we form in our mind, that is to say the way in which the body appears to ourselves. There are sensations which are given to us. We see parts of the body-surface. We have tactile, thermal, pain impressions. There are sensations which come from the muscles and their sheaths, indicating the deformation of the muscle; sensations coming from the innervation of the muscles (energy sense, von Frey); and sensations coming from the viscera. Beyond that there is the immediate experience that there is a unity of the body. This unity is perceived, yet it is more than a perception. We call it a schema of our body or bodily schema, or, following Head, who emphasizes the importance of the knowledge of the position of the body, postural model of the body. The body schema is the tri-dimensional image everybody has about himself. We may call it "body-image." The term indicates that we are not dealing with a mere sensation or imagination. There is a self-appearance of the body. It indicates also that, although it has come through the senses, it is not a mere perception. There are mental pictures and representations involved in it, but it is not mere representation. Head writes:

But, in addition to its function as an organ of local attention, the sensory cortex is also the storeroom of past impressions. These may rise into consciousness as images, but more often, as in the case of special impressions, remain outside of central consciousness. Here they form organized models of ourselves, which may be termed "schemata." Such schemata modify the impressions produced by incoming sensory impulses in such a way that the final sensation of position, or of locality, rises into consciousness charged with a relation to something that has happened before. Destruction of such "schemata" by a lesion of the cortex renders impossible all recognition of posture or of the locality of a stimulated spot in the affected part of the body.

Previously he had stated:

But in both cases the image, whether it be visual or motor, is not the fundamental standard against which all postural changes are to be measured. Every recognizable change enters into consciousness already charged with its relation to something that has happened before, just as on a taximeter the distance is represented to us already transformed into shillings and pence. So the final product of the tests for the appreciation of posture or passive movement rises into consciousness as a measured postural change.

For this combined standard, against which all subsequent changes of posture are measured before they enter consciousness, we propose the word "schema." By means of perpetual alterations in position we are always building up a postural model of ourselves, which constantly changes. Every new posture or movement is recorded on this plastic schema, and the activity of the cortex brings every fresh group of sensations evoked by altered posture into relation with it. Immediate postural recognition follows as soon as the relation is complete.

One of our patients had lost his left leg some time before the appearance of the cerebral lesion which destroyed the power of recognizing posture. After the amputation, as in so many similar cases, he experienced movements in a phantom foot and leg. But these ceased immediately on the occurrence of the cerebral lesion; the stroke which abolished all recognition of posture destroyed at the same time the phantom limb.

In the same way, recognition of the locality of the stimulated spot demands the reference to another "schema"; for a patient may be able to name correctly, and indicate on a diagram or on another person's hand, the exact position of the spot touched or pricked, and yet be ignorant of the position in space of the limb upon which

SOURCE. Paul Schilder, *The Image and Appearance of the Human Body,* New York: International Universities Press, 1935; 1950 edition, pp. 11–13, 213–216, 223–226, 234–236, 257 (title), and 267. Copyright 1935. Reprinted by permission of International Universities Press, Inc.

it lies. This is well shown in Hn. (case 14), who never failed to localize the stimulated spot correctly, although he could not tell the position of his hand. This faculty of localization is evidently associated with the existence of another schema or model of the surface of our bodies, which also can be destroyed by a cortical lesion. The patient then complains that he has no idea where he has been touched. He knows that a contact has occurred, but he cannot tell where it has taken place on the surface of the affected part.

It is to the existence of these "schemata" that we owe the power of projecting our recognition of posture, movement, and locality beyond the limits of our own bodies to the end of some instrument held in the hand. Without them we could not probe with a stick, nor use a spoon unless our eyes were fixed upon the plate. Anything which participates in the conscious movement of our bodies is added to the model of ourselves and becomes part of these schemata: a woman's power of localization may extend to the feather in her hat.

When a leg has been amputated, a phantom appears; the individual still feels his leg and has a vivid impression that it is still there. He may also forget about his loss and fall down. This phantom, this animated image of the leg, is the expression of the body schema.

The body-image expands beyond the confines of the body. A stick, a hat, any kind of clothes, become part of the body-image. The more rigid the connection of the body with the object is, the more easily it becomes part of the body-image. But objects which were once connected with the body always retain something of the quality of the body-image on them. I have specifically pointed out the fact that whatever originates in or emanates out of our body will still remain a part of the body-image. The voice, the breath, the odour, faeces, menstrual blood, urine, semen, are still parts of the body-image even when they are separated in space from the body. (Cf. Roheim.) The patient who felt torn by anxiety felt the parts of his body flying around. All these instances, different though they may be in detail and in their deepest mechanism, have one thing in common; the space in and around the postural model is not the space of physics. The body-image incorporates objects or spreads itself into space.

Anna R., 42 years old, admitted to Bellevue Hospital on May 6th, 1932, had, according to her own and her daughter's report, already been in the hospital seven years ago. A year before this first admission one of her children

had been run over by a truck. After the accident she heard people talk about her and believed that they knew everything that was going on in the house. She then came to Bellevue Hospital and a little later was for a year and a half in the State Hospital. She was never quite free from hallucinations. This time she entered the hospital voluntarily because she felt that she was being hounded by enemies who talked about her and sent electricity into her. In the clinic she complained in a vivid and often agitated manner about the persecution she had to stand. But one could always establish good relations with her.

When the street-cleaner used to sweep the street I felt as if he was sweeping over my genitals. It felt as if he was tearing me. It was terrible pain. It made be shiver. I was on the fifth floor and he was in the street. They were killing my girl. She began to shiver; her face had red streaks and her eyes turned up. I saw a man from the street. He upset my nerves with electricity. I don't know what it means. He was in front of my face. He took my breath. He hurt my heart. He breathes my breath. Right now, it hurts me here (pointing to her pelvis); it is in the womb. Anyone in here does it; anybody here can kill me. This morning a doctor walked on top of me; he was stepping on my body (he was not near me, but it hurt me). They break my legs with electricity. They stop my thinking, my breathing, my eating. Whatever I say here everybody knows. They even hear what I think. They come and call me S.O.B. They show me a man's action when they pass on the street. When a man passed he looked down and said "look." He did not take out his genitals but I could see them as if he was naked. People in the street were running after me to kill me. When you talk naturally it is all right. But when you talk unnaturally you hurt me here and there. You just coughed on me and you touched me with your cough (the patient coughs). When I cough I do not do it on you. When you move your shoulder I feel it too. There is electricity all over where I am. I had a neighbour who left a smell in my house. They used it again on me in another house. It was killing my blood. They used to make me stink. A boy used to make on me a dirty woman's smell. I smell now a fresh green smell like a tree-smell. That woman (pointing to the street) makes signs as if I want to go to the toilet. Everybody works on me . . . men, women, children, crazies. They used to let people into my bedroom and they tore my sex organ. And they burn me. They used to put a sort of red paint in me. Maybe they worked on me. I am like a radio. They can work on me. When a kid makes a grabbing motion of pointing I feel it in my blood and bones. They say such dirty things all day.

Whatever I do, for instance if I buy meat, they talk all day and night about me and make jokes. The butcher comes at night and he talks hard words at me which kill and stick. I could not eat anything. Every butcher did it. He put his hands on me like electricity and tore my sex-parts. He made my stomach swell. They used to stop up my bowels. When somebody laughed it went through me like an electric machine. A policeman told him to do it. Through my knees and everywhere I get it. They do the same thing in the Ward. I don't go to the toilet; they locked up my womb. A boy of 14 used to live with me as man and wife. He was downstairs; he did it through electricity. It was terrible, I had pain, I was ashamed. For years my faeces do not smell right. When I walk they make me vomit if they want to.

We see that the patient connects herself with everybody. When a person breathes it is her breath. When a person moves his shoulders she feels it in her shoulders. In other words, she takes the postural models of others into her own. Their spatial difference does not exist any more. By magic she is forced to imitate. It is passive imitative magic. When a man sweeps the street she feels the movement on her genitals. When somebody walks by she feels him walk on herself. The actions which go on in the outside world are felt in her body-image. The difference in space between her body-image and the outside world has been changed. One may say that her libido attracts other persons nearer to her. A boy who lives downstairs has sexual relations with her, "by electricity."

Magic action is an action which influences the body-image irrespective of the actual distance in space. It influences, not only in this case, the sex organs in particular. It seems that the psychological space around the sex organs has its special characteristics.

The specific space around the body-image may either bring the objects nearer to the body or the body nearer to the objects. The emotional configuration determines the distances of objects from the body.

There is a community between my picture, my image in the mirror, and myself. But are not my fellow human beings outside myself also a picture of myself? A simple experiment may emphasize again that the community between the body-image outside and the body exists already in the sphere of perception. I sit about ten feet away from a mirror holding a pipe or a pencil in my hand and look into the mirror. I press my fingers tightly against the pipe and have a clear-cut feeling of pressure in my fingers. When I look intently at the picture of my hand in the mirror I now feel clearly that the sensation of pressure is not only in my fingers in my own hand, but also in the hand which is twenty feet distant in the mirror. Even when I hold the pipe in such a way that only the pipe is seen and not my hand, I can still feel, though with some difficulty, the pressure on the pipe in the mirror. This feeling is therefore not only in my actual hand but also in the hand in the mirror. One could say that the postural model of the body is also present in my picture in the mirror. Not only is it the optic picture but it also carries with it tactile sensation. My postural model of the body is in a picture outside myself. But is not every other person like a picture of myself? One sees again how strong is the influence of the optic sphere on the postural model of the body. We meet again the dependence of the image on the body which we encountered in our discussion of Stratton's experiment and experiments concerning the doubling of one's own finger by double vision.

The sensations felt in the above experiment cannot be attributed to projection. The experience of the sensation in the mirror is as immediate and original as the experience in the real hand. It is at least very probable that part of these experiences are given when we see the bodies of others, especially when one considers how little the optic experience concerning one's own body-image differs from the experiences we have concerning the optic image of the bodies of others. Further, one may compare the important investigations made by Landis and his co-workers with the conclusions deduced from our own experiences. Landis has found that the expression of emotions is very often misunderstood. He has taken photographs of persons in actual emotional situations. People who looked at these photographs often misinterpreted their meaning. But it is not justifiable to select one part only out of a whole situation. The emotion cannot be separated from the sequences of motility, and the object which provokes an emotion is a part of the emotional situation. Landis' interesting investigations show therefore that we understand emotional situations only as wholes and not in parts, even when the snapshot catches the climax of the emotional situation. (Landis himself comes to very similar conclusions.)

The close relation between one's own body and the bodies of others also comes into the foreground in a series of interesting investigations made by David Levy. He has studied body interest in children. All the children examined presented evidence of physical disease. There were many responses indicating special interest in or sensitivity to a part of the body, which they considered inferior. The problems were chiefly aesthetic. Only three can be interpreted as interfering with the functions (knock-knees, flat feet, squint). Many of the children complained about the skull; its funny shape; its being big, long, and narrow. But particular interest was also displayed in length and strength, for instance in the length of the fingers. Of all parts of the body the visible area was most productive of sensitivity. A number of boys under the age of 12 objected to the idea of body hair, one accepted it only on the face, another had no objection to body hair if light.

It is of special interest in this connection that sensitivity to a discovery on one's own body may draw special attention to the corresponding part in the bodies of others. A boy with inverted nipples was especially observant of women's breasts. But in Levy's material it comes out clearly that children find out about their own body by the talk and observation of others. The attitude of the parents towards scars and the observation of others provoke a great interest in the child's own body. Family conversations about health, appearance, or illness in the family may also increase the child's interest in its own body.[1]

It is obvious that interest in particular parts of one's own body provokes interest in the corresponding parts of the bodies of others. Between one's own body and the bodies of others there exists a connection. We may emphasize again our previous observation that patients found out about their own bodies with the help of others. It is remarkable that interest in others and interest in oneself run in some way parallel to each other. In a case in which a mutilation of the hand took place, the patient at first took an enormous interest in the people with whom he came into contact. But his interest in his surroundings soon decreased and with it also his self-consciousness concerning the change. A person's own interest in the body and the social interest of others concerning the body run parallel to each other. When we try to assess the value of Levy's material we have,

of course, to take into consideration that he does not deal with primary changes in a postural model of the body, but that we deal with special interest in the body and the adjustments which are based upon this interest. There is also the intellectual and emotional interest of others concerning the body of the child.

We should not forget that the postural image of the body, although it is primarily an experience of the senses, provokes attitudes of an emotional type, and that these emotional attitudes are inseparable from the sensory experience. The judgment concerning the body is derived from both sources, and is only possible on the basis of the underlying sensory and emotional factors. The same levels can be distinguished when we see the body of another person. We first get a sensory impression about the other person's body. This sensory impression gets its real meaning by our emotional interest in the various parts of his body, and finally we come to a judgment relating to the different parts of the other's body. But even this threefold sub-division does not give the full importance of the body-image. Just as one's own body-image gains its full meaning only by its motion and by its function, which expresses itself again in a sensory way, the motion of another person's body-image, its changes concerning function, and its prospects concerning action, give the body-image a deeper meaning.

SOCIAL RELATIONS OF BODY-IMAGES. THE SOCIAL DISTANCE

There now arises the question what is our own body and what is the body of others? Which does one perceive first? Is the one secondary to the other? Do we perceive them at the same time? According to the dogmatic formulation of analysis, the child knows first about his own body. But our whole discussion shows clearly that our own body is not nearer to us than the outside world, at least in important parts. The optic impressions concerning our own body, which are so important for the formation of the body-image, are in no way different from the optic impressions we have concerning the bodies of others. It is not possible to say that we gain our knowledge of outside bodies and their images by projecting our own body into the outside world. But we are also not justified in taking the opposite view, and saying that we gain the knowledge of our own body by introjecting the body-images of others into ourselves. The body-image is not a product of the appersonization

---

[1] In a further paper Levy has studied these attitudes in connection with the individual life problems of the children.

of the bodies of others, although we may take parts of the body-images of others into our postural model. It is also not gained by identification with the body-images of others, although we may enrich our body-image perception by such identifications. There is no other way out than to formulate that our own body-image and the body-images of others are primary data of experience, and that there is from the beginning a very close connection between the body-image of ourselves and the body-images of others. We take parts of the body-images of others into others, and push parts of our body-images into others. We may push our own body-images completely into others, or in some way there may be a continuous interplay between the body-images of ourselves and the persons around us. This interplay may be an interplay of parts or of wholes.

There is no question that there are from the beginning connecting links between all body-images, and it is important to follow the lines of body-image intercourse. We meet here the question of the way in which distance in space influences these lines. There is no doubt that the far-distant body will offer less possibility of interplay. If we put our body into an imaginary centre we may measure the spatial distance of other bodies when we want to determine the relation between the body-images. To be close in space increases the possibility of an interrelation between the body-images, and besides other things contact between two bodies must afford a greater possibility of the melting together of the body-images. We must also consider sexual contact between two bodies from the point of view of spatial nearness. It is true that when two bodies come very near each other, optic distinction becomes more difficult and there will be a greater possibility of a complete melting and reconstructing of one's own body-image as well as the body-image of the other person. It must also not be forgotten that every touch given or received will, as the discussion in the first and second parts show, immediately produce new and interesting problems concerning the structure of one's own body-image as well as of the body-image of the other person. The factor of spatial distance is at first an optic factor and becomes finally a factor of touch.[2] Besides the factor of spatial

distance we have to consider that every emotion concerning the other person brings the body-image of this other person nearer to us.

We have therefore the factor of the emotional distance. Language throws considerable light on this relation. We say of a person with whom we are in emotional relations that he is near to us. We could describe the relations between the body-images of different persons under the metaphor of a magnetic field with stream-lines going in all directions.

But it would be wrong to conclude that the metaphorical distance between the various images of the body is the same in the case of all parts of the body. Parts which have an erotic interest are nearer to each other than parts which are less important from an erotic point of view. It might almost be said that the erogenic zones of the various body-images are closer to each other than the other parts of the body, or that the intercourse between the body-images takes place especially through the erogenic zones. I purposely use this word which has a double meaning because sexual intercourse is certainly a very complete melting together of body-images, and if we ever have a psychology of intercourse (we are pretty far from that) it will be based on the relation of body-images in intercourse.

* * *

When we try to come to more general formulations we can make the following propositions: (1) Body-images are never isolated. They are always encircled by the body-images of others. (2) The relation to the body-images of others is determined by the factor of spatial nearness and remoteness and by the factor of emotional nearness and remoteness. (3) Body-images are nearer to each other in the erogenic zones and are closely bound together in the erogenic zones. (4) The transfer of erogenic zones will reflect itself also in the social relation to other body-images. (5) Erotic changes in the body-image are always social phenomena and are accompanied by corresponding phenomena in the body-images of others. (6) Body-images are on principle social. Our own

---

[2] It is a well known trick on the vaudeville stage for two comedians to intertwine their legs so closely that they are apparently unable to determine the ownership.

I was once present at a conference in which the question was discussed with a friend of a patient whether the patient should stay in the hospital or not. The patient was present. The friend took the patient's part. I wondered what was the connection between these two? Why was this other man so much interested in the fate of this other person sitting nearby?

body-image is never isolated but is always accompanied by the body-images of others. (7) Our own body-image and the body-image of others are not primarily dependent upon each other; they are equal, and the one cannot be explained by the other. (8) There is a continuous interchange between parts of our own body-image and the body-images of others. There is projection and appersonization. But in addition the whole body-image of others can be taken in (identification) or our own body-image can be pushed out as a whole. (9) The body-images of others and their parts can be integrated completely with our own body-image and can form a unit, or they can be simply added to our own body-image and then merely form a sum. (10) We have always emphasized that the postural model of the body is not static, that it changes continually according to the life circumstances. We have considered it as a construction of a creative type. It is built up, dissolved, built up again. An important part in this continuous process of construction, reconstruction, and dissolution of the body-image, is played by the processes of identification, appersonization, and projection. When the body-image has once been created according to our needs and tendencies it does not remain unchanged; it is in a continual flow, and a crystallization is immediately followed by a plastic stage from which new constructions and new efforts are possible according to the emotional situation of the individual. Moreover, there is not only the continual change in our own body-image but also the continual changes in its spatial relations, emotional relations of the body-images of others and the construction of the body-images of others. Also the social relation of the body-images is not a fixed "gestalt." But we have a process of forming a "gestalt," "gestalting," or creative construction in the social image.

* * *

BEAUTY AND BODY-IMAGE

Our own body is an image, and is built up in ourselves in accordance with our instinctive attitudes. An actual change in the appearance can therefore only have a limited result. It is true that a cosmetic operation may occasionally change not only the body but also the body-image. We may build up the body-image again. We may look into the mirror and project the mirror-image into ourselves. We may also study the changed attitude of others and transfer it to our body-image. But all these factors will not have a decisive influence when they are not able to change the psychic attitude of the individual. These considerations also explain the special difficulties in plastic operation, which will set in motion so many of the deep-lying pregenital activities.

We should not underrate the importance of actual beauty and ugliness in human life. Beauty can be a promise of complete satisfaction and can lead up to this complete satisfaction. Our own beauty or ugliness will not only figure in the image we get about ourselves, but will also figure in the image others build up about us and which will be taken back again into ourselves. The body-image is the result of social life. Beauty and ugliness are certainly not phenomena in the single individual, but are social phenomena of the utmost importance. They regulate the sex activities in human relations, and not only the manifest heterosexual activities, but also the homosexual ones which are so important for the social structure. In the case of our patient, the admiration for his friends who were, in his opinion, better endowed than himself, plays an enormous part. Our own body-image and the body-images of others, their beauty and ugliness, thus become the basis for our sexual and social activities. We like to believe that our standards of measurement of beauty are absolute.

The unprejudiced study of the ideas of the human body in different societies offers considerable difficulties for this point of view. When we leave the borders of our own cultural race, it is very difficult to keep up the standards of beauty. It is sometimes impossible to appreciate the beauty standard of primitive races, but even when we compare our own beauty standard with the beauty standard of the yellow, brown, or black races, the integration into a general law is not a simple task. It is difficult for us to understand that the crippling of the feet in the Chinese is considered by them to increase their beauty. We need not even go so far for an example. It is hard for us now to understand that the crippling of the female figure by a tight corset ever conformed with the general ideas of beauty. Tattooing, pulling out the lips, and many other disfigurements which are supposed to be decorations in primitive societies are other instances of this kind.

We understand the actual changes which different societies perform on their bodies when we study the instinctive desires and drives. The ideal of beauty and the measurement of beauty will always be the expression of the libidinous situation in society. This libidinous situation is necessarily changeable. I do not want to give the impression that I adhere to a relativistic idea of beauty. There are laws of libidinous structures, but the libidinous structure changes its manifestations according to the whole social situation, and in this way the manifestation of beauty will also change.

Body-images and their beauty are not rigid entities. We construct and reconstruct our own body-image as well as the body-images of others. In these perpetual processes we interchange parts of our images with the images of others, or, in other words, there is a continual socialization of body-images. It is one phase in the continual stream of libidinous desires, a phase where we feel that no immediate responsible action, either social or sexual, is forced upon us, where the action can remain an unaccomplished germ, or where the action may be a play. The treacherous character of beauty is based upon this. We are, after all, not able to perceive without acting. We are not able to maintain the attitude of merely perceiving without acting. Action is not something added to the passive reception of the experiences of the world; action and reception are an inseparable unit. There is no play which is only play, there is some responsibility in every play. We like to deceive ourselves with the thought that we may dispense with actions and that we may act not as personalities as a whole but may reserve our final inner commitment. But we know in the core of our personality that the real beauty of life lies in its inexorability and seriousness.

* * *

In discussing the beauty of the body, we have so far only considered the body at rest. But this is a great schematization of the problem. The fact that we have so far considered the beauty of the form more than the beauty of the function has a deeper meaning. As soon as we leave the state of rest and start movement, it is much more difficult to remain in the attitude of what Kant has called, "Interesseloses Wohlgefallen." We are immediately stirred up to a more energetic action. It is true that when we build up our own body-image and the body-image of others, we always tend to build up something static and then to dissolve it again. We always return to the primary

positions of the body. When we think about a person running, we see him changing from one primary position into another primary position. Primary positions are positions of relative rest. The positions in between the two primary positions are neglected and even the movement is neglected as such. To use a simile taken from physics, we may say that we are less interested in what is going on in the field, we are not interested in the continual flow, but more or less in the quantums, the crystallized units of the postural model. We should, however, realize that our own body-image and the body-image of others is not only a body-image at rest but a body-image in movement. But beauty is especially connected with the body-image at rest. It is owing to this that we are so astonished when we see a single phase of any movement in a photograph. It does not seem to be natural. The process of the human being in motion is reconstructed by ourselves according to the laws of the body-image.

* * *

Plastic art necessarily neglects the colour of the human body. But there is no question that colour is of enormous importance in the image of the human body. Although one might think that it should be very simple to know the colour of the human body, yet nothing is more changeable, more elusive, than this very colour. It is true that the configuration of the human body, the changing lights will provoke many variations. But there is, in addition, the ever varying play of movements, which gives an additional life to the surface of the body. There are also the continual variations of the tone of the skin, its turgidity connected with the variation in the blood supply and the water absorption. But even when we consider these factors, it remains unexplained why the colour of the human body is again and again a surprise to us. Painters have incessantly tried to catch this colour. The nude body and bathers are the eternal problems of painting. They reflect the surprise we feel again and again when seeing the various colours of human bodies. It may be said that this is due to our social habits which generally hide the body. But the colour of the human face is not less mysterious. And when one sits in a stadium and looks about, one wonders about the mysterious appearance of the faces of thousands.

The same difficulties that we have in building up the postural image of the body arise when we try to build up a deeper knowledge of the colour of the human body. There is no question that an explanation is only possible when we keep in mind how many interfering libidinous tendencies are attached to the image of our body. And the uncertainty concerning the colours of the body, our never flagging curiosity concerning the body, emphasize the dynamic character of our knowledge of the human body and of our body-images. It would be a fascinating problem to go through the history of painting and study the various ways in which the different ages have seen the human body and especially its colour. All these different interpretations reflect our change in attitudes towards the body and its colours and different stages in our libidinous development. Our own body is in no way better known to us than the bodies of others. We should not use the mirror so eagerly if it were otherwise. The interest we have in mirrors is the expression of lability of our own postural model of the body, of the incompleteness of the immediate data, of the necessity of building up the image of our body in a continual constructive effort.

* * *

One last remark about the dead body in its relation to the body-image. Since the body-image is a creation which uses raw experience only as material, death does not destroy the body-image of another person. We build up also in the dead person the body-image of a living person. Since the body-image and its parts are so often interchangeable, we understand that every part of the body of a dead person remains connected with him. Even his clothes retain a part of his personality. It has often been emphasized that dreams about dead persons add to the belief in their immortality. I have mentioned that the body of a fellow-being is built up and constructed like a picture of imagination and like a picture of a dream. The continuation of the body-image in dream and phantasy retains, therefore, an important part of what we actually perceive in fellow human beings. The dead, therefore, do not disappear from the community of the living. They remain in this community as long as their pictures are revived in any members of the community.

I have repeatedly emphasized that every isolated psychological study is necessarily artificial. The body-image does not exist *per se,* it is a part of the world. And even if we suppose that in some stages of development the whole world consists of parts of bodies, still the outside world is also there in a less structured form. This outside world becomes, however, clearer in the developed experience of the fully conscious mind. On the other hand, there is not only an outside world of a structure different from the body-image, but there is also a personality, the whole world of psychic life, as far as it is the expression of an ego, of a subject. But it is true that in every experience the body-image is present. It is one side of the full experience which comprises the personality (the true ego), the body, and the world. We have merely taken the body as one of the three spheres of experiences which constitute life and existence.

Chapter 11 Self-Conceptions: Configurations of Content*

CHAD GORDON

ORIENTING CONCERNS

As long as there have been attempts to understand and explain human conduct, there have been formulations of the nature of "the one who" perceives, thinks, feels, chooses, remembers, imagines, or acts. Concepts such as soul, reason, mind, drives, personality trends, conscience, and ego are based upon different views of the nature of man, and they are linked to different theories regarding the motivation and direction of conduct. Yet they share as their core meaning a reference to a single self, a bounded unit of being, an enduring particle of existence which is itself at least partly *aware* of that existence.

Philosophical analysis of human consciousness now constitutes a fascinating and extensive literature.[1] In particular, there are some indications that the perspectives of phenomenology and existentialism may provide substantial assistance to the social scientist.[2]

William James' early discrimination of the experiencing *I* from the experiecned *Me* as fundamental aspects of self-process still remains viable and has served to structure much of the later theory and research.[3] If it is assumed that this *I*, or continuing process of individual experience, establishes the perspective and contextual ground for much of the person's perception and interpretation, the features of the self-as-experiencer offer almost unlimited opportunities for the student of cognitive processes.

The *Me*, or self-as-experienced, is of more direct social-psychological concern. Beyond the central presupposition of symbolic interactionism that the very genesis of the self is to be found in the processes of communicative interaction, many specific aspects of the individual's past socialization concern development of his self-conceptions. The person's present self-conceptions and self-evaluations

SOURCE. This paper was prepared originally for this volume.

* The investigations on which this report is based have been supported by the National Science Foundation, the research fund of the University of California at Los Angeles, the Laboratory of Social Relations at Harvard, and the Clarke Fund for faculty research at Harvard. This support is gratefully acknowledged, and reference is made to the author's doctoral dissertation *Self-Conception and Social Achievement*, Ann Arbor: University Microfilms, 1964; small portions of this dissertation have been adapted for use in the present paper. I wish to thank Erving Goffman, Kenneth Gergen and Thomas Cottle for their valuable criticisms and suggestions.

[1] Two recent examples are Maurice Merleau-Ponty, *Phenomenology of Perception,* London: Routledge and Kegan Paul, 1962; and Aron Gurwitsch, *The Field of Consciousness,* Pittsburgh, Pa.: Duquesne University Press, 1964.

[2] For the classical phenomenological position, see Edmund Husserl, *Ideas: General Introduction to Pure Phenomenology,* translated by W. R. Boyce Gibson, New York: The Macmillan Company, 1931; published in German, 1913; from a more

sociological point of view, though philosophically derived from Husserl, see Alfred Schutz, "Common Sense and Scientific Interpretation of Human Action," *Philosophy and Phenomenological Research,* **14** (September 1953), reprinted in Volume I of Schutz's *Collected Papers,* edited by Maurice Natanson, The Hague: Martinus Nijhoff, 1964, pp. 3–47. Also, Edward A. Tiryakian in two recent papers, "Existential Phenomenology and the Sociological Tradition," *American Sociological Review,* **30** (October 1965), pp. 674–688, and "The Existential Self and the Person," Chapter 7 of the present volume, has indicated some of the major relevances of the phenomenological and existential philosophical perspectives for a radically more fundamental social theory of the lived world of everyday life. The leading exponent of this approach to the formulation of sociological theory is Harold Garfinkel, "Studies of the Routine Grounds of Everyday Activities," *Social Problems* (Winter 1964), pp. 225–250; also "Conditions of Successful Degradation Ceremonies," *The American Journal of Sociology,* **61** (March 1956), pp. 420–424.

[3] William James, *Psychology: The Briefer Course,* New York: Henry Holt, 1892, pp. 176–216.

are hypothesized to be intimately connected to his sense of well-being and may be at the root of important categories of pathology. There is the further assertion that some of the person's self-conceptions play an important part in determining the courses of future conduct he selects from among those he sees as available.[4]

However, these relationships can never be substantiated convincingly until the nature of self-conception is more clearly formulated and connected to operational methods of empirical investigation. The central objective of this chapter is to present one such conceptualization and operational approach to investigating typical configurations of self-conception content.

SOME THEORETICAL AND METHODOLOGICAL ISSUES

An adequate program of research on self-conception must come to terms with a number of general theoretical issues as well as with the difficulties of particular operational techniques. The first requirement is a relatively rigorous definition by which to orient the entire enterprise of specifying the relevant properties of the self-process:

The self is *not* a thing; it is a complex *process* of continuing interpretive activity—simultaneously the person's located subjective stream of *consciousness* (both reflexive and nonreflexive, including perceiving, thinking, planning, evaluating, choosing, etc.) *and* the resultant accruing *structure of self-conceptions* (the special system of self-referential meanings available to this active consciousness).

Formulation of self-conceptions as constituting a *system* facilitates raising important but very difficult questions concerning the elements and their interrelations as well as the patterns of their change over time.

The very fact of conceptualization in terms of a multiplicity of available meanings leads to investigation of the actually encountered *types* of meanings and the relative frequencies of their occurrence. The plural view also leads away from the simplistic notion of "the self concept" of an individual, toward determination of the relative *consistency* of the elements. The idea of a structure of available meanings encourages inquiry as to their *organization,* perhaps along the lines of central versus peripheral elements, or in terms of a hierarchy of impact on perception and action.[5]

Since we are dealing with meanings, questions of *clarity* to the person immediately arise and suggest consideration of the dimension of conscious/preconscious/unconscious, in addition to the more familair problem of the factors shaping relevance and salience.

Change in the elements of the person's structure of self-conceptions occurs during their *formation* in early socialization, and in *transformations* after childhood. The overall *temporal orientation* of the person's self-process includes the reverie of focus on the "self I used to be," the current perspective of those attuned to "being," and the prospective future selves of those engaged in thoughts of becoming.

Successful exploration of these and many other similar questions could lead to consideration of the associated social factors which help to shape these configurations, priorities of relevance, transformations, and so forth. Further, we could then ascertain the degree to which there is congruence between a respondent's structure of self-conceptions and the conceptions of him held by significant others, and we could explore the implications of varying degrees of disparity or incongruity.

But before these interesting questions can be addressed empirically, there must be some method for translating the respondent's self-conceptions (available only to him) into *self-representations* available to the researcher. Thus we may work with the self-descriptions or self-ratings which the respondent is willing and able to give us in order to make inferences concerning his inner experience. Even if we

---

[4] The basic statements on the relations of consciousness and self to symbolic interaction are found in George Herbert Mead's *Mind, Self, and Society,* C. W. Morris (ed.), Chicago, Ill.: University of Chicago Press, 1934, and his "Development of the Self and Social Control," *International Journal of Ethics,* **25** (1924–25), pp. 251–277. Much more comprehensive analyses of socialization, social control, and self esteem from the same general perspective are contained in Tamotsu Shibutani, *Society and Personality,* Englewood Cliffs, N.J.: Prentice-Hall, 1961.

[5] A very similar conceptualization of the self-referential meanings is Carl Rogers' use of "self-structure." See in particular "A Theory of Therapy, Personality, and Interpersonal Relationships, as Developed in the Client-Centered Framework," in Sigmund Koch (ed.), *Psychology: The Study of A Science,* Vol. III, *Formulations of the Person and the Social Context,* New York: McGraw-Hill, 1959, pp. 184–256, esp. 200–206.

use an indirect approach and go from observed behavior to the conceptions the person "must" be using, or from his responses to projective and disguised tests, we never have direct access to his shifting fields of consciousness.

Since there is no external criterion to use in assessing predictive validity, the problem of construct validity for any particular aspect of self-conception is an extremely difficult one. For the present, we should adopt a pragmatic and provisional approach. Some assurance that obtained representations are at least rough approximations of actual conceptions may be gleaned from seeking instruments of "reasonable" face validity and then checking with the respondent in a less stylized manner to see if he "recognizes" himself as accurately depicted. In some situations indirect procedures can be used to determine whether very favorable outcomes on more direct measures are the result of ego defense mechanisms or such factors as compensation for actually felt unfavorability and the desire for approval. Most important, verification of validity may be attempted by relation of obtained measures to other variables suggested by our rudimentary theoretical hunches.

When we turn to the specific problems of chosen methods for collecting self-representations, we find little guidance regarding the manner in which respondents interpret the research tasks facing them. There is not the slightest doubt that all kinds of more or less extraneous factors such as social desirability of the items, approval motivation of the respondent, response set, and experimenter bias in the testing situation are operating in current data collection procedures. Certainly steps should be taken to eliminate, minimize, or at least take account of these factors. Yet overly severe standards of methodological purity applied too early in the process of investigation can lead to paralysis, and can prevent the accretion of valuable insights into ways of increasing the validity to the desired level of assurance.

Although methodologically imperfect, a given procedure may allow one to organize the data into patterns which are themselves meaningful and which yield substantial relations to appropriate external variables.

With these questions and cautions in mind, we may now turn to consideration of four methodological issues that have important bearing on the operational procedures suggested in this paper. These issues concern the category-attribute problem, the question of tense, the evaluation of self-representations, and the determination of relative importance.

The Category-Attribute Problem: Social Identity and Personal Characteristics

Investigators describing the phenomena of self-consciousness have often used the ambiguous circumlocution, "the individual becomes an object to himself."[6] We are told that this peculiar "object" is perceived, interpreted, judged, and so on. But, as is the case with any object of consciousness, this self may be perceived in either categorical or attributive terms. The relevant *categories* denote the "kind of thing" the object is, whereas the *attributes* describe the object in terms of qualities that differentiate it from others of its kind. Thus an object in the environment may be interpreted by consciousness as an *instance* of the category "man," and it may perhaps be further characterized as "tall, dark, and handsome."

The categories tend to have relatively clear boundaries and are inferred according to the logic of membership, inclusion, and exclusion. The attributes, on the contrary, are generally matters of degree or intensity. Properties (such as tall-ness or dark-ness) may be imagined in the abstract but are presented to consciousness only as the attributes of objects (a dark man, a dark secret, etc.). Neither the man nor the secret is likely to be viewed as an "instance" of "darkness."

It is clear from introspection that the ordinary member of the society conceives of himself in terms of both categories and attributes simultaneously. He knows, for example, that he belongs in the category "foreman" in his factory, and therefore stands in certain definite relations to the production manager, the secretaries in the front office, and the members of his work crew. All such role identifications, formal or informal, establish just this categorical mode of thought.[7] The ascribed characteristics (sex, age, ethnicity, nationality, etc.) function in the same manner, to the

---

[6] See, for example, Mead, *Mind, Self, and Society, op. cit.,* p. 136.

[7] Ralph Turner, "Role-Taking: Process Versus Conformity," A. M. Rose (ed.), *Human Behavior and Social Processes,* Boston, Mass.: Houghton-Mifflin, 1962; Orrin E. Klapp, *Heroes, Villains, and Fools,* Englewood Cliffs N.J.: Prentice-Hall, 1962; Alfred Schutz, "Common-Sense and Scientific Interpretation of Human Action," *Collected Papers,* Vol. I, *op. cit.,* esp. pp. 15–19.

degree that they have come to carry role-like characteristics of their own or serve as major categories of person necessitating special forms of behavior. Thus our Foreman conceives of himself as also a Male, an Adult, an American, a Catholic, a Leader, and the like. Linguistically, these categories typically are designated by nouns or noun-like forms. Each of these noun forms refers to a culturally provided *social type,* which is likely to imply several specific behavior patterns and attributes.

But our Foreman also conceives of himself as (among a great many other things) quite honest, fairly smart, not very religious, physically strong, and unusually lucky. Self-representations in terms of these kinds of adjectival attributes are also very likely to have an impact on his conduct, especially in shaping his expectations regarding the likelihood of favorable outcomes in different kinds of encounters.

The category-attribute dichotomy is not a logical problem for the individual. He knows that everyone is characterized by both sets of references at once. Furthermore, he knows that some attributes are "appropriate" to certain categories (the wisdom of the judge, the responsibility of the father, etc.), whereas others would constitute serious problems or perhaps would be irrelevant free variants. The logical difficulties are inflicted on the investigator who attempts to move toward adequate operationalization of the various concepts lurking about in the self-conception literature. Some decision must be made on whether to approach self-conception in terms of categorical noun-forms or attributive adjectival forms, or to attempt an integration of the two.

Social Identity: the individual's major role and social-type categorizations are here conceptualized as his social identity. This social identity can then be portrayed as the combination of a number of categorical meanings designating socially recognizable types. Thus in our example we may have the social identity: Adult, Male, American, Leader, Foreman, Catholic, Father, and so on. Analyses could then proceed to determine priorities of relevance according to which the individual's own self-conceived social identity is constituted, the degree to which these categories are similar to those used by the persons with whom he interacts in important contexts, and to assess the evaluation which the person places on this combination of categorical representations.[8]

Personal Attributes. Far more frequent than analyses of categorical meanings is description in terms of dimensional atttributes. These properties are almost always expressed as adjectives or adjectival forms. The attributes assessed are usually "personality traits," typical interpersonal styles, evaluative dimensions, sensed impressions made on others, and the like.

A common method for tapping personal attributes is the adjective checklist, on which the respondent indicates as "generally true" of him any number of atttributes from among as many as 200 items such as "responsible," "dominant," and "trusting."[9] Some inference of degree or intensity is possible with the use of the semantic differential technique with its set of 10 to 20 paired opposites (strong-weak, good-bad, etc.) rated along scales representing some qualification such as "slightly," "quite," and "extremely."[10] A still more elaborate approach to the problem of relative applicability is Stephenson's Q-sort technique, in which the respondent sorts a very large number (sometimes more than 100) of adjectival phrases into piles according to the degree to which he feels each is accurately descriptive of him.[11]

---

[8] This conceptualization of social identity is very similar to that proposed by Erving Goffman in *Stigma: Notes on the Management of Spoiled Identity,* Englewood Cliffs, N.J.: Prentice-Hall Spectrum Books, 1963, esp. pp. 2–3.
[9] Theodore Sarbin's adjective checklist approach may be seen in his article with Bernard G. Rosenberg, "Contributions to Role-Taking Theory: IV. A Method for Obtaining a Qualitative Estimate of the Self," *Journal of Social Psychology,* **42** (1955), pp. 71–81. Timothy Leary's Interpersonal Check List (ICL) and other methods based on dichotomous applicability of descriptive words or phrases can be found in his *Interpersonal Diagnosis of Personality,* New York: Ronald Press, 1957, esp. pp. 456–457.
[10] Charles E. Osgood, George J. Suci, and Percy H. Tannenbaum, *The Measurement of Meaning,* Urbana, Ill.: University of Illinois Press, 1957; S. F. Miyamoto and Sanford Dornbusch, "A Test of the Symbolic Interactionist Hypothesis of Self-Conception," *American Journal of Sociology,* **61** (1956), pp. 399–403; and Leo G. Reeder, G. A. Donahue, and Arturo Biblarz, "Conceptions of Self and Others," *American Journal of Sociology,* **45** (1960), pp. 153–159.
[11] William Stephenson, *The Study of Behavior,* Chicago, Ill.: University of Chicago Press, 1953. John M. Butler and Gerard V. Haigh have provided a frequently used set of 100 Q-sort statements, "Changes in the Relation Between Self-Concepts and Ideal Concepts Consequent upon Client-Centered Counseling," in Carl R. Rogers and Rosalind F. Dymond (eds.), *Psychotherapy and Personality Change,* Chicago, Ill.: University of Chicago Press, 1954, pp. 55–75.

The vast majority of psychological studies of self-conception have utilized these adjectival approaches to characterize the respondent's current views of himself, his "ideal self," or the ways in which he feels he is seen by other persons. Also quite frequent is the use of discrepancies between descriptions of "the way I really am" and "the way I'd most like to be" as measures of self-regard or self-acceptance.[12]

There are important advantages to be gained from rapid and economical collection of easily scored information that is more or less comparable over large numbers of respondents. Obviously, this kind of approach becomes more appropriate as investigators develop clearer conceptualizations of important theoretical variables.

Yet it is equally obvious that since there are no noun-like forms included in the checklist, semantic differential, or Q-sort techniques, there can be no assessment of the respondent's self-conceptions in terms of roles, memberships, activities, or loyalties. The adjectival approach can only describe an individual as he is differentiated from others along segmental properties. It cannot discover what "type" of person he considers himself to be, nor the social and idea systems in which he feels implicated.

These considerations argue for a comprehensive view of self-conception. This must include both the *social identity* represented by the combination of primarily noun-like social categories telling what the individual shares with others in those categories *and* the *personal attributes* that distinguish him from others. If this more comprehensive view is adopted, I would suggest that operationalization of self-conceptions can be approached most meaningfully through a relatively unstructured spontaneous-response technique which will allow either categories or attributes to be expressed, in any order, as these are called up by the respondent himself. This free-response approach does require a very comprehensive coding scheme in order to capture at all adequately the major themes in the rich and subtle data produced. But it also allows inferences about the respondent's utilization

of an additional aspect of self-conception to which we now turn: the tenses of self.

The Tenses of Self

Since William James' day there have been many attempts to analyze self-conceptions according to their time perspective. Early analyses were cast in totalistic terms, such as James' relatively remote "potential social Me" as distinguished from the immediate present Me and from the Me of the past.[13] Later attempts at empirical investigation of self-conceptions have frequently used multi-attribute adjectival approaches such as semantic differentials or Q-sorts on "the way I really am" and some noncurrent self, such as "the way I would most like to be." These techniques may yield measurements sufficiently valid for many purposes, but they share the central difficulty of all fixed-dimension approaches. Since the investigator supplies the stimulus for distinction between the time perspectives, he cannot infer anything about the respondent's own tendency to think of himself in the different time senses.

Even more serious is confusion between time reference and actuality level, and insufficient attention to their interaction in conceptions of self. In addition to distinguishing retrospective and prospective elements from those meanings felt to be currently applicable, members of our culture also categorize their actions and states of being according to degree of perceived *actuality*. This perceived actuality reaches a maximum in those self-referential meanings the person feels are really true of him in the sense of factually having come to pass. Decreasing in sensed actuality or "likelihood" are "realistic" expectations, intentions, and "possible" potentials. Least actual are conceptions of ideal conditions. Thus persons may differ a great deal in their propensity to conceive of themselves in terms of past, present, and future time; and (within the future category) they may also differ in their use of expectations, intentions, potentials, and ideals. Differences of both sorts may be associated with important differences in coping styles, life satisfaction, aspirations, and courses of conduct selected.

Since the distinctions between types of time reference and actuality levels are exactly those made in ordinary English language usage, I am conceptualizing these two dimensions as jointly

---

[12] Ruth Wylie has recently compiled a very comprehensive review of this large and interesting literature, *The Self Concept: A Critical Survey of Pertinent Research Literature*, Lincoln, Neb.: University of Nebraska Press, 1961, esp. pp. 69–107.

[13] James, *op. cit.*, pp. 58–59.

The Tenses of Self		Exemplar Meaning
Past	Reflective past	"I could have been ——— if only ———."
	Completed past	"I used to be ———."
Present	Past-continuing, into present	"I was and still am ———."
	Current, present self	"I now am, I have become ———."
Future	Prospective, intended self	"I want, am trying, planning, hoping, to be ———."
	Actually expected outcome	"I probably will be ———."
	Potential, possible self	"I could be, might be ———."
Timeless value	Ideal, most desirable self	"I should be ———."

constituting the *tenses of self*.[14] These tenses may be used to characterize each element of self-representation, as in the table above.

As was shown in the discussion of the category-attribute issue, a very open approach is required if the investigator is to use the actual representations to make inferences about the individual's spontaneous use of dimensions such as the tenses of self. There is one method that has the required features of allowing the respondent to represent himself in any framework he pleases, in terms of noun-like categories or adjectival attributes, in any order, and in any tense. This solution, which also possesses at least a plausible face validity for operationalizing self-conceptions, involves eliciting repeated answers to the open question "Who am I?"

The Who Am I? Method

Bugenthal and Zelen[15] were among the first to suggest that the respondent simply be allowed to *describe* himself. They merely provided the respondent with a blank piece of paper and asked him to give three answers to the question "Who are you?" These answers were then classified by mention of name, status characteristics, affective quality, and the like. Somewhat later, Kuhn and McPartland offered techniques for analyzing an expanded version of this procedure.[16] They asked respondents

to give 20 answers to the question "Who am I?" in a period of 12 minutes, calling this technique the Twenty Statements Test.

The rich revealingness of the Who Am I method and the value of tense coding are perhaps best communicated by direct presentation of actual protocols. Consider, for example, these two self-descriptions written 6 months apart by Clarie, a 17-year-old girl who was recently a freshman at Los Angeles City College. In both cases the Who Am I appeared as the first section of a take-home questionnaire and carried these instructions:

There are fifteen numbered blanks on the page below. Please write fifteen different answers to the simple question "Who am I?" in the blanks, answering as if you were giving the answers to yourself, not to somebody else. Write the answers in the order that they occur to you. Don't worry about "logic" or "importance." Please do not take more than six or seven minutes for this part.

Three categories of social identity are clear and prominent. Sex (as inferred from the name, as Clarie would expect us to do), race, and religion are mentioned immediately and serve to "position" her in relation to three of the most important dimensions of our society's "social space." They are all past-continuing in tense, and serve as stable points of social anchorage. Thus we are dealing with a person who represents herself as standing in the area of intersection of three major categories: Female-Negro-Catholic.

Change in self-conception may occur in categories or in attributes, although it is somewhat more likely in the attributes. These attributes are limitless in number, and often concern states of mind (such as "shy" or "intelligent") which permit subtle shades of intensity. Our attention is often called to either type of change by the appearance of representations which are completed-past or current in tense. Clarie's answers illustrate these indicators.

[14] I am indebted to Victoria Steinitz for suggesting this term. A very similar formulation of the tenses of action can be found in Alfred Schutz, "On Multiple Realities," in Vol. I of *Collected Papers, op. cit.,* esp. pp. 214 ff.

[15] J. F. T. Bugental and S. L. Zelen, "Investigations into the Self-Concept," *Journal of Personality,* **18** (1950), pp. 483–498.

[16] Manford H. Kuhn and Thomas S. McPartland, "An Empirical Investigation of Self-Attitudes," *American Sociological Review,* **19** (1954), pp. 68–76; Manford H. Kuhn, "Self-Attitudes by Age, Sex, and Professional Training," *Sociological Quarterly,* **9** (Jan. 1960), pp. 39–55.

Who Am I?
(October)

I am:	Category/	Attribute	Tense
1. ...Clarie M. ————	(×)	×	past-continuing
2. ...5 feet 5 inches tall.		×	current
3. ...a Negro.	×		past-continuing
4. ...Catholic (religion).	×		past-continuing
5. ...118 (weight).		×	current
6. ...interested in sports.		×	past-continuing
7. ...not conceited.		×	past-continuing
8. ...honest with people.		×	past-continuing
9. ...not one who always criticizes.		×	past-continuing
10. ...interested in all types of music.		×	past-continuing
11. ...one who likes to dance.		×	past-continuing
12. ...sometimes easy to get angry.		×	past-continuing
13. ...considered attractive.		×	past-continuing
14. ...easy to talk with strangers.		×	past-continuing
15. ...quick to respond to some emotions.		×	past-continuing

Who Am I?
(March)

I am:	Category/	Attribute	Tense
1. ...Clarie M. ————	(×)	×	past-continuing
2. ...a Negro.	×		past-continuing
3. ...Catholic by religion.	×		past-continuing
4. ...considered attractive.		×	past-continuing
5. ...built rather shapely.		×	past-continuing
6. ...five feet four and one-half inches tall.		×	current
7. ...very friendly.		×	past-continuing
8. ...now eighteen years old.		×	current
9. ...not a virgin anymore.	×		completed past
10. ...now feeling very depressed.		×	current
11. ...one who knows how it feels to have loved and lost.		×	current
12. ...interested in all types of music.		×	past-continuing
13. ...one who likes to be alone sometimes.		×	past-continuing
14. ...one who is interested in all types of sports.		×	past-continuing
15. ...interested in people in general.		×	past-continuing

She tells us in the second protocol that she is "now eighteen years old" (she was seventeen at the time she filled out the first "Who Am I?" but apparently did not then think of age as a particularly relevant attribute).

Change indicated by a completed-past reference to fundamental social category is often a very important event, one of the "transformations of identity" analyzed by Anselm Strauss.[17] In Clarie's case, the reference to being "not a virgin anymore" is graphic demonstration of the importance of analysis in terms of categories and tenses and also helps to counter the charge that little really meaningful information can be gathered by "pencil and paper" techniques.

Detailed analysis of differential use of the various tenses and relations to other aspects of the respondent's life will be reported in another paper. For the present, it is perhaps sufficient to indicate that across several diverse pilot study groups (high school students, schizophrenic and alcoholic patients, students at Los Angeles City College, and Harvard-Radcliffe undergraduates), about 75% of the self-representation elements were in the past-continuing

---

[17] Anselm Strauss, *Mirrors and Masks: The Search for Identity,* Glencoe, Ill.: Free Press, 1959, esp. Chapter 4.

tense, and approximately 20% were current references. Intentions, completed past, expectations, potentials, and ideal standards occur in approximately that order within the remaining 5%. Reflective past is rare in youth.

The relative preponderance of past-continuing and current responses is not surprising, considering that the stimulus is the stem "I am ————." More interesting are the facts that the various groups differed a good deal in the proportion of respondents who used each tense at all, and that some individuals used a particular tense a great many times.

Naturally, the analysis of the tenses of self-representations should not be completely divorced from the actual content of the elements, and this content will be discussed in a following section. The idea of checking the tense of each representation separately permits more fine-grained analysis of tense patterns for each individual, provides important indicators of change over time, and allows investigation of dominant and variant patterns of connection between particular categories of content and the tenses assigned them by important types of respondent.

Evaluation of Elements

The very general evaluative dimension of self-conception is usually termed self-esteem or self-regard.[18] This kind of global self-evaluation, or "preponderant feeling tone," as William James described it, has a respectable although perhaps overrated position in the conceptual literature. At least it seems to be much closer to actual feelings held by individuals than are holistic conceptions of ideal-self-in-all-its-aspects and the like. Three points will be advanced here in favor of also assessing *each element* of free-response self-representations for its evaluative character.

After separate evaluation has been accomplished (either by the investigator's imputation, or better, by the respondent himself), we may choose to make some kind of summary assess-

ment of the overall evaluation. Consideration of the separate evaluations makes possible the discrimination of "middling" levels of self-esteem that are the result of some kind of weighted balance between extreme positive and extreme negative elements from middling self-esteem that is simply the result of compounded middling elements. Second, when used in relation to a direct self-esteem scale, this approach permits exploration of systems of determining appropriate weights for the individual's positive and negative items. Third, separate evaluation makes possible the analysis of patterns of evaluation for a given category of content among different types of individuals. Thus the meaning of "I am a Jew" may differ markedly for people contented with life in a solidary ethnic community as against those seeking advancement in occupations where discrimination is still practiced.

In exploratory studies now in progress, each Who Am I meaning element is rated according to whether it may reasonably be interpreted as (1) strongly negative, a problem or shame to the respondent, (2) moderately negative, mildly displeasing, (3) neutral or unascertainable as to evaluation, (4) moderately positive, a pleasing good point, or (5) strongly positive, a source of definite satisfaction or pride. Approximately 40% of the students' references are clearly either positive or negative, whereas the alcoholics (52%) and schizophrenics (70%) are considerably higher in use of these affect-laden items.

When the mean of the separately rated representations for each individual is calculated, we find that the composite means for the school groups fall at the center of the scale and do not differ appreciably from each other. The alcoholic patients scored lowest, with frequent use of such low evaluation self-representations as "I am nothing," or "nobody, hopeless, helpless, selfish, mean, hateful, no good, cruel, foolish, and impulsive." The schizophrenics fell in between the school and alcoholic groups. They were the most variable, ranging from "my mind is no more" to "excellent in life." These patterns of group differences are one further indication that the Who Am I method can elicit valid and important information.

A further advantage of evaluating each element in the self-description is the possibility of determining typical patterns in the ordering of favorable, neutral, and negative elements. When we compute the proportion of responses

---

18 See, for example, Morris Rosenberg, *Society and the Adolescent Self-Image,* Princeton, N.J.: Princeton University Press, 1965, for a very comprehensive use of a self-esteem scale, including attempts at construct-validity assessment in relation to reported neurotic symptoms, etc. The term self-regard is perhaps most closely associated with the work of Carl Rogers. For example, "The Significance of the Self-Regarding Attitudes and Perceptions," in R. Reymert (ed.), *Feelings and Emotions: The Moosehart Symposium,* New York: McGraw-Hill, 1950, pp. 374–382.

at each position which are of each valence, we find the following configuration: Contrary to the folk injunctions to "put your best foot forward" and to "make a good first impression," the vast bulk of the early responses are neutral in evaluation (their actual content will be discussed presently). Among the 265 Los Angeles City College students, for example, the proportion of neutral elements declines from a high of 80% for the first responses to 29% at the twelfth. Negative elements stay fairly close to their average of approximately 10%, ranging from a low of 3% to a high of 18%. The large and steady increase in positives from 15% at first to 47% at twelfth position balances the decline in neutral references. A very similar pattern is observed in the protocols of the 157 high school students.

Importance Ranking of Who Am I Self-Representations

Kuhn and McPartland consider order-position in the set of self-representations to be a measure of the salience or readiness to respond in terms of that particular category. They further assert that salience is reasonably interpreted as an indicator of the importance of that representation to the individual.[19] This is in contrast to the familiar position of psychoanalysis and other depth psychologies, which hold that the most important, authentic, or "real" aspects of mental life are just those that are *least* open to conscious public display. A more complex interpretation may view the Who Am I method as similar in many ways to a projective technique. Thus the *repeated-stimulus* format first tends to exhaust the respondent's supply of easy-access identifications, then calls forth word associations connected in subtle ways to less available, semi-unconscious, or actually repressed material. In order to bring some empirical data to bear on these interpretations, I have asked respondents in several studies to rank each of their self-representations in terms of importance.

In the Who Am I protocols of the 157 high school students, the hypothesis of order as an indication of importance is clearly supported. The mean importance rank (with a possible range of 1.0 to 10.0, since 10 statements were requested of these students) moves quite evenly from an indication of highest average importance for the first response (3.1) to

lowest average importance (6.3) at the thirteenth meaning element. For 53 Harvard and Radcliffe students, however, the pattern is different. In this group, which was asked to give 15 responses rather than 10, there is a definite suggestion of a more complex curve. Relatively low average importance was assigned to references 1 and 9, with increasing average importance rankings up to the thirteenth meaning element.

Probably at least two factors are at work to produce the difference between the high school and elite-college patterns. First, the 10-statement version of the Who Am I may not sufficiently challenge those taking it to require the inclusion of items which are usually not recognized by the person because of the ego defense mechanisms, but which are seen as important when revealed. The greater tendency toward introspection of the Harvard-Radcliffe students produces a much greater proportion of responses concerning such personal characteristics as competences, psychic and interpersonal styles, and judgments. All of these tend to be rated as high in importance, but typically occur in the "early middle" or quite late in the protocol.

The patterns of importance and position of the proposed content categories will be presented in the next section; the present discussion can be concluded with the suggestion that order and importance are probably differently related in different populations, for different content categories. Consider that Lyndon Johnson once said of himself:

> I am a free man, an American, a United States Senator and a Democrat, in that order. I am also a liberal, a conservative, a Texan, a taxpayer, a rancher, a businessman, a consumer, a parent, a voter, and not as young as I used to be nor as old as I expect to be—and I am all those things in no fixed order.

A SYSTEM FOR ANALYSIS OF FREE-RESPONSE SELF-REPRESENTATIONS

At this point I wish to focus on the actual content of the self-representations as they are typically given in the Who Am I protocols, with the goal of introducing a system of ordered coding categories with which to capture the main dimensions of the data's meaning.

Kuhn has used a five-category qualitative coding scheme,[20] and McPartland, Cumming and Garretson have been able to predict some

---

[19] Kuhn and McPartland, *op. cit.*, pp. 72–72 and n. 10.

[20] Kuhn, *op. cit.*, pp. 39–55.

forms of behavior among psychiatric patients using a very interesting procedure based on discerning the respondent's most frequently used type of response.[21] In a series of unpublished papers, Theodore Kemper (with Orville Brim and Leonard Cottrell) has been developing a much more comprehensive set of categories for manifest content of self-representations, and a psychologically oriented self-conception dictionary has recently been constructed at Harvard for use with the General Inquirer system of computer-assisted content analysis.[22] The method of analysis proposed here was designed to consolidate many of the features of this previous work to tap more fully the categories of social identity and to provide a theoretical rationale for some of the more important response attributes.

The system is intended to capture the major varieties of concrete self-representation, including four more general or systemic senses of self to be proposed shortly. The categories are organized into a series of major rubrics, moving from the basic elements of social identity (the ascribed social locators and other social types), through abstract allegiances and connections, to particular interests, activities, and objects, and finally up to the major personal characteristics of self and psyche.

In the course of analysis each meaning element in the respondent's Who Am I protocol is coded for four things: its category designation; its tense; its evaluation; and the importance rank assigned to it by the respondent. Some references inherently carry more than one categorical meaning. Thus the self-representation "a boy" is simultaneously a sex reference *and* an age reference, since the

respondent could have said "a male" if he meant only gender. Similarly, "a son" is both a kinship role and a sex reference, and "a teenager" is both a reference to age and to an abstract category. Thus a single word of self-description may yield two or even three codable meaning elements.

The following sections describe the content of each coding dimension, indicate those typically composed of categorical rather than attributive references, and give the percentage of the 157 high school students who were coded as using a given dimension at least one time. In a subsequent section, the category-attribute designation will be related to other features of self-conception.

Detailed Categories With Typical Examples

A. Ascribed Characteristics. Fundamental to the idea of social identity used in this chapter are the ascribed role and category designations conferred on the individual at birth, which typically remain with him throughout his lifetime. They may well be viewed as one set of major "structural locators" that serve to position the individual with regard to the major axes of differentiation in his society. The coding categories for the ascribed characteristics follow.

	Per Cent of High School Students Mentioning at least once ($N = 157$)
1. *Sex:* a man, a boy, a son, clear name, etc. (almost always categorical).	74%
2. *Age:* 15 years old, a boy, young, a teenager, a freshman, etc. (at least public if not exactly categorical).	82%
3. *Name:* John Jones, Clarie M., etc. (at least public and partly categorical).	17%
4. *Racial or National Heritage:* a Negro, white; a Chinese (meaning ancestry or race, not current citizenship); of Italian, Irish ancestry; an immigrant, etc. (usually categorical).	7%
5. *Religious Categorization:* a Catholic, Protestant, Methodist; Jewish, etc. (not just "Christian," "atheist," etc., must be definite religious group) (predominantly categorical).	11%

[21] Thomas S. McPartland, John H. Cumming and Wynona S. Garretson, "Self-Conception and Ward Behavior in Two Psychiatric Hospitals," *Sociometry,* **24** (June 1961), pp. 111–124.

[22] Barry S. McLaughlin, *Identity and Personality,* unpublished doctoral dissertation, Harvard University, 1965, esp. pp. 93–100, 276–293. The present conceptual categories have been built into the McLaughlin dictionary, which has been expanded by Robert Aylmer, Jr. and Lane K. Conn, and thoroughly revised by Barry Wellman, the new dictionary containing about 5000 words and idioms in 99 concept categories, is presently in use at Harvard with the General Inquirer content analysis system developed by Philip Stone: P. J. Stone, D. C. Dunphy, and D. M. Ogilvie, *The General Inquirer: A Computer Approach to Content Analysis,* Cambridge, Mass.: M.I.T. Press, 1967, esp. Chapter 18: "The Who Am I dictionary and self-perceived identity in college students."

Two of these categories require further comment. An individual's current age is not strictly an ascribed aspect, but the date of his birth is; thus in relation to others he is always put into categories such as baby, child, teenager, adult, "old man," and the like. Here we have an interesting case of changing ascription. Second, an individual's name at first does not seem to represent a category. Yet at the same time that it serves as his more or less unique "identity peg," it also locates him in his family and serves as a handy indication of his sex. References to clearly one-sex names are also coded as a sex reference, since most respondents feel that they have already made clear their sex if they have given such a name.

B. Roles and Memberships. The other basic set of social identity elements is comprised of roles and categorical designations which are to an appreciable degree under the control of the individual. This element of choice is important because it implies that the person who has entered these categories or social types has voluntarily chosen to do so, and can thus be held accountable or responsible. Clarification is needed regarding the territoriality category. Being "an American" is usually an ascribed characteristic and thus belongs in the first set. But among younger respondents there is a more common form of response regarding territoriality. Many protocols contain a reference to current residence locale, conveying a distinctly temporary flavor (now living in the Back Bay area, etc.). Others give a mixed heritage and current "turf" answer (a Bostonian, etc.). The responses in this category are generally less "structural" and "fixed" than were those of the ascribed characteristics.

6. *Kinship Role:* a son, mother, sister, aunt, housewife, etc. (also coded as sex references), engaged, going steady, married, etc. (generally categorical).   17%

7. *Occupational Role:* specific occupation, employed, working part-time, hoping to become a doctor, etc. (mainly categorical).   5%

8. *Student Role:* a student, at South Boston High, getting bad grades, going to Harvard, taking 4 courses, trying to get into a good college, etc. (mainly categorical).   80%

9. *Political Affiliation:* a Democrat, an Independent, other clear party (*not* liberal, conservative, etc.) (almost always categorical).   1%

10. *Social Status:* from a poor family, an elite neighborhood, middle class, an aristocrat, of an old-line family etc. (somewhat more frequently attributive).   1%

11. *Territoriality, Citizenship:* now a Cambridge resident, living on Oak St., a Bostonian, from Alabama, an American, a German (current citizenship, not "heritage"), a foreign student, etc. (usually categorical).   16%

12. *Membership in Actual Interacting Group:* on the football team, in the science club, at a specific school, a friend, in a clique or fraternity, member of a certain family, etc. (almost always categorical).   17%

C. Abstract Identifications. A very interesting set of three dimensions contains those that (although often categorical rather than attributive) are usually too abstract or too private to serve as distinct social identity elements. The first of these portrays the individual as a unique, irreducible particle of Being, not definable by reference to anything outside himself. The second type places the person in some universal or very large and abstract category, without implication of interaction among members. The third form associates the person with some relatively comprehensive idea system, whether theoretical, philosophical, idealogical, religious, or more narrowly political.

13. *Existential, Individuating:* me, an individual, an existing being, myself, nothing, unique, undefinable, etc. (generally the denial of categories).   29%

14. *Membership in an Abstract Category:* a person, a human, a voter, a teenager (also an age reference), a speck in the cosmos, etc. (almost exclusively categorical by definition).   41%

15. *Ideological and Belief*

References: a liberal, a conservative, a Christian, very religious, a Marxist, against the war in Viet Nam, a pacifist, not prejudiced, etc. (somewhat more frequently categorical).   18%

D. Interests and Activities. It is often very difficult to distinguish among the various forms of personal connection to objects outside the self, and the cognitive, cathectic, and active modes are frequently blurred. Nevertheless, there are good grounds for distinguishing references to judgments of quality, concern over intellectual questions of meaning and substance, and actual participation in activities. In particular, the separation of intellectual and artistic references from the others was an attempt to verify hypotheses relating these kinds of self-conceptions to school performance and the qualitative nature of the career chosen by the respondent.

16. *Judgments, Tastes, Likes:* one who likes abstract art, hates rock'n'roll, a jazz fan, loves Bach, etc. (usually attributive).   27%

17. *Intellectual Concerns:* interested in literature, trying to understand modern theater, a reader, getting an education, a thinker, an intellectual, etc. (generally the verb-form of an attribute).   1%

18. *Artistic Activities:* a dancer, painter, poet, musician, singer, cello player, etc. (usually a category reference, the noun form of a verb).   4%

19. *Other Activities:* a football player, a hiker, a stamp collector, a moviegoer, one who dates a lot, a good swimmer, etc. (categorical on the whole).   27%

E. Material References. There have always been references to the body as a primary object of self-conscious awareness, but William James was among the first to point out the importance of other material objects as elements of identification. I have included both varieties, but have preserved separate coding.

20. *Possessions, Resources:* a car owner, one who has pretty clothes, hoping for a

secure future, one who never has enough money, etc. (usually categorical).   5%

21. *Physical Self, Body Image:* good-looking, pretty, strong, tall, 5'10", too thin, blonde, healthy, ugly, 112 lbs., etc. (preponderantly attributive).   36%

F. Four Systemic Senses of Self. Categories 1 to 21 of this coding scheme are designed to encapsulate the meaning of relatively specific self-representations. Yet the literature on self-conception contains a number of potentially very important theoretical dimensions that refer to levels of the person's functioning which are at middle levels of generality, being somewhat less global than such very comprehensive variables as self-esteem or the sense of autonomy.

Examination of relevant theory indicates that there is at least one conceptual framework that was designed to cope with this middle level of functioning of any kind of system: the general theory of action, as formulated principally by Talcott Parsons.[23] This framework asserts that every system (whether at the cultural, social, personality, or organismic level) must in some fashion solve four problems—adaptation, goal-attainment, integration, and pattern maintenance—if it is to function and survive.

The central argument of this section is that the action theory perspective can be extended to order in a meaningful manner some of the person's subjective experience at this middle level of self-conception. This extension is possible because each of the four functional problems has a corresponding "sense of self" available to consciousness—the individual's interpretation of his standing with regard to that system problem. To outline briefly, in the following analysis I suggest the correspondence

[23] A clear and concise formulation for the social system level appears as Chapter II, "Outline of the Social System," in Talcott Parsons, Edward Shils, Kaspar D. Naegele, and Jesse R. Pitts (eds.), *Theories of Society,* Vol. I, Glencoe, Ill.: Free Press, 1961; and, for the psychological level, see Talcott Parsons, "An Approach to Psychological Theory in Terms of the Theory of Action," in Sigmund Koch, *Psychology: The Study of a Science,* New York: McGraw-Hill, 1959, Vol. III, pp. 612–711; and his most recent work on this level, "The Position of Identity in the General Theory of Action," Chapter 1 of the present volume.

of the sense of *competence* to the problem of adaptation, the sense of *self-determination* to goal-attainment, the sense of *unity* to integration, and the sense of *moral worth* to pattern maintenance.[24]

The Sense of Moral Worth: Pattern Maintenance at the Person Level. There seems to be one essential feature of James' treatment of pride versus shame and mortification, Baldwin's formulation of the ethical socius, Cooley's discussion of self-feelings, Mead's idea of self-respect, and many recent treatments of guilt.[25] This is the person's sensed degree of adherence to a valued code of moral standards transcending him.

Now it is just this legitimation of standards for action by moral norms and values, institutionalized and shared in the person's social systems, which constitutes the core of the pattern maintenance problem at the person level.[26] As highly generalized cultural symbols, these universalistic value standards are used by others in morally evaluating the actions and attributes of the individual in particular social situations.

The point of articulation to self-conception is seen in the fact that the person generally evaluates his *own* attributes and actions in terms of these same moral standards and therefore has a continuingly available sense of greater or less moral worth. Thus I am suggesting that the individual's sense of *moral worth* may well be viewed as his subjective interpretation of how he stands in relation to the problem of pattern maintenance.

Once more it should be emphasized that this coding system records each of the respondent's utilizations of the particular dimensions, while the corresponding evaluation codes are used to retain these references as positive, neutral, or negative. The two may then be used together (or even with the tense and importance) to characterize the respondent's meanings more accurately.

25. *The Sense of Moral Worth:* self-respecting, a sinner, bad, good, honest, reliable, trustworthy, responsible, evil, a thief, etc. (preponderantly attributive).   22%

The Sense of Self-Determination: Goal-Attainment at the Person Level. Every system must provide at least minimal gratification of the basic requirements of its constituent elements if it is to remain in operation. Yet the interchange processes in specific situations make such heavy demands on the resources of the system that it is never able to provide continuous gratification for all elements. These disruptions of consummatory relations with objects in the environment plus the competing demands made by the internal elements concerning the plurality of goal objects add to the complexity of the goal-attainment problem. Fulfilling the goal-attainment function requires complex processes which establish priorities among the goal objects, allocate facilities, and distribute rewarding resources among the internal elements.

At the level of the person, there is a well established tendency to optimize gratification through selecting goals and instrumental steps for their attainment. Parsons, among others, has also pointed out the additional importance of volition toward achievement in these interchanges between the psychological and social systems. He focuses on the concepts of agency, decision making, and commitment to attainment of high-priority goals.[27]

One of the most sensitive psychological analysts concerned with consummatory gratification at this more complex symbolic level is Abraham Maslow. His delineation of the characteristics of the "self-actualizing" person contains many features that the action theory perspective can subsume under the problem of goal attainment at the level of the individual:

So far as motivational status is concerned, healthy people have sufficiently gratified their basic needs for safety, belongingness, love, respect and self-esteem so that they are motivated primarily by trends to self-actualization (defined as

---

[24] The conceptualization on which this section is based was largely worked out in the spring of 1965, in connection with guiding the honors thesis, "Mental Health, Occupational Choice, Self-Concept," of Linwood Laughy, then a senior in Harvard College. I am indebted to Mr. Laughy for many valuable suggestions.

[25] William James, *op. cit.,* esp. p. 106; James M. Baldwin, *Social and Ethical Interpretations in Mental Development,* New York: The Macmillan Co., 1897, esp. Chapter 1; Charles H. Cooley, *Human Nature and the Social Order,* New York: Charles Scribner's Sons, 1902, esp. Chapter 6; and, for example, Helen Merrell Lynd, *On Shame and the Search for Identity* (1958), New York: Science Editions, 1961.

[26] Parsons, "An Approach to Psychological Theory in Terms of the Theory of Action," *op. cit.,* esp. 657.

[27] Parsons, *ibid.,* esp. pp. 632, 652.

ongoing actualization of potentials, capacities and talents), as fulfillment of mission (or call, fate, destiny, or vocation). . . .[28]

Yet, as Maslow clearly indicates, only a tiny fraction of any society's members are able to make much sense of Nietzsche's directive, "Become what thou art!" A concept is needed which does *not* have a built-in requirement that the person possess a superior degree of certainty and insight regarding his "true self" and inherent destiny. Yet it *must* retain the essential features of *sensed ability* to select one's own goals and determine their relative priorities, initiate and vigorously pursue necessary lines of action, and act with freedom from control by others. This second systemic sense of self might well be called *self-determination*.

23. *The Sense of Self-Determination:* trying to get ahead, deciding things for myself, ambitious, hardworking, not my own boss, a self-starter, etc. (almost always attributive).   23%

The Sense of Unity: Integration at the Person Level. The problem of system integration concerns the internal harmony of the constituent elements. At the social system level this is the problem of solidarity or cohesion among units despite their differentiated functions. At the person level, we are concerned with the degree of conflict or inconsistency among personality dispositions, social roles, priorities or goal objects, loyalties, transcendent value standards, and the like.[29]

Erik Erikson's formulations of various aspects of identity are among the most subtle and insightful in the literature. Writing as a psychoanalyst with anthropological experience and an interest in the impact of historical contexts, he uses ego, self, and identity concepts as keys to social-psychological processes of development throughout the life-cycle.[30]

The concept Erikson terms "the sense of ego identity" (in ideally healthy individuals) is actually a kind of grand congruence of three personal meanings. This congruence is conceptualized as the achievement of a sense of *unity* among the person's own self-conceptions, plus the sense of *continuity* of the attributes over time, plus the sense of *mutuality* between that individual's conceptions of himself and those which significant others hold of him.[31]

Erikson's conceptualization certainly does capture the recurrent theme of interconnection between self and others. In its most complete form this interconnection seems to erase the borders of the self. Instances include the total, joyful intimacy with another, the "peak experiences" and "oceanic mergings" of Maslow's self-actualizing people,[32] and perhaps some forms of psychedelic experiences.

It is therefore not surprising that Erikson makes the developing sense of ego identity the basis of self-esteem, the most general evaluative dimension of self. Ideally, this will occur if the individual is able to overcome the adolescent identity crisis, with its common problem of identity diffusion. Resolution of the identity crisis often requires a "psychosocial moratorium" of relatively free and unthreatening role experimentation before the individual can learn to experience intimacy and achieve a meaningful connection between self and a small, unitary set of occupational, professional, ideological, membership, family, and interpersonal roles. Identity diffusion is epitomized by Biff's words in *Death of a Salesman,* "I just can't take hold, Mom, I can't take hold of some kind of a life."[33]

---

[28] Abraham H. Maslow, "Deficiency and Growth Motivation" (1955), reprinted in Maslow's *Toward a Psychology of Being,* Princeton, N.J.: D. Van Nostrand, 1962, p. 23. See also Chapter 12, "Self-Actualizing People: A Study of Psychological Health," in his *Motivation and Personality,* New York: Harper and Brothers, 1954.

[29] Parsons, "Psychological Theory . . . ," *op. cit.,* p. 636. An interesting attempt at partial reconciliation of the psychoanalytic and symbolic interactionist perspective by means of the mechanisms of defense may be found in Tamotsu Shibutani, *Society and Personality, op. cit.,* esp. p. 438 ff.

[30] See, for example, Erik H. Erikson, *Childhood and Society,* New York: W. W. Norton, 1950, and the papers "Growth and Crises of the Healthy Personality" (1950) and "The Problem of Ego Identity" (1956), in *Identity and the Life Cycle* [*Psychological Issues,* **1**(1), 1959]. A valuable addition to the literature in this field is a recent interpretive work largely devoted to consideration of Erikson's theory of identity: David J. deLevita, *The Concept of Identity,* Paris: Mouton and Co., 1965.

[31] Erikson, "Healthy Personality . . . ," *op. cit.,* p. 89.

[32] Abraham H. Maslow, "Cognition of Being in the Peak-Experiences" and "Peak Experiences as Identity Experiences," in his *Toward a Psychology of Being, op. cit.,* pp. 67–96 and 97–108.

[33] Clear analyses of identity diffusion and the

Parsons' treatment of the intricacies of system integration at the personality level is far more complex than the simple version that heads this section. Further, he is not explicitly dealing with the kinds of self-representations formulated by Erikson. Yet I believe that the first of the three elements drawn from Erikson can be proposed as the individual's interpretation of his standing with regard to the problem of personality level system integration: *the sense of internal unity.*

24. *The Sense of Unity:* in harmony, mixed up, ambivalent, a whole person, straigthened out now, etc. (predominantly attributive). 5%

The Sense of Competence: Adaptation at the Person Level. The last of the system problems concerns development of general coping facilities, resources, and capacities. Parsons conceptualizes adaptation in this way:

As distinguished from goal attainment, adaptation is the degree to which a system has developed a *generalized* capacity to meet the exigencies imposed by an unstable and varying situation, without reference to any one particular goal interest.[34]

This theme of generalized capacity has a direct equivalent in the recent work of Robert White.[35] White has proposed that both the

Freudian libidinal model and the neo-Freudian interpersonal model need to be supplemented by a *competence* model before the stages of human development can be successfully interpreted in a way that squares with the realities of normal functioning. As White presents the major concepts:

I therefore introduce competence to describe a person's existing capacity to interact effectively with his environment. . . . *Sense of competence* describes the subjective side of one's actual competence. . . . We can reserve the term *feeling of efficacy* for what is experienced in each individual transaction, using *sense of competence* for the accumulated and organized consequences in later stages of ego development.[36]

White[37] argues that the sense of competence is the basis for the more general dimension, self-esteem. This view contrasts with that of Erikson, who sees the basis of overall evaluation in what I have called congruence of personal meanings: harmonious, stable, and consensually supported self-conceptions.

Let us select Robert White's concept of the *sense of competence* as the individual's reflexive interpretation regarding the system problem of adaptation, since it refers to just the generalized capacity put forward by Parsons as adaptation's core meaning.

25. *Sense of Competence:* intelligent, talented, creative, skillful, low in ability, good at many things, always making mistakes, etc. (primarily attributive). 36%

Summary. This section has presented a proposal for conceptualizing four systemic senses of self, intermediate in degree of generality between the concrete descriptive contents of the first twenty-one categories and the most general dimensions of self-esteem or autonomy. Under one name or another, each of these four senses has had a long and substantial history in the literature of self theory. Further reports will describe efforts to move beyond Who Am I coding to treatment of the senses as problems in self-attitude scale construction. These studies

---

example of Biff's plea may be found in "Healthy Personality . . . ," pp. 91–94, and "Ego Identity . . . ," pp. 122–146. Another problem which would also cripple the individual's self-esteem but is not explicitly dealt with by Erikson points up the "integration bias" built into his concept of the sense of ego identity. What happens when the highly congruent match between individual and significant others concerns mutual agreement on *negatively* valued attributes (unattractiveness, low intelligence, limited competence, immorality or traitorous activity, etc.)? Here there would likely be high agreement, but low self-satisfaction.
34 Parsons, "Psychological Theory . . . ," p. 633 (emphasis in original).
35 Robert W. White, "Motivation Reconsidered: The Concept of Competence," *Psychological Review,* **66** (1959), pp. 297–333; "Competence and the Psychosexual Stages of Development," in M. Jones (ed.), *Nebraska Symposium on Motivation,* Lincoln, Neb.: University of Nebraska Press, 1960, pp. 97–141; and *Ego and Reality in Psychoanalytic Theory (Psychological Issues,* Monograph 11, 1963), especially the papers, "A Way of Conceiving of Independent Ego Energies: Efficacy and Competence," pp. 24–43, and "Self-esteem, Sense of Competence, and Ego Strength," pp. 125–150.

---

36 White, "Efficacy and Competence," *op. cit.,* p. 39 (emphases in original).
37 White, "Self-esteem, Sense of Competence, and Ego Strength," *op. cit.,* esp. pp. 129–136; and "Competence and the Psychosexual Stages of Development," *op. cit.,* pp. 126–127.

System Function	Corresponding Personal Sense of Self
Adaptation	The sense of competence
Goal-attainment	The sense of self-determination
Integration	The sense of unity
Pattern-maintenance	The sense of moral worth

use other aspects of general action theory to provide direct indexing of the four senses as continuous variables.

For the present, this portion of the coding scheme can be summarized as the formulation of a subjective sense of self to match each of the four functions held in action theory to be essential features of every system (listed above).

G. Personal Characteristics. As we move from the categories and roles of social identity through the interests, activities, material references and the senses of self, there is a large and interesting set of more general self-descriptions which refer to the individual's typical manner of *acting* and his typical style of *psychic functioning*.

26. *Interpersonal Style (how I typically act):* friendly, fair, nice, shy, introverted, hard to get along with, affable, quiet, demanding, good with children, affectionate, cool, etc. (almost exclusively attributes).   59%

27. *Psychic Style, Personality (how I typically think and feel):* happy, sad, moody, a daydreamer, in love, depressed, confident, "crazy," lonely, curious, calm, searching for love, mature, objective, optimistic, etc. (predominantly adjectival attributes).   52%

H. External Meanings. Two remaining categories of relatively infrequent Who Am I elements refer not to the individual himself in any typical or continuing manner, but rather to the impression he feels that he makes on others, or to the immediate testing situation itself. References to the impressions or attitudes of others toward the respondent are actually representations of *them*, not him. This is the imputed, generalized *Social Me* of James and Cooley.

28. *Judgments Imputed to Others:* popular, respected, well-liked, well thought of, loved, etc. (preponderantly attributive).   18%

We use the term "situational reference" to denote the other major escape from self-description in terms of enduring, typical categories and attributes: fleeting reference to the person's immediate situation and activities at the moment of filling out the questionnaire.

29. *Situational References:* tired, hungry, bored, filling out this questionnaire, going on a date tonight, late for dinner, finished, etc. (usually attributive).   9%

These "situational" elements should not be confused with the valuable new concept of *situational self-image* introduced by Ralph Turner to capture the individual's sense of how well or how badly he is portraying his attributes over the moment-to-moment course of a particular interaction episode.[38] Turner's development of this sensed outcome of the processes of presentation of self that Goffman had analyzed from the perspective of the omniscient observer[39] was a precursor of the present attempt to provide the senses of self as the phenomenal or subjective side of the objective system problems.

The last category includes all those self-representations that are not codable under one or more of the previous rubrics. Across the various pilot groups studied, only about 4% of the respondents give even one uncodable reference. None of the Harvard-Radcliffe students did so, whereas 6% of the City College students mentioned at least one. Even among this City College group, only 38 out of 4240 responses were uncodable by this system, representing an insignificant 0.9%.

30. *Uncodable Responses:* superman, President of the U.S., a flower, the sea, a shell on the beach, etc. (usually categorical, if decipherable at all).   4%

---

[38] Ralph H. Turner, "The Self-Conception in Social Interaction," Chapter 9 of the present volume.

[39] Erving Goffman, *Presentation of Self in Everyday Life,* Garden City, N. Y.: Doubleday Anchor Books, 1959; and *Behavior in Public Places,* New York: Free Press, 1963.

Sometimes this is simply a matter of illegible handwriting, or of misunderstanding the questionnaire instructions. Another possibility is that these references are idiosyncratic flights of fancy indicating a very active imagination, fantasy careers, defenses against "real" answers, or even clues to latent mental difficulties.

Examples of the more imaginative and metaphoric usages from a 22-year-old girl at Los Angeles City College who had previously studied in three other colleges: I am . . . "a mean witch, a flower, a troll, an invisible person, a cloud," and so on.

There is no opportunity at present to discuss the technical aspects of the proposed system for coding each self-representation according to its category, tense, evaluation, and importance rank. The inter-rater reliability, stability over time, and sensitivity to change are being given serious attention and seem to be acceptable for most purposes. More difficult are problems of relations between Who Am I configurations and the more traditional measures of differentiation and evaluation derived from projective and other techniques. These questions will be dealt with in subsequent reports on the features of respondents' social backgrounds or major life ambitions that have been found to be related substantially to patterns of self-representation, and on the ways in which the relevance of differing self-conceptions is affected by various forms of interaction.

ILLUSTRATIVE OUTCOMES

The distributions and interrelations of some of the coding scheme's aspects are illustrated in the following sections by reference to the Harvard-Radcliffe and Los Angeles City College data. These findings are in no way intended as normative standards or precise estimates of population parameters, since the protocols were collected under varying conditions from available pilot groups which are not really representative samples of rigorously specifiable populations. The outcomes obtained from these preliminary investigations do provide some general indication of the system's plausibility, since they can be assessed in relation to what is known about the students' situations.

Configurations of Category Usage

Figure 1 shows for each category the percentage of respondents in the City College and Harvard-Radcliffe study groups who described themselves *at least once* in terms of that category's meanings. Since the category usage profile of the 157 high school students (presented

in the course of describing the coding scheme) is very similar to that of the City College group, it is possible to suggest that the configuration described by the solid line in Figure 1 gives a rough approximation to what a representative sample of high school and college respondents would yield.

Most frequently mentioned by the City College students (72%) is the large cluster of characteristics describing interpersonal style (shy, friendly, etc.). Next are the solid "social locators," sex (70%) and age (69%). These are very large proportions considering that only a very few words or phrases will qualify as age or sex references, unlike the thousands of terms for interpersonal styles. The near equality of proportions mentioning either age or sex is partially an artifact of the coding convention that terms such as "boy" are scored as reference to both sex and age.

Next in proportion of City College students mentioning at least once (66%) is psychic style, or personality characteristics. Since there are an unlimited number of these attributes from which to choose, an interesting question reserved for a future paper is the nature of the 34% who do *not* use at least one personality description. General defensiveness is one plausible interpretation for avoidance of this and other attributive references.

Three content categories fall into a middle usage position: the student role (59%); physical or body image (55%); and the sense of self-determination (55%). Two of the other senses of self—moral worth (38%) and competence (30%)—are the last of the more frequently mentioned categories.

Noticeably *in*frequent in the City College Who Am I protocols are references to political affiliation (4%), social status (3%), and intellectual concerns (2%). Older respondents would probably use these dimensions of self-representation more frequently. As mentioned previously, uncodable references were given by only 6% of the students and accounted for less than 1% of the total number of self-representations.

Comparison of the Los Angeles City College and Harvard-Radcliffe groups is helpful in making a rough assessment of the validity of the scheme. Since these groups "feel" very different to one who has known both, the system should be able to differentiate them on relevant dimensions. Although both groups were asked for 15 responses, the Harvard-Radcliffe students frequently gave more complex answers and so were coded as providing a slightly higher

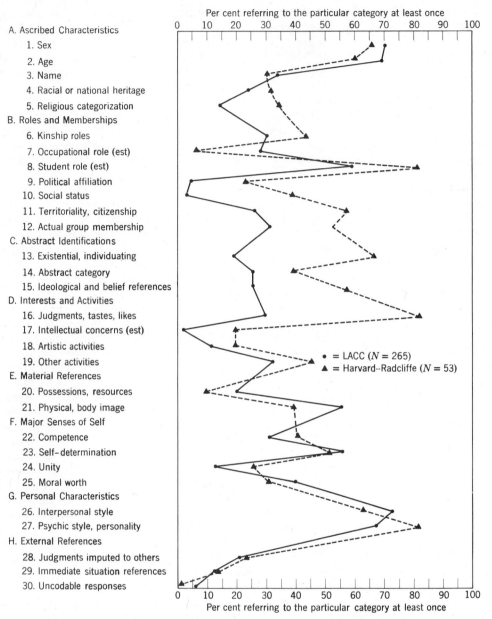

A. Ascribed Characteristics
   1. Sex
   2. Age
   3. Name
   4. Racial or national heritage
   5. Religious categorization
B. Roles and Memberships
   6. Kinship roles
   7. Occupational role (est)
   8. Student role (est)
   9. Political affiliation
   10. Social status
   11. Territoriality, citizenship
   12. Actual group membership
C. Abstract Identifications
   13. Existential, individuating
   14. Abstract category
   15. Ideological and belief references
D. Interests and Activities
   16. Judgments, tastes, likes
   17. Intellectual concerns (est)
   18. Artistic activities
   19. Other activities
E. Material References
   20. Possessions, resources
   21. Physical, body image
F. Major Senses of Self
   22. Competence
   23. Self–determination
   24. Unity
   25. Moral worth
G. Personal Characteristics
   26. Interpersonal style
   27. Psychic style, personality
H. External References
   28. Judgments imputed to others
   29. Immediate situation references
   30. Uncodable responses

• = LACC ($N = 265$)
▲ = Harvard–Radcliffe ($N = 53$)

Per cent referring to the particular category at least once

Figure 1. Configuration of content categories; self-conceptions in the "Who Am I?" responses. (est) = estimated from sample of protocols after later change in coding procedures. Solid circle = Los Angeles City College ($N = 265$). Solid triangle = Harvard-Radcliffe ($N = 53$).

number of separate self-representations (a mean of 18.7 compared to 16.0 for Los Angeles City College). Thus on probability grounds alone we would expect the Los Angeles City College students to have a somewhat lower proportion giving at least one reference to any particular category.

The data of Figure 1, however, indicate that the Los Angeles City College students are somewhat *more* likely to give self-representa-

tions in terms of sex, age, occupational role, possessions, body characteristics, the senses of self-determination and moral worth, and interpersonal style. These differences are each quite small, but taken together they support the interpretation suggested by the obvious differences in the two situations. The individual backgrounds and capabilities of the Los Angeles City College students, their college context, and the general Los Angeles milieu are probably at work to produce a somewhat greater reliance on the external, concrete dimensions and on the mobility orientation regarding occupations seen as close at hand.

Further confirmation may be found in the configuration of categories in which the Harvard-Radcliffe students have the higher proportion of mentioners. These were religious categorization, the kinship and student roles, political affiliation, social status, territorial locale or background, actual interaction groups, existential individuating references, the abstract category references, ideologies and beliefs, intellectual concerns, psychic style, and (most strongly) the dimension of judgments and tastes. This pattern gives a fairly clear picture of a more individuated and introspective group of students, somewhat conscious of family, but defining themselves primarily by reference to their own ways of thinking and the values encouraged by the university.

Other studies using this category system for Who Am I coding are now in progress, and are directed to somewhat more representative samples of students, adults, and very old persons. Much more solid comparative configurations will be reported elsewhere, as will analyses of the categories' typical patterns of tense, evaluation, and importance. But for the present it seems that the coding system does provide meaningful dimensions of self-representation.

Configurations of the Categories' Order and Importance

Kuhn and McPartland in the paper previously cited proposed two generalizations regarding the order of self-representations in the Who Am I protocols. The first asserts that respondents will tend to exhaust all their "consensual" references, then switch to describing themselves in terms of "subconsensual" references. This distinction concerns the presence or absence of relatively clear boundaries. Thus "a male" and "a college student" are consensual representations, having a publicly ascertainable character. "Too thin" or "trying to do better in school" are subconsensual, since they are judgmental or in some sense private, requiring extensive interpretation by the respondent himself. Kuhn and McPartland conceived of the number of consensual references given by a respondent as his "locus score," which they assert indicates in a rough way the degree of social anchorage that individual experiences.

The idea of social anchorage seems to be a

valid one, but it may better be indicated by the use of categorical versus attributive responses. The validity of this procedure is supported by the fact that the categorical or noun-like representations typically associate the respondent *with others,* as in references to his sex, ethnic group, role relations, interaction group memberships, and allegiances. The attributes generally serve to distinguish the respondent *from* others or at least describe him individualistically.

Consideration of the differing functions of categories and attributes in self-description suggests that a very old principal of definition may be at work here. Consider Aristotle's approach to classification, which stresses primacy of substantive categories over the qualities that differentiate a particular instance from others in the same genus: "Substance is primary in definition, in knowledge, and in time."[40]

The first hypothesis regarding order configuration would thus assert that use of categorical references will tend to precede use of attributive references.

The responses of the 53 Harvard and Radcliffe students are arrayed in Figure 2 so as to provide some test of this hypothesis. The vertical dimension represents the ordering of references according to the mean response position of all those using the particular dimension at all. The horizontal dimension is the mean importance rank assigned to the particular type of reference by those using it.[41] The types of reference that are preponderantly categorical are indicated by a *C* in the column at the left. Predominantly attributive types of reference are indicated by an *A.*

The hypothesis of "categories first, then attributes" is supported by the data. Of the fifteen types having the earliest mean response positions, only two (competence and physical characteristics) are generally attributive. Two other types (name and age) appear quite early

---

[40] *Metaphysics,* Ross translation, 1028a30.
[41] The order positions of the various categories are obtained by computing for each individual the mean response position (as coded) for each content category he used at all. The mean of these average category positions may then be used to rank order the categories according to their position among the meaning elements for this group of respondents. This procedure yields conservative results since the *mean* position of coded elements is used rather than the first mention. It should be noted that the numbers of cases on which these means are computed (shown at the right-hand side of the figure) vary a good deal, and are often quite small.

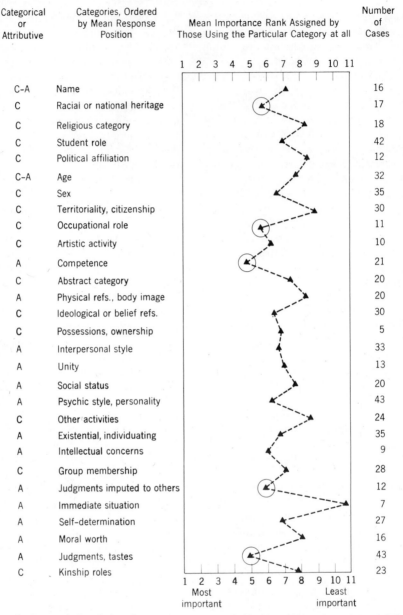

Categorical or Attributive	Categories, Ordered by Mean Response Position	Mean Importance Rank Assigned by Those Using the Particular Category at all	Number of Cases
C-A	Name		16
C	Racial or national heritage		17
C	Religious category		18
C	Student role		42
C	Political affiliation		12
C-A	Age		32
C	Sex		35
C	Territoriality, citizenship		30
C	Occupational role		11
C	Artistic activity		10
A	Competence		21
C	Abstract category		20
A	Physical refs., body image		20
C	Ideological or belief refs.		30
C	Possessions, ownership		5
A	Interpersonal style		33
A	Unity		13
A	Social status		20
A	Psychic style, personality		43
C	Other activities		24
A	Existential, individuating		35
A	Intellectual concerns		9
C	Group membership		28
A	Judgments imputed to others		12
A	Immediate situation		7
A	Self-determination		27
A	Moral worth		16
A	Judgments, tastes		43
C	Kinship roles		23

Figure 2. Categories' relative importance, assessed by the Harvard and Radcliffe students (N = 53).

if used at all, but these are attributive nearly as often as they are categorical. The later fifteen response types contain only three categorical dimensions. "Other activities" (defined as nonintellectual and nonartistic), group memberships, and kinship roles are the dimensions which are out of position, and none of these receive high average importance rankings. Among these students, activities are not likely to be strong identity bases. Groups are not what they once were, and the son or daughter role is being shucked off before the husband,

wife, father, or mother roles have been acquired.

Second, Kuhn and McPartland assert that the earlier a reference comes in the Who Am I protocol, the greater its importance. This has previously been discussed in general terms, where it was pointed out that although it did fit the data from the high school students, Harvard-Radcliffe students on the average showed a kind of S-curve of importance: medium→high→low→high. Since their configuration of category use is also quite different from that of the high school students, there is the immediate suggestion of a more complex interaction between category content and importance in shaping the order of presentation. Now that the categories of the present system have been introduced, the relation of order to both content and importance ranking can be illustrated.

A more general interpretation of the interrelations among content dimensions, order positions, and importance rankings is suggested from data of previous exploratory studies, and is based on two principals drawn from the perspective of symbolic interactionism. First, self-conceptions are assumed to be intimately related to the courses of conduct in which persons engage. Second, if we tentatively adopt the assumption that persons generally attempt to interpret meaning within their symbolic environments, we can formulate the following hypothesis:

A person giving free-response self-representations will generally assign relatively high importance to aspects of his total symbolic environment which render his past, present, and future courses of conduct meaningful and understandable, both to himself and to significant others.

Consider once again the data presented in Figure 2, representing the mean importance rank assigned to a given response dimension by all respondents who used that dimension at all. There are many complexities in interpreting data of this kind because of the widely fluctuating number of persons utilizing each dimension, and because of the tenuous nature of our understanding of the meaning of order and importance ranking operations. Yet I believe that these data provide some support for the hypothesis of positive association between a dimension's relevance for interpreting major courses of conduct and the importance rank assigned to that dimension.

Five of the coding dimensions received unusually high mean importance ranks, and all five are quite directly connected to interpretation of the person's projects of action. In order of descending importance rank they are: judgments, competence, judgments imputed to others, occupational role, and racial or national heritage. Consideration of these dimensions in relation to their average order position within the protocols and their classification as being typically categorical or attributive suggests a more comprehensive perspective on the question of interpretability.

Perhaps interpretability may be attempted by first specifying the relevant features of one's external situation and then providing the relevant internal information.

External interpretability may be constructed out of at least three types of material. First are references to the actual project of action underway or the state of affairs to be brought about (in this case, references to current or prospective occupational role such as "going to become a lawyer"; less frequently by reference to an artistic activity such as "a pianist"). Second are references to the "logical" instrumental steps leading toward the accomplishment of the action program (such as student role mentions, or the somewhat less frequent ideological references to being "a liberal," etc.). The third element in external interpretability seems to be any particularly relevant condition that specifies starting location or special facilitations or disadvantages in pursuing the project (e.g., "a Negro," "a female," "a member of a wealthy family," etc.). These three sets of external interpreters are drawn from the ascriptive and achieved categories of social identity, and their typically early appearance may help to explain the prevalence of noun-like forms in the first half of the Who Am I protocols. Together they allow the respondent to indicate who he is and what he is trying to do.

Internal interpretability is apparently constructed from references to subjective or "private" dimensions which also seem to fall into three sets. First come the person's assessments of his ability (in this case his perceived degree of competence, but also his psychic and interpersonal styles of action, and probably his body image in other populations). Second is a set of references to his values, judgments, and concerns (here judgments are assigned the highest importance, followed by intellectual concerns). Finally, we have the person's assessment of the outcomes of his previous (and eventually of his current) projects of action in terms of the judgments about him he imputes to significant others ("respected," "popular," etc.). These dimensions of internal interpretability are approached mainly through adjectival attributes, and this may help to account for preponderance of attributive forms in the last half of the typical protocol.

Much more research on relations among content, linguistic form, order position, and importance ranking must be carried out on diverse populations before there could be anything approaching a solid conclusion concerning the general formulation set out above. Until that time, the discussion will have to close with a restatement of the relation's plausibility: order and importance assessment among Who Am I self-representations may be explained in part by the principle of interpretability. According to this principle, projects of action are rendered interpretable by first using the noun-like categories of social identity to specify the external context of action, then using the adjectival personal attributes to specify internal competence, motivations, and assessments of the outcomes.

CONCLUSION

Self as a process rather than a thing; simultaneity of self-as-experiencer and self-as-experienced; self-conceptions as an accruing structure of available reflexive meanings; social identity as the combination of categorical or noun-like conceptions versus personal characteristics as the combination of adjectival attributes; the tenses of self; a content coding system (including competence, self-direction, unity, and moral worth as middle-level senses of self corresponding to the system problems posited in the general theory of action); and exploratory empirical materials illustrating some of the interrelations among content, order position, linguistic form, and importance ranking of free response self-representations—these and other themes have been introduced in this chapter but dealt with in only the most cavalier fashion.

Possibilities for both theoretical and methodological extension exist in many directions. Already in progress are efforts to standardize a fixed-dimension self-rating procedure designed to tap the four senses of self in a more systematic manner. A set of semantic differential scales has been worked out to provide an assessment of change in interpersonal and psychic styles during such processes as socialization, therapy, or severe role alterations.

On the theoretical side, the action theory framework with its stress on system resources and interchange processes has led to the design of research in which the four senses of self are being examined as possible determinants of two more global senses: self-esteem and the sense of personal autonomy.

It is perhaps an appropriate closing note to a paper which has argued for the importance of continued investigation of aspects of self-process to reach back some 300 years for a very explicit formulation of the resource core of autonomy:

> A *freeman* is he that in those things which by his strength and wit he is able to do, is not hindered to do what he has a will to do.
>
> Thomas Hobbes, *Leviathan* (1651)[42]

It is interesting to note the parallels to a theory of system resources and their subjective interpretation: strength and wit are forms of competence; refusing to be hindered is basic to the integrity aspect of moral worth; and having the will for decisive action is the crux of active self-determination.

---

[42] Thomas Hobbes, *Leviathan,* (1651), Part II, Ch. 21, par. 2. Personal autonomy is the main concept being used in my current study of self-conception changes over the course of retirement.

Chapter 12 The Social Self: On the Varieties of Self-Feeling

CHARLES HORTON COOLEY

In Mr. Roget's *Thesaurus* may be found about six pages devoted to words denoting "Extrinsic personal affections, or personal affections derived from the opinions or feelings of others," an expression which seems to mean nearly the same as is here meant by social self-feeling of the reflected or looking-glass sort. Although the compiler fishes with a wide net and brings in much that seems hardly to belong here, the number of words in common use indicating different varieties of this sort of feeling is surprising and suggestive. One cannot but think, What insight and what happy boldness of invention went to the devising of all these terms! What a psychologist is language, that thus labels and treasures up so many subtle aspects of the human mind!

We may profitably distinguish, as others have done, two general attitudes—the aggressive or self-assertive and the shrinking or humble. The first indicates that one thinks favorably of himself and tries to impose that favorable thought on others; the second, that he accepts and yields to a depreciating reflection of himself, and feels accordingly diminished and abased. Pride would, of course, be an example of the first way of feeling and acting, humility of the second.

But there are many phases of the aggressive self, and these, again, might be classified something as follows: first, in response to imagined approval we have pride, vanity, or self-respect; second, in response to imagined censure we have various sorts of resentment; and the humble self might be treated in a similar manner.

Pride and vanity are names which are commonly applied only to forms of self-approval that strike us as disagreeable or egotistical; but

they may be used in a somewhat larger sense to indicate simply a more or less stable attitude of the social self toward the world in which it is reflected; the distinction being of the same sort as that between unstable and rigid egotism already suggested.

These differences in stability, which are of great importance in the study of social personality, are perhaps connected with the contrast between the more receptive and the more constructive types of mind. Although in the best minds reception and construction are harmoniously united, and although it may be shown that they are in a measure mutually dependent, so that neither can be perfect without the other, yet as a rule they are not symmetrically developed, and this lack of symmetry corresponds to divergences of personal character. Minds of one sort are, so to speak, endogenous or ingrowing in their natural bent, while those of another are exogenous or outgrowing; that is to say, those of the former kind have a relatively strong turn for working up old material, as compared with that for taking in new; cogitation is more pleasant to them than observation; they prefer the sweeping and garnishing of their house to the confusion of entertaining visitors; while of the other sort the opposite of this may be said. Now, the tendency of the endogenous or inward activities is to secure unity and stability of thought and character at the possible expense of openness and adaptability; because the energy goes chiefly into systematization, and in attaining this the mind is pretty sure to limit its new impressions to those that do not disturb too much that unity and system it loves so well. These traits are, of course, manifested in the person's relation to others. The friends he has "and their acceptance tried" he grapples to his soul with hooks of steel, but is likely to be unsympathetic and hard toward influences of a novel character. On the other hand, the exogenous or outgrowing mind, more active near the periphery than

SOURCE. Charles Horton Cooley, *Human Nature and the Social Order,* New York: Charles Scribner's Sons, 1902, pp. 198-222. Copyright 1902. Reprinted by permission of Charles Scribner's Sons, Inc.

toward the centre, is open to all sorts of impressions, eagerly taking in new material, which is likely never to get much arrangement; caring less for the order of the house than that it should be full of guests, quickly responsive to personal influences, but lacking that depth and tenacity of sympathy that the other sort of mind shows with people congenial with itself.

Pride, then, is the form social self-approval takes in the more rigid or self-sufficient sort of minds; the person who feels it is assured that he stands well with others whose opinion he cares for, and does not imagine any humiliating image of himself, but carries his mental and social stability to such a degree that it is likely to narrow his soul by warding off the enlivening pricks of doubt and shame. By no means independent of the world, it is, after all, distinctly a social sentiment, and gets its standards ultimately from social custom and opinion. But the proud man is not *immediately* dependent upon what others think; he has worked over his reflected self in his mind until it is a steadfast portion of his thought, an idea and conviction apart, in some measure, from its external origin. Hence this sentiment requires time for its development and flourishes in mature age rather than in the open and growing period of youth. A man who is proud of his rank, his social position, his professional eminence, his benevolence, or his integrity, is in the habit of contemplating daily an agreeable and little changing image of himself as he believes he appears in the eyes of the world. This image is probably distorted, since pride deceives by a narrowing of the imagination, but it is stable, and because it is so, because he feels sure of it, he is not disturbed by any passing breath of blame. If he is aware of such a thing at all he dismisses it as a vagary of no importance, feeling the best judgment of the world to be securely in his favor. If he should ever lose this conviction, if some catastrophe should shatter the image he would be a broken man, and, if far gone in years, would perhaps not raise his head again.

In a sense pride is strength; that is, it implies a stable and consistent character which can be counted on; it will do its work without watching, and be honorable in its dealings, according to its cherished standards; it has always a vigorous, though narrow, conscience. On the other hand, it stunts a man's growth by closing his mind to progressive influences, and so in the long run may be a source of weakness. Burke said, I believe, that no man ever had a point

of pride that was not injurious to him; and perhaps this was what he meant. Pride also causes, as a rule, a deeper animosity on the part of others than vanity; it may be hated but hardly despised; yet many would rather live with it than with vanity, because, after all, one knows where to find it, and so can adapt himself to it. The other is so whimsical that it is impossible to foresee what turn it will take next.

Language seldom distinguishes clearly between a way of feeling and its visible expression; and so the word vanity, which means primarily emptiness, indicates either a weak or hollow appearance of worth put on in the endeavor to impress others, or the state of feeling that goes with it. It is the form social self-approval naturally takes in a somewhat unstable mind, not sure of its image. The vain man, in his more confident moments, sees a delightful reflection of himself, but knowing that it is transient, he is afraid it will change. He has not fixed it, as the proud man has, by incorporation with a stable habit of thought, but, being immediatey dependent for it upon others, is at their mercy and very vulnerable, living in the frailest of glass houses which may be shattered at any moment; and, in fact, this catastrophe happens so often that he gets somewhat used to it and soon recovers from it. But the image which the proud person contemplates is fairly consistent, and, though distorted, has a solid basis in his character, so that he will not accept praise for qualities he does not believe himself to possess; vanity has no stable idea of itself and will swallow any shining bait. The person will gloat now on one pleasing reflection of himself, now on another, trying to mimic each in its turn, and becŏming, so far as he can, what any flatterer says he is, or what any approving person seems to think he is. It is characteristic of him to be so taken up with his own image in the other's mind that he is hypnotized by it, as it were, and sees it magnified, distorted, and out of its true relation to the other contents of that mind. He does not see, as so often happens, that he is being managed and made a fool of; he "gives himself away"—fatuity being of the essence of vanity. On the other hand, and for the same reason, a vain person is frequently tortured by groundless imaginings that some one has misunderstood him, slighted him, insulted him, or otherwise mistreated his social effigy.

* * *

It is the obnoxious, or in some way conspicuous, manifestations of self-feeling that are likely to receive special names. Accordingly, there are many words and phrases for different aspects of pride and vanity, while a moderate and balanced self-respect does not attract nomenclature. One who has this is more open and flexible in feeling and behavior than one who is proud; the image is not stereotyped, he is subject to humility; while at the same time he does not show the fluttering anxiety about his appearance that goes with vanity, but has stable ways of thinking about the image, as about other matters, and cannot be upset by passing phases of praise or blame. In fact, the healthy life of the self requires the same co-operation of continuity with change that marks normal development everywhere; there must be variability, openness, freedom, on a basis of organization: too rigid organization meaning fixity and death, and the lack of it weakness or anarchy. The self-respecting man values others' judgments and occupies his mind with them a great deal, but he keeps his head, he discriminates and selects, considers all suggestions with a view to his character, and will not submit to influences not in the line of his development. Because he conceives his self as a stable and continuing whole he always feels the need to *be,* and cannot be guilty of that separation between being and seeming that constitutes affectation.

* * *

With some, then, the self-image is an imitative sketch in the supposed style of the last person they have talked to; with others, it is a rigid, traditional thing, a lifeless repetition that has lost all relation to the forces that originally moulded it, like the Byzantine madonnas before the time of Cimabue; with others again it is a true work of art in which individual tendencies and the influence of masters mingle in a harmonious whole; but all of us have it, unless we are so deficient in imagination as to be less than human. When we speak of a person as independent of opinion, or self-sufficient, we can only mean that, being of a constructive and stable character, he does not have to recur ever day to the visible presence of his approvers, but can supply their places by imagination, can hold on to some influences and reject others, choose his leaders, individualize his conformity; and so work out a characteristic and fairly consistent career. The self must be built up by the aid of social suggestions, just as all higher thought is.

Honor is a finer kind of self-respect. It is used to mean either something one feels regard-

ing himself, or something that other people think and feel regarding him, and so illustrates by the accepted use of language the fact that the private and social aspects of self are inseparable. One's honor, as he feels it, and his honor in the sense of honorable repute, as he conceives it to exist in the minds of others whose opinion he cares for, are two aspects of the same thing. No one can permanently maintain a standard of honor in his own mind if he does not conceive of some other mind or minds as sharing and corroborating this standard. If his immediate environment is degrading he may have resort to books or memory in order that his imagination may construct a better environment of nobler people to sustain his standard; but if he cannot do this it is sure to fall. Sentiments of higher good or right, like other sentiments, find source and renewal in intercourse. On the other hand, we cannot separate the idea of honor from that of a sincere and stable private character. We cannot form a habit of thought about what is admirable, though it be derived from others, without creating a mental standard.

* * *

In point of fact, a man's honor, as he conceives it, is his self in its most immediate and potent reality, swaying his conduct without waiting upon any inquiry into its physiological antecedents. The preference of honor to life is not at all a romantic exception in human behavior, but something quite characteristic of man on a really human level.

* * *

In modern life we see the same subordination of sensation to sentiment among soldiers and in a hundred other careers involving bodily peril—not as a heroic exception but as the ordinary practice of plain men. We see it also in the general readiness to undergo all sorts of sensual pains and privations rather than cease to be respectable in the eyes of other people. It is well known, for instance, that among the poor thousands endure cold and partial starvation rather than lose their self-respect by begging. In short, it does not seem too favorable a view of mankind to say that under normal conditions their minds are ruled by the sentiment of Norfolk:

Mine honor is my life: both grow in one;
Take honor from me and my life is done.

If we once grasp the fact that the self is primarily a social, ideal, or imaginative fact, and not a sensual fact, all this appears quite natural and not in need of special explanation.

In relation to the highest phases of individuality self-respect becomes self-reverence, in the sense of Tennyson, when he says:

> Self-reverence, self-knowledge, self-control,
> These three alone lead life to sovereign power.

or of Goethe when, in the first chapter of the second book of Wilhelm Meister's Wanderjahre, he names self-reverence—*Ehrfurcht vor sich selbst*—as the highest of the four reverences taught to youth in his ideal system of education. Emerson uses self-reliance in a similar sense, in that memorable essay the note of which is "Trust thyself, every heart vibrates to that iron string," and throughout his works.

Self-reverence, as I understand the matter, means reverence for a higher or ideal self; a real "I," because it is based on what the individual actually is, as only he himself can know and appropriate it, but a better "I" of aspiration rather than attainment; it is simply the best he can make out of life. Reverence for it implies, as Emerson urges, resistance to friends and counsellors and to any influence that the mind honestly rejects as inconsistent with itself; a man must feel that the final arbiter is within him and not outside of him in some master, living or dead, as conventional religion, for instance, necessarily teaches. Nevertheless this highest self is a social self, in that it is a product of constructive imagination working with the materials which socal experience supplies. Our ideals of personal character are built up out of thoughts and sentiments developed by intercourse, and very largely by imagining how our selves would appear in the minds of persons we look up to. These are not necessarily living persons; any one that is at all real, that is imaginable, to us, becomes a possible occasion of social self-feeling; and idealizing and aspiring persons live largely in the imagined presence of masters and heroes to whom they refer their own life for comment and improvement. This is particularly true of youth, when ideals are forming; later the personal element in these ideals, having performed its function of suggesting and vivifying them, is likely to fade out of consciousness and leave only habits and principles whose social origin is forgotten.

Resentment, the attitude which an aggressive self takes in response to imagined depreciation, may be regarded as self-feeling with a coloring of anger; indeed, the relation between self-feeling and particular emotions like anger and fear is so close that the latter might be looked upon as simply specialized kinds of the former.

* * *

If a person conceives his image as depreciated in the mind of another; and if, instead of maintaining an aggressive attitude and resenting that depreciation, he yields to it and accepts the image and the judgment upon it; then he feels and shows something in the way of humility. Here again we have a great variety of nomenclature, indicating different shades of humble feeling and behavior, such as shame, confusion, abasement, humiliation, mortification, meekness, bashfulness, diffidence, shyness, being out of countenance, abashed or crestfallen, contrition, compunction, remorse, and so on.

Humility, like self-approval, has forms that consist with a high type of character and are felt to be praiseworthy, and others that are felt to be base. There is a sort that goes with vanity and indicates instability, and excessive and indiscriminate yielding to another's view of one's self. We wish a man to be humble only before what, from his own characteristic point of view, is truly superior. His humility should imply self-respect; it should be that attitude of deference which a stable but growing character takes in the presence of whatever embodies its ideals.

* * *

Humility of this sort goes with self-reverence, because a sense of the higher or ideal self plunges the present and commonplace self into humility. The man aims at "so high an ideal that he always feels his unworthiness in his own sight and that of others, though aware of his own desert by the ordinary standards of his community, country, or generation." But a humility that is self-abandonment, a cringing before opinion alien to one's self, is felt to be mere cowardice and servility.

Books of the inner life praise and enjoin lowliness, contrition, repentance, self-abnegation; but it is apparent to all thoughtful readers that the sort of humility inculcated is quite consistent with the self-reverence of Goethe or the self-reliance of Emerson—comes, indeed, to much the same thing.

* * *

No healthy mind can cast out self-assertion and the idea of personal freedom, however the form of expression may seem to deny these things . . . . Where there is no self-feeling, no ambition of any sort, there is no efficacy or significance. To lose the sense of a separate, productive, resisting self, would be to melt and merge and cease to be.

Healthy, balanced minds, of only medium sensibility, in a congenial environment and occupied with wholesome activity, keep the middle road of self-respect and reasonable ambition. They may require no special effort, no conscious struggle with recalcitrant egotism, to avoid heart-burning jealousy, arrogance, anxious running after approval, and other maladies of the social self. With enough self-feeling to stimulate and not enough to torment him, with a social circle appreciative but not flattering, with good health and moderate success, a man may go through life with very little use for the moral and religious weapons that have been wrought for the repression of a contumacious self. There are many, particularly in an active, hopeful, and materially prosperous time like this, who have little experience of inner conflict and no interest in the literature and doctrine that relate to it.

But nearly all persons of the finer, more sensitive sort find the social self at times a source of passion and pain. In so far as a man amounts to anything, stands for anything, is truly an individual, he has an ego about which his passions cluster, and to aggrandize which must be a principal aim with him. But the very fact that the self is the object of our schemes and endeavors makes it a centre of mental disturbance: its suggestions are of effort, responsibility, doubt, hope, and fear. Just as a man cannot enjoy the grass and trees in his own grounds with quite the peace and freedom that he can those abroad, because they remind him of improvements that he ought to make and the like; so any part of the self is, in its nature, likely to be suggestive of exertion rather than rest. Moreover, it would seem that self-feeling, though pleasant in normal duration and intensity, is disagreeable in excess, like any other sort of feeling. One reason why we get tired of ourselves is simply that we have exhausted our capacity for experiencing with pleasure a certain kind of emotion.

As we have seen, the self that is most importunate is a reflection, largely, from the minds of others. This phase of self is related to character very much as credit is related to the gold and other securities upon which it rests. It easily and willingly expands, in most

of us, and is liable to sudden, irrational, and grievous collapses. We live on, cheerful, self-confident, conscious of helping make the world go round, until in some rude hour we learn that we do not stand so well as we thought we did, that the image of us is tarnished. Perhaps we do something, quite naturally, that we find the social order is set against, or perhaps it is the ordinary course of our life that is not so well regarded as we supposed. At any rate, we find with a chill of terror that the world is cold and strange, and that our self-esteem, self-confidence, and hope, being chiefly founded upon opinions attributed to others, go down in the crash. Our reason may tell us that we are no less worthy than we were before, but dread and doubt do not permit us to believe it. The sensitive mind will certainly suffer, because of the instability of opinion. *Cadit cum labili.* As social beings we live with our eyes upon our reflection, but have no assurance of the tranquillity of the waters in which we see it. In the days of witchcraft it used to be believed that if one person secretly made a waxen image of another and stuck pins into the image, its counterpart would suffer tortures, and that if the image was melted the person would die. This superstition is almost realized in the relation between the private self and its social reflection. They seem separate but are darkly united, and what is done to the one is done to the other.

If a person of energetic and fine-strung temperament is neither vain nor proud, and lives equably without suffering seriously from mortification, jealousy, and the like; it is because he has in some way learned to discipline and control his self-feeling, and thus to escape the pains to which it makes him liable. To effect some such escape has always been a present and urgent problem with sensitive minds, and the literature of the inner life is very largely a record of struggle with the inordinate passions of the social self. To the commoner and somewhat sluggish sorts of people these passions are, on the whole, agreeable and beneficent. Emulation, ambition, honor, even pride and vanity in moderation, belong to the higher and more imaginative parts of our thought; they awaken us from sensuality and inspire us with ideal and socially determined purposes. The doctrine that they are evil could have originated only with those who felt them so; that is, I take it, with unusually sensitive spirits, or those whom circumstances denied a normal and wholesome self-expression. To such the thought of self becomes painful, not because of any lack of self-feeling; but, quite the reverse, because, being too sensitive and tender, it becomes overwrought, so that this thought sets in vibration an emotional chord already strained and in need of rest. To such minds self-abnegation becomes an ideal, an ideal of rest, peace, and freedom, like green pastures and still waters. The prophets of the inner life, like Marcus Aurelius, St. Paul, St. Augustine, Thomas à Kempis, and Pascal, were men distinguished not by the lack of an aggressive self, but by a success in controlling and elevating it which makes them the examples of all who undergo a like struggle with it. If their ego had not been naturally importunate they would not have been forced to contend with it, and to develop the tactics of that contention for the edification of times to come.

The social self may be protected either in the negative way, by some sort of withdrawal from the suggestions that agitate and harass it, or in the positive way, by contending with them and learning to control and transform them, so that they are no longer painful; most teachers inculcating some sort of a combination of these two kinds of tactics.

Physical withdrawal from the presence of men has always been much in favor with those in search of a calmer, surer life. The passions to be regulated are sympathetic in origin, awakened by imagination of the minds of other persons with whom we come in contact. As Contarini Fleming remarks in Disraeli's novel, "So soon as I was among men I desired to influence them." To retire to the monastery, or the woods, or the sea, is to escape from the sharp suggestions that spur on ambition; and even to change from the associates and competitors of our active life into the company of strangers, or at least of those whose aims and ambitions are different from ours, has much the same effect. To get way from one's working environment is, in a sense, to get away from one's self; and this is often the chief advantage of travel and change. I can hardly agree with those who imagine that a special instinct of withdrawal is necessary to explain the prominence of retirement in the ordinances of religion. People wish to retire from the world because they are weary, harassed, driven by it, so that they feel that they cannot recover their equanimity without getting away from it. To the impressible mind life is a theatre of alarms and contentions, even

when a phlegmatic person can see no cause for agitation—and to such a mind peace often seems the one thing fair and desirable, so that the cloister or the forest, or the vessel on the lonesome sea, is the most grateful object of imagination. The imaginative self, which is, for most purposes, the real self, may be more battered, wounded, and strained by a striving, ambitious life than the material body could be in a more visible battle, and its wounds are usually more lasting and draw more deeply upon the vitality. Mortification, resentment, jealousy, the fear of disgrace and failure, sometimes even hope and elation, are exhausting passions; and it is after a severe experience of them that retirement seems most healing and desirable.

A subtler kind of withdrawal takes place in the imagination alone by curtailing ambition, by trimming down one's idea of himself to a measure that need not fear further diminution. How secure and restful it would be if one could be consistently and sincerely humble! There is no sweeter feeling than contrition, self-abnegation, after a course of alternate conceit and mortification. This also is an established part of the religious discipline of the mind. Thus we find the following in Thomas:

> Son, now I will teach thee the way of peace and of true liberty. . . . Study to do another's will rather than thine own. Choose ever to have less rather than more. Seek ever the lower place and to be subject to all; ever wish and pray that the will of God may be perfectly done in thee and in all. Behold such a man enters the bounds of peace and calm.

In other words, lop off the aggressive social self altogether, renounce the ordinary objects of ambition, accustom yourself to an humble place in others' thoughts, and you will be at peace; because you will have nothing to lose, nothing to fear. No one at all acquainted with the moralists, pagan or Christian, will need to be more than reminded that this imaginative withdrawal of the self from strife and uncertainty has ever been inculcated as a means to happiness and edification.

Many persons who are sensitive to the good opinion of others, and, by impulse, take great pleasure in it, shrink from indulging this pleasure because they know by experience that it puts them into others' power and introduces an element of weakness, unrest, and probable mortification. By recognizing a favorable opinion of yourself, and taking pleasure in it, you in a measure give yourself and your peace of mind into the keeping of another, of whose attitude you can never be certain. You have a new source of doubt and apprehension. One learns in time the wisdom of entering into such relations only with persons of whose sincerity, stability, and justice one is as sure as possible; and also of having nothing to do with approval of himself which he does not feel to have a secure basis in his character.

Chapter 13 Self-Acceptance and Self-Evaluative Behavior: A Critique of Methodology*

DOUGLAS P. CROWNE AND MARK W. STEPHENS

"Self-acceptance" has become a popular concept in psychological literature. Along with "rigidity," "authoritarianism," and "conformity," it has come to particular prominence in the last decade, perhaps reflecting an evolution in value systems in American culture. Concepts pertaining to the self have been given considerable space in the writings of personality theorists and social-personality psychologists and inevitably have found their way into psychological research.

Self-acceptance has been particularly identified with Rogers' personality theory and is accorded the status in that system of a major therapeutic goal. Phenomenological research on self-acceptance dates from the classic study of Raimy (1948). However, very similar concepts have played dominant roles in other theories— e.g., Snygg and Combs (1949), Horney (1950), and Sullivan (1953). More important, self-acceptance seems to have been pre-empted for less systematic, eclectic usage by a great many practicing clinicians and researchers (Cowen, 1956; Cowen, Heilizer, Axelrod, and Alexander, 1957; Zuckerman, Baer, and Monashkin, 1956; Zukerman and Monashkin, 1957). The major portion of the research on self-acceptance derives from Rogers' self-theory, but studies based on other theories (Block and Thomas, 1955; Sarbin and Rosenberg, 1955) and the generally empirical investigations referred to above attest to the breadth

SOURCE. Douglas P. Crowne and Mark W. Stephens, "Self-acceptance and Self-evaluative Behavior: A Critique of Methodology," from *Psychological Bulletin*, 58 (No. 2, 1961), pp. 104–115 and 117–119. Copyright 1961, *Psychological Bulletin*. Reprinted by permission of the American Psychological Association.

* The authors would like to express their indebtedness to the following persons, who critically read this paper and made a number of valuable suggestions: Donald Campbell, Shephard Liverant, Julian Rotter, Lee Sechrest, Charles Smock, and Janet Taylor.

of current interest in the behaviors subsumed under this broadly interpreted construct.

While no single definition of self-acceptance would be accepted by all who use the term, the phenomenological view of Rogers seems to represent at least a common point of departure. From the definition of a *self-concept* construct the concept of self-acceptance is derived, referring, at least operationally, to the extent to which this self-concept is congruent with the individual's description of his "ideal self."

The majority of self-acceptance tests have followed this model (cf. Rogers and Dymond, 1954; Bills, 1958; Zuckerman and Monashkin, 1957; Brownfain, 1952). A somewhat different psychometric model has been proposed by Gough (1955), in which self-acceptance is inferred from the ratio of "favorable" self-descriptive statements to the total number of self-descriptive statements made by the subject.

A common denominator in the definition of self-acceptance, judging from the operations employed in its assessment, would seem to be the degree of self-satisfaction in self-evaluation. This definitional consensus, however, is achieved at the level of operations, and other meanings may be implied by self-acceptance *constructs*. Phenomenological theorists, for example, appear to be interested in an "internal" phenomenal state. Other theorists (Block and Thomas, 1955) have formulated self-acceptance as a function of an ego-control construct. The phenomenological concept of Rogers and the psychoanalytic set of meanings implied by Block and Thomas' construct of ego control probably diverge in important respects. The purpose here, however, is merely to illustrate the point that emphasis on definitional clarity achieved at an operational level tends to ignore the probably significant differences in the implied theoretical meanings of self-acceptance.

Reflecting in part the widespread interest in self-acceptance are the numerous instruments which have been devised to measure the construct. A striking phenomenon of research in this area is that these tests, characterized by a diversity of both theoretical and psychometric models, have apparently been assumed to be interchangeable. Thus, characteristic of self-acceptance research appears to be a basic conception that measures of this construct possess face validity; that is, in a simple denotative sense, the tests are viewed as being manifestly similar (Peak, 1953).

Criterion validation of self-acceptance tests is, of course, logically impossible, and attempts at construct validation do not lend much faith in the validity even of a particular test, much less of all the different tests. Face validity, however, has apparently been assumed without question. The acceptance of face validity—that is, manifest similarity—implies adherence to a further assumption incorporated in phenomenological theory—that of the validity of self-reports (Rogers, 1951, p. 494). In terms of these assumptions, a self-acceptance test is valid if it looks like a self-acceptance test and is similar to other tests, and what a person says about himself self-evaluatively is accepted as a valid indication of how he "really" feels about himself.

The acceptance of these assumptions whether acknowledged or implicit, has definite implications for the assessment of self-acceptance and for the interpretation of experimental results in this area. This paper will show that there are four major problems in the measurement of this construct and that, in view of the common adherence to these assumptions, the results of studies on self-acceptance are rendered highly ambiguous. These issues seem, despite their essential pertinence to research on self-acceptance, to have been sufficiently ignored to warrant exposition in this paper.

* * *

EQUIVALENCE OF OPERATIONS

As observed above, the diverse tests of self-acceptance have been assumed to be equivalent operations for measuring behaviors subsumed under the construct. The failure of experimenters to consider the problem of the equivalence of assessment operations in published reports (Bills, Vance, and McLean, 1951; Block and Thomas, 1955; Calvin and Holtzman, 1953; Cowen, Heilizer, and Axelrod, 1955; Hillson and Worchel, 1957; Phillips, 1951) raises the question of the basis on which the findings of individual studies employing different measuring operations are generalized and incorporated

in the larger body of self-acceptance research. The basis of generalization, in view of the absence of explicit consideration of the question, must be inferred to lie in the assumption of face validity as defined above. Even statements implying differences among self-acceptance tests fail to deal with the logically sequential question of the extent to which these differences may mean that self-acceptance as measured by Test 1 is not the same as self-acceptance as measured by Test 2.

* * *

Writers do not make clear what relationship obtains between classes of self-acceptance tests (tests yielding discrepancy scores versus self-concept rating devices) or, more basically, how phenomenological personality theory can lead to operations that apparently can satisfy certain predictions in the case of one class of instruments but requires different operations to obtain positive results from other hypotheses based on the same construct.

According to the notion of face validity, what looks like a test of self-acceptance *is* such, by definition. All the test constructor is required to do, in terms of this criterion, is to elicit self-evaluative statements from subjects. All measures that conform to this requirement achieve validity and are therefore equivalent. By this procedure the test itself becomes the construct, in the sense of the narrowest kind of operational definition.

An operational definition stating what is measured by a given device or procedure in terms of specified measurement operations is, of course, a perfectly legitimate and necessary procedure in scientific investigation *as long as the interpretation of results is strictly confined to the particular test or measurement procedure.* A problem arises, however, when an attempt is made to generalize from experimental findings with a particular test to results obtained by *different* assessment operations. The problem similarly occurs in another case when a certain test is applied to an experimental problem and negative results are interpreted as disconfirming the hypotheses relating the construct to observables. As Jessor and Hammond (1957) have pointed out, in the absence of an explicit, logical relationship between the superordinate construct and the operations designed to assess it, conclusions cannot be made concerning the validity of the hypotheses since invalid measurement operations could equally account for negative findings.

The point at issue is that tests of self-acceptance (or for that matter, of any construct) which are based on different construct systems and in the development of which different procedures and items have been employed are not equivalent *in the absence of empirical demonstration of their relationships;* they must be shown to be either highly related to each other or similarly related to other constructs in the nomological net. Further, in the absence of demonstrated equivalence, experimental results cannot be generalized to findings with a different instrument. This seems to be so obvious a consideration that explication here is redundant. The fact remains, however, that the equivalence of self-acceptance tests has been assumed despite their independent derivation and despite the relative lack of empirical demonstration that there is a high degree of common variance among them.

* * *

DEFINITION OF THE CONSTRUCT
Specifying Parameters

The ability to reach generalized conclusions from current self-acceptance research seems to be limited by a failure to give adequate definitions to the construct itself. As Rotter (1954) has pointed out, it is important to distinguish between ideal, theoretical, and operational definitions of a given construct. An experimenter can define self-acceptance, for example, as the behavior sample (or as the "internal" phenomenal state *reflected* by the behavior sample) obtained on a particular test. But he is usually not interested in restricting his interpretation of his findings (if any) to this limited behavior sample, and he seeks to place his results in the larger context of research by other investigators and to generalize his findings to "real life" situations such as those encountered in clinical practice. By a narrow interpretation of operationism, the experimenter has made it logically indefensible to relate his findings to a theoretical system, to results obtained with other measurement devices, or to "real life" situations. When nothing more than an operational definition is offered, the parameters defining the variable are not specifiable, and there is no basis for generalization of the results.

At the other extreme, definitions of self-acceptance at an abstract level, not specifically articulated with other variables in a theory or tied to a specific test, are apt to be semantically loose and to be subject to differing interpretations. It is true, of course, that definitions of variables at this level transcend any particular set of operations and can usually be applied to an infinite variety of situations and behaviors. The looseness of such definitions, however, precludes rigorous tests of hypotheses and makes precise communication impossible. In self-acceptance research there have been few if any definitions of the construct which are not either rigidly operational or highly abstract.

The deduction from an abstract definition, with all its surplus meanings, to specific operations is likely to be a tenuous one and, perhaps more often than not, as a private, nonrepeatable process. An intervening step is necessary in which the construct is broadly defined in terms of specific behavioral referents and preferably in relation to other variables in a specific theory. A "working definition," as Rotter has defined it, clearly represents an attempt to specify the parameters of the variable in question so that both generality and precise communication are gained. Self-acceptance research appears to have lacked such definitions.

Although this paper is chiefly concerned with pointing out certain methodological pitfalls in research on self-acceptance, some clarification may be achieved by defining briefly this intermediate theoretical step and attempting to relate the logic of contruct validation to the more general theoretical problem. Rotter's working definition could be described as a definition at the construct level. In terms of this view, the behavioral referents and the hypothesized relationships of the construct are described as part of its definition—that is, the implied meanings of the term are publicly specified. In effect, specifying the behavioral referents and hypothesized relationships reduce to the same thing: locating the construct in a nomological net. In the language of test construction, Cronbach and Meehl (1955) write:

> Construct validation takes place when an investigator believes that his instrument reflects a particular construct to which are attached certain meanings. The proposed interpretation generates specific testable hypotheses, which are a means of confirming or disconfirming the claim. . . . To validate a claim that a test measures a construct a nomological net surrounding the concept must exist (pp. 290–291).

The logic of construct validation cannot be invoked to justify the identification of a particular set of operations as unique to a given construct, nor does it support the view that a construct is "validated" by the confirmation of a single hypothesis. The establishment of a single relationship belongs more properly in the domain of criterion oriented validity, as Cronbach and Meehl point out. With construct validation procedures clearly at issue, it would seem to be desirable to specify in advance the referents of self-acceptance. When the situations in which the behaviors subsumed under the construct and the behaviors themselves are identified, some idea of the generality and functional unity of self-acceptance is afforded, and relationships to other constructs, situations, and measurement operations can be suggested at a logical level.

* * *

Self-acceptance research is in need of clear construct-level definitions in which the relationships of the construct to other variables are explicitly stated. These definitions must refer primarily to the relationship of self-acceptance to other variables in the general theory in which the construct is embedded. Depending upon the particular theory, definitions might specify the nature of the relationship of self-acceptance to adjustment; to such personality variables as creativity, neuroticism, and defensiveness; to interpersonal variables such as acceptance of others; to environmental, social, and cultural variables, as, for example, the role of cultural sanctions in self-evaluation, or the influence of the experimental (or therapeutic) context on self-appraisal.

Representative Sampling

A second problem associated with the definition of the parameters of self-acceptance concerns the representative sampling of self-acceptance test items. As applied to the construct of self-acceptance, the problem of representative sampling is involved in the systematic sampling of some specified universe of self-evaluative behaviors. Assuming that one has defined this population theoretically, it is then of importance to draw one's sample of test items in such a way as to represent their occurrence in the population. The achievement of representative sampling in this respect means that generalization can reasonably be attempted to other situations and/or behaviors than those of a particular experiment or test. Although the behavioral referents of self-acceptance might seem obvious, on closer scrutiny it appears that there is notable confusion resulting from a lack of consensus as to what these referents are.

Some examples from published research may illustrate what is implied by failure to sample representatively a population of self-evaluative behaviors. Butler and Haigh (1954) begin with Rogers' abstract definition of the self-concept. Then, they write:

A set of one hundred [self-reference] statements was taken at random from available therapeutic protocols. (Actually, the statements were selected on the basis of accidental, rather than random, sampling) (p. 57).

The population of relevant self-percepts was therefore restricted to those verbalized by some sample of clients in client centered therapy, the basis for sampling was accidental, and thus there is no precise definition of self-acceptance in terms of what particular self-percepts define its parameters. The finding that changes in self-acceptance were demonstrated to occur as a function of client centered therapy is thereby limited to the particular conditions of this experiment, the subject population used, and the particular items employed in the Q sort measure. For example, it is quite possible (but unknown) that the statements used comprise a sample biased in favor of client centered counseling as perceived and defined by the judges (presumably Butler and Haigh) who selected the items.

A second example can be seen in the development of the IAV (Bills et al., 1951). The items (adjectives) in the IAV were drawn from Allport and Odbert's (1936) list of 17,953 traits. The basis of selection was the frequent appearance of the adjective in question in client centered interviews and whether it presented a "clear example of self-concept definition." Self-evaluation on the IAV, then, pertains only to the Allport and Odbert traits mentioned frequently in client centered interviews, and generalization to other self-evaluative situations, or traits, would be tenuous.

* * *

With such lists of traits or items it is necessary to assume either that they truly represent *all* self-percepts, or at least that they represent the most important ones. But, especially for the phenomenologist, must it not be assumed that these are different for different subjects and/or subject populations? Must not this list, then, be tailor-made to the subject to be truly representative for him (a totally idiographic procedure)? Perhaps what is required is that the subject generate his own list of self-descriptions, or a self-description, and the values he attaches to the separate elements and to the composite.

* * *

SOCIAL DESIRABILITY

The third general issue to raise concerns the extent to which self-evaluative responses are influenced by "defensive behavior" (Butler and Haigh, 1954; Zuckerman and Monashkin, 1957), "self-protective response tendencies" (Crowne, 1959), or "social desirability" (Edwards, 1957; Kenny, 1956).

* * *

Butler and Haigh, and also Zuckerman and Monashkin, conclude that subjects who are unwilling to attribute undesirable characteristics to themselves or confess self-dissatisfaction are by that very fact maladjusted, and presumably therefore self-dissatisfied. This, however, is obviously an hypothesis for investigation, and not necessarily true by definition. Self-acceptance tests do not directly indicate whether the subject is *willing* to express self-discontent, but only whether he *does* express it. Zuckerman and Monashkin have also suggested, in fact, that subjects giving more socially undesirable responses may have a different conception of what *is* socially desirable, and thus they implicitly suggest that these subjects may actually *not* differ in terms of their *need* to respond in a socially desirable fashion. Such a difference in conception of what is socially desirable might be expected to be associated with maladjustment, but it would certainly be a less direct indication of self-dissatisfaction per se.

Four separate hypotheses could be advanced concerning the relationship between social desirability and responses on self-acceptance (or any other self-report) tests. Each of these is capable in some degree of being tested.

Hypothesis I. Social desirability has no effect on test responses. This is essentially the assumption of validity of self-reports: that what the subject says about himself is a valid and direct indication of what he feels or thinks at least at the time, about himself. This, incidentally, seems to be a necessary *assumption* for phenomenologists, although it is a testable proposition.

Hypothesis II. Social desirability factors account for equal variance in all subjects test scores. This assumption is tenable from Edwards' approach and could be held even in

the face of most of the research to be reported below. It posits, in effect, that once one has accounted for variance due to nomothetically determined social desirability in any subject's test score, what is *left* indicates the subject's true self-feelings.

Hypothesis III. Social desirability, while it may or may not be an important factor for all subjects, accounts for *more* of the variance for some subjects than for others. This corresponds to the suggested differences in *need* to perform in a socially desirable way, protect the self, and disguise self-discontent. It is interesting that such need has been supposed to be an important variable only for those who show relatively high self-acceptance or social desirability scores: the rebel, or the individual seeking succorance, may produce very *low* scores, as a result of a complementary need to perform in a socially *undesirable* way, and still not necessarily differ from others in terms of overall adjustment *or* "true" self-acceptance. In any case, such a conception as this suggests research determining the correlates of this need to perform in a socially desirable, or to perform in a socially undesirable, way.

Hypothesis IV. Variance associated with a nomothetically determined social desirability factor reflects differences in the conception of what *is* socially desirable. This hypothesis is not necessarily in conflict with Hypothesis III. Both factors could operate simultaneously, although separating the variance due to each might be quite difficult. This, as well as Hypothesis III, is definitely incompatible with Hypotheses I and II.

With the above distinctions in mind, then, the results of some investigations of the relationship of the social desirability variable to self-acceptance test scores can be examined. Kenny (1956) gave 25 self-descriptions previously employed in a study by Zimmer (1954) to a group of judges for social desirability scaling. Three independent samples of subjects then responded to these items in the form of a questionnaire, a self-descriptive rating scale, and a *Q* sort. The correlations between the social desirability scale values and the scores obtained on the questionnaire, rating scale, and *Q* sort were .82, .81, and .66, respectively. The last two correlation coefficients are based on a "real self" scores. Social desirability correlated .82 with the "ideal self" rating scale score and .59 with the "ideal" self *Q* sort.

Edwards (1955, 1957) and Edwards and

Horst (1953) have also shown that *Q* sorts are highly influenced by the social deirability variable. In a study reported in 1955 and reviewed in 1957, Edwards found correlations of .84 and .87 for males and females, respectively, between item placement on a *Q* sort and the social desirability scale values of the items. In this case, the items were those employed in the development of the Edwards Personal Preference Schedule (1953).

* * *

While studies of the effect of the social desirability variable on many of the commonly employed tests of self-acceptance have not been done, the results of the investigations discussed above would suggest that self-evaluative tests are particularly susceptible to criticism on social desirability grounds. A common denominator in research findings on self-acceptance may well be the variable of social desirability. Edwards (1957) and Jackson and Bloomberg (1958) have made a similar analysis with respect to the Taylor anxiety scale (Taylor, 1953). Systematic investigation of both the parameters and the effects on test behavior of social desirability would clearly seem to be in order. That self-acceptance tests are influenced by factors other than the manifest content of the items, however, seems beyond dispute.

THE GENERALITY OF SELF-ACCEPTANCE

To this point the issues discussed have been pertinent strictly to psychometric and methodological problems in assessing self-acceptance. A further issue to be raised, although it certainly has methodological ramifications, is the primarily theoretical question of the generality of self-acceptance.

Generality involves two related problems, one empirical and the other a theoretical problem of interpretation. Empirically, there is need of evidence concerning the temporal stability of self-acceptance; the consistency of an individual's self-acceptance from one situation to another (for example, in friendly vs. hostile groups, or where self-effacement is rewarded or not rewarded); the generality of self-acceptance in reference to different aspects of the "self" (for example, in reference to morality vs. in reference to interpersonal effectiveness); and agreement of different kinds of *manifestation* of self-acceptance (for example, spontaneous self-appraisal vs. that manifested in an undisguised test such as the ACL vs. inferences drawn from a TAT protocol). The theoretical

question is simply how best to construe self-acceptance. If, as has been suggested (Rogers, 1951), the self-concept and self-acceptance can be considered to be relatively stable characteristics of a person, one should find that situational variables have only a negligible effect on self-acceptance, that measures of self-acceptance taken in different social contexts are highly correlated, and that measures taken over temporal intervals are likewise highly stable. If these questions can be answered positively, it would be reasonable to construe the self-concept, from which the discrepancy notion of self-acceptance is derived, as a meaningful variable on which there are consistent differences between subjects, and it would be highly appropriate to think of individuals in terms of their characteristic levels of self-acceptance. To the degree that self-acceptance is a function of variables associated with specific situations or types of situations, however, it will be more fruitful to investigate self-evaluative behavior per se and its situational determinants.

The empirical evidence with respect to the generality of self-acceptance is rather scanty. The fact that studies have not attacked this question may be attributable to the general assumption that self-acceptance *is* consistent. Three investigations have been reported which do bear on this question. With respect to temporal stability, Taylor (1955) reports a test-retest correlation of .79 (presumably based on self-sort/ideal-sort discrepancy scores) over an interval of a week. Butler and Haigh (1954) report the correlations between self-sorts and ideal-sorts for each subject in a control group (*N*=16) not receiving therapy for two *Q* sort administrations separated by a considerable period of time. Although consistency was apparent, Butler and Haigh noted that

There are some sharp individual changes which indicate that alteration in self-ideal congruence does occur at times in the absence of therapy (p. 67).

Concerning the influence of situational variables of self-acceptance, a study by Thorne (1954) is relevant. Employing the IAV, Thorne found that following induced failure on a mirror drawing task, subjects whose initial level of self-acceptance was high tended to lower their self-ratings in the direction of a more realistic evaluation, while those originally having low self-acceptance scores showed concern over loss of self-esteem. The results of this study would suggest that self-acceptance is influenced by environmental events and that persons respond self-reflexively to perceived successes and failures.

It would appear, from this brief discussion, that studies should be devoted to the problem of the generality of self-evaluative behavior. Of particular interest are the questions of temporal stability, influence of situational variables, and the effect on self-evaluation of such factors as success, failure, and punishment.

SELF-ACCEPTANCE VERSUS SELF-EVALUATION BEHAVIOR

It has been necessary at several points in this discussion to point out differences between a phenomenological and a behavioristic approach to self-acceptance. Since these differences are basic to the research approaches—not to mention the way in which such research is construed—in this general area of inquiry, and since these differences seem not to have been fully appreciated by all who have written on the topic, some further discussion of them is in order.

A phenomenological approach to self-acceptance is concerned with self-acceptance itself, or "real" self-acceptance, as a totally private, subjective experience of the subject. By definition this is never observable by any other; the best that an experimenter or clinician can hope to do is make relatively accurate guesses, or inferences, concerning the existence or degree, of the variable as it "exists" in the subject. By such a definition, self-acceptance corresponds to MacCorquodale and Meehl's (1948) early conception of an "hypothetical construct"—something which cannot be observed but still is assumed to exist—except that there is little suggestion that self-acceptance even *can* be observed by anyone other than the subject himself. It is only with some difficulty, it would seem, that a phenomenologist can avoid the necessity of assuming the validity of self-reports. Representative sampling, and also an idiographic procedure for determining what are the most salient aspects of a subject's self-evaluation, would seem to be most important in a phenomenological approach to the assessment of self-acceptance. Social desirability, on the other hand, should be assumed *not* to be a factor in self-reports. To assume a high degree

of generality or consistency—temporal, situational, etc.—is not necessarily essential to a phenomenological approach; however, in any theory which posits generalized self-acceptance as an important dimension on which to compare people, empirically determined generality of the variable is, naturally, crucial.

A behavioristic concern with self-acceptance might more clearly be directed toward "self-evaluative behavior," on the other hand. The additional inference of some underlying, real if unobservable, phenomenological state is not essential to a study of self-evaluative behavior per se; and it might be pointed out that self-evaluative behavior is an interesting and perhaps important focus of interest in and of itself. In such an approach, the assumption of validity of self-reports is clearly not essential; a clear construct-level definition of self-evaluative behavior, on the other hand, is. Generality, representative sampling in test construction, and the related question of equivalence of assessment operations are crucial questions only if the goal is to approach self-evaluative behavior as a trait, or consistent behavioral tendency, by which to classify people in a generalized fashion. It is quite feasible to examine self-evaluative behavior as a situationally determined phenomenon, or as one determined by a situation-person interaction, rather than as a trait. Social desirability, defensiveness, etc., become merely other variables related (or unrelated) to self-evaluative behavior, and not components of error variance. And, most important, it becomes an empirical matter to determine correlates (such as "adjustment") of various forms of self-evaluative behavior, either in general or in specified contexts.

This discussion is not meant to imply that a phenomenological interest in self-acceptance is unsophisticated or unworthy. Theoretical understanding of phenomenal states is a problem of inference. A clearer conception of "internal" phenomenal states such as self-acceptance would seem to be best derived from the observable behaviors of the person—that is, his self-evaluative behaviors. Phenomenological research would appear, in fact, to involve complexities that do not attach to more behavioristic efforts.

REFERENCES

Allport, G. W., and Odbert, H. S. Trait names: A psycholexical study. *Psychol. Monogr.*, 1936, **62** (1, Whole No. 211).

Berger, E. M. The relation between expressed acceptance of self and expressed acceptance of others. *J. abnorm. soc. Psychol.*, 1952, **47**, 778–782.

Berger, E. M. Relationships among acceptance of self, acceptance of others and MMPI scores. *J. counsel. Psychol.*, 1955, **2**, 279–284.

Bills, R. E. Rorschach characteristics of persons scoring high and low in acceptance of self. *J. consult. Psychol.*, 1953, **17**, 36–38 (a).

Bills, R. E. A validation of changes in scores on the index of adjustment and values as measures of changes in emotionality. *J. consult. Psychol.*, 1953, **17**, 135–138 (b).

Bills, R. E. *Manual for the Index of Adjustment and Values. Form: Adult and high school senior.* Auburn: Alabama Polytechnic Institute, 1958.

Bills, R. E., Vance, E. L., and McLean, O. S. An Index of Adjustment and Values. *J. consult. Psychol.*, 1951, **15**, 257–261.

Block, J., and Thomas, H. Is satisfaction with self a measure of adjustment? *J. abnorm. soc. Psychol.*, 1955, **51**, 254–259.

Brownfain, J. J. Stability of the self-concept as a dimension of personality. *J. abnorm. soc. Psychol.*, 1952, **47**, 597–606.

Buss, A. H., and Gerjuoy, H. The scaling of terms used to describe personality. *J. consult. Psychol.*, 1957, **21**, 361–369.

Butler, J. M., and Haigh, G. V. Changes in the relation between self-concepts and ideal-concepts. In C. R. Rogers and Rosalind F. Dymond (Eds.), *Psychotherapy and personality change.* Chicago: Univer. Chicago Press, 1954.

Calvin, A. D., and Holtzman, W. H. Adjustment and discrepancy between self concept and inferred self. *J. consult. Psychol.*, 1953, **17**, 39–44.

Campbell, D. T., and Fiske, D. W. Convergent and discriminant validation by the multitrait-multimethod matrix. *Psychol. Bull.*, 1959, **56**, 81–105.

Cattell, R. B. The description of personality: II. Basic traits resolved into clusters. *J. abnorm. soc. Psychol.*, 1943, **38**, 476–507.

Cattell, R. B. *Description and measurement of personality.* Yonkers-on-Hudson, New York: World Book, 1946.

Cowen, E. L. An investigation of the relationship between two measures of self-regarding attitudes. *J. clin. Psychol.*, 1956, **12**, 156–160.

Cowen, E. L., Heilizer, F., and Axelrod, H. S. Self-concept conflict indicators and learning. *J. abnorm. soc. Psychol.*, 1955, **51**, 242–245.

Cowen, E. L. Heilizer, F., Axelrod, H. S., and Alexander, S. The correlates of manifest anxiety in perceptual reactivity, rigidity, and self concept. *J. consult. Psychol.*, 1957, **21**, 405–411.

Cowen, E. L., and Tongas, P. N. The social desirability of trait descriptive terms: Applications to a self-concept inventory. *J. consult. Psychol.*, 1959, **23**, 361–365.

Cronbach, L. J., and Meehl, P. E. Construct validity in psychological tests. *Psychol. Bull.*, 1955, **52**, 281–302.

Crowne, D. P. The relation of self-acceptance behavior to the social learning theory construct of need value. Unpublished doctoral dissertation, Purdue University, 1959.

Crowne, D. P., Stephens, M. W., and Kelly, R. The validity and equivalence of tests of self-acceptance. *J. Psychol.*, 1961, **51**, 101–112.

Edwards, A. L. *Manual for the Edwards Personal Preference Schedule.*
New York: Psychological Corporation, 1953.

Edwards, A. L. Social desirability and *Q* sorts. *J. consult. Psychol.,*
1955, **19**, 462.

Edwards, A. L. *The social desirability variable in personality assessment
and research.* New York: Dryden, 1957.

Edwards, A. L., and Horst, P. Social desirability as a variable in *Q* technique
studies. *Educ. psychol. Measmt.,* 1953, **13**, 620–625.

Gough, H. G. *Reference handbook for the Gough Adjective Check-List.*
Berkeley: Univer. California Institute of Personality Assessment and
Research, 1955. (Mimeo)

Hillson, J. W., and Worchel, P. Self concept and defensive behavior in the
maladjusted. *J. consult. Psychol.,* 1957, **21**, 83–88.

Horney, Karen. *Neurosis and human growth.* New York: Norton, 1950.

Jackson, D. N., and Bloomberg, R. Anxiety: Unitas or multiplex?
J. consult. Psychol., 1958, **22**, 225–227.

Jessor, R., and Hammond, K. R. Construct validity and the Taylor anxiety
scale. *Psychol. Bull.,* 1957, **54**, 161–170.

Kelly, G. A. *The psychology of personal constructs.* New York: Norton, 1955.

Kenny, D. T. The influence of social desirability on discrepancy measures
between real self and ideal self. *J. consult. Psychol.,* 1956, **20**, 315–318.

Kogan, W. S., Quinn, R. D., Ax, A. F., and Ripley, H. S. Some methodological problems in the quantification of clinical assessment by *Q*
array. *J. consult. Psychol.,* 1957, **21**, 57–62.

LaForge, R., and Suczek, R. F. The interpersonal dimension of personality:
III. An interpersonal check list. *J. Pers.,* 1955, **24**, 94–112.

MacCorquodale, K., and Meehl, P. E. On a distinction between hypothetical
constructs and intervening variables. *Psychol. Rev.,* 1948, **55**, 95–107.

McKinley, J. C., Hathaway, S. R., and Meehl, P. E. The MMPI: VI. The *K*
scale. *J. consult. Psychol.,* 1948, **12**, 20–31.

Nebergall, Nelda S., Angelino, H., and Young, H. H. A validation study
of the self-activity inventory as a predictor of adjustment.
J. consult. Psychol., 1959, **23**, 21–24.

Omwake, Katherine T. The relation between acceptance of self and
acceptance of others shown by three personality inventories.
J. consult. Psychol., 1954, **18**, 443–446.

Peak, Helen. Problems of objective observation. In L. Festinger and D. Katz
(Eds.), *Research methods in the behavioral sciences.* New York:
Dryden, 1953.

Phillips, E. L. Attitudes towards self and others: A brief questionnaire report.
J. consult. Psychol., 1951, **15**, 79–81.

Raimy, V. C. Self reference in counseling interviews. *J. consult. Psychol.,*
1948, **12**, 153–163.

Rogers, C. R. *Client-centered therapy.* Boston: Houghton-Mifflin, 1951.

Rogers, C. R., and Dymond, Rosalind F. (Eds.) *Psychotherapy and
personality change.* Chicago: Univer. Chicago Press, 1954.

Rotter, J. B. *Social learning and clinical psychology.* Englewood Cliffs, N.J.:
Prentice Hall, 1954.

Sarbin, T. R., and Rosenberg, B. G. Contributions to role-taking theory.
J. soc. Psychol., 1955, **42**, 71–81.

Snygg, D. S., and Combs, A. W. *Individual behavior: A new frame of
reference for psychology.* New York: Harper, 1949.

Sullivan, H. S. *The interpersonal theory of psychiatry.* New York:
Norton, 1953.

Taylor, D. M. Changes in the self concept without psychotherapy. *J. consult.
Psychol.,* 1955, **19**, 205–209.

Taylor, Janet A. A personality scale of manifest anxiety. *J. abnorm. soc.*
     Psychol., 1953, **48**, 285–290.
Taylor, Janet A. Drive theory and manifest anxiety. *Psychol. Bull.* 1956,
     53, 303–320.
Thorne, R. B. The effects of experimentally induced failure on self evaluation.
     Unpublished doctoral dissertation, Columbia University, 1954.
Underwood, B. J. *Psychological research.* New York: Appleton-Century-
     Crofts, 1957.
Zimmer, H. Self-acceptance and its relation to conflict. *J. consult. Psychol.,*
     1954, **48**, 447–449.
Zuckerman, M., Baer, N., and Monashkin, J. Acceptance of self, parents,
     and people in patients and normals. *J. clin. Psychol.,* 1956, **12**, 327–332.
Zuckerman, M., and Monashkin, J. Self-acceptance and psychopathology.
     J. consult. Psychol., 1957, **21**, 145–148.

Part IV The Development of Self

The centrality of self in social interaction has been discussed and numerous self-aspects have been examined, but little has been said about the growth and development of the self. How does the person come to know and identify himself? In what ways are the various aspects of self engendered? What processes are at stake in determining how the person comes to conceptualize himself? Understanding in such areas is pivotal on several counts. For one, much will be said in this volume on the multiple functions which self-conception may serve— ways in which various forms of social conduct are prohibited, discouraged, supported, or required by one's views of self. However, the functions of self-conception in normal conduct can be neither fully understood nor appreciated without a temporally sensitive appraisal. As continuously demonstrated in the area of human learning, the prediction of a person's behavior at any point in time is much enhanced by knowledge of his past experiences. To understand current behavior, one ideally needs an understanding of the developmental processes on which the present is based.

Patterns of social conduct also undergo many transitions as the person passes through life. To the extent that a person's behavior can be derived from his conceptions of self, a concentration on the development and modification of these conceptions is critical. Later in the volume much will also be said of maladaptive behavior that appears to be rooted in processes of self-conception. Such behavior may depend largely on inadequate or deficient developmental sequences. An understanding of "normal" development should thus appropriately set the stage for later discussions of the self and socially deviant behavior. Finally, nowhere is the dependency of self-conception on social interaction more vividly demonstrated than in an examination of the genesis of self.

If there is any one notion concerning the development of self that may be singled out as pre-eminent, it is that fostered by the symbolic interactionists. As developed in the writings of Cooley and Mead, the basic position holds that the person's self-conceptions are initially developed from the views taken toward him by significant others in his social environment. Through a process of assuming imaginatively the attitudes of others toward himself, the individual eventually incorporates what he feels to be the general view of others toward him. The original statement of this position appears in the preceding chapters by Mead (Chapter 4) and Cooley (Chapter 8). In view of the prevailing influence of this theoretical stance, the selections in this Part were chosen with two central intents: first, to illustrate a number of major extensions and derivations from the basic position; and, more important, to supplement its limitations. In the latter regard, these selections should serve to document the range of influential factors and complex processes involved in self-development. The intent is not at all to negate the symbolic interactionist position; it is rather to point out that any general theory of self-development must ultimately pay heed to an extremely wide range of factors.

DEVELOPMENT OF SELF-CONCEPTION OVER THE LIFE CYCLE

James Mark Baldwin's discussion of the development of self-consciousness in childhood (Chapter 14) was chosen primarily for the reasons just stated, but it was chosen also to help prevent the disappearance from the field of the important thinking of an early social-psychological pioneer. Baldwin's work was published in 1897, a time when research methodology was not adequate to meet the challenge provided by complex theory. Perhaps for this reason his thinking has been largely overlooked. At this point in time, however, his work presents a number of invigorating and empirically challenging ideas. One of the most important of these ideas concerns the close relationship between one's self-conception and his views of others. Essentially, Baldwin gives us a very social account of the dialectical processes of role playing and of imputing a self to others engaged in interaction. These socialization processes require the individual to consider his own capacities and actions in terms of how these are regarded by himself and others in relation to obligatory moral norms. Baldwin was also a precursor of the current emphasis on situational selves (cf. Turner, Chapter 9; Gergen, Chapter 30; Goffman, Chapter 31).

Perhaps the only conceptual relationship between Baldwin's work and the selection by Sullivan (Chapter 15) is the shared emphasis on the subjective world of the socially dependent child. Sullivan's work is certainly in no present danger of being buried in the sands of time, and, in fact, the included piece is often regarded as a classic of its kind. His contribution also picks up the recurring psychoanalytic theme confronted initially in the chapter by Parsons (Chapter 1). However, the dependency of self-conception on the quality of early bodily experiences is an emphasis unique to Sullivan. It also serves as an important adjunct to the symbolic-interactionist emphasis on social communication. The view of self as an organization of experiences created out of the necessity to avoid anxiety may also be fruitfully compared with Hilgard's views (Chapter 36).

Theodore Sarbin's work (Chapter 16) may be seen partly as a derivative of the symbolic interactionist perspective and partly as a sophisticated attempt to unify and amalgamate a number of important psychological insights. The chapter is thus closer to representing a general theory of self-development than is the symbolic interactionist approach. Particularly helpful is the way in which Sarbin has combined the views of Baldwin (Chapter 14) and James (Chapter 3) and extended them to include the relationship between self and role (cf. Preiss, Chapter 19; Backman and Secord, Chapter 28). In light of the distinction between self-as-knower and self-as-known, the reader will also appreciate Sarbin's attempt at a parsimonious solution.

Whereas all three of the initial contributions can be considered conceptually wealthy but in need of supporting evidence, much the opposite may be felt of the Bandura and Walters (Chapter 17) treatment of the development of self-control. In contrast to the others, their work is closer to the laboratory tradition in psychology, with its continuous attempt to build theory on a solid foundation of demonstrated fact. The Bandura and Walters discussion of modeling behavior is pivotal and may be seen in the larger context of the development of self through imitation (cf. Baldwin, Chapter 14). One should also take careful note of the subtle differences in the way the term "self" is used by Bandura and Walters as opposed to its use in the preceding chapters in this section. In this instance the subjective dimension of self, emphasized in the other contributions, is to some extent gratuitous, and self is considered largely synonymous with the individual's overt behavior.

The fact that this book does not include a chapter dealing with self-development in puberty does not represent a choice on the part of the editors, but rather reflects the dearth of material in this area. This may be one of the unfortunate backwashes of the Freudian emphasis in developmental psychology. However, on the brighter side of this ledger are the influential writings of Erik Erikson on the crisis of adolescent identity formation. Chapter 18 embodies portions of three Erikson papers on the syndrome of identity diffusion. This contribution is especially important in its focus on the relationship between self-development and structural aspects of society, and in this respect it represents a significant departure from the classic Freudian emphasis on internal dynamics.

Preiss (Chapter 19) amplifies this concern with social structure by examining the development of self-conception through role training. The research summarized by Preiss provides an excellent example of the pervasive influence of symbolic interactionist theory on current thinking and research. More significantly, it is a clear demonstration of the effects of formal role training on self-conception over time. This report may be considered a prelude to a more extensive analysis of a major long-term investigation on the effects of medical education on the self-conceptions of the medical student.[1]

The chapter by Helen Merrell Lynd is partly intended to counter the preceding emphasis on formal roles. Although it does not rely on the usual data sources of the behavioral sciences, her contribution is both eloquent and convincing in its treatment of more intrinsic psychological development. It is necessary to realize that this contribution has been excerpted from Lynd's larger work, *On Shame and the Search for Identity*,[2] and for a richer understanding of the distinction between shame (based on estimates of one's own capacities) and guilt (derived from one's relationship to social mores and laws) the reader should turn to that book. In any case, this distinction becomes particularly relevant to research defining self-esteem as the discrepancy between present self and ideal self (cf. Crowne and Stephens, Chapter 13).

Whereas Lynd's analysis has implications for identity development throughout the life span, the problem of long-term transitions is approached more formally in the chapter by Brim (Chapter 21). Particularly important is Brim's discussion of socialization in later life. As he points out, the socialization process, its contents, and its outcomes may differ at various stages of the life cycle. Values and motives may be emphasized during childhood, but the learning of most social roles occurs at a much later stage; still later, internal self-evaluation may abate. Such variable processes would suggest that dramatic changes in self-conception continue to occur during the entire life cycle, a view

---

[1] Although not included in this volume, a lively and interesting discussion of transformations in identity after childhood is contained in Anselm Strauss' *Mirrors and Masks,* Glencoe, Ill.: Free Press, 1959.
[2] Helen Merrell Lynd, *On Shame and the Search for Identity,* New York: Harcourt, Brace, 1958.

that challenges the traditional notion of childhood crystallization of personality.

Discussions of self-development during puberty are sparse, and matters are little improved when one turns to the period of late adulthood. Chapter 22 by Back and Gergen attempts to sketch a model dealing with a limited set of transitions occurring during these years. The reader should be sensitive in this case to the recurring emphasis on the somatic contribution to self-conception, an emphasis shared in the chapters by Allport (Chapter 2), Schilder (Chapter 10), Sullivan (Chapter 15), and Gordon (Chapter 11). The model's utilization of public opinion data is perhaps one of its unique features within this volume.

As an appropriate capstone to discussions of self-development through the life span, Lifton's chapter (Chapter 23) deals with the relationship of death and self. The article raises particular questions vis-à-vis the arguments presented by Back and Gergen. Their arguments stress the person's acceptance of a finite end to self, whereas Lifton pinpoints a number of ways in which persons attempt to bypass this terminus. It should be noted that space limitations necessitated deletion of Lifton's probing and poignant description of the survivors' views of the Hiroshima atom blast, a description from which his 'general principles' are partly derived.

DEVELOPMENT OF SELF-CONCEPTION IN UNIQUE OR PROBLEMATIC CIRCUMSTANCES

Although the chapters just discussed deal with processes of very general significance, it was felt that a discussion of self-development would be incomplete without attention being directed toward the effects of unique and problematic circumstances. Under such conditions, processes which may have general relevance are often etched with greater clarity. And too, understanding in such cases may be important in its own right. The Kardiner and Ovesey chapter (Chapter 24) illustrates this latter point in its examination of the effects of minority group oppression. The personality dynamics of Negroes have received considerable attention in recent years; the Kardiner and Ovesey chapter is of particular moment inasmuch as it represents one of the few attempts at integrating traditional psychoanalytic theory with work on self-conception. It should also be noted that this chapter is based on intensive case studies. One of the most important outcomes is the strong indication that psychodynamic patterns and processes may differ according to social class. The reader may also wish to compare their discussion of self-esteem with the papers by Fromm (Chapter 32), Cohen (Chapter 38), and Rogers (Chapter 44).

Goffman's discussion (Chapter 25) stands in direct contrast to the highly psychological treatment of Kardiner and Ovesey. This piece deftly reveals the traumatic and insidious effects of the "total institution" on self. Goffman's description of the various humiliations "inmates" are often forced to suffer is also interesting to view in light of Lynd's (Chapter 20) earlier discussion of the functions of shame and guilt in forming identity. Goffman's implied criticism of subjugation processes is also reiterated in the chapter by Laing (Chapter 42).

The final selection (Chapter 26), in which Maslow discusses the effects of "peak experiences" on the self, has received a high degree of acclaim. For present purposes it is useful to see this contribution against the backdrop of the selections in Part II (Self-as-Experiencer). Particularly important is the relationship between Maslow's emphasis on subjective experience and that of other writers who have benefited from the existentialist tradition (cf. Tiryakian, Chapter 7; and Laing, Chapter 42). Maslow's approach also serves as a useful antidote to theories overstressing the dependency of the self on social influence.

Given the range of concepts and phenomena discussed in these various contributions, the question remains as to the ultimate possibility of a general theory of self-development. It may be that models of limited range, designed to explain particular forms of behavior, will prove most useful for a good many years. It is true that recurring trains of thought appear in these and other chapters, and if one could overcome the semantic problems already well embedded in the discipline, it might be possible to specify a set of variables and multiple interrelationships. However, even this goal is some way off. Coming full circle, our position may be similar to that of James M. Baldwin: our capacity to spell out relationships in theory is not yet paralleled by our ability to demonstrate their truth value through empirical test.

Chapter 14 The Self-Conscious Person

JAMES M. BALDWIN

1. THE DIALECTIC OF PERSONAL GROWTH

One of the most interesting tendencies of the very young child in its responses to its environment is the tendency to recognize differences of personality. It responds to what have been called "suggestions of personality." As early as the second month it distinguishes its mother's or nurse's touch in the dark. It learns characteristic methods of holding, taking up, patting, and adapts itself to these personal variations. It is quite a different thing from the child's very first step toward a sense of the qualities which distinguish persons. The sense of uncertainty grows stronger and stronger in its dealings with persons. A person stands for a group of experiences quite unstable in its prophetic as it is in its historical meaning. This we may, for brevity of expression, assuming it to be first in order of development, call the *"projective stage"* in the growth of the child's personal consciousness.

Further observation of children shows that the instrument of transition from such a projective to a subjective sense of personality is the child's active bodily self, and the method of it is the *function of imitation*. When the organism is ripe for the enlargement of its active range by new accommodations, then he begins to be dissatisfied with "projects," with contemplation, and starts on his career of imitation. And of course he imitates persons.

Further, persons are bodies which move. And among these bodies which move, which have certain projective attributes, a very peculiar and interesting one is his own body. It has connected with it certain intimate features which all others lack—strains, stresses, resistances, pains, etc., an inner felt series added to the new imitative series. But it is only when a peculiar experience arises which we call effort that there comes that great line of cleavage in his experience which indicates the rise of volition, and which separates off the series now first really *subjective*. What has formerly been "projective" now becomes "subjective." This we may call the *subjective* stage in the growth of the self-notion. It rapidly assimilates to itself all the other elements by which the child's own body differs in his experience from other active bodies—all the passive inner series of pains, pleasures, strains, etc. Again it is easy to see what now happens. The child's subject sense goes out by a sort of return dialectic to illuminate the other persons. The "project" of the earlier period is now lighted up, claimed, clothed on with the raiment of selfhood, by analogy with the subjective. The subjective becomes *ejective;* that is, other people's bodies, says the child to himself, have experiences *in them* such as mine has. They are also *me's;* let them be assimilated to my me-copy. This is the third stage; the ejective, or social self, is born.

The "ego" and the "alter" are thus born together. Both are crude and unreflective, largely organic. And the two get purified and clarified together by this twofold reaction between project and subject, and between subject and eject. "My sense of myself grows by imitation of you, and my sense of yourself grows in terms of my sense of myself. Both *ego* and *alter* are thus essentially social; each is a *socius* and each is an imitative creation."[1]

This give-and-take between the individual and his fellows, looked at generally, we may call the *Dialectic of Personal Growth*. It serves as the point of departure for the main positions developed in the following pages; and the lines of the summary sketch will be filled in as we advance.

SOURCE. James Mark Baldwin, *Social and Ethical Interpretations in Mental Development,* New York: The Macmillan Company, 1897, pp. 7–12, 16–21, 23-24, 31-32, 34-37, and 44-50. Copyright 1897. Reprinted by permission of Mrs. Philip M. Stimson (Professor Baldwin's daughter).

[1] Quotation, somewhat condensed and revised, from the author's *Mental Development in the Child and the Race,* 2d ed., p. 335. A position similar to this has been taken by Professor Josiah Royce. Cf. also Avenarius, *Der menschl. Weltbegriff.* I have indicated in the earlier work (*Ment. Devel.,* p. 339) the relation of my position to Avenarius' theory of *Introjection.*

2. THE PERSON AS A SELF

The outcome serves to afford a point of departure for the view which we may entertain of the person as he appears to himself in society. If it be true, as much evidence goes to show, that what the person thinks as himself is a pole or terminus at one end of an opposition in the sense of personality generally, and that the other pole or terminus is the thought he has of the other person, the "alter," then it is impossible to isolate his thought of himself at any time and say that in thinking of himself he is not essentially thinking of the alter also.[2] What he calls himself now is in large measure an incorporation of elements that, at an earlier period of his thought of personality, he called someone else. The acts now possible to himself, and so used by him to describe himself in thought to himself, were formerly only possible to the other; but by imitating that other he has brought them over to the opposite pole, and found them applicable, with a richer meaning and a modified value, as true predicates of himself also. If he thinks of himself in any particular past time, he can single out what was then he, as opposed to what has since become he; and the residue, the part of him that has since become he, that was then only thought of—if it was thought of as an attribute of personality at all—as attaching to some one with whom he was acquainted. For example, last year I thought of my friend W. as a man who had great skill on the bicycle and who wrote readily on the typewriter; my sense of his personality included these accomplishments, in what I have called a "projective" way. My sense of myself did not have these elements, except as my thought of my normal capacity to acquire delicate movements was comprehensive. But now, this year, I have learned to do both these things. I have taken the elements formerly recognized in W.'s personality, and by imitative learning brought them over to myself. I now think of myself as one who rides a "wheel" and writes on a "machine." But I am able to think of myself thus only as my thought includes, in a way now called "subjective," the personal accomplishments of W., and with him of the more or less generalized alter which in this illustration we have taken him to stand for. So the truth we now learn is this: that very many of the particular marks which I now call mine, when I think of myself, have had just this origin. I have first found them in my social environment, and by reason of my social and imitative disposition, have transferred them to myself by trying to act as if they were true to me, and so coming to find out that they are true of me. And further, all the things I hope to learn, to acquire, to become, all—if I think of them in a way to have any clear thought of my possible future—are now, before I acquire them, possible elements of my thought of others, of the social alter, or of what considered generally we may call the "socius."

But we should also note that what has been said of the one pole of this dialectical relation, the pole of self, is equally true of the other also—the pole represented by the other person, the alter. What do I have in mind when I think of him as a person? Evidently I must construe him, a person, in terms of what I think of myself, the only person whom I know in the intimate way we call "subjective."

* * *

So my thought of any other man—or all other men—is, to the richest degree, that which I understand of myself, together with the uncertainties of interpretation which my further knowledge of his acts enables me to conjecture. I think him rational, emotional, volitional, as I am;[3] and the details of his more special characteristics, as far as I understand them at all, I weave out of possible actions of my own, when circumstances call me out in similar ways. But there is always the sense that there is more to understand about him; for, as we have seen, he constantly, by the diversities between us which I do not yet comprehend, sets me new actions to imitate or to avoid in my own growth.

So the dialectic may be read thus: my thought of self is in the main, as to its character as a personal self, filled up with my thought of others, distributed variously as individuals; and my thought of others, as persons, is mainly filled up with myself. In other words, but for certain minor distinctions in the filling, and for certain compelling distinctions between that which is immediate and that which is objective, *the ego and the alter are to our thought one and the same thing.*

* * *

---

[2] In isolating the "thought elements" in the self, I do not, of course, deny the organic sensation and feeling elements; but for our present purposes the latter may be neglected.

[3] Even temporary affective experiences tend to be "ejected." When I have a headache I cannot see a person riding, jumping, etc., without attributing to him the throbbing which such actions would produce in my own head.

Let us say that the sense of self always involves the sense of the other. And this sense of the other is but that of another "self," where the word "self" is equivalent to myself, and the meaning of the word "other" is that which prevents it from being myself. Now my point is that whatever I fancy, hope, fear, desire for self in general, with no qualification as to which self it is, remains the same whether afterwards I do qualify it by the word "my" or by the word "your." Psychologically there is a great mass of motor attitudes and reactive expressions, felt in consciousness as emotion and desire, which are common to the self-thought everywhere.

This is true just in so far as there is a certain typical other self whose relation to me has been that of the give-and-take by which the whole development of a sense of self of any kind has been made possible. And we find certain distinctions at different stages of the development which serve to throw the general idea of the social relationship into clearer light.

Let us look at the life of the child with especial reference to his attitudes to those around him; taking the most common case, that of a child in a family of children. We find that such a child shows, in the very first stages of his sense of himself as a being of rights, duties, etc., a very imitative nature. He is mainly occupied with the business of learning about himself, other people, and nature. He imitates everything, being a veritable copying-machine. He spends the time not given to imitating others very largely in practicing in his games what he has picked up by his imitations, and in the exploiting of these accomplishments. His two dominating characteristics are a certain slavishness, on the one hand, in following all examples set around him; and then, on the other hand, a certain bold aggressiveness, inventiveness, a showing-off, in the use he makes of the things he learns.

But it does not take very extended observation to convince us that this difference in his attitudes is not a contradiction: that the attitudes themselves really terminate upon different thoughts of self. The child imitates his elders, not from choice, but from his need of adaptation to the social environment; for it is his elders who know more than he does, and who act in more complex ways. But he is less often aggressive toward his elders; that is, toward those who have the character of command, direction, and authority over him. His aggressions are directed mainly toward his brothers and sisters; and even as toward them, he shows very

striking discriminative selection of those upon whom it is safe to aggress. In short, it is plain that the difference in attitude really indicates differences in his thought, corresponding to differences in the elements of the child's social environment. We may suppose the persons about him divided roughly into two classes: those from whom he learns, and those on whom he practices; and then we see that his actions are accounted for as adaptations toward these, in his personal development.

The facts covered by this distinction—probably the first general social distinction in the child's career—are very interesting. The stern father of the family is at the extreme end of the class he reveres with a shading of fear. The little brother and sister stand at the other extreme; they are the fitting instruments of his aggression, the practice of his strength, the assertion of his agency and importance. The mother usually stands midway; it seems, serving to unite the two aspects of personality in the youngster's mind. And it is pretty clear, when the case is closely studied, that the child has, as it were, two thoughts of his mother—two mothers, according as she on occasion falls into one or the other of these classes. He learns when, in what circumstances, she will suffer him to assert himself, and when she will require him to be docile and teachable. And although she is for the most part a teacher and example, yet on occasion he takes liberties with the teacher.

Now what does this mean, this sorting out, so to speak, of the persons of the family? It means a great deal when looked at in the light of the "dialectical movement" in the development of personality. And I may state my interpretation of it at the outset.

The child's sense of himself is, as we have seen, one pole of a relation; and which pole it is to be, depends on the particular relation which the other pole, over which the child has no control, calls on it to be. If the other person involved presents uncertain, ominous, dominating, instructive features, or novel imitative features, then the self is "subject" over against what is "projective." He recognizes new elements of personal suggestion not yet accommodated to. His consciousness is in the learning attitude; he imitates, he serves, he trembles, he is a slave. But on the other hand, there are persons to whom his attitude has a right to be different. In the case of these the dialectic has gone further. He has mastered all their features, he can do himself what they do, he anticipates no new developments in his intercourse with them; so he "ejects" them, as the psychological expression is: for an "eject" is a person whose consciousness has only those elements in it which the individual who thinks of that consciousness is able, out of his own store of experience, to read into it. It is ejective to him, for he makes it what he will, in a sense. Now this is what the brothers and sisters, notably the younger ones, are to our youthful hero. They are his "ejects"; he knows them by heart, they have no thoughts, they do no deeds, which he could not have read into them by anticipation. So he despises them, practices his superior activities on them, tramples them under foot.

Now at this earliest stage in his unconscious classification of the elements of his personal world, it is clear that any attempt to describe the child's interests—the things which he wants, as we have agreed to define "interests"—as selfish, generous, or as falling in any category of developed social significance, is quite beside the mark. If we say that to be selfish is to try to get all the personal gratification possible, we find that he does this only part of the time; and even on these occasions, not because he has any conscious preference for that style of conduct, but merely because his consciousness is then filled with the particular forms of personal relationship—the presence of his little sister, etc.— which normally issue in the more habitual actions which are termed "aggressive" in our social terminology. His action is only the motor side of a certain collection of elements. He acts that way, then, simply because it is natural for him to practice the functions which he has found useful. We see that it is natural; and on the basis of its naturalness, we are prone to call him selfish by nature.[4]

But that this is arguing beyond our facts— really arguing on the strength of the psychological ignorance of our hearers, and our own—is clear when we turn the child about and bring him into the presence of the other class of persons to whom we have seen him taking up a special attitude. We have but to observe him in the presence of his father, usually, or of some one else whom he habitually imitates and from whom he learns the lessons of life, to find out that he is just as pre-eminently social, docile,

accommodating, centered-outwardly, so to speak, as before we considered him unsocial, aggressive, and self-centered. If we saw him only in these latter circumstances, we should say possibly that he was by nature altruistic, most responsive to generous suggestion, teachable in the extreme. But here the limitation is the same as in the former case. He is not altruistic in any high social sense, nor consciously yielding to suggestions of response which require the repression of his selfishness. As a matter of fact, he is simply acting himself out; and in just the same natural way as on the occasion of his apparent selfishness. But it is now a different self which is acting itself out. The self is now at the receptive pole. It is made up of elements which are inadequate to a translation of the alter at the other pole of the relationship now established. The child's sense of self is now not that of a relatively completed self in relation to the alter before him; it was that in the earlier case, and the aggression of which he was then guilty showed as much. Now he feels his lack of adequate means of response to the personality before him. He cannot anticipate what the father will do next, how long approbation will smile upon him, what the reasons are for the changes in the alter-personality. So it is but to state a psychological truism to say that his conduct will be different in this case. Yet from the fact that the self of this social state is also in a measure a regular pole of the dialectic of personal growth, it often tempts the observer to classify the whole child, on the strength of this one attitude, in some one category of social and political description.

* * *

Now all these changes have meaning only as we realize the fact of the social dialectic, which is the same through it all. There are changes of attitude simply and only because, as the psychologist would express it, there are changes in the content of his sense of self. In more popular terms: he changes his attitude in each case because the thing called another, the alter, changes. His father is his object; and the object is the "father," *as the child thinks him,* on this occasion and under these circumstances, *right out of his own consciousness.* The father-thought is a part of the child's present social situation; and this situation in the child's mind issues in the attitude which is appropriate to it. If it be the father in wrath, the situation produces such a father out of the child's available social thought-material; and the presence of

---

[4] A good instance of this inadequacy of statement from a psychological point of view, is seen in Professor J. Sully's grave discussion as to whether infants are naturally immoral or not (*Studies of Childhood,* Chap. VII.).

the combination in the child's mind itself issues in the docile, fearful attitude. But if it then turn into the jovial father, the child does not then himself set about reversing his attitude. No, the father-thought is now a different father-thought, and of itself issues in the child's attitude of playful aggression, rebellion, or disobedience. The growing child is able to think of self in varying terms as varying social situations impress themselves upon him; so these varying thoughts of self, when made real in the persons of others, call out, by the regular process of motor discharge, each its own appropriate attitude.

But see, in this more subtle give-and-take of elements for the building up of the social sense, how inextricably interwoven the ego and the alter really are! The development of the child's personality could not go on at all without the constant modification of his sense of himself by suggestions from others. So he himself, at every stage, is really in part some one else, even in his own thought of himself. And then the attempt to get the alter stript from elements contributed directly from his present thought of himself is equally futile. He thinks of the other, the alter, as his *socius*, just as he thinks of himself as the other's *socius:* and the only thing that remains more or less stable, throughout the whole growth, is the fact that there is a growing sense of self which includes both terms, the ego and the alter.

In short, *the real self is the bipolar self, the social self, the socius.*

* * *

The family is, of course, the first place in which the child finds food for his own personal assimilation; but he does not long limit himself to the family diet. Nor is he from his early months entirely shut up to suggestions from within the family circle. His nurse comes in to stand as a member of his social company, and often the most important member from the point of view of the regularity and intimate character of her ministrations. She is part of the family to all intents and purposes. And other children from abroad who come often or at critical times to play, etc., are also "in it." Then again certain actual members of the home circle may see the child so seldom or in such a passing way that they practically are not, as far as the child's personal growth is concerned. So while the family is the theatre of this first stage of his growth, it still represents a rather flexible set of personal influences.

And his circle grows as he comes to have other relationships than those of his immediate and domestic life. When he begins to go to the kindergarten or school, the teacher in the first instance, then the pupils beside him there, or some of them, come to bear on his life in the same way that his family companions do. So gradually he widens out the sphere of the exploitation of his two selves—the receptive self, and no less, the aggressive self. In all the stretch of early childhood, pet animals, dolls, toys, etc., also play a part, especially as giving him now and then a more or less complete alter on which to wreak the performance of the new acts recently learned. And as he grows a little older, and the sense of personal agency arises to play its great part in the development of his activities, all mechanical tools, contrivances, building-blocks, sliced animals, etc., are valuable aids to the exercise of his understanding of the powers of himself and of others.

In this expansion of his interests—and with it, his enlarging sense of the sphere of personality realized in himself and in others, gradual as it is—we may mark off certain dividing lines. We may always say, no matter what the details of the boy's daily life are, that there is a circle within which his socius resides, understanding socius as we have above. His socius—to repeat —is the higher sense of commonalty, personal implication, mutual interest, which social intercourse arouses in him. This is always alive when events occur which involve persons in a larger or smaller circumference drawn about him. He has the sense of a socius, for example, when his own school is brought into rivalry with the school around the corner. . . .

3. THE PERSON AS AN ETHICAL SELF[5]

Looking back over the path we have already travelled, we see the two poles of the dialectic now familiar to us, standing prominently out: the child has, on one hand, a self which he ejects into the alter. This is the solidified mass of personal material which he has worked into a systematic whole by his series of acts. When he thinks of himself, this is very largely what his consciousness is filled with. Let us now call this the "self of habit," or the "habitual self"—terms which are common and which carry their ordinary meaning. But, on the other hand, we have found that the child has another self: the self that learns, that imitates, that ac-

---

[5] The substance of this paragraph has been printed in the *Philosophical Review,* May, 1897.

commodates to new suggestions from persons in the family and elsewhere. It is this self that is in part yet "projective," unfinished, constantly being modified by the influences outside, and, in turn, passing the new things learned over to the self of habit. Let us call this, for reasons also evident from the common significance of the term, the "accommodating self." Not that the child has at any time two distinct thoughts of himself existing side by side—that is not true—but that his one thought of self at any time is at one or the other pole, is *a self of habit or a self of accommodation*. Which it is to be, depends upon what kind of an alter is then at the other pole. But I trust this is now clear.

It is a further result that if we continue to ask at any time for a complete notion from outside of that boy's self, we cannot say that either the self of habit or the self of accommodation adequately expresses it. The only adequate expression of the boy is that which acquaints us with the whole dialectic of his progress, a dialectic which comprehends both these selves and the alter personalities which are progressive functions of his thoughts of himself; that is, *with the self of all the rich social relationships, or the "socius."*

It seems then a natural question to ask, whether the boy comes to have any sense of just this inadequacy of his thought of self when he is thinking of himself in either way, either in the way of the habitual or of the accommodating self. In other words, does he go on to reflect upon the "socius," as a larger bond of union to the different private thoughts of himself?[6] This is really the question of the evolution of the ethical sense put in closer psychological terms; and it may be worth while to see to what ethical conclusions this line of distinctions would lead. This conclusion has been anticipated in the following quotation:[7]

Whether *obedience* comes by suggestion or by punishment, it has this genetic value: it leads to another refinement in the sense of self. . . . The child finds himself stimulated constantly to deny his impulses, his desires, even his irregular sympathies, by conforming to the will of another. This other represents a regular, systematic, unflinching, but reasonable personality—still a person, but a very different person from the child's own. In the analysis of "personality suggestion," we found this stage of the child's apprehension of persons; his

sense of the regularity of personal character in the midst of the capriciousness that before this stood out in contrast to the regularity of mechanical movement in things. There are extremes of indulgence, the child learns, which even the grandmother does not permit; there are extremes of severity from which even the cruel father draws back. Here, in this dawning sense of the larger limits which set barriers to personal freedom, is the "copy" forming which is his personal authority, or law. It is "projective" because he cannot understand it, cannot anticipate it, cannot find it in himself. And it is only by imitation that he is to reproduce it, and so arrive at a knowledge of what he is to understand it to be. So it is a "copy for imitation." It is its aim—so may the child say to himself—and should be mine, if I am awake to it, to have me obey it, act like it, think like it, be like it in all respects. It is not I, but I am to become it. Here is my ideal self, my final pattern, my "ought" set before me. My parents and teachers are good because, with all their differences from one another, they yet seem to be alike in their acquiescence in this law. Only in so far as I get into the habit of being and doing like them in reference to it, get my character moulded into conformity with it, only so far am I good. And so, like all other imitative functions, it teaches its lesson only by stimulating to action. I must succeed in doing—he finds out, as he grows older and begins to reflect upon right and wrong—if I would understand. But as I thus progress in doing, I forever find new patterns set for me; and so my ethical insight must always find its profoundest expression in that yearning which anticipates but does not overtake the ideal.

My sense of moral ideal, therefore, is my sense of a possible perfect, regular will taken over *in me*, in which the personal and the social self—my habits and my social calls—are brought completely into harmony; the sense of obligation in me, in each case, is the sense of the actual discrepancies in my various thoughts of self, *as my actions and tendencies give rise to them.*

* * *

Turning now to the child and observing him in the period when his personal relationships are becoming complex, say along through the third year, the dawning moral sense is then caught as it were in the process of making. And in it we have a right to see, as I have had occasion to say in regard to other of the child's processes, the progress of the race depicted with more or less adequacy of detail.

The child begins to be dimly aware of such a presence, in his contact with others, as that which has been called in the abstract the *socius*. What this is to him is, of course, at this early stage simply an element of personal quality in the suggestions which he now gets from others;

---

[6] We saw that he has a sense of it, in his *esprit-de-corps.*

[7] *Mental Development,* pp. 334 f., somewhat revised and condensed.

an element which is not done justice to by either of the thoughts of self to which he is accustomed on occasion to react. He notes in the behaviour of his father and mother, whenever certain contingencies of the social situation present themselves, a characteristic which, in the development of "personality-suggestion," was termed the "regularity of personal agency."[8] He sees the father pained when he has to administer punishment; and he hears the words, "Father does not like to punish his little boy." He finds the mother reluctantly refusing to give a biscuit when it is her evident desire to give it. He sees those around him doing gay things with heavy hearts, and forcing themselves to be cheerful in the doing of things which are not pleasant. He sees hesitations, conflicts, indecisions, and from the bosom of them all he sees emerge the indications of something beyond the mere individual attitudes of the actor, something which stands toward these higher persons from whom he learns, as the family law, embodied possibly in the father, stands toward him.

Now I do not mean that the child sees all this in the terms in which I have described what he "sees." He does not see anything clearly. He simply feels puzzled at the richness of the indications of personal behaviour which pour in upon him. But the very puzzle of these situations is just the essential thing. It means that the categories of personality which he has so far acquired, the two selves which exhaust the possible modes of behaviour he is able to depict to himself in thought, are really inadequate. Here in these situations of his father and mother is more personal suggestion, which is still quite "projective." It is personal; things do not show it. But it is not yet understood. The self of habit, no less than the self of accommodation, is thrust aside, as he sees his mother's sorrow when she refuses him the biscuit; he cannot act aggressively toward her nor yet sympathetically. There must needs be some other type of personal behaviour, *some other thought of a self;* for if not, then character must after all remain to him a chaotic, capricious thing.

We way ask, before we attempt to find a way for the child to extricate himself from this confusion in his thoughts of personality, whether he have in his own experience any analogies which will help him to assimilate the new suggestive elements. And our observation is very superficial if we do not light upon an evident thing in his life; the thing he has come to under-

stand something about every time he *obeys.* This is so evidently a thing of value that psychologists long ago struck upon it. The "word of command" is to Professor Bain the schoolmaster to morality. By it the child gets the habit of personal subjection which, when he illustrates it reflectively, shows itself as morality. This, I think, is true as far as the function of the "schoolmaster" is concerned; but much more than this schoolmaster is needed to school the agent boy to morality. How it works, however, another appeal to the growing sense of self will serve to show.

Whenever he obeys, the boy has forced in upon him a situation which his thoughts of himself are not adequate to interpret. He is responding neither to his habitual self nor to his accommodating self. Not to the former, for if the thing he is told to do is something he does not want to do, his habits, his private preferences, are directly violated. And on the other hand he is not acting out his accommodating self simply, just in proportion as he is unwilling to do what he is told to do. If this self held all the room in his consciousness, then obedience would be companionship, and compliance would be no more than approval. No, it is really his private habitual self that is mainly present; the other being a forced product, unless by dint of schooling in submission his obedience has become free and unconstrained.

Besides these elements, his two selves, then, what more is there to the child? This: *a dominating other self, a new alter,* is there; that is the important thing. And what does it mean? It means, in the first instance, a line of conduct on his part which the obedience represents. But in this line of conduct we now have the real schoolmaster to the boy. It is just by it that he learns more about character, precisely as, by his spontaneous imitations at the earlier stage, he established lines of conduct which taught him more about character. At this stage also, his intelligence is not so rudimentary as at the earlier one. It does not take him long to learn certain great things. By the action he performs through obedience, he learns the meaning of these actions: how they feel, what good or evil results they lead to. And in all his learning by this agency, he learns above all the great lesson essential to the development of his thought of self: that there is a something always present, an atmosphere, a circle of common interest, a family propriety, a mass of accepted tradition. *This is his first realization to himself of what the socius means.* It comes by his growth as a

---

[8] *Mental Development,* p. 125.

personal self, but[9] the process of obedience greatly abbreviates his growth. For a long time it is embodied as a matter of course in the persons whom he obeys. But the social limitations which these persons respectively represent are not always coextensive or parallel. His father and mother often embody very different family spirits to him. And it is only after many tentative adjustments, mistaken efforts to please, excesses of duty in one direction, and instances of rebellion[10] in other directions, that he learns the essential agreements of the different persons who set law to him.

Now this is a new thought of self. How can it be otherwise when all its origin is from persons, and all its characters are learned only by the efforts of the struggling hero to realize their meaning by his own actions? Apart from the elements of a possible self, there is absolutely nothing. It is his own actions felt, then added to imitatively and made to illustrate the actions of others, with which he fills his consciousness when he thinks of it. And in each of his straining efforts to obey, to do what he is told to do, his success or failure is a further defining of the limitations of one or the other of his old selves, and in so far the creation of a new self which sets law to both of them.

Now this new self arises, as we have seen, right out of the competitions, urgencies, inhibitions of the old. Suppose a boy who has once obeyed the command to let an apple alone, coming to confront the apple again, when there is no one present to make him obey. There is his private, greedy, habitual self, eyeing the apple; there is also the spontaneously suggestible, accommodating, imitative self over against it, mildly prompting him to do as his father said and let the apple alone; and there is—or would be, if the obedience had taught him no new thought of self—the quick victory of the former. But now a lesson has been learned. There arises a thought of one who obeys, who has no struggle in carrying out the behests of the father. This may be vague; his habit may be

yet weak in the absence of persons and penalties, but it is there, however weak. And it is no longer merely the faint imitation of an obedient self which he does not understand. It carries within it, it is true, all the struggle of the first obedience, all the painful protests of the private greedy self, all the smoke of the earlier battlefield. But while he hesitates, it is now not merely the balance of the old forces that makes him hesitate; it is the sense of the new, better, obedient self hovering before him. A few such fights and he begins to grow accustomed to the presence of something in him which represents his father, mother, or in general, *the lawgiving personality.* So, as he understands the meaning of obedience better, through his own acting out of its behests in varied circumstances, the projective elements of the alter which thus sets law to him become subjective. The socius becomes more and more intimate as a law-abiding self of his own.

Then, with this self in him, he proceeds to do with it what we always do with our thoughts of self; he "ejects" it into all the other members of the family and of his social circle. He expects, and rightly too, that each brother and sister will have the same responsibility to the *Zeitgeist* that he has—will reverence the same Penates. He exacts from them the same obedience to father and mother that he himself renders. It is amusing to see the jealousy with which one child in a family will watch the others, and see that they do not transgress the law of the family. If the father makes an exception of one little being, he is quickly "brought up" by the protests of other little beings.[11] This is a pertinent piece of evidence to the essential truthfulness of the process depicted above, where it was said that the alter is one with the ego as a self, and that it is impossible for the child to attach predicates to the one without, *ipso facto,* attaching the same predicates to the other. To say that little brother need not obey, when I am called on to obey, is to say that little brother is in some way not a person, that is all. So we constantly have to explain to our children "the dollie cannot feel," "the leather elephant cannot eat," "the woolly dog need not be beaten when he gets in the way." "These things," in short, we say to our children, "are not selves; they have the shapes of possible selves, it may

---

[9] As he grows older his intellectual faculties are also exercised at their best upon those puzzling situations presented by the behaviour of others toward one another, in which a solution by his own action is not immediately required.

[10] The instances of violent rebellion, which become frantic and dramatic sometimes in young children, are emphasized by Sully (*Studies of Childhood,* Chap. VIII.) as impressive revelations to the child of the existence of law.

[11] Cf. the instances cited by Sully, *loc. cit.,* Chap. VIII., with his curious explanation of them as implying an "instinct for order" in the child (p. 284 *et seq.*).

be, and they have so far served as convenient alters for you to practice on, but they need not be expected to take up with you the responsibilities of family life."

So, once born in the fire and smoke of personal friction, the socius lives in the child, a presence of which he can never rid himself. It is the germ of the ideals of life, the measure of the life to come, both in this world and in the next; for it is this self that the child thereafter pursues in all his development, making it his only to find that it is further beyond him. He is "ever learning, but never able to come to the knowledge of the truth."

Chapter 15 Beginnings of the Self-System

HARRY STACK SULLIVAN

THREE ASPECTS OF
INTERPERSONAL COOPERATION

We have got our human animal as far, in the process of becoming a person, as the latter part of infancy, and we find him being subjected more and more to the social responsibilities of the parent. As the infant comes to be recognized as educable, capable of learning, the mothering one modifies more and more the exhibition of tenderness, or the giving of tenderness, to the infant. The earlier feeling that the infant must have unqualified cooperation is now modified to the feeling that the infant should be learning certain things, and this implies a restriction, on the part of the mothering one, of her tender cooperation under certain circumstances.

Successful training of the functional activity of the anal zone of interaction accentuates a new aspect of tenderness—namely, the additive role of tenderness as a sequel to what the mothering one regards as good behavior. Now this is, in effect—however it may be prehended by the infant—a *reward,* which, once the approved social ritual connected with defecating has worked out well, is added to the satisfaction of the anal zone. Here is tenderness taking on the attribute of a reward for having learned something, or for behaving right.

Thus the mother, or the parent responsible for acculturation or socialization, now adds tenderness to her increasingly neutral behavior in a way that can be called rewarding. I think that very, very often the parent does this with no thought of rewarding the infant. Very often the rewarding tenderness merely arises from the pleasure of the mothering one in the skill which the infant has learned—the success which has attended a venture on the toilet chair, or something of that kind. But since tenderness in general is becoming more restricted by the parental necessity to train, these incidents of straightforward tenderness, following the satisfaction of a need like that to defecate, are really an addition—a case of getting something extra for good behavior—and this is, in its generic pattern, a reward. This type of learning can take place when the training procedure has been well adjusted to the learning capacity of the infant. The friendly response, the pleasure which the mother takes in something having worked out well, comes more and more to be something special in the very last months of infancy, whereas earlier, tenderness was universal when the mothering one was around, if she was a comfortable mothering one. Thus, to a certain extent, this type of learning can be called learning under the influence of reward—the reward being nothing more or less than tender behavior on the part of the acculturating or socializing mothering one.

Training in the functional activity of the oral-manual behavior—that is, conveying things by the hand to the mouth and so on—begins to accentuate the differentiation of anxiety-colored siuations in contrast to approved situations. The training in this particular field is probably, in almost all cases, the area in which *grades of anxiety* first become of great importance in learning; as I have already stressed, behavior of a certain unsatisfactory type provokes increasing anxiety, and the infant learns to keep a distance from, or to veer away from, activities which are attended by increasing anxiety, just as the amoebae avoid high temperatures.

This is the great way of learning in infancy, and later in childhood—by the grading of anxiety, so that the infant learns to chart his course by mild forbidding gestures, or by mild states of worry, concern, or disapproval mixed with some degree of anxiety on the part of the mothering one. The infant plays, one might say, the old game of getting hotter or colder,

SOURCE. Harry Stack Sullivan, M.D., *The Interpersonal Theory of Psychiatry,* New York: W. W. Norton and Company, 1953, pp. 158–171. Reprinted by permission of W. W. Norton and Company, Inc. Copyright 1953 by The William Alanson White Psychiatric Foundation.

in charting a selection of behavioral units which are not attended by an increase in anxiety. Anxiety in its most severe form is a rare experience after infancy, in the more fortunate courses of personality development, and anxiety as it is a function in chronologically adult life, in a highly civilized community confronted by no particular crisis, is never very severe for most people. And yet it is necessary to appreciate that it is anxiety which is responsible for a great part of the inadequate, inefficient, unduly rigid, or otherwise unfortunate performances of people; that anxiety is responsible in a basic sense for a great deal of what comes to a psychiatrist for attention. Only when this is understood, can one realize that this business of whether one is getting more or less anxious is in a large sense the basic influence which determines interpersonal relations—that is, it is not the motor, it does not call interpersonal relations into being, but it more or less directs the course of their development. And even in late infancy there is a good deal of learning by the anxiety gradient, particularly where there is a mothering one who is untroubled, but still intensely interested in producing the right kind of child; and this learning is apt to first manifest itself when the baby is discouraged from putting the wrong things in the mouth, and the like. This kind of learning applies over a vast area of behavior. But in this discussion I am looking for where things are apt to start.

Training of the manual-exploratory function —which I have discussed in conection with the infant's getting his hands near the anus, or into the feces, or, perhaps, in contract with the external genitals—almost always begins the discrimination of situations which are marked by what we shall later discuss as *uncanny emotion.* This uncanny feeling can be described as the abrupt supervention of *severe anxiety,* with the arrest of anything like the learning process, and with only gradual informative recall of the noted circumstances which preceded the extremely unpleasant incident.

Early in infancy, when situations approach the "all-or-nothing" character, the induction of anxiety is apt to be the sudden translation from a condition of moderate euphoria to one of very severe anxiety. And this severe anxiety, as I have said before, has a little bit the effect of a blow on the head, in that later one is not clear at all as to just what was going on at the time anxiety became intense. The

educative effect is not by any means as simple and useful as is the educative effect in the other two situations which we have discussed, because the sudden occurrence of severe anxiety practically prohibits any clear prehension, or understanding, of the immediate situation. It does not, however, preclude recall, and as recall develops sufficiently so that one recalls what was about to occur when severe anxiety intervened—in other words, when one has a sense of what one's action was addressed to at the time when everything was disorganized by severe anxiety—then there come to be in all of us certain areas of "uncanny taboo," which I think is a perfectly good way of characterizing those things which one stops doing, once one has caught himself doing them. This type of training is much less immediately useful, and, shall I say, is productive of much less healthy acquaintance with reality, than are the other two.

GOOD-ME, BAD-ME, AND NOT-ME

Now here I have set up three aspects of interpersonal cooperation which are necessary for the infant's survival, and which dictate learning. That is, these aspects of interpersonal cooperation require acculturation or socialization of the infant. Infants are customarily exposed to all of these before the era of infancy is finished. From experience of these three sorts—with rewards, with the anxiety gradient, and with practically obliterative sudden severe anxiety—there comes an initial personification of three phases of what presently will be *me,* that which is invariably connected with the sentience of *my body*—and you will remember that *my body* as an organization of experience has come to be distinguished from everything else by its self-sentient character. These beginning personifications of three different kinds, which have in common elements of the prehended body, are organized in about mid-infancy—I can't say exactly when. I have already spoken of the infant's very early double personification of the actual mothering one as the good mother and the bad mother. Now, at this time, the beginning personifications of *me* are *good-me, bad-me,* and *not-me.* So far as I can see, in practically every instance of being trained for life, in this or another culture, it is rather inevitable that there shall be this tripartite cleavage in personifications, which have as their central tie—the thing that binds them ultimately into one, that always keeps them in very close relation—their relatedness to the growing conception of "my body."

Good-me is the beginning personification which organizes experience in which satisfactions have been enhanced by rewarding increments of tenderness, which come to the infant because the mothering one is pleased with the way things are going; therefore, and to that extent, she is free, and moves toward expressing tender appreciation of the infant. Good-me, as it ultimately develops, is the ordinary topic of discussion about "I."

Bad-me, on the other hand, is the beginning personification which organizes experience in which increasing degrees of anxiety are associated with behavior involving the mothering one in its more-or-less clearly prehended interpersonal setting. That is to say, bad-me is based on this increasing gradient of anxiety and that, in turn, is dependent, at this stage of life, on the observation, if misinterpretation, of the infant's behavior by someone who can induce anxiety.[1] The frequent coincidence of certain behavior on the part of the infant with increasing tenseness and increasingly evident forbidding on the part of the mother is the source of the type of experience which is organized as a rudimentary personification to which we may apply the term bad-me.

So far, the two personifications I have mentioned may sound like a sort of laboring of reality. However, these personifications are a part of the communicated thinking of the child, a year or so later, and therefore it is not an unwarranted use of inference to presume that they exist at this earlier stage. When we come to the third of these beginning personifications, *not-me,* we are in a different field—one which we know about only through certain very special circumstances. And these special circumstances are not outside the experience of any of us. The personification of not-me is most conspicuously encountered by most of us in an occasional dream while we are asleep; but it is very emphatically encountered by people who are having a severe schizophrenic episode, in aspects that are to them most spectacularly real. As a matter of fact, it is always manifest—not every minute, but every day, in every life—in certain peculiar absences of phenomena where there should be phenomena; and in a good many people— I know not what proportion—it is very striking in its indirect manifestations (dissociated behavior), in which people do and say things of which they do not and could not have knowledge, things which may be quite meaningful to other people but are unknown to them. The special circumstances which we encounter in grave mental disorders may be, so far as you know, outside your experience; but they were not once upon a time. It is from the evidence of these special circumstances—including both those encountered in everybody and those encountered in grave disturbances of personality, all of which we shall presently touch upon—that I choose to set up this third beginning personification which is tangled up with the growing acquaintance of "my body," the personification of *not-me.* This is a very gradually evolving personification of an always relatively primitive character—that is, organized in unusually simple signs in the parataxic mode of experience, and made up of poorly grasped aspects of living which will presently be regarded as "dreadful," and which still later will be differentiated into incidents which are attended by awe, horror, loathing, or dread.

This rudimentary personification of not-me evolves very gradually, since it comes from the experience of intense anxiety—a very poor method of education. Such a complex and relatively inefficient method of getting acquainted with reality would naturally lead to relatively slow evolution of an organization of experiences; furthermore, these experiences are largely truncated, so that what they are really about is not clearly known. Thus organizations of these experiences marked by uncanny emotion—which means experiences which, when observed, have led to intense forbidding gestures on the part of the mother, and induced intense anxiety in the infant—are not nearly as clear and useful guides to anything as the other two types of organizations have been. Because experiences marked by uncanny emotion, which are organized in the personification of not-me, cannot be clearly connected with cause and effect—cannot be

---

[1] Incidentally, for all I know, anybody can induce anxiety in an infant, but there is no use cluttering up our thought by considering that, because frequency of events is of very considerable significance in all learning processes; and at this stage of life, when the infant is perhaps nine or ten months old, it is likely to be the mother who is frequently involved in interpersonal situations with the infant.

dealt with in all the impressive ways by which we explain our referential processes later—they persist throughout life as relatively primitive, unelaborated, parataxic symbols. Now that does not mean that the not-me component in adults is infantile; but it does mean that the not-me component is, in all essential respects, practically beyond discussion in communicative terms. Not-me is part of the very "private mode" of living. But, as I have said, it manifests itself at various times in the life of everyone after childhood—or of nearly everyone, I can't swear to the statistics—by the eruption of certain exceedingly unpleasant emotions in what are called nightmares.

These three rudimentary personifications of *me* are, I believe, just as distinct as the two personifications of the objectively same mother were earlier. But while the personifications of me are getting under way, there is some change going on with respect to the personification of mother. In the latter part of infancy, there is some evidence that the rudimentary personality, as it were, is already fusing the previously disparate personifications of the good and the bad mother; and within a year and a half after the end of infancy we find evidence of this duplex personification of the mothering one as the good mother and the bad mother clearly manifested only in relatively obscure mental processes, such as these dreamings while asleep. But, as I have suggested, when we come to consider the question of the peculiarly inefficient and inappropriate interpersonal relations which constitute problems of mental disorder, there again we discover that the trend in organizing experience which began with this duplex affair has not in any sense utterly disappeared.

THE DYNAMISM OF THE SELF-SYSTEM

From the essential desirability of being good-me, and from the increasing ability to be warned by slight increases of anxiety—that is, slight diminutions in euphoria—in situations involving the increasingly significant other person, there comes into being the start of an exceedingly important, as it were, secondary dynamism, which is purely the product of interpersonal experience arising from anxiety encountered in the pursuit of the satisfaction of general and zonal needs. This secondary dynamism I call the *self-system*. As a dynamism it is secondary in that it does not have any particular zones of interaction, any particular physiological apparatus, behind it; but it literally uses all zones of interaction and all physiological apparatus which is integrative and meaningful from the interpersonal standpoint. And we ordinarily find its ramifications spreading throughout interpersonal relations in every area where there is any chance that anxiety may be encountered.

The essential desirability of being good-me is just another way of commenting on the essential undesirability of being anxious. Since the beginning personification of good-me is based on experience in which satisfactions are enhanced by tenderness, then naturally there is an essential desirability of living good-me. And since sensory and other abilities of the infant are well matured by now—perhaps even space perception, one of the slowest to come along, is a little in evidence—it is only natural that along with this essential desirability there goes increasing ability to be warned by slight forbidding—in other words, by slight anxiety. Both these situations, for the purpose now under discussion, are situations involving another person—the mothering one, or the congeries of mothering ones—and she is becoming increasingly significant because, as I have already said, the manifestation of tender cooperation by her is now complicated by her attempting to teach, to socialize the infant; and this makes the relationship more complex, so that it requires better, more effective differentiation by the infant of forbidding gestures, and so on. For all these reasons, there comes into being in late infancy an organization of experience which will ultimately be of nothing less than stupendous importance in personality, and which comes entirely from the interpersonal relations in which the infant is now involved—and these interpersonal relations have their motives (or their motors, to use a less troublesome word) in the infant's general and zonal needs for satisfaction. But out of the social responsibility of the mothering one, which gets involved in the satisfaction of the infant's needs, there comes the organization in the infant of what might be said to be a dynamism directed at how to live with this significant other person. The self-system thus is an organization of educative experience called into being by the necessity to avoid or to minimize incidents of anxiety.[2] The functional activity

---

[2] Since *minimize* in this sense can be ambiguous, I should make it clear that I refer, by minimizing, to moving, in behavior, in the direction which

of the self-system—I am now speaking of it from the general standpoint of a dynamism—is primarily directed to avoiding and minimizing this disjunctive tension of anxiety, and thus indirectly to protecting the infant from this evil eventuality in connection with the pursuit of satisfactions—the relief of general or of zonal tensions.

Thus we may expect, at least until well along in life, that the components of the self-system will exist and manifest functional activity in relation to every general need that a person has, and to every zonal need that the excess supply of energy to the various zones of interaction gives rise to. How conspicuous the "sector" of the self-system connected with any particular general need or zonal need will be, or how frequent its manifestations, is purely a function of the past experience of the person concerned.

I have said that the self-system begins in the organizing of experience with the mothering one's forbidding gestures, and that these forbidding gestures are refinements in the personification of the bad mother; this might seem to suggest that the self-system comes into being by the *incorporation* or *introjection* of the bad mother, or simply by the introjection of the mother. These terms, incorporation or introjection, have been used in this way, not in speaking of the self-system, but in speaking of the psychoanalytic superego, which is quite different from my conception of the self-system. But, if I have been at all adequate in discussing even what I have presented thus far, it will be clear that the use of such terms in connection with the development of the self-system is a rather reckless oversimplification, if not also a great magic verbal gesture the meaning of which cannot be made explicit. I have said that the self-system comes into being because the pursuit of general and zonal needs for satisfaction is increasingly interfered with by the good offices of the mothering one in attempting to train the young. And so the self-system, far from being anything like a function of or an identity with the mothering one, is an organization of experience for avoiding increasing degrees of anxiety which are connected with the educative process. But these degrees of anxiety cannot conceivably, in late

infancy (and the situation is similar in most instances at any time in life), mean to the infant what the mothering one, the socializing person, believes she means, or what she actually represents, from the standpoint of the culture being inculcated in the infant. This idea that one can, in some way, take in another person to become a part of one's personality is one of the evils that comes from overlooking the fact that between a doubtless real "external object" and a doubtless real "my mind" there is a group of processes—the act of perceiving, understanding, and what not—which is intercalated, which is highly subject to past experience and increasingly subject to foresight of the neighboring future. Therefore, it would in fact be one of the great miracles of all time if our perception of another person were, in any greatly significant number of respects, accurate or exact. Thus I take some pains at this point to urge you to keep your mind free from the notion that I am dealing with something like the taking over of standards of value and the like from another person. Instead, I am talking about the organization of experience connected with relatively successful education in becoming a human being, which begins to be manifest late in infancy.

When I talk about the self-system, I want it clearly understood that I am talking about a *dynamism* which comes to be enormously important in understanding interpersonal relations. This dynamism is an explanatory conception; it is not a thing, a region, or what not, such as superegos, egos, ids, and so on.[3] Among the things this conception explains is something that can be described as a quasi-entity, the personification of the self. The personification of the self is what you are talking about when you talk about yourself as "I," and what you are often, if not invariably, referring to when you talk about "me" and "my." But I would like to make it

is marked by diminishing anxiety. I do not mean, by minimize, to "make little of," because so far as I know, human ingenuity cannot make little of anxiety.

[3] Please do not bog down unnecessarily on the problem of whether my self-system ought to be called the superego or the ego. I surmise that there is some noticeable relationship, perhaps in the realm of cousins or closer, between what I describe as the personification of the self and what is often considered to be the psychoanalytic ego. But if you are wise, you will dismiss that as facetious, because I am not at all sure of it; it has been so many years since I found anything but headaches in trying to discover parallels between various theoretical systems that I have left that for the diligent and scholarly, neither of which includes me.

forever clear that *the relation of personifica-tions to that which is personified is always complex and sometimes multiple;* and that *personifications are not adequate descriptions of that which is personified.* In my effort to make that clear, I have gradually been com-pelled, in my teaching, to push the beginnings of things further and further back in the his-tory of the development of the person, to try to reach the point where the critical deviations from convenient ideas become more apparent. Thus I am now discussing the beginning of the terrifically important self-dynamism as the time when—far from there being a personifi-cation of the self—there are only rudimentary personifications of good-me and bad-me, and the much more rudimentary personification of not-me. These rudimentary personifications constitute anything but a personification of the self such as you all believe you manifest, and which you believe serves its purpose, when you talk about yourselves one to another in adult life.

THE NECESSARY AND UNFORTUNATE
ASPECTS OF THE SELF-SYSTEM

The origin of the self-system can be said to rest on the irrational character of culture or, more specifically, society. Were it not for the fact that a great many prescribed ways of doing things have to be lived up to, in order that one shall maintain workable, profitable, satis-factory relations with his fellows; or, were the prescriptions for the types of behavior in car-rying on relations with one's fellows perfectly rational—then, for all I know, there would not be evolved, in the course of becoming a person, anything like the sort of self-system that we always encounter. If the cultural prescriptions which characterize any particular society were better adapted to human life, the notions that have grown up about incorporating or intro-jecting a punitive, critical person would not have arisen.

But even at that, I believe that a human being without a self-system is beyond imagina-tion. It is highly probable that the type of education which we have discussed, even prob-ably the inclusion of certain uncanny experi-ence that tends to organize in the personification of not-me, would be inevitable in the process of the human animal's becoming a human being. I say this because the enormous capac-ity of the human animal which underlies human personality is bound to lead to ex-ceedingly intricate specializations—differentia-tions of living, function, and one thing and another; to maintain a workable, profitable, appropriate, and adequate type of relationship among the great numbers of people that can become involved in a growing society, the young have to be taught a vast amount before they begin to be significantly involved in so-ciety outside the home group. Therefore, the special secondary elaboration of the sundry types of learning—which I call the self-system —would, I believe, be a ubiquitous aspect of all really human beings in any case. But in an ideal culture, which has never been approxi-mated and at the present moment looks as if it never will be, the proper function of the self-system would be conspicuously different from its actual function in the denizens of our civilization. In our civilization, no parental group actually reflects the essence of the social organization for which the young are being trained in living; and after childhood, when the family influence in acculturation and social-ization begins to be attenuated and augmented by other influences, the discrete excerpts, you might say, of the culture which each family has produced as its children come into collision with other discrete excerpts of the culture— all of them more or less belonging to the same cultural system, but having very different ac-cents and importances mixed up in them: As a result of this, the self-system in its actual functioning in life in civilized societies, as they now exist, is often very unfortunate. But do not overlook the fact that the self-system comes into being because of, and can be said to have as its goal, the securing of necessary satisfaction without incurring much anxiety. And however unfortunate the manifestations of the self-system in many contexts may seem, always keep in mind that, if one had no pro-tection against very severe anxiety, one would do practically nothing—or, if one still had to do something, it would take an intolerably long time to get it done.

So you see, however truly the self-system is the principal stumbling block to favorable changes in personality—a point which I shall develop later on—that does not alter the fact that it is also the principal influence that stands in the way of unfavorable changes in per-sonality. And while the psychiatrist is skillful, in large measure, in his ability to formulate the self-system of another person with whom he is integrated, and to, shall I say, "intuit" the self-system aspects of his patient which tend to perpetuate the type of morbid living that the patient is showing, that still, in no sense, makes the self-system something merely to be regretted. In any event, it is always before us, whether we regret or praise it. This idea of the self-system is simply tremendously important in understanding the vicissitudes of interpersonal relations from here on. If we understand how the self-system begins, then perhaps we will be able to follow even the most difficult idea connected with its function.

Chapter 16 A Preface to a Psychological Analysis of the Self[1]

THEODORE R. SARBIN

The purpose of this preface is fourfold: *first,* to suggest that much of the undiagnosed confusion in the theory and practice of psychology is due to the multiplicity of meanings attached to the words self and ego; *second,* to sketch briefly a theory of self-development (which I have called epistemogenesis because it emphasizes cognitive factors); *third,* to illuminate the subject-object problem with the aid of this theoretical approach; and *fourth,* to formulate an illustrative hypothesis the testing of which would give at least initial validity to the theory.

Fifty years ago a psychological theorist would have found it hard going to write a psychology that did not deal in one way or another with the self. Such keen thinkers as James (15), Titchener (33), Hall (14), McDougall (21), Baldwin (3), and many others, posited a self or ego as a conception without which psychological theory just wouldn't make sense. Although they all agreed that such a concept was necessary, they differed amongst themselves as to the nature of the self, its development, and its function in various psychological processes. For example, Titchener declared simply that the "self is the sum total of conscious processes which run their course under conditions laid down by bodily tendencies" (33),

while William James in more complicated manner described the self or "me as an empirical aggregate of things objectively known. The [Ego or] I which knows them . . . is a *Thought,* at each moment different from that of the last moment . . ." (15).

Except for certain European psychologists, such as Stern (31) and Claparède (8), the psychoanalytic theorists, notably Freud (11) and Jung (17), and such sociologically oriented scholars as Cooley (9) and Mead (22), the self all but disappeared from learned psychology with the rise of behaviorism. The emphasis on the exclusively objective approach to psychological phenomena considered the self (with its soulful antecedents) not essential in formulating psychological theory.

The recrudescence of the self began with Allport's book on personality (1) and since that time the ego has become more and more popular in psychological discussions.[2] In fact, in 1943, Allport felt called upon to comment on the multiplicity of meanings attached to the term (2). In describing eight general meanings that were current, he suggested that one all-inclusive theory of the ego might account for the multiplicity of functions and characteristics attributed to it. Although beginnings have been made (7), the all-inclusive theory has yet to be advanced.

To begin this analysis, some of the main conceptions of the ego were reviewed and at least a dozen variants were discovered. Some of these are: the physical self, the material self, the interjecting ego, the empirical self, the projective self, the pure ego, the transcendental ego, the social self, the ethical self, the inferred self, and so on. In the contexts in which these expressions were used, each had some degree of validity, yet they were obviously not the same things. For example, one would have to stretch his credulity to equate the somatic self of the

SOURCE. Theodore R. Sarbin, "A Preface to a Psychological Analysis of the Self," from *Psychological Review,* No. 59 (1962), pp. 11–22. Copyright 1962, *Psychological Review.* Reprinted by permission of the American Psychological Association.

[1] No. 3 in a series of papers entitled *Contributions to Role-taking Theory.*

A somewhat abbreviated version of this preface was read at the 1950 meetings of the Western Psychological Association. For many stimulating comments I wish to thank the members of an informal graduate seminar: Messrs. N. Adler, D. R. Brown, N. S. Greenfield, M. Hyman, W. F. McCormack, and R. Taft. Mr. Greenfield should be credited with first suggesting the term "epistemogenesis." I am also grateful to Professor T. M. Newcomb for many valuable criticisms.

[2] Self and ego are here used synonymously.

neonate with the ethical self of a university professor struggling with the problem of signing or not signing a controversial document. It is unnecessary to labor the point further; a large number of terms are in use that appear to have a common signification, but communication on the subject is so lacking in unity, that confusion is often a result.

OUTLINE OF THE EPISTEMOGENIC THEORY

With the aforementioned multiple referents in the background, the formulation of a theory of the origins and development of the self is herewith essayed, being guided by the following informal postulates:

1. The human animal can regard itself as an object in the same way as it regards objects in the external world. Put in other terms, the interbehavioral field of the human can include perceptions and cognitions referable to objects in the external world, and perceptions and cognitions referable to his own body, to his own beliefs, his own statuses, and so on.

2. Behavior is organized around cognitive structures, the result of responses of the organism to stimulus-objects and residual stimuli. The self is one such cognitive structure or inference. Like all cognitive structures it is organized around substructures, here called empirical selves. These substructures are interrelated through some learning mechanism.

3. The self is empirically-derived, not transcendental; it is the resultant of experience, i.e., interaction with body-parts, things, persons, images, and so on.

4. The properties of these substructures at any given moment are determined by the total interbehavioral field of which the substructures are a part. Thus, any of the empirical selves may occupy the focus of the interbehavioral field at any given time.

5. The self (in common with other cognitive structures) is subject to continual and progressive change, usually in the direction from low-order inferences about simple perceptions to higher-order inferences about complex cognitions.

6. Organic maturation and reinforcement of selected responses contribute to changes in the empirical selves (substructures) and concurrently to changes in the total self-structure.

7. Change in cognitive structure is a function of (at least) two properties: (a) resistance to de-differentiation and (b) the breadth of the substructures. Resistance to de-differentiation may be defined in terms of the strength of the boundaries of a structure which, in turn, is related to overlearning. Breadth may be considered the dimension that determines how many structurally-dissimilar perceptions may be included in the same substructure. This view is similar to Frenkel-Brunswik's notion of ambiguity-tolerance (10).

With these guideposts set down, an initial problem is approached. Is the self as a cognitive structure to be considered an enduring structure, a momentary structure, or both? Calkins' definition of the self includes the notion that the self is an enduring structure:

The characters of the experienced self . . . are, first, its persistence or self-identity, second, its individuality or uniqueness, third, . . . it is fundamental . . . to its experiences, and finally, . . . it is related to its environment (6, pp. 493–494).

The self-structure as a cross-section in time can be inferred from G. Stanley Hall's statement:

The earliest parts of the physical self to attract attention are the hands and fingers. . . . Children of four and five months are described as attentively feeling of one hand with the other, each at the same time feeling and being felt, each subject and object to the other, and thus detaching them from the world of external things and labeling them with a mark which will enable the soul later to incorporate them into the plexus which forms the somatic ego (14, pp. 351–352).

Statements of this kind, which influenced the development of the postulates, stimulated the construction of a graphic model which allowed for the simultaneous presentation of the self as a longitudinal structure and as a cross-sectional structure (see Fig. 1).

The model is divided into sections so that the reader may more easily follow the argument. Figure 2 overlaps Fig. 1, Fig. 3 overlaps Fig. 2, etc. Figure 6 is a schematized outline of the part of the theory which is elaborated in this preface. Items of behavior are introduced along the continuum to illustrate how certain empirical data fit into the differentiated substructures. The age-references are approximate.

In this analysis five substructures are developed; these substructures, or empirical selves, may be regarded as stages of refinement in discrimination of stimuli, or as the development of differential reference-schemata. The second reference-schema, the receptor-effector

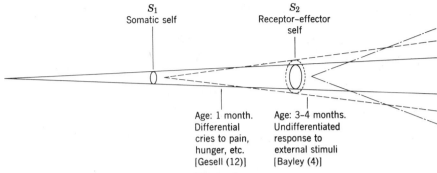

S_1
Somatic self

S_2
Receptor–effector
self

Age: 1 month.
Differential
cries to pain,
hunger, etc.
[Gesell (12)]

Age: 3–4 months.
Undifferentiated
response to
external stimuli
[Bayley (4)]

Figure 1.

self, is an emergent which is formed after some consolidation (fixing of boundaries) has taken place in the first reference-schema. Similarly, the third empirical self appears after the second is consolidated, etc. Overlearning (fixation) at any level may produce reference-schema whose boundaries are so rigid that all incoming stimuli are cognized in terms of those schema so far developed, at the same time inhibiting or delaying the formation of new cognitive structures.[3]

I. At the apex of the cone is the neonate. Because the stimulus field is probably made up exclusively of unorganized somatic sensations (see Fig. 1) any "inferences" or cognitions made by the infant would be unstable and of the most primitive and rudimentary variety. Available data indicate that CR's—which may be regarded as the most rudimentary type of inferential behavior—while possible, are difficult to establish during the first month and are easily extinguished (23). The first perceptual organization of the infant is probably in relation to the modes of restoring homeostatic balance at the physiological level. The *somatic self* becomes organized around responses initiated by stimuli to the somesthetic senses, kinesthesis, proprioception, and the cutaneous senses. Most of the infant's motility, for example, is accounted for by internal stimuli (25). That there is initially no differentiation of self from non-self may be inferred from casual observation of the neonate during the feeding period. What he grasps, for example, is a matter of indifference whether it be a body part or an object in the outside world. Thus the matrix of somesthetic sensations may be regarded as the infant's first reference schema.[4]

II. Tensions arising out of uncorrected homeostatic imbalances become part of the stimulus field of the infant. Receptor processes lead to tension reduction—the paradigm of these processes is the incorporation of nutriment. With the maturation of the organism and with its increased motility, other kinds of stimuli are mediated via the distance and other receptors. Concurrently, tensions introduced into the infant's stimulus field by the accumulation of waste products are reduced by motor activity of the skeletal muscles and sphincters. In the infant's reference-schemata there is probably no distinction between *objects* which are instrumental in tension-reduction and *persons* who are instrumental in tension-reduction. We might infer that to the infant certain perceptions are associated with tension-reduction. At this point, of course, tension-reduction is a mass-action or global affair—probably all the perceptual and motor apparatus is involved in any behavior segment. This substructure is labeled the *receptor-effector self*.[5]

Around this primary matrix, then, the infant at the primitive deductive (CR) level interacts only with the non-self which is instrumental in reducing or eliminating its tensions. This is the *Anlage* of the next-described cognitive structure which begins to differentiate between non-self objects and non-self persons (see Fig. 2).

III. The next level of development is labeled the *primitive construed self* (see Figs. 2 and 3). At the preceding level the cognitive structure is not sufficiently differentiated to perceive differences between *objects* which are instrumental in tension-reduction and *persons* who

----

[3] Only the main outlines of the cognitive structures are sketched. In the larger work to be published later, the several substructures are described more systematically and in greater detail.
[4] The cognitive development of the somatic self

into the more complex "body image" will be described in the fuller treatment of the theory.
[5] The names attached to these cognitive substructures are admittedly awkward. In seminar discussions the substitution of symbols S_1, S_2, S_3, S_4, and S_5 has been helpful.

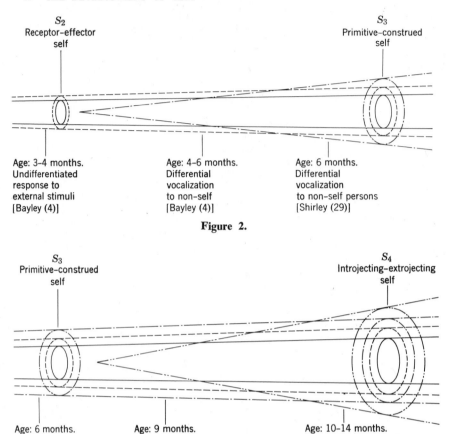

S_2
Receptor-effector
self

S_3
Primitive-construed
self

Age: 3-4 months.
Undifferentiated
response to
external stimuli
[Bayley (4)]

Age: 4-6 months.
Differential
vocalization
to non-self
[Bayley (4)]

Age: 6 months.
Differential
vocalization
to non-self persons
[Shirley (29)]

Figure 2.

S_3
Primitive-construed
self

S_4
Introjecting-extrojecting
self

Age: 6 months.
Differential
vocalization to
non-self persons
[Shirley (29)]

Age: 9 months.
Understands gestures
Waves Bye-Bye
[Buhler (5)]

Age: 10-14 months.
Responds to commands
[Bayley (4)]

Figure 3.

are instrumental in tension-reduction. Now, with increased physiological maturation and with the effects of reinforcement of certain responses selected by others, the cognitive organization differentiates *between objects and persons.* Apparent to the observer at this level is the differential reactivity of the infant. For example, he vocalizes pleasure, eagerness, and displeasure (4, 20). He is active, he attempts to touch, he discriminates tone and expression, he distinguishes persons (4, 20). The important distinction between this level of selfhood and the previous levels is that here the cognitive structure embraces perceptions of persons, who are selective, whimsical, and dynamic. The stimulus properties of persons are ever-changing affairs, as contrasted to the stimulus properties of things. Baldwin's analysis is apposite here.

. . . this is the child's very first step toward a sense of the qualities which distinguish persons. The sense of uncertainty grows stronger and stronger

in its dealings with persons. A person stands for a group of experiences quite unstable in its prophetic as it is in its historical meaning. This we may, . . . in assuming it to be the first in order of development, call the "projective stage" in the growth of the child's consciousness (3, p. 7).

Thus, the child's reference-schemata must now function to select the more perduring stimulus qualities from the more evanescent. Because of physiological maturation and also because of the acquisition and the consolidation of a schema for perceiving many objects, there now emerges a new cognitive substructure, a new reference-schema, a new self. This emergence is facilitated by non-self persons who, unlike objects which serve mainly on the stimulus side, interact with the child in *both* the stimulus and the response aspects. There is still relatively little binding of tension—no appreciable delay between sensory and motor aspects: Perception of stimuli and motor discharge are relatively

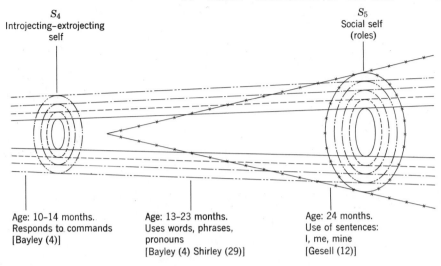

S_4
Introjecting–extrojecting
self

S_5
Social self
(roles)

Age: 10–14 months.
Responds to commands
[Bayley (4)]

Age: 13–23 months.
Uses words, phrases,
pronouns
[Bayley (4) Shirley (29)]

Age: 24 months.
Use of sentences:
I, me, mine
[Gesell (12)]

Figure 4.

continuous processes.[6] Available data indicate that delay, followed by responses indicating memory, is not more than one minute in the 10–11-month-old child (23). At 6–8 months, time-binding is probably much less. Perception is still of the physiognomic kind, literal perception depending upon greater differentiation in cognitive structures (35).

At this level, then, we can infer that the child has three main substructures or reference-schemata: the somatic self, the receptor-effector self, and the primitive construed self. These are all empirical—all derived from interaction with things, people, and perhaps simple signs. With these cognitive structures, the infant interacts with non-self objects and non-self persons both of which are instrumental in reducing tensions.[7]

---

[6] These tensions of course stimulate the mother or nurse to aid in tension-reduction. The cries, restlessness, etc., exhibited by the baby are treated as a signal by the adult. Since the ministrations of the adults which follow the child's "signals" have some regularity and organization, the infant might formulate—in a primitive way—a deductive inference which has a magical denotation such as the "superstitions" developed by Skinner's pigeons (30). This parallel between the "superstitions" of these pigeons and the magical thinking of adult persons whose self-structures are dominated by this empirical self is utilized in the illustrative hypothesis below.

[7] T. M. Newcomb (personal communication) suggests calling these three aspects of selfhood "pre-self" differentiations, reserving the term "self" for those later differentiations which depend on the more refined use of symbols. While this emendation would be more continuous with the traditional sociological usage of the term, it might be inter-

IV. Cognition becomes more varied, rich, and complex with the growth of non-verbal and verbal language structures. At the next level of the self, the substructures so far described are central to a new emergent—the *introjecting-extrojecting* self (see Figs. 3 and 4). The distinguishing feature here is the use of crude language devices in isolating, differentiating, and strengthening the cognitive structure *which the child communicates to others.* At the same time, development of motor skills, increased motility, postural changes, etc., increase the number and range of potential non-self objects and persons that can be responded to and integrated into the currently-forming cognitive structure. In addition, the child can now differentiate words, imitate words, cooperate in play, etc. (4, 20).

In the interbehavioral field are different persons whose responses to the child are variable. It is probably at this level that Baldwin's "dialectic of personal growth" (3) has its greatest applicability. The reactions to the multiple and shifting stimulus properties (acts) of others are introjected or assimilated (or they become "subjective" according to Baldwin) if congruent with the reference-schemata so far developed. Extrojection (Baldwin's "ejective consciousness") probably emerges simultaneously. The child's own responses to the

preted as signifying a discontinuous process. It should be emphasized that although the earlier cognitive structures are rooted in the more somatic aspects of behavior and are derived from interaction with signs, they serve as the *Anlage* for the later cognitive structures which involve interaction with symbols.

differential acts of other persons are organized into this substructure. By a primitive analogical process which develops with the increase in language structures the acts of others are perceived as the same as the child's own acts.[8]

Introjecting and extrojecting responses become more differentiated as a result [1] of increased locomotor and manipulative skills and [2] of the selection and reinforcement of certain types of responses by others. The most important developmental feature at this stage is the refinement in the use of the gesture (22). First, motoric gestures, "whole-body language" (19), and, later, vocal gestures become the instruments by which the child organizes this new reference-schema. The importance of language in concept formation needs no comment here. With language symbols, the acts of others can more readily be conceptualized as similar to one's own acts (projection) or one's acts can more readily be conceptualized as similar to the acts of others (identification).

The child has not learned to say I, although he does use his own name as others use it; he employs other gestural equivalents which are imitations of others' behavior in referring to him (12). Here we have the *Anlage* of the social self.

V. With the development of the first person personal pronoun, I, the child attains a more refined concept than formerly, at the same time acquiring a conventional symbol for self-reference (see Fig. 4). With I, mine, and me, he can categorize perceptions in a more sharply differentiated way than before. The *social self* thus emerges—a new cognitive substructure. The child has a reference-schema with which he can organize perceptions and cognitions of the organized behaviors of other persons. Now he can differentiate not only *discrete acts* of persons, but *organized acts* or *roles*.

The conventional role of mother and the conventional role of father, e.g., are easily differentiated. Differential roles are perceived and integrated into the cognitive structure. Roles are seen as differentiations of this subtructure because different roles in others call out different responses in the child.

Because perception of a stimulus and enactment (*motor discharge*) are so closely tied together in the development of the self up to

this point, *acting* the role of the other implies the concurrent or just prior *perception* of the role of the other. Later, *delay* is introduced between role-perception and role-enactment.[9] Acting the role of the other often means attaching adult values to perceptions of others and indirectly to perceptions of self. The further development of the self-structure into the "generalized-other" (22) could be represented by the emergence of another substructure. Because of the limitations imposed by the prefatory nature of this essay, a discussion of further development of the self will be deferred.

Like other models, this one has its deficiencies. Figure 5 shows the somatic self as the core of the self-structure with the other selves concentric to it. While the somatic self may be the central feature of the self-structure in early childhood, it probably becomes subordinated to other aspects of selfhood in later life. Therefore, a transformation is necessary. The various selves are best regarded as semi-independent substructures which later become overlaid with substructures of the social self—the roles (see Fig. 5).

This is not the terminus of the epistemogenic theory. In this essay we are content to point out the directions that must be taken. A more extended treatment of the theory will be made available later. In fact, the model represents only the beginning of the self-organization which becomes tremendously hypertrophied and complicated by further differentiations in the cognitive structure due to the role-taking process. Additional reference-schema are formed as a result of the interaction of the self with others. From this point on the epistemogenic theory is carried forward with the aid of role-taking concepts (22, 26, 27, 28). In a word, roles which are perceived as congruent with one's current self-organization are capable of enactment; roles which are incongruent with the structure of the self are distorted in enactment or delayed or rejected.

Subject or Object?

Current discussions of the self often distinguish between the knower and the known or between the subjective and objective aspects of the ego or self. William James (15) and Mead (22) both treated these as the "I" and the "me." This distinction is usually equated with private and public aspects of selfhood.

---

[8] Weiss has written a technical but readable description of these processes from the psychoanalytic viewpoint. Compare his concepts of introjection, extrojection and objectification with this portion of our analysis (34).

[9] A second paper will deal with this aspect of the self with special reference to motivational analysis.

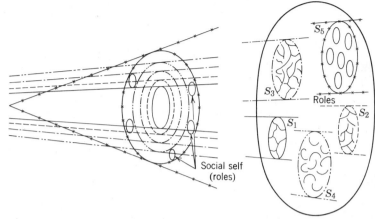

Figure 5. At this level the social self is normally the dominant self-structure. Roles are seen as differentiations of the social self. The drawing on the right illustrates increased differentiation and also the manner in which various substructures may be conceived. The somatic self is not necessarily central.

That this distinction is not valid is seen from this example: A person's fantasies, while private, and supposedly subjective, may be treated as an object. The person, by virtue of his cognitive organization, may identify and evaluate his fantasy reactions in the same way that he identifies and evaluates external objects. Therefore, to consider the self as made up of subjective and objective aspects is an oversimplification. A dualistic set of postulates is implied in such a formula. Most contemporary discussions, notably Symonds (32), are able to give a clear and straightforward presentation of the development of the self as object, but the self as subject, as knower, doer, thinker, etc., is considered a given or is not considered at all.

In the epistemogenic theory the I and the me are both handled in terms of a consistent set of postulates without having recourse to the old dualistic tradition. The self as I is seen as an *inference,* a high-order inference or cognitive structure, which develops as a result of and consists of lower-order inferences (or reference-schemata) which are here called empirical selves. To support the notion of its being a higher-order inference, that is to say, one which develops out of the matrix of lower-order inferences, we have only to mention again the studies of language development in children. The consistent use of the concept "I" occurs relatively late—about two years (12).

This theory takes its point of departure from James (15) and Pillsbury (24). Both of these writers saw the problem in terms of empirical selves as the "objects of awareness," and the I

or pure ego as "interpretations" (Pillsbury) or "Thought" (James). In terms of the present theory, when a person uses the term "I" the referent is a cognitive structure, an inference, the internal organization of which is characterized by substructures with varying properties of strength and breadth.

Thus, a patient with strong internal pressures for constant massage (somesthetic stimulation) might have a concept of self in which the earliest empirical self is the most developed substructure—the somatic self. His use of the pronoun "I" then is referable to a cognitive structure (a cross-section in the immediate present of the entire interbehavioral field) in which the somatic self is dominant. Similarly, when another person says, "I am always craving food," the I may have as its referent a conceptual organization in which the empirically-derived substructure known as the receptor-effector self is in focus. Or, when a person says "I can't understand why people are always losing patience with me," we might suggest that the referent for the I is a cognitive structure where the primitive construed self is in focus and where perception of tension release through the instrumentality of others is immediate. The neurotic patient who anxiously says: "I can't seem to do the right things to make friends," has as the referent for the I an inference whose structural organization places the empirically-derived introjecting-extrojecting self in the focus. Or finally, when a college student says: "When I stand up in front of a class, I imagine myself as a leader or a great teacher and I behave accordingly," the referent for the

I is the substructure designated as the social self which differentiates roles. The basis for these variants in cognitive organization is to be discovered in the conditions in early childhood which lead the formation of over-developed boundaries of particular empirical selves.

This set of suggestions is illustrative of the general proposition that the properties of the substructures are determined by the total interbehavior field. And the total interbehavioral field includes not only perceptions referable to objects in the external world but also perceptions referrable to the self.

AN HYPOTHESIS ARISING FROM THE THEORY

Here is one hypothesis that can be formulated from the foregoing paragraphs. When studied in terms of reference to the self, the inmates of a school for delinquent boys will fall into two classes: (1) those whose cognitive organizations are dominated by the primitive construed self (S_3), and (2) those whose cognitive organizations are dominated by the introjecting-extrojecting self (S_4). In both groups the social self (S_5), as a cognitive substructure, is absent or poorly developed, probably as the result of overlearning at earlier stages due to personal-social factors. Members of Group I respond to imbalance in the interbehavioral field at the level of the primitive construed self: immediate motor discharge (acting out) upon perception of a stimulus object or event. In Group 2 the cognitive structures of the members are dominated by the *Anlage* of the social self—the introjecting-extrojecting self—where there is some time-binding and tension-binding. At this level of self-organization, discrete acts of others are introjected, such as "Mama says no, no" or extrojected. The delinquent act committed by a member of Group 2 is usually incongruent with the child's inferences about self which are at the level where *acts* are differentiated in terms of approval-disapproval. A kind of rudimentary conscience is apparent.

The delinquent acts performed by Group 1 are consistent with the level of the inferred self whose main substructure is the primitive construed self. Members of Group 2 are able to evaluate acts in terms of parental approval-disapproval because of the strength of the introjecting-extrojecting self, and cannot easily take the role of the delinquent. From these sentences we can state a high probability that members of Group 1 have a poor prognosis

and will turn out to be recidivists, while members of Group 2 have a better prognosis and will become acceptable citizens. That is to say, they may develop a social self—which means skill in taking the role of the other, time-binding, etc. It is predicted that members of a third group, non-delinquents, will be characterized by inferences about self at the level of the social self. These boys do not take the role of the delinquent, nor do they commit serious delinquent acts, as do members of Groups 1 and 2, respectively. How can we test this in terms of the theory of self-organization? We begin with the question: what is the referent for the term "I"? We set up subtle tests designed to get at descriptions of the self in terms of time-binding characteristics, reliance on magic, failure to take the role of the other, physiognomic and literal perception, and other characteristics which are derived from the epistemogenic theory. My colleague, Harrison G. Gough, has advanced a similar theory (13) and has developed a scale of 50 self-reference items which are answered by the subject. On the basis of these and other descriptions of self, a behavior analyst can infer which substructures of the self are dominant and from these inferences he can formulate predictions of behavior.

Recapitulation

In this essay I take the position that a more careful and sophisticated analysis of the concept of the self (or ego) will help reduce the confusion in personality theory and clinical practice. The description of the self in terms of cognitive structures takes advantage of the most advanced conceptual schemata currently available (18). Because it leans so heavily on cognition, I have labeled the theory "epistemogenesis."

Through interaction with stimuli at different times in the maturational and personal series, various empirical selves or cognitive substructures are organized. These subtructures may have different properties of strength and breadth, thus accounting for some aspects of differential conduct. The referent for the "I" or Pure Ego is the cross-section in the present of the total cognitive organization that embraces those more-or-less enduring substructures, the empirical selves.

That the theory is not footless is demonstrated by informally deriving an illustrative

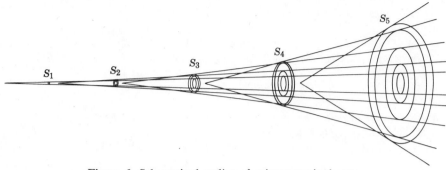

Figure 6. Schematized outline of epistemogenic theory.

hypothesis. The predictions from the hypothesis are testable by means of a set of experiments designed to estimate the "I's" or current self-organization of at least three classes of persons.

REFERENCES

1. Allport, G. *Personality, a psychological interpretation*. New York: Holt, 1937.
2. ———. The ego in contemporary psychology. *Psychol. Rev.,* 1943. **50**, 451–479.
3. Baldwin, J. M. *Social and ethical interpretations in mental development* (3rd ed.). New York: Macmillan, 1902.
4. Bayley, Nancy. Mental growth during the first three years. *Genet. Psychol. Monogr.,* 1933, **14**, No. 1.
5. Buhler, Charlotte. *The first year of life*. New York: Day, 1930.
6. Calkins, Mary W. The self in scientific psychology. *Amer. J. Psychol.,* 1915, **26**, 495–524.
7. Chein, I. The awareness of the self and the structure of the ego. *Psychol. Rev.,* 1944, **51**, 304–314.
8. Claparède, E. Note sur la localization du moi. *Arch. de Psychol.,* 1924, **19**, 172–182.
9. Cooley. C. H. *Human nature and the social order*. New York: Scribner, 1902.
10. Frenkel-Brunswick, Else. Intolerance of ambiguity as an emotional and perceptual personality variable. *J. Personality,* 1949, **18**, 108–143.
11. Freud, S. *A general introduction to psychoanalysis*. New York: Boni and Liveright, 1920.
12. Gesell, A. *The mental growth of the pre-school child: a psychological outline of normal development from birth to the sixth year, including a system of developmental diagnosis*. New York: Macmillan, 1925.
13. Gough, H. G. A sociological theory of psychopathy. *Amer. J. Sociol.,* 1948, **53**, 359–366.
14. Hall, G. S. Some aspects of the early sense of self. *Amer. J. Psychol.,* 1898, **9**, 351–395.
15. James, W. *Psychology, briefer course*. New York: Holt, 1915.
16. Jersild, A. T. *Child psychology*. New York: Prentice-Hall, 1940.
17. Jung, C. G. *Two essays on analytical psychology*. New York: Dodd, Mead, 1928.
18. Krech, D., and Crutchfield, R. *Theory and problems of social psychology*. New York: McGraw-Hill, 1948.

19. Latif, I. The physiological basis of linguistic developmental and of the ontogeny of meaning. Part I and II, *Psychol. Rev.*, 1934, **41**, 55–85, 153–176.

20. McCarthy, Dorothea. Language development in children. In *Manual of child psychology* (L. Carmichael, Ed.). New York: Wiley, 1946.

21. McDougall, W. *An introduction to social psychology*. Boston: Luce, 1921.

22. Mead, G. H. *Mind, self, and society*. Chicago: Univ. of Chicago Press, 1934.

23. Munn, N. Learning in children. In *Manual of child psychology* (L. Carmichael, Ed.). New York: Wiley, 1946.

24. Pillsbury, W. B. The ego and empirical psychology. *Phil. Rev.*, 1907, **16**, 387–407.

25. Pratt, K. C. The neonate. In *Manual of child psychology* (L. Carmichael, Ed.). New York: Wiley, 1946.

26. Sarbin, T. R. Contributions to role-taking theory. I: Hypnotic behavior. *Psychol. Rev.*, 1950, **57**, 255–271.

27. ———. The concept of role-taking. *Sociometry*, 1943, **6**, 273–285.

28. ———, and Farberow, N. L. Contributions to role-taking theory. II: A clinical study of self and role. (In press.)

29. Shirley, M. M. *The first two years: a study of 25 babies, Vol. II, Intellectual development*. Minneapolis: Univ. of Minnesota Press, 1933.

30. Skinner, B. F. "Superstition" in the pigeon. *J. exp. Psychol.*, 1948, **38**, 168–172.

31. Stern, W. *Psychology of early childhood*. New York: Holt, 1924.

32. Symonds, P. M. *Dynamic psychology*. New York: Appleton-Century-Crofts, 1949.

33. Titchener, E. B. *An outline of psychology*. New York: Macmillan, 1896.

34. Weiss, E. Projection, extrojection, and objectification. *Psychoanal. Quart.*, 1947, **16**, 357–377.

35. Werner, H. *Comparative psychology of mental development* (rev. ed.). Chicago: Follett, 1948.

Chapter 17 The Development of Self-Control

ALBERT BANDURA AND RICHARD H. WALTERS

The process of acquiring self-control has usually been described as one in which parental standards are incorporated, introjected, or internalized, a "superegro" is formed, or some inner moral agent that is a facsimile of the parents is developed to hold in check impulses that are "ego-alien." These descriptions are replete with terms that have considerable surplus meaning and that frequently personify the controlling forces. The superfluous character of the constructs becomes evident when one examines laboratory studies in which animals are trained not to exhibit behavior that the experimenter has arbitrarily selected as deviant. For example, Whiting and Mowrer (1943), using a socialization paradigm, taught rats, as a result of punishment, to take a circuitous route to a food reward instead of a considerably shorter and more direct one; the rats maintained this behavior for some time after punishments were withdrawn. The substitution of less direct, more effortful, and more complicated ways of obtaining reward exhibited by the animals parallels changes in children's behavior that result from social training and are ordinarily regarded as indices of the development of self- or impulse-control. However, no one would say that the rats in the Whiting and Mowrer study had internalized the superego of the experimenters or had introjected their standards.

Numerous attempts have been made to identify differences among fear, guilt, and shame as determinants of social control and even to characterize cultures in terms of the modal inhibitory forces that maintain social conformity (Benedict, 1946; Mead, 1950; Piers and Singer, 1953; Whiting, 1959). Two criteria have been advanced for distinguishing guilt from shame. The first of these assumes a dichotomy between

SOURCE. Albert Bandura and Richard H. Walters, *Social Learning and Personality Development,* New York: Holt, Rinehart and Winston, 1963, pp. 162–165, 172–174, 175–176, 177–183, and 188–191. Copyright © 1963 by Holt, Rinehart and Winston, Inc. All rights reserved.

external and internal sanctions and regards shame as a reaction to actual or anticipated disapproval by an audience and guilt as a negative self-evaluation resulting from a deviation from an internalized moral standard. Somewhat similar bases for distinction are Riesman's (1950) contrast between inner-directed and outer-directed persons and the public-private dimension of Levin and Baldwin (1959).

It is reasonable to believe that both external and internal sanctions are instrumental in maintaining social control in almost every society and individual (Ausubel, 1955). Indeed, the requirement that in case of guilt the intrapsychic self-evaluative response should occur without reference to any actual or fantasied reactions of external agents is probably very rarely, if ever, met. This requirement presupposes that guilt is mediated by an internal moral agent, which originated and developed from sanctions imposed by the parents or other primary socializing agents, but which is now completely independent of an individual's current social experiences. To the extent that a person selects a reference group whose members have standards that are similar to his own, his self-evaluations undoubtedly involve an assessment of how these members would react to his behavior. The size of the group by reference to which a particular person evaluates his behavior may vary considerably; when a person's immediate reference group is small and select and does not share the values of the majority of persons of his social class, it may sometimes appear that he is making an independent self-evaluation and displaying "inner-directed" behavior, whereas he may be, in fact, highly dependent on the actual or fantasied approval or disapproval of a few individuals whose judgments he values highly.

A second criterion that has been proposed as a basis for distinguishing guilt and shame assumes that these are a function of degree of responsibility or voluntariness, which may be thought of in terms of a dichotomy between a transgression and a defect (Levin and Baldwin,

1959) or between a motive and an attribute (Piers and Singer, 1953). From this point of view, a person has little or no responsibility for a personal limitation and consequently can feel no guilt, but only shame, on account of his defect. It is true that persons may attempt to conceal intellectual and physical shortcomings in order to avoid negative reactions from others, but these do not necessarily involve a negative self-evaluation that could be described either as guilt or as shame. Let us imagine that a keen swimmer, as a result of an accident, acquires an unsightly scar that invokes reactions, such as staring, from others. He may forego swimming, thereby avoiding displaying his defect in public, but his giving up swimming would in this case be a means of avoiding aversive stimulation and not necessarily a shame, or a self-punitive guilt, reaction. This example highlights the difficulty of distinguishing between shame and fear of aversive responses from others. Of course, the former swimmer could negatively evaluate himself for concealing the defect, or attribute to himself responsibility for the injury.

It is evident that sharp distinctions such as those considered above give rise to semantic difficulties and do little to further the understanding of the acquisition and maintenance of self-control responses, which are undoubtedly a function both of fear of anticipated aversive reactions from others and of self-generated aversive stimulation. On the other hand, it is profitable to attempt to identify social influences that generate or intensify fear of others' disapproval or self-punitive responses for transgressions, and defects and factors that affect the size and nature of the groups that persons permit to influence their behavior.

* * *

ACQUISITION OF SELF-CONTROL THROUGH MODELING

Social-learning principles dealing with imitation and direct reinforcement can aid in the undertaking of all aspects of self-control, including the development of self-rewarding and self-punitive responses. The influence of modeling is most clearly apparent in those societies in which the majority of adults consistently display self-denying or self-indulgent behavior. In societies in which denial or indulgence is a cultural norm, the children have little opportunity to observe any other patterns of behavior and consequently are forced to model themselves after the prevalent self-control patterns. As research on the Hutterites (Eaton and Weil, 1955) show, patterns of self-denial may persist for many generations.

The transmission of self-indulgent patterns may be associated with a low level of technology and a precarious economic and social life, which persist in spite of contact with more provident social groups. Among the Siriono of Bolivia, for example, there are relatively few restrictions on the expression of sex and aggression, and there is no obligation for the younger and healthier members to care for the old and infirm, who are abandoned to die when the social group moves on to a new location, Holmberg (1950) attributes the "Siriono personality" to a chronic shortage of food; however, his description of Siriono life indicates that this shortage is largely due to lack of self-denial among the members of the society. On returning from a successful expedition, the Siriono hunter may enter his village empty-handed and signal to his wife to retrieve the game that he has surreptitiously set aside before his entry. He and his family then gorge themselves on the spoils, leaving nothing for a time of shortage. So extreme is this immediate self-indulgence that Siriono females characteristically have distended stomachs, which are, according to Holmberg, attributable to sporadic overeating.

Leighton and his associates (Hughes, Tremblay, Rapoport, and Leighton, 1960) present an account of life in a Nova Scotian county, in which both self-indulgent and self-denial subcultural patterns have co-existed for a number of generations. In "Lavallée," an Acadian community, children are strictly trained in the control of sexual, aggressive, and dependency behavior and are strongly pressured to achieve educational and vocational success. *"Evidently some of these demands are contagious, for the mothers say that their children demand teaching even before entering school"* (p. 133; italics not in original). Both parents spend a considerable amount of time in interacting with their children and thus in transmitting to them the adult patterns which predominate in this cohesive community. While the people of Lavallée emphasize material success, the wealthier members of the community are not expected to be self-indulgent; "the greater economic success a person has, the more he is expected to share it with his family, his church, and his community" (p. 157).

* * *

Further evidence for the influence of parent models in the development of children's habits of self-control comes from Mischel's investigations into self-imposed delay of reinforcement. Anthropological data indicate that adult Trinidadian Negroes are more impulsive and self-indulgent, and less likely to provide for the future, than Grenadian Negroes or Trinidadian Indians. Mischel (1958; 1961c) examined preferences for larger, delayed rewards, as opposed to smaller, immediate rewards, among children of families belonging to each of these three subcultural groups. Children from the highly self-indulgent Trinidadian Negro subculture showed the greatest degree of preference for immediate rewards. Moreover, children who came from homes in which the father was absent were likely to choose smaller, immediate rewards rather than to postpone gratification in order to obtain a larger reward. Assuming that a father's abandonment of his home reflects the family's lack of participation in a delayed-reward culture (Mischel, 1958), this latter finding may be regarded as providing further evidence of the influence of parent models on the self-control of children.

The influence of models in modifying resistance to deviation has been demonstrated in experimental studies having relevance to the problem of deviation. S. Ross (1962) employed a toy-store situation in which nursery-school children alternated in the roles of customer and storekeeper. For children in a deviant-model condition, a peer model, who served as the experimenter's confederate, informed the children that upon completing the game they could select a *single* toy only. The model then proceeded to help himself to three toys. In the conforming-model condition, the model took only one toy and thus exhibited behavior that was consistent with his verbal prohibition. Children in the control group simply received the verbal prohibition. In each condition the peer model left the room while the children made their selections. Relative to the subjects in the conforming-model and the control groups, children who observed the deviant model violated the prohibition more often and exhibited more conflictful behavior as reflected in moralistic comments, self-reassurances about the deviation, self-directed hostility, and concealment while performing the misdeed. Some evidence that a conforming model reinforces the observer's self-controlling tendencies, and thereby reduces conflict in temptation situations, is pro-

vided by the finding that control children displayed significantly more conflictful behavior than those who witnessed the conforming model, although both groups were equally conforming.

* * *

Observation of aggressive models may serve not only to reduce inhibitions but also to teach the observers new ways to deviate. Bandura, Ross, and Ross (1963b) demonstrated that children who observed a model who was rewarded for aggression exhibited imitative aggressive responses that had not previously appeared in their repertory. Moreover, an analysis of aggressive responses which were not precisely imitative revealed that boys and girls were differentially influenced by the behavior of the models and its response consequences. Boys were inclined to inhibit aggression when they either observed an aggressive model punished or had no exposure to displays of aggression, whereas observation of both highly expressive but nonaggressive models and rewarded aggressive models greatly enhanced the boys' aggressive behavior. By contrast, exposure to nonaggressive models had the greatest inhibitory effect on the girls' expression of aggression. These findings suggest that control over aggression can be vicariously transmitted through the influence of models either by the administration of punishment to the model or by the presentation of incompatible prosocial examples of behavior.

The differential effects of prosocial and deviant models on the control of aggression by boys and girls may be partly explained by the relative dominance of aggressive responses in the subjects' repertories. Thus, for boys, in whom physically aggressive responses are relatively strongly established, exposure to a punished model effectively inhibited aggressive behavior, whereas their observation of highly expressive nonaggressive or rewarded aggressive models produced substantial disinhibitory effects. Presumably, a general increase in the boys' activity following exposure to an expressive model resulted in the manifestation of their relatively dominant habits of aggression. On the other hand, girls, who generally exhibit little physical aggression, showed little increase in nonspecifically imitative aggression following exposure to the aggressive models, while exposure to nonaggressive models produced decrements in the girls' aggressive responses.

It is generally assumed that resistance to deviation results from the association of noxious stimuli with the commission of prohibited responses during the life history of an individual. However, as modeling studies demonstrate, children may acquire inhibitions without committing a prohibited act and without themselves receiving any punishment. There is thus considerable evidence that response inhibition and response disinhibition can be vicariously transmitted, particularly if the immediate consequences to the model are apparent or the model is a person who has evidently been competent or successful in life.

The influence of models in transmitting patterns of self-rewards and self-punishments has received attention in only one experimental study (Bandura and Kupers, 1963). Children participated in a bowling game with an adult or a peer model, the scores, which could range from 5 to 30, being controlled by the experimenter. At the ouset of the game, the children and their models were given access to a plentiful supply of candy, from which they could help themselves as they wished. Under one experimental condition the model set a high standard for self-reinforcement; on trials in which the model obtained or exceeded a score of 20, he rewarded himself with candy and made self-approving statements, while on trials in which he failed to meet the adopted standard he took no candy and berated himself. In the other experimental condition, the model exhibited a similar pattern of self-reward and self-disapproval, except that he adopted the standard of 10, a relatively low level of performance. After exposure to their respective models, the children played a series of games on the bowling apparatus in the absence of the models. During these trials the children received a wide range of scores, and the performances for which they rewarded themselves with candy and self-approval were recorded.

It was found that the children's patterns of self-reinforcement closely matched those of the model to which they had been exposed; moreover, they tended to reproduce the self-approval and self-critical comments of their model. Thus, although both groups had access to a plentiful supply of desired material reinforcers, the children who had adopted a high criterion for self-reinforcement through imitation utilized these resources sparingly and only when they achieved relatively high levels of performance, while children who were exposed to the low-standard model rewarded themselves generously even for minimal performance.

A comparison of the results obtained with adult and peer models revealed that children were more influenced by the standard-setting behavior and self-reinforcement patterns exhibited by adults. A control group of children, who had no exposure to models, set no standards for themselves, and tended to reward themselves for minimal performance. . . . This experiment demonstrates the influence of vicarious reinforcement, in the form of rewards and punishments *self-administered* by the model, on the process of imitative learning; it thus indicates clearly one manner in which self-control may be acquired through observational learning.

Demonstrations that inhibitions and self-evaluative responses may be learned without the mediation of direct reinforcement are consistent with common-sense thinking. Socialization agents, for example, parents and teachers, frequently make use of exemplary models and from time to time reward or punish children in front of others in the expectation that the positive or negative reinforcement will influence the future behavior of the observers. Indeed, the administration of well-publicized rewards and penalties is a frequently employed social-influence procedure, whereby those who occupy power positions in society attempt to modify the behavior of many by rewarding and penalizing the behavior of individuals who are already socially visible or who become so as a result of the publicity.

ACQUISITION OF SELF-CONTROL THROUGH DIRECT REINFORCEMENT

The literature on achievement behavior indicates that parental reinforcement patterns play an important part in determining the extent to which children will make efforts, often involving a good deal of self-denial, in order to attain standards which they have learned to accept for themselves. Rosen and D'Andrade (1959) investigated the manner in which mothers of boys who displayed a great deal of self-reliance and effort responded to their sons' attempts to master a number of tasks. In comparison to mothers of boys who showed less achievement-oriented behavior, the former group of mothers set higher performance standards for their sons, more readily gave approval when their sons' performance was good, and were more critical when the boys' performance failed to reach the desired standards. The effect of positive reinforcement of achievement behavior is also apparent in a study by Crandall, Preston, and Rabson (1960), who found that mothers who spontaneously rewarded and praised their children's efforts to achieve had children who displayed strong and frequent achievement efforts outside the home.

A study by Winterbottom (1953) provides further evidence of the effect of parental training on children's achievement behavior and at the same time suggests a relationship between the development of self-reliance and the attainment of self-control. Winterbottom reported that mothers who trained their children to exhibit little task-oriented dependency, while rewarding person-oriented dependency, had sons who gave a relatively high number of achievement-oriented responses to thematic test stimuli. Winterbottom's findings probably reflect the fact that socially acceptable achievement behavior requires consideration for others, perhaps an outcome of parental fostering of person-oriented dependency and thus of affiliative behavior, as well as regulative self-direction in the pursuit of long-term goals.

In a number of investigations, the severity of parents' socialization pressures has been related to the extent to which children demonstrate self-control in temptation or achievement situations. The findings, though far from consistent, in general suggest that children who experience relatively early or severe socialization pressures tend to exhibit greater self-control than children who are more leniently trained (W. Allinsmith, 1960; Burton, Maccoby, and Allinsmith, 1961; Cox, 1962; Heineke, 1953; Whiting and Child, 1953). Assuming that severity-of-socialization measures largely reflect the extent to which parents dispense rewards for conformity with parental standards and punish noncompliance, these results provide indirect evidence that patterns of parental reinforcement are important determinants of the habit strength of the self-control responses of children.

Laboratory studies of reward of aggressive responses provide the only experimental demonstrations of the effects of direct positive reinforcement on the occurrence of socially disapproved responses. Similarly, the role of punishment in the development of response inhibition, although sometimes over-emphasized in theoretical expositions, has rarely been explored in experimental studies of human behavior in social situations. The available evidence suggests that punishment may have very diverse effects, depending on its timing, intensity, and nature, and on the status of the punitive agent.

* * *

REINFORCEMENT PATTERNS AND DISCIPLINARY TECHNIQUES

The influence of reinforcement patterns on the development and maintenance of self-controlling responses has been indirectly investigated, within the context of disciplinary methods, in a number of field studies. Considerable attention has, in fact, been paid to the differential effects on children's behavior of disciplinary practices such as physical punishment, verbal attack or criticism, deprivation of privileges, threat of loss of love, isolation, or reasoning. These practices have been sometimes classified under two main headings, psychological and material discipline, on the assumption that self-control is more readily achieved if psychological disciplinary methods predominate. Generally speaking, physical punishment has been considered the prototype of material or nonlove-oriented discipline, and reasoning and threat of loss of love as prototypes of the psychological or love-oriented type. However, there is far from perfect agreement among child psychologists concerning the categorization of other types of disciplinary practices (Bandura and Walters, 1959; Heineke, 1953; Miller and Swanson, 1960; Sears, Maccoby and Levin, 1957). One reason for disagreement may be that each type of discipline can involve several components and that the accompanying reactions of the disciplinary agent may be crucial in determining the kinds of effect that the discipline has on the child.

Any disciplinary act may involve in varying degrees at least two operations, the presentation of a negative reinforcer and the withdrawal or withholding of positive reinforcement. For example, threats of loss of love in which the parents depict disastrous consequences to their health resulting from the child's behavior predominantly consist in the presentation of fear-arousing noxious stimuli, whereas threats of loss of love in which the restoration of parental affection and approval is made contingent on the child's conformity to parental wishes involves the withholding of positive reinforcement but little aversiveness. Similarly, a parent who inflicts little pain while impersonally administering mild physical punishment to a child obtains his effects primarily through the withholding of positive reinforcers, whereas a parent who administers very severe physical punishment while assuring the child of his love is dispensing positive reinforcers at the same time as he administers noxious stimuli. Moreover, some parents exhibit pain and self-critical reactions while physically punishing their children, and subsequently apologize to the child or otherwise attempt to make restitution; in such cases, the primary effect may be to model guilt reactions concerning aggression.

Parental modeling of pain and other emotional reactions during the course of disciplinary interventions may in other ways contribute to the development of self-control and so have effects that have been generally attributed to psychological disciplinary practices. The manner in which vicariously acquired emotions may motivate avoidance responses was illustrated in an experiment by Miller, Banks, and Ogawa (1962). Rhesus monkeys were trained to avoid a shock by pressing a bar whenever a stimulus light appeared. The animals were then seated face to face, with the stimulus panel attached to one monkey's chair and the bar to the chair in which the second monkey was seated. The apparatus was wired in such a way that shocks would be simultaneously received by each of the monkeys.

The task confronting the animals is obvious. The monkey with the light had no means of performing the instrumental response which could avoid the noxious shock stimulus. The second monkey could perform the response but had no stimulus to inform him when a response was appropriate. However, if the animal with the stimulus was able to communicate to his partner by means of expressive cues the information that the conditioned stimulus (CS) was being presented, the second monkey could then make the appropriate instrumental response which would enable both animals to avoid shock (p. 344).

From our point of view, the most interesting data were obtained from the testing of a pair of monkeys over a twenty-two day period, during which the monkey to whom the stimulus light was presented failed to receive shocks on account of an apparatus defect. Nevertheless, during this period the monkey with the bar learned to avoid shock by attending to the emotional responses of the monkey with the stimulus light. The monkey with the light observed the startle and leg-withdrawal responses of his partner whenever the latter received a shock and reproduced them so precisely that the experimenters failed to detect the fault in their

equipment. After eight days of testing, the monkey with the light was behaving emotionally before the shock was delivered, *even though he himself received no shock,* and thus was emitting responses that served as a signal for the other monkey to make an avoidance response. In a similar manner, parents may exhibit anticipatory pain reactions to their children's deviant behavior before their disciplinary actions are carried out. If, at this stage, the child learns to react to his parents' emotional responses by ceasing disapproved activities or complying with parental demands, psychological control of the child's behavior has been largely achieved, no matter what form of discipline the parents originally preferred. Moreover, children often rely on the magnitude of parental emotional arousal to provide the main discriminative cues that compliance is expected and that noncompliant behavior is likely to be punished. In this way, children's behavior comes under the control of emotional-intensity cues that their parents, usually unwittingly, provide.

Experimental studies with children suggest that the immediate effects of presenting a noxious stimulus and of withdrawing or withholding a positive reinforcer may be diametrically opposite. Verbal criticism has been shown to lead to a decrease in both aggressive and dependency behavior in the presence of the disciplinary agent (Hollenberg and Sperry, 1951; Nelsen, 1960) and withholding of rewards to an increase in the strength of instrumental responses (Beller and Haeberle, 1961a, 1961b; Haner and Brown, 1955; Holton, 1961; Olds, 1956). Therefore, the prediction of what effect a particular type of discipline will have is dependent on knowing which operation has predominated. In general, such methods of discipline as threats of withdrawal of love and isolation—usually regarded as examples of psychological discipline—seem to involve predominantly the withholding of positive reinforcers, whereas physical and verbal punishments consist primarily in the presentation of negative reinforcers. Consequently, it is not surprising that some investigators (B. B. Allinsmith, 1960; Burton, Maccoby, and Allinsmith, 1961; Heineke, 1953; MacKinnon, 1938; Unger, 1962) have found that psychological and nonpsychological methods of discipline have differential effects; however, the lack of consistency of results concerning the outcome of these types of discipline and the generally low correlations between parental use of psychological disciplinary methods and the extent to which children show self-control (W. Allinsmith, 1960; Grinder, 1962; Sears, Maccoby, and Levin, 1957) suggest that attention might be more profitably focused on such variables as intensity and timing of presentation of noxious stimuli and completeness and timing of withdrawal of positive reinforcers.

REFERENCES

Allinsmith, Beverly B. Expressive styles: II. Directness with which anger is expressed. In D. R. Miller and G. E. Swanson (Eds.). *Inner conflict and defense.* New York: Holt, 1960, pp. 315–336.

Allinsmith, W. The learning of moral standards. In D. R. Miller and G. E. Swanson (Eds.). *Inner conflict and defense.* New York: Holt, 1960, pp. 141–176.

Ausubel, D. P. Relationships between shame and guilt in the socializing process. *Psychol. Rev.,* 1955, **62**, 378–390.

Bandura, A., and Kupers, Carol J. The transmission of patterns of self-reinforcement through modeling. *J. abnorm. soc. Psychol.,* in press.

Bandura, A., Ross, Dorothea, and Ross, Shiela A. Vicarious reinforcement and imitation. *J. abnorm. soc. Psychol.,* 1963, in press (b).

Bandura, A., Ross, Dorothea, and Ross, Shiela A. A comparative test of the status envy, social power, and the secondary-reinforcement theories of identificatory learning. *J. abnorm. soc. Psychol.,* 1963, in press (c).

Bandura, A., and Walters, R. H. *Adolescent aggression.* New York: Ronald, 1959.

Bandura, A., and Walters, R. H. Aggression. In *Child psychology: The sixty-second yearbook of the National Society for the Study of Education,* Part 1. Chicago: The National Society for the Study of Education, 1963, pp. 364–415.

Beller, E. K., and Haeberle, Ann W. Dependency and the frustration-aggression hypothesis. Unpublished manuscript, Child Develpm. Center, New York City, 1961 (a).

Beller, E. K., and Haeberle, Ann W. Dependency and the frustration-aggression hypothesis: II. Paper read at the Annual Meeting of the Eastern Psychol. Assoc., Philadelphia, 1961 (b).

Benedict, Ruth. *The chrysanthemum and the sword: Patterns of Japanese culture.* Boston: Houghton Mifflin, 1946.

Burton, R. V., Maccoby, Eleanor E., and Allinsmith, W. Antecedents of resistance to temptation in four-year-old children. *Child Develpm.,* 1961, **32**, 689–710.

Cox, F. N. An assessment of children's attitudes toward parent figures. *Child Developm.,* 1962, **33**, 821–830.

Crandall, V. J., Preston, Anne, and Rabson, Alice. Maternal reactions and the development of independence and achievement behavior in young children. *Child Develpm.,* 1960, **31**, 243–251.

Eaton, J. W., and Weil, R. J. *Culture and mental disorders.* New York: Free Press, 1955.

Grinder, R. E. Parental childrearing practices, conscience, and resistance to temptation of sixth-grade children. *Child Develpm.,* 1962, **33**, 803–820.

Haner, C. F., and Brown, Patricia A. Clarification of the instigation to action concept in the frustration-aggression hypothesis. *J. abnorm. soc. Psychol.,* 1955, **51**, 204–206.

Heineke, C. M. Some antecedents and correlates of guilt and fear in young boys. Unpublished doctoral dissertation, Harvard Univer., 1953.

Hollenberg, Eleanor, and Sperry, Margaret. Some antecedents of aggression and effects of frustration in doll play. *Personality,* 1951, **1,** 32–43.

Holmberg, A. R. *Nomads of the long bow.* Washington, D.C.: U.S. Govt. Print. Off., 1950.

Holton, Ruth B. Amplitude of an instrumental response following the withholding of reward. *Child Develpm.,* 1961.

Hughes, C. C., Tremblay, M., Rapoport, R. N., and Leighton, A. H. *People of cove and woodlot: Communities from the viewpoint of social psychiatry.* New York: Basic Books, 1960.

Levin, H., and Baldwin, A. L. Pride and shame in children. In M. R. Jones (Ed.). *Nebraska symposium on motivation.* Lincoln: Univer. of Nebraska Press, 1959, pp. 138–173.

MacKinnon, D. W. Violations of prohibition. In H. A. Murray et al. *Explorations in personality.* New York: Oxford Univer. Press, 1938, pp. 491–501.

Mead, Margaret. Some anthropological considerations concerning guilt. In M. L. Reymert (Ed.). *Feelings and emotions.* New York: McGraw-Hill, 1950, pp. 362–373.

Miller, D. R., and Swanson, G. E. (Eds.). *Inner conflict and defense.* New York: Holt, 1960.

Miller, R. E., Banks, J. H., and Ogawa, N. Communication of affect in "cooperative conditioning" of Rhesus monkeys. *J. abnorm. soc. Psychol.,* 1962, **64,** 343–348.

Mischel, W. Preference for delayed reinforcement: An experimental study of a cultural observation. *J. abnorm. soc. Psychol.,* 1958, **56,** 57–61.

Mischel, W. Father-absence and delay of gratification: Cross-cultural comparisons. *J. abnorm. soc. Psychol.,* 1961, **63,** 116–124 (c).

Nelsen, E. A. The effects of reward and punishment of dependency on subsequent dependency. Unpublished manuscript, Stanford Univer., 1960.

Olds, J. *The growth and structure of motives.* New York: Free Press, 1956.

Piers, G., and Singer, M. B. *Shame and guilt.* Springfield, Ill.: Thomas, 1953.

Riesman, D. *The lonely crowd.* New Haven: Yale Univer. Press, 1950.

Rosen, B., and D'Andrade, R. The psychosocial origins of achievement motivation. *Sociometry,* 1959, **22,** 185–218.

Ross, Shiela A. The effect of deviant and nondeviant models on the behavior of preschool children in a temptation situation. Unpublished doctoral dissertation, Stanford Univer., 1962.

Sears, R. R., Maccoby, Eleanor E., and Levin, H. *Patterns of child rearing.* New York: Harper, 1957.

Unger, J. M. On the functioning of guilt potential in a conflict dilemma. *Amer. Psychologist,* 1962, **17,** 303 (abstract).

Whiting, J. W. M. Sorcery, sin, and the superego. In M. R. Jones (Ed.). *Nebraska symposium on motivation.* Lincoln: Univer. of Nebraska Press, 1959, pp. 174–195.

Whiting, J. W. M., and Child, I. L. *Child training and personality.* New Haven: Yale Univer. Press, 1953.

Whiting, J. W. M., and Mowrer, O. H. Habit progression and regression—a laboratory study of some factors relevant to human socialization. *J. comp. Psychol.,* 1943, **36,** 229–253.

Winterbottom, Marian R. The relation of childhood training in independence to achievement motivation. Unpublished doctoral dissertation, Univer. of Michigan, 1953.

Chapter 18 Identity and Identity Diffusion

ERIK H. ERIKSON

With the establishment of a good relationship to the world of skills and to those who teach and share the new skills, childhood proper comes to an end. Youth begins. But in puberty and adolescence all sameness and continuities relied on earlier are questioned again because of a rapidity of body growth which equals that of early childhood and because of the entirely new addition of physical genital maturity. The growing and developing young people, faced with this physiological revolution within them, are now primarily concerned with attempts at consolidating their social roles. They are sometimes morbidly, often curiously, preoccupied with what they appear to be in the eyes of others as compared with what they feel they are and with the question of how to connect the earlier cultivated roles and skills with the ideal prototypes of the day. In their search for a new sense of continuity and sameness, some adolescents have to refight many of the crises of earlier years, and they are never ready to install lasting idols and ideals as guardians of a final identity.

The integration now taking place in the form of the ego identity is more than the sum of the childhood identifications. It is the inner capital accrued from all those experiences of each suc-

SOURCES. This chapter is composed of a number of selections from the works of Erik H. Erikson. Pages 88–90 from "The Growth and Crises of the Healthy Personality," in *Psychological Issues: Identity and the Life Cycle*, Volume I, No. 1, 1959, pp. 50–100. Copyright 1959. Reprinted by permission of International Universities Press, Inc. Pages 147–150 from "The Problem of Ego Identity," in *Psychological Issues: Identity and the Life Cycle*, Volume I, No. 1, 1959, pp. 101–166. This paper was originally published in *The Journal of the American Psychoanalytic Association*, Volume 4, 1956, pp. 56–121. Copyright 1956, American Psychoanalytic Association. Reprinted by permission of International Universities Press, Inc. and the American Psychoanalytic Association. "The Growth and Crises of the Healthy Personality," *op. cit.*, pp. 91–94. Pages 100–104 from *Young Man Luther*, New York: W. W. Norton, 1958. Reprinted by permission of W. W. Norton and Company, Inc. Copyright © 1958 by Erik H. Erikson. "The Problem of Ego Identity," *op. cit.*, pp. 110–114.

cessive stage, when successful identification led to a successful alignment of the individual's *basic drives* with his *endowment* and his *opportunities*. In psychoanalysis we ascribe such successful alignments to "ego synthesis"; I have tried to demonstrate that the ego values accrued in childhood culminate in what I have called *a sense of ego identity*. The sense of ego identity, then, is the accrued confidence that one's ability to maintain inner sameness and continuity (one's ego in the psychological sense) is matched by the sameness and continuity of one's meaning for others. Thus, self-esteem, confirmed at the end of each major crisis, grows to be a conviction that one is learning effective steps toward a tangible future, that one is developing a defined personality within a social reality which one understands. The growing child must, at every step, derive a vitalizing sense of reality from the awareness that his individual way of mastering experience is a successful variant of the way other people around him master experience and recognize such mastery.

In this, children cannot be fooled by empty praise and condescending encouragement. They may have to accept artificial bolstering of their self-esteem in lieu of something better, but what I call their accruing ego identity gains real strength only from wholehearted and consistent recognition of real accomplishment, that is, achievement that has meaning in their culture. On the other hand, should a child feel that the environment tries to deprive him too radically of all the forms of expression which permit him to develop and to integrate the next step in his ego identity, he will resist with the astonishing strength encountered in animals who are suddenly forced to defend their lives. Indeed, in the social jungle of human existence, there is no feeling of being alive without a sense of ego identity. To understand this would be to understand the trouble of adolescents better, especially the trouble of all those who cannot just be "nice" boys and girls, but are desperately seeking for a satisfactory sense of belonging, be it in cliques and gangs here in our country or in inspiring mass movements in others.

* * * * * *

It has not escaped the reader that the term identity covers much of what has been called the self by a variety of workers, be it in the form of a self-concept (George H. Mead, 1934), a self-system (Harry S. Sullivan, 1946–1947), or in that of fluctuating self-experiences described by Schilder (1934), Federn (1927–1949), and others.[1] Within psychoanalytic ego psychology, Hartmann, above all, has circumscribed this general area more clearly when in discussing the so-called *libidinal cathexis of the ego in narcissism,* he comes to the conclusion that it is rather a self which is thus being cathected. He advocated a term *"self-representation,"* as differentiated from "object representation" (Hartmann, 1950). This self-representation was, less systematically, anticipated by Freud in his occasional references to the ego's "attitudes toward the self" and to fluctuating cathexes bestowed upon this self in labile states of "self-esteem" (Freud, 1914). In this paper, we are concerned with the *genetic continuity* of such a self-representation —a continuity which must lastly be ascribed to the work of the ego. No other inner agency could accomplish the selective accentuation of significant identifications throughout childhood and the gradual integration of self-images in anticipation of an identity. It is for this reason that I have called identity, at first, ego identity. But in brashly choosing a name analogous to "ego ideal," I have opened myself to the query as to what the relationship of these two concepts is.

Freud assigned the *internalized perpetuation* of cultural influences to the functions of the "superego or ego ideal" which was to represent the commands and the prohibitions emanating from the environment and its traditions. Let

us compare two statements of Freud's which are relevant here.

. . . the super-ego of the child is not really built up on the model of the parents, but on that of the parents' super-ego; it takes over the same content, it becomes the vehicle of tradition and of all the age-long values which have been handed down in this way from generation to generation. You may easily guess what great help is afforded by the recognition of the super-ego in understanding the social behavior of man, in grasping the problem of delinquency, for example, and perhaps, too, in providing us with some practical hints upon education. . . . Mankind never lives completely in the present; the *ideologies of the super-ego*[2] perpetuate the past, the traditions of the race and the people, which yield but slowly to the influence of the present and to new developments, and, so long as they work through the super-ego, play an important part in man's life (Freud, 1932, pp. 95–96).

Freud, it is to be noted here, speaks of the "ideologies of the super-ego," thus giving the superego ideational content; yet he also refers to it as a "vehicle," i.e., as a part of the psychic system through which ideas work. It would seem that by ideologies of the superego Freud means the superego's specific contributions to the archaic, to the magic in the inner coerciveness of ideologies.

In a second statement Freud acknowledges the social side of the ego ideal.

The ego ideal opens up an important avenue for the understanding of group psychology. In addition to its individual side, this ideal has a social side; it is also the common ideal of a family, a class or a nation (1914, p. 101).

It would seem that the terms superego and ego ideal have come to be distinguished by their different relation to phylogenetic and to ontogenetic history. The superego is conceived as a more archaic and thoroughly internalized representative of the evolutionary principle of morality, of man's *congenital proclivity* toward the development of a primitive, categorical conscience. Allied with (ontogenetically) early introjects, the superego remains a rigidly vindictive and punitive inner agency of "blind" morality. The ego ideal, however, seems to be more flexibly bound to the ideals of the particular *historical period* and thus is closer to the ego function of reality testing.

Ego identity (if we were to hold on to this

---

[1] I am not yet able to establish the systematic convergencies and divergencies between the work of the so-called "Neo-Freudians" and that which I am trying to formulate. It will be seen, however, that in individuals as well as in groups I prefer to speak of a "sense of identity" rather than of a "character structure" or "basic character." In nations, too, my concepts would lead me to concentrate on the conditions and experiences which heighten or endanger a national sense of identity rather than on a static national character. An introduction to this subject is offered in my book, *Childhood and Society* (1950). Here it is important to remember that each identity cultivates its own sense of freedom—wherefore a people rarely understands what makes other peoples feel free. This fact is amply exploited by totalitarian propaganda and underestimated in the Western World.

[2] My italics.

term and to this level of discourse) would in comparison be even closer to *social reality* in that as a subsystem of the ego it would test, select, and integrate the self-representations derived from the psychosocial crises of childhood. It could be said to be characterized by the more or less *actually attained but forever-to-be-revised* sense of the reality of the self within social reality; while the imagery of the ego ideal could be said to represent a set of *to-be-strived-for but forever-not-quite-attainable ideal* goals for the self.

However, in using the word self in the sense of Hartmann's self-representation, one opens the whole controversy to a radical consideration. One could argue that it may be wise in matters of the ego's perceptive and regulative dealings with its self to reserve the designation "ego" for the subject, and to give the designation "self" to the object. The ego, then, as a central organizing agency, is during the course of life faced with a changing self which, in turn, demands to be synthesized with abandoned and anticipated selves. This suggestion would be applicable to the *body ego,* which could be said to be the part of the self provided by the attributes of the organism, and, therefore, might more appropriately be called the *body self;* it would also concern the ego ideal as the representative of the ideas, images, and configurations, which serve the persistent comparison with an *ideal self;* and finally, it would

apply to what I have called *ego identity*. What could consequently be called the self-identity emerges from all those experiences in which a sense of temporary self-diffusion was successfully contained by a renewed and ever more realistic self-definition and social recognition. *Identity formation thus can be said to have a self-aspect, and an ego aspect.* It is part of the ego in the sense that it represents the ego's synthesizing function on one of its frontiers, namely, the actual social structure of the environment and the image of reality as transmitted to the child during successive childhood crises. (The other frontiers would be the id, and the demands made on the ego by our biological history and structure; the superego and the demands of our more primitively moralistic proclivities; and the ego ideal with its idealized parent images.) Identity, in this connection, has a claim to recognition as the adolescent ego's most important support, in the task of containing the postpubetal id, and in balancing the then newly invoked superego as well as the again overly demanding ego ideal.

Until the matter of ego versus self is sufficiently defined to permit a terminological decision, I shall use the bare term identity in order to suggest a social function of the ego which results, in adolescence, in a relative psychosocial equilibrium essential to the tasks of young adulthood.

*   *   *

*   *   *

The emerging ego identity, then, bridges the early childhood stages, when the body and the parent images were given their specific meaning, and the later stages, when a variety of social roles becomes available and increasingly coercive. A lasting ego identity cannot begin to exist without the trust of the first oral stage; it cannot be completed without a promise of fulfillment which from the dominant image of adulthood reaches down into the baby's beginnings and which creates at every step an accruing sense of ego strength.

The danger of this stage is *identity diffusion;* as Biff puts it in Arthur Miller's *Death of a Salesman,* "I just can't take hold, Mom, I can't take hold of some kind of a life." Where such a dilemma is based on a strong previous doubt of one's ethnic and sexual identity, delinquent and outright psychotic incidents are not uncommon. Youth after youth, bewildered by

some assumed role, a role forced on him by the inexorable standardization of American adolescence, runs away in one form or another; leaving schools and jobs, staying out all night, or withdrawing into bizarre and inaccessible moods. Once "delinquent," his greatest need and often his only salvation, is the refusal on the part of older friends, advisers, and judiciary personnel to type him further by pat diagnoses and social judgments which ignore the special dynamic conditions of adolescence. For if diagnosed and treated correctly, seemingly psychotic and criminal incidents do not in adolescence have the same fatal significance which they have at other ages. Yet many a youth, finding that the authorities expect him to be "a bum" or "a queer," or "off the beam," perversely obliges by becoming just that.

In general it is primarily the inability to settle on an occupational identity which disturbs young people. To keep themselves together they temporarily over-identify, to the point of apparent complete loss of identity, with the heroes of cliques and crowds. On the other hand, they become remarkably clannish, intolerant, and cruel in their exclusion of others who are "different," in skin color or cultural background, in tastes and gifts, and often in entirely petty aspects of dress and gesture arbitrarily selected as *the* signs of an in-grouper or out-grouper. It is important to understand (which does not mean condone or participate in) such intolerance as the necessary *defense against a sense of identity diffusion,* which is unavoidable at a time of life when the body changes its proportions radically, when genital maturity floods body and imagination with all manners of drives, when intimacy with the other sex approaches and is, on occasion, forced on the youngster, and when life lies before one with a variety of conflicting possibilities and choices. Adolescents help one another temporarily through such discomfort by forming cliques and by stereotyping themselves, their ideals, and their enemies.

It is important to understand this because it makes clear the appeal which simple and cruel totalitarian doctrines have on the minds of the youth of such countries and classes as have lost or are losing their group identities (feudal, agrarian, national and so forth) in these times of world-wide industrialization, emancipation, and wider intercommunication. The dynamic quality of the tempestuous adolescences lived through in patriarchal and agrarian countries (countries which face the most radical changes in political structure and in economy) explains the fact that their young people find convincing and satisfactory identities in the simple totalitarian doctrines of race, class, or nation. Even though we may be forced to win wars against their leaders, we still are faced with the job of winning the peace with these grim youths by convincingly demonstrating to them (by living it) a democratic identity which can be strong and yet tolerant, judicious and still determined.

But it is increasingly important to understand this also in order to treat the intolerances of our adolescents at home with understanding and guidance rather than with verbal stereotypes or prohibitions. It is difficult to be tolerant if deep down you are not quite sure that you are a man (or a woman), that you will ever grow together again and be attractive, that you will be able to master your drives, that you really know who you are,[3] that you know what you want to be, that you know what you look like to others, and that you will know how to make the right decision without, once for all, committing yourself to the wrong friend, sexual partner, leader, or career.

Democracy in a country like America poses special problems in that it insists on *self-made identities* ready to grasp many chances and ready to adjust to changing necessities of booms and busts, of peace and war, of migration and determined sedentary life. Our democracy, furthermore, must present the adolescent with ideals which can be shared by youths of many backgrounds and which emphasize autonomy in the form of independence and initiative in the form of enterprise. These promises, in turn, are not easy to fulfill in increasingly complex and centralized systems of economic and political organization, systems which, if geared to war, must automatically neglect the "self-made" identities of millions of individuals and put them where they are most needed. This is hard on many young Americans because their whole upbringing, and therefore the development of a healthy personality, depends on a certain degree of *choice,* a certain hope for an individual *chance,* and a certain conviction in freedom of *self-determination.*

We are speaking here not only of high privileges and lofty ideals but also of psychological necessities. Psychologically speaking, a gradually accruing ego identity is the only safeguard against the *anarchy of drives* as well as the *autocracy of conscience,* that is, the cruel over-conscientiousness which is the inner residue in the adult of his past inequality in regard to his parent. Any loss of a sense of identity exposes the individual to his own childhood conflicts—as could be observed, for example, in the neuroses of World War II among men and women who could not stand the general dislocation of their careers or a variety of other special pressures of war. Our adversaries, it seems, understand this. Their psychological warfare consists in the determined continuation of general conditions which permit them to indoctrinate mankind within their orbit with the simple and yet for them undoubtedly effec-

---

[3] On the wall of a cowboys' bar in the wide-open West hangs a saying: "I ain't what I ought to be, I ain't what I'm going to be, but I ain't what I was."

tive identities of class warfare and nationalism, while they know that the psychology, as well as the economy, of free enterprise and of self-determination is stretched to the breaking point under the condition of long-drawn-out cold and lukewarm war. It is clear, therefore, that we must bend every effort to present our young men and women with the tangible and trustworthy promise of opportunities for a rededication to the life for which the country's history, as well as their own childhood, has prepared them. Among the tasks of national defense, this one must not be forgotten.

I have referred to the relationship of the problem of trust to matters of adult faith; to that of the problem of autonomy to matters of adult independence in work and citizenship. I have pointed to the connection between a sense of initiative and the kind of enterprise sanctioned in the economic system, and between the sense of industry and a culture's technology. In searching for the social values

which guide identity, one confronts the problem of aristocracy, in its widest possible sense which connotes the conviction that the best people rule and that that rule develops the best in people. In order not to become cynically or apathetically lost, young people in search of an identity must somewhere be able to convince themselves that those who succeed thereby shoulder the obligation of being the best, that is, of personifying the nation's ideals. In this country, as in any other, we have those successful types who become the cynical representatives of the "inside track," the "bosses" of impersonal machinery. In a culture once pervaded with the value of the self-made man, a special danger ensues from the idea of a synthetic personality; as if you are what you can appear to be, or as if you are what you can buy. This can be counteracted only by a system of education that transmits values and goals which determinedly aspire beyond mere "functioning" and "making the grade."

*   *   *   *   *   *

That extreme form of identity diffusion which leads to significant arrest and regression is characterized most of all by a mistrustful difficulty with mere living in time. Time is made to stand still by the device of ignoring the usual alternation of day and night, of more active and less active periods, of periods given more to work and talk with other people and of those given over to isolation, rumination, and musical receivership. There also may be a general slowing up that can verge on catatonic states. It is as if the young person were waiting for some event, or some person, to sweep him out of this state by promising him, instead of the reassuring routine and practice of most men's time, a vast utopian view that would make the very disposition of time worthwhile. Unless recruited outright, however, by an ideological movement in need of needy youths, such an individual cannot sustain any one utopian view for long. . . .

There is, of course, also a tortuous self-consciousness, characterized at one time by shame over what one is already sure one is, and at another time by doubt as to what one may become. A person with this self-consciousness often cannot work, not because he is not gifted and adept, but because his standards preclude any approach that does not lead to being outstanding; while at the same time these standards do not permit him to compete, to defeat others. He thus is excluded from ap-

prenticeships and discipleships which define duties, sanction competition and, as it were, provide a status of moratorium. . . .

Most of all, this kind of person must shy away from intimacy. Any physical closeness, with either sex, arouses at the same time both an impulse to merge with the other person and a fear of losing autonomy and individuation. In fact, there is a sense of bisexual diffusion which makes such a young person unsure about how to touch another person sexually or affectionately. The contrast between the exalted sexual fusion of his autoerotic dreams and the complete sense of isolation in the presence of the other sex is catastrophic. Here again, whatever sexual moratorium the society's mores offer most young people in a given setting cannot be shared by the patient, whether it is determined abstinence, sexual play without genital encounter, or genital engagement without affection or responsibility. . . .

Finally, the use of sharp repudiation, so eagerly indulged in by intolerant youth in an effort to bolster its collective identity with a harsh denunciation of some other "kind," be it on a religious, racial, or social basis, is blunted in such a person. He alternates between extreme self-repudiation and a snobbish disdain for all groups—except perhaps, for memberships whose true roots and obligations are completely outside his reach. One thinks of the "classical" yearnings of young Europeans or of the appeal which foreign totalitarian parties have for some young Americans, as do the lofty teachings of Eastern mystics. Here the need to search for total and final values can often be met only under the condition that these values be foreign to everything one has been taught. . . . We will call all self-images, even those of a highly idealistic nature, which are diametrically opposed to the dominant values of an individual's upbringing, parts of a *negative identity*—meaning an identity which he has been warned *not* to become, which he can become only with a divided heart, but which he nevertheless finds himself compelled to become, protesting his wholeheartedness. Obviously such rebellion can serve high adventure, and when joined to a great collective trend of rebellion . . . can rejuvenate as it repudiates. In malignant cases, however, the search for a negative identity soon exhausts social resources; in fact, no rebellious movement, not even a self-respecting delinquent gang, would consider taking such an individual as a member. For he rebels and surrenders on the spur of the moment, and cannot be relied on to be honestly asocial unto death.

When such young people become patients, they illustrate the depth of regression which can ensue from an identity-crisis, either because the identity-elements they were offered as children were not coherent—so that one may speak of a defect in this connection—or because they face a perplexing set of present circumstances which amounts to an acute state of ideological undernourishment. The most dramatic characteristic of work with such patients is their tendency to make intense and yet contradictory demands of the psychotherapist. In this they truly regress; for either openly or covertly they expect from the therapist the kind of omniscience an infant attributes to his mother when he seems to assume that she should have prevented the table from hitting him, or at any rate from being hard and sharp; or that she should be able to hold him firmly and to let him go freely at the same time, that is, at a time when he himself does not know which he wants. But even the paradoxical form which the patient's demands, to his own chagrin, can take concerns his very essence as an individual. He wants to have the right to act like nobody, and yet to be treated as quite a somebody; he wants to fuse with the therapist in order to derive from him everything the parents were or are not; yet he is afraid to be devoured by an identification

with the therapist. The outstanding quality of these patients is *totalism,* a to be or not to be which makes every matter of differences a matter of mutually exclusive essences; every question mark a matter of forfeited existence; every error or oversight, eternal treason. All of this narrows down to something like Jacob's struggle with the angel, a wrestling for a benediction which is to lead to the patient's conviction that he is an alive person, and, as such, has a life before him, and a right to it. For less, such patients will not settle. I have called this the "rock-bottom" attitude, and explained it as the sign of a perverted and precocious integrity, an attempt to find that immutable bedrock on which the struggle for a new existence can safely begin and be assured of a future. The patient desperately demands that the psychotherapist become for him as immediate and as close, as exclusive and as circumspect, as generous and as self-denying, a counterplayer as only a mother of an infant child can be. It is clear that these patients want to be reborn in identity and to have another chance at becoming once-born, but this time on their own terms. Needless to say, we can offer the patient nothing but our willingness to jointly face the odds that are the lot of all of us.

Where so-called schizophrenic processes take over, the rock-bottom attitude is expressed in a strange evolutionary imagery. Total feeling becomes dehumanized, and eventually even de-mammalized. These patients can feel like a crab or a shellfish or a mollusk, or even abandon what life and movement there is on the lowest animal level and become a lonely twisted tree on the ledge of a stormy rock, or the rock, or just the ledge out in nowhere. I must leave the psychiatric discussion of this to another publication; here it suffices to say, that at no other time in life can severe regression to a play with nothingness appear in such systematized form, and yet be, as it were, experimental, an adventure in reaching inner rock bottom to find something firm to stand on. Here the therapist cannot be optimistic enough about the possibility of making contact with the patient's untapped inner resources; on the other hand, it is also true that he cannot be pessimistic enough in the sustained apprehension that a mishap might cause the patient to remain at the rock bottom, and deplete the energy available for his re-emergence.

Other patients cling to a make-believe order of compulsive scrupulosity and of obsessive rumination. They insist on what seems like almost mock order for the world of man, a caricature of logic and consistency. . . . The eyes of such young people are often lifeless and out of contact; then they suddenly scan your face for its sincerity or even its mere presence; these patients, who according to popular judgment could be said to be "not quite there" most of the time, are all too suddenly and flamingly there. They can appear as remote, as lifeless, as impenetrable, as they say they feel; and yet, there are those moments of mutual recognition when they do seem to trust themselves and you, and when their smile can be as totally present and rewarding as only an

infant's first smiles of seeming recognition. But at this point the struggle just begins—as, indeed, does the infant's.

In this brief and impressionistic picture I have, for the sake of their common symptoms, lumped together men of different times and of different types. . . . But I wonder whether many readers will have read this account without having a sense of recognition. Either they themselves have felt and acted like this at one time, or they have been such a person's counterplayer: his parent or teacher, his friend or young spouse.

*　　*　　*　　　　*　　*　　*

Adolescence is the last and the concluding stage of childhood. The adolescent process, however, is conclusively complete only when the individual has subordinated his childhood identifications to a new kind of identification, achieved in absorbing sociability and in competitive apprenticeship with and among his agemates. These new identifications are no longer characterized by the playfulness of childhood and the experimental zest of youth: with dire urgency they force the young individual into choices and decisions which will, with increasing immediacy, lead to a more final self-definition, to irreversible role pattern, and thus to commitments "for life." The task to be performed here by the young person and by his society is formidable; it necessitates, in different individuals and in different societies, great variations in the duration, in the intensity, and in the ritualization of adolescence. Societies offer, as individuals require, more or less sanctioned intermediary periods between childhood and adulthood, institutionalized *psychosocial moratoria,* during which a lasting pattern of "inner identity" is scheduled for relative completion.

In postulating a "latency period" which precedes puberty, psychoanalysis has given recognition to some kind of *psychosexual moratorium* in human development—a period of delay which permits the future mate and parent first to "go to school" (i.e., to undergo whatever schooling is provided for in his technology) and to learn the technical and social rudiments of a work situation. It is not within the confines of the libido theory, however, to give an adequate account of a second period of delay, namely, adolescence. Here the sexually matured individual is more or less retarded in his psychosexual capacity for intimacy and in the

psychosocial readiness for parenthood. The period can be viewed as a *psychosocial moratorium* during which the individual through free role experimentation may find a niche in some section of his society, a niche which is firmly defined and yet seems to be uniquely made for him. In finding it the young adult gains an assured sense of inner continuity and social sameness which will bridge what he *was* as a child and what he is *about to become,* and will reconcile his *conception of himself* and his *community's recognition* of him.

If, in the following, we speak of the community's response to the young individual's need to be "recognized" by those around him, we mean something beyond a mere recognition of achievement; for it is of great relevance to the young individual's identity formation that he be responded to, and be given function and status as a person whose gradual growth and transformation make sense to those who begin to make sense to him. It has not been sufficiently recognized in psychoanalysis that such recognition provides an entirely indispensable support to the ego in the specific tasks of adolescing, which are: to maintain the most important ego defenses against the vastly growing intensity of impulses (now invested in a matured genital apparatus and a powerful muscle system); to learn to consolidate the most important "conflict-free" achievements in line with work opportunities; and to resynthesize all childhood identifications in some unique way, and yet in concordance with the roles offered by some wider section of society—be that section the neighborhood block, an anticipated occupational field, an association of kindred minds, or, perhaps (as in Shaw's case) the "mighty dead."

Linguistically as well as psychologically, identity and identification have common roots. Is identity, then, the mere sum of earlier identifications, or is it merely an additional set of identifications?

The limited usefulness of the *mechanism of identification* becomes at once obvious if we consider the fact that none of the identifications of childhood (which in our patients stand out in such morbid elaboration and mutual contradiction) could, if merely added up, result in a functioning personality. True, we usually believe that the task of psychotherapy is the replacement of morbid and excessive identifications by more desirable ones. But as every cure attests, "more desirable" identifications tend to be quietly subordinated to a new, a unique Gestalt which is more than the sum of its parts. The fact is that identification as a mechanism is of limited usefulness. Children, at different stages of their development, identify with those *part aspects* of people by which they themselves are most immediately affected, whether in reality or fantasy. Their identifications with parents, for example, center in certain overvalued and ill-understood body parts, capacities, and role appearances. These part aspects, furthermore, are favored not because of their social acceptability (they often are everything but the parents' most adjusted attributes) but by the nature of infantile fantasy which only gradually gives way to a more realistic anticipation of social reality. The final identity, then, as fixed at the end of adolescence is superordinated to any single identification with individuals of the past: it includes all significant identifications, but it also alters them in order to make a unique and a reasonably coherent whole of them.

If we, roughly speaking, consider introjection-projection, identification, and identity formation to be the steps by which the ego grows in ever more mature interplay with the identities of the child's models, the following psychosocial schedule suggests itself:

The mechanisms of *introjection and projection,* which prepare the basis for later identifications, depend for their relative integration on the satisfactory mutuality (Erikson, 1950) between the *mothering adult(s) and the mothered child.* Only the experience of such mutuality provides a safe pole of self-feeling from which the child can reach out for the other pole: his first love "objects."

The fate of *childhood identifications,* in turn, depends on the child's satisfactory interaction with a trustworthy and meaningful hierarchy of roles as provided by the generations living together in some form of *family.*

Identity formation, finally, begins where the usefulness of identification ends. It arises from the selective repudiation in a new configuration, which in turn, is dependent on the process by which a *society* (often through subsocieties) *identifies the young individual,* recognizing him as somebody who had to become the way he is, and who, being the way he is, is taken for granted. The community, often not without some initial mistrust, gives such recognition with a (more or less institutionalized) display of surprise and pleasure in making the acquaintance of a newly emerging individual. For the community, in turn, feels "recognized" by the individual who cares to ask for recognition; it can, by the same token, feel deeply—and vengefully—rejected by the individual who does not seem to care.

While the end of adolescence thus is the stage of an overt identity *crisis,* identity *formation* neither begins nor ends with adolescence: it is a lifelong development largely unconscious to the individual and to his society.

REFERENCES

Erikson, E. H. (1950), *Childhood and Society.* New York: Norton.

Federn, P. (1927-1949), *Ego Psychology and the Psychoses.* New York: Basic Books, 1952.

Freud, S. (1914), "On Narcissism: An Introduction." *Standard Edition,* 14 (1957), pp. 73-102.

Freud, S. (1932), *New Introductory Lectures on Psychoanalysis.* Lecture 31; "The Anatomy of the Mental Personality." New York: Norton, 1933.

Hartmann, H. (1950), "Comments on the Psychoanalytic Theory of the Ego." *The Psychoanalytic Study of the Child, 5,* pp. 74-96. New York: International Universities Press.

Mead, G. H. (1934), *Mind, Self, and Society.* Chicago: University of Chicago Press.

Schilder, P. (1934), *The Image and Appearance of the Human Body.* New York: International Universities Press.

Sullivan, H. S. (1946-1947), *The Interpersonal Theory of Psychiatry.* New York: Norton, 1953.

Chapter 19 Self and Role in Medical Education

JACK J. PREISS

Forty years ago, George Herbert Mead challenged us to regard personality primarily as a product of social-psychological rather than biological variables. Under Mead's influence, many behavioral scientists have been attempting to devise methods of social process analysis to meet the challenge. One essential task has been to analyze the ways in which the elements of the social environment are combined into behavior patterns (usually labeled "roles") which the community ("significant others" in Mead's terms) can recognize consistently. Reciprocally, the learning and filling of roles provides an individual with an internal self-image which reflects and coheres with the external role system in the community. In Mead's view, social identity and self-image become the two interactive sides of the personality coin.

One of the major procedural problems of the interactionist perspective has been that of reliably following the emergence of self as a result of acquiring and performing a role. We can often purposively survey and compare the characteristics, opinions, and attitudes of people at particular points in time. Sometimes we can arrange before-and-after investigations involving the presumed effect of the introduction of controlled stimuli into a group setting. However, neither of these approaches can take account of the time dimension satisfactorily. A better pattern of handling group change over time would seem to be offered by the panel and cohort designs.[1] These permit a continuous examination of relatively stable groups at systematic intervals in their life cycle. Incorporation of the time factor as a major element

in the design usually requires a relatively long research program. In practice, this requirement is frequently met by using two or more groups rather than following a single group through the entire series of stages.[2] For example, in tracing the course of student development through a four-year college experience, one might utilize the four different class groups simultaneously in a given year. This would be much more rapid and economical than following one class for four years. The main question, obviously, is whether the interclass variation is great enough to alter the findings significantly beyond the intraclass variations from year to year. Obviously, the single class design eliminates the type of error variance which would be involved in the multiple class approach. Nevertheless, the potential for interclass variations exists in a panel study of several classes. If we decide to employ a single class design, we usually assume that interclass variations are not important.

These issues are relevant for the study discussed in this chapter. The study is focused upon the development of self in terms of an occupational structure. The central importance of occupation as a means of self-identity and self-evaluation in Western society needs no elucidation. Clearly, the extensive division of labor and functional demarcation of many occupations have increased the requirements for recruitment and performance which must be met by candidates for such roles. Although this high specialization limits broad theoretical

---

SOURCE. This paper was prepared originally for this volume.

[1] One of the earlier (1948) and best known panel studies was Lazarsfeld, Berelson, and Gaudet's *The People's Choice,* a study of voting behavior. Cohort analysis over time has been extensively used in demographic research utilizing census data. The chief problem in panel design is, of course, attrition of subjects and their replacement.

[2] Two major studies of medical education have utilized the multiple group approach. In Merton, Reader, and Kendall (eds.), *The Student-Physician,* Cambridge: Harvard University Press, 1957, students in different classes (and sometimes different schools) were frequently compared with one another in different years. In Becker, Green, Hughes, and Strauss, *Boys in White,* Chicago, University of Chicago Press, 1961, a random sample of the medical student body in a given year provided much of the empirical data discussed in the book. Neither study employed a systematic panel design in following a particular student class through the training program.

generalization in some respects, it does provide concrete and well-defined procedures which can be used to study specific types of self-development. The numerous studies of occupational systems that have been undertaken in recent years are evidence of this potential. The heavy emphasis has been in the area of the professions and the profession-aspiring occupations.[3] This emphasis is understandable because the specificity of the self-development process is most clear-cut in these occupations. Their entrance qualifications, levels of training, and standards for licensure are usually high by comparison with other occupational systems. The stability and visibility of the professional training system are attractive to the researcher because they permit some control of the time dimension as well as a concrete definition of system boundaries. The formal preparation in the professions is also extensive enough to allow attitudinal changes to emerge and to be classified before the training period is completed.

The utility of the professional occupations for research in the processes of self-formation has been especially evident in the health professions, such as nursing and medicine. Expanding national interest in both health programs and the behavior of those who implement them has stimulated research investigation in these areas. As part of this trend, the study which provides the data for this chapter is centered upon the ways in which medical students become physicians as a consequence of their medical training. The design is an effort to deal with the problems of time and generalizability.

RESEARCH DESIGN

Three contiguous classes of students at a southeastern medical school were followed through their entire four-year course.[4] Further

data collection is also possible for an indefinite period[5] beyond this basic course. The design permits exploration of the variation among the three classes on many questionnaire items, such as background variables, career patterns, and attitudes. If the interclass variation were generally significant, we would have to conclude that the classes were probably not comparable to begin with, and that the training process was confounded by differences in antecedent factors. However, if the significant differences could be explained by changes from year to year rather than by interclass variation, more confidence could be placed upon the training process itself as the source of such differences. Preliminary comparisons among the three classes on the variables used in the study indicated that differences among classes were infrequent. Where they did occur, no pattern was discernible, in that no one class was noticeably more variant than the other two. Therefore it would seem that the three classes may properly be analyzed as a single group which was affected[6] in a consistent manner by the training program. Thus we shall accept the most important process variable as stage of training rather than class of entry.

Obviously, it will be feasible in this paper to deal with only a few dimensions of the image formation process. However, it is hoped that the discussion will illustrate the efficacy of this research design insofar as it helps meet the challenge of Mead's theory of the social self.

---

[3] In addition to the two studies of physicians already mentioned, examples are Gross, Mason, and McEachern, *Explorations in Role Analysis: Studies of the School Superintendency Role,* New York: John Wiley and Sons, 1958; Taves, Corwin, and Haas, *Role Conception and Vocational Success and Satisfaction: A Study of Student and Professional Nurses,* Monograph No. 112, Bureau of Business Research, Columbus, Ohio: The Ohio State University, 1963; J. E. Carlin, *Lawyers' Ethics: A Survey of the New York City Bar,* New York: Russell Sage Foundation, 1966: Preiss and Ehrlich, *An Examination of Role Theory: The Case of the State Police,* Lincoln, Nebraska: University of Nebraska Press, 1966.

[4] At this writing, the study is one year from completion in terms of four years of medical school.

Therefore data on the senior year of the third class are not yet available. However, a recent decision was made to continue following these three classes as far into their medical careers as is possible. Therefore we have been accumulating data on the first class in their internship. As we extend our efforts beyond medical school, the percentage of participation in the study by the several classes will probably decrease. However, it has been gratifying that so far two-thirds of the first class has responded to the internship questionnaire.

[5] Ordinarily, after the pretraining questionnaire was administered on the day of orientation for freshmen, the questionnaires were given in May or June of each year. Since some students began to accelerate (utilizing summer quarters) and others to lengthen (via added research quarters) training after the sophomore year, questionnaires had to be administered at additional times during the junior and senior years. Although the data collection process thus became more difficult, it maintained contact with each student when he actually finished a year's work.

[6] A cautionary word here is that no claim is to be made concerning causation. The differences which appear can only be noted as such in relation to the years in which they occur.

TABLE I

Doubts about Occupational Choice during Medical Training (Per Cent)

Doubt	Stage of Training				
	Pretraining	First Year	Second Year	Third Year	Fourth Year
No Doubt	41	57	64	68	70
Some Doubt	59	43	36	32	30
	$(N = 237)$	$(N = 205)$	$(N = 211)$	$(N = 157)$	$(N = 155)$

We shall be concerned with questions dealing with the relationships among self-doubts, competence, feelings of self as a physician, and career preference.[7]

In addition to the questionnaires, performance data consisting of yearly and cumulative grade point averages were obtained for the three classes. These were rank ordered and divided into quartiles.

From the preceding questions it can be seen that the development of self-image as a physician may be examined relative to such factors as actual and imagined performance in medical school, medical career preference, and satisfaction with occupational choice. All of these relationships can be viewed in the time perspective of the training program.

EXAMINATION OF THE DATA

Doubt about Occupational Choice

When an individual has been accepted by a medical school and agrees to attend, it can be said that he has made the first real commitment to the occupation. This commitment is confirmed by registration at the beginning of the freshman year. In all probability, many freshmen approach training with some trepidation and uncertainty. Their expectations are

derived mostly from secondary sources[8] since they have no experiential basis for such judgments. Under these circumstances, one might anticipate a greater amount of doubt about correctness of occupational choice early in training, with a lessening of such doubt as role preparation proceeds. Table I generally confirms this anticipation, although several other features are worth noting. First, it should be stated that medicine exhibits little flexibility in terms of student shifts to other occupations. Very few students resign or flunk out despite the extent and rigor of the course. This fact could be interpreted at some length,[9] but we mention it only to confirm the stability of the study population. The most striking feature of the table is that the dissipation of doubt which does occur takes place quite early in training and changes little after the second year. Furthermore, the size of the doubt group remains rather high. Given this sizable doubt group, we can further investigate those factors which may be related to its persistence.

Doubt about Occupational Choice and Actual Performance

An important factor influencing occupational doubt is the extent to which actual performance matches initial expectations of success in the role. During training, the performance criterion resides primarily in the assessments of the student by the faculty, functioning as role trainers and as a community of "significant others." These assessments are usually represented by grades given the student in specific courses and clinical rotations.[10] Presumably,

---

[7] Following are the specific items used in this analysis: (1) During your ——— year of medical training have you had any doubts that this is the right field for you? Serious doubts, what? ———; Slight doubts, what? ———; No doubts. (2) What is your realistic appraisal of how well you have done in your ——— year compared with other members of your class? Considerably better than average, Somewhat better than average, About average, Below average, Don't know. (3) When do you expect that you will first come to think of yourself as a physician? I already do, During my first year, During my second year, During my third year, During my fourth year, During my internship, During my residency, Haven't given it any thought. (4) At the present time, what is your career preference in medicine? General practice, Specialization . . field ———, Research . . type ———, Medical Education, Public health and preventive medicine.

[8] Among these sources are relatives and friends, published material such as bulletins and books, and personal experience as patients or as nonprofessional workers in medical settings.

[9] In a later paper, we shall venture into such interpretation by developing a concept of "entrapment" as it applies throughout the hierarchy of occupations in our society.

[10] It should be pointed out that formal grades are not the total evaluation of the student. Faculty committees and individuals do make additional

TABLE II

Distribution of Doubts about Occupational Choice in Relation to Levels of Actual Work Performance (as measured by grades)

Students Having Some Doubts about Occupational Choice (Per Cent)

Training Stage	Grade Quartiles							
	Quartile 1		Quartile 2		Quartile 3		Quartile 4	
	N^a	%	N	%	N	%	N	%
Pretraining[b]	(56)	46	(53)	58	(59)	61	(59)	68
First year	(53)	30	(47)	40	(51)	51	(47)	51
Second year	(48)	31	(48)	33	(55)	36	(43)	39
Third year	(58)	26	(52)	33	(56)	39	(59)	39
Fourth year	(40)	25	(35)	33	(46)	24	(33)	39

[a] N represents total N of quartile.
[b] Distribution made on basis of first-year grades.

the student would regard his grades as evidence of his success in acquiring the role. Consequently, he could compare his performance with initial expectations of success and this comparison could, in turn, affect some aspects of his self-image. If this chain of reasoning is valid, it would be expected that high performance would lessen doubts about occupational choice and hasten the formation of the physician self-image.

Table II examines the relationship between performance and doubt about occupational choice. Here we see that grades are not markedly related to doubts about occupational choice. Surprisingly, the pretraining distribution, which occurred prior to any work performance, shows the most clear-cut differences in terms of the grade quartiles. In subsequent years, the presence of occupational doubt becomes increasingly uniform among the quartiles. The quartiles columns in Table II show a decrease of doubt for all levels of performance through the second year, with less during the clinical years.

The most obvious interpretation of this material is that comparatively weak performance does not appear to increase a student's doubt about his occupational choice.[11] Even if weak

performance represents poor evaluation in the eyes of a "significant other" (faculty), this is not translatable into doubt about acquiring the role of physician.

Self-Evaluation of Performance and Actual Performance

We can pursue the matter further by asking whether the student's self-evaluation is, in fact, related to his actual performance as reflected in his grades.

Table III indicates that upon entrance to medical school, about one-fourth of the students anticipate low performance, whereas about one-sixth are uncertain. These distributions shift markedly after the first and second years of training, when more than one-half of the students rate themselves as low. After the third and fourth years, the pattern shifts again, this time toward the high category. Although the original level of optimism, as expressed by the ratio of high to low, is never regained, the fourth year distribution is closest to that of pretraining.

These shifts suggest that judgments of actual performance may significantly influence self-

evaluations for special purposes such as awards, admission to special programs, and promotion. The methods used in these latter evaluations are not standardized and therefore will not be included as part of the evaluation process being considered here.

11 Some clarification is necessary here regarding the term "weak performance." This term is used only in a relative sense because there are actually very few real failures for academic reasons. In spite of this academic security, students are quite

grade-conscious and there is a good deal of subvert competition for marks, especially in the first two years. The feeling among students that high grades will influence choice assignments in later years, especially for internships, persists throughout training. Although grades are often publicly shrugged off, few students seem able to discount them as being important in the eyes of the faculty. In the clinical years, students become less clear as to how grades are determined, and many feel that objective criteria become less important than subjective factors, such as compatibility and personal habits (punctuality, cheerfulness, etc.).

TABLE III

Students' Self-Evaluation of Performance during Four Years of Medical School

Training Stage	Self-Evaluation of Performance (Per Cent)[a]				
	High	Low	Don't Know		Total N
Pretraining[b]	60	23	17	100%	(233)
First year	44	55	1	100%	(207)
Second year	45	54	1	100%	(208)
Third year	58	41	1	100%	(155)
Fourth year	60	39	1	100%	(155)

[a] The self-evaluation distributions were derived by combining "considerably better than average" and "somewhat better than average" frequencies into a *High* category and "average" and "below average" into a *Low* category. Each student presumably was rating himself in terms of other medical students.

[b] The pretraining responses, of course, reflected expectations of performance rather than actual performance.

evaluation. This would certainly follow the logic of interactionist theory in which self-image and significant other-image of one's role performance would tend to coincide. Consequently, the relationship between self-evaluation and grade quartiles for each year was examined (see Table IV).

Table IV is interesting in several ways. First, it shows that pretraining expectations of performance are almost a perfect random distribution over the grade quartiles. Thus those with high pretraining expectations lacked power to predict level of first year performance. However, when we move to the next four stages in the table, the relationship becomes highly significant (at the .001 level), and it would seem that grades did markedly influence self-evaluation of performance. This "reality" factor, however, is not a static one, as closer scrutiny of the stages will reveal. Despite the continuous high significance of the relationship, its relative strength declines each year.[12] The source of this decline shows up in the high-expectation category, where an increasing number of high self-evaluators are found in the low quartiles, especially in the third and fourth years. The low self-evaluators remain much more realistic.

This internal trend in Table IV can now be combined with the data in Table III, which showed that the high self-evaluation category jumped sharply in the third and fourth years. These observations suggest that over the training program an increasing number of students claim a high self-image even though such an image is not supported by their actual perfor-

mance. One of two explanations seems likely. Either some students rationalize or delude themselves about their grades, or grades themselves become less important criteria of self-evaluation during training. These and other explanations remain to be tested by further data analysis.[13]

Self-Evaluation of Performance and Doubt about Occupational Choice

Let us now consider the relationship between self-evaluation of performance and doubt about occupational choice, for it is here that a crucial linkage between self and role may emerge.

Table V makes it obvious that students with high expectations of performance were also inclined to have less doubt about occupational choice than students with low performance expectations. Although there is no significant difference between the high and low groups, doubt about occupational choice is preponderant for both at entry into medical school. From then on, there is a growing disparity between the groups, with a strong statistical difference appearing during the third and fourth years.[14] Of course, we need to keep in mind

[12] The Chi-squares, in yearly sequence, are 118, 102, 80, 70.

[13] For example, if the trend we have just discussed continues, we would anticipate that subsequent time (i.e., internship) in the role would further increase the proportion of high self-evaluation among physicians regardless of grade-type criteria. It may also be true that many students conclude that the faculty, as a "significant other," either does not have or does not adhere to instrumental criteria of performance, either in determining grades or in weighting their importance.

[14] A modest difference (.05) between the groups was present in the first year but disappeared in the second.

TABLE IV

Relationship between Students' Self-Evaluation of Performance and Actual Performance (Grades) during Four Years of Medical School (Per Cent)

			Self-Evaluation of Performance								
	Pretraining[a]			First Year		Second Year		Third Year		Fourth Year	
Grade Quartiles	High (N[b] = 135)	Low (52)	Don't Know[c] (37)	High (86)	Low (109)	High (87)	Low (103)	High (129)	Low (92)	High (92)	Low (61)
First quartile	30	17	19	54	5	44	8	39	5	41	3
Second quartile	22	29	24	29	19	36	17	30	14	28	16
Third quartile	22	33	20	11	38	19	35	19	34	25	38
Fourth quartile	26	21	37	6	38	1	40	12	37	6	43
	100%	100%	100%	100%	100%	100%	100%	100%	100%	100%	100%

[a] Pretraining comparison was made with quartiles for first year grades.
[b] N represents total N of High, Low, Don't Know, respectively.
[c] This subcategory becomes numerically insignificant after pretraining.

TABLE V

Relationship between Having Doubts about Occupational Choice and Self-Evaluation of Performance

	Students Having Some Doubts about Occupational Choice (Per Cent)			
	Level of Self-Evaluation			
	High		Low	
Training Stage	Total N^a	%	Total N	%
Pretraining	(138)	53[b]	(56)	71
First year	(86)	30	(112)	54
Second year	(89)	32	(116)	40
Third year	(87)	21	(67)	45
Fourth year	(91)	19	(62)	47

[a] Each percentage is based on total N in high and low categories, respectively.
[b] Expressed as expectations of performance rather than actual performance.

that the percentage of career doubters declined steadily during medical training (see Table I). Yet those who retained doubt were increasingly those who had a low self-evaluation. The connection between grades and low self-evaluation was pointed out in the discussion of Table IV. Therefore it would appear that those with a low self-evaluation derive it from their low performance, and that this combination probably solidified doubt about career choice.

We have also established the fact that a sizable number of students have a high self-evaluation despite their relatively low performance. Apparently this group maintains satisfaction with occupational choice as a function of self-evaluation rather than performance.

We may conclude from these different patterns of role development that several role perspectives are available for medical students. The patterns can be represented schematically as follows:

(a) High Actual Performance→High Self-Evaluation→Low Occupational Doubt
(b) Low Actual Performance→Low Self-Evaluation→High Occupational Doubt
(c) Low Actual Performance→High Self-Evaluation→Low Occupational Doubt

Returning again to the logic of Mead's theory, we would expect patterns (a) and (b) to ensue as a direct effect of self-other interaction. However, the emergence of pattern (c) would appear to run counter to the "reality" principle inherent in the interactionist point of view. We have suggested previously that performance criteria other than grades or some other intervening variables may explain pattern (c). In any event, it seems clear that the relationship between performance and self-evaluation in the training process for the physician role is not a simple positive correlation for many students.

It is possible to investigate the doubt factor a bit further at this point. As part of one question, those who had doubts were asked to enumerate them. Most students supplied this information, which was classified primarily into two categories. One centered around the features of the role itself, such as work content, work environment, length of training, and reactions to patients. The other focused upon the student himself, principally his assessment of his capability and enthusiasm to perform in the role. Thus we have the contrast between an external role-doubt and an internal self-doubt.

The significant feature of Table VI resides in the comparison between role-type and self-type doubts. It can be seen clearly that during the first three years of training, doubt decreases over-all, but does so more rapidly in the self-type. The dramatic change occurs in the fourth year, when the combined doubt in the two categories increases. This is due entirely to rise in role-doubt offsetting a decline in self-doubt.

It would appear that those students who doubt their occupational choice increasingly shift in the locus of doubt from themselves to the nature of the role itself. Psychologically, this shift would support our finding that many students tend to have a high self-evaluation in the face of evidence of modest performance. This would reinforce our interpretation that many of the poorer performers may rationalize the reality of their performance by taking issue with and criticizing certain features of the role rather than questioning their ability to function adequately in it. There are many

TABLE VI

Distribution of Types of Doubt about Occupational Choice during Medical Training (Per Cent)

Type of Doubt	Training Stage				
	Pre-training	First Year	Second Year	Third Year	Fourth Year
None	41	57	64	68	70
Role	23	15	13	13	21
Self	25	16	9	7	3
Other and not specified	10	9	13	12	5
No answer	1	3	1	0	1
	100%	100%	100%	100%	100%
	$N = 154$	$N = 130$	$N = 139$	$N = 158$	$N = 156$

possible permutations involving this syndrome of response, but these will have to be explored elsewhere. However, it is obvious that the time dimension is an important one in the crystallization of doubt patterns.

Expectations of Self-Image as a Physician

When a student expects to feel like a physician is obviously a speculative and somewhat ambiguous matter, particularly in the early stages of role training. He may have expectations which are met earlier or later than he imagines, and he may change these anticipations during the training process. Preliminary examination of the data for this question (see format given previously) revealed that some of the year-by-year frequencies could be combined, including those periods which extended beyond the four years of medical training.

In Table VII we have an overview of students' expectations of acquiring the self-image of physician. Obviously, very few expect to acquire the role in the first two years.

Only 8% had such expectations at entrance, and this increased modestly to 12% who actually did claim they felt like physicians or expected to do so near the end of the first two years (combining columns 1 and 4). Fifty-six per cent said they already felt like physicians or expected to feel that way at the end of the fourth year (combining columns 1, 2 and 4). This percentage is almost identical with the 57% who, at entrance, anticipated acquiring the physician self-image while in medical school. However, this quantitative congruence of expectations is not uniform over the whole training process. While the "Don't Know" category consistently declines, the "After Medical School" category fluctuates in nonlinear fashion and finally shows as net gain over the entire course. Nevertheless, one cannot assume that the increase in column 3 is derived directly from the decrease in column 5. Column 6 does show that after the second year there is a clear postponement of expectations on the part of many students, the drop being

TABLE VII

Students' Expectations and Identification of Self-Image as a Physician during Medical Training (Per Cent)

Training Stage	When Expect to Feel Like a Physician						
	In First Two Years	In Second Two Years	After Med. School	Already Do	Don't Know[a]	In Med. School	N
Pretraining	8	49	34	0	9	(57%)	(137)
First year	9	48	31	3	9	(60%)	(118)
Second year	2	30	49	11	8	(43%)	(125)
Third year	0	9	57	32	2	(41%)	(148)
Fourth year	0	6	43	50	1	(56%)	(154)

[a] Columns 1-5 add to 100% across rows.

TABLE VIII

Relationship of Self-Identification as a Physician with Actual Work Performance
at End of Second and Fourth Years (Per Cent)

	Self-Identification as a Physician						
	End of Second Year			End of Fourth Year			
	(1) In First Two	(2) Hasn't Identi-		(3) In First Two	(4) In Second Two	(5) Hasn't Identi-	
Performance	Years	fied	N^a	Years[b]	Years	fied	N^a
High	12	88	(59)	8	43	49	(74)
Low	9	91	(68)	5	40	55	(80)

[a] N represents total N of high and low categories, respectively.
[b] Difference between columns (1) and (3) represents those who changed their minds between
the second and fourth years.

17% during the second year. This postponement increases slightly during the third year
but shifts decisively again in the fourth year
toward an earlier level of expectation. Thus
it can be seen that the apparent stability of
expectations between entrance and graduation
does indeed overlook considerable variation
during the training program. The postponement of expectations may be related to the
students' sense of the size and variety of his
intellectual and clinical tasks in terms of the
time and energy available to him. Thus he
pushes achievement of his role image farther
into the future. During the fourth year, however, the imminence of graduation and the

actual achievement of the M.D. degree and
license to practice medicine probably accelerate his role identification more rapidly than
his personal sense of attainment would permit
on its own.

We may now examine students' identity as
a physician with actual performance in medical
school. We can simplify the matter by using
the combined categories of identification with
a cumulative performance category for two-
year and four-year time spans.

Table VIII indicates that high-performance
students are not much more likely to see themselves as physicians during their medical training than are low-performance students. As with

TABLE IX

Relationship between Self-Evaluation of Performance and Self-Image as a
Physician (Per Cent)

		When Expect to Feel Like a Physician					
Training Stage	Self-Evaluation	First Two Years	Second Two Years	After Med. School	Already Do	Don't Know	N^a
Pretraining	High	11	49	31	1	8	(139)
	Low	11	48	36	0	5	(56)
First year	High	14	48	25	8	5	(88)
	Low	7	50	27	2	14	(113)
Second year	High	2	32	50	14	2	(56)
	Low	1	32	49	6	12	(76)
Third year	High	0	7	51	41	1	(84)
	Low	0	11	63	22	4	(64)
Fourth year	High	0	8	32	60	0	(44)
	Low	0	3	60	37	0	(62)

[a] N represents total N of high and low categories, respectively.

other variables we have discussed, high grades do not seem to hasten the perceived process of role development.

Now we turn to self-evaluation of performance (see Table IX), as distinct from grades, to discover whether high or low estimates affect the pace of role identification.

The trend illustrated in Table IX reflects an emergent difference in self-identification as a physician between high and low self-evaluators. The difference is not manifest until after the third year, and it becomes highly significant (.001) in the fourth year. Thus we may say that at the conclusion of medical school, self-evaluation is strongly related to role identification. As before, we would add that quite a few low performers academically will probably identify themselves as physicians if, at the same time, they possess a high self-evaluation.

The question of doubt about occupational choice may also be asked in terms of self-identification as a physician.

The essence of Figure 1 is that the "No Doubt" group always is more optimistic about achieving self-identification as a physician during medical school than is the "Some Doubt" group. yet both groups show a similar pattern of responses with low points in the second and third years. The only significant difference (.05) between the two groups occurs in the third year. Both groups regain their optimism

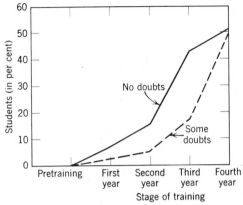

Figure 2. Medical students who already identify themselves as physicians (per cent). Solid line = those who have no doubts about occupational choice. Dashed lines = those who have some doubts about occupational choice.

in the fourth year, with the "Some Doubt" group making the more striking recovery.

Figure 2 illustrates the differences between the doubt groups more intensively by focusing on those students who actually said they felt like physicians at the several stages of training. As might be anticipated, groups diverge slowly during the first two years. In the third year, the disparity is dramatic in the expected direction, yet it almost disappears again in the fourth year. The interesting development here is not the third year increase of the "No Doubt" group, but the even greater increase of the "Some Doubt" group in the fourth year. Our current interpretation is not definitive, but we seem to be witnessing a belated effort by the doubters to identify with the physician role. This may reflect their need, at the conclusion of training, to express role identity even though many did not feel such an identity. The apparent dissonance of many of the doubters needs to be further investigated, since there may be factors which can be uncovered as effective dissonance reducers.

Career Choice within the Role

A considerable amount of previous research[15] on medical training has dealt with career selection within medicine, particularly with respect to choice of clinical specialty. Attempts have been made to show how the

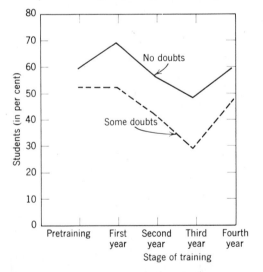

Figure 1. Medical students who identify or expect to identify themselves as physicians during medical school (per cent). Solid line = those who have no doubts about occupational choice. Dashed line = those who have some doubts about occupational choice.

---

15 An example of this type of research is H. Boverman, "Senior Student Career Choices in Retrospect," in *The Journal of Medical Education*, **40** (February 1965), pp. 161–165.

students are eventually distributed in terms of academic performance and other training factors. It was desirable, for comparative purposes, to check the current data along similar lines. At present, it is possible to comment only in a broad way regarding careers within medicine. It is of interest to know whether students select primarily clinical or academic/research medicine. If they choose clinical medicine, is it general practice or a specialty field? Admittedly, it is becoming more difficult to demarcate types of physicians, since many of them have multiple subroles within the profession. However, the preferences can be ascertained in the following manner by stages of training.

Table X reveals that more than four-fifths of the students have a basically clinical orientation to medicine, and that an overwhelming number of such students intend to practice a specialty. General practice has scanty appeal at the conclusion of medical training, although during the first and second years a fair number of students thought they would enter this area. Only a residual 5% of students were undecided in the fourth year. The proportion of those with an academic and/or research career orientation held relatively constant over the course as a whole, showing a slight net increase between pretraining and graduation. We may certainly conclude that when three-fourths of the graduating medical students perceive themselves in careers of clinical specialization, as compared with less than one-half having this perception at entrance, the training program has either permitted or actually fostered such perceptions. In any event, for the classes in this study, the field of general practice has all but disappeared as a career preference within medicine. The academic and/or research field

seems on the verge of growth, although its precise strength is uncertain on current evidence.

If we relate the other variables used in this presentation to medical career preference, we do not find any of these variables consistently connected to the clear pattern exhibited in Table X. We may summarize these computations by saying that the occupational doubt, self-evaluation, actual performance, and self-image as physican variables were not statistically significant as factors involving medical career preference.

There was a tendency for low performers and low self-evaluators to be slightly more undecided about career choice. Since these groups take slightly longer to identify themselves as physicians, it also is not surprising that they would select a medical career line somewhat later. However, the real emphasis should be on the fact that role-image and self-image factors did not affect the pattern of career preference or the time at which such preference was expressed.

CONCLUDING DISCUSSION

Although the data presented in the body of this chapter do not constitute a full-scale examination of the interactionist conception of personality, they do concern several prominent aspects of that theory.

From the methodological standpoint, the time dimension has proved valuable in adding systematic material on role acquisition during the period of formal training in medicine. It has been clearly superior to a before-after design in terms of process analysis.

This process analysis of selected role variables in the training of medical students has important implications both for medical edu-

TABLE X
Career Preference within Medicine during Medical Training (Per Cent)

| Stage of training | Medical Career Preference | | | | Total | N |
	General Practice	Clinical[a] Specialty	Academic/ Research[a]	Unde-cided		
Pretraining	10	47	10	33	100%	(237)
First year	19	54	13	14	100%	(211)
Second year	16	60	17	7	100%	(211)
Third year	10	66	18	6	100%	(157)
Fourth year	6	75	14	5	100%	(184)

[a] Although these areas can be subdivided more specifically, this would require a more detailed analysis than we shall attempt here. This detailed analysis will be carried out and reported in subsequent papers.

cation and for general interactionist theory. To review the matter, a rather complex network of relationships was found to be involved in the analysis of even the few variables which were chosen. We discovered that a sizable group (about 30%) of graduating medical students had doubts about their occupational choice. However, these doubts frequently were not related to actual performance (a "self" measure) but were shifted over time from self-doubt to role-doubt. Even more significant was the fact that actual performance did affect self-evaluation of performance in a variety of ways. In interactionist terms (following G. H. Mead), high performance should produce high self-evaluation, which consequently should remove doubt about occupational choice. Low performance should produce the reverse. For many medical students, this logic appears sound. But we did find that some students reacted to their low performance with a high self-evaluation and with no doubt about choice of occupation. Thus we seem to have at least three modes of self-role interaction instead of the two a "black and white" reading of Mead would suggest.

The existence of the low-performance and high self-evaluation (which was labeled "unrealistic" or "dissonant") group was further compounded by the finding that although high self-evaluation usually did produce an earlier self-identity as a physician, the "Some Doubt" group did identify as physicians nearly as strongly as the "No Doubt" group in the fourth year of training. Thus a low self-evaluation may delay but not prevent a student from identifying himself as a physician during medical school.[16]

At this stage of analysis we are not prepared to further unravel these relationships or to explore additional patterns of role-self interaction. It seems clear, however, that the interactionist theory of socialization should not be oversimplified. It is probably true, if this analysis of medical student education is at all representative of adult socialization, that while Mead's approach is correct for most people in a given context, there are substantial variations in the process. These variations seem incongruent with the expected sequence of self-image development in a role as a function of clear-cut responses by "significant others." However, before dismissing Mead, it will be necessary to find out whether the "dissonant" patterns of socialization that have come to light can still be explained within the basic theory, or a recognizable modification of it.[17] It is hoped that further analysis in this study and in others which deal with socialization in the perspective of role acquisition will aid in resolving this issue.

---

[16] We have previously alluded to the fact that few medical students actually leave medical school for other occupations. Bona fide academic failures are rare. The selection and admission process is assumed by the faculty to have screened out the potential failures from among the group of applicants who have already been self-screened. There-fore it is difficult for both students and faculty to acknowledge deficiencies in a student which would disqualify him for the role of physician. This view tends to ignore the fact that many students enter medicine for diverse reasons, some of which are peripheral to the physician role itself (i.e., having a father who is a physician, seeking status in the society, not having a strong preference for another occupation, etc.). Such reasons are not often given to admission committees, who may tend to see achievement motivation and service aspiration in places where they may not be present. A student's real feelings and perceptions of himself may remain locked in the hidden social environment from which he comes.

[17] Recent studies of Mead's formulations have begun to raise issues about his central ideas, many of which have become assumptions rather than hypotheses to be tested. See, for example, T. D. Kemper, "Reference Set and Self-Concept Among Business Executives," paper delivered at the ASA meetings, Los Angeles, August, 1963. It is the development and test of such hypotheses which seem to offer the most productive paths for research on the interactionist position in personality theory.

Chapter 20 Shame, Guilt, and Identity beyond Roles

HELEN MERRELL LYND

I

The idea of entering fully into the conflicts of our historical period and living in terms of a wider range of possibilities in oneself and in one's society raises the question of what more than the combination of prescribed social roles enables an individual to say: This is I.

Three further questions arise here:

What are the processes by which certain aspects of identifications with parents and with cultural roles are accepted and others rejected, and by which those accepted are woven into a new *Gestalt?*

What enables some individuals more than others to endure frustration, to forego identifications with their immediate society, and to find identifications with wider, longer-range, and more diversified human values?

Are there identifications that derive less from the particular features of the society in which an individual has been bred than from characteristics and aspirations both more particular to individuals and more common to humanity?

Attempts to answer these questions go into largely undiscovered country. Recent social theory, particularly the work of Durkheim, Parsons, and Merton, has taken note of deviance and *anomie.* But it remains true that in psychology and in social science in general more attention is still given to adaptation and adjustment to approved social roles and values than to deviation from them. And deviance is far too readily codified in oversimplified terms of genius or of rebellion or, even, of individual pathology.

All that has been said about shame as a revealing of one's society as well as of oneself

points beyond complete cultural relativism toward the possibility of more universal human values. There seem to be indications of aspirations of the self that go beyond the demands of society, requirements of oneself that exceed social demands, perspectives against which one places the demands of one's own society.

In one form or another, the question of how one forms one's own idiom has been recurrent throughout our history. How do we explain Amos, Socrates, Tycho Brahe, Galileo, Martin Luther, Freud, Cézanne, Rilke, Stephen Hero, Black Boy—or prophets, rebels, artists, or other innovators whose names are unknown—whose sense of self is related to ideals that they conceive as widely human and at the same time peculiarly their own?

Heraclitus asserted man's moral autonomy in opposition to religious belief in a tutelary spirit; he distinguished life as individuated in men from other life processes by its capacity for heightening its own status. This heightening of oneself beyond cultural demands is precisely what is involved in discovery of identity.

In Aristotle's view the life of each individual was governed by a law of its own through the unfolding of which each person attained his own separate individuality, his own "true" nature. This conception of development influenced such a very different person as St. Augustine and, in more recent times, Ortega y Gasset.

Keats sought to account for the varieties of differentiation from the culture in terms somewhat closer to our own:

Man is originally "a poor forked creature" . . . subject to the same mischances as the beasts of the forest. . . . Call the world . . . "The vale of soul-making." . . . There may be intelligence or sparks of the divinity in millions—but they are not souls until they acquire identity, till each one is personally itself. . . . I will call the *world* a School instituted for the purpose of teaching little children to read—I will call the *human heart* the *horn Book* read in that School—and I will call

SOURCE. Helen Merrell Lynd, *On Shame and the Search for Identity,* New York: Science Editions, Inc., 1961, pp. 226–241. Copyright 1958 by Helen Merrell Lynd.

the *Child able to read, the Soul* made from that *School* and its *hornbook. . . .* Not merely is the Heart a Hornbook, it is the Mind's Bible, it is the Mind's experience, it is the text from which the mind or intelligence sucks its identity. As various as the Lives of Men are—so various become their Souls . . . what are the provings of [man's] heart but fortifiers and alterers of his nature? and what is his altered nature but his soul?—and what was his Soul before it came into the world and had these provings and alterations and perfectionings? —An intelligence—without Identity—and how is this Identity to be made? Through the medium of the Heart? and how is the Heart to become this Medium but in a world of Circumstances?[1]

Some men and women as they grow older become less differentiated from, more and more replicas of, or masks formed by, their society. This can be seen from their successive portraits and from their literary and artistic work. Advancing years mean to them more need of the protection of being like others, less of the risk involved in the search for their own way of life. Others develop with added years more sureness and deep-rootedness in themselves in relation to the world. Their faces, their letters, and their published writings or artistic productions become more forthright, more genuinely individual as they grow older. This was true of Goethe, of T. H. Huxley, of Yeats, of Einstein.

The larger-than-immediate roles and values with which one can identify include the nonpersonal as well as the personal world. Work, relationship to, and discovery in, the nonpersonal world is not only or always a compensation or substitute for frustrated personal or sexual impulses. As the child begins to distinguish himself from the world around him and to acquire a growing sense of himself and of his own desires, this sense of self grows step by step with interest in the reality of the external world. The discovery of what is reality in nonpersonal things in themselves not related to one's personality is an indispensable part of discovering what is one's personality.

Piaget has described the child's early lack of distinction between inner and outer, subject and object, psychological and physical, living and nonliving. Schilder and Schachtel have amplified the account of the slow development of the sense of self as something different from the world of other people and of things, as this outer world at the same time becomes recognizable as something different from oneself.

Schachtel speaks of the importance of "the variety of the playful approach, as contrasted with the narrow directedness of the need-driven approach" in developing a child's sense of the world of social demands and of objects and of himself as related to, but distinct from, both.[2]

Curiosity, the desire for knowledge, the wish to orient oneself in the world one lives in—and finally the posing of man's eternal questions, "Who am I?" "What is this world around me?" "What can I hope for?" "What should I do?"—all these do not develop under the pressure of relentless need or of fear for one's life. They develop when man can pause to think, when the child is free to wonder and to explore. . . . They represent man's distinctive capacity to develop *interest*—the autonomous interest which alone permits the full encounter with the object.[3]

The child's reflective focussing on his own feelings and experiences constitutes the last step in the development of focal attention, and accompanies the development of the idea of "I" and the autobiographical memory—that is, the concept of the continuity of the self.[4]

In the discovery and creation of oneself in relation to and differentiated from social codes, both one's self-image, the picture of what one is, and one's self-ideal, the picture of what one would like to be, are involved. Different degrees and kinds of congruence between the two and between both and the life-style approved by the culture emerge in the process of developing identity.

There is much confusion about these terms, about the parts of the self they denote, and the ways in which these parts function in the developing personality. The superego of Freud is relatively clear. It is a prohibiting, restraining, guilt-producing part of the self compounded from instinctual drives, desire for parental approval, and parental threats and prohibitions which have become internalized through identification with the parents or with the parents' ideals. The self-ideal in Piers' sense is concerned, not with violation of taboos, but with long-term purposes and goals.[5]

There is need to explore further, not only the

[1] Letter to George and Georgiana Keats, Feb., Mar., Apr., 1819. Maurice Buxton Forman, ed., *The Letters of John Keats,* Oxford University Press, 1931, Vol. II, pp. 361–4.

[2] "The Development of Focal Attention," p. 320.
[3] *Ibid.*
[4] *Ibid.,* p. 313.
[5] The self-ideal is also sometimes used to include the prohibiting aspects of the superego, Horney's derogatory view of a romanticized self-ideal, and the incorporation of prescribed social roles.

sources of the idea of self and of the self-ideal, but also the kinds of relations there may be between them. One basis for distinction between different kinds of relations between the self and the self-ideal is the difference between a sense of identity formed primarily on what I have called the guilt axis (in Piers' words, formed in terms of the prohibiting superego) and a sense of identity formed primarily on what I have called the shame axis (in Piers' words, formed in terms of the ego-ideal). Individuals tend to find continuity in their lives either by means of basic emphasis on what others have taught them they should do and— more especially—should not do, or by means of emphasis on discovering their own lines of direction. Learning to know oneself is in part the ability to distinguish between these two ways of growth. In our society a person is inclined to be more specifically conscious of behavior on the guilt axis, of transgressions that are culturally defined and redeemable, and of their counterparts that add up role by role to a righteous, mature, adjusted life. He can perhaps at relatively small emotional expense fulfill the requirements society makes of him. But identity built on the guilt axis may be less enduring, more likely to break down into its parts. If its loyalties are based mainly on social requirements, the sense of self may change if these requirements shift.

Identity based more on the shame axis may go deeper and be more of a continuous process of creation with less easily dissipated *Gestalts*. Shame, while touched off by a specific, often outwardly trivial, occurrence initially felt as revealing one's own inadequacies, may also confront one with unrecognized desires of one's own and the inadequacy of society in giving expression to these desires. There is a natural tendency to seek cover from such experiences since the culture has little place for revelations of the inmost self or of the central dynamics of the society. But it is the whole purpose of oneself and of one's society that invites reexamination in the light of these experiences. Selective fulfilling of social roles when it occurs then becomes part of a continuing process rather than a series of isolable acts. Stubborn and minute control is replaced by the unfolding of the spirit. In a society more directly and variously expressive of human desires the guilt axis and the shame axis, role fulfillment and personal fulfillment, might more nearly coincide.

Although in many experiences both guilt and

shame are involved, at times the differences between adaptation to the social roles demanded by society and the demands of one's own life appear in sharp contrast. Of Aleksei Aleksandrovitch, Tolstoy says:

> [He] was now standing face to face with life, with the possibility that his wife was in love with someone else . . . and this seemed to him very senseless and incomprehensible, because it was life itself. All his life he had lived and labored in a round of official duties concerned with the reflections of life. And whenever he came in contact with life itself he was revolted by it. Now he experienced a sensation such as a man feels, who, passing calmly over a bridge above a precipice, suddenly discovers that the arch is broken, and that the abyss yawns beneath his feet. This abyss was actual life; the bridge—the artificial life he had been living.[6]

Confronting, instead of quickly covering, an experience of shame as revelation of oneself and of society—facing "actual life"—requires an ability to risk, if necessary to endure, disappointment, frustration, and ridicule. Commitment to any position or to any loyalty, like commitment to another person, involves the risk of being wrong and the risk of being ridiculous. It is *relatively* easy to take even difficult action if one is sure that one is right, that one has grasped the truth of a situation; it is relatively easy to entertain multiple possibilities of truth and of right action if one remains a spectator on the side-lines. Far more difficult than either is to give everything one is in supporting all the truth that one can see at any given time, with full awareness that there are other possibilities and that further knowledge may enlarge and revise the hypotheses on which one has risked everything. Engagement with life and with history—self-discovery and further discovery of the world—has always involved just such risks.

There is no easy way to distinguish between elements of dissolution and of promise in an era of the destruction of an old order and the birth of a new, between chaos that is only destructive and chaos that heralds the future, or even between that which is appropriately called order and that which is called disorder. Many people thought that they were living in a society of order and secure values in England at a time when children were working twelve hours a day in the mines and the mills.

But the culture within which one may dis-

---

[6] *Anna Karenina*, p. 168.

cover identifications is more than a geographical unit, more than a national concept, more than a particular historical period. History is more than the present, more than aspects of the past now dominant; it has other available traditions and various possible futures. The values associated with the importance of individual idiom, with human relations, freedom, and democracy, which we cherish as our cultural identifications, may be found in new forms in other parts of the world. We may extend the range of selectivity that inheres in any social situation to include wider areas, longer historical perspectives, closer examination of varied possibilities and of actual options within the present.

Harder than our own difficulties in living in such wider perspectives is contemplating such difficulties for the next generation. We would have them encounter what the world can be at the time they are living in it. But we shrink from what this encounter involves. We do not want their lives to be subject to the hazards of our own—or of their own—beliefs.

But we cannot have it this way. We want them to be intelligent and discerning. And we know that it is often the persons who have the greatest intelligence and awareness who are also most vulnerable to the inhumanities and hypocrisies of society and the least ready to make the compromises necessary for adjustment. They have a selectivity that does not allow them to accept passively.[7] How do we meet the perplexities of our children? How do we respond to the questions of our students about what it is to be mature, how one decides when to stand fast to a loyalty, when to modify and to con-

form[8]—all their contemporary versions of Kant's three questions: How can I know? What can I hope? What should I do? How and when do we prepare our children and our students for transition from the kind of personal responsiveness and support for their expectations that home and college may offer to a more impersonal and contradictory world? And how help them to discover wider identifications through which they can find continuities?

If greater awareness may make them more unprotected against the impact of the contradictions in society it may also give them more sturdy capacity, in Heraclitus' words, to heighten their own stature and to discern and ally themselves with men and values over wider ranges of time and space. The sense of identity that may be the outcome of the confrontation of the implications of shame is a lifelong process of discovery. Nor is it an even or a continuous process of discovery.

This again is truer the more intelligent, the more responsive, and hence the more aware and vulnerable the person is. Freud speaks of the "repeated adolescence" of creative minds which he ascribes to himself as well as to his friend Fliess. Goethe believed that while most people are young only once, there are some—and these the most gifted—who experience their youth repeatedly.[9] Such individuals must recurrently face what those who adapt more easily to social requirements settle in late adolescence.

The "normal" individual combines the various prohibitions and challenges of the ego-ideal in a sober, modest, and workable unit, well anchored in a set of techniques and in the roles that go with them. The restless individual must, for better or for worse . . . [continually reassert] his ego identity.[10]

Although the realization of identity is something more than and different from identification with parents and with social roles approved by society, the ways in which it is different from these identifications can be too simply conceived. Some restatements of the individual-

---

[7] Erikson says of Darwin, "I do not wish to speculate here on the dynamics of a psychoneurosis in a man like Darwin. But I do know that a peculiar malaise can befall those who have seen too much, who, in ascertaining new facts in a spirit seemingly as innocent as that of a child who builds with blocks, begin to perceive of the place of these facts in the moral climate of their day . . . a creative man has no choice. He may come across his supreme task almost accidentally. But once the issue is joined, his task proves to be at the same time intimately related to his most personal conflicts, to his superior selective perception, and to the stubbornness of his one-way will: he must . . . test . . . whether the established world will crush him, or whether he will disestablish a sector of this world's outworn fundaments and make place for a new one." ("The First Psychoanalyst," *The Yale Review,* Vol. XLVI, No. 1, Sept. 1956, pp. 42–3.)

[8] Adolescents in our society frequently go through difficulties of "role diffusion," a taking over of a variety of cultural roles in an attempt to find in them a confirmation of, or even a substitute for, inner design. (Erikson, *Childhood and Society,* pp. 227–8.)

[9] Barker Fairley, *A Study of Goethe,* p. 231.

[10] See Erikson, "The Dream Specimen of Psychoanalysis," in Knight and Friedman, *Psychoanalytic Psychiatry and Psychology,* Vol. I, p. 169.

group relation assume something like polar opposites between individuation and being a part of humanity.

Plato, Aristotle, and Kant believed that the most significant characteristic of men is their capacity for reason, and that affect, desire, and feeling are less important "accidental" features. They then drew the conclusion that only those aspects of human behavior that have to do with reason can be studied or are worth studying. Many philosophical, psychological, and social theories have been built on this assumption of the basic rationality of man. Freud in some sense reversed it, making emotion rather than reason basic in human beings, then attempting to classify emotions and to trace developmental stages that are alike, or differ only in quantitative distribution, for all men.

Like Freud, although with different wording and emphasis, Harry Stack Sullivan bases his theory and his therapy on the observation that we are all "more simply human" than we are healthy or diseased, normal or abnormal.[11] But Sullivan contrasts being more simply human with individual uniqueness.[12] Common humanity and individual uniqueness are not, I believe, Platonic opposites, as Sullivan suggests, but Hegelian opposites, in the sense that each is part of and necessary to the other.

An awareness of unique, precise detail as a universalizing as well as an individualizing experience appears in the great novelists and poets. The shape of Dmitri's toes, Dorothea's experience in Rome,[13] the particular quality of Flora's relation to her father,[14] were peculiar to them; no other human being ever had precisely these characteristics or experiences. The expression on the face of the little Princess, Prince Andrey's wife, in childbirth; the approaches and withdrawals in the conversations between Andrey and Pierre; Marya's blushes; the length of Natasha's skirt at her first ball; Natasha's changes of mood at the opera; Prince Andrey's feeling as he listened to Natasha sing; Petya's love of raisins—nothing could be more particular to the individuals involved, yet is it not just these things that make *War and Peace* universally human?

Every individual has some qualities and ways

of experiencing that are his own, and it is this fact as well as things that can be called common, shared human characteristics that make him a member of humanity. It is in part the very uniqueness of every individual that makes him, not only a member of a family, race, nation, or class, but a human being.

II

It is not necessary to go as far as Sullivan does, in saying that what one *is* is one's personal relations, to recognize the crucial importance in the search for identity of the way one views and engages with other individuals. Relations with other persons are something different from selective identifications with aspects of one's immediate social situation or with wider values. Both are involved, but neither comprehends all of person-to-person relations.

In personal relations, as in other phases of life, guilt-axis and shame-axis orientations are frequently interwoven in a particular experience. But to a person who lives and views experience primarily along the guilt-righteousness axis other persons tend to be primarily external and instrumental to himself or— another version of the same thing—he instrumental to them. This is true whether he regards them (or himself in relation to them) as indulgent or depriving agents administering pleasure or pain, as representing certain social roles, or as members of an audience who mete out approval or scorn. To a person oriented more to the shame-identity axis, other persons, the They, or at least some of them, are parts of himself as he is part of them.

The first tends to regard both others and himself as instruments, remaining external to each other. He must always weigh and appraise and be on guard against committing himself. From others, he should seek approval, indulgence, contributions to his pleasure. For others, he should do the right thing, meet the appropriate standards, fulfill the designated social roles. He should never lose sight of what they will think of what he does and how that will affect him. Appraisal tends to be always present. Trust is in abeyance.

In our society "emotional" is frequently used as a derogatory term. Developing emotional maturity is more often conceived in terms of training a child in what he should *not* feel and in controlling the expression of his feelings

---

11 *Conceptions of Modern Psychiatry,* p. 47.
12 See, for example, "The Illusion of Personal Individuality," *Psychiatry,* Vol. 13, No. 3, Aug. 1950.
13 *Middlemarch,* pp. 187–91.
14 *Chance.*

than in extending the range and depth of his emotions and their expression.[15]

A person who lives more on the shame-identity or shame-freedom axis, and who opens himself to his own emotions, faces other difficulties and other possibilities. There is not only more question of what I think of what I do and how it will affect others. Much more important, there is more ability to see the world through the eyes of another person, with another instead of myself as the center. The "I" is both more separate from, and more related to, other persons.

The blunting of the discovery by individuals of their own identity and their use of other persons as instrumental objects was the basis of Marx's indictment of capitalist industrialism, which, with varying degrees of explicitness, Fromm, Erikson, Marcuse, as well as some social scientists, follow.

Only in community with others has each individual the means of cultivating his gifts in all directions. . . . In the real community the individuals obtain their freedom in and through their association.

Competition makes individuals, not only the bourgeois but still more the workers, mutually hostile, in spite of the fact that it brings them together.[16]

Marx believed that present society "generates those false selves which make of our lives comedies and tragedies of mistaken identity." In the situation Marx hoped for, "No longer is each individual haunted by an alien 'I' detached from his daily life . . . the drama of the socialist revolution—and its pathos—is a drama of self-creation. . . . Making oneself would seem to be a different process from recognizing oneself as an already existing, if hidden, 'I.' "[17]

Much depends upon whether one believes that isolation and alienation are inevitable in man's fate or that openness of communication between persons, mutual discovery, and love are actual possibilities. But even if one faces in the direction of trust and the possibility of discovery, the development of relations of mutuality is not easy.

When Freud says that human relations almost always end in disappointment and a cutting down of hopes to meet reality,[18] he is describing what does happen in many, if not most, personal relations in our society. Rarely, perhaps, do the particular personal qualities of individuals that can bring the greatest mutual fulfillment coincide with the appropriate, socially approved roles. Certain parts of the personality often have to be submerged for the fulfillment of others. This is why, even in our society, which ostensibly gives great importance to love as the basis for marriage, counselors who give advice on marriage tend to warn against reliance on romantic love and to stress companionship, comparable background, and socially approved roles as a firmer foundation for marital happiness. This is already a denial in advance of certain possibilities.

It may be that in any known society mutuality and trust that make possible profound openness between persons, and the finding of oneself in and through others, are all but impossible. To some extent limitations of mutuality because of the nature of human beings and of circumstances, as well as loss through death, are part of the human lot. Just as in one lifetime only a limited range of a person's possible ways of expression may be fulfilled, so in any one relation it may be that only some ranges of mutual love that each person brings to it can be realized.

But with all the inevitable limitations, it is questionable whether loneliness and the substitution of roles for mutual openness need to characterize person-to-person relations as largely as they do at present. Questions about other possibilities cut to the roots of assumptions about human nature and personal relations. Assumptions about the outgrowth of intimacy and assumptions about the effect of

---

[15] Scheler points out that the term "sympathy" is often wrongly confined to pity or compassion. Sympathy with suffering (*Mitleid*) and sympathy with joy (*Mitfreude*) are two different things often confused, and the second is frequently neglected in the study of the first. (V. J. McGill, "Scheler's Theory of Sympathy and Love," "Symposium on the Philosophy of Max Scheler," *Philosophy and Phenomenological Research,* Vol. II, No. 3, Mar. 1952, p. 276.)

[16] Marx and Engels, *The German Ideology,* pp. 74–8 and p. 58, and "Alienated Labor."

[17] Harold Rosenberg, "The Pathos of the Proletariat," *Kenyon Review,* Vol. XI, No. 4, Autumn 1949, pp. 610, 611–13.

[18] Edith Weigert adds that repeated disappointment of expectation leads even to a denial of the expectations themselves. ("Existentialism and Its Relations to Psychotherapy," *Psychiatry,* Vol. 12, No. 4, Nov. 1949.) Meerloo believes that for many persons today fear of human relations is greater than fear of death; they are afraid to take the emotional responsibility of having an emotional involvement with their fellow beings. *The Rape of the Mind,* World Publishing Co., 1956, pp. 163–4.

the passage of time are separately involved but related. Time necessarily brings changes in any relation, and one must be prepared to recognize these changes and to grow and change with time. But if one can believe that it is possible for the greater knowledge that two persons may acquire of each other in the course of time to bring also greater respect and love, then—beyond the inevitabilities of human life cycles—one need not fear time. Can one have faith that with certain other persons greater openness can increase understanding, respect, and love? That with them increasing intimacy can be, not a corroding, but a deepening and enriching process?

E. M. Forster points out the contrast between Proust's lack of faith and Dante's faith in the possibilities in human intimacy.[19] Proust believed that the fonder we are of people the less we understand and respect them; Dante that the fonder we are of people the greater is our understanding. To Dante increased knowledge was love, love knowledge. For Proust, as for Freud, time eventually destroys love; for Dante expansion of time makes love more possible.[20] Love can become an intensification of seeing, a looking into hidden possibilities.

Recognizing the extent to which people do use other persons as objects for their own satisfaction and security, and to which greater intimacy and the passage of time do diminish love, we still find exceptions, and it is important to try to discover the nature of these exceptions and of the conditions that seem to permit or foster them.[21]

Enlarging the possibilities of mutual love depends upon risking exposure. This risk of exposure can come about only with respect for oneself, respect for the other person, and recognition of nonpersonal values and loyalties that both persons respect. Through such love one comes to know the meaning of exposure without shame, and of shame transformed by being understood and shared. Aristotle distinguishes between feeling ashamed of things shameful "according to common opinion" and things shameful "in very truth."[22] In love there can be the exploring together of the meaning of things shameful "in very truth."

Then shall the fall further the flight in me

In mutual trust and love there can be no incongruous or inappropriate words or behavior. Dropping the protection of role-playing, letting oneself go freely in risking incongruity and inappropriateness is one of the delights of trusted love. Exposure can be exposure of the diversity of the good, the hopeful, the tender, as well as of what may be in other circumstances accounted shameful.

Love casts out fear. Shakespeare shares this Biblical emphasis. Unlike Freud, he contrasts love, not with hate, but with fear. Love is strong and unshaken; fear is weak, palehearted, shuddering, trembling. Fear casts out love. Mutual love is incompatible with desire for power over other persons. Macbeth's retribution was the retreat of love before fear following desire for power.

> Those he commands move only in command,
> Nothing in love . . .[23]
> . . . I am cabin'd, cribb'd, confin'd, bound in
> To saucy doubts and fears.[24]

Richard II saw that

> The love of wicked men converts to fear,
> That fear to hate . . .[25]

For Donne love encompasses fear as well as space and time.

> And now good-morrow to our waking souls,
> Which watch not one another out of fear;
> For love all love of other sights controls,
> And makes one little room an every where.

The experience of deep engagement with and commitment to another person can be enhanced by time.

---

[19] E. M. Forster, "Proust," in *Abinger Harvest,* Harcourt, Brace, 1936, p. 100.

[20] Sartre, like Freud and Proust, believes that intimacy and satisfaction of desire tends to diminish love and to diminish oneself: ". . . the amorous intuition is . . . an ideal out of reach. The more I am loved, the more I lose my *being.* . . . In the second place the Other's awakening is always possible; at any moment he can make me appear as an object—hence the lover's perpetual insecurity. In the third place love is an absolute which is perpetually *made relative* by others . . . pleasure is the death and the failure of desire. It is the death of desire because it is not only its fulfillment but its limit and its end . . . pleasure . . . is *attention to the incarnation of the For-itself which is reflected-on* and by the same token it is forgetful of the Other's incarnation, *Being and Nothingness,* Philosophical Library, 1956, pp. 337, 397.

[21] Cf. Erikson, "The Problem of Ego Identity," pp. 80–83, 118.

[22] *Nicomachean Ethics,* Book IV, Chap. 9.

[23] *Macbeth,* V, ii, 19–20.

[24] *Ibid.,* III, iv, 24–5.

[25] *Richard II,* V, i, 66–7.

Love surfeits not, Lust like a glutton dies.[26]

It is a constant rebirth of surprise that the world can hold something so beyond imagination that is at the same time a familiar homecoming. It is a fullness of joy that entirely outruns any explanation in terms of the pleasure principle, or of the threat of time. Past and future unite in making the immediacy of the present moment what it is.

. . . immediate reality is transcended in any kind of joy . . . we have to distinguish between *pleasure by release of tension*, and the *active feeling of enjoyment* and freedom so characteristic of joy. . . . Pleasure may be a necessary state of respite. But it is a phenomenon of standstill. . . . It separates us from the world and the other individuals in it; it is equilibrium, quietness. In joy there is disequilibrium . . . disequilibrium, leading toward fruitful activity and a particular kind of self-realization.[27]

Openness to relatedness with other persons and the search for self-identity are not two problems but one dialectical process; as one finds more relatedness to other persons one discovers more of oneself; as the sense of one's own identity becomes clearer and more firmly rooted one can more completely go out to others. It is not a loss of oneself, an "impoverishment," but a way of finding more of oneself when one means most to others whom one has chosen. Nor must complete finding of oneself, as Fromm and others sometimes seem to imply, precede finding oneself in and through other persons. Identity is never wholly realized. Love is never perfect. Strength to apprehend love that is beyond anxiety, beyond the need to use other persons for one's own security, beyond desire for power over others is never complete, but may grow throughout life. Like identity and mutuality with others it is a lifetime process of discovery.

. . . in the struggle for existence in a world ruled by anxiety . . . the surrender to the . . . experience of Love appears softening and therefore weakening. . . . Love is deeply taboo. . . . Sex without love belongs in the sphere of power operations. . . . In the transcendence of Love their is no . . . struggle for self-assertion, for in the weness the Self is received as a gift of grace. . . . The fight for right, entitlement . . . becomes superfluous, for . . . Love experiences space as bountiful, infinite. . . .[28]

Love increasingly transcends power, anxiety, and shame. A person who cannot love cannot reveal himself. Exposure in love is beneficent.

---

26 *Venus and Adonis*, 803.
27 Goldstein, "The Effect of Brain Damage on the Personality," p. 251; cf. *The Organism*, pp. 317, 392, and Piers and Singer, *Shame and Guilt*, pp. 11, 16.

28 Weigert, "Existentialism and Its Relation to Psychotherapy," p. 405.

Chapter 21 Socialization through the Life Cycle*

ORVILLE G. BRIM, JR.

Socialization refers to the process by which persons acquire the knowledge, skills, and dispositions that make them more or less able members of their society. It is apparent that the socialization experienced by a person in childhood cannot prepare him for all the roles he will be expected to fill in later years. People move through a sequence of different positions in society, in accord with different stages of the life cycle. Changes in the demands upon them arise from their mobility, both geographic and social, and from the customs of their society which may vary during their lifetimes. A half century of important research on socialization of the child has described the development of children's personalities and social behavior; there has been much less work, almost none in comparison, on socialization at later stages of the life cycle. Moreover, neither those studying child socialization nor those studying adult socialization have yet realized the full extent of the similarity of their research interests, concepts, and procedures.

This essay is concerned with the characteristics of socialization at different times in the individual life span and is focused on the question of whether the fundamental components of socialization differ in important ways in different stages of the life cycle—in particular, whether there are differences between socialization in childhood and socialization in adulthood. Throughout, the objective has been to speculate, to try to identify topics warranting further study, and generally to open up the field of inquiry rather than to partition it into areas.

SOURCE. Orville G. Brim, Jr., "Socialization through the Life Cycle," in Orville G. Brim, Jr., and Stanton Wheeler, *Socialization after Childhood: Two Essays*, New York: John Wiley and Sons, 1966, pp. 3–7, 12–23, 24–33 and 46.

* The author wants to thank Leonard S. Cottrell, Jr., Norman Goodman, and Theodore D. Kemper, his colleagues on several studies of personality and social structure, for their contributions to the development of the ideas expressed here.

Personality in Relation to Society

There are two great traditions in the study of personality in relation to society. One is the interest in how individuals adjust to society and how in spite of the influence of society upon them they manage to be creative and gradually to transform the social order in which they have been born. The other is the interest in how society socializes the individual—how it transforms the raw material of biological man into a person suitable to perform the activities of society. The study of socialization falls into the latter tradition: its starting place is to ask the fundamental question of how it is possible for a society to endure and to continue to develop. The inquiry at all times is concerned with how society changes the natural man, not how man changes his society.

An individual is prepared, with varying degrees of success, to meet the requirements laid down by other members of society for his behavior in a variety of situations. These requirements are always attached to one or another of the recognized positions or statuses in this society, such as husband, son, employee, and male adult. The behavior required of a person in a given position or status is considered to be the prescribed role, and the requirements themselves can be called "role prescriptions."

The prescriptions for roles in any social system are directed to the successful discharge of the function of that system for society. Role prescriptions essentially are efforts on the part of society's members to regulate the behavior of other members so that certain consequences will follow. Role prescriptions, then, are based on theories, implicit or not, about human behavior. The prescriptions are for the behavior belived by society to be the instrumental means to the achievement of some desired result, that is, some specified function of the social system. It follows that changes in role prescriptions occur when the theories of human nature which underlie the prescriptions change, or when there is a change in the ends to be achieved by the social system. (7)

In simplest terms, the individual acquires the culture of his group(s) through socialization, which includes for our purposes two main divisions. One acquires an understanding of the recognized statuses—the traditional positions—in his society, learning the names so that he is able to locate other individuals in the social structure, as well as to identify himself. Not as much attention has been given to this aspect of the content of socialization; indeed, beyond the basic terms for age, sex, and a few others, we do not have any standard theoretical set of concepts that describe these positions. Secondly one learns, of course, role prescriptions and role behavior, with the associated modes of feeling. To summarize, the function of socialization is to transform the human raw material of society into good working members; the content can be considered analytically to include an understanding of the society's status structure and of the role prescriptions and behavior associated with the different positions in this structure.

In saying this, a few remarks are needed to avoid naïveté. A view of socialization as a process by which society creates persons suitable to carry out its functional requirements does not deny that sometimes the existing requirements of society are unrealistic and, according to one or another set of moral standards, unjust. Nor does it deny that sometimes the demands of society may limit, if not make impossible, the personal satisfactions of most of its members; or that the demands may be so irrational as to cause the disintegration of the society itself. Studies of the utility and of the morality of the demands of a given society upon its members are, of course, basic inquiries that go back as far as we have written records. This is not, however, the concern of the student of socialization. He asks how the work of society gets done and how the necessary manpower is trained, motivated, kept alive and functioning throughout the life cycle so that the specified roles are performed. His concern is not to understand how society is changed to fit man's nature better, or to improve his personal adjustment and satisfaction, but rather to understand how man is taught to get the work of society done. In the end, of course, what he learns from one line of inquiry pertains to the other. The analysis of socialization leads finally to the question of what is the desirable society.

Socialization into Social Roles

Our emphasis is on the acquisition of the habits, beliefs, attitudes, and motives which enable a person to perform satisfactorily the roles expected of him in his society. The acquisition of roles is not viewed as the entire content of socialization, but role learning is the segment of socialization that we propose to analyze, and role acquisition is probably the most important aspect of adult socialization.

Only recently has systematic attention been given in socialization studies to the acquisition of roles by children. Most work in the study of personality development has not had this specific phrasing of the problem or focus of interest. Although it has dealt with acquiring skills in social interaction, it has not concentrated on how an individual develops those organized, reciprocal, socially regulated interactions with other human beings which are role prescribed, or how he comes to distinguish between the important statuses in his society. Recently, Maccoby (21) has brought this question to the fore in child development research, and Sewell (27) has provided an up-to-date review of the few studies that have been made.

The emphasis in child development research, for several years after its beginning in the child welfare stations established soon after 1920, was more on maturation than socialization, more on development than learning. The major output has been studies of mental and physical development; only to a much lesser extent has there been research on the social and emotional aspects of development. The stimulus for much of the current work on socialization came from a different source: the work of Freud and related theories of personality. The effect of early-life experiences on the development of personality traits which were believed to be fundamental and enduring characteristics of the individual was the focus of study. It was later on, around 1930, that concepts emerging from cultural anthropology, especially the idea of cultural relativity and the plasticity of human nature, extended the scope of studies of personality and led to a convergence of the interests mentioned earlier. The traditional work on child development, combined with concepts stemming from clinical theories of personality and enhanced by cross-cultural perspectives, evolved into some notable studies of socialization. Even so, this work, for all of its contribution to our knowledge, did not concentrate on role learning as the content of socialization.

Throughout the history of child development research, the few studies which were being made of adult socialization—of personality change in later life, one might say—were different in their focus. They conceptualized socialization as learning new roles, and as the individual's adaptation to society's demands for changes in his social behavior as he moved from one position to the next. This is one of the most important reasons that convergence between child development research and adult socialization studies did not occur. Stating the problems involved in socialization as those of how social roles are learned may provide a focus for both child and adult studies and a meeting ground for those engaged in the two lines of research.

*   *   *

"I-Them," "They-Me," and "I-Me" Relationships

The relationships between a person and other people are the raw material for that part of the personality with which we are concerned. Analytically, personality is a set of learned self-other relationships or systems, themselves constituted of thousands and thousands of remembered expectations, appraisals of one's own performance by self and others, the resultant perceived conformity or deviance (or success or failure) of the action, and the consequent rewards or disapprovals given by society. A basic classification of the resulting self-other systems is expressed by the grammatical contruction which describes the relationship. In any thoughts or statements descriptive of one's relations with others either the person is the subject, and the other the object—or the reverse is true. Thus, there are subject and object aspects of any specific component of the self-other system, centering, of course, on some social episodes involving expectations, performance, and appraisals, and including the person and a significant other or others.

This gives rise, therefore, to two major kinds of relations. The first is the "they-me" relationship, in which the person is the object of another's actions, expectations, or attitudes, such as "He doesn't want me to do that," "She approves of what I have just done," "My brother always got along well with me." The second is the "I-them" type, where the object is some other person. Here we find statements or observations of this kind: "I do not think they are fair," "I demand that he do that," "I will be angry if he fails to live up to his promise," and so on.

Two other possible relationships come to mind. One of these is the "they-them" type, where others are both the subject and the object. This is not constitutive of the self-other system, since it involves interaction in which the person is neither subject nor object.

It is the other logical possibility, where the person himself is both the subject and the object, that captures the imagination. What of the general class of relationships of the "I-me" type? Examples are: "I am content with myself," "I expect that I will be able to do this," "I should not demand so much of myself." Perhaps at first glance this does not appear to be part of the self-other system as described above. In fact, it has been recognized as a most fundamental part.

How does the "I-me" component of the self-other system develop? The individual, when looking or acting toward himself as an object, must initially do so from the point of view of some significant other person. For several reasons, this viewpoint becomes dissociated from any specific person, and the "I-me" component of the self thus is generated over time from a number of "they-me" relationships.

How would the situation develop in which the person is no longer able to recall or identify the other in the interpersonal relation, that is, the other who was involved? It appears that both generalization and the inability to discriminate are sources of the "I-me" type of relationship. The "I-me" relationship is the product of a body of learning generalized from interaction with a number of reference figures now nameless because their identity has been lost in countless learning trials. In the most frequent case the information derived about one's self from interaction with others has been given by a great many people so that no specific individual remains linked to this self-other relationship. This is true about basic components of the self such as size, sex, ability, or appearance, and also one's conformity to and deviance from norms widely shared in society. This is one source, then, of the "generalized other" as described by Mead: that which is generalized is no longer identified with any specific other.

Secondly, there is a companion process also leading to generalization, namely, a lack of ability to discriminate on the part of the child in his early interactions with his parents. In these interactions a child's experience has been so limited that he has no basis for differentiating (discriminating) between the reactions of his parents and their demands upon him and the reactions and demands of the entire objective world. In largest part this inability to discriminate exists because communication between parent and infant is perverbal, and the infant lacks symbolic tools to facilitate discrimination between sources of reward and punishment. What is learned from parents thus is viewed as inherent in the world at large, that is, in the generalized social order. It follows that elements of personality thus acquired provide a good foundation upon which the further process of generalization mentioned above may proceed. For these two reasons, then, the child develops a major component of his personality consisting of self-other relationships of the "I-me" type.

The question of identity, or what might be called the "core periphery" issue can now be analyzed. Every person experiences some part of his personality that he feels is more truly his than are other parts. How is one to explain this universal feeling? It seems that there are components of the personality—certain groupings of self-other relationships—that are highly determining of the individual's behavior. In view of the foregoing discussion it appears that these would be primarily of the "I-me" type, in which the perception of one's self in relation to others has been laid down early and frequently, both from powerful figures such as parents and also from a broad and diverse group of human beings, so that these come to constitute his sense of identity. The interchanges and expectations with other specific persons may be of less significance. One is willing to put on a front for them; but their demands are viewed as superficial, and, when in conflict with the "true self," conformity to these relationships—primarily of the "I-them" or "they-me" type—is set aside and the "I-me" set of expectations dominates.

It is not suggested, and it does not follow, that the "I-me" components of personality bear any necessary relationship to components of personality that are repressed and constitute the unconscious aspects of the self-other systems. The fact is that, in the course of interaction with other persons controlling rewards and punishments, experiences occur in which the individual is punished for failure to live up to the expectations of others about his performance—or to his own expectations for his performance where these have been dissociated from the original reference figures (as in the "I-me" relationship in which the individual punishes himself). In these cases the anticipation of failure and punishment may lead to the repression of thoughts of this

specific relationship and its concomitants. In this sense, this specific self-other unit of the personality is lost from the conscious repertoire; it is not part of the self-reportable area of personality.

Of course, the components of the personality which are repressed and the components which constitute the "I-me" type *may* overlap; the degree of overlap would vary from one individual to the next. But there should be no confusion between these two distinct aspects of personality. Whether or not the early and generalized learning of the kind leading to "I-me" systems becomes repressed depends on the characteristics of the interaction process, that is, the type of situation in which the generalized material was learned. To repeat, the "I-me" and the repressed components of personality are not necessarily correlated.

Motivation and Role Behavior

What are the implications of the point of view advanced above for motivation and behavior? The answer is simple and straightforward. The individual, because of his previously acquired desire to conform to others' expectations, is motivated to live up to these standards, and his sense of well-being or satisfaction depends on such conformity. The self-other relationship leads to an individual's appraisal of himself as being good or bad, according to the degree to which he lives up to another's expectation. The importance of the self-appraisal to the individual varies according to the significance of the other person's evaluation of him, which, in turn, is based, in the last analysis, on the degree to which the other controls (or once controlled) rewards and punishments. The consequence of self-appraisal and of perceived adequacy or inadequacy is to increase or decrease an individual's self-esteem or self-respect.

It is evident that we are not talking about all motivation, or even all social motivation. However, a significant part of motivated activity in social situations is triggered by the individual's perception of present discrepancies between expectations and his own level of performance or, secondly, his perception of anticipated discrepancies. Where these are anticipated the individual believes that he will be unable to conform to others' standards for him, and the result is fear of or anxiety over possible failure.

Specific kinds of behavior, and motives inferred therefrom, such as a desire for dominance, achievement, or affiliation, frequently will depend on the demands for such behavior by others and the specific self-other relationships which are generating the concern of the individual about his performance. Thus, where achievement is concerned, the expression of behavior from which an "achievement motive" can be named may depend on the existence of a set of reference figures whose expectations for performance in a given context, for example, in school, are to reach a high level of success relative to others.

It must be understood that this powerful source of individual motivation does not come only from the pressures of the immediate or local social system. The general concept identifying those persons to whom an individual refers his behavior to check on its appropriateness and its value is the reference set.[1] The fundamental question in understanding motivation is the degree to which the members of an individual's reference set are those whose presence is immediate and proximate, and with whom he is engaged in day-to-day interaction, as contrasted with more distant figures. Indeed, we might refer to this as the proximal-distal characteristic of self-other systems. The assumption that the individual seeks social approval and that persons move in the direction of resolving the demands upon them by conformity to the greatest pressures does not refer solely to the impact of the local social system. The analysis of local expectancies is but the first step, the first appraisal of demands with which one is concerned in his analysis of behavior. He is next concerned with the impact of reference figures who are not present in the immediate social system, with those persons from an earlier part of life, from another year or another place, with the different drummers some men march to, with the influence of dead poets and distant heroes.[2]

Many men have as members of their reference set persons other than their immediate family or peer group—individuals or groups who are not presently living, such as fictional or religious figures who are far beyond the local social system. Any individual's gallery of reference figures is populated by representatives from a vast range of possibilities—earlier friends, great figures in history, spirits, men yet to be born.

Moreover, most of the significant others who generate motivation are those whose actual relationship to the self has been forgotten or generalized into "I-me" relationships. The major body of motivation coming from "I-me" relationships can be described as a maintenance of self-esteem; it is the pursuit of an adequate or superior performance of some expected task for which the significant appraiser of the outcome has become one's own self. The early, generalized learning described previously leaves the person deeply dependent on self-appraisal for his sense of satisfaction; being true to his core identity is fundamental to his self-esteem.

Thus we see that the vast range of significant others and their demands free the individual from purely immediate pressures of the local social system and provide a much broader basis for his actions.

SOCIALIZATION IN LATER LIFE
Need for Socialization after Childhood

The socialization that an individual receives in childhood cannot be fully adequate as preparation for the tasks demanded of him in later years. As individuals mature, they move through a sequence of statuses corresponding to different stages in the life cycle (12). Even though some of the expectations of society are relatively stable through the life cycle, many others change from one age to the next. We know that society demands that the individual meet these changed expectations, and demands that he alter his personality and behavior to make room in his life for newly significant persons such as his family members, his teachers, his employers, and his colleagues at work.

The effectiveness of childhood socialization certainly is greater in relatively unchanging societies. Cultural prescriptions of a powerful nature define the usual sequence of statuses and roles that individuals are to assume during their life span. The process of development and differentiation goes along in step with physical maturation—increases in stature, strength, capacity—that permits the individual to meet

---

[1] This concept, developed by Kemper (17), incorporates the earlier idea of the reference group as set forth by Sherif (28) and by Kelley (16) with the concept of role set as advanced by Merton (22). It refers to that multiple set of figures (persons or groups) to whom, in whatever role, the individual refers his behavior.
[2] See Robert N. Wilson's study of poets' reference sets (30).

the enlarged demands upon him associated with new statuses. The increased demands are timed according to age or growth and may be thought of as developmental tasks. Further advances of the individual to greater differentiation of his relationships with others occur according to certain schedules which integrate his capabilities with age-graded requirements of the society. For example, enrollment in school may occur at the age when the child's physical, linguistic, and social skills enable him to deal with the formal educational system.

Also, in such quiet societies, stability comes from the continuity over time of the significant others with whom one is evolved. The earliest groups of significant persons remain on the scene through much of one's life. Parents may live on through one's middle years; friendships may persist through much of the life span; one marries into a homogamous group whose expectations are similar to those of prior reference figures. All of this enables socialization to be developmental in nature, that is, to occur in a regular progression from infancy through old age, and for anticipatory socialization for later-life roles to be more effective.

However, even in such relatively unchanging societies one cannot be socialized in childhood to handle successfully all of the roles he will confront in the future. Socialization in later years builds on attitudes and skills acquired earlier, using them as a foundation for later, more demanding learning. It is also true that for reasons fundamental to social organization individuals at certain age periods cannot be socialized completely for roles they may occupy in the future; socialization into the marital role is a case in point. There will be, also, some cultural discontinuities, as Benedict has pointed out (5), so that successive roles to be learned do not build upon each other and even may conflict with what was learned earlier.

The situation for most men is much more difficult, because they live in complex and changing societies. The inadequacies of early socialization for the role the person will play during his lifetime are much greater. The geographical mobility associated with the modern age and the social mobility characteristic of the achievement-oriented open-class society both contribute to the characteristically unforeseeable career pattern of modern man. The heterogeneity of subcultures in complex modern societies compounds the effects of mobility by the novel and unpredictable role demands placed on the individual. So, also, do the rapid social changes occurring during a lifetime render inadequate much childhood learning: technological obsolescence in one's occupation, shifts in sexual folkways, opportunities for equality in employment for minority group members, are but a few of a myriad of examples that might be set forth. Discontinuities between what is expected in successive roles are greater; the inabilities of the socializing agents to do an effective job rise as the rate of change increases; subgroups with deviant values emerge which do not prepare the child for performance of the roles expected of him by the larger society. Agents may be missing, as in broken homes, or key institutions or agencies lacking, as in the absence of an educational system in counties in Virginia when the public schools were closed; the parent himself may be inadequate to the task because he no longer cares or understands.

Faced with these challenges, complex and changing societies might try to lay the groundwork for the necessary learning in later life, when the child will be confronted with adult roles as yet only dimly seen, by providing the individual with initiative, creativity, the power of self-determination, insight, flexibility, and intelligent response to new conditions; to move, that is, away from indoctrination and habit formation toward development of broadly useful traits and skills enabling him to meet a variety of social demands. This, of course, is a familiar educational theory, deriving from changes introduced by John Dewey and others in the past fifty years. From the sociological viewpoint these changes are seen as an attempt by American society to provide for effective socialization of its members through life without being dependent on societal stability.

This is desirable but not sufficient; modern societies must provide for resocialization into roles for which the person has not been developmentally prepared. Societal institutions evolve that are specifically devoted to resocialization of the child or adult, much as the school and family are devoted to developmental socialization. Newly visible deficiencies in training are met by new resocialization efforts, good illustrations being the marital and parental roles. Poor developmental socialization is caused by inattention on the part of the child's parents, the absence of many siblings in the home, general decreased responsibility of children for helping parents in their duties, and so on. As a consequence, programs and institutions are emerging which are devoted to parent and family life education.

Limits of Later-Life Socialization

Given the need for adult socialization, what are the potentialities for new learning, and for change in personality, of the individual after his formative childhood years? The limits of socialization in later life are set by the biological capacities of an individual and by the effects of earlier learning or the lack of it. The effectiveness of later-life socialization is a consequence of the interaction of these two restrictions with the level of technology achieved by the society in its socialization methods. The latter depend primarily on the knowledge available about human behavior and to a lesser extent on mechanical developments; the remarks that follow assume a given level of socialization technology.

A substantial portion of the human raw material of society that is biologically inadequate in one respect or another is removed from natural progression through the life cycle by one of several methods and hence does not appear in the usual later-life socialization situations. By and large, the demands of a society upon adults are tailored to the capacities of the average man, and socialization proceeds without interference from biological limitations.

There are, nevertheless, two ways in which biological restrictions lead to limitations on later-life socialization. The first of these occurs primarily in an open-class society with a high level of achievement motivation. Here upward mobility into ever more demanding roles may lead an individual to positions in which he is unable to meet the challenges because of limited intelligence, strength, or other biological attributes. The second occurs when war or another disaster destroys the protection given to individuals by society from the direct impact of nature, and persons biologically adequate for the roles they will meet in the course of their normal civilized life cycle may suddenly find themselves unable to live under new and primitive conditions.

The effects of earlier learning, or the lack of them, are the other limits on later-life socialization. First we must recognize the durable qualities of early childhood learning. Socialization occurring during childhood correctly receives primary emphasis in research and theory. The potency and durability of the learning that occurs during this period are assumed on the basis of the frequency of learning situations, their primacy in the career of the organism, and the intensity of the rewards and punishments administered. Moreover, what is learned in childhood is difficult to change because much of it was learned under conditions of partial reinforcement.

In addition, it is held by many (and believed to be of utmost importance) that during early socialization the bulk of the unconscious material of the personality is accumulated, and the inertia established in the individual personality by its unconscious components, relatively inaccessible as they are to change through simple socialization procedures, is the cause of its manifest continuity. One might add that probably the characteristic modes of defense also are established early, thus painting the basic colors of personality for the life span.

Granted that there are enduring qualities to childhood learning, the effects of such learning on later-life socialization are more complicated than they may seem to be on quick consideration. It is not only that early learning interferes with and limits later learning. This is just one of several effects. Rather, it is the relationship of earlier learning, or its absence, to later learning which determines whether it will limit or facilitate adult socialization.

In some cases there is discontinuity and conflict between earlier and later learning. Later-life socialization requires replacement of the earlier with the later, of the old with the new, rather than building upon the existing personality base; the contrast in the premarital and postmarital roles of the American middle-class female is an outstanding example of this discontinuity.

In other instances, the childhood learning may facilitate later learning, if the elements learned first are compatible with what is to be learned in later life. As is pointed out later, adult socialization frequently consists of creating new combinations of old response elements; if these elements have been well learned, they may facilitate learning the adult role.

Sometimes it is the absence of certain childhood learning that affects later-life socialization. Here, at first glance, we would think that the absence of childhood learning would provide a clean slate for the later-life socialization effort, and that the absence of possibly competing responses would make the adult's learning tasks much easier. Training the new bride how to cook, or teaching a manual trade to the previously untutored adolescent, seems easier than changing skills that may already exist. This is true in many cases, but we should be cautious. It is doubtful that one comes on a role in later life without any fragments at all of relevant socialization; the inexperienced mother may seem to know little, but she knows something, and, even more, she has response elements for the role performance that are not manifest at the conscious level.

The absence of early learning clearly will hinder later-life socialization when something that should have been acquired as a basis for learning in later years in fact was not. It has been suggested (10) that the occurrence of critical periods in the life cycle, now demonstrated in subhuman species, may also characterize human development. If there are certain things that must be learned by human beings at specific stages in their development, then failure to learn this material at the appropriate period makes subsequent learning impossible. Such early deficiencies may even affect the learning ability itself. Although we know little as yet about possible critical periods in learning, we can speculate about adulthood; for example, learning certain attitudes during the formative middle years may lay the necessary basis for satisfactory socialization into the old-age role.

* * *

CHANGES IN CONTENT OF
SOCIALIZATION

The substantive content of socialization differs, of course, in important ways at different stages of the life cycle and in different major social institutions. People learn different things at different times and places in their lives.

It is uncertain, however, whether the types as opposed to the substance of the content differ throughout the life cycle. Still the needs for socialization and the effects of learning and biological characteristics in any given case would seem to dictate the nature of the socialization process; and since these vary by life-cycle stages, with the needs and limits of adult socialization being different from those of childhood, it is probable that the types of content vary accordingly. Six such probable changes in content will be discussed.

The most important change, perhaps, is the shift in content from a concern with values and motives to a concern with overt behavior.[3]

Some other changes are described in other aspects of socialization content. These are as follows: from acquisition of new material to a synthesis of the old; from a concern with idealism to a concern with realism; from teaching expectations to teaching how to mediate conflict among expectations; from a concern with general demands of society to a concern with role-specific expectations; and finally, a change from "I-me" components of personality to other components.

Values and Motives versus Overt Behavior

There are three things a person requires before he is able to perform satisfactorily in a role. He must know what is expected of him (both in behavior and in values), must be able to meet the role requirements, and must desire to practice the behavior and pursue the appropriate ends. It can be said that the purposes of socialization are to give a person knowledge, ability, and motivation.

A simple cross-classification of these three concepts with values and behavior establishes a paradigm which helps to analyze changes in the content of socialization through the life cycle. In this paradigm six cells are indicated by letters for simplicity of reference:

	Behavior	Values
Knowledge	A	B
Ability	C	D
Motivation	E	F

Cells A and B indicate respectively that the individual knows what behavior is expected of him and what ends he should pursue; E and F indicate that the individual is motivated to behave in the appropriate ways and to pursue the designated values; C and D indicate that the individual is able to carry out the behavior and to hold appropriate values.[4]

With respect to changes during the life cycle, the emphasis in socialization moves from motivation to ability and knowledge, and from a concern with values to a concern with behavior.

[3] An analysis of adult socialization in terms of the

relative emphasis on these two role components was introduced to the Social Science Research Council Conference by Irving Rosow in his paper, "Forms and Functions of Adult Socialization." See also Merton (23).
[4] The question of being able or unable to hold values may at first seem somewhat peculiar, but the inability involved here arises from conflict within the personality. This instance of inability as a source of deviance in role performance is discussed in greater detail later on.

The highest priority in childhood socialization is represented by Cell F, namely, to take the basic drives of the infant and transform them over time into desires for recognition and approval and finally to the pursuit of more specific cultural values. Early-life socialization thus emphasizes the control of primary drives, while socialization in later stages deals with secondary or learned motives generated by the expectations of significant others. Except in rare and extreme conditions, adult socialization does not need to teach the individual to control and regulate the gratification of primary drive systems.[5]

The usual concern of adult socialization is represented by Cell A. Society assumes that the adult knows the values to be pursued in different roles, that he wants to pursue them with the socially appropriate means, and that all that may remain to be done is to teach him what to do. This is illustrated by the case of a military recruit. The training program starts at about the level of "This is a gun" and "This is how it is fired." If there are some things the individual is unable to do (Cell C), the training program seeks to upgrade his ability—for example, by instruction designed to reduce illiteracy. If he is unwilling to carry out his various tasks (Cell D), then motivational training occurs through administration of special rewards and punishments. If it appears that education about values is needed (Cell B), the individual is enrolled in a general orientation course on American values and the purpose of the wars; the "why we fight" training programs are instituted to provide an understanding of the appropriate ends to be sought. If the individual has serious conflicts within himself but does his best, therapeutic procedures are instituted to solve this problem, which lies in Cell D. Only in the last analysis, when other possible types of deficiencies in socialization have been ruled out, is it assumed that there is a problem in motivation toward the appropriate values, the case represented

by Cell F. Such men are critical of the value system of their society; in our country they may be pacifists, Communists, or members of other groups which reject traditional American values. Sometimes resocialization efforts are launched in such cases, but more often retraining of these individuals is considered to be an impossible task, and they are jailed, ignored, or relegated to marginal, inconsequential positions.

In general, then, socialization after childhood deals primarily with overt behavior in the role and makes little attempt to influence motivation of a fundamental kind or to influence basic values. Society is willing to spend much less time in redirecting the motivation and values of adults than of children; for the latter it is understood that this is a necessary task of the institutions involved, such as the family, and they are organized to carry out this function.

Why should this difference exist? Probably it stems directly from the limitations on learning in later life, which makes impractical any attempt at thorough resocialization. Irving Rosow has asked if adult socialization can, in fact, generate suitable beliefs and attitudes, suitable motivation for certain types of performance, or whether the limitations on learning are such that the socializing agent must deal with overt performance only. It may be that the costs are too high and that it simply is not efficient from society's point of view to spend too much time on teaching an old dog new tricks. Perhaps an intensive and costly resocialization effort can be made for adults only when the need for a certain kind of manpower is unusually great and the question of efficiency becomes secondary to the demand for personnel.

Society has at least two major solutions to this possible problem. One is anticipatory: selection is made of candidates for an adult organization to screen out those who do not have appropriate motives and values for the anticipated roles. This procedure helps to assure that those who enter the organization will not present difficult problems for the socialization program. In this way adults probably get sorted out, more or less, and placed in social situations where they fit best in terms of the values and motives learned in their early-life socialization.

A second solution, which Rosow has pointed out, is that society may accept as evidence of satisfactory socialization conforming behavior

---

[5] The development of secondary motives oriented toward social approval (in a broad sense) and based on learning associated with the satisfaction of primary motives is a part of socialization but is not commensurate with it. It is true that sometimes one speaks of a person being unsocialized because of what appears to be a greater concern with the gratification of primary than of secondary motivation. But one also correctly calls unsocialized a person with deviant values and bizarre behavior, even when the primary drive system itself has been well socialized.

alone, foregoing any concern with value systems. This entails risk, as he indicates, for if the social system undergoes stress, the conformity, since it is superficial, may break down rapidly.

As a last resort, the remaining instances of deviance in need of resocialization—the genuinely tough cases where the appropriate values have not been internalized—can be processed through the special correctional institutions (prisons, hospitals, etc.) of the society at large.

Acquisition of New Material versus Synthesis of Old Material

As a person moves through the life cycle he accumulates an extensive repertoire of responses, both affective and behavioral. These are organized according to roles and, at a more specific level, by episodes within a role. These responses can be detached from the contexts in which they have been learned and used, and joined with others in new combinations suitable as social behavior responsive to the complex demands of adulthood. We can say, therefore, that the content acquired in adult socialization is not so much new material as it is the aggregation and synthesis of elements from a storehouse of already-learned responses, with perhaps the addition of several fragments that are newly learned when necessary to fill out the required social acts. The usual objective of socialization in the later-life stages is to get one to practice a new combination of skills already acquired, to combine existing elements into new forms, to trim and polish existing material, rather than to learn wholly new complexes or responses, as in the case of the relatively untrained child, for whom the socialization effort starts with little more than initial intelligence and primary drives.

Idealism and Realism

The third change in content is the transformation of idealism into realism. As the individual matures, society demands that he become more realistic and lay aside his childish idealism. Early learning encompasses the formal status structure; later learning takes into account the actual and/or informal status structure. One designates as cynical a person who doubts that the actual and the formal are the same. However, we think of a person as naive if he does not make this distinction. In socialization the child is shielded from contact with the informal systems of society—or,

at least, knowledge of these is not formally taught. This serves to maintain and legitimize the formal status differentiations and to protect them from change. But at later stages in the life cycle, for the system to work effectively, the realistic aspects of status differentiation also must be taught.

Closely related is learning to distinguish between ideal role prescriptions and what is actually expected of one in a role. Here, as in the foregoing, the inculcation of ideal role prescriptions results in a desirable idealism which strengthens and perpetuates the ideal of the society. As the child matures he is taught to realize that there is a distinction between the ideal and the real, and learns to take his part in society according to the realistic expectations of others, rather than attempting conformity to ideal norms.

Resolving Conflicts; Meta-prescriptions

The fourth type of change is to a greater concern with teaching the individual to mediate conflicting demands. As one moves through the life cycle, he is forced to develop methods of selecting among conflicting role prescriptions. The possible conflicts between the prescriptions of reference set members are classifiable into two basic types. First, there is intrarole conflict of two kinds. (*a*) the prescriptions of two or more individuals for the same aspect of a role may conflict: thus, the wife and the employer may differ in their prescriptions for the individual's job performance; (*b*) prescriptions of just one individual about different aspects of the role may be in conflict; the wife may expect her husband to be both companion with and taskmaster to his son.

Second, there is interrole conflict, again classifiable into two subtypes: (*a*) conflict between two or more individuals about two separate roles; for example, the employer's demands for job performance conflict with the wife's demands for familial performance; (*b*) conflict between the expectations of one individual for performance in two different roles, as in the case where the wife has conflicting expectations for her husband's behavior at home and on the job.

The need to learn how to handle such conflicts occurs to a greater extent in later life for at least two reasons. First, children tend to be shielded by society from the realities of life; and if the cultural norm is that children should be protected from seeing life's conflicts, then it follows that nothing will be taught about ways of mediating them. Second, in later life there are more roles and more complexity within roles, so that a much greater possibility exists of role conflict. To put it differently, the reference set of adults is considerably larger than that of children; their social systems are more extensive and more numerous. They have a past, for one thing; and they have occupational roles, as well as additional family roles gained through marriage. They are attuned more often to distant reference figures than they were as children, when their reference sets included mainly those near them.

Thus, as a person ages, he learns the ways of conflict resolution which Ralph Linton (20) has described so well: avoiding the situation, withdrawing acceptably from conflict, and scheduling conflicting demands in temporal sequence, so that the conflict diasppears. Also, as Howard Becker has pointed out, he learns another major method of conflict resolution, that is, to compromise between the opposing demands.

There is another important method of conflict resolution which may have been overlooked or at least has not been given formal conceptualization. In every society there are well-recognized prescriptions for solving certain kinds of conflicts that arise from the competing demands of reference set members. These prescriptions for mediating role conflict can be called *meta-prescriptions*. Such meta-prescriptions govern the resolution of conflict between demands on one's time and loyalties, and usually, although not always, pertain to interrole rather than intrarole conflict.[6] Examples of meta-prescriptions are "Do what your employer asks of you, even if it means that you have little time for your children," and "Side with your wife when she disciplines the children, even if you think she is wrong." Meta-prescriptions, therefore, guide the process of compromise and dictate whether the solutions should be one-sided, as in the two examples given above, or more on a half-and-half basis, such as "Save at least three nights a week for your family, even if there is work you should be doing." It seems that a noticeable change in the content of socialization in later-life periods is the attention given to ways of resolving conflict through such meta-prescriptions.

Increase in Specificity

The fifth characteristic of change in socialization content is along the dimension of generality-specificity; that is, whether what is taught applies to many social situations or to just a few. This dimension can be applied to both components, values and means, of role prescriptions. There is no reason to maintain that values necessarily are general, and that methods of achieving them are specific. This is noted only because of the tendency to define values as something general; the concept is not being used in this sense.

A child is trained both deliberately and unwittingly by socializing agents in the goals and behavior appropriate for his sex. There are male and female styles of doing many different things, and these are learned early. These characteristics are general, in the sense that they are required in a variety of situations he will confront in society, either as major components or as necessary coloring to other aspects of his behavior.

The case is similar for cultural differences in basic values, such as those related to achievement, to nature, to the family, and indeed for all those general value orientations, to use Florence Kluckhohn's phrase (18), which help to distinguish major cultural groups. They are acquired early (and, in contrast to sex roles, with perhaps less deliberate instruction), and they give shape and tone to the performance of many roles in society.

It also is true that a person is socialized for his socioeconomic position, a process that Charles E. Bidwell speaks of as socialization into a status level or a style of life.[7] Again, general skills and values are learned, appropriate to carrying out in a certain manner a number of specific role demands for behavior. The values and behavior appropriate to a social

---

[6] A current study of executive personality and achievement carried out by the author and his colleagues and mentioned in the Preface has collected substantial data on the meta-prescriptions for resolving role conflict between the demands of parents and children, one's boss and his work colleagues, wife and employer, and so on. These meta-prescriptions may differ from one person to the next, and result in relatively more or fewer conflict resolutions being made in, say, the direction of favoring the prescriptions of one's work environment as contrasted with his home. These appear to be fairly powerful predictors of differential achievement.

[7] Charles E. Bidwell, "Some Aspects of Pre-adult Socialization," paper prepared for the Social Science Research Council Conference.

class position, to a prestige level in life, usually are acquired in childhood; and, as was true with respect to sex roles and basic cultural values, some part of what is learned is gained outside of any deliberate formal training program.

One would have to say that these general values of one's culture are, on the whole, acquired in childhood. True, as Bidwell points out, there is some socialization into value systems of a given social class during the college age. He notes that one function of fraternities in certain colleges is to carry on this kind of socialization into a social class level higher than that of the individual's family or origin. The existence of formal socializing agencies with this recognized function is understood as a response to the "legitimate" need for resocialization resulting from the upward social mobility in American life in which the individual moves from one subculture to another, with corresponding differences in expectations.

Doubtless there are other occasions in which the general values are the content of socialization at later age periods, but these are not easy to identify. In most instances the content of later-life socialization tends to be role-specific, rather than general in nature.

Fewer "I-Me" Relationships

This final life-cycle comparison arises from the basic view presented earlier that part of personality consists of self-other systems. From what has been said, it follows that the content acquired in later stages of the life cycle would involve fewer of the "I-me" type of self-other relationships and more of the objective "they-me" and "I-them" components. Reviewing the reasons for the development of this kind of self-other system, one realizes that the causes for the lack of identification of the significant person or persons, and the resultant use of "I" in their place, exist to a much lesser degree in adulthood. At later ages the

source of the material which is acquired is more readily identifiable; the "they" involved usually is quite clear. Moreover, with the growth of power in maturity, one increases the degree to which he is the instigator of the action and consequently is engaged more frequently in, and thus thinks about himself as, the "I-them" relationship.

If one equates the "I-me" component of personality with the core personality, with "identity," as indicated in the discussion earlier, then he could say that identity tends to be laid down in largest part in early stages of the life cycle. This is true to a degree, of course, but as was said in considering the limiting effects of childhood experiences, it is overemphasized. Not uncommonly, dramatic shifts in identity do occur at later stages of the life cycle, since significant persons may have an unusual impact on a person's appraisal of his own basic characteristics.

* * *

In closing we have reached the intersection of the two great interests in the study of personality and social structure: how society manages to socialize the individual so that the work of society gets done, and how individuals manage gradually to transform the social system in which they live. The deviant person who cannot be resocialized is the source of innovation and change in the behavior and ideals of society. The fundamental problem to be solved by an enduring society is to train individuals to be responsible, and yet provide for the development of the free and creative person. A middle way must be taken between producing the undersocialized and the oversocialized person. A society must develop members who conform and fit into the existing order, as well as those who, although deviant now, are better equipped to live in the world to come. Social responsibility has been the concern of this work. Freedom, creativity, and revolution properly are the topics of a separate work.

REFERENCES

1. Becker, Howard S., Blanche Geer, Everett C. Hughes, and Anselm Strauss, *Boys in White: Student Culture in Medical School,* Chicago, Illinois: University of Chicago Press, 1961.
2. Becker, Howard S., *Outsiders,* Glencoe, Illinois: The Free Press, 1963.
3. Becker, Howard S., "Personal Change in Adult Life," *Sociometry, 27* (No. 1, 1964), pp. 40–53.
4. Becker, Wesley C., "Consequences of Different Kinds of Parental

Discipline," in *Review of Child Development Research,* Vol. 1, New York: Russell Sage Foundation, 1964.

5. Benedict, Ruth, "Continuities and Discontinuities in Cultural Conditioning," in *A Study of Interpersonal Relations,* Edited by Patrick Mullahy, New York: Heritage Press, 1949, pp. 297–308.

6. Borgatta, Edgar F., Leonard S. Cottrell, Jr., and Henry J. Meyer, "On the Dimensions of Group Behavior," *Sociometry, 19* (No. 4, 1956).

7. Brim, Orville G., Jr., "The Parent-Child Relation as a Social System: I. Parent and Child Roles," *Child Development, 28* (No. 3, 1957), pp. 345–346.

8. Brim, Orville G., Jr., *Education for Child Rearing,* New York: Russell Sage Foundation, 1959.

9. Brim, Orville G., Jr., David C. Glass, David E. Lavin, and Norman Goodman, *Personality and Decision Processes:* Studies in the Social Psychology of Thinking, Stanford, California: Stanford University Press, 1962.

10. Caldwell, Bettye M., "The Usefulness of the Critical Period Hypothesis in the Study of Filiative Behavior," *Merrill-Palmer Quarterly,* 8 (No. 4, October, 1962).

11. Clausen, John A., and Judith R. Williams, "Sociological Correlates of Child Behavior," in *Child Psychology:* The Sixty-Second Yearbook of the National Society for the Study of Education, Part I, Chicago, Illinios: University of Chicago Press, 1963, Chapter II.

12. Glick, Paul C., *American Families,* New York: John Wiley, 1957.

13. Goffman, Erving, *Asylums,* Garden City, New York: Anchor Books, Doubleday, 1961.

14. Goodman, Norman, "Communication and the Self-Image," Ph.D. Dissertation, New York University, New York City, 1963.

15. Inkeles, Alex, "Sociology and Psychology," in *Psychology:* A Study of a Science, Vol. 6, Edited by S. Koch, New York: McGraw-Hill, 1963, pp. 317–387.

16. Kelley, R. H., "Two Functions of Reference Groups," in *Readings in Social Psychology,* Edited by G. E. Swanson, T. M. Newcomb, and E. L. Hartley, New York: Holt, 1952, pp. 410–414.

17. Kemper, Theodore D., "The Relationship Between Self-Concept and the Characteristics and Expectations of Significant Others," Ph.D. Dissertation, New York University, New York City, 1963.

18. Kluckhohn, Florence, "Dominant and Variant Value Orientation," in *Personality in Nature, Society, and Culture,* Edited by C. Kluckhohn and H. A. Murray, Revised and Enlarged Edition, New York: Knopf, 1953, pp. 342–357.

19. LeVine, Robert, "Political Socialization and Culture Change," in *Old Societies and New States,* Edited by Clifford Geertz, Glencoe, Illinois: The Free Press, 1963, pp. 280–303.

20. Linton, Ralph, *The Cultural Background of Personality,* New York: Appleton-Century-Crofts, 1945.

21. Maccoby, Eleanor E., "The Choice of Variables in the Study of Socialization," *Sociometry, 24* (No. 4, December, 1961).

22. Merton, Robert K., "Contributions to the Theory of Reference Group Behavior" (with Alice S. Rossi) and "Continuities in the Theory of Reference Groups and Social Structure," in *Social Theory and Social Structure,* Revised and Enlarged Edition, Glencoe, Illinois: The Free Press, 1957, pp. 225–281.

23. Merton, Robert K., "Social Structure and Anomie" and "Continuities in the Theory of Social Structure and Anomie," in *Social Theory and*

Social Structure, Revised and Enlarged Edition, Glencoe, Illinois: The Free Press, 1957, pp. 131–161.

24. Neugarten, Bernice L., "Personality Changes during the Adult Years," in *Psychological Background of Adult Education,* Edited by Raymond G. Kuhlen, Chicago: Center for the Study of Liberal Education for Adults, 1963, pp. 43–76.

25. Parsons, Talcott, *The Social System,* Glencoe, Illinois: The Free Press, 1951.

26. Parsons, Talcott, "Family Structure and the Socialization of the Child," in *Family, Socialization and Interaction Process,* Edited by Talcott Parsons and Robert F. Bales, Glencoe, Illinois: The Free Press, 1955.

27. Sewell, William H., "Some Recent Developments in Socialization Theory and Research," in *The Annals of the American Academy of Political and Social Science,* Philadelphia, *349* (September, 1963), pp. 163–181.

28. Sherif, M., *An Outline of Social Psychology,* Revised Edition, New York: Harper, 1956.

29. Vincent, Clark E., "Socialization Data in Research on Young Marriers," in *Acta Sociologica, 8* (August, 1964).

30. Wilson, R. N., "The American Poet: A Role Investigation," Ph.D. Dissertation, Harvard University, Cambridge, Mass., 1952.

31. Wrong, Dennis H., "The Oversocialized Conception of Man in Modern Sociology," *American Sociological Review,* 26 (April, 1961), pp. 183–193.

Chapter 22 The Self through the Latter Span of Life*

KURT W. BACK AND KENNETH J. GERGEN

Once when he saw a wall of books, he had been sure that he would read
them all, someday. There had been nothing impossible in that assurance
because he knew that he would have the time—someday—when he would
get through with what he was doing. Now he knew he would never read
them all. The realization did not make him exactly sad. He had simply
grown sufficiently wise to know that there would eventually be an end to
himself and everything around him.

J. P. Marquand, *So Little Time*

Studies of the development of the human personality have largely centered on the early years of life. In part, this concentration is due to the profound influence of Freudian theory with its heavy emphasis on childhood experience. Freud's discovery of the many crucial factors and crises preceding the achievement of sexual maturity fostered the implicit assumption that personality is crystallized in this early period and few important changes occur thereafter. This influence has not only pervaded the various forms of psychoanalytic thinking but is also evident in work that has extended the scope of analytic theory to include the later periods of life. It is noteworthy that the writer who has done most in delineating and analyzing the later periods, Erik Erikson, has seen development during these periods as heavily dependent on experiences of the person during childhood (cf. Erikson, 1950, 1958). The influence of Freud on Parsons and other theorists has introduced essentially the same emphasis in much sociological thinking (Blenkner, 1965).

SOURCE: This paper was prepared originally for this volume.

* The research presented in this article was supported by a grant from the Ford Foundation on socioeconomic studies of aging, by a faculty grant from the Duke University Research Council, and by a National Science Foundation grant (GS 562). The theory and research presented in this chapter are based on Chapters 18–21, by the same authors, in Ida A. Simpson and John C. McKinney, *Social Aspects of Aging*, Durham, N.C.: Duke University Press, 1966.

However, interest has gradually been expanding to the development of the self and of personality in later years. One significant step in this direction has been the study of personality changes in the adolescent period, with its focus on such phenomena as the identity crisis and self-diffusion. Further studies have concentrated on self-development resulting from professional training, occupational role taking, and changes occurring in old age. Such investigations have all tended to embarrass the assumption of childhood crystallization of personality. This chapter stems from the position of noncrystallization in assuming that there are highly significant changes in personality intrinsic to passage through the life span. We shall discuss the development of two important aspects of the self throughout the latter stages of life and give special emphasis to the period of old age. First, a model which attempts to chart a number of important changes taking place during the life span will be outlined. The model is a basis for understanding a variety of phenomena occurring in middle and old age.

It should be noted at the outset that there are many objective difficulties in developing a model of age-related personality development. Most investigators dealing with earlier years of life have realized the complex interplay among physiological, psychological, cultural, and social factors which may affect childhood or adolescent behavior and have acknowledged the difficulties involved in developing a model that concentrates on age

241

development per se. In the older age groups these diverse factors have had a longer period of time to exert their influence and to modify whatever may exist in the way of "intrinsic" development through the life span. Along these lines, whether the disengagement or withdrawal of the individual from society in old age is the result of pressures from the society or a product of natural physical changes within the person has raised controversy. Each point of view can amass considerable evidence. On the one hand, the variability of withdrawal in different societies, and within different persons existing in varying groups in the same society, has been well documented. On the other, one can point to definite physiological and psychological changes during aging which would cause the person to interact less with those in his social environment. Of course, it is quite probable that all such influences operate simultaneously, and the exceedingly difficult problem remains of isolating their independent contribution to behavioral variability.

We shall proceed therefore in a somewhat different way. In a purely abstract and general manner, we shall concentrate on two dimensions of the self that appear to be of great significance during the life span. Based on these dimensions, we shall develop a model which may help to explain the development and modification of personal styles of behavior during the later periods of life. Second, in order to indicate the various behavioral domains in which this development may be expressed, we shall rely on data obtained from large numbers of persons representing a variety of population groups. Shifts in attitudes toward public affairs, personal concern, and morale will all receive attention. In this way we hope to relate the general model to a range of specific behaviors and sentiments, and to subsume a number of more specific influences at play in the process of aging. It should be noted that the present discussion rests on a number of earlier investigations, and should the reader wish a more detailed account of either theoretical points or data analyses, he may wish to consult the various sources indicated.

THE MODEL

The two crucial conceptions in our model rest on the distinction a person makes between his physical being and the events impinging on him from the outside world. The development of the capacity to make this distinction has been recognized as a basic achievement of infancy and early childhood (cf. Werner, 1948). Although this distinction continues to be a mainstay in the phenomenology of everyday life, it can be obliterated in certain forms of mystical experience. More centrally, as far as the person himself is concerned, not all of the world of which he is aware is equally relevant or salient to him. The person sees himself as capable of exerting action upon or being potentially affected by only certain arenas of facts or events. Such facts or events can also be said to exist for the person on both temporal and spatial dimensions. To few of us do facts about the world in the twenty-fifth century or life in Mongolia make a great difference. In terms of temporality, the question is one of how much of the past or future a person may think to be relevant to himself (cf. Back and Gergen, 1963a). With regard to space, we mean the extent of the area in which he may see himself acting or being acted upon. We shall use a single rough concept, the *life space,* as a variable to denote the extensity of both time and space perspective.[1]

The second major component of the model is also derived from this distinction between bodily self and "outer" world. While we have accounted for the outer world with the concept of life space, bodily self also continues in the life of the individual to be a crucial determinant of his behavior. What a person chooses to do is largely dependent upon that which he feels himself physically capable of doing. A person who views himself as physically weak will not generally commit himself to a life of manual labor, nor will a person who feels that his mental stamina is weak often choose the life of a scholar. More interesting, however, is the fact that although the person may continue to distinguish between body and life space, the two may be quite interrelated. Those aspects of the world which the person sees as "relevant" are largely those in which he may take action or which may have effects on his corporeal being. Further, if the world offers the individual widespread opportunity for action, he may alter his physical being in such a way that the opportunities may be seized.

Our basic model traces both the extensity of the life space and bodily well-being through the adult years. We have sketched in Figure 1 the hypothetical trajectories of the two self-aspects. It should be noted that the decision to

---

[1] For additional discussion of this and related concepts see Back and Gergen, 1963a, 1966b.

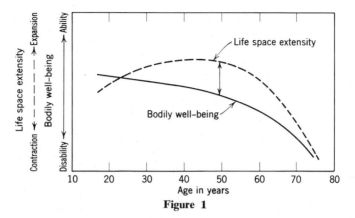

Figure 1

place the curves for both the life space and bodily well-being in the same two-dimensional plot is to some extent arbitrary. However, such an array does serve to point up the close interdependency of the two. In addition, later in this chapter we shall make use of the notion of magnitude of separation between the life space and body image trajectories.

The figure is of course in need of explanation, and the explanation is based on several lines of reasoning. First, as we have pointed out, there should be a close relationship between body image and life space. The range of time and space within which a person may see himself operating will depend, in part, on his perception of his physical well-being. The well and able person can simply act with regard to a greater expanse of time and space than the person who is sick or feels death approaching. As can be seen, we have traced a negatively accelerated curve to illustrate the decrement in physical well-being which occurs during the life span.[2] In this respect alone, the plot of the life space over time should parallel that of the body image: as the body image begins to reflect physical decrement, the life space should begin to constrict. A further reason for constriction of the life space during one's sixties can be traced to certain objective happenings in the person's environment. In Western culture, the person is often faced with forced retirement during this period, and certain parental functions may also be lost.[3] Such facts should serve further to constrict the life space, and they also

suggest that the trajectory we have offered may be quiet culture-bound.

It should be noted, however, that this reasoning does not adequately account for the entire trajectory of the life space, and more must be said. The first deviation from the life space curve, as reasoned above, occurs during adolescence. As the graph suggests, the life space is in a slightly constricted state during this period and is shown to expand during the twenties. Here again we are relying to some extent on cultural realities and, in this instance, on the fact that the educational and social institutions in Western society do not generally allow the adolescent broad freedom of action. For example, advanced schooling is often encouraged, parental influence is still much in evidence, voting rights are withheld, and means of personal transportation are not generally available to the adolescent. In addition, the adolescent is not often aware of what his options are in life, nor of what his potential for action is. Most of these restrictions are loosened for the person during his twenties, and it is at this point that the life space undergoes significant expansion.

In addition to this deviation from the general trajectory, it should also be noted that we have assumed a gradual expansion of the life space from the twenties through the late fifties. In part, this expansion can be attributed to the disappearance of the previously discussed restrictions in late adolescence. In addition, as the person develops an occupational role his latitude for potential action often increases. The structural features of most social institutions are such that status for a person is quite dependent on increased experience in the institution. Although occasionally debated (cf. Riecken and Homans, 1954), we are assuming that the higher the status within a social institution,

---

[2] For additional information concerning this decrement the reader may consult any number of sources, including Fisher and Birren, 1947; Bourlière, 1958; Anderson and Langham, 1959; and Weiss, 1959.

[3] See Cumming and Henry (1961) for a more detailed discussion of the ways in which the aged person becomes disengaged from those around him.

the greater the person's freedom and capacity for effective action (Jacques, 1956). As his livelihood and life's investments become more and more contingent on the fate of the social institutions in which he plays a role, the person should also come to broaden his awareness of the interdependence of these institutions with others in his society. In effect, the person is expanding the domain of events that may be considered personally relevant.

Although this reasoning may pertain more directly to males than to females, the same pattern of life space expansion during these years should apply to females. If we confine our argument to females functioning as wives and mothers, it can first be seen that to some extent their own world view will be quite related to the life situation faced by their spouses. In addition, rearing a child up to the time it reaches the early teens often has the effect of engaging the mother in a steadily expanding arena of social concerns. Later, when childhood dependency abates, the mother often has fewer restraints on her time and activities and may be free to engage in pursuits that are not family centered.

Thus far we have traced through later life the development of both the body image and life space and their relationship to each other. We may now turn to a number of derivations which can be made from these premises and to data relating to these derivations.

The data on which the following discussions rely were primarily the result of secondary analyses of public opinion surveys (e.g., Gallup and Roper). This method is highly advantageous in that it takes into account the responses of thousands of persons systematically selected to represent a cross section of the United States population. The range of generality of the results is thus considerable. Of course, the criticism can be raised that differences in responses as a function of age primarily reflect generational differences. However, we have attempted to meet this criticism in most cases by selecting data from various surveys taken over a 20- to 30-year period. One distinct liability of this method is that the items used on the surveys were not originally intended to assess the specific behavior of interest in the present paper. Thus we were sometimes obliged to rely on somewhat oblique measures and attempted to offset this difficulty by looking for similar patterns of results from several measures.

Attitudes toward Public Affairs

As will be recalled, one crucial point in our argument is that the life space, or that part of the world which is seen as self-relevant, is constricted during old age. We shall attempt to deal with life space constriction here by discussing in detail one of its consequences: a change in attitudes toward public affairs. A shift in attitudes might first result simply from an increased lack of interest in public affairs and the survey interview itself (cf. Gergen and Back, 1966). More important for present purposes, the amount of time or space a person takes into account may have considerable importance for the types of solutions to problems of public life which he prefers.[4] More specifically, when little future time is taken into account, more immediate and total solutions will be preferred. If the future is not relevant for an individual, then solving a problem in the present should be more appealing. In addition, looking into the future implies that a person will consider additional aspects of a problem. The more facets of a problem that are considered, the less extreme and complete can any solution be. One would expect, therefore, that constriction of life space would lead to a preference on the part of the elderly for more immediate or radical solutions than would be chosen by their younger counterparts. In the area of international conflict, the elderly may object to compromise or long-range solutions, while greater favor may be expressed for total annihilation of an adversary or denial that a threat exists. With domestic problems the aged may prefer punitive measures in dealing with problems, in preference to various long-range alternatives.

For examination of attitudes toward international relations, a set of public opinion items used around the time of the Korean War are relevant. In three Gallup surveys during the years 1948–1951, respondents were asked for solutions to then current issues of international conflict. The first question, in 1948, dealt with the possibility of engaging in all-out war with Russia. The second question, just at the outbreak of the Korean War, concerned the ideal policy

---

[4] It should be noted that the process of life space constriction described here does not account for the possibility that the aged may consider a greater segment of the past as being self-relevant. Whether periods of reverie may affect projects for action among the aged is a matter for future empirical concern.

to pursue in Korea. In the third survey, a year later, respondents were asked about expansion or abandonment of the war in Korea. For the first two questions there was a clear positive relationship between age and preference for an extreme solution, either expanding the war or complete pacifism, while preferences for moderate solutions declined correspondingly. In the third instance, the most extreme solutions were advocated by a middle-aged group with a very slight decline in the older group (over 60). However, in this same survey the oldest group did advocate, more than any other, bombing of Communist China by the United Nations forces. In addition, older people were found to be more opposed than the younger to foreign aid, a definite long-range means of addressing international issues. Thus the data tend to confirm the hypothesis that a restriction of life space in the aged leads to a preference for short-range solutions in the international sphere. Of course, other social conditions may well determine which short-range solution, either abandonment or expansion of aggression, a person may prefer.

A corresponding tendency was found in data dealing with national problems, Here again we took a variety of problems in order to eliminate, as much as possible, the influence of specific political ideologies. In this instance one question dealt with the problem of billboards, and one with outlawing boxing. A third focused on the extent to which government should control industry, and in this case the compromise solution of government control of only basic industries can be contrasted with no control of industry versus complete government ownership of all industry. In each of these instances there was an age-related increase in the preference for an extreme solution. The older respondent wanted to outlaw billboards, outlaw boxing, and preferred either complete or no government control of industry.

PUNITIVITY AND CAUSAL ATTRIBUTION

There is reason to suspect that although extreme aggression and nonaggression may both be preferred solutions for problems, extreme aggression may be the more compelling one. Almost all forms of aggression or punishment place an emphasis on immediate results, excluding consideration of the long-term effects and the more slow-working alternatives. How-

ever, another aspect of life space constriction leads to a similar preference. If the behavior of another is viewed against a backdrop in which few action-antecedents appear, this behavior is more likely to be seen as "internally" caused.[5] To illustrate, consider the case in which a person finds that his possessions have been stolen from his car. If he then sees the culprit with goods in hand, he is likely to view the robbery as stemming from some internal malevolence or criminal tendency on the part of the thief. Rapid punishment of the thief may be expected to follow. If, on the other hand, the victim finds that the thief comes from a broken home, has recently lost his job, and has experienced other forms of hardship, the causal attribution for the robbery shifts to the environment, and punishment becomes a difficult task at best. By definition, life space constriction involves a diminution in the number of events or facts considered in any instance. It would thus seem that one major result of life space constriction should be a general shift in causal attribution, and this shift should be accompanied by punishment or aggression as a preferred mode of reaction.

Evidence for this point of view comes from a mental health survey in which respondents were presented a series of situations in which people behaved in a maladjusted fashion. In each case, the respondent was asked to interpret the behavior and to give possible remedies. In general, the aged were much more likely to put the blame on the person and not attribute the causes of his behavior to environmental forces. Correspondingly, the aged were more likely to advocate punishment as a remedy as opposed to alternatives that would alter the environment. Three additional questions were found which dealt with preferred methods of social control. The elderly to a greater extent preferred to publish the names of juvenile first offenders, and advocated stricter discipline in both home and school. Although such coincidance is not conclusive by any means, it does suggest that further research in this area may be quite profitable.

Thus far we have seen that life space constriction may affect one's modes of relating to others. We are now in a better position to ask about the relationship between life space and attitudes towards one's own body.

---

[5] For additional discussion of this point and related evidence, see Gergen and Back, 1965.

CONCERN FOR BODILY SELF

The relationship between aging and the bodily self is complicated by several factors and therefore has to be specified in detail. One might speculate, for instance, that a constriction of life space would lead a person to closer interest in his own body. Further, the greater likelihood of diseases and ailments among older persons would almost force their attention to somatic matters. It may even be that exclusive concern with some physical deficiency or pain may fill out the entire life space and leave no room for other bodily or external matters.[6]

However, none of these inferences are necessarily warranted. The same physiological and psychological conditions that lead to a restriction of life space may also have an influence on the care given to the body. More specifically, when the life space is in a constricted state, one might expect less concern to be devoted to bodily states. In effect, when the environment offers few alternatives and little time for action, the need for bodily care is to some extent obviated. Thus, in spite of the common-sense notion that the aged should be more concerned with the body because of its more precarious state, our model leads us to exactly the opposite hypothesis.[7] The results from a series of surveys on attitudes, opinions, and expenditures provide an empirical basis for our position.

In looking at the findings we shall subdivide concern about the bodily self into two parts: the concern about how one's body appears to other persons, and the more intrinsic concern with one's own bodily state. With the constriction of the life space and the accompanying lack of concern for present and future relationships, it is not surprising that the aged express less interest in external care and grooming habits. In this case, results from a number of surveys demonstrated that concern with clothing declines with age. Further, among the criteria used in selecting clothing, beauty and style recede in importance, whereas considerations of practicality and utility tend to become predominant.[8] In addition, clothing becomes a less relevant criterion for judging others and is considered less likely to be relevant in the

way others judge oneself. Consumer surveys indicate that this attitude may be carried over to actual behavior. It has been shown, for example, that the aged spend a smaller percentage of their income on clothing, cosmetics, and items of personal ornament.

While the aged seem to be less concerned with the way they present themselves to others,[9] they also manifest less interest and concern over matters of physical well-being. Survey data demonstrated in this instance that age was associated with less concern about diet and nutrition, and about eating dietary supplements to keep oneself healthy. In a question that probably best summarizes this attitude, respondents were asked whether, in trying to keep healthy, it was more important to pay attention to what the appetite told them to eat or what modern science prescribed. There is a marked increase after age 60 in preference of the first alternative.

The most surprising finding related to our model was the lack of concern of the aged for medical care. Considering the objective fact that specific diseases and infirmities increase sharply after age 60, it is striking that data collected by the Public Health Service show only a minimal increase in number of visits to doctors with advancing age. This is true whether such visits are for treatment of diseases or for general checkups. Correspondingly, expeditures for medical service (pre-Medicare) do not increase with age, regardless of specific income group. As can be seen, the marked increase in disability associated with advancing age does not at all correspond to increased investment in medical care. These findings are buttressed by additional survey data indicating that the aged are little interested in preventive medicine or inoculations, even during such epidemics as that produced by Asia flu. They express, as well, less interest in exercise as a means of maintaining health, and when asked about reasons for not overeating, fewer reply with health-associated reasons.

Morale

In the young and middle aged, whose attitudes are dominant in our culture, detachment from bodily concern and general fatalism could

---

[6] This corresponds to the psychoanalytic theories of development of libido in pain and agony (Slater, 1964).

[7] For more detailed discussion of this argument and the data which follow, see Gergen and Back, 1966b.

[8] It should be well noted that for the analyses of these and other similar data, the appropriate controls for socioeconomic class have been taken into account.

[9] Additional data related to this point may be found in Back and Gergen, 1963b.

be said to be indicative of depression or low morale. For the aged, however, this is not necessarily so. We have sketched the relative trend of both bodily well-being and of the effective life space over time. We can also hypothesize that the value a person places upon himself will be partially dependent on the relationship between these trajectories. More explicitly, a person will value himself or possess high morale when his physical capacities are capable of matching the life space extensity.[10] Either a very extensive life space accompanied by a physical deficit, or physical vitality accompanied by an impoverished life space should engender low morale. For example, a person with grandiose plans for the future who finds that he has only a short time to live, or a person with marked aptitudes who finds that the paths of upward mobility are closed to him, may experience general feelings of apathy and depression. The major upshot of this argument is that the aging process may lead to a rather natural equilibrium of the two self-aspects: a point at which the life space has constricted to conform to the natural state of the body. Thus morale may not be expected to be substantially less during old age than in the mid-twenties.

It is also easy to understand why the younger person, operating in an extended spatiotemporal environment, interprets much of the behavior of the aged as indicative of low morale. Their conclusion is also confirmed by survey data which indicate that on a variety of opinion issues the aged are more pessimistic. Pessimistic responses increase uniformly with age on such questions as whether there will be war in the next five years, whether the United States is losing the Cold War, or whether cancer is curable. However, it remains an open question as to whether such responses are accompanied by negative affect or a pessimistic feeling about the world. What appears to be pessimism in such instances may reflect cognitive processes alone, or the outcome of a rational calculus developed over the years.

In contrast to such data, and confirming our view that there may not be a strong emotional attachment to the pessimistic responses, we found on an entire series of questions that the aged were more accepting of their condition and less willing to change. They enjoyed their work to a greater degree (housework in the case of most females); they said they would

not be happy in a different job, they enjoyed the kind of work they did more than any other, they would not be happy if they had more money, and that they would not like to live to be 150. In effect, the aged may reach a balanced perspective, normally seen as depression, but about which they are rather satisfied and uncaring for change. This condition is somewhat akin to successful disengagement as stated in current theory (Cumming and Henry, 1961), but it is not synonymous. It revolves around a balance between intrinsic motivation and environmental exigencies.

In a series of items more directly related to emotional feelings about the world, it was revealed that over a variety of topics the aged worry less than the younger group. These items concerned such matters as how much the respondent worried about health, income, and a place to live. It was found here, as in other cases, that the peak of stress or worry occurs in middle age and abates after the sixties. A similar pattern was found in the data on the desirability of bodily change. The greatest desire to change occurs when bodily features become objectively troublesome and the individual is still concerned with his social environment. If we do not control for actual body size we find that it is during the period preceding the sixties when individuals, especially women, wish they had less weight.

That the low point of morale seems to be reached during the fifties corresponds to our previous discussion of the differential trajectories of the life space and body image curves. As can be seen in Figure 1, the maximum discrepancy between these curves is reached at just about this time. As the life space remains extended, the bodily self declines continuously, and the two curves deviate most dramatically just before reaching the late stages of life. It may be said that the peak of worry and low morale occurs during that period in which the person has maximum freedom and control over his environment, but becomes aware of the finite and vulnerable aspects of his physical being. After this stage, a new balance point may be achieved.[11]

---

[10] For an earlier discussion of this point and the data which follow, see Back and Gergen, 1966b.

[11] It should be noted that both empirical and theoretical antecedents exist for this curvilinear relationship between age and morale. The reader may wish to consult, for example, Buhler, 1935; Linden and Courtney, 1953; Slotkin, 1954; Havighurst, 1954: Bloom, 1961; Reichard, Livson, and Petersen, 1962.

CONCLUSION

The model of self-change in aging presented in this chapter has attempted to underscore some of the psychological concerns confronted in the process of growing old. We are in no position to say that the processes we have sketched are ubiquitous in nature or even that they are necessarily normative. The secondary analyses of data from a number of national samples have suggested that such processes may have a widespread existence. However, it should be clear that many conditions and circumstances may modify the actual trend of self development. For example, education or other experiences involving symbol manipulation may counteract the constriction of the life space (cf. Back and Gergen, 1966a). Similarly, varying conditions of health and strength may alter reactions to the bodily self and indirectly influence the life space. Different environmental conditions may also exacerbate or ease the problems we have shown to be part of aging.

While positing a set of age-related changes in the structure of the self, we must also recognize that the manifestations of such changes may be of many varieties. This is to say that we do not feel that there is a basic hiatus between theories of single intrinsic aging processes and theories showing a variety of adjustments to the status of old age. Although similar factors may be involved for large numbers of people, depending on their exact operation for the individual, they may lead to quite different types of adjustment. For example, Riesman (1954) proposes three different types of aging which he calls autonomous, conformist, and anomic. For our framework this may suggest three basic patterns of body and life space relationships. The conformist may be more normative in terms of the model, with the other two types representing modifications. The

anomic may be seen to result from an imbalance between the bodily self and the life space, whereas the autonomous person may have been able to keep both his spatiotemporal perspective broad and his physical being in good condition, thus having accomplished equilibrium on a higher level than the regular process might warrant. Kastenbaum (1965) has proposed a similar classification of possible reactions to aging. In a searching study, measuring separately the effect of deprivation and withdrawal, Lowenthal and Boler (1963) have also shown that environmental conditions—deprivation—rather than withdrawal itself will affect morale. In our terms, it is possible to reach an equilibrium point on a restricted or deprived level, and a disturbance of either factor making up the equilibrium will lead to lowest morale.

These examples suggest a number of possible ways in which our model may be expanded and used as a basis for further research. From one vantage point, further derivations from the basic model could be made and different methods of testing might then be employed. Such an approach would seem particularly commendable inasmuch as the model developed thus far has by necessity excluded some factors and does not rely on a sufficiently precise data base. On the other hand, additional work could be devoted to studying ways in which the basic pattern may be modified, the consequences of such modification, and the conditions under which they may occur. To the extent that the model has a theoretical value in understanding personality development during the latter span of life, it should also have a potential for application. To the extent that we have an accurate picture of the problems which the older person must face, we are in a position to help him become beneficial to himself and to society.

REFERENCES

Anderson, E. C., and Langham, W. H. Average potassium concentration of the human body as a function of age. *Science* **130** (1959), pp. 713–714.

Back, Kurt W., and Gergen, Kenneth J. Apocalyptic and serial time orientation and the structure of public opinion. *Public Opinion Quarterly,* **27** (1963a), pp. 427–442.

Back, Kurt W., and Gergen, Kenneth J. Idea orientation and ingratiation in the interview: a dynamic model of response bias. *Proc. Am. Stat. Assn.* (1963b), pp. 284-288.

Back, Kurt W., and Gergen, Kenneth J. Cognitive and motivational factors in disengagement and aging. In J. McKinney and Ida Simpson (Eds.). *Social Aspects of Aging,* Durham, N.C.: Duke University Press, 1966a.

Back, Kurt W., and Gergen, Kenneth J. Personal orientation and morale of the aging. In J. McKinney and Ida Simpson (Eds.). *Social Aspects of Aging,* Durham, N.C.: Duke University Press, 1966b.

Blenkner, Margaret. Social work and family relationships in later life with some thoughts on filial maturity. In E. Shanas and G. F. Streib (Eds.). *Social Structure and the Family,* Englewood Cliffs, N.J.: Prentice-Hall, 1965.

Bloom, Kenneth. Age and the self concept. *A. J. Psychiatry,* **118** (1961), pp. 534–538.

Bourlière, Francois. *Genescence et Senilité,* Paris: Doin, 1958.

Buhler, Charlotte. The curve of life as studied in biographies. *J. Appl. Psych.* **19** (1935), pp. 405–409.

Cumming, Elaine, and Henry, William E. *Growing Old,* New York: Basic Books, 1961.

Erikson, Erik. *Childhood and Society,* 2nd Ed., New York: W. W. Norton and Co., 1950.

Erikson, Erik. *Young Man Luther,* New York: W. W. Norton and Co., 1958.

Fisher, M. B., and Birren, J. E. Age and strength. *J. of Appl. Psychol.,* **31** (1947), pp. 490–497.

Gergen, Kenneth J., and Back, Kurt W. Time perspective, aging and preferred solutions to international conflicts. *J. Confl. Resol.,* **9** (1965), pp. 177–186.

Gergen, Kenneth J., and Back, Kurt W. Cognitive constriction in aging and attitudes toward international issues. In J. McKinney and Ida Simpson (Eds.). *Social Aspects of Aging,* Durham, N.C.: Duke University Press, 1966a.

Gergen, Kenneth J., and Back, Kurt W. Aging and the paradox of bodily concern. In J. McKinney and Ida Simpson (Eds.). *Social Aspects of Aging,* Durham, N.C.: Duke University Press, 1966b.

Gergen, Kenneth J., and Back, Kurt W. Communication in the interview and the disengaged respondent. *Public Opinion Quarterly,* **30** (1966), pp. 385–398.

Havighurst, Robert J. Flexibility and the social roles of the retired. *A. J. Soc.,* **59** (1954), pp. 309–311.

Jacques, Elliot. *Measurement of Responsibility,* London: Tavistock, 1956.

Kastenbaum, Robert. Theories of human aging: the search for a conceptual framework. *Journal of Social Issues,* **21** (1965), pp. 13–36.

Linden, Maurice, and Courtney, Douglas. The human life cycle and its interruptions: a psychologic hypothesis. *A. J. Psychiatry,* **109** (1953), pp. 906–915.

Lowenthal, Marjorie F., and Boler, Deetje. Voluntary vs. involuntary social withdrawal. *Journal of Gerontology,* **20** (1963), pp. 363–371.

Marquand, John P. *So Little Time,* Boston: Little, Brown Co., 1943.

Reichard, Suzanne, Livson, Florine, and Petersen, Paul G. *Aging and Personality—A Study of Eighty-Seven Older Men,* New York: John Wiley and Sons, 1962.

Riecken, H. W., and Homans, G. C. Psychological aspects of social structure. In Gardner Lindzey (Ed.). *Handbook of Social Psychology, Vol. II,* Reading, Mass.: Addison-Wesley, 1954, pp. 786–832.

Riesman, David. *Individualism Reconsidered,* New York: The Free Press of Glencoe, 1954, pp. 484–491.

Slater, Philip E. Prolegomena to a psychoanalytic theory of aging and death. In R. Kastenbaum (Ed.). *New Thoughts on Old Age,* New York: Springer Publ. Co., 1964.

Slotkin, J. S. Life course in middle age, *J. Soc. Forces,* **33** (1954), pp. 171–177.

Weiss, A. D. Sensory functions. *Handbook of Aging and the Individual: Psychological and Biological Aspects,* Chicago, Ill.: University of Chicago Press, 1959.

Werner, Heinz. *Comparative Psychology of Mental Development,* Chicago, Ill.: Follet, 1948.

Chapter 23 On Death and Death Symbolism

ROBERT JAY LIFTON

The larger a human event, the more its significance eludes us. In the case of Hiroshima's encounter with the atomic bomb—surely a tragic turning point in man's psychological and historical experience—the meaning is perhaps only now, after 19 years, beginning to reveal itself. Yet the event has much to teach us that is of considerable value in our struggles to cope with a world altered much more than we realize, and made infinitely more threatening, by the existence of nuclear weapons. In this article I shall describe a portion of a larger study of the psychological effects of the atomic bomb in Hiroshima.[1] I shall focus upon what I believe to be the central psychological issue in both the actual disaster and its wider symbolism—the problem of death and dying. The work represents a continuation of an effort, begun ten years ago, to develop a modified psychoanalytic research approach to broad historical problems.

There are many reasons why the study of death and death symbolism has been relatively neglected in psychiatry and psychoanalysis: Not only does it arouse emotional resistances in the investigator—all too familiar, though extraordinarily persistent nonetheless—but it confronts him with an issue of a magnitude far beyond his empathic and intellectual capacities. Yet whatever the difficulties, the nuclear age provides both urgent cause and vivid stimulus for new efforts to enhance our understanding of what has always been man's most ineradicable problem. Certainly no study of an event like the Hiroshima disaster can be undertaken without some exploration of that problem.

I conducted the study over a six-month period, from April to September, 1962, mostly in Hiroshima itself. This was the last portion of a two and one-half years stay in Japan, the greater part of which was spent investigating psychological and historical patterns of Japanese youth.[2] The Hiroshima study consisted primarily of individual interviews with two groups of atomic bomb survivors: One group of 33 chosen at random from the list of more than 90,000 survivors (or *hibakusha*) kept at the Hiroshima University Research Institute for Nuclear Medicine and Biology; and an additional group of 42 survivors specially selected because of their prominence in dealing with atomic bomb problems or their capacity to articulate their experiences—including physi-

SOURCE: Robert Jay Lifton, "On Death and Death Symbolism: The Hiroshima Disaster," from *Psychiatry: Journal for the Study of Interpersonal Processes*, 27 (August 1964), pp. 191–192, 202–205, and 207–210. Reprinted by special permission of The William Alanson White Psychiatric Foundation, Inc. Copyright 1964 by The William Alanson White Psychiatric Foundation, Inc.

[1] The study was supported by research funds from the Department of Psychiatry, Yale University. Colleagues and friends from the various divisions of Hiroshima University (particularly the Research Institute for Nuclear Medicine and Biology), the Hiroshima City Office, and many other groups in the city lent indispensable help in making arrangements; and Miss Kyoko Komatsu and Mr. Kaoru Ogura provided skillful and dedicated research assistance throughout. I have published one earlier, more general paper on the work ["Psychological Effects of the Atomic Bomb in Hiroshima: The Theme of Death," *Daedalus* 92: (1963), pp 462–487], and the present article draws upon a more comprehensive book-length report now in preparation.

[2] Robert J. Lifton, "Youth and History: Individual Change in Postwar Japan," *Daedalus* 91: (1962), pp. 172–197; and "Individual Patterns in Historical Change: Imagery of Japanese Youth," in *Disorders in Communication*, Vol. 42, *Proceedings of the Assn. for Research in Nervous and Mental Disease*, edited by David McK. Rioch, Baltimore, Waverly, 1964 (forthcoming).

cians, university professors, city officials, politicians, writers and poets, and leaders of survivor organizations and peace movements.

Hibakusha is a coined word which is by no means an exact equivalent of "survivor" (or "survivors"), but means, literally, "explosion-affected person" (or people), and conveys in feeling a little more than merely having encountered the bomb, and a little less than having experienced definite physical injury from it. According to official definition, the category of *hibakusha* includes four groups of people considered to have had possible exposure to significant amounts of radiation: Those who at the time of the bomb were within the city limits then defined for Hiroshima, an area extending from the bomb's hypocenter to a distance of 4,000, and in some places up to 5,000 meters; those who were not in the city at the time, but within 14 days entered a designated area extending to about 2,000 meters from the hypocenter; those who were engaged in some form of aid to, or disposal of, bomb victims at various stations which were set up; and those who were *in utero,* and whose mothers fit into any of the first three groups. In addition to these interviews with *hibakusha,* I tried to learn all I could, from a variety of sources and in a variety of informal ways, about the extraordinary constellation of influences felt by the city and its inhabitants in relationship to the bomb during the 17-year period that had elapsed between the disaster itself and the time of my research.[3]

* * *

GENERAL PRINCIPLES

Through the experiences of Hiroshima survivors we have been thrust into the more general realm of the interrelationship between the anticipation of death and the conduct of life. It is an interrelationship that has been recognized and commented upon by generations of philosophers, though mentioned with surprising infrequency in psychiatric work. There are many signs that this psychiatric neglect is in the process of being remedied,[4]

and indeed the significance of problems in this area so impresses itself upon us in our present age that matters of death and dying could well serve as a nucleus for an entire psychology of life. But I will do no more than state a few principles which I have found to be a useful beginning for comprehending the Hiroshima experience, for relating it to universal human concerns, and for examining some of the impact upon our lives of the existence of nuclear weapons. Attempting even this much is audacious enough to warrant pause and examination of some rather restraining words of Freud, which are made no less profound by the frequency with which they have been quoted in the past:

It is indeed impossible to imagine our own death; and whenever we attempt to do so we can perceive that we are in fact still present as spectators. Hence the psychoanalytic school could venture on the assertion that at bottom no one believes in his own death, or, to put the same thing in another way, that in the unconscious every one of us is convinced of his own immortality.

These words, which were written in 1915, about six months after the outbreak of World War I,[5] have found many recent echoes (Merleau-Ponty, the distinguished French philosopher, has said, "Neither my birth nor my death can appear to me as *my* experiences . . . I can only grasp myself as 'already born' and 'still living'—grasping my birth and death only as pre-personal horizons."[6])

Profound as Freud's words are, it is possible that psychological investigations of death have been unduly retarded by them. For they represent the kind of insight which, precisely because

---

[3] A listing of relevant Japanese and American writings on the various aspects of the atomic bomb problem can be found in Lifton, "Psychological Effects of the Atomic Bomb in Hiroshima" (see footnote 1).

[4] Among recent psychiatric and psychological studies of death and death symbolism, see K. R. Eissler, *The Psychiatrist and the Dying Patient,* New York, Internat. Univ. Press, 1955; Herman Feifel, editor, *The Meaning of Death,* New York,

McGraw-Hill, 1959; and Norman O. Brown, *Life Against Death: The Psychoanalytical Meaning of History,* Middletown, Conn., Wesleyan Univ. Press, 1959. In addition, a good deal of research is now in progress. See, for instance, Avery Weisman, and Thomas P. Hackett, "Predilection to Death: Death and Dying as a Psychiatric Problem," *Psychosomatic Medicine* 23 (1961) pp. 232–256; and Edwin S. Shneidman, "Orientations Toward Death: A Vital Aspect of the Study of Lives," in Robert W. White, editor, *The Study of Lives,* New York, Atherton, 1963.

[5] Sigmund Freud, "Thoughts for the Times on War and Death," *Standard Edition of the Complete Psychological Works* 14:275–300, London, Hogarth, 1957, p. 289. . . .

[6] *Phénoménologie de la Perception;* pp. 249–250, as quoted and translated by Arleen Beberman in "Death and My Life," *Review of Metaphysics* 17:18–32, (1963) p. 31.

of its importance and validity must be questioned further and even transcended. I believe it is more correct to say that our own death—or at least our own dying—is not entirely unimaginable but can be imagined only with a considerable degree of distance, blurring, and denial; that we are not absolutely convinced of our own immortality, but rather have a need to maintain a *sense of immortality* in the face of inevitable biological death; and that this need represents not only the inability of the individual unconscious to recognize the possibility of its own demise but also a compelling universal urge to maintain an inner sense of continuous symbolic relationship, over time and space, to the various elements of life. Nor is this need to transcend individual biological life *mere* denial (though denial becomes importantly associated with it): Rather it is part of the organism's psychobiological quest for mastery, part of an innate imagery that has apparently been present in man's mind since the earliest periods of his history and prehistory. This point of view is consistent with the approach of Joseph Campbell, the distinguished student of comparative mythology, who has likened such innate imagery or "elementary ideas" to the "innate releasing mechanisms" described by contemporary ethologists. It also bears some resemblance to Otto Rank's stress upon man's longstanding need of "an assurance of eternal survival for his self," and to Rank's further assertion that "man creates culture by changing natural conditions in order to maintain his spiritual self."[7]

The sense of immortality of which I speak may be expressed through any of several modes. First, it may be expressed biologically—or, more correctly, biosocially—by means of family continuity, living on through (but in an emotional sense, *with*) one's sons and daughters and their sons and daughters, by imagining (however vaguely and at whatever level of consciousness) an endless chain of biological attachment. This has been the classical expression of the sense of individual immortality in East Asian culture, as particularly emphasized by the traditional Chinese family system, and to a somewhat lesser extent by the Japanese family system as well. But it is of enormous universal importance, perhaps the most universally significant of all modes. This mode of immortality never remains purely biological; rather it is experienced psychically and symbolically, and in varying degree extends itself into social dimensions, into the sense of surviving through one's tribe, organization, people, nation, or even species. On the whole, this movement from the biological to the social has been erratic and in various ways precarious; but some, like Julian Huxley and Pierre Teilhard de Chardin,[8] see it as taking on increasing significance during the course of human evolution. If this is so, individual man's sense of immortality may increasingly derive from his inner conviction, "I live on through mankind."

Second, a sense of immortality may be achieved through a theologically-based idea of life after death, not only as a form of "survival" but even as a "release" from profane life burdens into a "higher" form of existence. Some such concept has been present in all of the world's great religions and throughout human mythology. The details of life after death have been vague and logically contradictory in most theologies, since the symbolic psychological theme of transcending death takes precedence over consistency of concrete elaboration. Christianity has perhaps been most explicit in its doctrine of life after death, and most demanding of commitment to this doctrine; but intra-Christian debate over interpretation of doctrine has never ceased, with present thought tending toward a stress upon transcendent symbolism rather than literal belief.

Third, and this is partly an extension of the

[7] In developing his ideas on the "inherited image," Joseph Campbell, *The Masks of God: Primitive Mythology;* New York: Viking, 1959, pp. 30–49, 461–472 follows Adolf Bastian and C. G. Jung. Otto Rank, *Beyond Psychology;* New York: Dover, 1958, pp. 62–101 develops his concepts of man's quest for immortality through the literary and psychological concept of "The Double as Immortal Self." While I do not agree with all that Rank and Campbell say on these issues (I would, in fact, take issue with certain Jungian concepts Campbell puts forward), their points of view at least serve to open up an important psychological perspective which sees the quest for immortality as inherent in human psychology and human life.

[8] Huxley and Père Teilhard, of course, go further, and visualize the development of a unifying, more or less transcendent idea-system around this tendency. Huxley refers to this as "evolutionary humanism," *The Humanist Frame,* edited by Julian Huxley; New York: Harper, 1961, pp. 11–48 and Père Teilhard speaks of the "Omega point," at which a "hyperpersonal" level of advanced human consciousness may be attained, *The Phenomenon of Man,* New York: Harper, 1959, pp. 257–263.

first two modes, a sense of immortality may be achieved through one's creative works or human influences—one's writings, art, thought, inventions, or lasting products of any kind that have an effect upon other human beings. (In this sense, lasting therapeutic influences upon patients, who in turn transmit them to their posterity, can be a mode of immortality for physicians and psychotherapists.) Certainly this form of immortality has particular importance for intellectuals conscious of participating in the general flow of human creativity, but applies in some measure to all human beings in their unconscious perceptions of the legacy they leave for others.

Fourth, a sense of immortality may be achieved through being survived by nature itself: the perception that natural elements—limitless in space and time—remain. I found this mode of immortality to be particularly vivid among the Japanese, steeped as their culture is in nature symbolism; but various expressions of Western tradition (the romantic movement, for instance) have also placed great emphasis upon it. It is probably safe to say—and comparative mythology again supports this—that there is a universal psychic imagery in which nature represents an "ultimate" aspect of existence.

These psychological modes of immortality are not merely problems one ponders when dying; they are, in fact, constantly (though often indirectly or unconsciously) perceived standards by which people evaluate their lives. They thus make possible an examination of the part played by death and death symbolism during ordinary existence, which is what I mean by the beginnings of a death-oriented psychology of life. I shall for this purpose put forth three propositions, all of them dealing with death as a standard for, or test of, some aspect of life.

1.   Death is anticipated as a *severance of the sense of connection*—or the inner sense of organic relationship to the various elements, and particularly to the people and groups of people, most necessary to our feelings of continuity and relatedness. Death is therefore a test of this sense of connection in that it threatens us with that which is most intolerable: *total severance*. Indeed, all of the modes of immortality mentioned are symbolic reflections of that part of the human psychic equipment which protects us from such severance and isolation.

Another expression of the threat to the sense of connection represented by death is the profound ambivalence of every culture toward the dead. One embraces the dead, supplicates oneself before them, and creates continuous rituals to perpetuate one's relationship to them, and (as is so vividly apparent in the case of the Hiroshima survivors) to attenuate one's guilt over survival priority. But one also pushes away the dead, considers them tainted and unclean, dangerous and threatening, precisely because they symbolize a break in the sense of connection and threaten to undermine it within the living. These patterns too were strongly present in Hiroshima survivors (and can be found in general Japanese cultural practice), although less consciously acceptable and therefore more indirectly expressed. Indeed, in virtually every culture the failure of the living to enact the rituals necessary to appease the dead is thought to so anger the latter (or their sacred representatives) as to bring about dangerous retribution for this failure to atone for the guilt of survival priority.

2.   Death is a test of the meaning of life, of the symbolic integrity—the cohesion and significance—of the life one has been living. This is a more familiar concept, closely related to ideas that have long been put forth in literature and philosophy, as well as in certain psychoanalytic writings of Freud, Rank, and Jung; and it has a variety of manifestations. One is the utilization of a *way or style of dying* (or of anticipated dying) as an epitome of life's significance. An excellent example of this is the Japanese *samurai* code, in which a heroic form of death in battle on behalf of one's lord (that is, a death embodying courage and loyalty) was the ultimate expression of the meaning of life.[9] Various cultures and subcultures have similarly set up an ideal style of dying, rarely perfectly realized, but nonetheless a powerful standard for the living. The anticipation of dying nobly, or at least appropriately

---

[9] The *Hagakure,* the classical eighteenth-century compilation of principles of *Bushidō* (The Way of the Samurai), contains the famous phrase: "The essence of *Bushidō* lies in the act of dying." And another passage, originally from The *Manyōshū,* a poetic anthology of the eighth century: " 'He who dies for the sake of his Lord does not die in vain, whether he goes to the sea and his corpse is left in a watery grave, or whether he goes to the mountain and the only shroud for his lifeless body is the mountain grass.' This is the way of loyalty." Robert N. Bellah, *Tokugawa Religion,* Glencoe, Ill.: Free Press, 1957, pp. 90–98.

—of dying for a meaningful purpose—is an expression of those modes of immortality related both to man's works (his lasting influences) and his biosocial continuity. And I believe that much of the passionate attraction man has felt toward death can be understood as reflecting the unspoken sense that only in meaningful death can one simultaneously achieve a sense of immortality and articulate the meaning of life.

Apart from dramatically perfect deaths on the *samurai* model, timing and readiness play an important part. Can one visualize, in association with death, sufficient accomplishment to justify one's life? Or has life become so burdensome and devoid of meaning that death itself (whatever the style of dying) seems more appropriate? The latter was the case with a remarkable group of people undergoing surgery recently described by Avery Weisman and Thomas P. Hackett. These "predilection patients" were neither excessively anxious nor depressed, and yet correctly predicted their own deaths. For them, "death held more appeal . . . than did life because it promised either reunion with lost love, resolution of long conflict, or respite from anguish,"[10] and one is led to conclude that this psychological state interacted with their organic pathology and their reactions to surgical procedures to influence significantly the timing of their deaths. Their surrender to death was apparently related to their sense that they could no longer justify their continuing survival.

* * *

All of us who continue to live while people anywhere die are survivors, and both the word and the condition suggest a relationship which we all have to the dead. Therefore, the Hiroshima survivors' focus upon the dead as arbiters of good and evil, and invisible assigners of guilt and shame, is by no means as unique as it at first glance appears to be. For we all enter into similar commitments to the dead, whether consciously or unconsciously, whether to specific people who lived in the past or to the anonymous dead; or whether these commitments relate to theological or quasi-theological ideas about ties to the dead in another form of existence, or to more or less scientific ideas about a heritage we wish to affirm or a model we wish to follow. In fact, in any quest for perfection there is probably a significant

identification with the imagined perfection of the dead hero or heroes who lived in the golden age of the past. Most of our history has been made by those now dead, and we cannot avoid calling upon them, at least in various symbolic ways, for standards that give meaning to our lives.

3. And a last proposition: Death, in the very abruptness of its capacity to terminate life, becomes a test of life's sense of movement, of development and change—of sequence—in the continuous dialectic between fixed identity on the one hand and individuation on the other. To the extent that death is anticipated as absolute termination of life's movement, it calls into question the degree to which one's life contains, or has contained, any such development. Further, I would hold that a sense of movement in the various involvements of life is as fundamental a human need, as basic to the innate psychic imagery, as is the countervailing urge toward stillness, constancy, and reduction of tension which Freud (after Barbara Low) called the "Nirvana principle."[11] Freud referred to the Nirvana principle as "the dominating tendency of mental life" and related it to the "death instinct"; but I would prefer to speak instead of polarizing psychic tendencies toward continuous movement and ultimate stillness, both equally central to psychic function. Given the preoccupation with and ambivalence toward death since mankind's beginnings, Freud's concept of the death instinct may be a much more powerful one than his critics will allow. At the same time, it may yield greater understanding through being related to contemporary thought on symbolic process and innate imagery, rather than to older, more mechanistic views on the nature of instinct.[12]

[11] Sigmund Freud, "Beyond the Pleasure Principle," *Standard Edition of the Complete Psychological Works* **18**:55–56; London, Hogarth, 1955. Maryse Choisy, *Sigmund Freud: A New Appraisal,* New York: Philosophical Library, 1963 has pointed out that Freud (and presumably Barbara Low), in employing this terminology, misunderstood the actual significance of Nirvana— to which I would add that Nirvana (whether the ideal state or the quest for that state) probably involves various kinds of indirect activity and sense of movement, and not simply ultimate stillness.

[12] See, for instance, Joseph Campbell (footnote 7); Kenneth Boulding, *The Image: Knowledge in Life and Society,* Ann Arbor, Mich.: Univ. of Mich. Press, 1956; S. A. Barnett, " 'Instinct,' " *Daedalus* **92**: (1963) pp. 564–580; and Adolf Portmann, *New Paths in Biology,* New York: Harper & Row, 1964. . . .

[10] Avery Weisman and Thomas P. Hackett, "Predilection to Death" (see footnote 4); p. 254.

To express this human necessity for a sense of movement, I find it often useful to speak of "self-process" rather than simply of "self." And I believe that the perpetual quest for a sense of movement has much to do with the appeal of comprehensive ideologies, particularly political and social ones, since these ideologies contain organized imagery of wider historical movement, and of individual participation in constant social flux. Yet ideologies, especially when totalist in character, also hold out an ultimate vision of Utopian perfection in which all movement ceases, because one is, so to speak, *there*. This strong embodiment of both ends of the psychic polarity—of continuous movement as well as perfect stillness—may well be a fundamental source of ideological appeal. For in this polarity, ideologies represent a significant means of transcending linear time, and, at least symbolically, of transcending death itself. In the promise of an interminable relationship to the "Movement," one can enter into both a biosocial mode of immortality and a very special version of immortality through man's works, in this case relating to man's symbolic conquest of time. Nor is it accidental that ideologies appear and gather momentum during periods of cultural breakdown and historical dislocation, when there tends to be a sense of cessation of movement and of prominent death symbolism. For central to the revitalizing mission of ideologies is their acting out, in historical (and psychological) context, the classical mythological theme of death and rebirth.[13]

The psychic response to a threat of death, actual or symbolic, is likely to be either that of stillness and cessation of movement, or else of frenetic, compensatory activity. The former was by far the most prominent in the Hiroshima situation, though the latter was not entirely absent. The psychic closing-off which took place right after the bomb fell was, in an important sense, a cessation of psychic motion—a temporary form of symbolically "dying"—in order to defend against the threat of more lasting psychological "death" (psychosis) posed by the overwhelming evidence of actual physical death. And the same may be said of the later self-imposed restraint in living which characterizes the "identity of the dead,"

an identity whose very stillness becomes a means of carrying on with life in the face of one's commitment to death and the dead. But there were occasional cases of heightened activity, usually of an unfocused and confused variety, even at the time of the bomb. And later energies in rebuilding the city—the "frontier atmosphere" that predominated during much of the postwar period—may also be seen as a somewhat delayed intensification of movement, though it must be added that much of this energy and movement came from the outside.

Can something more be said about these propositions concerning death, and about the various modes of immortality, as they specifically apply to the nuclear age? I believe that from these perspectives we can see new psychological threats posed by nuclear weapons—right now, to all of us among the living.

Concerning the first proposition, that death is a test of our sense of connection, if we anticipate the possibility of nuclear weapons being used (as I believe we all do in some measure), we are faced with a prospect of being severed from virtually all of our symbolic paths to immortality. In the postnuclear world, we can imagine no biological or biosocial posterity; there is little or nothing surviving of our works or influences; and theological symbolism of an afterlife may well be insufficiently strong in its hold on the imagination to still inner fears of total severance. Certainly in my Hiroshima work I was struck by the inability of people to find adequate transcendent religious explanation—Buddhist, Shinto, or Christian—for what they and others had experienced. This was partly due to the relatively weak state of such theological symbolism in contemporary Japan, but perhaps most fundamentally due to the magnitude of the disaster itself. And whatever the mixed state of religious symbolism in the rest of the world, there is grave doubt as to whether the promise of some form of life after death can maintain symbolic power in an imagined world in which there are none (or virtually none) among the biologically living. This leaves only the mode of immortality symbolized by nature, which I found to be perhaps the most viable of all among Hiroshima survivors—as expressed in the Japanese (originally Chinese) proverb quoted to me by several of them: "The state may collapse but the mountains and rivers remain." And with

[13] For a discussion of psychological and historical aspects of ideology, and particularly of ideological extremism, see Lifton, *Thought Reform and the Psychology of Totalism: A Study of "Brain-washing" in China,* New York: Norton, 1961, Ch. 22.

all the other modes of immortality so threatened, we may raise the speculative possibility that, independent of any further use of nuclear weapons, one outcome of the nuclear age might be the development of some form of natural theology (or at least of a theology in which nature is prominent) as a means of meeting man's innate need for a sense of immortality.

Concerning the second proposition, relating to the meaning and integrity of life, we find ourselves even more directly threatened by nuclear weapons. As many have already pointed out, nuclear weapons confront us with a kind of death that can have no meaning.[14] There is no such thing as dying heroically, for a great cause, in the service of a belief or a nation—in other words, for a palpable purpose—but rather only the prospect of dying anonymously, emptily, without gain to others. Such feelings were prominent among Hiroshima survivors both at the time of their initial immersion in death and during the months and years following it. They could not view their experience as purposeful, in the sense of teaching the world the necessity for abandoning nuclear weapons, but rather saw themselves as scapegoats for the world's evil, "guinea pigs" in a historical "experiment," or else as victims of a war made infinitely more inhuman by the new weapon. Part of their problem was the difficulty they had in knowing whom, or what to hate, since, as one of my colleagues put it, "You can't hate magic." They did find in postwar Japanese pacifism an opportunity for organized rechanneling of resentment into a hatred of war itself; this was of considerable importance, but has by no means resolved the issue. The only consistent "meaning" survivors could find in all of the death and destruction around them was in the application of an everyday expression of East Asian fatalism—*"shikataganai"* ("It can't be helped") —which is a surface reflection of a profoundly important psychological tendency toward ac-

cepting whatever destiny one is given. But however great the psychological usefulness of this attitude, one can hardly say that it enabled survivors to achieve full mastery of their experience. And concerning the question of the "appropriateness" of anticipated death, Hiroshima survivors were the very antithesis of the "predilection patients" mentioned before: Rather than being ready for death, they found its intrusion upon life to be unacceptable, even absurd; and when seeming to embrace death, they were really clinging to life.

But considering the destructive power of present nuclear weapons (which is more than a thousandfold that of the Hiroshima bomb), and considering the impossibility of a meaningful nuclear death, is not life itself deprived of much of its meaning? Does not nuclear death threaten the deep significance of all of our lives? Indeed, the attraction some feel toward the use of nuclear weapons might be partly a function of this meaninglessness, so that in a paradoxical way they want to "end it all" (and perhaps realize their own end-of-the-world fantasies) as a means of denying the very emptiness of the nuclear death toward which they press. Here the principle of individual suicide as an attempt to deny the reality of death[15] is carried further to encompass nuclear suicide-murder as an attempt to deny the threat to meaningful human existence posed by these weapons.

And finally, in relationship to the proposition of death as a test of life's sense of movement, I think the matter is more ambiguous, though hardly encouraging. There is a sense in all of us, in greater or lesser degree, that nuclear weapons might terminate all of life's movement. Yet there is also, at least in some, a strange intensity and excitement in relationship to the confrontation with danger which nuclear weapons provide; and this, it might be claimed, contributes to a sense of movement in present-day life. But this exhilaration—or perhaps pseudo exhilaration—is less a direct function of the nuclear weapons themselves than of the universal historical dislocation accompanying a wider technolog-

---

[14] See, for instance, Hans J. Morgenthau, "Death in the Nuclear Age," *Commentary,* September, 1961. Among psychological studies, see Jerome D. Frank, "Breaking the Thought Barrier: Psychological Challenges of the Nuclear Age," *Psychiatry* **23**: (1960) pp. 245–266; *Some Socio-psychiatric Aspects of the Prevention of Nuclear War,* forthcoming report of the Committee on Social Issues of the Group for the Advancement of Psychiatry; and Lester Grinspoon, "The Unacceptability of Disquieting Facts," presented at the 1962 American Association for the Advancement of Science Symposium, to be published.

[15] K. R. Eissler (footnote 4; pp. 65–67) notes the frequently observed psychological relationship between suicide and murder, and goes on to speak of suicide as "the result of a rebellion against death," since "for most suicides the act does not mean really dying" but is rather a means of active defiance of, rather than passive submission to, death.

ical revolution. In other words, there is in our world an extraordinary combination of potential for continuously-enriching movement and development of self-process, side by side with the potential for sudden and absolute termination. This latter possibility, which I have called the *potentially terminal revolution,*[16] has not yet been seriously evaluated in its full psychological consequences; and whatever its apparent stimulus to a sense of movement, one may well suspect that it also contributes to a profound listlessness and inertia that lurk beneath.

I am aware that I have painted something less than an optimistic picture, both concerning the Hiroshima disaster and our present relationship to the nuclear world. Indeed it would

seem that we are caught in a vicious psychological and historical circle, in which the existence of nuclear weapons impairs our relationship to death and immortality, and this impairment to our symbolic processes in turn interferes with our ability to deal with these same nuclear weapons. But one way of breaking out of such a pattern is by gaining at least a dim understanding of our own involvement in it. And in studying the Hiroshima experience and other extreme situations, I have found that man's capacity for elaborating and enclosing himself in this kind of ring of destructiveness is matched only by his equal capacity for renewal. Surely the mythological theme of death and rebirth takes on particular pertinence for us now, and every constructive effort we can make to grasp something more of our relationship to death becomes, in its own way, a small stimulus to rebirth.

[16] Lifton, *Thought Reform and the Psychology of Totalism,* New York: Norton Library (paperback) Edition, 1963, Preface, pp. vii-ix.

Chapter 24 On the Psychodynamics of the Negro Personality

ABRAM KARDINER AND LIONEL OVESEY

It is a consistent feature of human personality that it tends to become organized about the main problems of adaptation, and this main problem tends to polarize all other aspects of adaptation toward itself. This central problem of Negro adaptation is oriented toward the discrimination he suffers and the consequences of this discrimination for the self-referential aspects of his social orientation. In simple words, it means that his self-esteem suffers (which is self-referential) because he is constantly receiving an unpleasant image of himself from the behavior of others to him. This is the subjective impact of social discrimination, and it sounds as though its effects ought to be localized and limited in influence. This is not the case. It seems to be an ever-present and unrelieved irritant. Its influence is not alone due to the fact that it is painful in its intensity, but also because the individual, in order to maintain internal balance and to protect himself from being overwhelmed by it, must initiate restitutive maneuvers in order to keep functioning—all quite automatic and unconscious. In addition to maintaining an internal balance, the individual must continue to maintain a social facade and some kind of adaptation to the offending stimuli so that he can preserve some social effectiveness. All of this requires a constant preoccupation, notwithstanding the fact that these adaptational processes all take place on a low order of awareness. Figure 1 is a diagram of a typical parallelogram of forces. In the center of this adaptational scheme stand the low self-esteem (the self-referential part) and the aggression (the reactive part). The rest are maneuvers

with these main constellations, to prevent their manifestation, to deny them and the sources from which they come, to make things look different from what they are, to replace aggressive activity which would be socially disastrous with more acceptable ingratiation and passivity. Keeping this system going means, however, being constantly ill at ease, mistrustful, and lacking in confidence. The entire system prevents the affectivity of the individual that might otherwise be available from asserting itself.

This is the adaptational range that is prescribed by the caste situation. This is, however, only a skeletal outline. Many types of elaboration are possible, particularly along projective or compensatory lines. For example, the low self-esteem can be projected as follows:

Low self-esteem =
self-contempt → idealization of the white →
frantic efforts to be white =

$$\text{unattainable} \begin{cases} \nearrow \text{hostility to whites} \\ \searrow \text{introjected white ideal} \rightarrow \end{cases}$$

self-hatred → projected on to other Negroes = hatred of Negroes.

The low self-esteem can also mobilize compensations in several forms: (1) apathy, (2) hedonism, (3) living for the moment, (4) criminality.

The disposition of aggression is similarly susceptible to elaboration. The conspicuous feature of rage lies in the fact that it is an emotion that primes the organism for motor expression. Hate is an attenuated form of rage, and is the emotion toward those who inspire fear and rage. The difficult problem for those who are constantly subject to frustration is how to contain this emotion and prevent its motor expression. The chief motive for the latter is to avoid setting in motion retaliatory aggression.

The most immediate effect of rage is, therefore, to set up a fear of its consequences. Fear

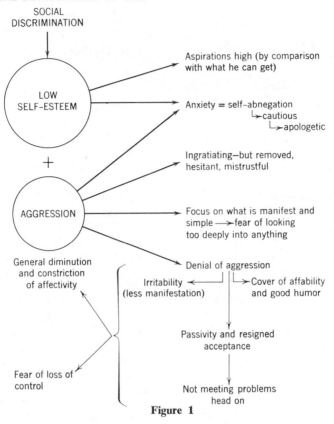

Figure 1

and rage become almost interchangeable. When the manifestations of rage are continually suppressed, ultimately the individual may cease to be aware of the emotion. In some subjects the *only* manifestation of rage may be fear.

The techniques for disposing of rage are varied. The simplest disposition is to suppress it and replace it with another emotional attitude—submission or compliance. The greater the rage, the more abject the submission. Thus, scraping and bowing, compliance and ingratiation may actually be indicators of suppressed rage and sustained hatred. Rage can be kept under control but replaced with an attenuated but sustained feeling—resentment. It may be kept under control, but ineffectively, and show itself in irritability. It may be kept under sustained control for long periods, and then become explosive. Rage may show itself in subtle forms of ingratiation for purposes of exploitation. It may finally be denied altogether (by an automatic process) and replaced by an entirely different kind of expression, like laughter, gaiety, or flippancy.

Rage may ricochet back on its author, as it does in some types of pain-dependent behavior (masochism). This is only likely to happen

when rage is directed toward an object that is loved; the rage is then accompanied by strong guilt feelings. In this case the only manifestion of rage may be depression.

The tensions caused by suppressed or repressed aggression often express themselves through psychosomatic channels. Headaches of the migrainous variety are often the expression of rage which is completely repressed. These are usually not accompanied by amorphous anxiety—though the latter may be the sole vehicle for this agression. Hypertension is another psychosomatic expression of the same, but predominantly suppressive, process.

In the case histories, we found all these varieties of the expression and control of rage. All kinds of combinations are possible. The two commonest end products of sustained attempts to contain and control aggression were low self-esteem and depression. These are merely the results of the continuous failure of a form of self-assertion.

The adaptational scheme we have charted above takes in the impact of discrimination but does not account for the integrative systems due to other conditions operative in the process of growth. This division is purely arbitrary for actually both series run concomitantly. There is no time in the life of the Negro that he is not actively in contact with the caste situation. The other personality traits derive, however, from the disturbances in his family life. This source gives rise to the following constellations: the affectivity range, the capacity for idealization and ideal formation, the traits derived from reactions to discipline, and conscience mechanisms. In these categories there is some difference as we proceed from the lower- to the upper-class Negro. Let us take up the lower-class Negro first.

Affectivity range means the range of emotional potential. In appraising the role of emotion in personal and social adaptation, we have both quantitative and qualitative features to take into account. The total adaptation of the individual will depend on how much and what kind of emotion he has in a given situation. Emotion in man's adaptation tends to operate on a mass action principle. That is, the predominance of one emotion tends to stifle all others.

Emotion has the function of orientation toward objects in the outer world that can be the source of frustration or gratifications. The individual responds to a frustrating object with the emergency emotions of fear and rage, and their derivatives of hate, suspicion, distrust, apprehensive anticipation, and the like. These functions are self-preservative in intent and gear the organism for defensive action. The feeling toward objects which are the source of gratifications is the wish to be near, to perpetuate the influence of, to love, to desire, to have anticipations of continued gratifications, to trust, to have confidence, to cooperate with.

We must stress the point from this inventory that the emotions most conducive to social cohesion are those that pertain to the categories of love, trust, and confidence. All creatures are natively endowed with the capacity for fear and rage. The positively toned feelings of love, trust, and confidence, however, must largely be cultivated by experience. Hence, when we refer to the affectivity potential of an individual, we do not mean the emergency functions of fear and rage. We mean rather the capacity for cooperative and affectionate relatedness to others.

None of these emotions functions in isolation; they have a continuous adaptive interplay during the entire process of growth and living. What counts in the individual are the types of emotional response that become habitual and automatic. These fixed patterns of emotion are not only adaptive, in the sense that they are reaction types to actual situations; they also play a dominant role in shaping anticipations and to a degree, therefore, influence how events will shape up. For example, a person trained to be suspicious will shape the actual events of his life in such a way that his suspicions appear warranted.

The emotions play a decisive role in determining the sociability (peaceful cooperation with others) of the individual through the development of conscience mechanisms and the formation of ideals. The desire on the part of the child to be loved and protected is the dominant incentive for the child to be obedient to his protectors. He needs this because he is helpless himself. The child thus becomes socialized in order to continue the boons of love and protection. He learns to anticipate the requirements for these returns by internalizing them and making them automatic. He also learns the methods of escaping blame and of devising techniques for reinstatement. Thus, the fear of punishment and the withdrawal of love exert a powerful restraining influence against antisocial behavior. The reward for conformity is a sense of pride in the social recognition of "good" behavior, while the fear of detection and punishment leads to guilty fear and either an anticipation of punishment or self-punishment.

However, in order for these positive emotional feelings and the functions of conscience to be instituted, certain behavior by the parents toward the child is required. Thus, we cannot expect the child to develop affection and dependence on the parent who is not constant in his care, who does not love in return for obedience, whose punishments are either disproportionate, or have no relation to the offense. In this instance, conformity is of no adaptive value at all. A child who is constantly abused by the parent cannot be expected to have pleasant anticipations or to idealize the parent or wish to be like him. A child exposed to this kind of behavior from the parent will not love, trust, or cooperate. It can take flight from the hostile environment and try to seek another more friendly one. Or it can stay and hate the parent, and suppress all the hostile feeling.

On the institutional side, the family structure of the lower-class Negro is the same as the white. However, in the actual process of living, the vicissitudes of the lower-class family are greater and its stability much less. This is where the broken family through early death of parents, abandonment or divorce, takes a heavy toll on the opportunities for developing strong affective ties to the parents. First, the needs for dependency are frustrated. This makes the mother a frustrating object, rather than one the child can depend on. This does not mean that it is the intention of the mothers to neglect or mistreat their children. Quite the contrary, the intention is the usual one, and many lower-class Negro mothers have strong maternal feelings, are exceedingly protective, and try to be good providers. This is not, however, what one hears from the subjects. They tell chiefly the story of frustration and of arbitrary discipline by mothers. Not infrequently there is also the constant story of beating and cursing as disciplinary reinforcements. The rivalry situation between siblings in the lower classes is greatly enhanced by the general scarcity in which they live. This situation, of course, is greatly magnified when the child is given to some other relative for custody, as a consequence of a broken home. These children fare worse than any of the others. They are the ones who, because of mistreatment, decide at the age of 10 or 12 to run away and shift for themselves. In these children, some of whom we studied, the premature independence hardly works to the advantage of the personality in the long run. They become shrewd and adjustable, but at the cost of complete mistrust in everyone.

The result of the continuous frustrations in childhood is to create a personality devoid of confidence in human relations, of an eternal vigilance and distrust of others. This is a purely defensive maneuver which purports to protect the individual against the repeatedly traumatic effects of disappointment and frustration. He must operate on the assumption that the world is hostile. The self-referential aspect of this is contained in the formula "I am not a lovable creature." This, together with the same idea drawn from the caste situation, leads to a reinforcement of the basic destruction of self-esteem.

Thus, many of the efforts of the lower-class Negro at emotional relatedness are canceled out by the inner mistrust in others, the conviction that no one can love him for his own sake, that he is not lovable. Under these conditions, not much real social relatedness is possible. It is, however, very significant that

the lower-class Negro is an inveterate "joiner" in one kind of social voluntary organization or another, of clubs and cliques with high-sounding names and with much ritualism in initiation rites. In these organizations, which have a very short life span, there is continuous discord, jockeying for position and prestige, and insistence that each member must have his own way. In other words, through these clubs and associations, the Negro tries to compensate for his lack of relatedness. But for the greater part, he fails. The intrapsychic mistrust and need for dominance destroy the effectiveness of these compensatory efforts. This is a noteworthy feature of Negro life, because the social organizations are supposed to facilitate cooperative endeavor and to give the members the satisfaction of belonging to something, to diminish their isolation. This end is not accomplished because most of the energy of these "associations" is taken up with overcoming mutual distrust and very little energy goes into the mutual supportive aspects of the organization.

Closely related to the question of the affectivity potential is the capacity for idealization. This trait is a general human characteristic, and is rooted in the biological make-up of man. It is the most powerful vehicle for the transmission of culture. During his helpless state man must place his trust in the parent who is his support. If this support and affection aid the individual in his adjustment, the natural tendency is to magnify the powers of the parent to magical proportions. This projection of magical attributes on the parent is the most powerful implement the parent has in enforcing discipline, because the threat of withdrawal of this support creates anxiety in the child. It follows, therefore, that the idealized parent is the satisfying parent whose authority is less enforced than it is delegated, and the acquiescence to discipline is a method the child has for perpetuating those boons he has already enjoyed in the past and hence expects to enjoy in the future.

The formation of ideals to pursue is a corollary of the idealization of the parent. It is easy to identify oneself with the idealized parent if the expectations from him have been realized. If these expectations are frustrated, then there may develop a reactive ideal or the opposite to the one experienced. This is generally a rare phenomenon, where a mistreated child becomes an ideal parent by living the opposite of what he has experienced. It does indeed happen. But it is far from the rule. The commonest outcome of this situation is that despite the hatred to the parent, the child takes on and identifies himself with the hated and frustrating attributes and becomes the replica of the frustrating parent. Here one must draw the line between an activating ideal and the unconscious identification. The activating ideal may be "I will be a provident parent"; the unconscious identification, however, may be with the frustrating parent. In some instances, the mistreated child when it becomes the parent is actuated by the idea: "Why should I give you what I never had myself?" These are the cases in which the frustrated dependency cravings interfere with the protective parental role.

The question of Negro-ideal formation is hardly limited to the parental role. The "ideal" answers the question: "Whom do I want to be like?" This is where the Negro encounters a great deal of difficulty. The parent is a member of a despised and discriminated-against group. Hence, this ideal is already spoiled because it carries with it a guarantee of external and reflected hatred. No one can embrace such an ideal. Furthermore, until very recently the Negro has had no real culture heroes (like Joe Louis and Jackie Robinson) with whom he could identify. It is therefore quite natural that the Negro ideal should be *white*. However, accepting the white ideal is a recipe for perpetual self-hatred, frustration, and for tying one's life to unattainable goals. It is a formula for living life on the delusional basis of "as if." The acceptance of the white ideal has acted on the Negro as a slow but cumulative and fatal psychological poison. Its disastrous effects were due to the fact that the more completely he accepted the white ideal, the greater his intrapsychic discomfort had to become. For he could never become *white*. He had, therefore, to settle for the delusion of whiteness through an affectation of white attributes or those that most closely resembled them. This also means the destruction of such native traits as are susceptible of change (kinky hair, etc.). In its most regressive form, this ideal becomes the frantic wish to be reborn white. Pride in oneself could not, therefore, be vested in attributes one had, but in attributes one aspired to have, that is to say, on borrowed ideals. This maneuver, calculated as a restitutive one, ends by being destructive of self-esteem.

The reactions to discipline and the dynamics of conscience mechanisms are closely interrelated, and these in turn are related to the general affectivity potential and ideal formation.

In general, there are several factors operating on the parental side of the induction of disciplines which differ from the situation among whites. The Negro parent has no authority in the social world in which he lives. It is, therefore, a strong temptation for the Negro parent to tend to be authoritative in the only place where he can exercise it, namely in his own home. Hence, we get repeated stories of children being subjected to disciplines that are both arbitrary, instantaneous, and inconsistent, depending often on whim, and at the same time without the ability to offer the child the appropriate rewards for obedience and conformity. Children recognize these rewards chiefly in terms of need satisfactions. These the parent, more often than not, cannot implement. They often fail on the sheer subsistence level. Such a parent cannot have much delegated authority or inspire much dependence. Hence, the authority of the parent is destroyed. A second factor occurs especially in those cases where the mother works. She has no time to be the careful and provident mother. After a day's work, during which time the child often shifts for itself, she is inclined to be tired and irritable which accounts for much of her impatience and insistence on immediate and unqualified obedience.

As between mother and father, many factors conspire to make the mother the chief object of such dependency as is possible under the circumstances. The male as provider and protector definitely suffers disparagement. The mother's objective—since she has so little time—is to make the child as little nuisance as possible. This makes her both an object to be feared and at the same time the only one that can be relied upon.

In passing, we must mention here the place of street life for the Negro child and adolescent. In many ways this street life is no different from corresponding street life in lower-class whites. The crowded home is not a happy place for the growing child, especially when parents are so often away. Since the family does not implement its disciplines with appropriate rewards, the children tend to get their ideals and pattern their amusements on the opportunities of the street, with its values, its heroism, its ideals, and its factionalism. They differ from corresponding white groups in the quantity of the savagery of their mutual aggression, in which the boys get seriously hurt and in some instances killed. Part of this street life pattern is the result of sheer boredom and the irrelevancy of education. Hence, they cannot be attentive at school or get the feeling that they are engaged in a meaningful and ego-enhancing activity. Many of these high school boys have been to bed with women the age of their female teachers and the disciplines and obligations of school life make no sense to them. In consequence, school is treated as a meaningless routine. The street, on the other hand, offers adventure, struggle for dominance, mock and real hostilities. It is, in other words, a better training for life—according to their sights—than education. Delinquency among adolescents runs high for very good reasons.

In this general setting we can evaluate the effects of the socializing disciplines.

We have seen but little evidence of rigid anal training in childhood. There is no serious contest of will between parent and child over this aspect of socialization. It is largely neglected, and in those who came from the South, there was little emphasis on order, neatness, or systematization. Hence, in this group we would not expect much adventitious use of the anal zone for elaborate constellations about expulsion and retention. If there are any compulsive traits in the Negroes of this group, they do not derive from this source.

A more important aspect of socializing discipline is in the sexual domain. Here the picture is very confused. In the lower classes, the sex morality taught is of the Victorian variety. However, there is but little effort made to implement it. There is, on the whole, much less anxiety introduced into sexual disciplines than is the case with the white middle classes. The result is actually more sexual freedom among lower-class Negro children than among whites. And it is by no means unusual for boys and girls to be inducted into sexual activity quite early (7 to 13). It is therefore highly unlikely that potency troubles in both males and females of this group derive from anxieties introduced into the picture by parental threats. In those cases observed these difficulties usually arose from another source. They came from the confusion in the sociosexual roles of male and female. The male derives these difficulties from his inability to assume the effective masculine role according to white ideals, as against the dominant position of the female, first in

the dominant mother and later in the dominant wife. The economic independence of the female plays havoc with the conventional male-female roles, and this in turn, influences the potency of the males. In the case of the female, her sociosexual role is reversed. She is dominant, and rebels against the passive and dependent role. Thus, the sexuality of the Negro in the lower classes is confused by the sexual significance of the social role.

Contrary to expectations, the sexual drive of the adult Negro is relatively in abeyance. We saw no evidence of the sex-craved and abandoned Negro. This playing down of sex is the result of the socioeconomic hardship and the confusion in the sexual roles.

What kind of conscience mechanisms can be integrated under these conditions? This situation is, if anything, more complex than in the white. Basically, the tonicity of the conscience mechanisms depend on the ability of the parent to act as provider of satisfactions. Hence, in the lower-class Negro, we cannot expect strong internalized conscience. If we add to this the disastrous effects of the caste system, then the lower-class Negro, in his hatred for the white, is robbed of any incentive for developing a strong conscience. However, the effects of the caste system are such that they inspire a great deal of fear. Therefore, antisocial tendencies would be held in rigid check by fear of detection. In fact, we can say that conscience in the lower-class Negro is held in tow by his general vigilance over his hatred and aggression, and that the fear of detection of his aggression and antisocial tendencies are both governed by the same control mechanisms. The great danger for the lower-class Negro is that these control devices may occasionally and impulsively be overwhelmed—a factor that is of enormous concern to every lower-class Negro.

This group of constellations sets up in the Negro a strong need for compensatory activities, to help establish some semblance of internal harmony. These compensatory activities have the function of (a) bolstering self-esteem, (b) narcotizing the individual against traumatic impact, (c) disparaging the other fellow, (d) getting magical aid for status improvement.

Among the activities for bolstering self-esteem are flashy and flamboyant dressing, especially in the male, and the denial of Negro attributes, such as doing away with kinky hair.

Narcotizing the individual against traumatic influences is effected largely through alcohol and drugs. In these activities, the males predominate. Alcoholic psychoses in Negroes occur with twice the frequency that they do in whites.[1] Narcotics have a wide use among Negroes, but their high cost makes alcohol much more available.

Disparaging the other fellow is widespread among urban Negroes. It is of a vindictive and vituperative kind and derives largely from the status strivings. The street corner and candy store are favorite places for malicious gossip.

In the domain of magical aid to self-esteem, gambling takes a high place. This takes the form of card playing but more often of participation in the numbers racket. Here everyone has a chance at beating fate, of being the favored one, if only for a day. The lure of this tantalizing game must be very high, judging from the vast fortune spent annually by the bulk of the Negro population.

In addition to these, there are occasional outlets, chiefly by males, which stem from their inability to plan or have any confidence in a future. Since the general tendency is to live from day to day, explosive spending when they have money is not infrequent. An occasional illusion of plenty and luxury can thus be created, even if to do so means to mortgage one's energy for months ahead to pay for the luxury.

This psychological picture is to some extent changed in the middle and upper classes. Here the family organization corresponds more closely to the middle-class white group. The emphasis shifts from subsistence problems to status problems. There is also a shift from female to male dominance in the family. The chief conflict area is that concerned with status. In general, the benefits derived from better parental care, better induction of affectivity, better ideal formation and more tonic conscience mechanisms are to a large extent canceled out by the enormous increase in status conflict caused by the caste situation.

In appraising the adaptation of the middle- and upper-class Negro, we encountered a good deal of difficulty in differentiating the real from the apparent. For example, the affectivity potential is much better in this group than in the lower class. But against this we must discount the fact that the representations of better

affectivity rest largely on a formal basis. Their marriages are more stable; they induct affectivity more appropriately, etc. But these features are due largely to the fact that the upper- and middle-class Negroes strive hardest to live and feel like the whites. They are more conventional, have more rigid sex mores, set more store by "respectability" than do lower-class Negroes. They know what the "right" feelings are for a given situation and they try very hard to have them. But whether they do or not depends on the quantity of the conflicts they have on the issues of skin color and status strivings, all of which tend to detract from the freedom of feeling.

In the specific integrative areas this group approximates the white. Parental care is good in the same sense and with the same incompatibilities as with whites. The affectivity potential is apparently higher than in lower-class Negroes and they have more capacity for relatedness. They have a high capacity for idealization, but what is idealized is white and not Negro. Here again the ideal formation in the Negro has two layers. The natural figure to idealize is the provident parent; but he is a disparaged figure. Introjecting this object means to hate it to the accompaniment of perpetual guilt. The substitution of a white object as the source of the ideal does not solve the problem. It, too, is hated and likewise must give rise to guilt. The Negro cannot win in either case. As one upper-class Negro observed: "The only thing black that I like is myself." Their ideal formation is of a high order, but founders on the rock of unattainable ideals. The fact that these ideals are relatively more capable of achievement than in the lower classes renders the conflict sharper. Thus, they tend to drive themselves harder, make greater demands on themselves for accomplishment, and are obligated to refuse the compensatory activities open to lower-class Negroes. This greatly augments the internal self-hatred and makes it more difficult to accept the Negro status. I could love myself "if" is all the more tantalizing because they can almost make the grade, but for skin color. They are therefore more vulnerable to depressed self-esteem than the lower class.

The need to conform to white standards of middle-class respectability gives the upper classes a harder time with their control of aggression. And this in turn has a constricting effect on all their affectivity.

In view of the good parental care, one would

[1] See Malzberg, Benjamin, "Mental Disease Among American Negroes: A Statistical Analysis," in Klineberg, Otto (ed.), *Characteristics of the American Negro,* New York: Harper, 1944.

expect that their tendencies to passivity would be accentuated. But this is countered by the strong pressure against any form of passivity or subordination especially to other Negroes—since they cannot avoid subordination to the white. This constellation would be very valuable to follow through in Negro homosexuals. As we saw in the biographies, the conflict about passivity in the males was enormous.

The points where the intrapsychic conflicts are sharpened for the middle- and upper-class Negro, then, are in the disposition and compensations for lowered self-esteem, the disposition of aggression, and in the uncompromising acceptance of white ideals.

The self-hatred of this group takes the usual form of projection on both white and on Negroes lower than themselves. However, they have more guilt about their Negro hatred than is the case with lower classes. To the whites, the formula is hatred + control = disguise; to the Negro the formula is hatred + guilt = anxiety of retaliation. Thus, every middle- and upper-class Negro has increased competitiveness with whites, but his psychological task is merely one of control and concealment. The hatred to the Negro has a way of ricocheting back on its source. Every Negro who is higher than lower class has a sense of guilt to other Negroes because he considers success a betrayal of his group and a piece of aggression against them. Hence, he has frequently what might be called a "success phobia," and occasionally cannot enjoy the fruits of his achievements.

In his acceptance of white ideals, the Negro often overshoots the mark. He overdoes the sex mores so that the incidence of frigidity in the women is very high. In his acceptance of the white man's cleanliness obsession, the Negro ends by identifying himself with feces, and becomes extraordinarily clean and meticulous. However, the obstructions to the accomplishments of white ideals lead to increase in aggression, anxiety, depression of self-esteem, and self-hatred. This compels him to push harder against the social barriers, to drive himself

harder, and ends with more frustration and more self-hatred. This vicious circle never ends.

Thus, as we stated above, it is difficult to appraise the advantages and disadvantages of the upper classes as regards their intrapsychic effects. The shift from female to male orientation at least saves this group from the confusion of social and sexual roles. It is one of male dominance and clear definition of sexual role. However, they overdo the rigidity of sexual restrictions, and this affects the female more than the male. The marriages are more stable, but the importance of conventionality is very high; hence the impression remains that as an average the marriages are not more happy. Affectivity is better; but its betterment is largely on the formal side.

The chief outcome of the psychological picture is that the upper classes of Negro society have so much controlling to do of their psychic life, that they must be extremely cramped and constricted and unspontaneous. There is too little self-contentment for true abandonment, and too much self-hatred and mutual mistrust for effective social relatedness. They must constantly choose the lesser evil between spontaneity and getting hurt by retaliation. Hence, they prefer not to see things as they are, or to enter too deeply into anything to the accompaniment of apathy and resignation.

Is there such a thing as a basic personality for the Negro? This work proves decidedly that there is. Though he lives in American culture, the Negro lives under special conditions which give this personality a distinctive configuration. Taking as our base line the white middle class, the conditions of life for the Negro are so distinctive that there is an actual alteration of the pressures to which he must adapt. Hence, he develops a distinctive personality. This basic Negro personality is, however, a caricature of the corresponding white personality, because the Negro must adapt to the same culture, must accept the same social goals, but without the ability to achieve them. This limitation in social opportunities accounts for the difference in personality configuration.

Chapter 25 The Inmate World

ERVING GOFFMAN

INTRODUCTORY NOTE

A total institution may be defined as a place of residence and work where a large number of like-situated individuals, cut off from the wider society for an appreciable period of time, together lead an enclosed, formally administered round of life. Prisons serve as a clear example, providing we appreciate that what is prison-like about prisons is found in institutions whose members have broken no laws. This analysis deals with total institutions in general and one example, mental hospitals, in particular. The main focus is on the world of the inmate, not the world of the staff. A chief concern is to develop a sociological version of the structure of the self.

I

It is characteristic of inmates that they come to the institution with a "presenting culture" (to modify a psychiatric phrase) derived from a "home world"—a way of life and a round of activities taken for granted until the point of admission to the institution. (There is reason, then, to exclude orphanages and foundling homes from the list of total institutions, except insofar as the orphan comes to be socialized into the outside world by some process of cultural osmosis, even while this world is being systematically denied him.) Whatever the stability of the recruit's personal organization, it was part of a wider framework lodged in his civil environment—a round of experience that confirmed a tolerable conception of self, and allowed for a set of defensive maneuvers, exercised at his own discretion, for coping with conflicts, discreditings, and failures.

Now it appears that total institutions do not substitute their own unique culture for some-thing already formed; we deal with something more restricted than acculturation or assimilation. If cultural change does occur, it has to do, perhaps, with the removal of certain behavior opportunities and the failure to keep pace with recent social changes on the outside. Thus if the inmate's stay is long, what has been called "disculturation"[1] may occur—that is, an "untraining" which renders him temporarily incapable of managing certain features of daily life on the outside, if and when he gets back to it.

The full meaning for the inmate of being "in" or "on the outside" does not exist apart from the special meaning to him of "getting out" or "getting on the outside." In this sense, total institutions do not really look for cultural victory. They create and sustain a particular kind of tension between the home world and the institutional world and use this persistent tension as strategic leverage in the management of men.

II

The recruit, then, comes into the establishment with a conception of himself made possible by certain stable social arrangements

SOURCES. Introductory Note: from *Asylums,* New York: Doubleday Anchor, 1961, p. xiii. Reprinted by permission of Doubleday and Company, Inc. Erving Goffman, "On the Characteristics of Total Institutions: The Inmate World," from Donald R. Cressey, ed., *The Prison,* New York: Holt, Rinehart and Winston, Inc., 1961, pp. 22–31, 33–39, and 44–47, copyright © 1961 by Holt, Rinehart and Winston, Inc. All rights reserved.

[1] A term employed by Robert Sommer, "Patients Who Grow Old in a Mental Hospital," *Geriatrics,* **14** (1959), pp. 586–587. The term "desocialization," sometimes used in this context, would seem to be too strong, implying loss of fundamental capacities to communicate and cooperate.

in his home world. Upon entrance, he is immediately stripped of the support provided by these arrangements. In the accurate language of some of our oldest total institutions, he begins a series of abasements, degradations, humiliations, and profanations of self. His self is systematically, if often unintentionally, mortified. He begins some radical shifts in his *moral career,* a career composed of the progressive changes that occur in the beliefs that he has concerning himself and significant others.

The processes by which a person's self is mortified are fairly standard in total institutions;[2] analysis of these processes can help us to see the arrangements that ordinary establishments must guarantee if members are to preserve their civilian selves.

The barrier that total institutions place between the inmate and the wider world marks the first curtailment of self. In civil life, the sequential scheduling of the individual's roles, both in the life cycle and in the repeated daily round, ensures that no one role he plays will block his performance and ties in another. In total institutions, in contrast, membership automatically disrupts role scheduling, since the inmate's separation from the wider world lasts around the clock and may continue for years. Role dispossession therefore occurs. In many total institutions, the privilege of visiting away from the establishment or having visitors come to the establishment is completely withheld at first, ensuring a deep initial break with past roles and an appreciation of role dispossession. A report on cadet life in a military academy provides an illustration:

This clean break with the past must be achieved in a relatively short period. For two months, therefore, the swab is not allowed to leave the base or to engage in social intercourse with non-cadets. This complete isolation helps to produce a unified group of swabs, rather than a heterogeneous collection of persons of high and low status. Uniforms are issued on the first day, and discussions of wealth and family background are taboo. Although the pay of the cadet is very low, he is not permitted to receive money from home. The role of cadet must supersede other roles the individual has been accustomed to play. There are few clues left which will reveal social status in the outside world.[3]

I might add that when entrance is voluntary, the recruit has already partially withdrawn from his home world: what is cleanly severed by the institution is something that had already started to decay.

Although some roles can be re-established by the inmate if and when he returns to the world, it is plain that other losses are irrevocable and may be painfully experienced as such. It may not be possible to make up, at a later phase of the life cycle, the time not now spent in educational or job advancement, in courting, or in socializing one's children. A legal aspect of this permanent dispossession is found in the concept of "civil death": prison inmates may face not only a temporary loss of the rights to will money and write checks, to contest divorce or adoption proceedings, and to vote, but may have some of these rights permanently abrogated.[4]

The inmate, then, finds that certain roles are lost to him by virtue of the barrier that separates him from the outside world. The process of entrance typically brings other kinds of loss and mortification as well. We very generally find what are called admission procedures, such as taking a life history, photographing, weighing, fingerprinting, number-assigning, searching, signing away of personal possessions, undressing, bathing, disinfecting, haircutting, issuing institutional clothing and instruction as to rules, and assigning to quarters.[5] Admission procedures might better be called "trimming" or "programming" because in thus being squared-away the new arrival allows himself to become shaped and coded into the kind of object that can be fed into the administrative machinery of the establishment, to be worked on smoothly by routine operations. Many of these procedures depend upon attributes such as weight or fingerprints which the individual possesses merely because he is a member of the largest

---

[2] An example of the description of these processes may be found in Gresham M. Sykes, *The Society of Captives,* Princeton: Princeton University Press, 1958, Ch. 4, "The Pains of Imprisonment," pp. 63–83.

[3] Sanford M. Dornbusch, "The Military Academy

as an Assimilating Institution," *Social Forces,* **33** (1955), p. 317. For an example of initial visiting restrictions in a mental hospital see, D. McI. Johnson and N. Dodds, eds., *The Plea for the Silent,* London: Christopher Johnson, 1957, p. 16. Compare the rule against having visitors which has often bound domestic servants to their total institution. See J. Jean Hecht, *The Domestic Servant Class in Eighteenth-Century England,* London: Routledge, Kegan Paul, 1956, pp. 127–128.

[4] A useful review in the case of American prisons may be found in Paul W. Tappan, "The Legal Rights of Prisoners," *The Annals,* **293** (May, 1954), p. 99–111.

[5] See, for example, J. Kerkhoff, *How Thin the*

and most abstract of social categories, that of the human being. Action taken on the basis of such attributes necessarily ignores most of his previous basis of self-identification.

Because a total institution deals with so many aspects of its inmates' lives, with the consequent complex squaring away at admission, there is a special need to obtain initial cooperativeness from the recruit. Staff often feel that a recruit's readiness to be appropriately deferential in his initial face-to-face encounters with them is a sign that he will pliantly take the role of the routinely pliant inmate. The occasion on which staff members first tell the inmate of his deference obligations may be structured to challenge the inmate to balk or to hold his peace forever. Thus these initial moments of socialization may involve an "obedience test" and even a will-breaking contest: an inmate who shows defiance receives' immediate visible punishment, which increases until he openly "cries uncle" and humbles himself.

* * *

Admission procedures and obedience tests may be elaborated into a form of initiation that has been called "the welcome," where staff or inmates, or both, go out of their way to give the recruit a clear notion of his plight.[6] As part of this rite of passage he may be called by a term, such as "fish" or "swab," which tells him that he is merely an inmate, and, what is more, that he has a special low status even in this low group.

The admission procedure may be characterized as a leaving off and a taking on, with the midpoint marked by physical nakedness. Leaving off, of course, entails a dispossession of property, important here because persons invest self-feelings in their possessions. Perhaps the most significant of these possessions is not physical at all, that is, one's full name; whatever one is thereafter called, loss of one's name can be a great curtailment of the self.[7]

Once the inmate is stripped of his possessions, at least some replacements must be made by the establishment, but these take the form of standard issue, uniform in character and uniformly distributed. These substitute possessions are clearly marked as really belonging to the institution and in some cases are recalled at regular intervals to be, as it were, disinfected of identifications. With objects that can be used up, for example pencils, the inmate may be required to return the remnants before obtaining a re-issue.[8] Failure to provide inmates with individual lockers, and periodic searches and confiscations of accumulated personal property[9] reinforce property dispossession. Religious orders have appreciated the implications for self of such separation from belongings. Inmates may be required to change their cells once a year so as not to become attached to them.

* * *

One set of the individual's possessions has a special relation to self. The individual ordinarily expects to exert some control over the guise in which he appears before others. For this he needs cosmetic and clothing supplies, tools for applying, arranging, and repairing them, and an accessible, secure place to store these supplies and tools—in short, the individual will need an "identity kit" for the management of his personal front. He will also need access to services offered by barbers and clothiers.

On admission to a total institution, however, the individual is likely to be stripped of his usual appearance and of the equipment and services by which he maintains it, thus suffering a personal defacement. Clothing, combs, needle and thread, cosmetics, towels, soap, shaving sets, bathing facilities—all these may be taken away or denied him, although some may be kept in accessible storage, to be returned if and when he leaves. In the words of Saint Benedict's Holy Rule:

Then forthwith he shall, there in the oratory, be divested of his own garments with which he is

Veil: A Newspaperman's Story of His Own Mental Crackup and Recovery, New York: Greenberg, 1952, p. 110; Elie A. Cohen, *Human Behaviour in the Concentration Camp,* London: Jonathan Cape, 1954, p. 120; Eugen Kogon, *The Theory and Practice of Hell,* New York: Berkeley, 1950, pp. 63–68.
[6] For a version of this process in concentration camps, see Cohen, *op. cit.,* p. 120, and Kogon, *op. cit.,* pp. 64–65. For a fictionalized treatment of the welcome in a girls' reformatory see, Sara Norris, *The Wayward Ones,* New York: Signet Books, 1952, pp. 31–34. A prison version, less explicit, is

found in George Dendrickson and Frederick Thomas, *The Truth About Dartmoor,* London: Gollancz, 1954, pp. 42–57.
[7] For example, Thomas Merton, *The Seven Storey Mountain,* New York: Harcourt, Brace and Company, 1948, pp. 290–91; Cohen, *op. cit.,* pp. 146–47.
[8] Dendrickson and Thomas, *op. cit.,* p. 85; also, *The Holy Rule of St. Benedict,* Ch. 55.
[9] Kogon, *op. cit.,* p. 69.

clothed and be clad in those of the monastery. Those garments of which he is divested shall be placed in the wardrobe, there to be kept, so that if, perchance, he should ever be persuaded by the devil to leave the monastery (which God forbid), he may be stripped of the monastic habit and cast forth.[10]

As suggested, the institutional issue provided as a substitute for what has been taken away is typically of a "coarse" variety, ill-suited, often old, and the same for large categories of inmates. The impact of this substitution is described in a report on imprisoned prostitutes:

> First, there is the shower officer who forces them to undress, takes their own clothes away, sees to it that they take showers and get their prison clothes—one pair of black oxfords with cuban heels, two pairs of much-mended ankle socks, three cotton dresses, two cotton slips, two pairs of panties, and a couple of bras. Practically all the bras are flat and useless. No corsets or girdles are issued.
> There is not a sadder sight than some of the obese prisoners who, if nothing else, have been managing to keep themselves looking decent on the outside, confronted by the first sight of themselves in prison issue.[11]

In addition to personal defacement that comes from being stripped of one's identity kit, there is personal disfigurement that comes from such direct and permanent mutilations of the body as brands or loss of limbs. Although this mortification of the self by way of the body is found in few total institutions, still, loss of a sense of personal safety is common and provides a basis for anxieties about disfigurement. Beatings, surgery, or shock therapy—whatever the intent of staff in providing these services for some inmates—may lead many inmates to feel that they are in an environment that does not guarantee their physical integrity.

At admission, then, loss of identity equipment can prevent the individual from presenting his usual image of himself to others. After admission, the image of himself he presents is attacked in another way. Given the expressive idiom of a particular civil society, certain movements, postures, and stances will convey

lowly images of the individual and be avoided as demeaning. Any regulation, command, or task that forces the individual to adopt these movements or postures may thus mortify the self. In total institutions, such physical indignities abound. In mental hospitals, for example, patients may be forced to eat all food with a spoon.[12] In military prisons, inmates may be required to stand at attention whenever an officer enters the compound.[13] In religious institutions, there are such classic gestures of penitence as the kissing of feet,[14] and the posture required of an erring monk—that he must

> lie prostrate at the door of the oratory in silence; and thus, with his face to the ground and his body prone, let him cast himself at the feet of all as they go forth from the oratory.[15]

In some penal institutions, we find the humiliation of bending over to receive a birching.[16]

Just as the individual can be required to hold his body in a humiliating pose, so he may have to provide humiliating verbal responses. An important instance of this is the forced deference pattern of total institutions; inmates are often required to punctuate their social intercourse with staff by verbal acts of deference, such as saying "Sir." Another instance is the necessity to beg, importune, or humbly ask for little things such as a light for a cigarette, a drink of water, or permission to use the telephone.

Corresponding to the indignities of speech and action required of the inmate are the indignities of treatment others accord him. The standard examples here are *verbal or gestural profanations:* staff or fellow inmates call the individual obscene names, curse him, point out his negative attributes, tease him, or talk about him or his fellow inmates as if he were not present.

Whatever the form or the source of these various indignities, the individual has to engage in activity whose symbolic implications are incompatible with his conception of self. A more diffuse example of this kind of mortification occurs when the individual is required to under-

---

10 *The Holy Rule of St. Benedict,* Ch. 58.
11 John M. Murtagh and Sara Harris, *Cast the First Stone,* New York: Pocket Books, 1958, pp. 239–240. On mental hospitals see, for example, Kerkhoff, *op. cit.,* p. 10. Mary Jane Ward in *The Snake Pit,* New York: New American Library, 1955, p. 60, makes the reasonable suggestion that men in our society suffer less defacement in total institutions than do women.

12 Johnson and Dodds, *op. cit.,* p. 15; for a prison version see Alfred Hassler, *Diary of a Self-Made Convict,* Chicago: Regnery, 1954, p. 31.
13 L. D. Hankoff, "Interaction Patterns Among Military Prison Personnel," *U.S. Armed Forces Medical Journal,* **10** (1959), p. 1419.
14 Kathryn Hulme, *The Nun's Story,* London: Muller, 1957, p. 52.
15 *The Holy Rule of St. Benedict,* Ch. 44.
16 Dendrickson and Thomas, *op. cit.,* p. 76.

take a daily round of life that he considers alien to him—to take on a disidentifying role. In prisons, denial of heterosexual opportunities can induce fear of losing one's masculinity.[17] In military establishments, the patently useless make-work forced on fatigue details can make men feel their time and effort are worthless.[18] In religious institutions there are special arrangements to ensure that all inmates take a turn performing the more menial aspects of the servant role.[19] An extreme is the concentration-camp practice requiring prisoners to administer whippings to other prisoners.[20]

There is another form of mortification in total institutions; beginning with admission a kind of contaminative exposure occurs. On the outside, the individual can hold objects of self-feeling—such as his body, his immediate actions, his thoughts, and some of his possessions—clear of contact with alien and contaminating things. But in total institutions these territories of the self are violated; the boundary that the individual places between his being and the environment is invaded and the embodiments of self profaned.

There is, first, a violation of one's informational preserve regarding self. During admission, facts about the inmate's social statuses and past behavior—especially discreditable facts—are collected and recorded in a dossier available to staff. Later, in so far as the establishment officially expects to alter the self-regulating inner tendencies of the inmate, there may be group or individual confession—psychiatric, political, military, or religious, according to the type of institution. On these occasions the inmate has to expose facts and feelings about self to new kinds of audiences. The most spectacular examples of such exposure come to us from Communist confession camps and from the *culpa* sessions that form part of the routine of Catholic religious institutions.[21] The dynamics of the process have been explicitly considered by those engaged in so-called milieu therapy.

New audiences not only learn discreditable facts about oneself that are ordinarily concealed but are also in a position to perceive some of these facts directly. Thus prisoners and mental patients cannot prevent their visitors from seeing them in humiliating circumstances.[22] Another example is the shoulder-patch of ethnic identification worn by concentration camp inmates.[23] Medical and security examinations often expose the inmate physically, sometimes to persons of both sexes. Collective sleeping arrangements cause a similar exposure, as do doorless toilets.[24] An extreme here, perhaps, is the situation of the mental patient who is stripped naked for what is felt to be his own protection and placed in a constantly-lit seclusion room, into whose judas-window any person passing on the ward can peer. In general, of course, the inmate is never fully alone; he is always within sight and often within earshot of someone, if only his fellow-inmates.[25] Prison cages with bars for walls fully realize such exposure.

Perhaps the most obvious type of contaminative exposure is the directly physical kind—the besmearing and defiling of the body or of other objects closely identified with the self. Sometimes this involves a breakdown of the usual environmental arrangements for insulating oneself from one's own source of contamination, as in having to empty one's own slops[26] or having to subject one's evacuation to regimentation.

* * *

I have suggested that the inmate undergoes mortification of the self by contaminative exposure of a physical kind, but this must be amplified: when the agency of contamination is another human being, then the inmate is in addition contaminated by forced interpersonal contact and, in consequence, a forced social relationship. (Similarly, when the inmate loses control over who observes him in his predicament, or who knows about his past, he is being

---

[17] Sykes, *op. cit.*, pp. 70–72.

[18] For example, T. E. Lawrence, *The Mint*, London: Jonathan Cape, 1955, pp. 34–35.

[19] *The Holy Rule of St. Benedict*, Ch. 35.

[20] Kogon, *op. cit.*, p. 102.

[21] Hulme, *op. cit.*, pp. 48–51.

[22] Wider communities in Western society, of course, have employed this technique too, in the form of public floggings and public hangings, the pillory and stocks. Functionally correlated with the public emphasis on mortifications in total institutions is the commonly found strict ruling that staff is not to be humiliated by staff in the presence of inmates.

[23] Kogon, *op. cit.*, pp. 41–42.

[24] Brendan Behan, *Borstal Boy*, London: Hutchinson, 1958, p. 23.

[25] For example, Kogon, *op. cit.*, p. 128; Hassler, *op. cit.*, p. 16. For the situation in a religious institution, see Hulme, *op. cit.*, p. 48. She also describes a lack of aural privacy: thin cotton hangings are used as the only door closing off the individual sleeping cells (p. 20).

[26] Anthony Heckstall-Smith *Eighteen Months*, London: Allan Wingate, 1954, p. 21; Dendrickson and Thomas, *op. cit.*, p. 53.

contaminated by a forced relationship to these people—for it is through such perception and knowledge that relations are expressed.)

The model for interpersonal contamination in our society is presumably rape; although sexual molestation certainly occurs in total institutions, there are many other less dramatic examples. Upon admission, one's on-person possessions are pawed and fingered by an official as he itemizes and prepares them for storage. The inmate himself may be frisked and searched to the extent—often reported in the literature—of a rectal examination.[27] Later in his stay he may be required to undergo searchings of his person and of his sleeping-quarters, either routinely or when trouble arises. In all these cases it is the searcher as well as the search that penetrates the private reserve of the individual and violates the territories of his self. Even routine inspections can have this effect, as Lawrence suggests:

> In the old days men had weekly to strip off boots and socks, and expose their feet for an officer's inspection. An ex-boy'd kick you in the mouth, as you bent down to look. So with the bath-rolls, a certificate from your N.C.O. that you'd had a bath during the week. One bath! And with the kit inspections, and room inspections, and equipment inspections, all excuses for the dogmatists among the officers to blunder, and for the nosy-parkers to make beasts of themselves. Oh, you require the gentlest touch to interfere with a poor man's person, and not give offence.[28]

Further, the practice of mixing age, ethnic, and racial groups in prisons and mental hospitals can lead an inmate to feel he is being contaminated by contact with undesirable fellow-inmates. A prisoner, describing his admission to prison, provides an example:

> Another warder came up with a pair of handcuffs and coupled me to the little Jew, who moaned softly to himself in Yiddish.[29]

> Suddenly, the awful thought occurred to me that I might have to share a cell with the little Jew and I was seized with panic. The thought obsessed me to the exclusion of all else.[30]

*   *   *

One routine instance of this contaminative contact is the naming system of inmates. Staff and fellow-inmates automatically assume the right to employ an intimate form of address or a truncated formal one: for a middle class person, at least, this denies the right to hold himself off from others through a formal style of address.[31] When the individual has to eat food he considers alien and polluted, this contamination sometimes derives from other persons' connection with the food.

*   *   *

A more thoroughgoing version of this type of contaminative exposure occurs in institutionally-arranged confessions. When a significant other must be denounced, and especially when this other is physically present, confession of the relationship to outsiders can mean an intense exposure and contamination of self.

*   *   *

A parallel example can be found in highly professionalized mental hospitals devoted to intensive milieu therapy, where patient-pairs conducting an affair may be obliged to discuss their relationship during group meetings.

In total institutions, exposure of one's relationships can occur in even more drastic forms, for there may be occasions when an individual must witness a physical assault upon someone to whom he has ties, and suffer the permanent mortification of having taken no action. Thus we learn of a mental hospital:

> This knowledge [of shock therapy] is based on the fact that some of the patients in Ward 30 have assisted the shock team in the administration of therapy to patients, holding them down, and helping to strap them in bed, or watching them after they have quieted. The administration of shock on the ward is often carried out in full sight of a group of interested onlookers. The patient's convulsions often resemble those of an accident victim in death agony and are accompanied by choking gasps and at times by a foaming overflow of saliva from the mouth. The patient slowly recovers without memory of the occurrence, but he has served the others as a frightful spectacle of what may be done to them.[32]

*   *   *

The extreme of this kind of *experiential mortification* is found of course in the concentration camp literature:

> A Jew from Breslau named Silbermann had to stand by idly as SS Sergeant Hoppe brutally tor-

---

[27] For example, Murtagh and Harris, *op. cit.*, p. 240; Lowell Naeve, *A Field of Broken Stones,* Glen Gardner: Libertarian Press, 1950, p. 17; Kogon, *op. cit.*, p. 67; Holley Cantine and Dachine Rainer, Eds., *Prison Etiquette,* Bearsville, N.Y.: Retort Press, 1950, p. 46.
[28] Lawrence, *op. cit.*, p. 196.
[29] Heckstall-Smith, *op. cit.*, p. 14.
[30] *Ibid.*, p. 17.

[31] For example, see Hassler, *op. cit.*, p. 104.
[32] Belknap, *op. cit.*, p. 194.

tured his brother to death. Silbermann went mad at the sight, and late at night he precipitated a panic with his frantic cries that the barracks was on fire.[33]

* * *

In concluding this description of the processes of mortification, three general issues must be raised.

First, total institutions disrupt or defile precisely those actions that in civil society seem to have the special role of attesting to the actor and to those in his presence that he has some command over his world—that he is a person with "adult" self-determination, autonomy, and freedom of action. A failure to retain this kind of adult executive competency, or at least the symbols of it, can produce in the inmate the terror of feeling radically demoted in the age-grading system.[34]

A margin of self-selected expressive behavior—whether of antagonism, affection, or unconcern—is one symbol of self-determination. This evidence of one's autonomy is weakened by such specific obligations as having to write one letter home a week, or having to refrain from expressing sullenness. It is further weakened when this margin of behavior is used as evidence concerning the state of one's psychiatric, religious, or political conscience.

There are certain bodily comforts significant to the individual that tend to be lost upon entrance into a total institution—for example, a soft bed,[35] or quietness at night.[36] Loss of this set of comforts is apt to reflect a loss of self-determination, too, for the individual tends to ensure these comforts the moment he has resources to expend.[37]

Loss of self-determination seems to have been ceremonialized in concentration camps; thus we have atrocity tales of prisoners being forced to roll in the mud,[38] stand on their heads in the snow, work at ludicrously useless tasks, swear at themselves[39] or, in the case of

Jewish prisoners, sing anti-Semitic songs.[40] A milder version is found in mental hospitals where attendants have been observed forcing a patient who wanted a cigarette to say "pretty please," or to jump for it. In all such cases the inmate is made to display a giving up of his will. Less ceremonialized, but just as extreme, is the embarrassment to one's autonomy that comes from being locked in a ward, placed in a tight wet-pack, or tied up in a camisole, and thereby denied the liberty of making small adjustive movements.

Another clear-cut expression of personal inefficacy in total institutions has to do with inmates' use of speech. One implication of using words to convey decisions about action is that the recipient of an order is seen capable of receiving a message and acting under his own power to complete the suggestion or command. Executing the act himself, he can sustain some vestige of the notion that he is self-determining. Responding to the question in his own words, he can sustain the notion that he is somebody to be considered, however slightly. And since it is only words that pass between himself and the others, he succeeds in retaining at least physical distance from them, however unpalatable the command or statement.

The inmate in a total institution can find himself denied this kind of protective distance and self-action. Especially in mental hospitals and political training prisons, the statements he makes may be discounted as mere symptoms, and the non-verbal aspects of his reply attended to.[41] Often he is considered to be of insufficient ritual weight to be given even minor greetings, let alone listened to.[42] Or the inmate may find that a kind of rhetorical use of language occurs: questions such as, "Have you washed yet?" or "Have you got both socks on?" may be accompanied by a simultaneous searching action by staff which physically discloses the facts, making their verbal questions superfluous. And instead of being told to move in a particular direction at a particular rate, he may find himself pushed along by the guard, or pulled (in the case of overalled mental patients), or frog-marched. And finally, the inmate may find that a dual language exists, with the disciplinary facts of his life given a

---

[33] Kogon, *op. cit.*, p. 160.

[34] *Cf.* Sykes, *op. cit.*, pp. 73–76, "The Deprivation of Autonomy."

[35] Hulme, *op. cit.*, p. 18 George Orwell, "Such, Such Were the Joys," *Partisan Review 19* (1952), p. 521.

[36] Hassler, *op. cit.*, p. 78; Johnson, and Dodds *op. cit.*, p. 17.

[37] This is one source of mortification that civilians practice on themselves during camping vacations, perhaps on the assumption that a new sense of self can be obtained by voluntarily foregoing some of one's previous self-impregnated comforts.

[38] Kogon, *op. cit.*, p. 66.

[39] *Ibid.*, p. 61.

[40] *Ibid.*, p. 78.

[41] See A. Stanton and M. Schwartz, *The Mental Hospital*, New York: Basic Books, 1954, pp. 200, 203, 205–206.

[42] For an example of this non-person treatment see Johnson and Dodds, *op. cit.*, p. 122.

translated ideal-phrasing by staff that mocks the normal use of language.

The second general consideration is the rationale that is employed for assaults upon the self. This issue tends to place total institutions and their inmates into three different groupings.

In religious institutions, the implications environmental arrangements have for self are explicitly recognized:

That is the meaning of the contemplative life, and the sense of all the apparently meaningless little rules and observances and fasts and obediences and penances and humiliations and labors that go to make up the routine of existence in a contemplative monastery: they all serve to remind us of what we are and Who God is—that we may get sick of the sight of ourselves and turn to Him: and in the end, we will find Him in ourselves, in our own purified natures which have become the mirror of His tremendous Goodness and of His endless love . . .[43]

The inmates, as well as the staff, actively seek out these curtailments of the self, so that mortification is complemented by self-mortification, restrictions by renunciations, beatings

by self-flagellations, inquisition by confession. Because religious establishments are explicitly concerned with the processes of mortification, they have a special value for sociological study.

In concentration camps, and to a lesser extent, prisons, some mortifications seem to be arranged solely or mainly for their mortifying power, as when a prisoner is urinated on, but here the inmate does not embrace and facilitate his own destruction of self.

In many of the remaining total institutions, mortifications are officially rationalized on other grounds, such as sanitation (in connection with latrine duty), responsibility for life (in connection with forced feeding), combat capacity (in connection with Army rules for personal appearance), "security" (in connection with restrictive prison regulations).

In total institutions of all three varieties, however, the various rationales for mortifying the self are very often merely rationalizations, generated by efforts to manage the daily activity of a large number of persons in a small space with a small expenditure of resources. Further, curtailments of the self occur in all three, even in the case where the inmate is willing and the management has ideal concerns for his well-being.

[43] Merton, *op. cit.*, p. 372.

Chapter 26 Peak-Experiences as Acute Identity-Experiences

ABRAHAM H. MASLOW

As we seek for definitions of identity, we must remember that these definitions and concepts are not now existing in some hidden place, waiting patiently for us to find them. Only *partly* do we discover them; partly also we create them. Partly identity is whatever we say it is. Prior to this of course should come our sensitivity and reception to the various meanings the word already has. At once we find that various authors use the word for different kinds of data, different operations. And then of course we must find out something of these operations in order to understand just what the author means when *he* uses the word. It means something different for various therapists, for sociologists, for self-psychologists, for child psychologists, etc., even though for all these people there is also some similarity or overlap of meaning. (Perhaps this similarity is what identity "means" today.)

I have another operation to report, on peak-experiences, in which "identity" has various real, sensible and useful meanings. But no claim is made that these are *the* true meanings of identity; only that we have here another angle. Since my feeling is that people in peak-experiences are *most* their identities, closest to their real selves, most idiosyncratic, it would seem that this is an especially important source of clean and uncontaminated data; i.e., invention is reduced to a minimum, and discovery increased to a maximum.

It will be apparent to the reader that all the "separate" characteristics following are not really separate at all, but partake of each other in various ways, e.g., overlapping, saying the same thing in different ways, having the same

meaning in a metaphorical sense, etc. The reader interested in the theory of "holistic analysis" (in contrast to atomistic, or reductive, analysis) is referred to [8]. I shall be describing in a holistic way, not by splitting identity apart into quite separate components which are mutually exclusive, but rather by turning it over and over in my hands and gazing at its different facets, or as a connoisseur contemplates a fine painting, seeing it now in this organization (as a whole), now in that. Each "aspect" discussed can be considered a partial explanation of each of the other "aspects."

1. The person in the peak-experiences feels more integrated (unified, whole, all-of-a-piece), than at other times. He also looks (to the observer) more integrated in various ways (described below), e.g., less split or dissociated, less fighting against himself, more at peace with himself, less split between an experiencing-self and an observing-self, more one-pointed, more harmoniously organized, more efficiently organized with all his parts functioning very nicely with each other, more synergic, with less internal friction, etc.[1] Other aspects of

---

[1] This is of special interest to therapists not only because integration is one of the main goals of all therapy, but also because of the fascinating problems involved in what we may call the "therapeutic dissociation." For therapy to occur from insight, it is necessary to experience and to observe simultaneously. For instance, the psychotic who is totally experiencing but not detached enough to observe his experiencing is unimproved by this experiencing, even though he may have been right in the middle of the unconscious that is so hidden to neurotics. But it is also true that the therapist must split in the same paradoxical way, since he must simultaneously accept and not-accept the patient; that is, on the one hand, he must give "unconditional positive regard" [12], he must identify with the patient in order to understand him, he must put aside all criticisms and evaluations, he must experience the patient's Weltanschauung, he must fuse with him in an I-Thou encounter, he must in

SOURCE. Abraham H. Maslow, "Peak-Experiences as Acute Identity-Experiences," from *American Journal of Psychoanalysis*, Volume 21 (1961), pp. 254–260. Copyright, 1961, *American Journal of Psychoanalysis*. Reprinted by permission of the Association for the Advancement of Psychoanalysis.

integration and of the conditions upon which it rests are discussed below.

2. As he gets to be more purely and singly himself he is more able to fuse with the world,[2] with what was formerly not-self, e.g., the lovers come closer to forming a unit rather than two people, the I-Thou monism becomes more possible, the creator becomes one with his work being created, the mother feels one with her child, the appreciator *becomes* the music (and it becomes *him*) or the painting, or the dance, the astronomer is "out there" with the stars (rather than a separateness peering across an abyss at another separateness through a telescope-keyhole).

That is, the greatest attainment of identity, autonomy, or selfhood is itself simultaneously a transcending of itself, a going beyond and above selfhood. The person can then become relatively egoless.[3]

3. The person in the peak-experiences usually feels himself to be at the peak of his powers, using all his capacities at the best and fullest. In Rogers' [13] nice phrase, he feels "fully-functioning." He feels more intelligent, more perceptive, wittier, stronger, or more

---

a broad Agapean sense, love him, etc. And yet, on the other hand, he is also implicitly disapproving, not-accepting, not-identifying, etc. because he is trying to improve him, to make him better than he is, which means something other than he is right now. These therapeutic splits are quite explicitly a basis of therapy for Deutsch and Murphy [2].

But here, too, the therapeutic goal is, as with multiple personalities, to fuse them into an unsplit harmonious unity, both in the patient and in the therapist. One may also describe it as becoming more and more a purely experiencing ego with self-observation always available as a *possibility*, preconsciously perhaps. In the peak-experiences, we become much more purely experiencing egos.

[2] I realize that I am using language which "points" to the experience, i.e., it will communicate meaning only to those who themselves have not repressed, suppressed, denied, rejected or feared their own peak-experiences. It is possible, I believe, to communicate meaningfully with "non-peakers" also, but this is very laborious and lengthy.

[3] This meaning can be communicated easily enough, I think, by calling it the total loss of that self-consciousness or self-awareness or self-observation which is normally with us but which we feel to lower in any absorption or interest or concentration or distraction, or being taken "out of ourselves," whether on the high level of peak-experiences, or on the lower level of becoming so interested in a movie or a novel or a football game as to become forgetful of oneself and one's minor pains, one's appearance, one's worries, etc. This is practically always felt as a pleasant state.

---

graceful than at other times. He is at his best, at concert pitch, at the top of his form. This is not only felt subjectively but can be seen by the observer. He is no longer wasting effort fighting and restraining himself; muscles are no longer fighting muscles. In the normal situation, part of our capacities are used for action, and part are wasted on restraining these same capacities. Now there is no waste; the totality of the capacities can be used for action. He becomes like a river without dams.

4. A slightly different aspect of fully-functioning is effortlessness and ease of functioning when one is at one's best. What takes effort, straining and struggling at other times is now done without any sense of striving, of working or laboring, but "comes of itself." Allied to this often is the feeling of grace and the look of grace that comes with smooth, easy, effortless fully-functioning, when everything "clicks," or "is in the groove," or is "in overdrive."

One sees then the appearance of calm sureness and rightness, as if they knew exactly what they were doing, and were doing it wholeheartedly, without doubts, equivocations, hesitations or partial withdrawal. There are then no glancing blows at the target or softened blows, only full hits. The great athletes, artists, creators, leaders, and executives exhibit this quality of behavior when they are functioning at their best.

(This is less obviously relevant to the concept of identity than what has gone before, but I think it should be included as an epiphenomenal characteristic of "being one's real self" because it is external and public enough to be researchable. Also I believe it is needed for the full understanding of the kind of godlike gaiety (humor, fun, foolishness, silliness, play, laughter) which I think to be one of the highest B-values of identity.) ["B" stands for Being].

5. The person in peak-experiences feels himself, more than at other times, to be the responsible, active, creating center of his activities and of his perceptions. He feels more like a prime mover, more self-determined (rather than caused, determined, helpless, dependent, passive, weak, bossed). He feels himself to be his own boss, fully responsible, fully volitional, with more "free will" than at other times, master of his own fate.

He also looks that way to the observer, for instance, becoming more decisive, looking more strong, more single-minded, more apt to scorn or overcome opposition, more grimly sure of himself, more apt to give the impression that it would be useless to try to stop him. It is as if now he had no doubts about his worth or about his ability to do whatever he decided to do. To the observer he looks more trustworthy, more reliable, more dependable, a better bet. It is often possible to spot this great moment—of becoming responsible—in therapy, in growing up, in education, in marriage, etc.

6. He is now most free of blocks, inhibitions, cautions, fears, doubts, controls, reservations, self-criticisms, brakes. These may be the negative aspects of the feeling of worth, of self-acceptance, of self-love-respect. This is both a subjective and an objective phenomenon and could be described further in both ways. Of course this is simply a different "aspect" of the characteristics already listed and those to be listed below.

Probably these happenings are in principle testable, for objectively these are muscles fighting muscles, instead of muscles synergically helping muscles.

7. He is therefore more spontaneous, more expressive, more innocently behaving (guileless, naive, honest, candid, ingenuous, childlike, artless, unguarded, defenseless), more natural (simple, relaxed, unhesitant, plain, sincere, unaffected, primitive in a particular sense, immediate), more uncontrolled and freely flowing outward (automatic, impulsive, reflexlike, "instinctive," unrestrained, unselfconscious, thoughtless, unaware).[4]

8. He is therefore more "creative" in a particular sense. His cognition and his behavior, out of greater self-confidence and loss of doubts, can mold itself in a non-interfering, Taoistic way, or in the flexible way that the Gestalt psychologists have described, to the problematic or unproblematic situation in *its* intrinsic, "out there" terms or demands (rather than in ego-centered or self-conscious terms), in terms set by the *per se* nature of the task, or the duty (Frankl), or the game. It therefore

is more improvised, extemporized, impromptu, more created out of nothing, more unexpected, novel, fresh, not-stale, non-canting, untutored, unhabitual. It is also less prepared, planned, designed, premeditated, rehearsed, afore-thought, to the extent that these words imply prior time and planning of any sort. It is therefore relatively unsought, non-desired, unneeded, purposeless, unstriven for, "unmotivated," or undriven, since it is emergent and newly created and doesn't come out of prior time.

9. All this can be phrased in still another way as the acme of uniqueness, individuality or idiosyncracy. If all people are different from each other in principle, they are *more* purely different in the peak-experiences. If in many respects (their roles), men are interchangeable, then in the peak-experiences, roles drop away and men become least interchangeable. Whatever they are at bottom, whatever the word "unique self" means, they are more that in the peak-experiences.

10. In the peak-experiences, the individual is most here-now [11], most free of the past and of the future in various senses, most "all there" in the experience. For instance, he can now listen better than at other times. Since he is least habitual and least expectant, he can fully listen without contamination by dragging in expectations based on past situations (which can't be identically like the present one), or hopes or apprehensions based on planning for the future (which means taking the present only as means to the future rather than as end in itself). Since also he is beyond desire, he needn't rubricize in terms of fear, hate or wish. Nor does he have to compare what is here with what is not here in order to evaluate it [4].

11. The person now becomes more a pure psyche and less a thing-of-the-world living under the laws of the world. That is, he becomes more determined by intra-psychic laws rather than by the laws of non-psychic reality insofar as they are different. This sounds like a contradiction or a paradox but it is not, and even if it were, would have to be accepted anyway as having a certain kind of meaning. B-cognition of the other is most possible when there is simultaneously a letting-be of the self *and* of the other; respecting-loving myself *and* respecting-loving the other each permit, support, and strengthen each other. I can grasp the non-self best by non-grasping, i.e., by letting it be itself, by letting it go, by permitting

---

[4] This aspect of authentic identity is so important, has so many overtones, and is so difficult to describe and communicate, that I append the following partial synonyms with their slightly overlapping meanings. Unintentional, of its own accord, free, unforced, unreasoning, undeliberate, impetuous, unreserved, non-withholding, self-disclosing, frank, non-dissembling, open, undissimulating, unpretending, unfeigning, forthright, unsophisticated, not artificial, unworried, trusting. I leave aside here the question of "innocent cognition," of intuition, B-cognition, etc.

it to live by its own laws rather than by mine, just as I become most purely myself when I emancipate myself from the not-me, refusing to let it dominate me, refusing to live by *its* rules, and insisting on living only by the laws and rules intrinsic to me. When this has happened, it turns out that the intra-psychic (me) and the extra-psychic (other) are not so terribly different after all, and *certainly* are not *really* antagonistic. It turns out that both sets of laws are very interesting and enjoyable and can even be integrated and fused.

The easiest paradigm to help the reader to understand this maze of words is the relationship of B-love between two people but any other of the peak-experiences can also be used. Obviously at this level of ideal discourse (what I call the B-realm) the words freedom, independence, grasping, letting go, trust, will, dependence, reality, the other person, separateness, etc., all take on very complex and rich meanings which they don't have in the D-realm of everyday life, of deficiencies, wants, needs, self-preservation and of dichotomies, polarities and splits. ["D" stands for deficiency.]

12. There are certain theoretical advantages in stressing now the aspect of non-striving or non-needing and taking it as the centering-point (or center of organization) of the something we are studying. In various ways described above, and with certain delimited meanings, the person in the peak-experience becomes unmotivated (or undriven), especially from the point of view of the deficiency needs. In this same realm of discourse, it makes similar sense to describe highest, most authentic identity as non-striving, non-needing, non-wishing, i.e., as having transcended needs and drives of the ordinary sort. He just is. Joy has been attained which means a temporary end to the *striving* for joy.

Something of the sort has already been described for the self-actualizing person. Everything now comes of its own accord, pouring out, without will, effortlessly, purposelessly. He acts now totally and without deficiency, not homeostatically or need-reductively, not to avoid pain or displeasure or death, not for the sake of a goal further on in the future, not for any other end than itself. His behavior and experience becomes per se, and self-validating, end-behavior and end-experience, rather than means-behavior or means-experience.

At this level, I have called the person godlike because most gods have been considered to have no needs or wants, no deficiencies, nothing lacking, to be gratified in all things. The characteristics and especially the actions of the "highest," "best" gods have then been deduced as based upon not-wanting. I have found these deductions very stimulating in trying to understand the actions of human beings when *they* act from non-wanting. For instance, I find this a very illuminating base for the theory of god-like humor and amusement, the theory of boredom, the theory of creativeness, etc. The fact that the human embryo also has no needs is a fertile source of confusion between the high Nirvana and the low Nirvana.

13. Expression and communication in the peak-experiences tend often to become poetic, mythical and rhapsodic, as if this were the natural kind of language to express such states of being. I have only recently become aware of this in my subjects and in myself so shouldn't say much about it. The implication for identity theory is that more authentic persons may, by that very fact, become more like poets, artists, musicians, prophets, etc.[5]

14. All peak-experiences may be fruitfully understood as completions-of-the-act in David M. Levy's sense [5], or as the Gestalt psychologists' closure, or on the paradigm of the Reichian type of complete orgasm, or as total discharge, catharsis, culmination, climax, consummation, emptying or finishing [9]. Contrast is with the perseveration of incompleted problems, with the partially emptied breasts or prostate gland, with the incomplete bowel movement, with not being able to weep away grief, with the partial satiation of hunger in the dieter, with the kitchen that never gets fully clean, with coitus reservatus, with the anger which must remain unexpressed, with the athlete who has had no exercise, with not being able to straighten the crooked picture on the wall, with having to swallow stupidity, inefficiency or injustice, etc. From these examples, any reader should be able to understand phenomenologically how important completion is, and also why this viewpoint is so helpful in enriching the understanding of non-striving, integration, relaxation and everything else that has gone before. Completion seen out in the world is perfection, justice, beauty, end

---

5 "Poetry is the record of the best and happiest moments of the happiest and best minds." P. B. Shelley.

rather than means, etc. [9]. Since the outer and inner world are to some extent isomorphic and are dialectically related ("cause" each other), we come to the edge of the problem of how the good person and the good world make each other.

How does this bear on identity? Probably the authentic person is himself complete or final in some sense; he certainly experiences subjective finality, completion or perfection at times; and he certainly perceives it in the world. It *may* turn out that *only* peakers can achieve full identity; that non-peakers must always remain incomplete, deficient, striving, lacking something, living among means rather than among ends; or if the correlation turns out not to be perfect, I am certain at least that it is positive, between authenticity and peak-experiencing.

As we consider the physical and psychological tensions and perseverations of incompleteness, it seems plausible that they may be incompatible not only with serenity, peacefulness and psychological well-being, but also with physical well-being. We may also have a clue here to the puzzling finding that many people report their peak-experiences as if they were somehow akin to (beautiful) death, as if the most poignant living had a paradoxical something of eager or willing dying in it, too. It may be that any perfect completion or end is metaphorically, mythologically or archaically a death, as Rank implies [3, 10].

15. I very strongly feel that playfulness of a certain kind is one of the B-values. Some of the reasons for thinking so have already been touched upon. One of the most important is that it is fairly often reported in the peak-experiences (both within the person and perceived in the world) and also can be perceived by the investigator from outside the person reporting.

It is very hard to describe this B-playfulness since the English language falls far short here (as *in general* it is unable to describe the "higher" subjective experiences). It has a cosmic or a godlike, good-humored quality, certainly transcending hostility of any kind. It could as easily be called happy joy, or gay exuberance or delight. It has a quality of spilling over as of richness or surplus (not D-motivated). It is existential in the sense that it is an amusement or delight with both the smallness (weakness) and the largeness (strength) of the human being, transcending the dominance-subordinance polarity. It has a certain quality of triumph in it, sometimes perhaps also of relief. It is simultaneously mature and childlike.

It is final, Utopian, Eupsychian, transcendent in the sense in which Marcuse [7] and Brown [1] have described. It could also be called Nietzschean.

Intrinsically involved with it as part of its definition are ease, effortlessness, grace, good fortune, relief from inhibitions, restraints and doubts, amusement-with (not -at) B-cognition, transcendence of ego-centering and means-centering, transcendence of time and space, of history, of localism.

And finally, it is in itself an integrator, as beauty is, or love, or the creative intellect. This is in the sense that it is a resolver of dichotomies, a solution to many insoluble problems. It is one good solution of the human situation, teaching us that one way of solving a problem is to be amused by it. It enables us to live simultaneously in the D-realm and in the B-realm, to be at the same time Don Quixote and Sancho Panza.

16. People during and after peak-experiences characteristically feel lucky, fortunate, graced. A not uncommon reaction is "I don't deserve this." Peaks are not planned or brought about by design; they happen. We are "surprised by joy" [6]. The reaction of surprise, of unexpectedness, of the sweet "shock of recognition" are very frequent.

A common consequence is a feeling of gratitude, in religious persons to their God, in others to Fate, to Nature, to people, to the past, to parents, to the world, to everything and anything that helped to make this wonder possible. This can go over into worship, giving thanks, adoring, giving praise, oblation, and other reactions which fit very easily into a religious framework. Clearly any psychology of religion, either supernatural or natural, must take account of these happenings, as also must any naturalistic theory of the origins of religion.

Very often this feeling of gratitude is expressed as or leads to an all-embracing love for everybody and everything, to a perception of the world as beautiful, and good, often to an impulse to do something good for the world, an eagerness to repay, even a sense of obligation.

Finally, it is quite probable that we have here the theoretical link to the described facts of humility and pride in self-actualizing, authentic persons. The lucky person could hardly take full credit for his luck, nor could the awed person, nor the grateful person. He must ask himself the question "Do I deserve this?" Such people resolve the dichotomy between pride and humility by fusing them into a single, complex, superordinate unity, that is, by being proud (in a certain sense) and humble (in a certain sense). Pride (tinctured with humility) is not *hubris* or paranoia; humility (tinctured with pride) is not masochism. Only dichotomizing them pathologizes them. B-gratitude enables us to integrate within one skin the hero and the humble servant.

CONCLUDING REMARK

I wish to underscore one main paradox I have dealt with above (number 2) which we must face even if we don't understand it. The goal of identity (self-actualization, autonomy, individuation, Horney's real self, authenticity, etc.) seems to be simultaneously an end-goal in itself, and also a transitional goal, a rite of passage, a step along the path to the transcendence of identity. This is like saying its function is to erase itself. Put the other way about, if our goal is the Eastern one of ego-transcendence and obliteration, of leaving behind self-consciousness and self-observation, of fusion with the world and identification with it (Bucke), of homonomy (Angyal), then it looks as if the best path to this goal for most people is via achieving identity, a strong real self, and via basic-need-gratification rather than via asceticism.

Perhaps it is relevant to this theory that my young subjects tend to report *two* kinds of physical reaction to peak-experiences. One is excitement and high tension ("I feel wild, like jumping up and down, like yelling out loud"). The other is relaxation, peacefulness, quietness, the feeling of stillness. For instance, after a beautiful sex experience, or esthetic experience or creative furor, *either* is possible; either continued high excitement, inability to sleep, or lack of wish for it, even loss of appetite, constipation, etc. Or else, complete relaxation, inaction, deep sleep, etc. What this means I don't know.

REFERENCES

[1] Brown, N., *Life Against Death*, Random House, 1959.
[2] Deutsch, F., and Murphy, W., *The Clinical Interview*, International Universities Press, 1955.
[3] Kempf, F. B., *The Psychology and Psychotherapy of Otto Rank*, Philosophical Library, 1953.
[4] Lee, D., *Freedom and Culture*, Prentice-Hall, 1959.
[5] Levy, D. M., Personal communication.
[6] Lewis, C. S., *Surprised by Joy*, Harcourt, Brace, 1956.
[7] Marcuse, H., *Eros and Civilization*, Beacon Press, 1955.
[8] Maslow, A. H., *Motivation and Personality*, Harper, 1954.
[9] Maslow, A. H., "Peak-Experiences as Completions," (to be published).
[10] Munroe, R. L., *Schools of Psychoanalytic Thought*, Dryden Press, 1955.
[11] Perls, F., Hefferline, R., and Goodman, P., *Gestalt Therapy*, Julian Press, 1951.
[12] Rogers, C. R., "A Theory of Therapy, Personality and Interpersonal Relationships as Developed in the Client-Centered Framework," *Psychology: A Study of Science*, Vol. III, McGraw-Hill, 1959.
[13] Rogers, C. A., *On Becoming a Person*, Houghton Mifflin, 1961.

Part V Self-Conception and the Determination of Behavior

In Part IV self-conception was viewed largely as an effect rather than a cause. Various growth changes, social processes, and situational factors were examined in light of their impact on the person's developing views of self. Self-conception has contributed largely to the spectrum of dependent variables in such work, yet its theoretical utility is hardly limited to this function, and numerous investigators have focused on self-conception in its capacity to motivate and direct behavior. Such an emphasis is of obvious importance, for if variations in self-conception could not be used successfully to explain and predict differential conduct, they would be of limited value in the behavioral sciences. In the behavioral context, self variables operate in a fashion similar to a host of other personality variables used in social-psychological research. Although we do not subscribe to the extreme position that *all* behavior can be explained or predicted on the basis of the person's view of himself at a given time, Part V provides a good indication of the value of self variables in shaping social conduct.

SELF-CONCEPTION, MOTIVATION, AND THE DIRECTION OF CONDUCT

The first group of chapters in this Part are intended both to suggest the range of behaviors which potentially may be affected by self-conceptions and to outline a number of underlying processes. The initial selection, by Thorstein Veblen, is excerpted from his now classic *The Theory of the Leisure Class* (1899), and needs little introduction to students of economics or sociology. Here Veblen hypothesizes a direct causal relation between the struggle for increased self-esteem and the acquisition and conspicuous consumption of goods. It is interesting, however, that in spite of the broad implications of this hypothesis, it has yet to be verified in any systematic way. As we shall see, this emphasis on the relationship between economic behavior and self-conception is renewed in the contribution by Marx (Chapter 39).

Chapter 28 also attempts to bridge the gap between psychological processes and broad-scale social behavior. In this original paper, Backman and Secord utilize a psychologically based theory of congruency or consistency-striving, and successfully demonstrate the relationship between self-conception and the selection of occupational roles. This chapter may be seen to play a complementary function to Preiss' contribution in Chapter 19. Backman and Secord point up the fact that not only do occupational roles shape self-conception but that self-conception is quite important in determining role behavior.

The consistency theme is magnified in the selection by Prescott Lecky (Chapter 29). Although Lecky's published contributions are scarce, they were seminal in their influence. Not only were they to have an important effect on the theorizing of Carl Rogers (cf. Chapter 44), but they formed the groundwork for the theories of cognitive consistency now dominating the literature on social influence. Although most personality theorists would agree that Lecky overstates his case, his discussion of consistency-striving as the core process in personality functioning deserves serious attention.

The two contributions that follow both deal with the self as it affects the person's public personality. The original paper by Gergen (Chapter 30) is based on a number of controlled experiments which demonstrate the marked shifts that may take place in a person's public definition of self. The major thrust of the paper, however, is toward challenging the notion of self-consistency, either as an explanatory construct or as an ethical presumption. Gergen's emphasis on the self as altered by specific others in a situation may also be fruitfully compared with James' discussion of the "social self" (Chapter 3) and Baldwin's speculations concerning the development of self (Chapter 14).

Erving Goffman's acute observations on "face-work" (Chapter 31) foster an appreciation for the more subtle ways in which public definition of self may be generated and supported by the structure of social relationships. Goffman's emphasis on the ritualistic processes and tactical maneuvers involved in socially defining oneself and others in social situations is both fresh and invigorating. The theme of ritualization may also be profitably compared with the chapters by Schutz (Chapter 5) and Garfinkel (Chapter 6). It should be noted that Goffman's usage of the concept of self differs considerably from that occurring throughout much of the remainder of this volume. Essentially, Goffman's approach is to define self in terms of the particular "line" of conduct and "face" that the person attempts to present in an interaction episode. Thus problems having to do with defining or specifying psychological processes are avoided. This approach is not entirely dissimilar to that taken in the behavioristically oriented chapter of Bandura and Walters (Chapter 17).

SELF-CONCEPTION, EVALUATION, AND JUDGMENT

The second group of chapters in this section deals with ways in which self-conception may influence one's evaluations or judgments of others. Erich Fromm's paper "Selfishness and Self-Love" (Chapter 32) is perhaps the most widely known of the group. His statement of the relationship between self-love and love of others has had widespread repercussions in the field of psychiatry as well as in formal research settings. The recent spate of research on the relationship between self-acceptance and acceptance of others owes much to Fromm's theorizing. On the pessimistic side, Fromm tacitly suggests that those most in need of social acceptance and support may be least capable of securing them. The emphasis of the chapter is additionally underscored when seen in conjunction with the work of Carl Rogers and Arthur Cohen (Chapters 44 and 38).

Morris Rosenberg's essay on processes of selectivity in the formation of self-esteem (Chapter 33) makes exceptionally good use of correlational data in raising a set of broadly relevant issues. Whereas earlier accounts of self-development and self-esteem have tended to emphasize the influence of the social environment, Rosenberg's analysis suggests that the individual engages in a wide range of mental gymnastics to maintain and enhance a positive evaluation of himself. For example, it is seen that the person may come to value those attributes at which he considers himself good, distort the meaning of evidence pertaining to self, select goals that allow for success, and select associates who will bolster his self-esteem. The last point is particularly interesting as a contrast to the position of Backman and Secord (Chapter 28), who maintain that the person desires accuracy from others. In any case, Rosenberg's analysis again underscores the significance of self-esteem in the life of the person.

With the chapter by Pepitone (34) "An Experimental Analysis of Self-Dynamics," we move to factually based model building. In this case, perhaps the most important contribution to this series of papers derives from Pepitone's discussions of self-validation and its relationship to needs for self-esteem and judgments of others. The need for receiving "valid" information concerning self has been touched upon earlier, in the chapter by Backman and Secord (Chapter 28). However, Pepitone makes it clear that one must ultimately be able to account for multiple processes and their interrelationships. This stance presages the eventual demise of concentration on single variables or single causal relationships.

The chapter by Ossario and Davis (Chapter 35) ostensibly extends this emphasis on judgments to the area of reactions to evaluations of self made by others. However, the basic intent of the paper is quite different in character. Much in harmony with the current linguistic trend in philosophy, these authors develop the notion of "person," as used in ordinary language, and from this discussion derive their arguments concerning self and evaluations of self by others. Clearly their most challenging arguments concern the shortcomings of empirical research. They attempt to demonstrate that research neither validates hypotheses nor establishes a factual basis for theory. Rather, Ossario and Davis assert, our understanding of "persons" in general and "selves" in particular is based on concepts or language usage, and such usage is not subject to empirical tests. However, from their point of view, a close examination of language usage can tell us much about the structure of social relationships. Within the present volume this chapter provides a minority report, but one with far-reaching implications.

SELF-CONCEPTION, DEFENSE, AND SOCIAL CONTROL

The last three contributions in Part V deal with the function of self-conception in processes of social adaptation and control. In this area the major issues concern the ways in which self-conception may enhance or impede the individual's efforts to adapt and become autonomous in his social world. In "Human Motives and the Concept of the Self" (Chapter 36) Ernest Hilgard attempts to integrate the concept of the self with Freud's classic work on the mechanisms of psychological defense, and to emphasize how self-conception may motivate the individual toward certain ends. Although Hilgard's background is more closely allied with experimental psychology, it is of interest to compare his work with the work of others in this volume who have found the psychoanalytic soil a fertile one (cf. Erikson, Chapter 18; Kardiner and Ovesey, Chapter 24; Horney, Chapter 40; Sullivan, Chapter 15; and Fromm, Chapter 32). At the same time, Hilgard's notion of the "inferred self" may be found an exceedingly useful one, particularly for those who do not share the subjective point of departure developed in Part II.

Stemming from the symbolic interactionist approach, Shibutani's work in Chapter 37 attempts to trace the orderly and stable components of social conduct to a basis in self-conception. In so doing, he reintroduces a line of thought appearing in earlier chapters by Mead (Chapter 4), Turner (Chapter 9), and Bandura and Walters (Chapter 17). However, he expands on the earlier work in a significant way by exploring levels of self-consciousness. Self-control and control by others are, of course, opposite sides of the same coin. Thus, although it stems from a tradition far removed from Shibutani's, Cohen's paper (Chapter 38) plays a complementary role to its immediate forerunner. Working again from the laboratory setting, Cohen is able to demonstrate convincingly the potency of the self-esteem variable in predicting attempts to influence and susceptibility to social influence. The paper is also an excellent examplar of the extensive empirical literature on these relationships. Useful comparisons can also be made between this approach and the work of others in this book who have focused on the correlates of self-esteem (cf. Crowne and Stephens, Chapter 13; Kardiner and Ovesey, Chapter 24; Fromm, Chapter 32; and Rogers, Chapter 44). Each of the selections in this subsection also forms a useful bridge to the volume's epilogue, in which David Riesman discusses the problem of autonomy.

Chapter 27 On Pecuniary Emulation

THORSTEIN VEBLEN

Gradually, as industrial activity further displaces predatory activity in the community's everyday life and in men's habits of thought, accumulated property more and more replaces trophies of predatory exploit as the conventional exponent of prepotence and success. With the growth of settled industry, therefore, the possession of wealth gains in relative importance and effectiveness as a customary basis of repute and esteem. Not that esteem ceases to be awarded on the basis of other, more direct evidence of prowess; not that successful predatory aggression or warlike exploit ceases to call out the approval and admiration of the crowd, or to stir the envy of the less successful competitors; but the opportunities for gaining distinction by means of this direct manifestation of superior force grow less available both in scope and frequency. At the same time opportunities for industrial aggression, and for the accumulation of property by the quasi-peaceable methods of nomadic industry, increase in scope and availability. And it is even more to the point that property now becomes the most easily recognized evidence of a reputable degree of success as distinguished from heroic or signal achievement. It therefore becomes the conventional basis of esteem. Its possession in some amount becomes necessary in order to have any reputable standing in the community. It becomes indispensable to accumulate, to acquire property, in order to retain one's good name. When accumulated goods have in this way once become the accepted badge of efficiency, the possession of wealth presently assumes the character of an independent and definitive basis of esteem. The possession of goods, whether acquired aggressively by one's own exertion or passively by transmission through inheritance from others, becomes a conventional basis of reputability. The possession of wealth, which was at the outset valued simply as an evidence of efficiency, becomes, in popular apprehension, itself a meritorious act. Wealth is now itself intrinsically honorable and confers honor on its possessor. By a further refinement, wealth acquired passively by transmission from ancestors or other antecedents presently becomes even more honorific than wealth acquired by the possessor's own effort; but this distinction belongs at a later stage in the evolution of the pecuniary culture and will be spoken of in its place.

Prowess and exploit may still remain the basis of award of the highest popular esteem, although the possession of wealth has become the basis of commonplace reputability and of a blameless social standing. The predatory instinct and the consequent approbation of predatory efficiency are deeply ingrained in the habits of thought of those peoples who have passed under the discipline of a protracted predatory culture. According to popular award, the highest honors within human reach may, even yet, be those gained by an unfolding of extraordinary predatory efficiency in war, or by a quasi-predatory efficiency in statecraft; but for the purpose of a commonplace decent standing in the community these means of repute have been replaced by the acquisition and accumulation of goods. In order to stand well in the eyes of the community, it is necessary to come up to a certain, somewhat indefinite, conventional standard of wealth; just as in the earlier predatory stage it is necessary for the barbarian man to come up to the tribe's standard of physical endurance, cunning and skill at arms. A certain standard of wealth in one case, and of prowess in the other, is a necessary condition of reputability, and anything in éxcess of this normal amount is meritorious.

Those members of the community who fall short of this, somewhat indefinite, normal degree of prowess or of property suffer in the esteem of their fellowmen; and consequently they suffer also in their own esteem, since the usual basis of self-respect is the respect accorded by one's neighbors. Only individuals with an aberrant temperament can in the long run retain their self-esteem in the face of the disesteem of their fellows. Apparent exceptions to the rule are met with, especially among people with strong religious convictions. But these apparent exceptions are scarcely real exceptions, since such persons commonly fall back on the putative approbation of some supernatural witness of their deeds.

So soon as the possession of property becomes the basis of popular esteem, therefore, it becomes also a requisite to that complacency which we call self-respect. In any community where goods are held in severalty it is necessary, in order to ensure his own peace of mind, that an individual should possess as large a portion of goods as others with whom he is accustomed to class himself; and it is extremely gratifying to possess something more than others. But as fast as a person makes new acquisitions, and becomes accustomed to the resulting new standard of wealth, the new standard forthwith ceases to afford appreciably greater satisfaction than the earlier standard did. The tendency in any case is constantly to make the present pecuniary standard the point of departure for a fresh increase of wealth; and this in turn gives rise to a new standard of sufficiency and a new pecuniary classification of one's self as compared with one's neighbors. So far as concerns the present question, the end sought by accumulation is to rank high in comparison with the rest of the community in point of pecuniary strength. So long as the comparison is distinctly unfavorable to himself, the normal, average individual will live in chronic dissatisfaction with his present lot; and when he has reached what may be called the normal pecuniary standard of the community, or of his class in the community, this chronic dissatisfaction will give place to a restless straining to place a wider and ever-widening pecuniary interval between himself and this average standard. The invidious comparison can never become so favorable to the individual making it that he would not gladly rate himself still higher relatively to his competitors in the struggle for pecuniary reputability.

In the nature of the case, the desire for wealth can scarcely be satiated in any individual instance, and evidently a satiation of the average or general desire for wealth is out of the question. However widely, or equally, or "fairly," it may be distributed, no general increase of the community's wealth can make any approach to satiating this need, the ground of which is the desire of everyone to excel everyone else in the accumulation of goods. If, as is sometimes assumed, the incentive to accumulation were the want of subsistence or of physical comfort, then the aggregate economic wants of a community might conceivably be satisfied at some point in the advance of industrial efficiency; but since the struggle is substantially a race for reputability on the basis of an invidious comparison, no approach to a definitive attainment is possible.

What has just been said must not be taken to mean that there are no other incentives to acquisition and accumulation than this desire to excel in pecuniary standing and so gain the esteem and envy of one's fellowmen. The desire for added comfort and security from want is present as a motive at every stage of the process of accumulation in a modern industrial community; although the standard of sufficiency in these respects is in turn greatly affected by the habit of pecuniary emulation. To a great extent this emulation shapes the methods and selects the objects of expenditure for personal comfort and decent livelihood.

Besides this, the power conferred by wealth also affords a motive to accumulation. That propensity for purposeful activity and that repugnance to all futility of effort which belong to man by virtue of his character as an agent do not desert him when he emerges from the naïve communal culture where the dominant note of life is the unanalyzed and undifferentiated solidarity of the individual with the group with which his life is bound up. When he enters upon the predatory stage, where self-seeking in the narrower sense becomes the dominant note, this propensity goes with him still, as the pervasive trait that shapes his scheme of life. The propensity for achievement and the repugnance to futility remain the underlying economic motive. The propensity changes only in the form of its expression and in the proximate objects to which it directs the man's activity. Under the regime of individual ownership the most available means of visibly achieving a purpose is that afforded by the acquisition and accumulation of goods; and as the self-regarding antithesis between man and man reaches fuller consciousness, the propensity for achievement—the instinct of workmanship—tends more and more to shape itself into a straining to excel others in pecuniary achievement. Relative success, tested by an invidious pecuniary comparison with other men, becomes the conventional end of action. The currently accepted legitimate end of effort becomes the achievement of a favorable comparison with other men; and therefore the repugnance to futility to a good extent coalesces with the incentive of emulation. It acts to accentuate the struggle for pecuniary reputability by visiting with a sharper disapproval all shortcoming and all evidence of shortcoming in point of pecuniary success. Purposeful effort comes to mean, primarily, effort directed to or resulting in a more creditable showing of accumulated wealth. Among the motives which lead men to accumulate wealth, the primacy, both in scope and intensity, therefore, continues to belong to this motive of pecuniary emulation.

In making use of the term "invidious," it may perhaps be unnecessary to remark, there is no intention to extol or depreciate, or to commend or deplore any of the phenomena which the word is used to characterize. The term is used in a technical sense as describing a comparison of persons with a view to rating and grading them in respect of relative worth or value—in an aesthetic or moral sense—and so awarding and defining the relative degrees of complacency with which they may legitimately be contemplated by themselves and by others. An invidious comparison is a process of valuation of persons in respect of worth.

Chapter 28 The Self and Role Selection

CARL W. BACKMAN AND PAUL F. SECORD

The concepts of self and role have long been theoretically and empirically linked in the literature of socialization. This linkage has for the most part taken the form of role as the independent and self as the dependent variable. Such a sequence is implicit in the concept of the looking-glass self and in the dictum that the self is social. Occupation of a role category by an individual not only defines his own behavior but also the behavior of other persons toward him, including the kinds of characteristics they will attribute to him. As he moves through various positions in the social structure, attributes appropriate to these role categories are incorporated into his self concept. This relation between self and role is called the *fashioning effect*.

The fashioning effect views the causal sequence between role and self from one direction only. The self theorist who relies exclusively on it places himself in the relatively untenable position of treating the individual as passive, molded in a chameleon-like fashion by movement through the social structure and by social and other perhaps accidental determinants of association with other persons. The reverse of this fashioning of self by role may take two forms: *role selection* and *role portrayal*. In role selection, a person chooses roles that allow him to behave in a manner compatible with self; in role portrayal, when the role provides wide latitude for enactment, he favors the portrayal that is most consistent with self.

The interaction between these processes explains the amount and direction of change which accompanies socialization. The formation of new relations through the process of role selection and portrayal determines the direction of fashioning which, in turn, biases selection at the next choice point. Both the direction and degree of change in personality depend on factors that determine whether fashioning or selection effects predominate. To

SOURCE. This article was prepared originally for this volume.

the degree that selection prevails, stability is enhanced; where fashioning presides, change ensues.

Although earlier empirical work on vocational choice is related to role selection and fashioning, none of it has been conducted within the theoretical framework outlined here. The purpose of this report is to present the results of a series of investigations concerned with role selection. These have been guided by a social-psychological approach to personality, which assumes that stability or change in an individual's behavior over time is a function of stability or change in his relations with other persons (Secord and Backman, 1961; 1965). Stability in these relations has two sources. One lies in the institutional and subinstitutional regularities that constrain the individual's overt behavior, his perceptual, cognitive, and affective processes, and those of the persons with whom he interacts. Institutional regularities refer to systems of cognitive expectations regarding the behavior and attributes of individuals, systems that are shared by those in interaction. For example, an individual occupies a position in a family. Both he and other members of the family, by virtue of their positions, are expected to behave in certain ways and to have certain attributes. These expectations constrain the behavior of family members in the direction of role expectations appropriate to family interaction. Subinstitutional regularities are less formalized and more primitive. They include three relatively stable characteristics of relations among persons: feelings of like or dislike, relative control of one person over another, and evaluations of the relative worth or value of each party to the interaction. These relatively stable aspects of relations among persons may be termed the affect, power, and status structures, respectively. Once established, these properties of interpersonal relations have an enduring quality. They tend to perpetuate themselves by providing mutual reinforcement for the actions of participating individuals.

The second source of stability lies in the individual's active efforts to maintain congruency in spite of external forces disruptive of this state. Forces toward congruency exist between the elements of interpersonal systems, which consist of an aspect of the individual's self concept, his interpretation of those elements of his behavior related to that aspect, and his perception of related aspects of alter's behavior. A state of congruency exists when his behavior and that of alter imply definitions of self congruent with aspects of his self concept.

Two forms of congruency may be illustrated: congruency by implication and congruency by validation. In congruency by implication, S may perceive that O sees him as possessing a particular characteristic corresponding to an aspect of his self concept. A girl who regards herself as beautiful may perceive that another person also thinks she is beautiful. In congruency by validation, the behavior or other characteristics of O allow or call for behavior on the part of S that confirms a component of self. For example, a person who regards himself as strong and protective is especially able to behave in this fashion when he interacts with a person who is dependent (Secord and Backman, 1964a). These are illustrations of cognitive congruency. The theory also posits a similar tendency toward affective congruency. A state of affective congruency exists when the individual believes that alter feels toward him as he feels toward himself. These feelings may pertain to him as a whole or to some limited aspect of his self concept or behavior.

To maintain congruency, the individual actively uses a number of techniques to stabilize his interpersonal environment. He may misperceive or reinterpret his own actions and those of others so as to maintain congruent relations. He may deprecate aspects of self that are involved in incongruent relations. He may more frequently interact with and like more those persons whose behavior and other attributes provide congruency. He may become adept at evoking congruent responses from others. A number of these mechanisms, cognitive restructuring, selective interaction, selective evaluation of others, and response evocation, have been the focus of other reports and thus will not be discussed in detail here. (Backman and Secord, 1962; Backman, Secord, and Peirce, 1963; Secord and Backman, 1964a; Secord, Backman, and Eachus, 1964; Secord

and Backman, 1965.) Some of these mechanisms, however, are involved in role selection. An individual may select a role that enables him to interact with those persons who will attribute congruent characteristics to him or who will engage in behavior that validates aspects of self. Elsewhere we have attempted to delineate the conditions under which congruency will be maintained, through role selection and portrayal as well as other mechanisms, and under which the fashioning effect will prevail and result in change (Secord and Backman, 1965).

Constraints on role selection and portrayal stem from certain rigidities in the institutional and subinstitutional structure that fix the personnel in the individual's environment and restrict their behavior toward him and his toward them. One such limiting factor is the position of the role in question on the achievement-ascription continuum. Where position occupancy is a matter of ascription, role selection is excluded as a method of maintaining congruency. A second and related factor is the degree to which the associated role expectations allow latitude for varying role portrayals. To illustrate, status passage through the age-sex structure of a society is a matter of ascription rather than achievement. Such movement may be speeded or slowed, within limits; however, short of death it is inevitable. Although it may be possible to seek out some persons from whom one can evoke responses congruent with elements of self held while one was in a younger age category, this becomes increasingly difficult as one moves further into the next age category. Eventually the individual is forced to accept the role attributes ascribed to him with increasing uniformity by other persons. One can delay acceptance of being middle-aged only so long. Margaret Mead noted long ago that American society allows less latitude for portrayal of age-sex roles than many other societies. Such latitude appears to have increased in recent years; however, limits for portrayal are still comparatively narrow.

The several investigations reported in this chapter focus on occupational and marital roles as loci for studying the processes of role selection and role portrayal, respectively.

Study I: Preference for Type of Marital Role

This investigation was an attempt to determine whether the order of preference for three kinds of marital female roles was a function of congruency between the self concept and the role image. The three roles were drawn from Kirkpatrick's (1955) distinction between the wife-and-mother role, the companion role, and the partner role, described by him as follows.

The *wife-and-mother role* is the traditional role of the married woman. Its privileges include security, the right to support, alimony in case of divorce, respect as a wife and mother, a certain amount of domestic authority, loyalty of husband to the mother of his children, and sentimental gratitude from husband and children. Corresponding obligations include bearing and rearing children, making a home, rendering domestic service, loyal subordination of self to the economic interests of the husband, acceptance of a dependent social and economic status, and tolerance of a limited range of activity.

The *companion role* is essentially a leisure-class phenomenon. The privileges pertaining to this role include pleasures shared with the husband, a more romantic emotional response, admiration, funds adequate for dress and recreation, leisure for social and educational activity, and chivalrous attentions. On the other hand, it implies as obligations the preservation of beauty under the penalty of marital insecurity, the rendering of ego and erotic satisfaction to the husband, the cultivation of social contacts advantageous to him, the maintenance of intellectual alertness, and the responsibility for exorcising the demon of boredom.

The *partner role* corresponds to a new emergent definition of family relationships. The role entails the privilege of economic independence, equal authority in regard to family finances, acceptance as an equal, the exemption from one-sided personal domestic service to the husband, equal voice in determining the locality of residence, and equality in regard to social and moral freedom. The obligational side of the balance sheet would include renouncing of alimony save in the case of dependent children, an economic contribution in proportion to earning ability, acceptance of equal responsibility for the support of children, complete sharing of the legal responsibilities of the family, willingness to dispense with any appeal to chivalry, abrogation of special privileges in regard to children, and equal responsibility to maintain the family status by success in a career.

Fifty-two women enrolled in an introductory psychology course were asked to indicate their relative preference for these roles, ranking

them from 1 to 3. They were also told that if it was extremely difficult to decide between any two of them, they could assign an equal rank to these two roles; for example, 1,2,2; or, 1, 1, 2. This material was presented to them as part of a study of social roles. On a different occasion, in connection with another study, these women described themselves in terms of a 70-item, fixed distribution ranking procedure developed by Block (1961). This consisted of 70 descriptive adjectives, such as absent-minded, affected, ambitious, bossy, calm, or cautious, which were printed in three columns on a single page. Ten adjectives had to be assigned to each rank from 1 to 7.

To provide an image or profile in similar quantitative terms for each occupational role, three graduate students in social psychology served as judges. They read each role described by Kirkpatrick, and using the same 70-adjective instrument, completed one set of rankings for each role. The rank closest to the mean rank of each trait for the three judges was used to represent the role profile.

The specific hypothesis tested was that an individual would most prefer the marital role having a trait profile most similar to her own self profile. To measure similarity between self and each role, for each adjective the difference between the rank assigned to self and the rank representing the role was determined. Each difference was squared, and the total of the differences between the role and self profiles was obtained by summing across the traits. This procedure yielded a measure of similarity between self and each of the three roles, for each person.

Taking two roles at a time, similarity between self and each role profile was compared with the preference ranks assigned to these roles by the subject. For example, if a girl preferred the companion role to the partner role, her self profile was expected to be more similar to the companion role than to the partner role. To clarify this exposition, sample raw data for comparing the companion role with the partner role for the first four girls are illustrated in Table I.

The differences in the last column are positive if the difference between the two roles is in the direction predicted by the preferences; a minus sign is entered for the opposite direction. The column is left blank if no prediction is possible because of tied preferences.

Table II summarizes the material from this last column for all three comparisons, pre-

TABLE I

Subject	Order of Preference for Companion and Partner Role	Sum D^2 for Self and Companion Role	Sum D^2 for Self and Partner Role	Difference between Sum D^2's
1	2–1	454	364	110
2	1–2	601	531	−70
3	2–2	560	428	——
4	3–2	476	282	194

TABLE II
Agreement between Self-Role Congruency and Role Preference

Role Comparison	Number of Predictions Confirmed	Number of Predictions Not Confirmed	P[a]
Companion versus partner	18	25	>.05
Companion versus wife-mother	31	10	.001
Partner versus wife-mother	28	18	.03

[a] P was determined by the Wilcoxon signed-ranks test. One-tailed values are reported.

senting the number of subjects for whom predictions were confirmed and disconfirmed. Although the hypothesis was not confirmed for the comparison between the companion and partner roles, comparisons between the wife-mother role and the companion role, and the wife-mother role and the partner role, were in the predicted direction.

This first study demonstrates that, when given a choice of several ways of portraying a role, most individuals chose the portrayal that most closely resembled their self description.

Study II: Preference for Occupational Roles

The second investigation compared the occupational preferences of college students with the degree of congruency between self and the traits attributed to persons in each of the occupations. An individual was expected to prefer the role category most congruent with his self description. He anticipates that in that role he would be treated in a manner most congruent with his self concept.

Procedure. The following forms were administered to 43 male and 32 female college students: a preference ranking of ten occupations, a self-ranking form, and an occupational-ranking form. Ten occupations were ranked according to preference by the male students, disregarding considerations of training and aptitude: business executive, artist, engineer, lawyer, college professor, scientist, personnel director, accountant, doctor, and industrial

manager. The ten occupations ranked by females were: office manager, artist, housewife, accountant, news reporter, social worker, laboratory technician, school teacher, nurse, and personnel director.

The same self-ranking form was used for both males and females. With the aid of a study of occupational stereotypes (O'Dowd and Beardslee, 1960), fifteen traits likely to show maximum variation among the ten occupations were chosen: confident, attentive to people, rational, colorful, adaptable in habits, cautious, sociable, intelligent, self-sufficient, persevering, unselfish, responsible, stable, sensitive, and individualistic. Each individual ranked himself from 1 to 15, assigning a *1* to his most prominent trait and a *15* to his least prominent trait. Finally, subjects were given occupational booklets. Each page consisted of a list of the fifteen traits, with the title of an occupation at the top. They were told that people have impressions of what persons in various occupations are like, and were asked to rank the traits from 1 to 15 according to their own views of traits characterizing persons in that occupation.

Data were analyzed independently for each subject. The hypothesis tested was that the smaller the difference between rankings of self and rankings of an occupational image, the greater the preference for that occupation. Congruency between self and each occupational image was obtained by determining the difference between the self ranking and the

TABLE III
Self-Role Congruency and Role Preference

Males			Females	
.76	.32	−.01	.85	.24
.68	.31	−.01	.72	.19
.66	.30	−.08	.70	.10
.65	.28	−.09	.68	.03
.62	.26	−.10	.64	.02
.60	.25	−.12	.60	.02
.60	.20	−.13	.55	.01
.59	.19	−.28	.52	−.03
.55	.18	−.36	.50	−.04
.53	.18	−.37	.48	−.07
.45	.15	−.45	.47	−.13
.42	.12		.38	−.14
.39	.10		.37	−.19
.39	.10		.35	−.28
.39	.08		.26	−.50
.36	.05		.26	−.70

Note: Correlations reported are Spearman's Rho.

occupational ranking on each trait, and squaring the differences. These squared differences for the fifteen traits were then summed, yielding a congruency score for self versus a particular occupational image. Each subject had ten congruency scores of varying sizes, one for each of ten occupations. He had also independently ranked these occupations in order of preference from 1 to 10. A Spearman Rho was computed for these two sets of ranks to determine the amount of association between congruency and occupational preference.

Rhos for the 72 subjects are given in Table III. Since the majority of these are positive, and most of the negative ones generally small, the hypothesis may be regarded as confirmed. For some individuals, however, it is apparent that congruency and occupational preference is not associated; and for a few, there was an appreciable negative association. Possibly, however, the failure to confirm the hypothesis for all individuals may in part result from the limited measure of self (which included only fifteen traits, for convenience in ranking) and the highly selected list of occupations. For some individuals, these occupations may be relatively unimportant, and most of the fifteen traits may not be salient. An occasional high negative Rho may possibly be due to an inadvertent reversal of the numbers used in ranking: a few individuals may have mistakenly interpreted *15* as representing the most prominent trait, and *1* the least prominent.

One alternative interpretation of the positive findings is that subjects may have chosen self traits *and* occupational traits mainly on the basis of social desirability, creating spurious Rhos. An additional analysis controlling for social desirability through partial correlation, however, failed to reduce materially the Rhos obtained. We may conclude that, for most individuals, preference for an occupational role is in part a function of its congruency with their self description.

Study III: Selection of College Major

Data pertaining to role selection are also available from a study of college majors. Unlike the previous two studies, the individual here has taken the first step toward entering the occupation: he has chosen a college major directly associated with an occupational career. The hypothesis tested was that students in a major describe themselves as more like the trait image of the related occupation than do nonmajors.

The 70-item self-instrument previously described in the study of three female roles was administered to 221 males and 222 females. On another occasion 333 males and 184 females, a small minority of whom also belonged to the first two groups, were presented with the same 70 adjectives, with instructions to describe members of one of the following occupational groups: male public school teacher, female public school teacher, engineer, nurse, and artist. Since all 70 adjectives would be unlikely to be relevant to each of the occupations, and since various response sets (such as notions about people in general) modify ranking patterns, the image for each occupation was obtained in terms of those traits that appeared to be most distinctive of the occupation. Before describing the procedure for identifying these distinctive traits, we should point out that there was little difference in rankings of an occupation by control individuals and by persons in a major field related to the occupation. For example, mean rankings of the role of female public school teacher, by females not majoring in education, and those majoring in education, were compared. Only one of the 70 adjectives yielded a mean difference significant at the .01 level. Consequently, such groups were combined: occupational profiles are based upon rankings provided by control persons and by a sample of students from the related major field.

The distinctive characteristics of each occupational image were obtained by examining the difference between the mean self-rankings of individuals not in a relevant major and the mean rankings of the occupation on each trait. Those traits on which the occupational image differed from the self concept of the control subjects to a degree significant at the .01 level were regarded as distinctive of the occupation. This procedure has the advantage of identifying the distinctive characteristics of an occupational image, and it does not include those traits that are shared by college students in general. For example, compared with control self descriptions of college students, artists were viewed as significantly higher in such traits as affected, disorderly, dissatisfied, dramatic, hostile, imaginative, rebellious, self-indulgent, touchy, unconventional, and withdrawn, and lower in cautious, considerate, cooperative, dependent, easily embarrassed, fair-minded, friendly, reasonable, sense of humor, sentimental, sincere, and sympathetic.

In this investigation several analyses of congruency were conducted. Freshmen and sophomore majors were compared with nonmajors and with juniors and seniors majoring in the same subject.

First, data were examined to determine whether freshmen and sophomores in a major field had a self concept more like that of the corresponding occupational image than did freshmen and sophomores not in the major field. On each trait distinctive of the occupational image, the self-ranking of the freshmen and sophomores in the major field was compared with that of the freshmen and sophomores in the control group to see which group was more similar to the image. To illustrate this comparison, the first three traits of the artist image may be considered. These were: affected, disorderly, and dissatisfied. Compared with the control group of 105 freshmen and sophomores majoring in a variety of fields, the 15 art student majors ranked themselves .56 scale points *less* affected, 1.2 scale points *more* disorderly, and .34 scale points *more* dissatisfied. Thus on the first of these traits, they do not evaluate themselves as more like the image of artist than do freshmen and sophomores on their own self-evaluation, but on the other two sample traits, art majors do evaluate themselves as more like artists than do the controls.

Table IV summarizes the findings for the four major fields studied. Considering only the distinctive traits belonging to each occupation, the freshmen and sophomore majors in each field were compared with the freshmen and sophomore controls to determine whether their self-evaluations were in the direction of the

TABLE IV

Congruency and Selection of Major Field by Freshmen and Sophomores

Occupation	Number of Persons Having Majority of Self Traits in Direction of Image	Number of Persons *Not* Having Majority of Self Traits in Direction of Image	Ties	*P*
Male teacher	21	9	3	.028
Female teacher	22	10	5	.035
Male engineer	34	11	3	.00003
Female nurse	20	3	0	.00003

Note. In computing one-tailed sign tests of significance, ties were divided equally between the predicted and nonpredicted frequencies, as recommended by Bradley (1960).

occupational image. Clearly, for most subjects the majority of traits attributed to self by majors are in the direction of the occupational image corresponding to the major. This suggests a strong process of self selection, whereby those who perceive themselves in terms of traits commonly attributed to persons in an occupation chose a major corresponding to it.

Another analysis compares the self profiles of freshmen and sophomores majoring in a particular field with juniors and seniors majoring in the same subject. Both the fashioning and selection processes could operate to make upper-division majors more like their corresponding occupational image. Freshmen and sophomores who have a self concept that is markedly incongruent with their chosen major should tend to transfer to some other major field or to drop out of college. Those who pursue the same major, however, should repeatedly and increasingly be exposed to expectations that they behave more and more like the fully trained individual in the occupation to which the major leads. These pressures should produce change in their behavior and also in their concept of themselves, in the direction of the occupational image.

Table V compares lower- and upper-division majors, reporting the degree to which traits are in the direction of or away from the occupational image. Although all four occupations show that upper division majors are more like the occupational image, not all of these differences are significant. In the case of nurses this may result from marked differences between the lay image and the professional image of nurses. The image used in the present study is primarily a lay image since it is obtained mainly from college students not majoring in nursing; but, if there is a quite different professional image, nursing majors may gradually become familiar with it and move in that direction rather than toward the lay image.

An inspection indicates only slight differences for engineering and for female nursing majors, but a rather substantial difference in the direction of the hypothesis for both education majors. It is difficult to interpret these data; they lack sufficient specification. For example, students might drop out for financial reasons rather than incongruency, dropouts could have transferred to other institutions, or they might later re-enroll in the same field. In some instances, those who changed majors might have switched to a major that is still compatible with their self concept.

DISCUSSIONS AND CONCLUSIONS

The relation between self and role has been discussed in terms of two theoretical principles: the *fashioning effect* and *role selection*. The fashioning effect emphasizes the shaping of an individual's views of himself by virtue of occupying a role category. Occupying a role not only defines an individual's behavior, but also defines the behavior of other persons toward him, including the kinds of characteristics they will attribute to him. To the degree that his ideas of self initially deviate from the role prescriptions, the individual is apt to modify them toward the views of his role partners.

Congruency may also be maintained by the converse process of role selection, whereby an individual's choice of role is guided by his concept of self. A role is chosen because it is

TABLE V

Comparison of Lower- and Upper-Division Majors

Occupation	N_s	Upper-Division Students Net Number of Traits in Direction of Occupation	Lower-Division Students Net Number of Traits in Direction of Occupation	Difference	P
Male teacher	33,34	6.06	3.39	2.67	.04
Female teacher	37,48	6.33	3.57	2.76	.07
Male engineer	34,48	5.68	4.40	1.28	>.10
Female nurse	9,23	5.89	5.78	0.11	>.10

Note. The net number of traits in the direction of the occupation was computed by subtracting, for each person, the number of traits rated less like the occupational image from the number of traits rated more like the occupational image. From these figures mean differences were obtained.

associated with expectations for behavior that are congruent with the individual's self concept and because in that role he would be endowed with attributes like those of his self concept. A variant of this process is *role portrayal;* this is possible when a role allows a wide range of behavior: the individual is apt to portray it in a manner most consistent with self. Whether fashioning or role selection predominates in particular situations is in part a function of the position of the role on the achievement-ascription continuum. Certain roles, such as age-sex categories, are *ascribed* to the individual; he has no choice, and fashioning is apt to predominate. Sometimes, however, an ascribed role allows a fairly wide range of behavior; in that instance, the individual may portray it in a manner most congruent with self. Other roles, such as occupational categories, are more toward the achievement end of the continuum, and the individual may use the process of role selection to minimize change in self.

The several investigations reported demonstrated the operation of these principles. In one investigation, college students were shown to prefer those occupations commonly associated with personality characteristics most like their own. In another study, illustrating role portrayal, female college students were shown to choose a type of marital role most compatible with their self concept. A third study demonstrated that college students who had chosen a major had self concepts more like the occupational image associated with the major than were the self concepts of students not choosing that major. This investigation demonstrated further that upper division students in a major field had self concepts more like the relevant occupational image than freshmen and sophomores in the same major. This finding could be explained by either the fashioning effect, or role selection, or both.

The investigations reported here should be regarded primarily as demonstration studies. It is not contended that congruency processes are the only explanation for the findings; various other interpretations could be offered. But it is clear that the data are at least consistent with congruency theory. When they are taken in conjunction with data from other studies reported earlier, they provide substantial support for this theoretical approach to stability and change in personality.

REFERENCES

Backman, C. W., and Secord, P. F. Liking, selective interaction, and misperception in congruent interpersonal relations. *Sociometry,* **25** (1962), pp. 321–335.

Backman, C. W., Secord, P. F., and Peirce, J. R. Resistance to change in the self concept as a function of perceived consensus among significant others. *Sociometry,* **26** (1963), pp. 102–111.

Block, J. *The Q-sort method in personality assessment and psychiatric research.* Chicago, Ill.: C. C. Thomas, 1961.

Bradley, J. V. Distribution-free statistical tests. *USAF WADD tech Rep.,* 1960, No. 60–661.

Kirkpatrick, C. *The family as process and institution.* New York: Ronald, 1955.

O'Dowd, D. D., and Beardslee, D. C. College student images of a selected group of professions and occupations. Cooperative Research Project No. 562 (8142), Wesleyan Univer., April, 1960.

Secord, P. F., and Backman, C. W. Personality theory and the problem of stability and change in individual behavior: An interpersonal approach. *Psychol. Rev.,* **68** (1961), pp. 21–32.

Secord, P. F., and Backman, C. W. Interpersonal congruency, perceived similarity, and friendship. *Sociometry,* **27** (1964), pp. 115–127.

Secord, P. F., and Backman, C. W. An interpersonal approach to personality. In B. Maher (Ed.), *Progress in experimental personality research.* Vol. 2. New York: Academic Press, 1965, pp. 91–125.

Secord, P. F., Backman, C. W., and Eachus, T. Effects of imbalance in the self concept on the perception of persons. *J. abnorm. soc. Psychol.,* **68** (1964), pp. 442–446.

Chapter 29 The Theory of Self-Consistency

PRESCOTT LECKY

We conceive of the mind or personality as an organization of ideas which are felt to be consistent with one another. Behavior expresses the effort to maintain the integrity and unity of the organization. The point is that all of an individual's ideas are organized into a single system, whose preservation is essential. In order to be immediately assimilated, the idea formed as the result of a new experience must be felt to be consistent with the ideas already present in the system. On the other hand, ideas whose inconsistency is recognized as the personality develops must be expelled from the system. There is thus a constant assimilation of new ideas and the expulsion of old ideas throughout life.

The nucleus of the system, around which the rest of the system revolves, is the individual's idea or conception of himself. Any idea entering the system which is inconsistent with the individual's conception of himself cannot be assimilated but instead gives rise to an inconsistency which must be removed as promptly as possible.

By way of illustration, let us consider the interpretation of why a person feels insulted or has his feelings hurt. An insult is a valuation of the individual by others which does not agree with the individual's valuation of himself. Such a contradictory valuation cannot be assimilated, and when thrust into a person's experience acts as a foreign body whose elimination is essential.

The conflict provoked by the inconsistency may lead to several different kinds of behavior. The usual method of handling the problem is to strike back and try to inflict an equal injury upon the person responsible for the insult. It is necessary that the injury given be equal to the injury received if the conflict is to be dissolved completely. Ancient codes of justice emphasize this necessity—an eye for an eye, a tooth for a tooth. The demand for vengeance

is especially apparent in children because of their inability to unify on any other basis. The inconsistency may also be removed by an apology, again provided that the apology be equal to the insult.

Still another method is to reinterpret the disturbing incident in such a manner that it can be assimilated. For example, a child was deeply wounded when he failed to be invited to a schoolmate's birthday party. He was asked how many children he expected to invite the next time he gave a party. Looking at the situation in this new perspective, it was apparent that since the number of guests was limited by necessity, there was no occasion to regard the omission as a personal slight. His mental suffering was thereupon relieved.

Finally, it is sometimes necessary to alter the opinion one holds of oneself. This is difficult, for the individual's conception of himself is the central axiom of his whole life theory. Nevertheless, a gradual change in the concept of self is imperative to normal development and happiness.

There is thus a constant compulsion to unify and harmonize the system of ideas by which we live. It is only when a person is unable to rid himself of inconsistencies that psychological problems arise. The difficulty is to make him realize the nature of the inconsistency. For when an inconsistency is clearly recognized, the individual can be depended upon to make the problem his own and endeavor to alter the system in such a way that consistency is restored. In constructing his personal theory of life, in other words, the individual follows the same method precisely as the scientist constructing his theory of the world. In both cases the resistance to disturbance of the existing organization is readily observable.

As we have already pointed out, the various so-called emotional states cannot be treated independently, but must be regarded as different aspects of a single motive, the striving for unity. For example, love is the emotion subjectively experienced in reference to a person

SOURCE. Prescott Lecky, *Self-Consistency: A Theory of Personality,* Long Island, New York: The Island Press, 1945, Appendix III. Copyright 1945.

or object already assimilated and serving as a strong support to the idea of the self. Grief is experienced when the personality must be reorganized due to the loss of one of its supports. Hatred is an impulse of rejection felt towards unassimilable objects. Love may turn to hate if the accepted idea of a person turns out to be false in the light of later experience, and instead of serving as a support, becomes a threat to the integrity of the organization as a whole.

The emotion of horror appears when a situation arises suddenly which we are not prepared to assimilate, such as the sight of a ghastly accident. Experiences which increase the sense of psychological unity and strength give rise to the emotion of joy. Occasionally a person's own behavior may violate his conception of himself, producing feelings of remorse and guilt. In that case, the insult to himself, as it were, may be eliminated by seeking punishment sufficient to equalize the insult. Fear is felt when no adequate solution of a problem can be found, and disorganization impends.

Of special importance from the standpoint of the school is the phenomenon of resistance. The problem of resistance has heretofore received very little attention in educational psychology, which conceives learning in terms of habit formation. In psychiatry, on the other hand, resistance is regarded as a device to protect the neurosis, and hence as belonging to abnormal psychology. Yet the very fact that we strive to be true to ourselves involves resistance to the acceptance of that which is inconsistent. Thus resistance must be recognized as normal and necessary. Indeed, a unified organization could not be maintained without it. Nevertheless, there are always present in the system a certain number of ideas accepted on insufficient evidence, whose inconsistency has not yet been demonstrated. These ideas give rise to resistances which are likely to be detrimental to the individual in the long run, and which would not be retained if carefully re-examined.

A therapeutic technique which aims to bring about the re-examination and dissolution of this type of resistance has been successfully applied in the treatment of students who encounter difficulty both in academic work and in social situations.

Sensitiveness, inability to make friends, etc., are due to definitions which are difficult to support in the existing situation. The individual's definitions often formed as the result of excessive attention in childhood, are no longer supported by the persons with whom he comes in contact. The behavior of his associates does not confirm the conception of himself which he is committed to maintain. Unconsciously demanding more recognition than he commonly receives, he feels that he is being neglected or pushed aside. Furthermore, he defines himself in passive terms, as some one whose place it is to be assisted, invited, or admired, rather than in active terms, as someone who assists, invites and admires others. To take a socially active role, even to the extent of speaking first to another person, for him is out of character.

The maintenance of such a passive definition is not, of course, an easy task in the competitive adult world. Social support is a matter of exchange, in which one receives in proportion as he gives. The therapy must therefore aim to make the subject aware of the self-valuation which prevents assimilation of the existing situation. The task is not really as difficult as it seems, for the reason that he cannot escape from his environment and is constantly having more unassimilable situations thrust upon him, and is therefore already occupied with the problem before we offer our help. His passive definition, which is the real source of his difficulties, now appears as a useless burden to be thrown off rather than an asset to be justified and retained. In order to induce the student to accept the problem as his own, of course, criticism must be carefully avoided.

Since each personality is an organized system in which every idea is related to every other, it is obvious that any attempt to force the issue and remove the resistance by attacking it misses the point completely. For this reason the consultant will probably be more successful if he does not try too hard. Parents and teachers, whose own peace of mind is affected by the child's success or failure, usually cannot set aside their personal interest in the matter and are likely to become impatient. We may with advantage remind ourselves that only the individual himself can solve his problem, and he must necessarily solve it in his own way.

Chapter 30 Personal Consistency and the Presentation of Self*

KENNETH J. GERGEN

I

The world of social perception tends to be a stable one. Through our abilities to conceptualize, the complex flux is simplified and rendered comprehensible. As a person is exposed to facts about another, such facts are ordered and assimilated. Noting a person's abrasive speech or brusque treatment of others, for example, may lead one to conceptualize this person as "aggressive." The concept is thus used to encapsulate a series of observations, and the conceptualization of a body of observations forms the cornerstone for what we know as "understanding" of the other. Once such judgments are formed they tend to remain intact and unchanging. On the one hand, new information about a person may simply be assimilated into the already existing conceptual structure. As often demonstrated in a laboratory setting, the initial information received about another may substantially color the interpretation one makes of facts revealed at a later time. On the other hand, if later information grossly violates the once crystallized judgment of the other, it may be either distorted or misperceived. Research has shown, for example, that when persons receive contradictory information about another, they often misperceive entire sets of facts in order to develop an internally consistent view of the person.[1] In these ways, persons tend to be seen as stable and consistent. One may say that David is friendly and kind, that Charles is domineering and unsympathetic, and the words or concepts used to describe these persons operate as if to indicate something about their personalities across time and across situations.

Once conceptions of another are developed, they also form the basis of social expectancy. If on a given day David were "unfriendly" or "unkind," such behavior would be surprising and one might be inclined to wonder why David was "not himself today." In effect, we come to perceive, expect, and assume personal consistency on the part of others in our social environment. One may well ask, however: How accurate is this assertion of personal consistency? What are its consequences in social life and in the behavioral sciences? In this chapter, we take a close look at such issues, for they are intimately linked to the notion of the self and to the development of human potentiality.

Consistency and the Behavioral Sciences

The conceptual bracketing of an individual's personality is no less true in the arena of everyday life than it is in the laboratory of the behavioral scientist. Research in personality, for example, largely rests on the assumption of personal consistency. If a person fills out a questionnaire in a particular way or judges a stimulus configuration in a given manner, he may be classified as having certain personality characteristics. Certain responses are said to be indicative of high self-esteem, others of a strong achievement orientation, and so on. On the assumption that the person acts consistently, and that the personality traits found in the testing situation universally characterize the person's style of life, predictions are made and tested concerning the person's behavior under a variety of conditions. This research tactic is, of course, a quite common one and lies at the heart of the "trait" approach to personality. As MacKinnon has pointed out, in its extreme form this approach assumes that behavioral traits, "operate as fixed attributes of an organism as stable and unchanging as a finger print or birth mark."[2]

SOURCE. This paper was prepared originally for this volume.

* The research represented in this paper was made possible through a grant from the National Science Foundation (GS 562).

[1] Gollin, E. S., Forming impressions of personality, *Journal of Personality*, **23** (1954), pp. 65–76.

[2] MacKinnon, D. W., The structure of personality, in J. McV. Hunt (Ed.), *Personality and the*

Theorists interested in the self-concept have largely supported this conception of personality. Even the term "self-concept" implies that a person has a singular way of conceiving of himself, and that he may view all his actions as either confirming or being inconsistent with this concept. Carl Rogers has suggested, for example, that "all perceptions of the qualities, abilities, impulses, and attitudes of the person, all perceptions of himself in relation to others are accepted into the organized conscious concept of the self."[3] We find a similar approach in theories on personal identity. Erikson, Allport, and others, for example, equate the notion of identity with inner sameness or continuity. It is often supposed that the universal question for the person is "who am I," and the grammatical form of the question itself suggests that the answer should be in a singular form.

Over the past decade personal consistency has also come to play a cardinal role in models developed to explain processes of social influence. Festinger's[4] model of cognitive dissonance is a good case in point, inasmuch as the entire theory rests on the premise that a person continuously strives for consistency among his thoughts. Inconsistency is said to produce discomfort or to be noxious, and many of the experiments in this tradition have attempted to demonstrate the irrational measures taken by persons in reducing inconsistency. It should also be noted that the consistency assumption has proved to be an empirically useful one in research on both personality and social influence.

The Consistency Ethic

Perhaps one reason for the viability of the consistency assumption is that the ethical sanctions in Western culture tend to reinforce consistent behavior. That such sanctions do exist might be inferred from such Biblical statements as, "a double-minded man is unstable in all his ways," and, "no man can serve two masters."[5] In his *Outline of Western History,* H. G. Wells also remarks on the foibles of man by noting that "not one is altogether noble nor altogether trustworthy nor altogether consistent; and not one is altogether vile."[6] It may be said that we not only see people as being all of a piece, but we treat them as if they are, and we often punish them if they are not. If a person is seen acting in ways that violate our conceptions of him, we may often disdainfully characterize his conduct as "a facade," "superficial," or "insincere." A study conducted by Gergen and Jones[7] demonstrated, for example, that over a variety of conditions a predictable person comes to be liked and an unpredictable one produces a negative reaction. The concept of "trust," with all of its evaluative loading, is in part based on one's being able to assume that a person will not contradict that which he *seems* to be. Similarly, the common exhortation to be "true to self" may largely rest in the desire to have others act in ways that are consistent with that we conceive them to be. The longstanding odium attached to the acting profession or to that of the politician may stem from the fact that inconsistency is often an occupational hazard or necessity for persons thus employed. It also seems plausible that the great fear evoked by masks in many primitive cultures may result from the fact that the mask itself casts doubt on the validity of the wearer's outward visage.

And there is certainly good reason for the social value placed on consistency. For one, it is simply less taxing and perhaps less anxiety-provoking if the social environment is not in constant and capricious flux. More important, to a large extent we base our behavior toward another on our conceptions of him, and the adaptiveness of this behavior may be in direct proportion to the correctness of these conceptions. "Correct" conceptions depend on another's acting consistently. Personal security is also based on the behavioral coherency of others. On a broad social level one might even say that social order is to some extent dependent on consistent behavioral patterns among members of a society. If all acted spontaneously and unexpectedly from moment to moment, chaos would soon erupt.

Behavior Disorders, Vol. 1, New York: Ronald Press, 1944, pp. 3–48.

[3] Rogers, C. R., Some observations on the organization of personality, *American Psychologist,* **2** (1947), pp. 358–368.

[4] Festinger, L., *A Theory of Cognitive Dissonance,* Evanston, Ill.: Row, Peterson, 1957.

[5] For these quotations, I am indebted to Gordon Allport's *Pattern and Growth in Personality,* New York: Holt, Rinehart and Winston, 1961.

[6] Wells, H. G., *Outline of Western History,* Garden City, N. J.: Garden City Books, 1961.

[7] Gergen, K. J. and Jones, E. E., Mental illness, predictability, and affective consequences as stimulus factors in person perception, *Journal of Abnormal and Social Psychology,* **67** (1963), pp. 95–104.

The Ethic in the Behavioral Sciences

Behavioral scientists themselves are products of their culture, so it is no surprise to find in their work a certain moralistic cast placed on personal consistency. William James was perhaps the first to lend a strong voice in this direction. He differentiated between the basically healthy person whose inner constitution is "harmonious and well balanced from the outset" and the "sick souls" whose "spirit wars with their flesh, they wish for incompatibles, wayward impulses interrupt their most deliberate plans, and their lives are one long drama of repentance and of effort to repair misdemeanors and mistakes."[8] For James the only salvation for these "divided selves" lay in the "normal evolution of character," which consisted of the "straightening out and unifying of the inner self." Whereas the *Zeitgeist* of objectivity later reduced the occurrence of such baldly ethical statements, the implicit ethic has nevertheless remained in various forms. In Prescott Lecky's work[9] we find, for example, that the "normally" functioning human being strives for consistency in all aspects of his life. Mental imbalance and suffering are equated with blockage of consistency-striving, and therapy is largely envisioned as a tool to remove such blocks. The value of "inner sameness" has also been stressed by theorists discussing identity formation. Rogers has stated that integration of various aspects of the person into a unified concept of self "is accompanied by feelings of comfort and freedom from tension,"[10] and again unity becomes a goal of psychotherapy.

It has thus far been pointed out that behavioral scientists have found the assumption of personal consistency a highly useful one, and that as cultural exemplars they, too, may value consistent behavior. One may well question at this point the possibility of a causal link between these two tendencies. Is it possible that the utility of the consistency assumption is based not so much on its reflection of inner needs and overriding personal dispositions as on the fact that consistent behavior is sanctioned no less forcibly in the psychological clinic or research laboratory than in other realms of daily life? In effect, the demands for consistency in such settings may well engender behavior that validates the basic assumptions. Personal consistency in these settings may itself be fostered by the social situation in which the behavioral scientist plays a significant role.

To illustrate the plausibility of this argument, let us consider first the case of the individual who has been classified as mentally ill. Such a person may, in fact, be capable of much normal behavior. However, the classification of "mentally ill" may itself be encapsulating in that it serves to orient the behavior of others toward him. Perceiving the person as "sick," the attendant in a mental institution may effectively reinforce "sick" behavior and fail to encourage conduct that is inconsistent with this perception.[11] In a challenging description of the "moral career" of the mental patient, Goffman points out that "the setting and the house rules press home to the patient that he is, after all, a mental case who has suffered some kind of social collapse on the outside, having failed in some over-all way, and that he is of little social weight, being hardly capable of acting like a full-fledged person at all."[12] Of course, the goal of the institution is ultimately to bring the person into a "well" status, but the current conception of recovery from mental illness is that it is a gradual process, and this conception may have self-fulfilling properties.

The influence of the consistency assumption may be no less operative in the social psychological laboratory. Dissonance theory, as a case in point, is almost entirely based on laboratory research, and a noteworthy study by Aronson and Carlsmith[13] may serve to illustrate the present argument. In this particular experiment, subjects were caused to fail continuously in a task and then suddenly to find that they had succeeded. Based on the assumption that sudden success would be dissonant with the person's continued failure, it was predicted that in order to restore a consistent state, subjects would purposely engage in behavior which would cause them to fail once again. The pre-

8 James, W., *The Varieties of Religious Experience,* New York: The New American Library of World Literature, 1958.
9 Lecky, P., *Self-consistency, a Theory of Personality,* New York: Island Press, 1945.
10 Rogers, C. R., *op. cit.*

11 Interesting in this regard are recent findings communicated to me by Dr. Murray Melbin, to the effect that mental patients demonstrate greater symptomology during those times when a greater number of hospital staff members are within range of observation.
12 Goffman, E., *Asylums,* New York: Doubleday Books, 1961, pp. 151–152.
13 Aronson, E. and Carlsmith, J. M., Performance expectancy as a determinant of actual performance, *Journal of Abnormal and Social Psychology,* **65** (1962), pp. 178–182.

diction was verified. It might be asked, however, what function the experimenter served in the experimental situation? The test on which the subject had continuously received a low score was one that the experimenter had publicly proclaimed to be a valid indicator of social sensitivity. Was it possible that the subject, feeling that the experimenter would be disappointed if his test failed to yield consistent results, attempted to do poorly in order to prevent the experimenter's discomfort? A later study,[14] in which the experimenter denigrated the validity of the social sensitivity test, failed to replicate the original findings, and strongly suggests that experimenter sanction of consistent behavior does produce effects.

To recapitulate the basic line of reasoning up to this point, it has been said that in daily life the assumption is often made that persons are basically consistent, and that this assumption is buttressed by ethical sanctions. It has further been pointed out that this assumption has been widely adopted and equally sanctioned in the behavioral sciences, and that such sanctions may produce the very behavior predicted on other grounds. It is now appropriate to take a more critical look at the assumption of personal consistency. To what extent is it supported by current evidence? How valid is it in describing or explaining social interaction? What limitations must be placed on its generality? And what problems are created for the person by the existing ethic? The remainder of this paper attempts to treat such issues and their relevance to the self. The empirical evidence is first reviewed with particular focus on recent studies in the psychology of self-presentation. Finally, we will be in a position to return to the question of the ethical underpinnings of personal consistency.

II

Empirical work tending to embarrass an assumption of behavioral consistency has been on the scene for a good many years. One of the earliest and most extensive studies in this line was that of Hartshorne and May.[15] Utilizing a large sample of school children, correlations among a variety of measures designed to assess tendencies toward being deceitful were found to be quite meager. In effect, a child who lied was neither more nor less likely to engage in other deceitful forms of behavior than one who avoided lying. The conclusion was thus reached that these various behaviors represent situationally specific habits rather than general or consistent traits. Unfortunately, the study leaves unclear whether the lack of correlation among measures was due to the subjects' lack of personal consistency or to the insensitivity of the measures employed. The data have also been criticized on a number of other grounds. Allport has pointed out that dishonesty, for one, may not be a general trait, and that children may also constitute a poor sample for demonstrating consistency.[16]

Many other studies attempting to reveal behavioral inconsistency have emerged in the area of public opinion and attitude assessment. The classic in this realm is La Pierre's 1934 study in which the amount of anti-Chinese prejudice expressed by restaurant and hotel-motel owners on a mail out questionnaire was found to be far less than that found when they were actually confronted by a Chinese couple.[17] In the same vein, it has been found that interviewers who "look" Jewish and have Jewish names elicit fewer anti-Semitic attitudes than those who don't appear to be Jewish.[18] Katz reports that middle-class interviewers are more likely to elicit pro-conservative responses from low-income respondents than are working-class interviewers.[19] Many similar findings are reported in Hyman's penetrating discussion of bias in the survey interview.[20]

Although such findings serve to document inconsistency on the level of overt behavior, inconsistency on the covert or psychological level is yet another matter. These findings initially suggest that attitudes, conceived as psychological dispositions, have little cross-situational generality. However, such a conclusion seems unwarranted on the basis of this type of evidence alone. As Campbell has correctly pointed out, attitudinal dispositions vary in strength,

[14] Ward, W. D. and Sandvold, K. D., Performance expectancy as a determinant of actual performancy: a partial replication, *Journal of Abnormal and Social Psychology,* **67** (1963), pp. 293–295.
[15] Hartshorne, H. and May, M. A., *Studies in Deceit,* New York: Macmillan, 1928.

[16] Allport, G. W., *Pattern and Growth in Personality,* New York: Holt, Rinehart and Winston, 1961.
[17] La Pierre, R. T., Attitudes vs. actions, *Social Forces,* **13** (1934), pp. 230–237.
[18] Robinson, D. and Rohde, S., Two experiments with an anti-Semitism poll, *Journal of Abnormal and Social Psychology,* **51** (1946), pp. 136–144.
[19] Katz, D., Do interviewers bias polls? *Public Opinion Quarterly,* **6** (1942), pp. 284–288.
[20] Hyman, H., *Interviewing in Social Research,* Chicago, Ill.: University of Chicago Press, 1954.

and the public espousal of a position that seems discrepant from underlying feelings may simply reflect the fact that the feelings are not sufficiently intense to be expressed regardless of circumstances.[21] That an anti-Semite will not admit his feelings to a Rabbi, for example, may only mean that he does not feel strongly enough about his convictions to risk censure in such a situation. It does not mean that his underlying feelings are necessarily inconsistent with each other.

The same reasoning is also germane to the notion of the self-concept. Everyone is probably aware of circumstances that are inimical to his behaving as he truly feels himself to be, and responding to the dictates of such situations does not necessarily imply an inconsistent self-picture. Of course, this as well as the earlier examples have dealt with situations in which the person is attempting to avoid punishment. However, the preceding arguments apply equally to behavior stemming from what have been termed pro-active motives, or motives directed toward a positive goal state. For example, almost anyone who has worked in a new or different occupation has no doubt experienced a peculiar alienation from his behavior, an alienation fostered by the discrepancy existing between his time-worn conceptions of self and his current role-adoptive behavior. In essence, the attempt to achieve a desired goal has caused the person to behave inconsistently with his basic feelings about self. However, one may not infer on these grounds alone that his conceptions of self are contradictory.

Inconsistencies such as those described seem relegated to rather unusual or novel circumstances. Under normal conditions a person shuns those situations in which active dissimulation is required either in order to avoid punishment or to achieve a goal. What about the "average" sorts of events in a man's life, those which predominate in the day-to-day world of social relationships?

Perhaps the most sensitive and compelling treatment of the inconsistencies of everyday life has been provided by Erving Goffman.[22] Working from his own experiences and from a wide number of literary sources, Goffman underscores the subtle and often hidden variations in a person's behavior as he moves from one social situation to another. The picture of man resulting from these sketches is not a particularly laudible one. The Goffmanian man is a perpetual mummer, and all social relationships are made up of performances well calculated by the actor to achieve optimal returns. Certainly the ingredients of the "normal" personality, as served up by personality theorists discussed previously, could stand a dash or two of this robust flavor. However, for present purposes Goffman's treatment is insufficient. Goffman provides a discerning view of the chameleon-like behavior of individuals, but little attention is given to the ramifications of such behavior for underlying psychological structure. Essentially, in Goffman's work there is little in the way of a subjective sense of self for the person to present or reveal in behavior. His analysis also tends to place too heavy an emphasis on consciously calculated performances, while giving short shrift to behavior felt by the person to be "authentic." In addition, literary allusion and personal observation provide a shaky ground on which to establish conclusions. The case must ultimately rest on the controlled demonstration of both the antecedents and consequences of inconsistency.

Self-Presentation Research

Over the past several years a number of experimental studies of self-presentation have been conducted, and inroads have been made into a number of the issues we have discussed. For present purposes we can confine ourselves to a brief description of several investigations which demonstrate the effects of (a) other persons, (b) the interaction environment, and (c) motivation, on the self-picture provided to others. First an attempt is made to show that behavioral inconsistencies can be elicited in rather systematic fashion. In most instances, such studies have involved the assessment of the same individual's behavior under two differing conditions. However, as noted earlier, contradictions in overt behavior may not be indicative of inconsistency in underlying feelings about self. Thus the central focus is on evidence dealing with covert feelings about oneself and one's presentation to others.

The Other Person

As a person moves from one relationship to another, he is exposed to others who vary widely in behavioral style and disposition. Is

[21] Campbell, D. T., Social attitudes and other acquired behavioral dispositions, in Sigmund Koch (Ed.), *Psychology: a Study of a Science,* Vol. VI, New York: McGraw-Hill, 1963.

[22] Goffman, E., *The Presentation of Self in Everyday Life,* New York: Doubleday, 1959.

it possible to maintain a consistent stance in a constantly changing social evironment? For example, how does one react when confronted by a person who is boastful and egotistical as opposed to one who emphasizes his shortcomings? In a study conducted by Gergen and Wishnov,[23] subject groups found themselves interacting with just such persons. Subjects had filled out a series of self-ratings almost a month prior to the experiment. During the experiment they again described themselves along the same dimensions, but this time for a partner who was perceived to be either egotistical or humble. In terms of expressed level of self-esteem, subjects paired with the egotist became significantly more positive; subjects confronted by humility began to emphasize their own shortcomings. In other words, level of expressed self-esteem did not remain stable, but changed in either direction depending on the characteristics of the other person in the situation.

Since these results demonstrate changes in overt presentation only, subjects were also asked about how honest and open they felt they had been during the information exchange. Over two-thirds felt they had been completely open or that responses during the exchange were essentially no different from those of the prior testing session. Further, when ratings of honesty were correlated with amount of self-esteem change, virtually no relationship was found. In effect, the behavioral changes in the situation did not seem to depend on conscious precalculation but appeared to reflect habitual and unconscious modes of relation to others.

In addition to the other's personality, his *behavior* toward a person may also produce marked changes in social identity. As a prime example, G. H. Mead and the many who have followed in his footsteps have long maintained that a person's concept of self is primarily dependent on the expressed view of others toward the self. By and large, the literature in this area has discussed the self-concept as if it were a single entity representing the combined attitudes of several significant others toward a person. Such a position is, of course, quite compatible with the assumption of personal consistency. On the other hand, as a person moves through his social world he may encounter others who see him in strikingly different ways. The traits sought out and rein-

forced by an employer, for example, are probably not those with which a man's children will resonate. Do a person's underlying feelings about himself shift along with his behavior as he moves from one relationship to another? A second study strongly suggests that they do.

In this instance[24] female undergraduates rated themselves on a large number of items designed to tap self-esteem. Several weeks later they were interviewed by a trainee in a large interviewing project. They were told that the trainee's major task was to learn to be honest and spontaneous with the respondent. During the interview the subject was asked to respond to the same self-esteem items administered earlier. As the subject rated herself on each item, the interviewer, a confidante of the experimenter, subtly began to indicate her feelings toward the subject. She smiled, nodded her head, and gave minimal verbal reinforcement each time the subject rated herself positively; she displayed minimal signs of disagreement whenever the subject gave a negative self-opinion. During the interview, the subjects' overt level of self-esteem underwent a marked increase, an increase substantially higher than that occurring in a control group of nonreinforced subjects.

In order to shed light on the relationship between the overt expression of self-esteem and the covert feelings, additional self-esteem tests were administered after the interview. Subjects were told to be as honest as possible in completing these measures, and that the interviewer would not have access to their answers. The results showed that the enhanced level of self-esteem, produced by the reinforcement procedure, carried over into the postexperimental period and remained significantly above the level found in the control group. It seems, then, that the interaction was successful in producing at least temporary changes in the way the subject viewed herself in the situation.

The Interaction Environment

Judgments of another's behavior are seldom unaffected by the environmental context in which they are made. A person's smile may be interpreted quite differently if others in the situation are suffering as opposed to sharing in the conviviality. In the same way, the en-

[23] Gergen, K. J. and Wishnov, B., Others' self-evaluations and interaction anticipation as determinants of self-presentation, *Journal of Personality and Social Psychology*, **2** (1965), pp. 348–358.

[24] For a complete description of this investigation, see Gergen, K. J., Interaction goals and personalistic feedback as factors affecting the presentation of self, *Journal of Personality and Social Psychology*, **1** (1965), pp. 413–424.

vironmental context of a relationship offers many cues which may affect one's presentation of self. Results from two studies serve to illustrate such effects.

In most social relationships the participants are aware of and may be affected by the apparent duration of their acquaintanceship. A relationship which is seen to be short-lived, for example, may sometimes allow greater freedom of action and spontaneity than one in which behavior may have long-term consequences.[25] In the Gergen and Wishnov study, one group of subjects faced a partner who was neither egotistical nor humble, but who attributed to herself strong as well as weak points. Half the subjects interacting with this person were led to anticipate a long-term relationship with the partner; the remaining half were told that after the interchange the circumstances would not allow a continued acquaintanceship. In subsequently describing themselves to their partners, subjects who anticipated further interaction became significantly more self-revealing, whereas those who did not expect a further relationship described themselves in essentially the same way they had a month earlier. While these findings demonstrate the effects of perceived duration, they of course raise questions about the "greater freedom of action" supposedly found in short-lived relationships. However, subjects in both conditions predominantly felt honest and unchanged, and the intensity of these feelings was unrelated to their actual behavior.

A second study attempts to isolate differences in self-presentation stemming from variation in task demands.[26] In what way, it asks, is a person's social identity altered by a task in which productivity is the major goal as opposed to one in which social compatibility or solidarity is stressed? In order to answer this and other questions, members of a naval training program participated in an experiment in which half were confronted with the former type of task and half with the latter. In the task emphasizing productivity, subjects were to work on maneuvering a mock ship out of danger when confronted by much complex information. In the solidarity task, the primary objective of the subjects was to be compatible and understanding in working out some maneuvering arrangements. Each participant was further led to believe that he would be working with a person who was either higher or lower in rank than himself. After one of the two tasks had been explained, he was asked to describe himself to his partner. The results revealed that regardless of the relative rank of the partner, subjects in the productivity condition became significantly more positive in their ratings of self, whereas those attempting to be compatible began to emphasize more negative aspects of self. When subsequently asked about their honesty in the situation, over three-quarters of the subjects indicated that they felt their self-ratings to be virtually the same as those made along the same dimensions a month earlier. In terms of subjective experiences of the subjects, these results quite closely parallel those of the Gergen and Wishnov study previously described.

Motivation

It was reasoned earlier in this chapter that changes in self-presentation resulting from active goal seeking do not necessarily bear on the issue of internal consistency. However, a number of studies have demonstrated ways in which a person will alter his social visage in order to gain another's regard, and results from two of these shed important light on the problem of internal consistency.

In the first of these investigations,[27] females were to be interviewed by a trainee in Clinical Psychology. Prior to the interview, half were asked to describe themselves during the interview in any way they saw fit to gain the interviewer's favor, while the remainder were told to be as honest as possible during the proceedings. Self-ratings made during the interview indicated, as expected, that self-description in the former group was significantly more positive than that found in the latter. More important, after the interview had been completed half the subjects in each of the groups found that the interviewer had reacted favorably toward them, whereas the remainder were led to believe that the trainee had been unimpressed. Subjects were then asked to assess the honesty of their self-ratings during the interview.

25 Thibaut, J. W. and Kelley, H. H., *The Social Psychology of Groups,* New York: John Wiley and Sons, 1959.
26 Gergen, K. J. and Gibbs, Margaret G., Social expectancy and self-presentation in a status hierarchy. Paper presented at the 1965 meetings of the American Psychological Association.
27 Jones, E. E., Gergen, K. J., and Davis, K. E., Some determinants of reactions to being approved or disapproved as a person, *Psychological Monographs,* 1962, Whole No. 521.

The results revealed that those subjects who had both engaged in dissimulation and been favorably received felt their self-descriptions had been quite honest. Their honesty ratings did not differ from those made by subjects who had originally been asked to be honest, and differed significantly from the ratings made by the ingratiating subjects who had incurred disfavor. In essence, the findings strongly suggest that one's perception of his own identity in a situation may be quite affected by extrinsic influences. In this case, subjects seemed to distort their feelings about what constituted authentic behavior in a highly pragmatic way. That which produced the more positive results was felt to be the "real self."

A second study[28] penetrated such influences more directly. In this case, subjects were asked to formulate a talk about themselves which would gain the positive regard of a prospective employer. They were further encouraged to inflate this self-picture as much as needed in order to be successful. Half the participants subsequently delivered these speeches, and the others remained silent. Following the speech-making (and active role-playing for half the subjects) all were asked to rate themselves as honestly as possible on a self-esteem measure. This measure had also been administered some weeks prior to the experiment. An examination of self-esteem change revealed that both groups experienced an equally enhanced state of self-esteem, and for both groups such changes exceeded those found in a nonspeech-making control group. In effect, the subjective rehearsal of a given presentation, whether or not buttressed by active behavior, may alter a person's feelings about himself in a situation.

Scanning the results of the various studies described, what common threads can be identified? In light of the arguments developed in earlier sections of this paper, the work on self-presentation would strongly suggest the following:

1. The prevalent view that the normal behavior of individuals tends toward consistency is misconceived. If anything, the studies cited indicate the extreme ease with which a person can be caused to contradict himself. And we are not speaking here of differences in kind or type of behavior. A person's dishonesty in one

situation is not necessarily inconsistent with his affability in another, nor does his occupational role necessarily contradict his role as father. Rather, we have seen that along the single and very central dimension of self-esteem, a person will shift in either a more positive or negative direction depending on situational influence.

Of course it is quite possible that our daily perceptions of others as consistent are not entirely erroneous. It seems quite likely, however, that to some degree we perceive consistency because with most social relationships we provide a constant stimulus value. Depending on the way we perceive a given person and the circumstances surrounding the relationship, we may provide a self-picture which remains relatively stable and coherent. This self-picture may have constant effects on the other's behavior. Remembering that an identical process may characterize the other's behavior at the same time, relationships may be subject to a process of mutual jockeying and crystallization of social identities. Once out of the relationship, however, the "personality" of each participant may be unrecognizable.

2. The view that a person has a consistent and stabilized image of himself, and will always recognize behavior which is discrepant from this image as alien, is in need of modification. To be sure, there are instances in which a person may discern that his actions and feelings are incompatible. However, the circumstances provoking such experiences may have to involve rather dramatic social dislocation.

The above research does suggest that transitions from one relationship to another may be accompanied by a process of *self-adaptation*. Such a process would cause a person's subjective feelings of identity to become adapted to and cohere with the circumstances of any new relationship. The person's own behavior, his thoughts about his behavior, and reinforcement received from others may all contribute to this type of adaptation. The net result is a reduction in the potential descrepancy between covert feelings and overt behavior, and thus of alienation from behavior. Such a process would allow for behavioral inconsistency without parallel feelings on the subjective level.

3. The popular notion of the self-concept as a unified, consistent, or perceptually "whole" psychological structure is possibly ill-conceived. Such a notion is simply not supported

[28] Gergen, K. J. and Gibbs, Margaret G., Role playing and modifying the self-concept. Paper presented at the 1965 meetings of the Eastern Psychological Association.

by the findings related to the above described process of self-adaptation. A revision of the construct of self seems in order, and such a revision might profitably be directed toward a theory of *multiple selves*. In lieu of *the* self-concept, a process of self-conception will ultimately be necessary.

III

Having reviewed a body of evidence which strongly suggests that consistency, either in thought or action, does not constitute the normal state of affairs, we are now in a better position to return to the problem of ethics. As pointed out earlier, both people in general and behavioral scientists in particular are prone to view consistency as a desirable state, and to reward others' behavior accordingly. What costs are incurred through the perpetuation of such and ethic? What are the repercussions of such sanctions for the psychological state of the individual? Several considerations loom as important.

For one, a demand for thoroughgoing consistency would fly in the face of a major mode of social adaptation. In would essentially freeze the individual personality in such a way that the person would fail to meet the requisites of a changing social environment. To be continuously serious, light-hearted, understanding, domineering, or the like, will reduce one's option for behavior and limit his potential for being within situations which require the opposite characteristics. Ludwig[29] has even pointed out that active dissimulation and lying may be occasionally necessary and ethically permissible. And this is also to say that a prevailing need for achievement, need for positive regard, need for cognitive clarity, or any other of a host of needs or traits posited by personality theorists, will only be adaptive within a delimited set of relationships. Even the designation that a person is higher or lower on such and such a trait is mistaken if meant to imply that he does not often manifest the potential for the obverse of the designation.

It should be understood, however, that this is not to advocate a simple, chameleon-like approach to social interaction. Rather, it is to rely on the human capacity for rich and varied behavior, and on the fact that antithetical behavior may be enacted without losing one's feelings of honesty with self or with others.

It also seems that the more "natural" state of the organism is one which includes numerous disparities and contradicting tendencies. Freud came very close to making the same point in positing the *id,* that teeming repository of irrational and incompatible motives, as the basic given in personality structure. Of course, the argument need not be confined to a basic set of instincts. For any capacity possessed by the person, be it love, pain, lust, trust, nurturance, and so on, there exists the capacity and in some cases the need for its opposite. And too, polar capacities and feelings may exist coincidentally in the same relationship. From this point of view any strain toward consistency would appear to exist as an artificial overlay, fostered perhaps by a series of culturally specific learning experiences. Although being consistent may certainly be functional in some situations, in its most stringent form the overlay may well prevent the person from thoroughly partaking of the range and intensity of experiences potentially available to him.

If inconsistency can be considered a more intrinsically "natural" state, one wonders about the degree of frustration and emotional consternation generated in the attempt to bend oneself to the ethic. During the period of adolescence, for example, the individual may be particularly sensitive to the incompatibles in his life. Might it not be better to teach acceptance of the paradoxical than to require as a "mark of maturity" that the individual hang his identity on a limited set of his capacities for being? It also seems that internal demands and guilt feelings in the service of a consistency principle may constitute an appropriate context for generating repression. For example, it seems clear that the great anxiety many persons have about homosexuality is based on the assumption that one is *either* heterosexual *or* homosexual. If a person is unable to cope with or tolerate personal diversities, repression of its source could well result.

These arguments are, of course, quite tentative and should not be understood as advocating the abolishment of all consistent behavior. Of course, the commitment made to certain kinds of relationships demands consistency in certain realms of behavior. Many of a person's dearest experiences hinge on the establishment of trust within a relationship. And, as pointed out earlier, if everyone were

29 Ludwig, A. M., *The Importance of Lying,* Springfield, Ill.: Charles C. Thomas, 1965.

at all times acting unpredictably, what we know as "organized society" would cease to exist. However, personal consistency and stability may well be the by-products of most viable relationships—at least, within the relationships themselves. It is the expectation and demand for consistency across relationships which looms as most damaging to the individual. Quite probably persons vary with respect to their adherence to a principle of consistency. In light of these various arguments, future research might well be directed toward understanding the consequences of variations in this orientation.

Chapter 31 On Face-Work: An Analysis of Ritual Elements in Social Interaction*

ERVING GOFFMAN

Every person lives in a world of social encounters, involving him either in face-to-face or mediated contact with other participants. In each of these contacts, he tends to act out what is sometimes called a *line*—that is, a pattern of verbal and nonverbal acts by which he expresses his view of the situation and through this his evaluation of the participants, especially himself. Regardless of whether a person intends to take a line, he will find that he has done so in effect. The other participants will assume that he has more or less willfully taken a stand, so that if he is to deal with their response to him he must take into consideration the impression they have possibly formed of him.

The term *face* may be defined as the positive social value a person effectively claims for himself by the line others assume he has taken during a particular contact.[1] Face is an image of self delineated in terms of approved social attributes—albeit an image that others may share, as when a person makes a good showing for his profession or religion by making a good showing for himself.

A person tends to experience an immediate emotional response to the face which a contact with others allows him; he cathects his face; his "feelings" become attached to it. If the encounter sustains an image of him that he has long taken for granted, he probably will have few feelings about the matter. If events establish a face for him that is better than he might have expected, he is likely to "feel good"; if his ordinary expectations are not fulfilled, one expects that he will "feel bad" or "feel hurt."

In general, a person's attachment to a particular face, coupled with the ease with which disconfirming information can be conveyed by himself and others, provides one reason why he finds that participation in any contact with others is a commitment. A person will also have feelings about the face sustained for the other participants, and while these feelings may differ in quantity and direction from those he has for his own face, they constitute an involvement in the face of others that is as immediate and spontaneous as the involvement he has in his own face. One's own face and the face of others are constructs of the same order; it is the rules of the group and the definition of the situation which determine how much feeling one is to have for face and how this

SOURCE. Erving Goffman, "On Face-Work: An Analysis of Ritual Elements in Social Interaction," from *Psychiatry: Journal for the Study of Interpersonal Processes,* **18** (August 1955), pp. 213–231. Reprinted by special permission of The William Alanson White Psychiatric Foundation, Inc. Copyright 1955 by The William Alanson White Psychiatric Foundation, Inc.

* This paper was written at the University of Chicago; for financial support in writing it, I am indebted to a U. S. Public Health Grant [No. M702(6) MH(5)] for a study of the characteristics of social interaction of individuals, headed by Dr. William Soskin of the Department of Psychology, University of Chicago.
[1] For discussions of the Chinese conception of face, see the following: Hsien Chin Hu, "The Chinese Concept of 'Face,'" *Amer. Anthropologist,* **46** (1944), pp. 45–64. Martin C. Yang, *A Chinese Village,* New York, Columbia Univ. Press, 1945, pp. 167–172. J. Macgowan, *Men and Manners of Modern China,* London, Unwin, 1912, pp. 301–312. Arthur H. Smith, *Chinese Characteristics,* New York, Fleming H. Revell Co., 1894, pp. 16–18. For a comment on the American Indian conception of face, see Marcel Mauss, *The Gift* (Ian Cunnison, tr.), London, Cohen and West, 1954, p. 38.

feeling is to be distributed among the faces involved.

A person may be said to *have,* or *be in,* or *maintain* face when the line he effectively takes presents an image of him that is internally consistent, that is supported by judgments and evidence conveyed by other participants, and that is confirmed by evidence conveyed through impersonal agencies in the situation. At such times the person's face clearly is something that is not lodged in or on his body, but rather something that is diffusely located in the flow of events in the encounter and becomes manifest only when these events are read and interpreted for the appraisals expressed in them.

The line maintained by and for a person during contact with others tends to be of a legitimate institutionalized kind. During a contact of a particular type, an interactant of known or visible attributes can expect to be sustained in a particular face and can feel that it is morally proper that this should be so. Given his attributes and the conventionalized nature of the encounter, he will find a small choice of lines will be open to him and a small choice of faces will be waiting for him. Further, on the basis of a few known attributes, he is given the responsibility of possessing a vast number of others. His coparticipants are not likely to be conscious of the character of many of these attributes until he acts perceptibly in such a way as to discredit his possession of them; then everyone becomes conscious of these attributes and assumes that he willfully gave a false impression of possessing them.

Thus while concern for face focuses the attention of the person on the current activity, he must, to maintain face in this activity, take into consideration his place in the social world beyond it. A person who can maintain face in the current situation is someone who abstained from certain actions in the past that would have been difficult to face up to later. In addition, he fears loss of face now partly because the others may take this as a sign that consideration for his feelings need not be shown in future. There is nevertheless a limitation to this interdependence between the current situation and the wider social world: an encounter with people whom he will not have dealings with again leaves him free to take a high line that the future will discredit, or free to suffer humiliations that would make future dealings with them an embarrassing thing to have to face.

A person may be said to *be in wrong face* when information is brought forth in some way about his social worth which cannot be integrated, even with effort, into the line that is being sustained for him. A person may be said to *be out of face* when he participates in a contact with others without having ready a line of the kind participants in such situations are expected to take. The intent of many pranks is to lead a person into showing a wrong face or no face, but there will also be serious occasions, of course, when he will find himself expressively out of touch with the situation.

When a person senses that he is in face, he typically responds with feelings of confidence and assurance. Firm in the line he is taking, he feels that he can hold his head up and openly present himself to others. He feels some security and some relief—as he also can when the others feel he is in wrong face but successfully hide these feelings from him.

When a person is in wrong face or out of face, expressive events are being contributed to the encounter which cannot be readily woven into the expressive fabric of the occasion. Should he sense that he is in wrong face or out of face, he is likely to feel ashamed and inferior because of what has happened to the activity on his account and because of what may happen to his reputation as a participant. Further, he may feel bad because he had relied upon the encounter to support an image of self to which he has become emotionally attached and which he now finds threatened. Felt lack of judgmental support from the encounter may take him aback, confuse him, and momentarily incapacitate him as an interactant. His manner and bearing may falter, collapse, and crumble. He may become embarrased and chagrined; he may become shamefaced. The feeling, whether warranted or not, that he is perceived in a flustered state by others, and that he is presenting no usable line, may add further injuries to his feelings, just as his change from being in wrong face or out of face to being shamefaced can add further disorder to the expressive organization of the situation. Following common usage, I shall employ the term *poise* to refer to the capacity to suppress and conceal any tendency to become shamefaced during encounters with others.

In our Anglo-American society, as in some others, the phrase "to lose face" seems to mean to be in wrong face, to be out of face, or to be shamefaced. The phrase "to save one's face" appears to refer to the process by which the person sustains an impression for others that he has not lost face. Following Chinese usage, one can say that "to give face" is to arrange for another to take a better line than he might otherwise have been able to take,[2] the other thereby gets face given him, this being one way in which he can gain face.

As an aspect of the social code of any social circle, one may expect to find an understanding as to how far a person should go to save his face. Once he takes on a self-image expressed through face he will be expected to live up to it. In different ways in different societies he will be required to show self-respect, abjuring certain actions because they are above or beneath him, while forcing himself to perform others even though they cost him dearly. By entering a situation in which he is given a face to maintain, a person takes on the responsibility of standing guard over the flow of events as they pass before him. He must ensure that a particular *expressive order* is sustained— an order which regulates the flow of events, large or small, so that anything that appears to be expressed by them will be consistent with his face. When a person manifests these compunctions primarily from duty to himself, one speaks in our society of pride; when he does so because of duty to wider social units, and receives support from these units in doing so, one speaks of honor. When these compunctions have to do with postural things, with expressive events derived from the way in which the person handles his body, his emotions, and the things with which he has physical contact, one speaks of dignity, this being an aspect of expressive control that is always praised and never studied. In any case, while his social face can be his most personal possession and the center of his security and pleasure, it is only on loan to him from society; it will be withdrawn unless he conducts himself in a way that is worthy of it. Approved attributes and their relation to face make of every man his own jailer; this is a fundamental social constraint even though each man may like his cell.

Just as the member of any group is expected to have self-respect, so also he is expected to sustain a standard of considerateness; he is expected to go to certain lengths to save the feelings and the face of others present, and he is expected to do this willingly and spontaneously because of emotional identification with the others and with their feelings.[3] In consequence, he is disinclined to witness the defacement of others.[4] The person who can witness another's humiliation and unfeelingly retain a cool countenance himself is said in our society to be "heartless," just as he who can unfeelingly participate in his own defacement is thought to be "shameless."

The combined effect of the rule of self-respect and the rule of considerateness is that the person tends to conduct himself during an encounter so as to maintain both his own face and the face of the other participants. This means that the line taken by each participant is usually allowed to prevail, and each participant is allowed to carry off the role he appears to have chosen for himself. A state where everyone temporarily accepts everyone else's line is established.[5] This kind of mutual accep-

---

[2] See, for example, Smith, reference footnote 1; p. 17.

[3] Of course, the more power and prestige the others have, the more a person is likely to show consideration for their feelings, as H. E. Dale suggests in *The Higher Civil Service of Great Britain,* Oxford, Oxford Univ. Press, 1941, p. 126*n.* "The doctrine of 'feelings' was expounded to me many years ago by a very eminent civil servant with a pretty taste in cynicism. He explained that the importance of feelings varies in close correspondence with the importance of the person who feels. If the public interest requires that a junior clerk should be removed from his post, no regard need be paid to his feelings: if it is a case of an Assistant Secretary, they must be carefully considered, within reason; if it is a Permanent Secretary, his feelings are a principal element in the situation, and only imperative public interest can override their requirements."

[4] Salesmen, especially street "stemmers," know that if they take a line that will be discredited unless the reluctant customer buys, the customer may be trapped by considerateness and buy in order to save the face of the salesman and prevent what would ordinarily result in a scene.

[5] Surface agreement in the assessment of social worth does not, of course, imply equality; the evaluation consensually sustained of one participant may be quite different from the one consensually sustained of another. Such agreement is also compatible with expression of differences of opinion between two participants, provided each of the disputants shows "respect" for the other, guiding the expression of disagreement so that it will convey an evaluation of the other that the other will be willing to convey about himself. Extreme cases are provided by wars, duels, and barroom fights, when these are of a gentlemanly kind, for they can be conducted under consensual auspices, with each protagonist guiding his action according to the rules of the game, thereby making it possible for his action to be interpreted as an expression of a fair player openly in combat with a fair opponent. In fact, the rules and etiquette

tance seems to be a basic structural feature of interaction, especially the interaction of face-to-face talk. It is typically a "working" acceptance, not a "real" one, since it tends to be based not on agreement of candidly expressed heartfelt evaluations, but upon a willingness to give temporary lip service to judgments with which the participants do not really agree.

The mutual acceptance of lines has an important conservative effect upon encounters. Once the person initially presents a line, he and the others tend to build their later responses upon it, and in a sense become stuck with it. Should the person radically alter his line, or should it become discredited, then confusion results, for the participants will have prepared and committed themselves for actions that are now unsuitable.

Ordinarily, maintenance of face is a condition of interaction, not its objective. Usual objectives, such as gaining face for oneself, giving free expression to one's true beliefs, introducing depreciating information about the others, or solving problems and performing tasks, are typically pursued in such a way as to be consistent with the maintenance of face. To study face-saving is to study the traffic rules of social interaction; one learns about the code the person adheres to in his movement across the paths and designs of others, but not where he is going, or why he wants to get there. One does not even learn why he is ready to follow the code, for a large number of different motives can equally lead him to do so. He may want to save his own face because of his emotional attachment to the image of self which it expresses, because of his pride or honor, because of the power his presumed status allows him to exert over the other participants, and so on. He may want to save the others' face because of his emotional attachment to an image of them, or because he feels that his coparticipants have a moral right to this protection, or because he wants to avoid the hostility that may be directed toward him if they lose their face. He may feel that an assumption has been made that he is the sort of person who shows compassion and sympathy toward others, so that to retain his own face, he may feel obliged to be considerate of the line taken by the other participants.

of any game can be analyzed as a means by which the image of a fair player can be expressed, just as the image of a fair player can be analyzed as a means by which the rules and etiquette of a game are sustained.

By *face-work* I mean to designate the actions taken by a person to make whatever he is doing consistent with face. Face-work serves to counteract "incidents"—that is, events whose effective symbolic implications threaten face. Thus poise is one important type of face-work, for through poise the person controls his embarrassment and hence the embarrassment that he and others might have over his embarrassment. Whether or not the full consequences of face-saving actions are known to the person who employs them, they often become habitual and standardized practices; they are like traditional plays in a game or traditional steps in a dance. Each person, subculture, and society seems to have its own characteristic repertoire of face-saving practices. It is to this repertoire that people partly refer when they ask what a person or culture is "really" like. And yet the particular set of practices stressed by particular persons or groups seems to be drawn from a single logically coherent framework of possible practices. It is as if face, by its very nature, can be saved only in a certain number of ways, and as if each social grouping must make its selections from this single matrix of possibilities.

The members of every social circle may be expected to have some knowledge of face-work and some experience in its use. In our society, this kind of capacity is sometimes called tact, *savoir-faire,* diplomacy, or social skill. Variation in social skill pertains more to the efficacy of face-work than to the frequency of its application, for almost all acts involving others are modified, prescriptively or proscriptively, by considerations of face.

If a person is to employ his repertoire of face-saving practices, obviously he must first become aware of the interpretations that others may have placed upon his acts and the interpretations that he ought perhaps to place upon theirs. In other words, he must exercise perceptiveness,[6] But even if he is properly alive to symbolically conveyed judgments and is

[6] Presumably social skill and perceptiveness will be high in groups whose members frequently act as representatives of wider social units such as lineages or nations, for the player here is gambling with a face to which the feelings of many persons are attached. Similarly, one might expect social skill to be well developed among those of high station and those with whom they have dealings, for the more face an interactant has, the greater the number of events that may be inconsistent with it, and hence the greater the need for social skill to forestall or counteract these inconsistencies.

socially skilled, he must yet be willing to exercise his perceptiveness and his skill; he must, in short, be prideful and considerate. Admittedly, of course, the possession of perceptiveness and social skill so often leads to their application that in our society terms such as politeness or tact fail to distinguish between the inclination to exercise such capacities and the capacities themselves.

I have already said that the person will have two points of view—a defensive orientation toward saving his own face and a protective orientation toward saving the others' face. Some practices will be primarily defensive and others primarily protective, although in general one may expect these two perspectives to be taken at the same time. In trying to save the face of others, the person must choose a tack that will not lead to loss of his own; in trying to save his own face, he must consider the loss of face that his action may entail for others.

In many societies there is a tendency to distinguish three levels of responsibility which a person may have for a threat to face that his actions have created. First, he may appear to have acted innocently; his offense seems to be unintended and unwitting, and those who perceive his act can feel that he would have attempted to avoid it had he foreseen its offensive consequences. In our society one calls such threats to face *faux pas, gaffes,* boners, or bricks. Secondly, the offending person may appear to have acted maliciously and spitefully, with the intention of causing open insult. Thirdly, there are incidental offenses; these arise as an unplanned but sometimes anticipated by-product of action—action which the offender performs in spite of its offensive consequences, although not out of spite. From the point of view of a particular participant, these three types of threat can be introduced by the participant himself against his own face, by himself against the face of the others, by the others against their own face, or by the others against himself. Thus the person may find himself in many different relations to a threat to face. If he is to handle himself and others well in all contingencies, he will have to have a repertoire of face-saving practices for each of these possible relations to threat.

THE BASIC KINDS OF FACE-WORK

The Avoidance Process

The surest way for a person to prevent threats to his face is to avoid contacts in which these threats are likely to occur. In all societies one can observe this in the avoidance relationship[7] and in the tendency for certain delicate transactions to be conducted by go-betweens.[8] Summarily, in many societies, members know the value of voluntarily making a gracious withdrawal before an anticipated threat to face has had a chance to occur.[9]

Once the person does chance an encounter, other kinds of avoidance practices come into play. As defensive measures, he keeps off topics and away from activities which would lead to the expression of information that is inconsistent with the line he is maintaining. At opportune moments he will change the topic of conversation or the direction of activity. He will often present initially a front of diffidence and composure, suppressing any show of feeling until he has found out what kind of line the others will be ready to support for him. Any claims regarding self may be made with belittling modesty, with strong qualifications, or with a note of unseriousness; by hedging in these ways he will have prepared a self for himself that will not be discredited by exposure, personal failure, or the unanticipated acts of others. And if he does not hedge his claims about self, he will at least attempt to be realistic about them, knowing that otherwise events may discredit him and make him lose face.

Certain protective maneuvers are as common as these defensive ones. The person shows respect and politeness, making sure to extend to others any ceremonial treatment which might be their due. He employs discretion; he leaves unstated facts which might implicitly or explicitly contradict and embarrass the positive

---

[7] In our own society an illustration of avoidance is found in the middle- and upper-class Negro who avoids certain face-to-face contacts with whites in order to protect the self-evaluation projected by his clothes and manner. See, for example, Charles Johnson, *Patterns of Negro Segregation,* New York, Harper, 1943, ch. 13. The function of avoidance in maintaining the kinship system in small preliterate societies might be taken as a particular illustration of the same general theme.
[8] An illustration is given by K. S. Latourette, *The Chinese: Their History and Culture,* New York, Macmillan, 1942: "A neighbor or a group of neighbors may tender their good offices in adjusting a quarrel in which each antagonist would be sacrificing his face by taking the first step in approaching the other. The wise intermediary can effect the reconciliation while preserving the dignity of both" (vol. 2: p. 211).
[9] In an unpublished paper Harold Garfinkel has suggested that when the person finds that he has lost face in a conversational encounter, he may feel a desire to disappear or "drop through the

claims made by others.[10] He employs circumlocutions and deceptions, phrasing his replies with careful ambiguity so that the others' face is preserved even if their welfare is not.[11] He employs courtesies, making slight modifications of his demands on or appraisals of the others so that they will be able to define the situation as one in which their self-respect is not threatened. In making a belittling demand upon the others, or in imputing uncomplimentary attributes to them, he may employ a joking manner, allowing them to take the line that they are good sports, able to relax from their ordinary standards of pride and honor. And before engaging in a potentially offensive act, he may provide explanations as to why the others ought not to be affronted by it. For example, if he knows that it will be necessary to withdraw from the encounter before it has terminated, he may tell the others in advance that it is necessary for him to leave, so that they will have faces that are prepared for it. But neutralizing the potentially offensive act need not be done verbally; he may wait for a propitious moment or

---

floor," and that this may involve a wish not only to conceal loss of face but also to return magically to a point in time when it would have been possible to save face by avoiding the encounter.

[10] When the person knows the others well, he will know what issues ought not to be raised and what situations the others ought not to be placed in, and he will be free to introduce matters at will in all other areas. When the others are strangers to him, he will often reverse the formula, restricting himself to specific areas he knows are safe. On these occasions, as Simmel suggests, ". . . discretion consists by no means only in the respect for the secret of the other, for his specific will to conceal this or that from us, but in staying away from the knowledge of all that the other does not expressly reveal to us." See *The Sociology of Georg Simmel,* Kurt H. Wolff, tr. and ed., Glencoe, Ill., Free Press, 1950, pp. 320–332.

[11] The Western traveler used to complain that the Chinese could never be trusted to say what they meant but always said what they felt their Western listener wanted to hear. The Chinese used to complain that the Westerner was brusque, boorish, and unmannered. In terms of Chinese standards, presumably, the conduct of a Westerner is so gauche that he creates an emergency, forcing the Asian to forgo any kind of direct reply in order to rush in with a remark that might rescue the Westerner from the compromising position in which he had placed himself. (See Smith, reference footnote 1; ch. 8, "The Talent for Indirection.") This is an instance of the important group of misunderstandings which arise during interaction between persons who come from groups with different ritual standards.

natural break—for example, in conversation, a momentary lull when no one speaker can be affronted—and then leave, in this way using the context instead of his words as a guarantee of inoffensiveness.

When a person fails to prevent an incident, he can still attempt to maintain the fiction that no threat to face has occurred. The most blatant example of this is found where the person acts as if an event which contains a threatening expression has not occurred at all. He may apply this studied nonobservance to his own acts—as when he does not by any outward sign admit that his stomach is rumbling—or to the acts of others, as when he does not "see" that another has stumbled.[12] Social life in mental hospitals owes much to this process; patients employ it in regard to their own peculiarities, and visitors employ it, often with tenuous desperation, in regard to patients. In general, tactful blindness of this kind is applied only to events which, if perceived at all, could be perceived and interpreted only as threats to face.

A more important, less spectacular kind of tactful overlooking is practiced when a person openly acknowledges an incident as an event that has occurred, but not as an event that contains a threatening expression. If he is not the one who is responsible for the incident, then his blindness will have to be supported by his forbearance; if he is the doer of the threatening deed, then his blindness will have to be supported by his willingness to seek a way of dealing with the matter which leaves him dangerously dependent upon the cooperative forbearance of the others.

Another kind of avoidance occurs when a person loses control of his expressions during an encounter. At such times he may try not so much to overlook the incident as to hide or conceal his activity in some way, thus making it possible for the others to avoid some of the difficulties created by a participant who has not maintained face. Correspondingly, when a person is caught out of face because he had not expected to be thrust into interaction, or because strong feelings have disrupted his expressive mask, the others may protectively turn away from him or his activity for a moment, to give him time to assemble himself.

---

[12] A pretty example of this is found in parade-ground etiquette which may oblige those in a parade to treat anyone who faints as if he were not present at all.

The Corrective Process

When the participants in an undertaking or encounter fail to prevent the occurrence of an event that is expressively incompatible with the judgments of social worth that are being maintained, and when the event is of the kind that is difficult to overlook, then the participants are likely to give it accredited status as an incident—to ratify it as a threat that deserves direct official attention—and to proceed to try to correct for its effects. At this point one or more participants find themselves in an established state of ritual disequilibrium or disgrace, and an attempt must be made to re-establish a satisfactory ritual state for them. I use the term *ritual* because I am dealing with acts through whose symbolic component the actor shows how worthy he is of respect or how worthy he feels others are of it. The imagery of equilibrium is apt here because the length and intensity of the corrective effort is nicely adapted to the persistence and intensity of the threat.[13] One's face, then, is a sacred thing, and the expressive order required to sustain it is therefore a ritual one.

The sequence of acts set in motion by an acknowledged threat to face, and terminating in the re-establishment of ritual equilibrium, I shall call an *interchange*.[14] Defining a message or move as everything conveyed by an actor during a turn at taking action, one can say that an interchange will involve two or more moves and two or more participants. Obvious examples in our society may be found in the sequence of "Excuse me" and "Certainly," and

in the exchange of presents or visits. The interchange seems to be a basic concrete unit of social activity and provides one natural empirical way to study interaction of all kinds. Face-saving practices can be usefully classified according to their position in the natural sequence of moves which comprise this unit. Aside from the event which introduces the need for a corrective interchange, four classic moves seem to be involved.

There is, first, the challenge, by which participants take on the responsibility of calling attention to the misconduct; by implication they suggest that the threatened claims are to stand firm and that the threatening event itself will have to be brought back into line.

The second move consists of the offering, whereby a participant, typically the offender, is given a chance to correct for the offense and re-establish the expressive order. Some classic ways of making this move are available. On the one hand, an attempt can be made to show that what admittedly appeared to be a threatening expression is really a meaningless event, or an unintentional act, or a joke not meant to be taken seriously, or an unavoidable, "understandable" product of extenuating circumstances. On the other hand, the meaning of the event may be granted and effort concentrated on the creator of it. Information may be provided to show that the creator was under the influence of something and not himself, or that he was under the command of somebody else and not acting for himself. When a person claims that an act was meant in jest, he may go on and claim that the self that seemed to lie behind the act was also projected as a joke. When a person suddenly finds that he has demonstrably failed in capacities that the others assumed him to have and to claim for himself—such as the capacity to spell, to perform minor tasks, to talk without malapropisms, and so on—he may quickly add, in a serious or unserious way, that he claims these incapacities as part of his self. The meaning of the threatening incident thus stands, but it can now be incorporated smoothly into the flow of expressive events.

As a supplement to or substitute for the strategy of redefining the offensive act or himself, the offender can follow two other procedures: he can provide compensations to the injured—when it is not his own face that he has threatened; or he can provide punishment, penance, and expiation for himself. These are

---

[13] This kind of imagery is one that social anthropologists seem to find naturally fitting. Note, for example, the implications of the following statement by Margaret Mead in her "Kinship in the Admiralty Islands," *Anthropological Papers of the American Museum of Natural History,* **34,** pp. 183–358: "If a husband beats his wife, custom demands that she leave him and go to her brother, real or officiating, and remain a length of time commensurate with the degree of her offended dignity" (p. 274).

[14] The notion of interchange is drawn in part from Eliot D. Chapple, "Measuring Human Relations," *Genetic Psychol. Monographs,* **22** (1940), pp. 3–147, especially pp. 26–30, and from A. B. Horsfall and C. A. Arensberg, "Teamwork and Productivity in a Shoe Factory," *Human Organization,* **8** (1949), pp. 13–25, especially p. 19. For further material on the interchange as a unit see E. Goffman, "Communication Conduct in an Island Community," unpublished Ph.D. dissertation, Department of Sociology, University of Chicago, 1953, especially chs. 12 and 13, pp. 165–195.

important moves or phrases in the ritual interchange. Even though the offender may fail to prove his innocence, he can suggest through these means that he is now a renewed person, a person who has paid for his sin against the expressive order and is once more to be trusted in the judgmental scene. Further, he can show that he does not treat the feelings of the others lightly, and that if their feelings have been injured by him, however innocently, he is prepared to pay a price for his action. Thus he assures the others that they can accept his explanations without this acceptance constituting a sign of weakness and a lack of pride on their part. Also, by his treatment of himself, by his self-castigation, he shows that he is clearly aware of the kind of crime he would have committed had the incident been what it first appeared to be, and that he knows the kind of punishment that ought to be accorded to one who would commit such a crime. The suspected person thus shows that he is thoroughly capable of taking the role of the others toward his own activity, that he can still be used as a responsible participant in the ritual process, and that the rules of conduct which he appears to have broken are still sacred, real, and unweakened. An offensive act may arouse anxiety about the ritual code; the offender allays this anxiety by showing that both the code and he as an upholder of it are still in working order.

After the challenge and the offering have been made, the third move can occur: the persons to whom the offering is made can accept it as a satisfactory means of re-establishing the expressive order and the faces supported by this order. Only then can the offender cease the major part of his ritual offering.

In the terminal move of the interchange, the forgiven person conveys a sign of gratitude to those who have given him the indulgence of forgiveness.

The phases of the corrective process—challenge, offering, acceptance, and thanks—provide a model for interpersonal ritual behavior, but a model that may be departed from in significant ways. For example, the offended parties may give the offender a chance to initiate the offering on his own before a challenge is made and before they ratify the offense as an incident. This is a common courtesy, extended on the assumption that the recipient will introduce a self-challenge. Further, when the offended persons accept the corrective offering, the offender may suspect

that this has been grudgingly done from tact, and so he may volunteer additional corrective offerings, not allowing the matter to rest until he has received a second or third acceptance of his repeated apology. Or the offended persons may tactfully take over the role of the offender and volunteer excuses for him that will, perforce, be acceptable to the offended persons.

An important departure from the standard corrective cycle occurs when a challenged offender patently refuses to heed the warning and continues with his offending behavior, instead of setting the activity to rights. This move shifts the play back to the challengers. If they countenance the refusal to meet their demands, then it will be plain that their challenge was a bluff and that the bluff has been called. This is an untenable position; a face for themselves cannot be derived from it, and they are left to bluster. To avoid this fate, some classic moves are open to them. For instance, they can resort to tactless, violent retaliation, destroying either themselves or the person who had refused to heed their warning. Or they can withdraw from the undertaking in a visible huff —righteously indignant, outraged, but confident of ultimate vindication. Both tacks provide a way of denying the offender his status as an interactant, and hence denying the reality of the offensive judgment he has made. Both strategies are ways of salvaging face, but for all concerned the costs are usually high. It is partly to forestall such scenes that an offender is usually quick to offer apologies; he does not want the affronted persons to trap themselves into the obligation to resort to desperate measures.

It is plain that emotions play a part in these cycles of response, as when anguish is expressed because of what one has done to another's face, or anger because of what has been done to one's own. I want to stress that these emotions function as moves, and fit so precisely into the logic of the ritual game that it would seem difficult to understand them without it.[15] In fact, spontaneously expressed feelings are likely to fit into the formal pattern

---

[15] Even when a child demands something and is refused, he is likely to cry and sulk not as an irrational expression of frustration but as a ritual move, conveying that he already has a face to lose and that its loss is not to be permitted lightly. Sympathetic parents may even allow for such display, seeing in these crude strategies the beginnings of a social self.

of the ritual interchange more elegantly than consciously designed ones.

MAKING POINTS—THE AGGRESSIVE USE OF FACE-WORK

Every face-saving practice which is allowed to neutralize a particular threat opens up the possibility that the threat will be willfully introduced for what can be safely gained by it. If a person knows that his modesty will be answered by others' praise of him, he can fish for compliments. If his own appraisal of self will be checked against incidental events, then he can arrange for favorable incidental events to appear. If others are prepared to overlook an affront to them and act forbearantly, or to accept apologies, then he can rely on this as a basis for safely offending them. He can attempt by sudden withdrawal to force the others into a ritually unsatisfactory state, leaving them to flounder in an interchange that cannot readily be completed. Finally, at some expense to himself, he can arrange for the others to hurt his feelings, thus forcing them to feel guilt, remorse, and sustained ritual disequilibrium.[16]

When a person treats face-work not as something he need be prepared to perform, but rather as something that others can be counted on to perform or to accept, then an encounter or an undertaking becomes less a scene of mutual considerateness than an arena in which a contest or match is held. The purpose of the game is to preserve everyone's line from an inexcusable contradiction, while scoring as many points as possible against one's adversaries and making as many gains as possible for oneself. An audience to the struggle is almost a necessity. The general method is for the person to introduce favorable facts about himself and unfavorable facts about the others in such a way that the only reply the others will be able to think up will be one that terminates the interchange in a grumble, a meager excuse, a face-saving I-can-take-a-joke laugh, or an empty stereotyped comeback of the "Oh yeah?" or "That's what you think" variety. The losers in such cases will have to cut their losses,

tacitly grant the loss of a point, and attempt to do better in the next interchange. Points made by allusion to social class status are sometimes called snubs; those made by allusions to moral respectability are sometimes called digs; in either case one deals with a capacity at what is sometimes called "bitchiness."

In aggressive interchanges the winner not only succeeds in introducing information favorable to himself and unfavorable to the others, but also demonstrates that as interactant he can handle himself better than his adversaries. Evidence of this capacity is often more important than all the other information the person conveys in the interchange, so that the introduction of a "crack" in verbal interaction tends to imply that the initiator is better at footwork than those who must suffer his remarks. However, if they succeed in making a successful parry of the thrust and then a successful riposte, the instigator of the play must not only face the disparagement with which the others have answered him but also accept the fact that his assumption of superiority in footwork has proven false. He is made to look foolish; he loses face. Hence it is always a gamble to "make a remark." The tables can be turned and the aggressor can lose more than he could have gained had his move won the point. Successful ripostes or comebacks in our society are sometimes called squelches or toppers; theoretically it would be possible for a squelch to be squelched, a topper to be topped, and a riposte to be parried with a counterriposte, but except in staged interchanges this third level of successful action seems rare.[17]

THE CHOICE OF APPROPRIATE FACE-WORK

When an incident occurs, the person whose face is threatened may attempt to reinstate the ritual order by means of one kind of strategy, while the other participants may desire or expect a practice of a different type to be employed. When, for example, a minor mishap

---

[16] The strategy of maneuvering another into a position where he cannot right the harm he has done is very commonly employed but nowhere with such devotion to the ritual model of conduct as in revengeful suicide. See, for example, M. D. W. Jeffreys, "Samsonic Suicide, or Suicide of Revenge Among Africans," *African Studies,* **11** (1952), pp. 118–122.

[17] In board and card games the player regularly takes into consideration the possible responses of his adversaries to a play that he is about to make, and even considers the possibility that his adversaries will know that he is taking such precautions. Conversational play is by comparison surprisingly impulsive; people regularly make remarks about others present without carefully designing their remarks to prevent a successful comeback. Similarly, while feinting and sandbagging are theoretical possibilities during talk, they seem to be little exploited.

occurs, momentarily revealing a person in wrong face or out of face, the others are often more willing and able to act blind to the discrepancy than is the threatened person himself. Often they would prefer him to exercise poise,[18] while he feels that he cannot afford to overlook what has happened to his face and so becomes apologetic and shamefaced, if he is the creator of the incident, or destructively assertive, if the others are responsible for it.[19] Yet on the other hand, a person may manifest poise when the others feel that he ought to have broken down into embarrassed apology—that he is taking undue advantage of their helpfulness by his attempts to brazen it out. Sometimes a person may himself be undecided as to which practice to employ, leaving the others in the embarrassing position of not knowing which tack they are going to have to follow. Thus when a person makes a slight *gaffe,* he and the others may become embarrassed not because of inability to handle such difficulties, but because for a moment no one knows whether the offender is going to act blind to the incident, or give it joking recognition, or employ some other face-saving practice.

COOPERATION IN FACE-WORK

When a face has been threatened, face-work must be done, but whether this is initiated and primarily carried through by the person whose

face is threatened, or by the offender, or by a mere witness,[20] is often of secondary importance. Lack of effort on the part of one person induces compensatory effort from others; a contribution by one person relieves the others of the task. In fact, there are many minor incidents in which the offender and the offended simultaneously attempt to initiate an apology.[21] Resolution of the situation to everyone's apparent satisfaction is the first requirement; correct apportionment of blame is typically a secondary consideration. Hence terms such as tact and *savior-faire* fail to distinguish whether it is the person's own face that his diplomacy saves or the face of the others. Similarly, terms such as *gaffe* and *faux pas* fail to specify whether it is the actor's own face he has threatened or the face of other participants. And it is understandable that if one person finds he is powerless to save his own face, the others seem especially bound to protect him. For example, in polite society, a handshake that perhaps should not have been extended becomes one that cannot be declined. Thus one accounts for the *noblesse oblige* through which those of high status are expected to curb their power of embarrassing their lessers,[22] as well as the fact

---

[18] Folklore imputes a great deal of poise to the upper classes. If there is truth in this belief it may lie in the fact that the upper-class person tends to find himself in encounters in which he outranks the other participants in ways additional to class. The ranking participant is often somewhat independent of the good opinion of the others and finds it practical to be arrogant, sticking to a face regardless of whether the encounter supports it. On the other hand, those who are in the power of a fellow-participant tend to be very much concerned with the valuation he makes of them or witnesses being made of them, and so find it difficult to maintain a slightly wrong face without becoming embarrassed and apologetic. It may be added that people who lack awareness of the symbolism in minor events may keep cool in difficult situations, showing poise that they do not really possess.

[19] Thus, in our society, when a person feels that others expect him to measure up to approved standards of cleanliness, tidiness, fairness, hospitality, generosity, affluence, and so on, or when he sees himself as someone who ought to maintain such standards, he may burden an encounter with extended apologies for his failings, while all along the other participants do not care about the standard, or do not believe the person is really lacking in it, or are convinced that he is lacking in it and see the apology itself as a vain effort at self-elevation.

[20] Thus one function of seconds in actual duels, as well as in figurative ones, is to provide an excuse for not fighting that both contestants can afford to accept.

[21] See, for instance, Jackson Toby, "Some Variables in Role Conflict Analysis" [*Social Forces,* **30** (1952), pp. 323–337]: "With adults there is less likelihood for essentially trivial issues to produce conflict. The automatic apology of two strangers who accidentally collide on a busy street illustrates the integrative function of etiquette. In effect, each of the parties to the collision says, 'I don't know whether I am responsible for this situation, but *if* I am, you have a right to be angry with me, a right that I pray you will not exercise.' By defining the situation as one in which both parties must abase themselves, society enables each to keep his self-respect. Each may feel in his heart of hearts, 'Why can't that stupid ass watch where he's going?' But overtly *each plays the role of the guilty party* whether he feels he has been miscast or not" (p. 325).

[22] Regardless of the person's relative social position, in one sense he has power over the other participants and they must rely upon his considerateness. When the others act toward him in some way, they presume upon a social relationship to him, since one of the things expressed by interaction is the relationship of the interactants. Thus they compromise themselves, for they place him in a position to discredit the claims they express as to his attitude toward them. Hence in response to claimed social relationships every person, of high estate or low, will be expected to exercise *noblesse oblige*

that the handicapped often accept courtesies that they can manage better without.

Since each participant in an undertaking is concerned, albeit for differing reasons, with saving his own face and the face of the others, then tacit cooperation will naturally arise so that the participants together can attain their shared but differently motivated objectives.

One common type of tacit cooperation in face-saving is the tact exerted in regard to face-work itself. The person not only defends his own face and protects the face of the others, but also acts so as to make it possible and even easy for the others to employ face-work for themselves and him. He helps them to help themselves and him. Social etiquette, for example, warns men against asking for New Year's Eve dates too early in the season, lest the girl find it difficult to provide a gentle excuse for refusing. This second-order tact can be further illustrated by the wide-spread practice of negative-attribute etiquette. The person who has an unapparent negatively valued attribute often finds it expedient to begin an encounter with an unobtrusive admission of his failing, especially with persons who are uninformed about him. The others are thus warned in advance against making disparaging remarks about his kind of person and are saved from the contradiction of acting in a friendly fashion to a person toward whom they are unwittingly being hostile. This strategy also prevents the others from automatically making assumptions about him which place him in a false position and saves him from painful forbearance or embarrassing remonstrances.

---

and refrain from exploiting the compromised position of the others.

Since social relationships are defined partly in terms of voluntary mutual aid, refusal of a request for assistance becomes a delicate matter, potentially destructive of the asker's face. Chester Holcombe, *The Real Chinaman* (New York, Dodd, Mead, 1895) provides a Chinese instance: "Much of the falsehood to which the Chinese as a nation are said to be addicted is a result of the demands of etiquette. A plain, frank 'no' is the height of discourtesy. Refusal or denial of any sort must be softened and toned down into an expression of regretted inability. Unwillingness to grant a favor is never shown. In place of it there is seen a chastened feeling of sorrow that unavoidable but quite imaginary circumstances render it wholly impossible. Centuries of practice in this form of evasion have made the Chinese matchlessly fertile in the invention and development of excuses. It is rare, indeed, that one is caught at a loss for a bit of artfully embroidered fiction with which to hide an unwelcome truth" (pp. 274–275).

Tact in regard to face-work often relies for its operation on a tacit agreement to do business through the language of hint—the language of innuendo, ambiguities, well-placed pauses, carefully worded jokes, and so on.[23] The rule regarding this unofficial kind of communication is that the sender ought not to act as if he had officially conveyed the message he has hinted at, while the recipients have the right and the obligation to act as if they have not officially received the message contained in the hint. Hinted communication, then, is deniable communication; it need not be faced up to. It provides a means by which the person can be warned that his current line or the current situation is leading to loss of face, without this warning itself becoming an incident.

Another form of tacit cooperation, and one that seems to be much used in many societies, is reciprocal self-denial. Often the person does not have a clear idea of what would be a just or acceptable apportionment of judgments during the occasion, and so he voluntarily deprives or depreciates himself while indulging and complimenting the others, in both cases carrying the judgments safely past what is likely to be just. The favorable judgments about himself he allows to come from the others; the unfavorable judgments of himself are his own contributions. This "after you, Alphonse" technique works, of course, because in depriving himself he can reliably anticipate that the others will compliment or indulge him. Whatever allocation of favors is eventually established, all participants are first given a chance to show that they are not bound or constrained by their own desires and expectations, that they have a properly modest view of themselves, and that they can be counted upon to support the ritual code. Negative bargaining, through which each participant tries to make the terms of trade more favorable to the other side, is another instance; as a form of exchange perhaps it is more widespread than the economist's kind.

A person's performance of face-work, extended by his tacit agreement to help others perform theirs, represents his willingness to abide by the ground rules of social interaction. Here is the hallmark of his socialization as an interactant. If he and the others were not

---

23 Useful comments on some of the structural roles played by unofficial communication can be found in a discussion of irony and banter in Tom Burns, "Friends, Enemies, and the Polite Fiction," *Amer. Sociol. Rev.,* **18** (1943), pp. 654–662.

socialized in this way, interaction in most societies and most situations would be a much more hazardous thing for feelings and faces. The person would find it impractical to be oriented to symbolically conveyed appraisals of social worth, or to be possessed of feelings— that is, it would be impractical for him to be a ritually delicate object. And as I shall suggest, if the person were not a ritually delicate object, occasions of talk could not be organized in the way they usually are. It is no wonder that trouble is caused by a person who cannot be relied upon to play the face-saving game.

THE RITUAL ROLES OF THE SELF

So far I have implicitly been using a double definition of self: the self as an image pieced together from the expressive implications of the full flow of events in an undertaking; and the self as a kind of player in a ritual game who copes honorably or dishonorably, diplomatically or undiplomatically, with the judgmental contingencies of the situation. A double mandate is involved. As sacred objects, men are subject to slights and profanation; hence as players of the ritual game they have had to lead themselves into duels, and wait for a round of shots to go wide of the mark before embracing their opponents. Here is an echo of the distinction between the value of a hand drawn at cards and the capacity of the person who plays it. This distinction must be kept in mind, even though it appears that once a person has gotten a reputation for good or bad play this reputation may become part of the face he must later play at maintaining.

Once the two roles of the self have been separated, one can look to the ritual code implicit in face-work to learn how the two roles are related. When a person is responsible for introducing a threat to another's face, he apparently has a right, within limits, to wriggle out of the difficulty by means of self-abasement. When performed voluntarily these indignities do not seem to profane his own image. It is as if he had the right of insulation and could castigate himself qua actor without injuring himself qua object of ultimate worth. By token of the same insulation he can belittle himself and modestly underplay his positive qualities, with the understanding that no one will take his statements as a fair representation of his sacred self. On the other hand, if he is forced against his will to treat himself in these ways, his face, his pride, and his honor will be seriously threatened. Thus, in terms of the ritual

code, the person seems to have a special license to accept mistreatment at his own hands that he does not have the right to accept from others. Perhaps this is a safe arrangement because he is not likely to carry this license too far, whereas the others, were they given this privilege, might be more likely to abuse it.

Further, within limits the person has a right to forgive other participants for affronts to his sacred image. He can forbearantly overlook minor slurs upon his face, and in regard to somewhat greater injuries he is the one person who is in a position to accept apologies on behalf of his sacred self. This is a relatively safe prerogative for the person to have in regard to himself, for it is one that is exercised in the interests of the others or of the undertaking. Interestingly enough, when the person commits a *gaffe* against himself, it is not he who has the license to forgive the event; only the others have that prerogative, and it is a safe prerogative for them to have because they can exercise it only in his interests or in the interests of the undertaking. One finds, then, a system of checks and balances by which each participant tends to be given the right to handle only those matters which he will have little motivation for mishandling. In short, the rights and obligations of an interactant are designed to prevent him from abusing his role as an object of sacred value.

SPOKEN INTERACTION

Most of what has been said so far applies to encounters of both an immediate and mediated kind, although in the latter the interaction is likely to be more attenuated, with each participant's line being gleaned from such things as written statements and work records. During direct personal contacts, however, unique informational conditions prevail and the significance of face becomes especially clear. The human tendency to use signs and symbols means that evidence of social worth and of mutual evaluations will be conveyed by very minor things, and these things will be witnessed, as will the fact that they have been witnessed. An unguarded glance, a momentary change in tone of voice, an ecological position taken or not taken, can drench a talk with judgmental significance. Therefore, just as there is no occasion of talk in which improper impressions could not intentionally or unintentionally arise, so there is no occasion of talk so trivial as not to require each participant to show serious concern with the way in which he handles himself and the others present. Ritual factors which are present in mediated contacts are here present in an extreme form.

In any society, whenever the physical possibility of spoken interaction arises, it seems that a system of practices, conventions, and procedural rules comes into play which functions as a means of guiding and organizing the flow of messages. An understanding will prevail as to when and where it will be permissible to initiate talk, among whom, and by means of what topics of conversation. A set of significant gestures is employed to initiate a spate of communication and as a means for the persons concerned to accredit each other as legitimate participants.[24] When this process of reciprocal ratification occurs, the persons so ratified are in what might be called a *state of talk*—that is, they have declared themselves officially open to one another for purposes of spoken communication and guarantee together to maintain a flow of words. A set of significant gestures is also employed by which one or more new participants can officially join the talk, by which one or more accredited participants can officially withdraw, and by which the state of talk can be terminated.

A single focus of thought and visual attention, and a single flow of talk, tends to be maintained and to be legitimated as officially representative of the encounter. The concerted and official visual attention of the participants tends to be transferred smoothly by means of formal or informal clearance cues, by which the current speaker signals that he is about to relinquish the floor and the prospective speaker signals a desire to be given the floor. An under-

standing will prevail as to how long and how frequently each participant is to hold the floor. The recipients convey to the speaker, by appropriate gestures, that they are according him their attention. Participants restrict their involvement in matters external to the encounter and observe a limit to involvement in any one message of the encounter, in this way ensuring that they will be able to follow along whatever direction the topic of conversation takes them. Interruptions and lulls are regulated so as not to disrupt the flow of messages. Messages that are not part of the officially accredited flow are modulated so as not to interfere seriously with the accredited messages. Nearby persons who are not participants visibly desist in some way from exploiting their communication position and also modify their own communication, if any, so as not to provide difficult interference. A particular ethos or emotional atmosphere is allowed to prevail. A polite accord is typically maintained, and participants who may be in real disagreement with one another give temporary lip service to views that bring them into agreement on matters of fact and principle. Rules are followed for smoothing out the transition, if any, from one topic of conversation to another.[25]

These rules of talk pertain not to spoken interaction considered as an ongoing process, but to *an* occasion of talk or episode of interaction as a naturally bounded unit. This unit consists of the total activity that occurs during the time that a given set of participants have accredited one another for talk and maintain a single moving focus of attention.[26]

The conventions regarding the structure of occasions of talk represent an effective solution to the problem of organizing a flow of spoken messages. In attempting to discover how it is that these conventions are maintained in force as guides to action, one finds evidence to suggest a functional relationship between the structure of the self and the structure of spoken interaction.

The socialized interactant comes to handle spoken interaction as he would any other kind,

[24] The meaning of this status can be appreciated by looking at the kinds of unlegitimated or unratified participation that can occur in spoken interaction. A person may overhear others unbeknownst to them; he can overhear them when they know this to be the case and when they choose either to act as if he were not overhearing them or to signal to him informally that they know he is overhearing them. In all of these cases, the outsider is officially held at bay as someone who is not formally participating in the occasion. Ritual codes, of course, require a ratified participant to be treated quite differently from an unratified one. Thus, for example, only a certain amount of insult from a ratified participant can be ignored without this avoidance practice causing loss of face to the insulted persons; after a point they must challenge the offender and demand redress. However, in many societies apparently, many kinds of verbal abuse from unratified participants can be ignored, without this failure to challenge constituting a loss of face.

[25] For a further treatment of the structure of spoken interaction see Goffman, reference footnote 14; part 4.
[26] I mean to include formal talks where rules of procedure are explicitly prescribed and officially enforced, and where only certain categories of participants may be allowed to hold the floor—as well as chats and sociable talks where rules are not explicit and the role of speaker passes back and forth among the participants.

as something that must be pursued with ritual care. By automatically appealing to face, he knows how to conduct himself in regard to talk. By repeatedly and automatically asking himself the question, "If I do or do not act in this way, will I or others lose face?" he decides at each moment, consciously or unconsciously, how to behave. For example, entrance into an occasion of spoken interaction may be taken as a symbol of intimacy or legitimate purpose, and so the person must, to save his face, desist from entering into talk with a given set of others unless his circumstances justify what is expressed about him by his entrance. Once approached for talk, he must accede to the others in order to save their face. Once engaged in conversation, he must demand only the amount of attention that is an appropriate expression of his relative social worth. Undue lulls come to be potential signs of having nothing in common, or of being insufficiently self-possessed to create something to say, and hence must be avoided. Similarly, interruptions and inattentiveness may convey disrespect and must be avoided unless the implied disrespect is an accepted part of the relationship. A surface of agreement must be maintained by means of discretion and white lies, so that the assumption of mutual approval will not be discredited. Withdrawal must be handled so that it will not convey an improper evaluation.[27] The person must restrain his emotional involvement so as not to present an image of someone with no self-control or dignity who does not rise above his feelings.

The relation between the self and spoken interaction is further displayed when one examines the ritual interchange. In a conversational encounter, interaction tends to proceed in spurts, an interchange at a time, and the flow of information and business is parcelled out into these relatively closed ritual units.[28]

The lull between interchanges tends to be greater than the lull between turns at talking in an interchange, and there tends to be a less meaningful relationship between two sequential interchanges than between two sequential speeches in an interchange.

This structural aspect of talk arises from the fact that when a person volunteers a statement or message, however trivial or commonplace, he commits himself and those he addresses, and in a sense places everyone present in jeopardy. By saying something, the speaker opens himself up to the possibility that the intended recipients will affront him by not listening or will think him forward, foolish, or offensive in what he has said. And should he meet with such a reception, he will find himself committed to the necessity of taking face-saving action against them. Furthermore, by saying something the speaker opens his intended recipients up to the possibility that the message will be self-approving, presumptuous, demanding, insulting, and generally an affront to them or to their conception of him, so that they will find themselves obliged to take action against him in defense of the ritual code. And should the speaker praise the recipients, they will be obliged to make suitable denials, showing that they do not hold too favorable an opinion of themselves and are not so eager to secure indulgences as to endanger their reliability and flexibility as interactants.

Thus when one person volunteers a message, thereby contributing what might easily be a threat to the ritual equilibrium, someone else present is obliged to show that the message has been received and that its content is acceptable to all concerned or can be acceptably countered. This acknowledging reply, of course, may contain a tactful rejection of the original communication, along with a request for modification. In such cases, several exchanges of messages may be required before the interchange is terminated on the basis of modified lines. The interchange comes to a close when it is possible to allow it to do so—that is, when everyone present has signified that he has been ritually appeased to a degree satisfactory to him.[29] A momentary lull between interchanges

---

[27] Among people who have had some experience in interacting with one another, conversational encounters are often terminated in such a way as to give the appearance that all participants have independently hit upon the same moment to withdraw. The disbandment is general, and no one may be conscious of the exchange of cues that has been required to make such a happy simultaneity of action possible. Each participant is thus saved from the compromising position of showing readiness to spend further time with someone who is not as ready to spend time with him.

[28] The empirical discreteness of the interchange unit is sometimes obscured when the same person who provides the terminating turn at talking in one

interchange initiates the first turn at talking in the next. However, the analytical utility of the interchange as a unit remains.

[29] The occurrence of the interchange unit is an empirical fact. In addition to the ritual explanation for it, others may be suggested. For example, when

is possible, for it comes at a time when it will not be taken as a sign of something untoward.

In general, then, a person determines how he ought to conduct himself during an occasion of talk by testing the potentially symbolic meaning of his acts against the self-images that are being sustained. In doing this, however, he incidentally subjects his behavior to the expressive order that prevails and contributes to the orderly flow of messages. His aim is to save face; his effect is to save the situation. From the point of view of saving face, then, it is a good thing that spoken interaction has the conventional organization given it; from the point of view of sustaining an orderly flow of spoken messages, it is a good thing that the self has the ritual structure given it.

I do not mean, however, to claim that another kind of person related to another kind of message organization would not do as well. More important, I do not claim that the present system is without weaknesses or drawbacks; these must be expected, for everywhere in social life a mechanism or functional relation which solves one set of problems necessarily creates a set of potential difficulties and abuses all is own. For example, a characteristic problem in the ritual organization of personal contacts is that while a person can save his face by quarreling or by indignantly withdrawing from the encounter, he does this at the cost of the interaction. Furthermore, the person's attachment to face gives others something to aim at; they can not only make an effort to wound him unofficially, but may even make an official attempt utterly to destroy his face. Also, fear over possible loss of his face often prevents the person from initiating contacts in which important information can be transmitted and important relationships re-established; he may be led to seek the safety of solitude rather than the danger of social encounters. He may do this even though others feel that he is motivated by "false pride"—a pride which suggests that the ritual code is getting the better of those whose conduct is regulated by it. Further, the "after you, Alphonse" complex can make the termination of an interchange difficult. So, too, where each participant feels that he must sacrifice a

little more than has been sacrificed for him, a kind of vicious indulgence cycle may occur— much like the hostility cycle that can lead to open quarrels—with each person receiving things he does not want and giving in return things he would rather keep. Again, when people are on formal terms, much energy may be spent in ensuring that events do not occur which might effectively carry an improper expression. And on the other hand, when a set of persons are on familiar terms and feel that they need not stand on ceremony with one another, then inattentiveness and interruptions are likely to become rife, and talk may degenerate into a happy babble of disorganized sound.

The ritual code itself requires a delicate balance, and can be easily upset by anyone who upholds it too eagerly or not eagerly enough, in terms of the standards and expectations of his group. Too little perceptiveness, too little *savoir-faire,* too little pride and considerateness, and the person ceases to be someone who can be trusted to take a hint about himself or give a hint that will save others embarrassment. Such a person comes to be a real threat to society; there is nothing much that can be done with him, and often he gets his way. Too much perceptiveness or too much pride, and the person becomes someone who is thin-skinned, who must be treated with kid gloves, requiring more care on the part of others than he may be worth to them. Too much *savoir-faire* or too much considerateness, and he becomes someone who is too socialized, who leaves the others with the feeling that they do not know how they really stand with him, nor what they should do to make an effective long-term adjustment to him.

In spite of these inherent "pathologies" in the organization of talk, the functional fitness between the socialized person and spoken interaction is a viable and practical one. The person's orientation to face, especially his own, is the point of leverage that the ritual order has in regard to him; yet a promise to take ritual care of his face is built into the very structure of talk.

FACE AND SOCIAL RELATIONSHIPS

When a person begins a mediated or immediate encounter, he already stands in some kind of social relationship to the others concerned, and expects to stand in a given relationship to them after the particular encounter ends. This, of course, is one of the ways in

---

the person makes a statement and receives a reply at once, this provides him with a way of learning that his statement has been received and correctly received. Such 'metacommunication' would be necessary on functional grounds even were it unnecessary on ritual ones.

which social contacts are geared into the wider society. Much of the activity occurring during an encounter can be understood as an effort on everyone's part to get through the occasion and all the unanticipated and unintentional events that can cast participants in an undesirable light, without disrupting the relationships of the participants. And if relationships are in the process of change, the object will be to bring the encounter to a satisfactory close without altering the expected course of development. This perspective nicely accounts, for example, for the little ceremonies of greeting and farewell which occur when people begin a conversational encounter or depart from one. Greetings provide a way of showing that a relationship is still what it was at the termination of the previous coparticipation, and, typically, that this relationship involves sufficient suppression of hostility for the participants temporarily to drop their guards and talk. Farewells sum up the effect of the encounter upon the relationship and show what the participants may expect of one another when they next meet. The enthusiasm of greetings compensates for the weakening of the relationship caused by the absence just terminated, while the enthusiasm of farewells compensates the relationship for the harm that is about to be done to it by separation.[30]

It seems to be a characteristic obligation of many social relationships that each of the members guarantees to support a given face for the other members in given situations. To prevent disruption of these relationships, it is therefore necessary for each member to avoid destroying the others' face. At the same time, it is often the person's social relationship with others that leads him to participate in certain

---

[30] Greetings, of course, serve to clarify and fix the roles that the participants will take during the occasion of talk and to commit participants to these roles, while farewells provide a way of unambiguously terminating the encounter. Greetings and farewells may also be used to state, and apologize for, extenuating circumstances—in the case of greetings for circumstances that have kept the participants from interacting until now, and in the case of farewells for circumstances that prevent the participants from continuing their display of solidarity. These apologies allow the impression to be maintained that the participants are more warmly related socially than may be the case. This positive stress, in turn, assures that they will act more ready to enter into contacts than they perhaps really feel inclined to do, thus guaranteeing that diffuse channels for potential communication will be kept open in the society.

encounters with them, where incidentally he will be dependent upon them for supporting his face. Furthermore, in many relationships, the members come to share a face, so that in the presence of third parties an improper act on the part of one member becomes a source of acute embarrassment to the other members. A social relationship, then, can be seen as a way in which the person is more than ordinarily forced to trust his self-image and face to the tact and good conduct of others.

THE NATURE OF THE RITUAL ORDER

The ritual order seems to be organized basically on accommodative lines, so that the imagery used in thinking about other types of social order is not quite suitable for it. For the other types of social order a kind of schoolboy model seems to be employed: if a person wishes to sustain a particular image of himself and trust his feelings to it, he must work hard for the credits that will buy this self-enhancement for him; should he try to obtain ends by improper means, by cheating or theft, he will be punished, disqualified from the race, or at least made to start all over again from the beginning. This is the imagery of a hard, dull game. In fact, society and the individual join in one that is easier on both of them, yet one that has dangers of its own.

Whatever his position in society, the person insulates himself by blindnesses, half-truths, illusions, and rationalizations. He makes an "adjustment" by convincing himself, with the tactful support of his intimate circle, that he is what he wants to be and that he would not do to gain his ends what the others have done to gain theirs. And as for society, if the person is willing to be subject to informal social control—if he is willing to find out from hints and glances and tactful cues what his place is, and keep it—then there will be no objection to his furnishing this place at his own discretion, with all the comfort, elegance, and nobility that his wit can muster for him. To protect this shelter he does not have to work hard, or join a group, or compete with anybody; he need only be careful about the expressed judgments he places himself in a position to witness. Some situations and acts and persons will have to be avoided; others, less threatening, must not be pressed too far. Social life is an uncluttered, orderly thing because the person voluntarily stays away from the places and topics and times where he is not wanted and where he might be disparaged for going. He cooperates to save his face, finding that there is much to be gained from venturing nothing.

, Facts are of the schoolboy's world—they can be altered by diligent effort but they cannot be avoided. But what the person protects and defends and invests his feelings in is an idea about himself, and ideas are vulnerable not to facts and things but to communications. Communications belong to a less punitive scheme than do facts, for communications can be by-passed, withdrawn from, disbelieved, conveniently misunderstood, and tactfully conveyed. And even should the person misbehave and break the truce he has made with society, punishment need not be the consequence. If the offense is one that the offended persons can let go by without losing too much face, then they are likely to act forbearantly, telling themselves that they will get even with the offender in another way at another time, even though such an occasion may never arise and might not be exploited if it did. If the offense is great, the offended persons may withdraw from the encounter, or from future similar ones, allowing their withdrawal to be reinforced by the awe they may feel toward someone who breaks the ritual code. Or they may have the offender withdrawn, so that no further communication can occur. But since the offender can salvage a good deal of face from such operations, withdrawal is often not so much an informal punishment for an offense as it is merely a means of terminating it. Perhaps the main principle of the ritual order is not justice but face, and what any offender receives is not what he deserves but what will sustain for the moment the line to which he has committed himself, and through this the line to which he has committed the interaction.

Throughout this paper it has been implied that underneath their differences in culture, people everywhere are the same. If persons have a universal human nature, they themselves are not to be looked to for an explanation of it. One must look rather to the fact that societies everywhere, if they are to be societies, must mobilize their members as self-regulating participants in social encounters.

One way of mobilizing the individual for this purpose is through ritual; he is taught to be perceptive, to have feelings attached to self and a self expressed through face, to have pride, honor, and dignity, to have considerateness, to have tact and a certain amount of poise. These are some of the elements of behavior which must be built into the person if practical use is to be made of him as an interactant, and it is these elements that are referred to in part when one speaks of universal human nature.

Universal human nature is not a very human thing. By acquiring it, the person becomes a kind of construct, built up not from inner psychic propensities but from moral rules that are impressed upon him from without. These rules, when followed, determine the evaluation he will make of himself and of his fellow-participants in the encounter, the distribution of his feelings, and the kinds of practices he will employ to maintain a specified and obligatory kind of ritual equilibrium. The general capacity to be bound by moral rules may well belong to the individual, but the particular set of rules which transforms him into a human being derives from requirements established in the ritual organization of social encounters. And if a particular person or group or society seems to have a unique character all its own, it is because its standard set of human-nature elements is pitched and combined in a particular way. Instead of much pride, there may be little. Instead of abiding by the rules, there may be much effort to break them safely. But if an encounter or undertaking is to be sustained as a viable system of interaction organized on ritual principles, then these variations must be held within certain bounds and nicely counterbalanced by corresponding modifications in some of the other rules and understandings. Similarly, the human nature of a particular set of persons may be specially designed for the special kind of undertakings in which they participate, but still each of these persons must have within him something of the balance of characteristics required of a usable participant in any ritually organized system of social activity.

Chapter 32 Selfishness and Self-Love

ERICH FROMM

Modern culture is pervaded by a taboo on selfishness. It teaches that to be selfish is sinful and that to love others is virtuous. To be sure, this doctrine is not only in flagrant contradiction to the practices of modern society but it also is in opposition to another set of doctrines which assumes that the most powerful and legitimate drive in man is selfishness and that each individual by following this imperative drive also does the most for the common good. The existence of this latter type of ideology does not affect the weight of the doctrines which declare that selfishness is the arch evil and love for others the main virtue. Selfishness, as it is commonly used in these ideologies, is more or less synonymous with self-love. The alternatives are either to love others which is a virtue or to love oneself which is a sin.

This principle has found its classic expression in Calvin's theology. Man is essentially bad and powerless. He can do nothing—absolutely nothing—good on the basis of his own strength or merits. "We are not our own," says Calvin,[1] "therefore neither our reason nor our will should predominate in our deliberations and actions. We are not our own; therefore, let us not propose it as our end, to seek what may be expedient for us according to the flesh. We are not our own; therefore, let us, as far as possible, forget ourselves and all things that are ours. On the contrary, we are God's; to him, therefore, let us live and die. For, as it is the most devastating pestilence which ruins people if they obey themselves, it is the only haven of salvation not to know or to want anything by oneself but to be guided by God who walks before us."[2] Man should not only have

the conviction of his absolute nothingness. He should do everything to humiliate himself. "For I do not call it humility," says Calvin, "if you suppose that we have anything left . . . we cannot think of ourselves as we ought to

tutio Christianae Religionis. Editionem curavit A. Tholuk. Berolini 1835, par. I, p. 445). The reason for this shift is that Allen's translation slightly changes the original in the direction of softening the rigidity of Calvin's thought. Allen translates this sentence: "For as compliance with their own inclinations leads men most effectually to ruin, so to place no dependency on our own knowledge or will, but merely to follow the guidance of the Lord, is the only way of safety." However, the Latin *sibi ipsis obtemperant* is not equivalent to "follow one's own inclinations" but "to obey oneself." To forbid following one's inclinations has the mild quality of Kantian ethics that man should suppress his natural inclinations and by doing so follow the orders of his conscience. On the other hand, forbidding to obey oneself is a denial of the autonomy of man. The same subtle change of meaning is reached by translating *ita unicus est salutis portis nihil nec sapere, nec velle per se ipsum* "to place no dependence on our knowledge nor will." While the formulation of the original straightforwardly contradicts the motto of enlightenment philosophy: *sapere aude*—dare to know, Allen's translations warns only of a dependence on one's own knowledge, a warning which is by far less contradictory to modern thought. I mention these deviations of the translation from the original which I came across accidentally, because they offer a good illustration of the fact that the spirit of an author is "modernized" and colored—certainly without any intention of doing so—just by translating him.

SOURCE. Erich Fromm, "Selfishness and Self-Love," from *Psychiatry: Journal for the Study of Interpersonal Processes,* **2** (1939), pp. 507–508 and 510–523. Copyright 1939 by The William Alanson White Psychiatric Foundation, Inc. Reprinted by special permission of The William Alanson White Psychiatric Foundation, Inc.

[1] Calvin, Johannes, *Institutes of the Christian Religion* [translated by John Allen]; Philadelphia, Presbyterian Board of Christian Education, 1928 (1:688 pp.)—in particular Book III, Chapter 7, ¶1, p. 619.
[2] From "For as it is . . . ." the translation is mine from the Latin original (Johannes Calvini *Insti-*

think without utterly despising everything that may be supposed an excellence in us. This humility is unfeigned submission of a mind overwhelmed with a weighty sense of its own misery and poverty; for such is the uniform description of it in the word of God."[3]

This emphasis on the nothingness and wickedness of the individual implies that there is nothing he should like about himself. This doctrine is rooted in contempt and hatred for oneself. Calvin makes this point very clear; he speaks of "Self-love" as of a "pest."[4]

If the individual finds something in himself "on the strength of which he finds pleasure in himself," he betrays this sinful self-love. This fondness for himself will make him sit in judgment over others and despise them. Therefore, to be fond of oneself, to like anything about oneself is one of the greatest imaginable sins. It excludes love for others[5] and is identical with selfishness.[6]

There are fundamental differences between Calvin's theology and Kant's philosophy, yet, the basic attitude toward the problem of love for oneself has remained the same. According to Kant, it is a virtue to want the happiness of others, while to want one's own happiness is ethically "indifferent," since it is something which the nature of man is striving for and a natural striving cannot have positive ethical sense.[7] Kant admits that one must not give up one's claims for happiness; under certain circumstances it can even be a duty to be concerned with one's happiness; partly because health, wealth, and the like, can be means which are necessary to fulfill one's duty, partly because the lack of happiness—poverty—can seduce a person from fulfilling his duty.[8] But love for oneself, striving for one's own happiness, can never be a virtue. As an ethical principle, the striving for one's own happiness "is the most objectionable one, not merely because it is false, . . . but because the springs it provides for morality are such as rather undermine it and destroy its sublimity. . . ."[9] Kant differentiates in egotism, self-love, *philautia*—a benevolence for oneself; and arrogance—the pleasure in oneself. "Rational self-love" must be restricted by ethical principles, the pleasure in oneself must be battered down and the individual must come to feel humiliated in comparing himself with the sanctity of moral laws.[10] The individual should find supreme happiness in the fulfillment of his duty. The realization of the moral principle—and, therefore, of the individual's happiness—is only possible in the general whole, the nation, the state. Yet, "the welfare of the state—*salus rei publicae suprema lex est*—is not identical with the welfare of the citizens and their happiness."[11]

*   *   *

The doctrine that selfishness is the arch-evil that one has to avoid and that to love oneself excludes loving others is by no means restricted to theology and philosophy. It is one of the stock patterns used currently in home, school, church, movies, literature, and all the other instruments of social suggestion. "Don't be selfish" is a sentence which has been impressed upon millions of children, generation after generation. It is hard to define what exactly it means. Consciously, most parents connect with it the meaning not to be egotistical, inconsiderate, without concern for others. Factually, they generally mean more than that. "Not to be selfish" implies not to do what one wishes, to give up one's own wishes for the sake of those in authority; i.e., the parents, and later

---

[3] Reference footnote 1; chapter 12, ¶6, p. 681.

[4] Compare reference footnote 1; chapter 7, ¶4, p. 622.

[5] It should be noted, however, that even love for one's neighbor, while it is one of the fundamental doctrines of the New Testament, has not been given a corresponding weight by Calvin. In blatant contradiction to the New Testament Calvin says: "For what the schoolmen advance concerning the priority of charity to faith and hope, is a mere reverie of a distempered imagination. . . ." Compare reference footnote 1; chapter 24, ¶1, p. 531.

[6] Despite Luther's emphasis on the spiritual freedom of the individual, his theology, different as it is in many ways from Calvin's, is pervaded by the same conviction of man's basic powerlessness and nothingness.

[7] Compare Kant, Immanuel, *Kant's Critique of Practical Reason and Other Works on the Theory of Ethics* [translated by Thomas Kingsmill Abbot]; London, New York, Longmans Greene, 1909 (xiv and 369 pp.)—in particular Part I, Book I, Chapter I, ¶VIII, Remark II, p. 126.

[8] Compare reference footnote 7—in particular Part I, Book I, Chapter III, p. 186.

[9] Reference footnote 7—in particular *Fundamental Principles of the Metaphysics of Morals;* second section, p. 61.

[10] Compare reference footnote 7—in particular Part I, Book I, Chapter III, p. 165.

[11] Kant, Immanuel, *Immanuel Kant's Werke*; Berlin, Cassierer, (8:xxix and 468 pp.)—in particular Der Rechtslehre Zweiter Teil I. Abschnitt, ¶49, p. 124. I translate from the German text, since this part is omitted in the English translation of *The Metaphysics of Ethics* by I. W. Semple [Edinburgh, 1871].

the authorities of society. "Don't be selfish," in the last analysis, has the same ambiguity that we have seen in Calvinism. Aside from its obvious implication, it means, "don't love yourself," "don't be yourself," but submit your life to something more important than yourself, be it an outside power or the internalization of that power as "duty." "Don't be selfish" becomes one of the most powerful ideological weapons in suppressing spontaneity and the free development of personality. Under the pressure of this slogan one is asked for every sacrifice and for complete submission: only those aims are "unselfish" which do not serve the individual for his own sake but for the sake of somebody or something outside of him.

This picture, we must repeat, is in a certain sense one-sided. Beside the doctrine that one should not be selfish, the opposite doctrine is propagandized in modern society: have your own advantage in mind, act according to what is best for you—and by doing so, you will also bring about the greatest advantage for all others. As a matter of fact, the idea that the pursuit of individual egotism is the basis for the development of general welfare is the principle on which competitive capitalism has been built. It may seem strange that two such seemingly contradictory principles could be taught side by side in one culture. Of the fact, there can be no doubt. One result of this contradiction of ideological patterns certainly is confusion in the individual. To be torn between the one and the other doctrine is a serious blockage in the process of integration of personality and has often led to neurotic character formation.[12]

One must observe that this contradictory pair of doctrines has had an important social function. The doctrine that everybody should pursue his individual advantage obviously was a necessary stimulus for private initiative on which the modern economic structure is built. The social function of the doctrine "don't be selfish" was an ambiguous one. For the broad masses of those who had to live on the level of mere subsistence, it was an important aid to resignation to having wishes which were unattainable under the given socio-economic system. It was important that this resignation should be

one which was not thought of as being brought about by external pressure, since the inevitable result of such a feeling has to be a more or less conscious grudge and a defiance against society. By making this resignation a moral virtue, such a reaction could to a considerable extent be avoided. While this aspect of the social function of the taboo on selfishness is obvious, another, its effect upon the privileged minority, is somewhat more complicated. It only becomes clear if we consider further the meaning of "selfishness." If it means to be concerned with one's economic advantage, certainly the taboo on selfishness would have been a severe handicap to the economic initiative of business men. But what it really meant, especially in the earlier phases of English and American culture was, as has been pointed out before: don't do what you want, don't enjoy yourself, don't spend money or energy for pleasure, but feel it as your duty to work, to be successful, to be prosperous.

It is the great merit of Max Weber[13] to have shown that this principle of what he calls *innerweltliche Askese* (innerworldly asceticism) was an important condition for creating an attitude in which all energy could be directed toward work and the fulfillment of duty. The tremendous economic achievements of modern society would not have been possible if this kind of asceticism had not absorbed all energy to the purpose of thrift and relentless work. It would transcend the scope of this paper to enter into an analysis of the character structure of modern man as he emerged in the 16th century. Suffice it to say here, that the economic and social changes in the 15th and 16th centuries destroyed the feeling of security and "belonging" which was typical of the members of medieval society.[14] The socio-economic position of the urban middle class, the peasantry and the nobility were shaken in their foundations;[15] impoverishment, threats to traditional

---

[12] This point has been emphasized by Horney, Karen, *The Neurotic Personality of Our Time*; New York, Norton, 1937 (xii and 290 pp.), and by Lynd, Robert S., *Knowledge for What?*; Princeton, Princeton University Press, 1939 (x and 268 pp.).

[13] Weber, Max, *The Protestant Ethic and the Spirit of Capitalism* [translated by Talcott Parsons]; London, Allan, 1930 (xi and 292 pp.).
[14] Harry Stack Sullivan has given particular emphasis to the need for security as one of the basic motivating forces in man, while orthodox psychoanalytical literature has not paid sufficient attention to this factor.
[15] Compare Pascal, R., *The Social Basis of the German Reformation*; London, Watts, 1933 (viii and 243 pp.). Kraus, Johann Babtist, *Scholastik, Puritanismus und Kapitalismus;* Munchen, Dunker, 1930 (329 pp.). Tawney, R. H., *Religion and the Rise of Capitalism*; London, John Murray, 1926 (xiii and 339 pp.).

economic positions as well as new chances for economic success arose. Religious and spiritual ties which had established a rounded and secure world for the individual had been broken. The individual found himself completely alone in the world, paradise was lost for good, his success and failure were decided by the laws of the market; the basic relationship to everyone else had become one of merciless competition. The result of all this was a new feeling of freedom attended, however, by an increased anxiety. This anxiety, in its turn, created a readiness for new submission to religious and secular authorities even more strict than the previous ones had been. The new individualism on the one hand, anxiety and submission to authority on the other, found their ideological expression in Protestantism and Calvinism. At the same time, these religious doctrines did much to stimulate and increase these new attitudes. But even more important than the submission to external authorities was the fact that the authorities were internalized, that man became the slave of a master inside himself instead of one outside. This internal master drove the individual to relentless work and striving for success and never allowed him to be himself and enjoy himself. There was a spirit of distrust and hostility directed not only against the outside world, but also toward one's own self.

This modern type of man was selfish in a twofold sense: he had little concern for others and he was anxiously concerned with his own advantage. But was this selfishness really a concern for himself as an individual, with all his intellectual and sensual potentialities? Had "he" not become the appendix of his socio-economic rôle, a cog in the economic machine, even if sometimes an important cog? Was he not the slave of this machine even if he subjectively felt as if he were following his own orders? Was his selfishness identical with self-love or was it instead rooted in the very lack of it?

*   *   *

The doctrine that love for oneself is identical with "selfishness," and that it is an alternative to love for others has pervaded theology, philosophy, and the pattern of daily life; it would be surprising if one would not find the same doctrine also in scientific psychology, but here as an allegedly objective statement of facts. A case in point is Freud's theory on narcissism. He says, in short, that man has a certain quantity of libido. Originally, in the infant, all this libido has as its objective the child's own person, *primary narcissism*. Later on, the libido is directed from one's own person toward other objects. If a person is blocked in his "object-relationships," the libido is withdrawn from the objects and returned to one's own person, *secondary narcissism*. According to Freud, there is an almost mechanical alternative between ego-love and object-love. The more love I turn toward the outside world the less love I have for myself, and vice versa. Freud is thus moved to describe the phenomenon of falling in love as an impoverishment of one's self-love because all love is turned to an object outside of oneself. Freud's theory of narcissism expresses basically the same idea which runs through protestant religion, idealistic philosophy, and the everyday patterns of modern culture. This by itself does not indicate that he is right or wrong. Yet, this translation of the general principle into the categories of empirical psychology gives us a good basis for examining the principle.

These questions arise: Does psychological observation support the thesis that there is a basic contradiction and the state of alternation between love for oneself and love for others? Is love for oneself the same phenomenon as selfishness, is there a difference or are they in fact opposites?

Before we turn to the discussion of the empirical side of the problem, it may be noted that from a philosophical viewpoint, the notion that love for others and love for oneself are contradictory is untenable. If it is a virtue to love my neighbor as a human being, why must not I love myself too? A principle which proclaims love for man but which taboos love for myself, exempts me from all other human beings. The deepest experience of human existence, however, is to have this experience with regard to oneself. There is no solidarity of man in which I myself am not included. A doctrine which proclaims such an exclusion proves its objective insincerity by this very fact.[16]

We have come here to the psychological premises on which the conclusions of this paper are built. Generally, these premises are: not only others, but also we ourselves are the

---

[16] This thought is expressed in the bibical: "Love thy neighbor as thyself!" The implication is that respect of one's own integrity and uniqueness, love for and understanding of one's own self, cannot be separated from respect, love and understanding with regard to another individual. The discovery of my own self is inseparably connected with the discovery of any other self.

"object" of our feelings and attitudes; the attitude towards others and toward ourselves, far from being contradictory, runs basically parallel.[17] With regard to the problem under discussion this means: Love for others and love for ourselves are not alternatives. Neither are hate for others and hate for ourselves alternatives. On the contrary, an attitude of love for themselves will be found in those who are at least capable of loving others. Hatred against oneself is inseparable from hatred against others, even if on the surface the opposite seems to be the case. In other words, love and hatred, in principle, are indivisible as far as the difference between "objects" and one's own self is concerned.

To clarify this thesis, it is necessary to discuss the problem of hatred and love. With regard to hatred one can differentiate between "reactive hatred" and "character-conditioned hatred." By reactive hatred I mean a hatred which is essentially a reaction to an attack on one's life, security, or ideals or on some other person that one loves and identifies oneself with. Its premise is one's positive attitude toward one's life, toward other persons and toward ideals. If there is a strong affirmation of life, a strong hatred necessarily is aroused if life is attacked. If there is love, hatred must be aroused if the loved one is attacked. There is no passionate striving for anything which does not necessitate hatred if the object of this striving is attacked. Such hatred is the counterpoint of life. It is aroused by a specific situation, its aim is the destruction of the attacker and, in principle, it ends when the attacker is defeated.[18]

Character-conditioned hatred is different. To be sure, the hatred rooted in the character structure once arose as reaction to certain experiences undergone by the individual in his childhood. It then became a character trait of the person; he *is* hostile. His basic hostility is observable even when it is not giving rise to manifest hatred. There is something in the facial expression, gestures, tone of voice, kind of jokes, little unintentional reactions which impress the observer as indications of the fundamental hostility, which also could be de-

scribed as a continuous *readiness* to hate. It is the basis from which active hatred springs if and when it is aroused by a specific stimulus. This hate reaction can be perfectly rational; as much so, as a matter of fact, as is the case in the situations which were described as arousing reactive hatred. There is, however, a fundamental difference. In the case of reactive hatred it is the situation which *creates* the hatred. In the case of character-conditioned hatred an "idling" hostility is *actualized* by the situation. In the case where the basic hatred is aroused, the person involved appears to have something like a feeling of relief, as though he were happy to have found the rational opportunity to express his lingering hostility. He shows a particular kind of satisfaction and pleasure in his hatred which is missing in the case of an essentially reactive hatred.

In the case of a proportionality between hate reaction and external situation, we speak of a "normal" reaction, even if it is the actualization of character-conditioned hatred. From this normal reaction to an "irrational" reaction found in the neurotic or psychotic person, there are innumerable transitions and no sharp demarcation line can be drawn. In the irrational hate-reaction, the emotion seems disproportionate to the actual situation. Let me illustrate by referring to a reaction which psychoanalysts have ample opportunity to observe; an analysand has to wait ten minutes because the analyst is delayed. The analysand enters the room, wild with rage at the offense done to him by the analyst. Extreme cases can be observed more clearly in psychotic persons; in those the disproportionality is still more striking. Psychotic hatred will be aroused by something which from the standpoint of reality is not at all offensive. Yet, from the standpoint of his own feeling it is offensive, and thus the irrational reaction is irrational only from the standpoint of external objective reality, not from the subjective premises of the person involved.

* * *

The decisive factors for arousing character-conditioned hatred may be stated to be all the different ways by which spontaneity, freedom, emotional and physical expansiveness, the development of the "self" of the child are blocked or destroyed.[19] The means of doing this are

---

[17] This viewpoint has been emphasized by Horney, Karen, *New Ways in Psychoanalysis,* New York, Norton, 1939 (313 pp.); in particular Chapters 5 and 7.
[18] Nietzsche has emphasized the creative function of destruction. Reference footnote 23; *Ecce Homo,* Stanza 2.

[19] In recent years, a number of psychologists were interested in the problem of uncovering the hostility, consciously or unconsciously, present in

manifold; they vary from open, intimidating hostility and terror, to a subtle and "sweet" kind of "anonymous authority," which does not overtly forbid anything but says: "I know you will or will not like this or that." Simple frustration of instinctual impulses does not create deep seated hostility; it only creates a reactive hate reaction. Yet, this was Freud's assumption and his concept of the Oedipus Complex is based on it; it implies that the frustration of sexual wishes directed toward the father or the mother creates hatred which in its turn leads to anxiety and submission. To be sure, frustration often appears as a symptom of something which does create hostility: not taking the child seriously, blocking his expansiveness, not allowing him to be free. But the real issue is not isolated frustration but the fight of the child against those forces which tend to suppress his freedom and spontaneity. There are many forms in which the fight for freedom is fought and many ways in which the defeat is disguised. The child may be ready to internalize the external authority and be "good," it may overtly rebel and yet remain dependent. It may feel that it "belongs" by completely conforming to the given cultural patterns at the expense of the loss of its individual self—the result is always a lesser or greater degree of inner emptiness, the feeling of nothingness, anxiety and resulting from all that a chronic hatred, and *ressentiment,* which

---

children. Some of them were very successful in demonstrating the presence of strong hostility in very young children. A method which proved to be particularly fruitful was to arrange play situations in which the children expressed their hostility very clearly. According to Bender, Lauretta, and Schilder, Paul, "Aggressiveness in Children," *Genetic Psychology Monographs,* **18** (1936) pp. 410-425, the younger the children were the more directly they expressed hostility, while with the older ones the hate-reaction was already repressed but could be clearly observed in a play situation. Compare also Levy, David M., *Studies in Sibling Rivalry V,* New York, American Orthopsychiatric Association, 1937 (96 pp.). L. Murphey and G. Lerner have found normal children who seem quite conventionally adjusted to the nursery-school play group, revealing intense aggression in a free play situation, alone with one adult. J. Louise Despert has come to similar conclusions: See her "A Method for the Study of Personality Reactions in Preschool Age Children by Means of Analysis of their Play," *J. Psychol.* **9** (1940) pp. 17-29. Hartoch, A., and Schachtel, E. have found expression of strong aggressiveness in Rorschach tests in two- to four-year-old children who did not show proportionate amount of manifest aggressiveness in their behavior.

Nietzsche characterized very well as *Lebensneid,* envy of life.

There is a slight difference, however, between hatred and this envy of life. The aim of hatred is in the last analysis the destruction of the object outside of my self. By destroying it I attain strength in relative, although not in absolute terms. In envy of life, the begrudging attitude aims at the destruction of others too; not, however, in order to gain relative strength, but to have the satisfaction that others are being denied the enjoyment of things which—for external or inner reasons—I cannot enjoy myself. It aims at removing the pain, rooted in my own inability for happiness, by having nobody else who by his very existence demonstrates what I am lacking.[20]

In principle, the same factors condition the development of chronic hatred in a group. The difference here as in general between individual psychology and social psychology is only to be found in this: while in individual psychology, we are looking for the individual and accidental conditions which are responsible for those character traits by which one individual varies from other members of his group, in social psychology we are interested in the character structure as far as it is common to and, therefore, typical of the majority of the members of that group. As to the conditions, we are not looking for accidental individual conditions like an overstrict father or the sudden death of a beloved sister, but for those conditions of life which are a common experience for the group as such. This does not mean the one or the other isolated trait in the whole mode of life, but the total structure of basic life experiences as they are essentially conditioned by the socio-economic situation of a particular group.[21]

The child is imbued with the "spirit" of a society long before it makes the direct acquaintance with it in school. The parents repre-

---

[20] It should be noted that sadism has to be differentiated from hatred. As I see it, the aim of sadism is not destruction of the subject, but a seeking to have absolute power over it, to make it an instrument of oneself. Sadism can be blended with hatred; in this case it will have the cruelty usually implied in the notion of sadism. It can also be blended with sympathy in which case the impulse is to have the object as an instrument and, at the same time, to further him in any way excepting in one: letting him be free.

[21] See, on the method of analytic social psychology: Fromm, Erich, "Zur Aufgabe und Methode einer analytischen Sozialpsychologie," *Zeitschr. f. Sozialforschung* [Leipzig] **1** (1932) pp. 28-54.

sent in their own character structure the spirit prevalent in their society and class and transmit this atmosphere to the child from the day of his birth onward. The family thus is the "psychic agency" of society.

The bearing on our problem of the differentiation in hatred will have become clear by now. While in the case of reactive hatred the stimulus which is at the same time the object, constitutes the "cause" for the hatred; in the case of character-conditioned hatred, the basic attitude, the readiness for hatred, exists regardless of an object and before a stimulus makes the chronic hostility turn into manifest hatred. As has been indicated, originally, in childhood, this basic hatred was brought into existence by certain people, but later it has become part of the personality structure and objects play but a secondary rôle. Therefore, in its case, there is, in principle, no difference between objects outside of myself and my own self. The idling hostility is always there; its outside objects change according to circumstances and it but depends on certain factors whether I myself become one of the objects of my hostility. If one wants to understand why a certain person is hated in one case, why I myself am hated in another case, one has to know the specific factors in the situation which make others or myself the object of manifest hatred. What interests us in this context, however, is the general principle that character-conditioned hatred is something radiating from an individual and like a searchlight focussing sometimes on this and sometimes on that object, among them myself.

*   *   *

While important thinkers clearly saw the strength of hostility in modern man, popular ideologies and the convictions of the average man tend to ignore the phenomenon. Only a relatively small number of people have an awareness of their fundamental dislike for others. Many have only a feeling of just having little interest or feeling for others. The majority are completely unaware of the intensity of the chronic hatred in themselves as well as in others. They have adopted the feelings that they know they are supposed to have: to like people, to find them nice, unless or until they have actually committed an act of aggression. The very indiscriminateness of this "liking people" shows its thinness or rather its compensatory quality a basic lack of fondness.

While the frequency of underlying distrust and dislike for others is known to many observers of our social scene, the dislike for oneself is a less clearly recognized phenomenon. Yet, this self-hatred may be considered rare only so long as we think of cases in which people quite overtly hate or dislike themselves. Mostly, this self-dislike is concealed in various ways. One of the most frequent indirect expressions of self-dislike are the inferiority feelings so widespread in our culture. Consciously, these persons do not feel that they dislike themselves: what they do feel is only that they are inferior to others, that they are stupid, unattractive or whatever the particular content of the inferiority feelings is.[22]

To be sure, the dynamics of inferiority feelings are complex and there are factors other than the one with which we are dealing. Yet, this factor is never missing and dislike for oneself or at least a lack of fondness for one's own person is always present and is dynamically an important factor.

A still more subtle form of self-dislike is the tendency toward constant self-criticism. These people do not feel inferior but if they make one mistake, discover something in themselves which should not be so, their self-criticism is entirely out of proportion to the significance of the mistake or the shortcoming. They must either be perfect according to their own standards, or at least perfect enough according to the standards of the people around them so that they get affection and approval. If they feel that what they did was perfect or if they succeed in winning other people's approval, they feel at ease. But whenever this is missing they feel overwhelmed by an otherwise repressed inferiority feeling. Here again, the basic lack of fondness for themselves is one source from which the attitude springs. This becomes more evident if we compare this attitude toward oneself with the corresponding one toward others. If, for example, a man who believes that he loves a woman should feel if she makes any mistake that she is no good, or if his feeling about her is entirely dependent on whether others criticize or praise her, we cannot doubt that there is a fundamental lack of love for her. It is the person who hates who seizes every opportunity to criticize another person and who does not miss any blunder.

---

[22] Industry, for instance, capitalizes the unconscious self-dislike by terrorizing people with the threat of "body odor." The unconscious dislike the average person has for himself makes him an easy prey for this suggestion.

The most widespread expression of the lack of fondness for oneself, however, is the way in which people treat themselves. People are their own slave drivers; instead of being the slaves of a master outside of themselves, they have put the master within. This master is harsh and cruel. He does not give them a moment's rest, he forbids them the enjoyment of any pleasure, does not allow them to do what they want. If they do so, they do it furtively and at the expense of a guilty conscience. Even the pursuit of pleasure is as compulsory as is work. It does not lead them away from the continual restlessness which pervades their lives. For the most part, they are not even aware of this. There are some exceptions. Thus, the banker, James Stillman, who, when in the prime of life, had attained wealth, prestige and power reached only by but few people said: I never in my life have done what I wanted and never shall do so.[23]

The rôle of "conscience" as the internalization of external authorities and as the bearer of deep seated hostility against oneself has been seen clearly by Freud in the formulation of his concept of the Super-Ego. He assumed that the super-ego contains a great deal of the basic destructiveness inherent in man and turns it against him in terms of duty and moral obligation. In spite of objections to Freud's Super-Ego theory, which cannot be presented here,[24] Freud undoubtedly has sensed keenly the hostility and cruelty contained in the "conscience" as it was conceived in the modern era.

What holds true of hostility and hatred holds also true of love. Yet, love for others and self-love is by far a more difficult problem to discuss; and this for two reasons. One is the fact that while hatred is a phenomenon to be found everywhere in our society and, therefore, an easy object for empirical observation and analysis, love is a comparatively rare phenomenon, which lends itself to empirical observation only under difficulties; any discussion of love, therefore, implies the danger of being unempirical and merely speculative. The other difficulty is perhaps even greater. There is no word in our language which has been so much misused and prostituted as the word "love." It has been preached by those who were ready to condone every cruelty if it served their purpose; it has been used as a disguise under which to force people into sacrificing their own happiness, into submitting their whole self to those who profited from this surrender. It has been used as the moral basis for unjustified demands. It has been made so empty that for many people *love* may mean no more than that two people have lived together for 20 years just without fighting more often than once a week. It is dangerous and somewhat embarrassing to use such a word. Yet a psychologist may not properly succumb to this embarrassment. To preach love is at best bad taste. But to make a cool and critical analysis of the phenomenon of love and to unmask pseudo-love—tasks which cannot be separated from each other—is an obligation that the psychologist has no right to avoid.

It goes without saying that this paper will not attempt to give an analysis of love. Even to describe the psychological phenomena which are conventionally covered by the term "love" would require a good part of a book. One must attempt, however, the presentation necessary to the main trend of thought of this paper.

Two phenomena closely connected with each other are frequently presented as love—the masochistic and sadistic *love*. In the case of masochistic *love*, one gives up one's self, one's initiative and integrity in order to become submerged entirely in another person who is felt to be stronger. Because of deep anxieties which give rise to the feeling that one cannot stand on one's own feet, one wants to be rid of one's own individual self and to become part of another being, thus becoming secure and finding a center which one misses in oneself. This surrender of one's own self has often been praised as the example of "the great love." It is actually a form of idolatry, and also an annihilation of the self. The fact that it has been conceived as love has made it the more seductive and dangerous.

The sadistic *love* on the other hand springs from the desire to swallow its object to make him a will-less instrument in one's own hands. This drive is also rooted in a deep anxiety and an inability to stand alone, but instead of finding increased strength by being swallowed, strength and security are found in having a limited power over the other person. The masochistic as well as the sadistic kind of love are expressions of one basic need which springs

[23] Compare Robeson [Brown], Anna, *The Portrait of a Banker: James Stillmann,* New York, Duffield, 1927 (x and 370 pp.).
[24] See my discussion of the Super-Ego in the psychological part of *Studien über Autoritat und Familie* [Max Horkheimer, ed.], Paris, Alcan, 1936 (xv and 947 pp.).

from a basic inability to be independent. Using a biological term, this basic need may be called a "need for symbiosis." The sadistic *love* is frequently the kind of love that parents have for their children. Whether the domination is overtly authoritarian or subtly "modern" makes no essential difference. In either case, it tends to undermine the strength of the self of the child and leads in later years to the development in him of the very same symbiotic tendencies. The sadistic love is not infrequent among adults. Often in relationships of long duration, the respective rôles are permanent, one partner representing the sadistic, the other one the masochistic pole of the symbiotic relationship. Often the rôles change constantly—a continuous struggle for dominance and submission being conceived as *love*.

It appears from what has been said that love cannot be separated from freedom and independence. In contradiction to the symbiotic pseudo-love, the basic premise of love is freedom and equality. Its premise is the strength, independence, integrity of the self, which can stand alone and bear solitude. This premise holds true for the loving as well as for the loved person. Love is a spontaneous act, and spontaneity means—also literally—the ability to act of one's own free volition. If anxiety and weakness of the self makes it impossible for the individual to be rooted in himself, he cannot love.

This fact can be fully understood only if we consider what love is directed toward. It is the opposite of hatred. Hatred is a passionate wish for destruction; love is a passionate affirmation of its "object."[25] That means that love is not an "affect" but an active striving, the aim of which is the happiness, development, and freedom of its "object." This passionate affirmation is not possible if one's own self is crippled, since genuine affirmation is always rooted in strength. The person whose self is thwarted, can only love in an ambivalent way; that is, with the strong part of his self he can love, with the crippled part he must hate.[26]

* * *

Love, like character-conditioned hatred, is rooted in a basic attitude which is constantly present; a readiness to love, a *basic sympathy* as one might call it. It is started, but not caused, by a particular *object*. The ability and readiness to love is a character trait just as is the readiness to hate.[27] It is difficult to say what the conditions favoring the development of this *basic sympathy* are. It seems that there are two main conditions, a positive and a negative one. The positive one is simply to have experienced love from others as a child. While conventionally, parents are supposed to *love* their children as a matter of course, this is rather the exception than the rule. This positive condition is, therefore, frequently absent. The negative condition is the absence of all those factors, discussed above, which make for the existence of a chronic hatred. The observer of childhood experiences may well doubt that the absence of these conditions is frequent.

* * *

One last question remains to be discussed. Granted that love for oneself and for others in principle run parallel, how do we explain the kind of *selfishness* which obviously is in contradiction to any genuine concern for others. The *selfish* person is only interested in himself, wants everything for himself, is unable to give with any pleasure but is only anxious to take; the world outside himself is conceived only from the standpoint of what he can get out of it; he lacks interest in the needs of others, or respect for their dignity and integrity. He sees only himself, judges everyone and everything from the standpoint of its usefulness to him, is basically unable to love. This selfishness can be manifest or disguised by all sorts of unselfish gestures; dynamically it is exactly the same. It seems obvious that with this type of personality there is a contradiction between the enormous concern for oneself and the lack of concern for others. Do we not have the proof here that there exists an alternative between concern for others and concern for oneself? This would certainly be the case if selfishness and self-love were identical. But this assumption is the very fallacy

---

[25] Object is put into quotation marks because in a love relationship the "object" ceases to be an object; that is, something opposite to and separated from the subject. Not accidentally do "object" and "objection" have the same root.
[26] Sullivan has approached this formulation in his lectures. He states that the era of preadolescence is characterized by the appearance of impulses in interpersonal relations which make for a new type of satisfaction in the pleasure of the other person (the chum). Love, according to him, is a situation in which the satisfaction of the loved one is exactly as significant and desirable as that of the lover.
[27] It would be most unfortunate to assume that these respective readinesses are characteristics of different personalities. Many people present concomitant readinesses of both varieties.

which has led to so many mistaken conclusions with regard to our problem. Selfishness and self-love far from being identical, actually are opposites.

Selfishness is one kind of greediness.[28] Like all greediness, it contains an insatiability, as a consequence of which there is never any real satisfaction. Greed is a bottomless pit which exhausts the person in an endless effort to satisfy the need without ever reaching satisfaction. This leads to the crucial point: close observation shows that while the selfish person is always anxiously concerned with himself, he is never satisfied, is always restless, always driven by the fear of not getting enough, of missing something, of being deprived of something. He is filled with burning envy of anyone who might have more. If we observe still closer, especially the unconscious dynamics, we find that this type of person is basically not fond of himself but deeply dislikes himself. The puzzle in this seeming contradiction is easy to solve. The selfishness is rooted in this very lack of fondness for oneself. The person who is not fond of himself, who does not approve of himself, is in a constant anxiety concerning his own self. He has not the inner security which can exist only on the basis of genuine fondness and affirmation. He must be concerned about himself, greedy to get everything for himself, since basically his own self lacks security and satisfaction. The same holds true with the so-called narcissistic person, who is not so much overconcerned with getting things for himself as with admiring himself. While on the surface it seems that these persons are very much in love with themselves, they actually are not fond of themselves, and their narcissism—like selfishness—is an overcompensation for the basic lack of self-love. Freud has pointed out that the narcissistic person has withdrawn his love from others and turned it toward his own person. While the first part of this statement is true, the second one is a fallacy. He neither loves others nor himself.[29]

It is easier to understand this mechanism when we compare it with overconcern and overprotectiveness for others. Whether it is an oversolicitous mother or an overconcerned husband, sufficiently deep observation shows always one fact: While these persons consciously believe that they are particularly fond of the child or husband, there actually is a deep repressed hostility toward the very objects of their concern. They are overconcerned because they have to compensate not only for a lack of fondness but for an actual hostility.

The problem of selfishness has still another aspect. Is not the sacrifice of one's own person the extreme expression of unselfishness, and, on the other hand, could a person who loves himself make that supreme sacrifice? The answer depends entirely on the kind of sacrifice that is meant. There is one *sacrifice,* as it has been particularly emphasized in recent years by Fascist philosophy. The individual should give himself up for something outside of himself which is greater and more valuable; the Leader, the race. The individual by himself is nothing and by the very act of self-annihilation for the sake of the higher power finds his destiny. In this concept, sacrificing oneself for something or someone greater than oneself is in itself the greatest attainable virtue. If love for oneself as well as for another person means basic affirmation and respect, this concept is in sharp contrast to self-love. But there is another kind of sacrifice: If it should be necessary to give one's life for the preservation of an idea which has become part of oneself or for a person whom one loves, the sacrifice may be the extreme expression of self-affirmation. Not, of course, an affirmation of one's physical self, but of the self in the sense of the kernel of one's total personality. In this case the sacrifice in itself is not the goal; it is the price to be paid for the realization and affirmation of one's own self. While in this latter case, the sacrifice is rooted in self-affirmation, in the case of what one might call the masochistic sacrifice, it is rooted in the lack of self-love and self-respect; it is essentially nihilistic.

The problem of selfishness has a particular bearing on psychotherapy. The neurotic individual often is *selfish* in the sense that he is blocked in his relationship to others or overanxious about himself. This is to be expected since to be *neurotic* means that the integration of a strong self has not been achieved successfully. To be *normal* certainly does not mean that it has. It means, for the majority of *well-adapted* individuals that they have lost their own self at an early age and replaced it completely by a *social self* offered to them by society. They have no neurotic conflicts

---

[28] The German word *Selbstsucht* (addiction to self) very adequately expresses this quality common to all *Sucht.*

[29] Since Freud thinks only in the framework of his instinctual concepts, and since a phenomenon like love in the sense used here does not exist in his system, the conclusions to which he comes are all but inevitable.

because they themselves, and, therefore, the discrepancy between their selves and the outside world has disappeared. Often the neurotic person is particularly *unselfish,* lacking in self-assertion and blocked in following his own aims. The reason for this *unselfishness* is essentially the same as for the *selfishness.* What he is practically always lacking is self-love. This is what he needs to become *well.* If the *neurotic* becomes well, he does not become *normal* in the sense of the conforming *social self.* He succeeds in realizing his self, which never had been completely lost and for the preservation of which he was struggling by his neurotic symptoms. A theory, therefore, as Freud's on narcissism which rationalizes the cultural pattern of denouncing self-love by identifying it with *selfishness,* can have but devastating effects therapeutically. It increases the taboo on self-love. Its effects can only be called *positive* if the aim of psychotherapy is not to help the individual to be himself; that is, free, spontaneous and creative—qualities conventionally reserved for *artists*—but to give up the fight for his self and conform to the cultural pattern peacefully and without the noise of a neurosis.

Chapter 33 Psychological Selectivity in Self-Esteem Formation

MORRIS ROSENBERG

The aim of this chapter is to describe how psychological selectivity may operate to sustain self-esteem. That selectivity is an important psychological mechanism is now widely recognized in attitude research. Studies have demonstrated that the mechanisms of selective memory (Edwards, 1941; Levine and Murphy, 1943), selective exposure (Lazarsfeld and Merton, 1943; Lazarsfeld, Berelson, and Gaudet, 1948), and selective interpretation (Cooper and Jahoda, 1947; Kendall and Wolf, 1949) often operate to maintain desired attitudes.

One problem in dealing with psychological mechanisms is that it is usually difficult to stipulate the *conditions* under which they will find expression. This is much less true of the mechanism of selectivity. Selectivity, we suggest, is particularly free to operate under two conditions: (1) where the situation is unstructured or ambiguous, and (2) where the range of options is wide. These conditions are particularly characteristic of self-evaluation.

Without laying claim to exhaustiveness, we wish to point to five types of selectivity that may influence self-attitudes: selectivity of values, of interpretation, of standards, of interpersonal relations, and of situations.

SELECTIVITY OF SELF-VALUES

Although widely overlooked in self-esteem studies, it is a fairly obvious point that a man's global self-esteem is not based solely on his assessment of his constituent qualities; it is based on his self-assessments of qualities that *count*. This point was emphasized with characteristic felicity by William James as far back as 1890. He observed:

I, who for the time have staked my all on being a psychologist, am mortified if others know much

more psychology than I. But I am contented to wallow in the grossest ignorance of Greek. My deficiencies there give me no sense of personal humiliation at all. Had I "pretensions" to be a linguist, it would have been just the reverse (1950, p. 310).

The relevance of self-values is easily demonstrated in our study of adolescents in New York State. Consider the quality "likeable." Some students think they are very likeable, whereas others think they are not. As we would anticipate, those who consider themselves likeable are more likely to think well of themselves in general—to have high global self-esteem. *But the strength of this relationship depends upon the importance attached to being likeable* (Rosenberg, 1965). As Table I shows, among those who *care* about being likeable, the relationship of the self-estimate to global self-esteem is very strong, whereas among those to whom this quality matters little, the relationship is much weaker.

It is especially interesting to consider those students who said they were "little" or "not at all" likeable. Among those who did *not* care about whether they were likeable, only 19 per cent had low global self-esteem, whereas among those who cared a great deal, fully 50 per cent had low self-esteem.

Lest one assume that this result is unusual, we have chosen the 16 qualities out of the 44 in our study which are most highly valued. Consider just those people who feel they are *poor* with regard to these qualities—they do *not* consider themselves likeable, or dependable, or intelligent, or conscientious, and so on. How many of these people have global low self-esteem? The answer is that it depends on how important each of these qualities is to the individual. Table II shows that with regard to 15 out of these 16 qualities, those who cared about the quality had lower self-esteem than those who considered each quality unimportant. Yet these people ranked themselves the same way.

SOURCE. Condensed from Carolyn W. Sherif and Merzafer Sherif (eds.), *Attitude, Ego-Involvement and Change,* New York: John Wiley, 1967, pp. 26-50.

TABLE I

Self-Estimate as "Likeable" and Global Self-Esteem, by Value Attached to Being "Likeable"

Global Self-Esteem	Care a Great Deal about Being "Likeable" (Self-Value)			Do Not Care a Great Deal about Being "Likeable" (Self-Value)		
	Actually Consider Oneself "Likeable" (Self-Estimate)					
	Very	Fairly	Little or Not at All	Very	Fairly	Little or Not at All
High	54%	45%	17%	46%	49%	31%
Medium	39	42	33	39	43	50
Low	7	13	50	15	8	19
Total per cent	100	100	100	100	100	100
Number	(345)	(569)	(52)	(41)	(133)	(34)

TABLE II

Low Self-Estimates and Self-Esteem among Those Varying in Self-Values

Qualities on which Respondents Rated Themselves *Poor*	Care about qualities listed (per cent with low self-esteem)	
	Great deal	Little or not at all
Good student in school	32	18
Likeable	50	19
Dependable and reliable	36	23
Intelligent, good mind	34	26
Clear-thinking, clever	34	22
Hard-working, conscientious	28	17
Easy to get along with	38	23
Realistic, able to face facts	30	17
Friendly, sociable, pleasant	29	24
Honest, law-abiding	42	21
Mature, not childish	29	31
Good sense, sound judgment	33	26
Kind and considerate	28	22
Get along well	39	21
Well-liked by many different people	35	23
Stand up for rights	27	26
Moral and ethical	32	25

To know that someone considers himself deficient with regard to a particular quality is plainly an inadequate indication of what he thinks of himself. We must also know how much he *values* this quality.

Now, with regard to self-values, the principle of selectivity is free to operate because the range of options is inordinately wide. Many years ago, Allport and Odbert (1936) compiled a list of over 17,000 adjectives by which objects could be characterized. Not all of them, to be sure, are applicable to individuals, but an enormous number are. There scarcely seems to be any limit to the types of qualities an individual may consider important in evaluating himself. He may consider it important to be generous, good at working with his hands, a third-generation American, popular, nonconformist, daring, moral, thoughtful, good at dancing, cute, ruthless, imaginative, and on and on.

Given this broad range of options, which values will the individual tend to select? The answer is obvious. He will be disposed *to value those things at which he considers himself good and to disvalue those qualities at which he considers himself poor.* As one illustration, consider the quality "good at working with your hands." Table III shows that among those who felt they possessed this skill, 68 per cent valued this quality highly, whereas among those who believed they lacked this quality, only 6 per cent attached that much importance to it. Indeed, if one considers the same 16 qualities mentioned earlier, one finds that, *without exception,* those who considered themselves good in terms of these qualities were more likely to value them than those who considered themselves poor. Self-values, we see, tend to be selected in a way that enables the individual to maintain a congenial self-picture.

If people are reasonably free to choose their own values, we are led to an interesting paradox of social life: almost everyone can consider himself superior to almost everyone else, as long as he can choose *his own* basis for judgment. Take four boys. One is a good scholar,

TABLE III

Self-Estimate and Self-Value for Quality "Good at Working With Your Hands"

Self-Value: Care about Working with Hands	Self-Estimate: Actually Consider Self "Good at Working with Hands"		
	Very	Fairly	Little or Not at All
Care a great deal	68%	27%	6%
Care some-what or little	32	73	94
Total per cent	100	100	100
Number	(224)	(392)	(533)

TABLE IV

Association Between School Grades and Self-Estimates With Regard to Various Aspects of Intellectual Competence

Relationship between School Average and Estimate of Oneself as . . .	Coefficient of contingency (C)
a good student in school	0.52
intelligent	0.40
clear-thinking and clever	0.16
logical and reasonable	0.16
know quite a bit about many different things	0.15
a person with good sense and sound judgment	0.14
imaginative and original	0.08

the second a good athlete, the third very handsome, and the fourth a good musician. As long as each focuses upon the quality at which he excels, each is superior to the rest. At the same time, each person may blithely acknowledge the superiority of the others with regard to qualities to which he himself is relatively indifferent.

SELECTIVE INTERPRETATION

In judging oneself, one must take account of the "facts." But "facts," as everyone knows, are amenable to highly varying interpretations. Take a soldier who, in the heat of battle, rushes into the enemy stronghold; taking them by surprise, he destroys or captures them. What he has done is an objective fact. But how shall his act be interpreted? Does it prove that he is a man of utmost courage, fearless to the core? Or does it mean that he is simply too stupid to recognize obvious danger when it stares him in the face? This man's act was clear, but whether the act reflects the quality of "courage" or of "foolhardiness" is a matter of interpretation.

Now let us consider an example closer to the high school student's experience—his grade average. Grades are an objective measure of performance. But what do grades mean? This, to a substantial extent, is up to the individual to decide. Consider a number of characteristics which reflect intellectual qualities: good student in school; intelligent, a person with a good mind; clear-thinking and clever; imaginative and original; know quite a bit about many different things; a person with good sense and sound judgment; a logical, reasonable type of person. Table IV reveals striking differences in

the *degree* of association between grade average and self-estimations on these qualities. The association of objective grades to the belief that one is a good student in school is 0.52, but the association of grades to the conviction that one is clear-thinking and clever is only 0.16, and the association of grades to the belief that one is imaginative and original is only 0.08.

In other words, most people agree that grades are a good indication of whether they are good students, but they are by no means convinced that grades tell much about whether they are "clear-thinking and clever" or "imaginative and original." In fact, nearly three-fourths of the students with D or F averages consider themselves very likely or fairly likely to be imaginative and original, and the same is true with regard to having good sense and sound judgment.

This is not a reflection of denial of reality. A D or F student knows that he has poor grades. But there are many aspects of intelligence, and there is nothing in the objective situation to compel the student to interpret his poor grades as relevant to these aspects of intelligence.

If the relevance of grades to intellectual abilities is so wrapped in uncertainty, how much more ambiguous must be the relevance of evidence regarding such characteristics as "moral," "interesting," and "easy to get along with." Here there are no report cards, no test scores, no class percentile ranks. There are no General College Entrance Examination scores for tact, consideration, or independence. Under these circumstances, the inflation of the self-estimates is to be anticipated.

Another factor introducing ambiguity into

the interpretation of evidence is the nature of trait language and the ease of linguistic selectivity. Traits are the main dimensions by which individuals are characterized (Murphy, 1947, p. 506). But the language of traits is simply shot through with evaluative overtones. Even a superficial glance at any list of adjectives shows that the vast majority are not simply descriptions but imply negative or positive judgments. To call a person kind is not a description; it is an accolade. To call him cruel is not to describe him but to condemn him.

What all this adds up to is the fact that *opposite* linguistic patterns are entirely appropriate to the description of the *same* behavior. For example, if one man calls us clever and thoughtful and another calls us shrewd and calculating, are they really describing anything different? If a friend says we are kind, warm, and generous, and an enemy says we are maudlin, syrupy, and prodigal, is there really any disagreement about what we are like? Indeed, both I and my critic may agree that I am bohemian and nonconformist, a term he employs to condemn a quality in which I take the utmost pride. Even though people may agree on the evidence, then, they assuredly do not agree on its meaning.

The fact that this process is so extreme, and yet so common, highlights the nature of self-evaluation perhaps more sharply than any other single thing. *There is scarcely any behavior which cannot be interpreted as admirable in some way* (the last resort is to say that "at least" one is not the opposite appalling extreme). And the individual who engages in "reverse interpretation" cannot clearly be proved wrong. In the silence of our minds, generally unimpeded by the intrusion of alternative interpretations, we are free to review and evaluate the evidence as our biases dictate, to shift perspectives until a congenial one emerges, and to settle on a comfortable conclusion.

Just as selectivity holds sway with regard to the interpretation of the meaning of evidence pertaining to the self, so does it have free rein when it comes to the *choice* of evidence in the first place. For the type of evidence relevant to a given characteristic is widely varied. On what basis shall a man judge his generosity— has he contributed to the Community Chest? has he recently given money to a beggar? did he buy his wife or child a birthday present? did he lend money to a friend? did he pick up the check at a restaurant for a party? He is not obliged to consider *all* these criteria; he

can choose one—any one he wants, any one that fits. And he is right; the situation is so unstructured that *there is no way to prove him wrong.* The same is obviously true of the vast range of qualities that characterize a man.

A high level of ambiguity and wide range of options thus make it possible for selectivity of interpretation, linguistic selectivity, and selectivity of evidence to obtain. That these mechanisms are effective is suggested by the data from our adolescent study. In this investigation the students were asked to rate themselves on 48 qualities which are generally considered desirable and which are not sex-linked. With regard to every quality but one, the subjects were more likely to rank themselves favorably than unfavorably. This result is clearly consistent with people's preferences for positive self-attitudes.

SELECTIVITY OF STANDARDS

In his trail-blazing discussion of the self, William James (1950) devised a most ingenious formula: self-esteem, he held, equals success over pretensions. It was but a small step for him to point out that it may be as blessed a relief for the individual to reduce the denominator as to increase the numerator.

The truth of this observation is apparent from the fact that it is not simply how good a person thinks he is with regard to some quality, but how good he *wants to be* that counts. In the realm of standards, too, the range of options is wide and the situation is extremely unstructured.

How good is "good enough?" Assume that people are satisfied to be fairly good students in school—a choice they can make unhindered. By this criterion, all of the A students, almost all of the B students, seven-tenths of the C students, and even nearly half of the D or F students in our study qualified. Using this moderate standard, most people meet it very well.

This is all the more true of standards with regard to much more ambiguous qualities. A man may want to be "considerate" or "dependable and reliable," but he is under no pressure to be *extremely* considerate or dependable; it is perfectly satisfactory if he is reasonably so. In view of the ease with which evidence can be selected and interpreted in a congenial way, one can reasonably assume that most people can meet the moderate standards they select for themselves.

People have a wide range of options in setting standards for themselves. One can aspire to the very pinnacle of achievement, to a good level of performance, to moderate accomplishment, or even to modest success. A man may aim to be a dominant figure in the world of business or politics, or to be a competent plumber or carpenter. This principle is all the more true of nonoccupational goals. One person may aspire to be the ultimate in sweetness, goodness, and kindness, whereas another is content just to be a decent fellow. One person may set a goal of being absolutely punctual, of never making an error, whereas another may be satisfied to be reasonably reliable. There is thus a great choice available in the setting of standards of performance in the great sweep of areas pertaining to the self.

Given these options, what standards do people select for themselves? If any single conclusion is suggested by the great body of level-of-aspiration literature appearing in the forties, it is that most people tend to set goals that they interpret as falling within reasonable range of their potential accomplishments. When college students are told that WPA workers, college students, and authors and literary critics have made certain scores on a test of literary acquaintance, and are asked how well they expect to do, their estimates center about the hypothetical college students' mean (Chapman and Volkmann, 1939). Similarly, when individual students are "graded" on a task, and then are asked how well they expect to do next time, their estimates change to conform to a new realistic assessment.

More recent surveys of occupational aspirations tend to confirm the laboratory findings. In a study (Rosenberg, 1957) of college students' values, a sample of respondents was asked: "What business or profession would you *most like* to go into?" and "What business or profession do you realistically think you are *most apt* to go into?" While in an abstract sense each student might ideally like to be a surgeon, corporation lawyer, or millionnaire, these young people did not choose these aspirations. Seventy-six per cent said they realistically expected to enter the occupation they most desired, and the course of time had the effect of bringing occupational aspirations and expectations still closer together. Most of the students had scaled down their aspirations to correspond to what they considered within the range of realistic fulfillment. The individual thus tends to select goals (standards, level of

performance, etc.) in accord with his assessment of his qualities. This selectivity enables him to achieve his personal goals, to consider himself "good enough," and to maintain a favorable opinion of himself.

It may be noted that many standards are normatively determined, and that the principle of selectivity of standards characterizes groups as well as individuals. One might call these "societal coping mechanisms." Such standards, it should be noted, are not always high.

For example, the occupational achievements of people of working-class origins are considerably lower than those raised in a middle-class environment. Does their lower success result in lower self-esteem? Not necessarily, because their aspirations (or "pretensions") are much lower. It is not necessary to repeat here Hyman's (1953) ample documentation of this fact. It is sufficient to observe that a working-class boy who wants to become a plumber is surely as likely to achieve his goal as a middle-class boy who wants to become a doctor.

INTERPERSONAL SELECTIVITY

One of the most consistent findings in mass communications research is that people elect to expose themselves to communications with which they agree. With regard to self-attitudes, of course, the mass media are largely irrelevant. What is most important is the communications we get from other people. But interpersonal communications, like impersonal communications, are highly selective. One may advance as a fundamental principle of social life the idea that people, when given the choice, will tend to associate with those who think well of them and to avoid those who dislike or despise them, thereby biasing the communications about themselves to which they are exposed in a favorable direction.

The outstanding case in point is *friendship*. Friendship is the purest illustration of picking one's propaganda. For it is characteristic of a friend that not only do we like him, but he likes us. To some extent, at least, it is probable that we like him *because* he likes us. Indeed, it is well-nigh impossible to be friends with someone who hates us, not only because we would have no taste for such a friendship, but because *he* would not allow the friendship to exist. The upshot of friendship selection is thus to expose people to implicit and explicit interpersonal communications which reflect well on themselves, whereas they hear much less from people who dislike them. All friendship, then, is at least to some extent a "mutual admiration society," whereby each partner helps to sustain the desired self-image of the other.

Perhaps one of the most important appeals of *romantic love* is the great intensity with which the mutual admiration is held. To be sure, love may be unrequited, but where it is mutually held, it is surely a great prop to self-esteem. To find that someone considers us the most beautiful girl in the world or the most wonderful boy is the kind of communication we will select to hear.

What is true of friends and lovers is equally true of *groups*. The avid search for social acceptance is one of the prime enterprises of youth. Young people are constantly in quest of environments where they will be accepted, whether it be the peer group, the beatnik group, Greenwich Village, or whatever. They rebel against their parents, who disapprove of their behavior, characteristics, or qualities—a disapproval offensive to self-esteem—and gravitate toward groups that accept and approve of them, thereby enhancing their self-esteem.

In addition to the individual's selection of interpersonal communications, a social selection, of normative character, holds sway. We might say that there exists a worldwide social conspiracy designed to elevate the general level of self-esteem. We are all part of that conspiracy. The secret, of course, is *tact*. "Tact is everything, talent nothing," it has been said. One of Webster's definitions of tact is a "peculiar ability to deal with others without giving offense." A person devoid of tact is rejected as a boor or a clod.

Men living in society are thus under pressure to protect one another's self-esteem. To imply that someone is stupid, immoral, or disagreeable is to give offense. This behavior is not only punished by the object of attack, but by everyone else as well, since it threatens a social norm which protects the self-esteem of all. Under certain social conditions, such as in the search for scientific truth, it is functionally indispensable to violate the norm. In ordinary social relations, however, it is acceptable to express our admiration and regard for another—although even this must be done in a normatively acceptable way—but not to express our disdain and disrespect. And to censor our disdain for another person is also the better part of valor, for we can be assured that the expression of such sentiments will stimulate in their object observations ill-designed to enhance our own self-esteem.

The communications about ourselves are thus either biased in a generally favorable direction or are so ambiguous that our own biases are free to operate. That this is the case is suggested by the responses of our adolescent subjects to the question: "What do most people think of you?" Nearly 97 per cent said that most people thought very well or fairly well of them, and only 3 per cent said fairly poorly or very poorly. Even two-thirds of those with low self-esteem attributed such benevolent attitudes to others. They may, of course, be right. It is possible that a vast wave of mutual love and good will engulfs the world. One cannot, however, evade the suspicion that, within the ambiguity inherent in determining another's attitudes, a great many people are giving themselves the benefit of the doubt.

SITUATIONAL SELECTIVITY

In a complex, multifaceted society, men are not always able to *make* their environments, but they are often able to *select* their environments. A major motivation in such selectivity is the desire to maintain a congenial self-image. In other words, the individual will tend to expose himself to experiences in which he excels rather than to those in which he is found wanting.

For example, if a person is good at dancing but poor at bowling, he will usually prefer to go to a dance, where his skill is appreciated, than to a bowling alley, where his ineptitude is deprecated. If he is witty rather than deep, he will be disposed to go to parties or social gatherings rather than to lectures and discussions. Similarly, it is well-known that college students tend to elect subjects in which they are strong and avoid those in which they are weak.

Occupational choice is a prime example of situational selectivity. Ginzberg, Ginsburg, Axelrad, and Herma (1951), in their study of occupational choice, accept it as axiomatic that a student will not select an occupation unless he expects to be good at it. When given the choice, then, men gravitate toward situations in which their skills will find expression and their talents will elicit appreciation.

In speaking to this issue of selectivity, we have at the same time been illustrating the pervasiveness and centrality of the self-esteem drive. It directs thought and action in a wide variety of areas. To an important extent it determines our values, our memory processes, our perspectives on and interpretations of facts, our standards of evaluation and reference points, our goals, our choice of friends, marital partners, groups, associations, occupations, or environments generally. As a pervasive influence, there are few factors which can match it. The maintenance of self-esteem is thus a highly constant and omnipresent aspect of our daily lives as well as of our longer-range aims.

LIMITATIONS ON SELECTIVITY

Due to the unstructuredness of the situation and the wide range of options, then, the mechanism of selectivity is very free to operate, forming one's self-attitudes in accord with one's desires. Perhaps the wonder, then, is that people do not all have favorable self-attitudes. Yet we know that many people have mild or moderate doubts about themselves, others serious doubts, and still others grave doubts, or are in fact firmly convinced of their unworthiness.

Such evidence does not mean that the principle of selectivity is wrong, but that there are certain conditions of human experience which are structured and which are characterized by a narrow range of options. In the realm of values, for example, men are largely bound by social role definitions and social group norms. In addition, many self-values are acquired long before the opportunity to test them adequately is at hand, and cannot easily be discarded later. Finally, since certain traits are relevant means for the attainment of certain goals, their importance to the individual, as long as the goals are maintained, cannot easily be dismissed.

A still greater restriction on the operation of the principle of selectivity is to be found in the interpersonal realm. It is in this area of paramount significance for self-esteem that the range of options is most limited. While we are relatively free to choose whom we wish as friends, the same is not true of parents, teachers, or children, and far less true of neighbors, employers or employees, colleagues, or clients. Thus, if our parents scold us, our teachers greet our remarks with sarcasm, our fellow workers laugh at us, our employer berates us, we are largely deprived of the option of avoiding their company or their criticism.

Probably the most significant limit on interpersonal selectivity, however, is this: that at the time of life especially important for self-esteem formation—from about the age of 4 on—the range of interpersonal and situational options is the most severely restricted. The main interpersonal communications about the self come from one's parents, and the child is stuck with them, for better or worse. If they love him, then he has a decisive basis for thinking well of himself. If they do not—if they disparage or reject him—then it is difficult to evade the conclusion that he is unworthy. With no options, there can be no selectivity.

The work of Hovland, Lumsdaine, and Sheffield (1949) as well as that of Sherif and Sherif (1956), and Berelson (1950) clearly shows that the attitudes that are easiest to change, shape, or form are those which are least structured. Now it is precisely in childhood that the self-image is most unformed and unstructured. The child emerging into the stage of self-consciousness has nothing upon which to base a self-estimate. Hence, with parents holding a virtual monopoly on communications, their attitudes have particularly powerful significance for his self-esteem.

The relative absence of interpersonal options for the child is matched by restrictions on situational selectivity. The child's environment is largely fixed. A child with musical skill in a lower-class family, where this quality is of no interest, cannot choose to move into an upper-middle-class family, where this talent is valued. Similarly, there is no assurance that one's characteristics will fit in with the norms of the neighborhood peer group. One gains no applause for talents disdained in the group, and one is powerless to select a different school or neighborhood.

Despite the generality and power of the principle of selectivity, then, it is easy to see why many people *do* have low or moderate self-esteem. These observations also highlight the central significance of childhood in self-esteem formation and the powerful role played by parents in self-esteem formation.

It would outstrip the scope of this paper to document the contention, yet the evidence is consistent in suggesting that, overall, people are more likely to hold favorable than unfavorable opinions of themselves. It seems reasonable to infer that family environments are generally more benign than malignant and that the mechanism of psychological selectivity, whose various expressions have formed the core of this discussion, is highly effective in enabling people to hold desired self-attitudes.

REFERENCES

Allport, G. W. and Odbert, H. S. Trait-names: a psycho-lexical study. *Psychol. Monogr.,* No. 211 (1936).

Berelson, B. Communications and public opinion. In B. Berelson and M. Janowitz, *Public opinion and communication.* Glencoe, Ill.: Free Press, 1950, pp. 448–462.

Chapman, D. W. and Volkmann, J. A social determinant of the level of aspiration. *J. abnorm. soc. Psychol.,* 34 (1939), pp. 225–238.

Cooper, E. and Jahoda, M. The evasion of propaganda: How prejudiced people respond to anti-prejudice propaganda. *J. Psychol.,* 23 (1947), pp. 15–25.

Edwards, A. L. Political frames of reference as a factor influencing recognition. *J. abnorm. soc. Psychol.,* 36 (1941), pp. 34–61.

Ginzberg, E., Ginsburg, S. W., Axelrad, S., and Herma, J. L. *Occupational choice.* New York: Columbia Univ. Press, 1951.

Hovland, C. I., Lumsdaine, A. A., and Sheffield, F. D. *Experiments on mass communication.* Princeton, N. J.: Princeton Univ. Press, 1949.

Hyman, H. H. The value systems of different classes: A social psychological contribution to the analysis of stratification. In R. Bendix and S. M. Lipset (eds.), *Class, status and power.* Glencoe, Ill.: Free Press, 1953, pp. 426–442.

James, W. *The principles of psychology.* New York: Dover, 1950.

Kendall, P. L. and Wolf, K. M. The analysis of deviant cases in communications research. In P. F. Lazarsfeld and F. N. Stanton (eds.), *Communications Research: 1948–49.* New York: Harper, 1949, pp. 152–179.

Lazarsfeld, P. F., Berelson, B., and Gaudet, H. *The people's choice.* New York: Columbia Univ. Press, 1948.

Lazarsfeld, P. F., and Merton, R. K. Studies in radio and film propaganda. *Trans. N. Y. Acad. Sci.,* 6 (1943), pp. 58–79.

Levine, J. M. and Murphy, G. The learning and forgetting of controversial material. *J. abnorm. soc. Psychol.,* 38 (1943), pp. 507–517.

Murphy, G. *Personality.* New York: Harper, 1947.

Rosenberg, M. *Occupations and values.* Glencoe, Ill.: Free Press, 1957.

Rosenberg, M. *Society and the adolescent self-image.* Princeton, N. J.: Princeton Univ. Press, 1965.

Sherif, M. and Sherif, C. W. *An outline of social psychology* (Rev. ed.). New York: Harper, 1956.

Chapter 34 An Experimental Analysis of Self-Dynamics

ALBERT PEPITONE

In the history of psychology, the self has been in and out of fashion like the style-changes of *haute couture*. In the early years, when psychology was breaking away from philosophy, the self often figured importantly in theoretical discussions. Indeed, the classic William James paper reprinted in this book (Chapter 3) is just such an example of the self's theoretical centrality and metatheoretical respectability. With the advent of behaviorism, however, the self went into a decline, and except for the psychoanalytic domain, where the ego has always been a basic self-related construct, the demise was progressive until just before World War II. Then there was a spurt of interest, largely in connection with level of aspiration research and theory (Lewin et al., 1944). But the interest was short-lived, and in the fifties the self looked as dead as the dodo bird. In very recent years, there has been a reawakening of interest—a stirring—due partly to existential philosophy and psychoanalysis and partly to disenchantment with psychological theories that ignore phenomenal experience. Such pithy observations as "the way a man looks at himself profoundly affects the way he behaves," "the man who failed became angry because he was ego-involved in the task," "self-interest underlies many instances of altruism," and "suicide is the end result of self-aggression" are intuitively compelling and as common as adages about home and family.

Despite this relatively recent flurry, the utility of the self as a focal point for theory and research is by no means unequivocal. What reliable data there are do not permit anything like a theoretical integration of self-dynamics. Perhaps research approaches involving the use of subjects selected by personality questionnaires rather than the experimental manipulations of conditions can partly be

blamed for this. But whatever the method, research can only be as penetrating as the concepts underlying it. And, in this connection, it seems fair to say that the analysis of the self and its functioning has been woefully simplistic (see the useful review by Wylie, 1961). Often, a single hypothesized function of the self has carried the entire explanatory burden. Thus self-actualization is seen as the driving force toward mental health, ego-involvement is the dominant work motivation, and so on. Such monolithic characterizations are valid under certain circumstances, but are surely oversimplified and incomplete. Even when the self is differentiated, the various characterizations and functions proposed are wholly descriptive—endowed with neither conceptual properties nor clear operational significance. Allport (1943), for example, listed several self-functions that have been reported in the literature: the ego as "knower," as "object of knowledge," as "primitive selfishness," as "fighter for ends," and as "a behavioral system." Although descriptively apt, such self-functions lack the operational specification that would be necessary to employ them in research. Psychoanalytic conceptions of the ego are also difficult to translate into operational terms. Freud conceived the ego to be the executive source of action, the organ that maintains contact with reality, the repressor of id impulses, and the mainspring of defense mechanisms generally. Although cogent theoretical distinctions are involved in the Freudian analysis, it is not clear how the different self-functions interact and how they are to be identified and manipulated in experiments.

The purpose of this chapter is to isolate several self-related functions and to describe some experimental data generated by such an analysis. We do not suppose, of course, that the self dynamisms considered are exhaustive or that they are precisely and inalterably defined. Further distinctions and modifications

SOURCE. This article was prepared originally for this volume.

347

will almost certainly be necessary with the accumulation of more refined experimental data.

SELF AND IDENTITY

In recent years, the importance of self-identity has been increasingly touted in the literature of personality and psychotherapy. This trend appears to originate in existential philosophy, and particularly in the philosophical phenomenology of Kierkegaard, Husserl, Heidegger, and Sartre. Although, because of its subjective and philosophical background, the psychological treatment of self-identity often sounds strange and obscure to empirical American ears, there is a core idea relevant to personality and social behavior that can be readily expressed: The essential problem of modern man is to realize and to feel his being and existence in a meaningless and absurd world. Due to urbanization, robotization, mass communication, the knowledge gap created by advances in science and technology, and so on, man has become isolated, alienated, rootless, a cog in a wheel within millions of wheels beyond his intellectual grasp. He suffers with questions like "Who am I?" "What am I doing?" In a word, modern man has lost his identity, and desperately needs a knowledge and feeling of self.

In theoretical and especially psychoanalytic treatments of self-identity, it has not been sufficiently recognized that there are multiple sources and levels of identity.[1] In the primitive biological sense, identity is presumably the consciousness of functioning as an organism, the feeling and awareness of need satisfaction, frustration, and fear. At the individual psychological unit of analysis, identity is the awareness and feeling of unique responsibility for choices and their consequences. At the interpersonal level, identity is the consciousness of having effects on the social environment and being individuated and affected by it. Presumably, being a differentiated member of a group adds to a person's identity, whereas being in a homogeneous mass detracts from it. There is a sense of paradox in noting that conforming to the distinctive standards of a group—achieving group identity—can foster individual self-identity.

There are two operational considerations concerning the concept of self-identity. First, the tendency of individuals to make themselves known to others in various verbal and nonverbal ways is not necessarily a reflector of a need for identity. The identification of the person by others is a necessary condition for his obtaining varied social and physical rewards which are mediated by the social environment. For example, the individual must be known so that materials can be given to him, stimuli can be presented to him, and communications can be directed toward him. Of course, such social transactions in the long run can result in a heightened sense of being a distinct individual and so, as a by-product, lead to a gain in self-identity. Second, individuating conditions and behaviors generated by a need for identity should not be confused with attention-seeking behaviors motivated by a need to augment self-esteem. There appears to be a class of behaviors which reflect both identity and esteem needs and thus cannot be an unequivocal definition of either one. For example, the dependent person who cannot assert himself typically suffers from poorly defined identity *and* from low self-esteem. It appears unlikely that a need for identity gives rise to any unique instrumental response. Certainly, such phenomenological characteristics of nonidentity as the feeling of numb isolation and emptiness would militate against specific, directed actions. Private verbal expressions of loneliness and the inability to feel and integrate experience are probably better measures than overt actions, decisions, and social communications.[2]

The pervasive and complex conditions of society which have supposedly weakened personal identity—automation, urbanization, and so forth—are not variables that can be manipulated easily in the laboratory, certainly not in their natural form. What the laboratory experiment can do is create conditions that contain some of the same ingredients in derivative form. For example, conditions like anonymity should tend to intensify the need for self-identity; the individual should display attempts to become individuated. Strong emotional states like anxiety and "excitement" can presumably be used to weaken identity and thus arouse a need for it. The individual should also seek identity when he is made part of a highly uniform social environment, when there are restrictions against making independent choices,

---

[1] An exception is Erikson (1956) who has made a most detailed analysis of the individual developmental and social sources of ego-identity.

[2] Inability to feel, however, may be due to massive inhibitions of powerful impulses like hostility.

and the like. But although these conditions can be created in the laboratory, present knowledge does not allow us to be sure if they affect identity only.

A consideration relevant to experimentation with self-identity is that existential personality theorists have probably exaggerated the negative character of the "human condition." The fact is that weakened self-identity is not always a phenomenologically unpleasant condition and certainly not a condition from which the individual invariably strives to escape. Indeed, individuals often appear to seek situations in which they cannot be clearly identified, and it is likely that, at least temporarily, anonymity is desirable (Festinger, Pepitone, and Newcomb, 1952). Under anonymity, painful responsibilities can be avoided or shared with others, and guilt-evoking impulses and emotions can be expressed with impunity. Thus crowds, mass situations, alcohol, and drugs can be attractive because they *weaken* self-identity. The need therefore is probably best conceived as an equilibrium point, with departures in either direction giving rise to symptomatic emotions and various corrective actions. At the present time, identity is the most difficult self-function to deal with experimentally, and it is no surprise that hardly any laboratory data on the conditions of its arousal and satisfaction are available.

SELF AS CAPACITY

The estimates individuals continually make concerning their ability to perform a task, to achieve goals, and to defend against danger are all essentially descriptions of the self in terms of capacity. The capacities of the self range from the general sense of mastery or "effectance," (White, 1959) masculinity, and the like, to specific abilities, skills, and resources which are relevant to concrete circumstances. Thus a man in a burning house is reflecting on himself when he estimates his chances of putting the fire out with a fire extinguisher and other means available to him. The fact that these cognitions refer to physical objects does not hide their essential function as abilities of the individual who perceives he can use them.

Manifestly, in problem-solving situations, the estimate of his capacity can powerfully affect the individual's performance, aspiration, and social behavior. However, the salutary effect of perceived competence and depressing effect of low ability are not inevitable in all circumstances. Self-confidence cannot work wonders

in performance if the ability is not objectively there. Equally, the capacity which the individual has may not be relevant to the problem at hand. And finally, the individual may not be motivated to achieve what he is capable of. The capacity function of the self is not strictly a motivation but a facilitator or hinderer of motivated behavior.

The role of the self as a perceived capacity can most clearly be seen in the classic level of aspiration experiment (Lewin et al., 1944). Here the individual is confronted with tasks which are hierarchically ordered in terms of difficulty. Just before each performance trial, he states the difficulty level at which he wants to perform. He then actually performs the task at that level and either succeeds or fails. There is substantial agreement among many studies that the level of aspiration rises with successful performance and falls with failure. Theoretically, actual performance affects the level of aspiration through the individual's estimate of the probability of success and failure at that level—in other words, his perception of his ability. In addition, the amount of reward and punishment contingent upon success and failure determine the level of aspiration on each subsequent trial. The effects of success and failure are mediated by a third function of the self.

SELF-ESTEEM

The rule that the greater the difficulty of a task on which one succeeds, the greater the psychological reward, reflects the operation of a social norm with respect to achievement. At least in so-called Western society, the greater reward value in achieving increasingly difficult goals is highly salient and strongly enforced (McClelland, 1961). The achievement norm presumably affects child-rearing practices which inculcate conformity tendencies over a wide range of achievement situations. Such internalized parental (and other societal agents') pressures to achieve are partly based on a need for self-esteem—the internalized need to win and retain the esteem of these agents. The achievement "drive" is also directly based on the desire to be positively evaluated (or to avoid negative evaluation) by the social environment—the desire to improve or to maintain status.[3] The striving toward higher self-esteem and status (or avoidance of loss of esteem and

---

[3] We ignore here the need to finish tasks, to master the environment and to solve problems and other "achievement" tendencies which appear to be independent of self-esteem.

status) must surely be counted as the most powerful and pervasive psychological motivations in man's repertoire. In general, these tensions are aroused in situations where the individual perceives he can succeed or fail, that is, where he perceives his esteem and status could change in either direction. When the task is too difficult, or when the individual has a secure or unchangeable status position or self-concept, such motivations are presumably weak or absent.

SELF-VALIDATION

Conformity to achievement norms in various performance situations is not motivated only by the need for status and self-esteem. Another basis is a cognitive pressure toward self-evaluation. According to one formulation of this idea (Festinger, 1954), the individual has a need to evaluate his ability, and where there are no objective tests for this purpose, he must rely on the social environment. What he does is "compare" his performance with the performance of others who are perceived to be relevant and comparable. The comparison process consists of trying to perform close to the performance level of this "measurement norm." For individuals whose performance is slightly below that of comparable others, the comparison process is reflected in competitive activity aimed at closing the gap. Thus coalition-formation in bargaining situations (Hoffman, Festinger, and Lawrence, 1954) and persistence in setting levels of aspiration (Dryer, 1954) are explainable by the "drive" to evaluate one's abilities. There is some evidence that individuals also attempt to evaluate their emotions by reference to the social environment. Given uncertainty about the quality or intensity of one's feelings—and since objective measures of emotional reactions do not exist in most arousal situations, this is prevailingly the case —there are tendencies to affiliate with others who have been subject to the same stimulus (Schachter, 1959).

It is important to note that, theoretically, it is not any kind of evaluation that the individual needs but one that corresponds with what he considers to be objective reality. In other words, the need is to *validate* various parts of the self and environment represented in the individual's cognitive structure. In a research program designed to test hypotheses derived from this cognitive postulate, it was shown that the attractiveness of the self and of others was determined by the validity of the evaluational

information available. Invalid information about another or self tends to modify one's evaluations in a way that makes them more valid (Pepitone, 1964).

The foregoing analysis points up the essential problem in doing laboratory research on the self: the necessity to take account of multiple self-related motives and functions. The research strategy in such circumstances might be to manipulate one aspect of the self while trying to hold the others constant, or it might vary two or more self-dynamics simultaneously by independent operations and observe the predicted interactive effects. It is clear in either case that not only do self-motives and functions interact independently to produce behavioral outcomes, but in all likelihood they affect each other in various ways. Perhaps the complexity can be illustrated by some concrete examples.

Both self-esteem and self-validation play roles in the personal, evaluative judgments individuals make about themselves and each other. If, for example, the individual is requested to evaluate himself along some personality dimension of which he is rather uncertain, that is, if he does not know whether he possesses the trait or how much of it he possesses, we can predict that his judgment will probably be close to the self-evaluation (along the same dimension) of another person whom he perceives to be comparable. He should have a tendency to "take over" that personality trait. Now, if the personality evaluation of the other is favorable, that is, if the trait is a positive one, the individual who compares himself not only obtains a subjectively valid self-evaluation but gains in self-esteem as well. On the other hand, if the comparable other person evaluates himself unfavorably in terms of a negative trait, then the individual who is under pressure to compare himself is in conflict: To attribute an unfavorable personality trait to himself would provide him with a valid self-evaluation but would simultaneously cause a lowering of his self-esteem.

The resolution of these "self-evaluation" conflicts is not easily predicted without a detailed knowledge of the resolution possibilities perceived by the individual. But one frequently possible solution would be to regard the other person as incomparable, that is, not a good validity criterion. Along the same lines, the individual who is constrained to accept the negative trait may be able to attribute other negative characteristics to the other person. By attributing more of these characteristics to the other person than to himself, he becomes relatively less negative on the whole. And if his "true" overall personality is less unattractive, he satisfies the validity pressure and removes the threat to his self-esteem at the same time. There are other possibilities, of course. If the trait of the comparison or "criterion" person is ambiguously negative, it may be easy to distort so that what the individual attributes to himself is not nearly so unfavorable.

Conflict between the two self-motives often seems to occur in inner psychodynamics. For example, the individual who has powerful chronic hostile impulses that are unacceptable when they threaten to enter his consciousness may tend to feel unworthy, depressed, hypochondriacal, and so on. Such tendencies toward self-devaluation obviously run counter to the need to maintain self-esteem but are perfectly in line with the need for a valid self-concept. In the interest of validity, his self-evaluation "wants" to change to be consistent with the judgment of his conscience, but it simultaneously resists the potential loss of self-esteem. The problem for the individual is how to deny the impulse or the transgressive behavior based on it. A frequent device is to delegitimatize the grounds for self-devaluation. Concretely, this may be done by seeking and accepting information which is self-justifying. Thus the person who is the target of the hostile impulse is seen to have "done" something or to possess a character blemish which makes him deserve punishment. If, on the other hand, the individual commits an unequivocal transgression against an unequivocally innocent party, he must accept the valid negative self and the loss of esteem that is tied to it. In general, how the conflict gets resolved seems to depend upon the ambiguity surrounding the arousal of a self-devaluation tendency.

Self-motives frequently affect the relative tendency to be cooperative or competitive. A situation that constrains the individual to share rewards may be perceived as a threat to self-esteem and degenerate into an attempt to maximize rewards in order to restore self-esteem. Such compulsive competitiveness would be characteristic of individuals who have chronic feelings of inferiority or who are insecure about their status. Individuals also, of course, compete on "rational" grounds—to win the contest, to obtain the larger amount of reward—where competition is demanded by the task and does not involve a self-esteem threat. But whatever the basis, competition may be affected by an opposing self-validation tendency which stems from the fact that the amount of reward to which an individual aspires is also governed by how much he thinks he is really worth. If the reward gained by the person with whom he interacts is taken as the amount he deserves, then the competitiveness of the individual would tend to be restrained in order for him to maintain a subjectively valid self-evaluation. We are not talking here of a competition conflict that is based on fear of punishment from the person with whom the individual competes but of the tendency for individuals to take from a situation the amount of reward which is consistent with their self-worth. This amount is almost always less than the maximum reward that can be obtained and, in the case where his true worth is based on objective information—where the other person is not used as a standard—can be less than the amount perceived to have been gained by the other person.

The foregoing discussion will perhaps suffice to illustrate the complex and subtle interrelationships that theoretically exist between two major self-motivations. We now proceed with a more detailed experimental analysis of the self-motive determinants of projection.

PROJECTION AND SELF-EVALUATION CONFLICT

The effects of self-motives on the cognitive processes are nowhere more evident than in the phenomenon of projection. Everyday experience tells us that the attribution of personal characteristics, including traits, motives, and values, to others is strongly determined by the person's evaluation of himself. In the orthodox psychoanalytic view, projection is restricted to characteristics that are unconscionable to the individual and therefore repressed in his unconscious. The tendency to attribute such characteristics arises when they threaten to reveal themselves to his consciousness. In more technical terms, projection is a defense mechanism initiated by the Ego in order to resolve the conflict between the impulses of the Id and the moral proscriptions of the Superego. In essence, the defense consists of a shifting of attention from the self to the social environment—a relocation of the source of evil against which a self-righteous moral crusade can then be made (cf. Fenichel, 1945, for a more complete analysis).

Alternatively, instead of conceiving projection to be based on a Superego-Id conflict, it is possible to view the phenomenon as the outcome of self-evaluation conflicts—conflicts between and among self-esteem and self-validation tendencies. In pursuing this view empirically, it is necessary to create self-evaluation conflicts while holding the Superego-Id conflict constant, so that it could not account for any predicted effects. An experimental design which accomplishes this objective was developed by Bramel (1962), and our own procedure is identical in fundamental respects (Pepitone, 1964).

Self-evaluation conflicts can be created by providing a person who has a positive self-evaluation with credible information about himself which is unequivocally negative, or by providing a person who has a negative self-evaluation with undeniably favorable information about himself. The person who is favorably disposed toward himself and who receives negative information from an objective, irrefutable source experiences two types of conflict. First, his true self-evaluation is equivocal. He does not know if he is an attractive or an unattractive person and there are oscillating tendencies for him to regard himself either way. Second, the negative information about himself (as well as the tendency to form a valid negative self-evaluation) threatens to bring about a loss of self-esteem. This threat activates a counter tendency to defend against such a loss of esteem. How does projection help resolve this set of self-validation and self-esteem conflicts?

Assuming that it is possible for the individual to employ projection in such a dual conflict situation—for example, in an experimental situation where the experimenter requests the subject to make personality ratings of his partner and himself—the individual can effect a solution by attributing unfavorable characteristics to someone else. The more of some unfavorable characteristic attributed to another person or group, the relatively less unattractive the individual regards himself. In other words, by implanting negative traits in others with whom he can compare himself, the individual eases the threats to his self-esteem created by the negative information. He solves the quandary of whether he's good or bad by making himself relatively good and thus weakens the negative validating tendency and the counter self-esteem tendency which it has aroused.

If the individual has a negative evaluation of himself to begin with, the negative information he receives poses no problem in validation; it serves to confirm his unfavorable self-opinion. And, although the unflattering information arouses a tendency to defend the self-esteem from being pushed even below its preexisting level, the total strength of conflict is less than for the individual whose preexisting self-evaluation is positive. Accordingly, the tendency to project negative traits should be weaker.

A similar analysis can be made of the case where the individual learns from an unimpeachable source that he possesses an important favorable characteristic. In this case, however, the individual with the preexisting negative self-evaluation suffers the stronger conflict and, consequently, projects to a greater degree. Presumably, such an individual harbors a chronic tendency to enhance his self-esteem. At the same time, there should be some question in his mind as to which evaluation is valid. By attributing negative characteristics to another, the individual becomes less unattractive in his own eyes. He thus alleviates the chronic threat to his self-esteem and removes the doubt about his true worth at the same time. For the individual with a preexisting positive self-evaluation, no conflict exists at all; there is no self-esteem threat or defense against it, and there is no conflict about a valid self-evaluation.

The foregoing analysis leads to the prediction of a statistical interaction: *Given a negative disclosure about the self, subjects with positive self-evaluation should attribute more of some negative characteristic to a partner (relative to themselves) than subjects who have a negative self-evaluation; but given a favorable disclosure about the self, those subjects with a negative self-evaluation should attribute relatively more of some negative characteristics than those who have positive pre-existing evaluations.*

In the experiment designed to test this hypothesis, a pair of male *S*'s who were strangers to each other observed a series of pictures either of female or male nudes after having received a confidential report of personality tests taken earlier. At this earlier session, one *S* was given a favorable report on such dimensions as hostility, maturity, efficiency and social sensitivity, whereas the other *S* was given an unfavorable report. A self-evaluation form including a variety of personality trait ratings administered after the High and Low Self-Evaluation induction confirmed the effectiveness of this induction.

The ostensible purpose of the experiment was to study human sexuality, and a physiological measure, the psychogalvanic skin response (GSR), was used to record the *S*'s' level of arousal to the pictures. Actually, the needle deflection on the microammeters in each *S*'s booth could be controlled by *E*. Strong reactions were communicated in this manner to viewers of both nude males and nude females. In the case of males the arousal meant latent homosexuality (Negative Information),[4] whereas for the pairs who viewed females the information was a sign of basic virility (Positive Information). For each of the 15 pictures in the Positive and Negative Information conditions, each *S* rated his own reaction on a 0-100 scale (in effect, he recorded the dial reading reflecting his degree of arousal) and the reaction of the other *S* of the pair. Projection was based on the sum of the 15 discrepancies between the two ratings made by each *S*. The greater the positive discrepancy (partner rated as more aroused than self) or the smaller the negative discrepancy (partner arousal weaker than self), the stronger the projection.

Following the GSR procedure, *S*'s were given a list of ten emotional reactions on each of which he rated himself and his partner on a seven-point scale labeled "Not at all" on the low end and "Very Strongly" on the high end. Projection of these emotional reactions (nervousness, shame, fear, anger, disgust, sexuality, pleasure) was measured the same way as the projection of sexuality, that is, by the discrepancy between the *S*'s rating of himself and his partner. The greater the positive discrepancy (partner rated more emotional than self) or the less the negative discrepancy (partner rated less than self) the stronger the projection.

Regarding sexuality projection in terms of GSR rating discrepancies, Table I shows that the results do not confirm the interaction hypothesis; that is, the negative discrepancy in the upper left cell is not smaller than it is in the lower left cell, and the positive discrepancy in the lower right cell is not reliably greater than the negative discrepancy in the upper right cell.

Significant interactions were obtained, how-

---

[4] To guard against panic reactions in the Negative Information condition, *S*'s were told about the bisexual nature of man and that the latent homosexual reactions were within normal limits. After the experimental session all *S*'s were given a thorough explanation of the purposes and procedures.

TABLE I

The Projection of Sexuality
(Masculinity and Homosexuality)

		Self Information	
		Negative	Positive
Initial self-	Positive	−2.6	−0.10
evaluation	Negative	−2.5	+0.45
Interaction *SE* × Information *F* ns			

ever, in the projection of two (out of ten) emotional reactions. These are unfavorable traits and from a psychoanalytic point of view highly relevant to the phenomenon on projection: shame and diffuse anger. These results are found in Table II.

There is thus partial support for the projection hypothesis and the theoretical analysis that led to it. However, it is not clear why the predicted effects failed to occur on all the characteristics which the *S*'s had an opportunity to project. Further specification of the negative value and the relevance of projectable characteristics is necessary.

We may conclude this discussion of self-dynamics with the *caveat* that the road ahead for experiment is fraught with technical difficulties. There are two paramount problems: (*a*) the development of independent operations which manipulate one and only one self-motive with sufficient strength; and (*b*) the identification and measurement of dependent variables which exclusively reflect the effects of the self-motives manipulated. But difficult or not there is no other way to obtain information about the self which can be scientifically useful.

TABLE II

Projection of Shame and Diffuse Anger

		Self-Information	
A. Shame		Negative	Positive
Initial self-	Positive	0.00	+0.10
evaluation	Negative	−0.30	+0.95
Interaction SE × Information $F = 6.74, p < 0.05$			

		Self-Information	
B. Diffuse Anger		Negative	Positive
Initial self-	Positive	−0.20	+0.05
evaluation	Negative	−0.15	+0.50
Interaction SE × Information $F = 4.78, p < 0.05$			...

REFERENCES

Allport, G. The ego in contemporary psychology. *Psychol. Bull.,* **50** (1943), pp. 451–478.

Bramel, D. A dissonance theory approach to defensive projection. *J. abnorm. soc. Psychol.,* **44** (1962), pp. 121–129.

Dryer, A. Aspiration behavior as influenced by expectation and group comparison. *Hum. Relat.,* **7** (1954), pp. 175–190.

Erikson, E. The problem of ego identity. *J. Amer. Psychoanal. Assoc.,* **4** (1956), pp. 56–121.

Fenichel, O. *The psychoanalytic theory of neuroses,* New York: Norton, 1945.

Festinger, Leon. A theory of social comparison processes. *Hum. Rel.,* **7** (1954), pp. 117–140.

Festinger, L., Pepitone, A., and Newcomb, T. Some consequences of de-individuation in groups. *J. abnorm. soc. Psychol.,* **47** (Supplement) (1952), pp. 382–389.

Hoffman, P., Festinger, L., and Lawrence, D. Tendencies toward group comparability on competitive bargaining. *Hum. Rel.,* **7** (1954), pp. 141–159.

Lewin, K., Dembo, T., Festinger, L., and Sears, P., Level of aspiration. In *Personality and the Behavior Disorders* (Ed. J. McV. Hunt), New York: Ronald Press, 1944.

McClelland, D. *The Achieving Society.* Princeton, N.J.: Van Nostrand, 1961.

Pepitone, A. *Attraction and Hostility.* New York: Atherton, 1964.

Schachter, S. *The Psychology of Affiliation.* Palo Alto, Cal.: Stanford, 1959.

White, R. Motivation reconsidered: the concept of competence. *Psychol. Rev.,* **66** (1959), pp. 297–333.

Wylie, Ruth. *The Self Concept: A Critical Survey of Pertinent Research Literature.* Lincoln, Univ. Nebraska, 1961.

Chapter 35 The Self, Intentionality, and Reactions to Evaluations of the Self[*]

PETER G. OSSORIO AND KEITH E. DAVIS

This paper involves several interrelated theses and expositions. The first thesis is that in its primary use (i.e., the nontechnical use which has motivated psychologists to develop "self" as a technical term in psychology), "self" is simply a locution for identifying a particular *person as such,* so that to understand the phenomena for which "self" terminology is used depends on a prior understanding of what it is to be an individual person. The second thesis is that the concept of "a person" is like the concept of "arithmetic": it is an articulated conceptual *system* in which distinctions and transitions are made which could not possibly be established empirically or justified by reference of evidence of any kind. Here a limited aspect of the concept of a person—the concept of one person *liking* another person—is delineated in sufficient detail to exhibit some of

the nonempirical connections which have a direct relevance for some psychological research. The third thesis is that a substantial portion of research in social psychology has been presented as a matter of establishing empirically the very relationships which are nonempirical and *could not* be established empirically (like announcing the "experimental finding" that six and four are ten or that bachelors are not married). The third thesis is upheld by a demonstration that brings together the prior discussions of "person," "self," and "liking," for it consists of showing that recent experiments dealing with persons' reactions to evaluations of them*selves* exemplify the attempt to demonstrate empirically relationships that are nonempirical from the start.

THE CONCEPT OF A PERSON

The formulation of the concept of a person represents a substantial departure from current psychological mores in many respects. To facilitate understanding and encourage responsible criticism, the following "position" points are noted briefly, though space does not permit the amplification they require:

1. The reality underlying the term "causes of behavior" is that people sometimes succeed in giving causal explanations. The reality underlying *that* is that people look for explanations and give explanations of various sorts, including causal accounts. The Person concept reflects the general phenomenon and explains it by means of a noncausal form of explanation of human behavior.

2. Looking for and giving explanations are inseparable from the more general phenomena of speaking and the use of concepts and descriptive terminology. Psychological descriptions of psychological phenomena (human behavior) are not taken to be less fundamental *in any sense* than, say, physical or physiological descriptions of any phenomena.

SOURCE. This article was prepared originally for this volume.

[*] We are indebted to a great number of psychologists and sociologists for giving us the benefit of their critical response to an earlier version of this paper. Unfortunately that list is so long that we can hardly acknowledge our gratitude individually. Davis' work on this paper was initially supported by a grant from the University of Colorado's Council on Research and Creative Work, and the revision was supported by NSF Grant GS-945. The present paper is one of a series of conceptually oriented and research oriented monographs and papers in which certain conceptual themes and methodological arguments are applied to various topic areas within Psychology. The central member of the series is the monograph *Persons* (Ossorio, 1965) which develops in substantially greater detail the logical and methodological characteristics of person concepts and applies the analysis to psycholinguistics, individual differences, research methods, and selected recent formulations of motivation and emotion within psychology. Copies of *Persons* may be obtained from the Linguistic Research Institute, Box 1294, Boulder, Colo., 80302. This article is publication No. 107 of the Institute of Behavioral Science, U. of Colorado.

3. The "assertion" that we have a prelinguistic access to reality (obviously, a "physical" or "phenomenological" reality) which we *then* baptize with words is taken to be not merely mistaken, but self-contradictory and unintelligible. The distinction between linguistic and nonlinguistic is a *linguistic* distinction, and so the separation of language from reality is a *linguistic* fiction.

4. But there is a basic, nonfictitious contrast *and relationship* between what is verbal and what is not. This is dealt with in the formulation of the Person concept.

5. The concept of a Person is nonempirical because *all* concepts are nonempirical. Complex concepts such as "arithmetic," "physical object," "person," and "chess" are also conceptual systems (they consist of conceptual components having *logically necessary* relationships to one another). It is only by virtue of our individual histories that we come to be able to use such concepts correctly, but we do not discover or establish those necessary relationships *empirically* (in the sense of an experiment, an investigation, or an inductive count).

A further caution is in order: The task of formulating the Person concept is like the task of axiomatizing arithmetic. The task is to exhibit the necessary relationships our familiar practices conform to, and not *merely* to summarize how we talk about what we do, so the talk may be strange, though apropos. The task is not to present statements that can be justified as being true but rather to communicate a set of instructions, *no one of which is sufficient by itself,* for performing effectively in the relevant domain (in the present case, explaining human behavior). It is the entire Person concept, not this or that portion of it, which is required for understanding persons, the "self," and human behavior. The Person concept is presented in the next four sections of this paper.

Language

"Saying something" is a form of human activity which is important because of the way it is bound up in other human activities. It is important because what we say makes a difference in what *else* we do. What we say about people makes a great deal of difference.

Schematically: To say that something is X is always to characterize it as being X *rather* than Y or Z (some set of not-X's). This requires that we have linguistic distinctions among X, Y, and Z, which requires that on particular occasions we are able to recognize which of these terms has been used. In order for uttering X to be a case of saying something, we also must be able to recognize what occasions are occasions for X rather than Y or Z. Further, there must be something that hinges on whether an occasion is an occasion for X rather than Y or Z. That is, there must be some one or more actions that are recognizable as cases of treating something as X rather than Y or Z. This involves both performance skills (knowing how to treat something as X) and observational skills (being able to tell when that is what has been done).

"P says X" is the irreducible unit for a pragmatic conceptualization of language. It is obviously a complex unit, since it requires reference to a repertoire of observational skills and both verbal and nonverbal performance skills in giving merely a descriptive account of even the simplest verbal behavior. The significance lies in pursuing these connections in the opposite direction: what gives language its crucial importance is that it does connect observation, speech, and nonverbal behavior in a nonempirical way, and so it codifies (systematizes and makes public) what people know how to do. For example, it connects (*a*) being able to distinguish being "afraid" from feeling some other way, (*b*) being able to tell someone about it, (*c*) being able to act in a way that is appropriate to being afraid, and (*d*) knowing what sort of things to expect from someone else who is afraid, and knowing what to do about that.

That a description may be incorrect is a logical prerequisite for the possibility of its being correct. Since an occasion for X must be distinguishable from an occasion for Y, it clearly is possible to utter X when the occasion is an occasion for Y, that is, to use X incorrectly. The fact that a description may be incorrect implies that we are able to agree sufficiently in our judgments as to whether it has been used correctly on particular occasions. Thus all of the performance standards codified by our language are *public* standards (although there is no single, universal "public" in this respect, but only various linguistic publics). We are tempted to assert an infallible, privileged access to some phenomena, for example, our own feelings. But if any phenomenon were a matter of one person's say so, there would be no difference between his being right and his being wrong, and so no sounds that he might utter could qualify as having said anything (cf. Rhees, 1954). Again, the temptation is to suppose that if I could not be wrong then I have the freedom to say *anything* ("Words mean what I want them to mean"), but that is a mistake. Without reality constraints those sounds have only the parasitical significance that we know what *we* would be saying if *we* uttered them, and we only know that by the virtue of the constraints for *us* on what constitutes an appropriate occasion. And if someone claimed that he had a feeling that had no relationship at all with his behavior, we should have to say that then there was no difference between his having that feeling and his not having it, and so there is no claim that *could* be a claim to having such a feeling.

What constitutes sufficient agreement with respect to the occasions for particular descriptions or locutions will vary according to the requirements of the human activities within which such performances have a point. Language and action are mutually supporting, and because of that they provide mutual checks. If it has no implications for nonverbal behavior, no verbal performance is a case of *saying* anything, and if no psychological description is applicable to a given event, that event is not a case of anyone *doing* anything.

"Our language" covers a number of *logically independent* descriptive systems. Each is anchored in human life, human knowledge, and human action, and that is enough. And, of course, a descriptive system implies a conceptual system—to have the competence to say that something is X is to have the concept of X.

No methodological backsliding is involved in references to concepts or conceptual systems. A concept is not an inner event, an invisible state or process, a hidden cause, or any of the peculiar entities endemic to causal explanations. To say that on a particular occasion (a) I am using the concept of an X, or (b) I am treating something as an X, or (c) the concept of an X guides my behavior, is to say one thing, not three, and it is to say that thing literally and precisely, not metaphorically or loosely. (For the purist: distinguishing the case of treating something as a non-X or a truth-function of X is not to the point here.) To say this is simply to classify my behavior on that occasion as being of one distinguishable kind rather than any other kind. *What* kind depends, of course, on the particular concept in question.

The use by a person of a particular descriptive system (conceptual system) provides the basis both for talking about particular kinds of "things" and for distinguishing a generic kind of behavior. For example, the use of the descriptive system "chess" provides the objective basis for talking about these heterogeneous "things," such as "pawn," "move," and "checkmate," which are the conceptual components of "chess." And it provides the objective basis for talking about "chess behavior." Similarly, the use of the descriptive system "Person" provides the objective, observable basis for talking about a heterogeneous set of "things" such as "feelings," "actions," "wants," "anger," "interest," "attitude," and "trait." It also provides the objective basis for talking about *"human behavior."*

There is no more fundamental basis than this for talking about "things" of particular kinds. There is no prelinguistic Reality by reference to which we might certify the existence of some things rather than others. Knowing what we do know, and what we do know how to do, and being able to say what we are able to say, it would be egregious and incoherent to ask whether there are *really* any such things as pawns (or physical objects, or persons, wants, actions, finesses, observations, etc.) in the Real world. If we tried that, we would fail to ask any question, for although the words in our "question" would be familiar, there would be no reality constraints to give them any significance.

Thus in the following presentation it should be kept in mind that references to concepts, conceptual systems, and descriptive systems are not references to things that are once-removed from reality and contrasted with reality, for our *use* of concepts and descriptive systems, and the constraints they reflect, represent our *direct* access to "the real world."

Intentional Action

The concept of intentional action is the basic conceptual element in the concept of a Person. "Intentional action" is itself a conceptual system articulated into four "structural" concepts, or "concept-types." These are designated as the "Want," "Know," "Know How," and "Overt Attempt" concept-types. These four are classificatory terms which subsume an indefinitely large number of particular wants, particular items of knowledge, particular skills, and particular performances or recognizable behaviors. To call these four "structural" concepts is to say that an intentional action logically requires particulars of all four kinds. Compare the structural description of a sandwich: "Two slices of bread and something edible in between." A particular sandwich must have a particular kind of bread and a particular comestible in between, but what makes it a sandwich is not the particular kind of bread and comestible, but, instead, the fact that it satisfies the structural description. Given that, the particulars make it a sandwich of a particular kind. This will also be the case for *types* of intentional action, referred to later. Acting from anger, guilt, or fear are three particular types of intentional action, just as "ham on rye," "hot turkey," and "hamburger" are three particular types of sandwich.

Thus in any intentional action, a person *necessarily* (*a*) is trying to accomplish something he wants or has a reason to do, (*b*) has the knowledge relevant to the attempt, (*c*) is recognizably doing the sort of thing one *would* do in order to accomplish this, and (*d*) his doing this is neither accident nor coincidence but exercise of skill or competence.

The four structural concepts are now briefly characterized.

Wants. The basic cases are those wants that are intelligible without reference to further wants. Among these are such biosocial wants as food, drink, sex, and physical comfort, and also a variety of artistic, recreational, occupational, and generally social activities or states of affairs. Other wants are intelligible as means to these "intrinsic" wants. A situation or activity can provide reason enough for what we do; for example, in a social context, a greeting provides reason enough for a greeting, and failure to respond in this way would call for a special explanation. Finally, we have standards of intelligibility for priorities among wants. We understand those priorities that are embodied in activities, social practices, and ways of life of which we have some knowledge.

Know. Intentional action is intelligibly ascribed only to sentient individuals. For a nonsentient individual there is no difference between acting and moving. At a minimum, a person who wants something must be able to distinguish between that thing and other things. Normally other knowledge is required too. The basic case of knowing (or believing) is that in which the person *knows what* he is distinguishing, so that he is able to say what it is. An important derivative case is that in which a person's awareness is reflected in what he does, although he cannot say what he is reacting to. "Selective perception," "unconscious motivation," and many cases of emotionally motivated

behavior involve the derivative case. In this case, the person does just the sort of thing he *would* do if he knew and could say what he was doing.

Overt Attempt. The overt attempt corresponds closely to what most psychologists would call "behavior" or "response." It is the objective, observable *psychological process* by which an intentional action is accomplished. Our terminology for identifying overt attempts is the same as that for identifying intentional actions, for example, "drinking a cup of coffee," "pressing a lever," "saying 'I do,'" "walking to the window." Identifying an overt attempt is noncommittal in the way that "the smell of bacon" may be noncommittal. The latter is a way of identifying a certain smell in the only way we know how: not by saying what smell it is, but by saying what it is the smell *of,* and we recognize that the smell may be present without the bacon being present. "Pressing a lever" identifies a behavioral process *in the only way we know how*—not by saying what process it is, but by saying what intentional action it is an appropriate process *for*. If the corresponding want, knowledge, and skill are present, then it *is* the intentional action "pressing a lever"; if they are not present, it is not, but the characterization of the overt attempt as such would not then be incorrect.

Know How. Whatever the overt attempt in an intentional action is, it must represent the exercise of some skill or skills (which implies learning), for otherwise its occurrence at that time would be a matter of accident or coincidence, and that would be incompatible with its being the expression of an intention or an *attempt* to achieve something wanted.

Not every combination of wants, knowledge, overt attempt, and skilled performance qualifies as an intentional action. Moreover, the specification of a particular intentional action will usually provide strong restrictions on which combinations of particular wants, and the like, qualify. Thus our knowledge of a person's actions is based on the convergence of (*a*) the wants, skills, and knowledge we have prior and independent reason for thinking he had, and (*b*) the wants, skills and knowledge required in order for something that he is apparently doing (the overt attempt) to be a case of intentional action.

Because of the conceptual complexity of intentional action, there are a great many ways in which intentional actions could be "the same." An important class of instances of classifying intentional actions as being of "the same kind" involves the use of "feeling" concepts as motivational concepts. For example, if we ask what are the minimum conditions under which "he did H because he was afraid of X" is intelligible, we find the following (Gosling, 1962):

1. He must have learned to discriminate some things as dangerous, in contrast to other non-dangerous things. [To see something as dangerous is to see it as something to be avoided.]

2. He must have learned some ways of avoiding some dangers.

3. He must have a learned tendency to take steps to avoid dangers without stopping to think. [This distinguishes fear from, e.g., caution or prudence.]

Thus to say that "He did H because he was afraid of X" is to say that (a) he appraised X as dangerous, (b) this gave him reason enough to want and to try to avoid X, (c) what he was apparently doing is the sort of thing one would do in an attempt to avoid X, and (d) his doing that was not accidental or coincidental, but represented the exercise of some set of skills. To give the foregoing analysis is to exhibit doing something out of fear as a case of intentional action. Similar analyses can be given for other feelings (e.g., anger, guilt, envy). Unconscious motivation can likewise be derived as a special case of intentional action (Ossorio, 1965).

Individual Persons

The concept of intentional action, articulated into its four structural concepts, is entirely general across persons, groups, and societies. This logical structure is the general form in which we explain and understand human behavior. It is this structure which, when whimsically cast in causal form, constitutes the basic "laws of behavior" formulated in S-R, cognitive, and other technical psychological theories (Ossorio, 1965). The delineation of intentional action provides the basis for the presentation of the concept of a Person.

The Person concept is what we use in describing individual persons and in distinguishing one person from another. It, too, is articulated into a set of structural concepts: *trait, value, style, attitude, interest, ability, state, status,* and *need*. These structural concepts will be referred to as "individual difference concepts," or "I.D. concepts." Each such concept subsumes an indefinitely large number of particular traits, attitudes, and so on.

Each individual difference concept (except the state, status, need cluster) has as its basic conceptual unit a distinguishable genus of intentional action. We have seen that intentional actions can be classified as being "of the same type" on the basis of similarity in regard to one or more of the parameters of intentional action, for example, the case of "fear." A genus of intentional action is one in which the similarity that serves as the basis for classification is at the level of a structural description of the action. For example, since "Want" is one of the structural concepts of intentional action, to identify "actions which are similar in terms of what is wanted" is to identify a genus of intentional action. In contrast, if the similarity basis were "wanting to avoid P," that would be a type or species of intentional action. A delineation of the I.D. concepts of "trait" and "attitude" in some detail follows, and the remaining I.D. concepts are very briefly characterized. Such a list makes for tedious reading, but some appreciation of the individual variety and collective scope of these individual difference concepts is essential to the understanding of the Person concept, for, collectively, they *are* the Person concept.

1. **Trait, Attitude.** Let type Y actions be cases of "P did it because he was afraid." The series Y' of type Y actions *in a person's life history* is a finite set; in contrast, the class of type Y actions is not a finite set. We have standards of appropriateness and frequency we apply to Y' and make judgments to the effect that Y' is a case of "overdoing" fear behavior, or a case of "underdoing" it, or neither. What it takes to overdo is what it takes to make a significant difference. We may also direct our attention to the "know" aspect of type Y actions and identify the objects or classes of objects, if any, toward which the action is directed. If in Y' these objects are significantly restricted to particular objects or classes of objects Q, and Y' is a case of overdoing, we have identified a "Y *attitude* toward Q"; if there is no such restriction, then we have established that "P has *trait* Y."

2. **Interest.** P has an interest in R when (a) Q is the totality of objects or classes of objects toward which P's actions which have no further end in view are directed, and (b) Q is significantly restricted to particular objects or classes of objects, and (c) R is one of those.

3. **Value.** The similarity basis is the priority of the "Want" involved in the action. Dominant values of a person are classes of high-priority wants.

4. **Ability.** Actions are classified in terms of

outcomes, or achievements, which are graded according to difficulty and restricted as to type (e.g., athletic, musical, intellectual). A high level of achievement of a given kind identifies an individual who has a high degree of that ability.

5. **Style.** Here, actions are classified according to distinguishable characteristics of the Overt Attempt (e.g., "expansive").

6. **State.** When a person is in a particular state (e.g., sick, drunk, bored, asleep, in pain, infatuated, expectant) there is a systematic change in the actions that are to be expected of him. In a few cases such as "asleep" or "unconscious," the state implies an observable similarity among people in that state; in most cases, it is the kind of change (the kind of difference it makes) which is similar. The states we identify are typically linked to changes in ability and the exercise of skills; for example, in an emotional state we expect a lessened ability to control impulsive expressions of feeling. A pathological state is one in which a person's ability to engage in intentional action is restricted to a significant degree.

7. **Need.** A need is a state of affairs the absence of which is injurious to the person. Needs are conceptually linked to pathological states. Needs have no necessary motivational implications.

8. **Status.** A status has the same logical characteristics as a state but is permanent, quasi-permanent, or irreversible (e.g., man, woman, child, mental defective, foreigner).

The concept of a Person is the concept of a type of individual whose history is a history of intentional action articulated into the conceptual format provided by the individual difference concepts. (Periods of nonaction, e.g., sleep or falling downstairs, are accommodated by the concept of a state or of an unsuccessful performance.) Intentional actions are episodes in a person's life. In addition to being exemplars of a type, they are *parts* of the hypothetical series by means of which we conceptualize the individual difference concepts. Intentional action and I.D. concepts are fundamentally different. Intentional actions reflect the logic of class membership and universal statements, whereas I.D. concepts reflect the logic of identity and part-whole structure. The parallel to "nomothetic" and "morphogenic" is not accidental.

Intentional actions are observable and they are the jointly exhaustive *parts* of the series which define individual difference concepts. Thus there is nothing about the series which is not observed, if the actions do occur. And if the actions do occur, the series does not then exist in some hidden realm such as "Reality." Since it does not usually make any sense to say

that we infer wholes from observing parts of them, the place of inference in characterizing persons is peripheral and exceptional, not customary and basic. It is only when we personify the whole-part relationship as an organizing causal influence that we generate the paradox of presuming to "infer" a forever-hidden entity which just for that reason could not possibly be inferred.

The ascription of particular traits, interests, and the like, to a person almost *never* involves predicting his behavior or ascribing causes to it. (Only in the mythology of personality theory are either of these regular occurrences.) The series in question are not guesses as to what he will do or has done—they are a way of *representing* what his life *now* is like. That is, they permit us to characterize the person *now* as one who would do those things if nothing operated to prevent it. What does happen when we formulate an individual difference description of a person is that we come to *expect* certain things and not others from him. That is a far cry from making predictions, for all it amounts to is that now certain things he might or might not do will surprise us (or dismay, elate, or disappoint us, etc.) where they would not have previously—and we may fail to be surprised even when what he does is entirely unforeseen ("Yes, he *would* do that"). What else happens when we give an individual difference description is that it becomes appropriate to treat him accordingly (to treat him as an X rather than a Y or a Z). In general, our need and inclination to predict is inversely proportional to the effectiveness of our actions —an omnipotent being would have *no* use for prediction. We are not omnipotent, but we are far from helpless, for we are not intrinsically strangers to one another. On the contrary, *the primary function of the concept of a Person is to guide the behavior of one Person with respect to another.* Thus the present delineation of the Person concept is an explicit, *systematic* formulation of what has in recent years come to be called "the Rule-Following Model" of human behavior (cf. Mischel, 1964).

In summary, the "Rule-Following Model" provides an explanation of human behavior in the following way:

1. The delineation of intentional action introduces the use of concepts as an essential *feature of* human behavior rather than, say, a special kind of behavior or the inner cause or hypothetical "determinant" of "visible" behav-

ior. It also provides the equivalent of "the laws of behavior."

2. The delineation of the Person concept provides the integrated conceptual system which is *used* in describing individual persons and distinguishing among them. Since intentional action is the uniquely important element in this conceptual system, there is no forced division, and no competition, either, between general (lawlike) features of behavior and individual behavior; on the contrary, each contributes something essential to the intelligibility and viability of the other.

3. The person concept provides an account of its own use; hence it requires no external methodological foundation. Given that the use of concepts is a logical component of the concept of intentional action and that the concept of intentional action is a logical component of the concept of a Person, we need only to add that the use of a particular concept —the concept of a Person—by an individual is what is required for that individual to *be* a Person. With this specification, the basic formal requirements for an adequate general account of human behavior are met.

4. If *P* does use the Person concept (if that concept guides his behavior), then he will qualify for recognition as a Person by any individuals *O* and *Q* who also use the Person concept. The participation of persons *P, O,* and *Q* in human interactions with one another is a consequence of the person-descriptive appraisals of each by each, and differences in the appraisals, for example, of *P* by *O* and *Q,* are themselves subsumed under the individual difference descriptions applicable to *O* and *Q.* It is because the behavior of *P, O,* and *Q* is guided by the same *complex* concept that the behavior of each is relevant to each and responsive to each, without being a duplicate of each. Thus human action and continuing interaction are exhibited as mutually intelligible among Persons and actually possible for them without any implication that there are underlying causal processes which *produce* that behavior or that there is something called "the objective Truth" about a Person which we have to guess at (but never really know) in order to have an effective basis or a rational basis for dealing with him. Both of these familiar myths are superfluous, because human behavior *as such* is already a lawful domain of objective, *observable* psychological processes, and it requires nothing outside of itself to make it so: It requires nothing to "make it go."

The Phenomena of "Self"

Given the complex conceptual articulation of "Person," the force of the first thesis, that "self" was merely a locution for identifying particular *persons as such,* may now be apparent. "Self" terminology serves to call our attention to certain aspects of human behavior of which it has seemed particularly important and been particularly difficult to give a coherent account. The way in which the Person concept provides such an account will now be illustrated briefly with several significant examples of "self" phenomena. The effect is cumulative in that what is said in connection with one example amplifies or lays the groundwork for what is said about another.

1. **Self-Concept.** We distinguish persons as individual Persons, that is, as individuals essentially characterized by the individual difference concepts presented previously. A person distinguishes himself as one such individual. Because he is well-placed for observing his behavior, he comes to know a good deal about himself. What he takes himself to be as a Person is his self-concept. Since he acts (intentionally) in the light of what he knows, what he knows about himself makes a difference in what he does. The main function of our references to "self-concept" appears to be to make this connection between what a person knows (believes) about himself and what he does. We elaborate that connection by correlating descriptions of persons' self-concepts with descriptions of their behavior. The structure of intentional action guarantees that the Person is *both* "Knower" and "Known."

2. **The Self as Agent.** An intentional action is what a Person *does.* Thus a Person is a paradigm of an "Agent" in the sense in which an agent is identified as the locus of freedom, choice, and responsibility. Since what a person does (with respect to others) depends on his person-descriptive appraisals of them, and since these are in part a function of his own person-characteristics, what a Person *does* reflects what he *is.* Therefore knowledge of what he does is a genuine basis for knowledge of what he is (the knower and the known). And a person's knowledge of what he does is not the observation of Overt Attempts, but the knowledge of his actions, and so his self-concept is no less the concept of an agent than of an object. Thus, for a person to recognize himself as a Person is for him to recognize himself as agent, knower, and known. Notably, the Person con-

cept exhibits all of these "mysterious" features without any paradox or conflict among them.

3. **The Unity of Self.** We use this phrase to call attention to (*a*) a psychological "whole" which is more than the sum of its "parts" and (*b*) the articulation of this "whole." The unity of the self is the unity of the *concept* of a Person. The latter is not a mere garden-variety concept, but is, instead, a universe of discourse, hence a comprehensive and significant *totality*. The unity of the self is the unity of any individual Person, since any *individual* is *ipso facto* a unity, and any such individual is *essentially* characterized by a set of concepts which are held together by the *logically necessary* interrelationships among the structural concepts within the Person concept. We can no more think of a fragmentary person than we can think of an inside without an outside.

4. **The Consistency of Self.** We use this phrase to call attention to the logical consistency or motivational coherence which we see in human behavior. But we use it, too, to express conviction and perplexity. For we commonly detect more consistency than we can put our finger on and have the conviction that somehow there is an *overall* consistency. (This overall consistency may now be seen as the "Unity of the Self.") The structural articulation of the Person concept makes clear the source of our perplexity: the consistency is systematic and therefore cannot be subsumed under any single description, not even a description at the level of structural concepts.

To illustrate, in terms of intentional action: (*a*) If I know myself to be of a certain kind (self-concept), I will treat myself as being of that kind. One way of doing this amounts to simply acting that way. (Compare: to treat myself as a landlord is simply to act like a landlord, without "putting on an act.") The decisive feature here is what I *know*. (*b*) But not every case of treating myself as what I know myself to be works in this way. For if I treat myself as a wrongdoer, I will not necessarily do that by further wrongdoing. On the contrary, I may punish or condemn myself. Here, the decisive feature is what I *want*: I want to do the right thing, and so what I know makes a different kind of difference in what I do. (*c*) I may believe myself to be a suave man of affairs; however, if I am *not* that, I will probably not know how to act like one. But I may have the ability to ignore the ways in which I fail to carry off the role, and so continue to "know" that I am that kind. Here the decisive

feature is what I *know how* to do, and so what I know and want operate differently also.

If I behave in all of these ways there is no single characterization that will directly describe what it is about my behavior that makes sense and is consistent in spite of obvious "inconsistencies." The answer will not be given by inventing a new trait name, or nonspecific "motive," or whatever. It is not at the level of structural concepts, but at the level of their collective *articulation* in the Person concept that that elusive consistency is to be found after all. It is *necessarily* there, and the concepts of disabilities, errors, and aberrant states protect us from the linguistic pressure to interpret "consistent" by analogy to "logic machine." Succumbing to that pressure only leads us into further distress when we see how "inconsistent" and "irrational" human beings can be *and still be human beings*.

5. **Self-Esteem.** Our "sense of worth" follows directly from the fact that the social practices in which we participate involve evaluations of individual difference characteristics. Because we are both "knower" and "known," we make appraisals of our own individual difference characteristics as we see them. In particular, our *abilities* are subject to evaluative criteria. Because of the "Unity of the Self," our appraisals of our I.D. characteristics one by one in accordance with public standards also come to a single overall self-evaluation. That evaluations stem from social practices does not imply uniformity of appraisals across persons, for conformity to evaluational standards (and ability to so conform) is itself an individual difference concept.

Examples could be multiplied indefinitely, and the examples given could be expanded in more rigorous detail, but the point that the Person concept makes explicit the logic of "self" should need no further demonstration here, and if that is the case, our first thesis is valid.

CLARIFICATION OF CONCEPTS AND REVIEW OF RESEARCH

Here we shall analyze in some detail the implications of liking another person and of being aware that one is liked, and then we shall apply this analysis to an experiment that typifies studies of reactions to evaluations of the self. Although our major aim will be the clarification of the conceptual issues involved in this research tradition, we shall make some brief comments on methodological and empirical issues.

Research Tradition

Perhaps the most informative way of characterizing this research tradition is to identify the investigators who have contributed to it and to describe the kinds of issues that they have considered important. Among those investigators who have conducted at least two studies in this area and who have made evaluations of the self a central focus of their theorizing are Deutsch (1960; 1961; and Deutsch and Solomon, 1959); Harvey (1962; Harvey, Kelley, and Shapiro, 1957); and Harvey and Clapp, 1965); Jones (1964; Jones, Gergen, and Davis, 1962; and Jones' students, Dickoff, 1961; and Gergen, 1965); and Secord and Backman (1961; Backman and Secord, 1959; 1962). In addition to the work of these investigators, a number of other important studies must be noted (Aronson and Linder, 1965; Haas and Maehr, 1965; Maehr, Mesing, and Nafzger, 1962; Videbeck, 1960; and Walster, 1965). There is also a recently published, very comprehensive review of the work on interpersonal attraction by Lott and Lott (1965).

A central characteristic of this research tradition has been its focus on two dependent variables: (*a*) evaluations (or changes in evaluations) of the person (the source) who evaluates the subjects in the study, and (*b*) evaluations (or changes in evaluations) of the self. Both of these dependent variables are viewed as a function of the source O's evaluation of the subject P in combination with other treatment effects. The evaluations that the Ps receive in these studies are typically global or complex assessments of their goodness, likeability, and competence. The dependent variables are usually quite global, too. Thus the central research questions have been (*a*) "Is the P's evaluation of the source more or less favorable?" or (*b*) "Is P's evaluation of himself more or less favorable?" Typically, the kinds of evaluations conveyed to P's lead both the experimenter and the subjects to talking about O's like or dislike for P.

Before going into the studies in any detail, it seems important then to examine the concept of "liking another person" and the implications of P's knowing that O likes him.

Liking Another Person

We want to suggest that a most important use of "P likes O" is a reply to the question "Why did P do that?" In reply to such "Why" questions, we customarily give one of two types of answers: (*a*) an answer specifying P's further end in view or reasons for doing X ("in order to get . . ."), or (*b*) an answer designed to show that we have reached the end point of explanation for such "Why" questions ("He likes, or enjoys doing that."). While the most fundamental and typical uses of liking and other "pleasure" concept types such as "enjoyment" and "pleasure" are as explanation stoppers (Manser, 1960–1961), there are some contexts in which one can say that P likes X only because X furthers his ends. To say that P gets pleasure from X or is pleased with Y invites the question "Why?" where the question is understood as a request for P's reasons (i.e., what he finds desirable about X or Y). Thus in this use, to say that P likes X or gets pleasure from X is not a way of saying what P's reason is and thus it does not function as an explanation-stopper. In the case of persons, as opposed to objects, such a use of liking is extremely rare and quite misleading unless it is appropriately qualified. If, for example, one is told that P likes O and then learns that P likes O only because he can use O to further his own ends, we are inclined to feel that we have been misled. We should have been told that P does not *really* like O even though P gets pleasure from being able to use O. Thus when P genuinely likes O, no further motive, reason, or end in view needs to be cited to explain P's friendliness toward O. Thus liking another person is conceptually similar to enjoying a particular object, sensation, or state of affairs (Taylor, 1963). But exactly what kinds of information are conveyed by statements such as "P likes O," and why are the concepts involved so useful in human affairs?

1. To explain that P did X because he likes O is not necessarily to describe an action but is to classify it. There are an almost unlimited number of specific acts that P coud have been doing. "Liking O," then, is a polymorphous dispositional concept (White, 1964, pp. 5–7). Just as saying that P is a farmer or is intelligent does not imply any one kind of activity on P's part, so to know that P likes O is not to know that P will do any one thing. Just as there is no one kind of activity by virtue of which P can be said to like O, there is no finite list of activities which, if they are all absent, prove that P does not like O. But the violation of our expectations about certain activities and liking

would require explanation. If, for example, *P* is said to like *O*, has the opportunity to associate with *O*, and yet does not want to associate with *O*, then we either demand further explanation or begin to doubt the original description. Of course, *P* may have a stronger reason for doing something else—going to court—or he may not be in the mood to want to see anyone, even the people he likes.

2. In order for *P* to do something because he likes *O*, he must have had some prior experience with *O*; for example, the kind of experience that would allow him to learn what it was like to be with *O*, and hence to learn that he liked or enjoyed being with *O*. Learning something about *O*'s characteristics is a precondition for trying to be with *O* simply because one likes *O*.

3. One cannot say of just any activity that *P* did *X* because he likes to do it. Only certain sensations, activities, events, and relationships are understandable as ends in themselves. (These may vary from culture to culture.) We cannot, for example, claim to use sand in our food just because we like it. But the fact that an activity is intelligible as an end in itself does not mean that on this occasion *P* actually has no further end in view. Rather, it is informative to know if the relationship is actually engaged in because *P* likes *O* rather than because *P* wants some favor that *O* can bestow. One very important kind of information is conveyed by knowing that *P* associates with *O* because he likes *O*: we expect him to treat *O* differently in any of numerous ways appropriate to genuine as opposed to exploitative relationships, and friendly as opposed to hostile relationships, and, furthermore, we (as observers) appraise further action of *P* in terms of this understanding of him and consequently guide our behavior toward P with this understanding.

P's Awareness That O Likes Him

In order to understand the implications of such knowledge, we must go to the full-blown case of reciprocal liking or friendship. (We do not suppose that there are no significant conceptual distinctions between liking and friendship, only that the differences are not central to any of the points we shall be making here.) Among those interpersonal activities that can be carried out with no further end in view are liking, friendship, love, duty, and moral behavior. The central question is whether or not *P* can enter into a relationship of liking or friendship unless *O* reciprocates. If *P* gives *O* assistance with a difficult exam problem because *P* likes *O*, then *P* has been used by *O* if *O* accepts the assistance simply because he wants to pass the course. *P* may start with the intention of entering into a friendly relationship, but he cannot succeed in that desire unless *O* makes the appropriate "moves" in return. In the preceding example, *O*'s treatment of the assistance must signify his friendship; otherwise *O* has refused to participate in the relationship of friendship.

Liking and friendship share with most social relationships the quality that they are essentially cooperative. One person cannot guarantee that the activities that take place will signify friendship; the other person must make the appropriate contributing moves for there to be a relationship of the type in question.

Liking and friendship are distinguished from relationships that require just cooperation by the further requirement that both parties participate in the relationship as an *end in itself*. The requirement that both parties want the relationship as an end in itself does not preclude their having additional, ulterior reasons for associating. Suppose that the relationship is heterosexual and that *P* wants sexual satisfaction in his relationship with *O*. What is essential, if the relationship is to be friendship, is that some of the activities that *P* and *O* engage in are ones that *P* would have done simply because he liked *O* regardless of any other reasons he may have had. Thus the point of saying that friendship is a relationship that can be entered into as an end in itself is that the relationship and the activities expressing it need no further justification, and typically these activities cannot be given any justification that is more basic than the relationship itself.

Knowledge that one is liked facilitates certain kinds of social interaction with the person who likes us. In effect, if *O* likes *P*, that validates some of *P*'s ways of behaving or appearing. The state of affairs of being liked is much more than the mere possibility of friendship; it marks the *genuine opportunity to become friends*. Of course, this state of affairs is not operative unless *P* is aware of it, but, when awareness is present, it serves as a go-ahead signal for the relevant interactions. Just as knowing how to add and subtract makes it reasonably likely that *P* can solve arithmetic problems involving these skills, so being aware that one is liked makes the development of friendship a genuine likelihood. For *P*, the central issue then becomes whether he wants to become friends with *O*. Since being friends is a relationship that needs no further justification, *P* will often want to become friends, but he need not. The desire to become friends may be absent when (*a*) *P* finds *O* despicable or disgusting, and thus does not really have the genuine opportunity of entering into a friendly relationship; or (*b*) when *P* is incapable of responding to liking and thus incapable of participating in genuine friendship. (This is to mention only two obvious cases.)

What has been established thus far? We may begin with the nonempirical point that being given the opportunity to gratify a desire is, *ipso facto,* to find the situation attractive. Since the importance of being liked by *O* is that *P* has a genuine opportunity to gratify a desire for friendship (except where *P* already finds *O* distasteful, despicable, or revolting), then being liked is necessarily a *basis for liking O*. And its being such a basis is not something that we could establish empirically, even though we could find out empirically whether the awareness of liking is a sufficient basis for liking to develop in any particular case. It follows therefore that when *P* knows that *O* likes him, *P* has a basis for finding *O* more attractive than he did prior to such knowledge. And in the absence of other factors, *P* will find *O* more attractive. At this point, however, we must add the qualifier, "unless some particular circumstances prevent this from happening." But such a qualification does not vitiate the conceptual point. In fact, it is formally analogous to the same qualification in the physical statement, "an object will move in the direction of an applied force, unless some particular other force is applied in a different direction." Other bases for liking (the other "forces") include *P*'s awareness of *O*'s other characteristics. If *O* is Negro, *P*, as a result of his social learning, may not be able to like *O*. This brings us to an important point. The connection between being aware of being liked and liking that person is strictly emiprical. *P*'s liking of *O* is a combined product of his knowledge of *O*'s characteristics. What is nonempirical is that various characteristics, such as being liked by *O* or finding *O* physically attractive, are bases for liking *O*. When the experimenters in the research tradition that we are commenting on reduce *P*'s access to information about *O*'s characteristics to a bare minimum, then what is fundamentally an empirical question can become a foregone conclusion.

Thus the statement that liking begets liking is uninformative. No empirical study has any bearing on the conceptual point that awareness of being liked is a basis for liking the person who likes us. And if one arranges the experiment so that considerations relevant to liking are seriously reduced or eliminated, then one can hardly learn anything that he did not already know. Empirically interesting questions arise when one puts the awareness of being liked into competition with other facts such as minority group status and physical appearance, which would ordinarily be basis for finding *O* unattractive. Such a procedure would allow the investigator (*a*) to make a profile for a group or culture of the relative strengths of various factors that serve as the basis for feelings of liking or disliking, (*b*) allow him to distinguish individuals for whom one basis clearly outweighed others, and (*c*) place him in a position to study the development of the different weights placed on being liked versus other characteristics of *O*. Thus to have nonempirical connections among concepts does not stop research, it opens up research questions. Furthermore, the asking and answering of such research questions does not depend on there being some so-called testable theory that would allow one to predict the results. The conceptual significance of the questions and results follows from the myriad connections that the concepts of liking and friendship have in our lives.

The Implications of Being Liked by O for P's Evaluation of Himself

The analysis here must start with the kinds of experience that would be a basis for *P* to change his evaluation of himself. Of necessity there must be experience in which *P* succeeds (or fails) in the light of criteria that he respects. While the particular kinds of accomplishments that an individual may recognize as worthwhile can vary from culture to culture, it is difficult to conceive of a culture in which friendship would not be seen as worthwhile. Even if there were such a culture, it remains true that in our culture one ground for evaluating oneself favorably is that others evaluate you favorably. Thus, if *P* takes *O*'s favorable evaluation to be sincerely given, then *P* has a basis for evaluating himself more favorably than he did prior to such knowledge. And, in the absence of competing grounds, *P* will evaluate himself more favorably. One of the significant competing circumstances is that *P* may be incapable of accepting positive evaluations as significant or as being sincerely given. Thus for such a *P*, no expression of liking would be a genuine opportunity for friendship, and he would be both incapable of becoming a friend to any *O* and incapable of changing his self-evaluation on the basis of being liked.

Whereas it is a strictly nonempirical matter that being liked by *O* is a basis for thinking highly of oneself, it is strictly an empirical question whether *P* does end up by thinking highly or more highly of himself after he learns that *O* likes him.

Again, however, it is possible to trivialize the issue. And most often the trivialization takes the form of assuming that there is a significant question concerning why *P* likes *O* when he knows that *O* likes him and assuming further that the why question requires a causal underlying process theory. No answer to the why question can be given other than one that shows exactly how the awareness of liking is a basis for evaluating the self more favorably. At least, none can be given that would *actually* count as an answer to the why question. Instead we ask "Why?" when *P* *fails* to see himself more favorably after learning that *O* likes him. The import of the question in these circumstances is: (*a*) Exactly what are the competing considerations that prevented the expected sequence from happening? or (*b*) How did *P* come to feel that way? And no *underlying* process explanation is needed for these questions either.

What is one of the significant research questions with regard to self-evaluation? For the subgroup of the population that is incapable of responding realistically to favorable (or unfavorable) evaluations of itself, there are two important questions: (*a*) What are the etiological circumstances that have rendered such persons incapable of responding realistically? and (*b*) What recipes, if any, can we devise to improve their capacity for responding realistically? To have the nonempirical knowledge that there are several bases for changing a person's self-evaluation in a positive direction —such as being liked by persons one respects and likes, or being favorably evaluated by experts, or having a set of consistently rewarding experiences with tasks that one sees as worthwhile—is still not to have a set of generally effective therapeutic techniques. But such knowledge is a starting place.

Some of the studies in this tradition make an indirect contribution to answering the second of the preceding questions (Gergen, 1965; Haas and Maehr, 1965; Harvey and Clapp, 1965; Maehr, Mensing, and Nafzger, 1962; and Videbeck, 1960). The contribution is only indirect, however, because there is no guarantee that the relative strengths will be the same for those people who characteristically do not respond realistically and because they provide no information about what else the therapist would need to do in order to make the positive evaluations—normally ineffective for this group —effective in changing their self-evaluations. Speculation about the characteristics of such a therapeutic invention are out of place here, but it is worth observing that the significance of the invention would not derive from the existence of any hypothetical "underlying causal processes" nor from the existence of any inferred entities such as "drives" or "egostrengths." The significance of such an invention would lie in the increased know-how that we would have, and such knowledge would probably be embodied in new conceptual distinctions and practices that would represent a further articulation of the person concept.

Research Case: Gain and Loss of Esteem and Determinants of Interpersonal Attraction

We have chosen the study by Aronson and Linder (1965) because it is commonly regarded as one of the best studies in the genre and because it goes beyond the demonstration that liking begets liking.[1] Their major hypothesis is: "If *O*'s behavior toward *P* was initially negative but gradually became more positive, *P* would like *O* more than he would have had *O*'s behavior been uniformly positive. This would follow even if, in the second case, the sum total of rewarding acts emitted by *O* were less than in the first case" (p. 156). This hypothesis was clearly supported for the "gut" expressions of liking.

Aronson and Linder see two entirely different possible "causes" of the observed pattern. "The existence of a prior negative drive state will increase the attractiveness of an individual who has both created and reduced this drive

---

[1] In an earlier version of the paper, we analyzed two other studies in some detail. These were studies by Harvey and Clapp (1965) and by Jones, Gergen, and Davis (1962). We have omitted these studies because of space limitations. Needless to say, the kinds of comments that we would make about any of the studies in this genre would vary only in detail. Furthermore, it should be noted that we have dealt with only part of the data from the Aronson and Linder study, but the omitted data present no special problem of analysis.

state" (p. 157). The experience of being criticized is presumed to arouse the negative drive state. On the other hand, it could well be that O's changed evaluation of P is "indicative of the fact that O has some discernment and that his evaluation is a considered judgment" (p. 167). Among subjects in the negative-to-positive treatment, those who report being very upset by the critical comments are presumed to be in a more negative drive state; thus the "drive-reduction" value of the final positive statements is greater. The data are consistent in that highly upset subjects like the interviewer considerably more than those who were not upset, and the discernment hypothesis receives less adequate support.

What does the subject P know about the source of evaluation O? Aronson and Linder arranged for P to think that O is a naïve subject in a verbal conditioning study and that P is to be the experimenter's helper. The experimenter E claims to be interested in learning about the generalization of a brief verbal conditioning of plural nouns from the conditioning topic to other discussion topics. But E needs some guise for getting O to talk about a new discussion topic. E then claims to have hit on the idea of presenting the study of O as a study of impression formation. In this way, E can justify having P and O interact and also justify having O talk about her evaluation of P. P believes that her task is to talk with O for three minutes on each of seven occasions as part of the experiment task, but that her real task is to record the number of plural nouns that O utters in talking with E about her impressions of P. After each discussion P leaves the room so that she can observe O (unknown to O).

This cover story nicely provides E with the opportunity to manipulate P's access to evaluations of herself. O is in fact not a naïve subject but a paid confederate of E's. Thus O gives her evaluation according to one of five prearranged schedules. O is either (a) consistently positive in her evaluation, (b) consistently negative in her evaluation, (c) begins in a very negative manner and gets progressively more positive, (d) reverses the order in (c), or (e) begins with neutral and ambivalent statements and gets progressively more positive. The experiment is followed by an interview in which the dependent variables are assessed.

Aronson and Linder comment on the results as follows: "During the interview many subjects spontaneously mentioned that, after hearing O describe them as dull and stupid, they tried hard to make interesting and intelligent statements in subsequent encounters with O. It is reasonable to suspect that they were gratified to find that these efforts paid off by inducing a change in O's evaluations. This raises an interesting theoretical question; it may be that the feeling of competence is not only a contributing factor . . . but may actually be a necessary condition" (p. 168).

If effect, Aronson and Linder use all four elements of the intentional action concept in interpreting the negative-to-positive evaluation condition. P's *know* that O thinks they are dull, uninteresting, or otherwise unattractive. Some P's (enough to make a statistical difference) *want* to convince O that they are not all that bad, and these P's *try to change* O's mind, a performance that requires competence or *skill*. Aronson and Linder's technique is a variant of one general technique for making people want something. The state of affairs—in this case being liked or respected—has to be something that is intelligible as an end in itself, and then the person's attention must be drawn forcefully to the fact that he does not have the potentially desirable thing; in this case, the other subject's favorable evaluation. Given that P places at least a modest value on O's evaluation of him —as indicated by being upset over a negative evaluation—and given that P has no stronger motive, then he will try to change O's evaluation. It is perfectly intelligible that some P's may not care enough about O's evaluation to do very much, but even these would be pleased if it changed in a more favorable direction. (And one could easily vary the proportion of P's who care by selecting O's who are more or less attractive.)

Finally, to return to the main hypothesis, we can now see that the "same" behavior (O's favorable comments) took on the significance of (a) O's having changed his mind about P and (b) of being an X-favorable attitude toward P in the negative-to-positive condition. (X merely indicates that it is some degree.) In the continuously positive condition, O's comments have only the significance of being an X-favorable attitude toward P. What alters the significance of these "same" behaviors (O's final favorable comments) is the context or experimental manipulations. Thus in the negative-to-positive condition P has *two bases* for changing his mind about O, whereas in the continuously positive condition, he has only one basis, and it is the *same basis* as one of those that P's had in the negative-to-positive condition. Therefore we can conclude that *P* has stronger grounds for liking *O* in the negative-to-positive condition than in the continuously positive condition. Thus we can say what the direction of the difference between conditions *must* be (assuming that there are no more qualifying cases in one condition than the other), even though we could not say exactly how large the difference would be. This conclusion can be translated into two forms—each of which is reflected in their original hypothesis: (*a*) it takes less of the "same behavior" under the negative-to-positive condition to produce the same degree of liking than under the positive only condition, and (*b*) since the differential provided under the negative-to-positive case is a finite quantity, there is a special range of cases where *less* of the "same behavior" (i.e., favorable comments) in the negative-to-positive condition produces *more* liking than more favorable comments do in the positive only condition. And, of course, this reasoning is strictly nonempirical and would not be changed regardless of the experimental outcomes; for the reasoning classifies the possibilities of empirical outcomes and provides the conceptual guides for making the various possibilities happen. Whether or not any particular investigator will have the talent to bring off the study is another matter.

In conclusion, we want only to remind the reader of our three central theses and to make the following observation by way of summary. The failure to distinguish conceptual from empirical issues has seriously hampered the development of a psychological science capable of making some contribution to human affairs and to our understanding of man. Such contributions to human understanding are the criteria of scientific success—not incidental by-products of success. To have human affairs or psychology as a subject matter means that we must already have a great deal of nonempirical knowledge—the kind of knowledge involved in knowing how to recognize that *X* is a case of anger or that *Y* is a means of dealing with *X* and thus participating in the wealth of conceptual distinctions and conceptual-behavioral linkages that constitute human affairs. One virtue of setting the clarification and codification of our nonempirical knowledge as a goal is that in doing this, we discover places where the absence of conceptual links creates a place for empirical knowledge and come to recognize the most efficient use of our empirical skills. To elaborate and to describe our new empirical discoveries in terms of person concepts is to take advantage of the skills that we already have and to assimilate these discoveries to what we already know. In contrast, programs that purport to erect a psychology or social science out of concepts such as "drives, causes, and underlying processes" run the risk of duplicating in an unintelligible jargon what we already know or of inventing an altogether new subject matter whose scientific status is uncertain and whose relation to human affairs is problematic.

REFERENCES

Anscombe, G. E. M. *Intention*. Ithaca, N.Y.: Cornell U. Press, 1963 (second edition); Oxford, England: Blackwells, 1957 (first edition).

Aronson, E., and Linder, D. Gain and loss of esteem as determinants of interpersonal attractiveness. *Journal of Experimental Social Psychology,* **1** (1965), pp. 156–171.

Backman, C., and Secord, P. The effect of perceived liking on interpersonal attraction. *Human Relations,* **12** (1959), pp. 379–384.

Backman, C., and Secord, P. Liking, selective interaction, and misperception in congruent interpersonal relations. *Sociometry,* **25** (1962), pp. 321–335.

Deutsch, M. The pathetic fallacy: an observer error in interpersonal perception. *Journal of Personality,* **22** (1960), pp. 317–322.

Deutsch, M. The interpretation of praise and criticism as a function of their social context. *Journal of Abnormal and Social Psychology,* **62** (1961), pp. 391–400.

Deutsch, M., and Solomon, L. Reactions to evaluations by others as influenced by self-evaluations, *Sociometry,* **22** (1959), pp. 93–112.

Dickhoff, H. Reactions to evaluations by another person as a function of self-evaluation and the interaction context. Unpublished Ph.D. Dissertation, Duke University, 1961.

Gergen, K. The effects of interaction goals and personalistic feedback upon the presentation of the self. *Journal of Personality and Social Psychology,* **1** (1965), pp. 413–424.

Gosling, J. Mental causes and fear. *Mind,* **71** (1962), pp. 289–306.

Haas, H., and Maehr, M. Two experiments on the concept of self and the reaction of others. *Journal of Personality and Social Psychology,* **1** (1965), pp. 100–105.

Harvey, O. J. Personality factors in the resolution of conceptual incongruities. *Sociometry,* **25** (1962), pp. 336–352.

Harvey, O. J., and Clapp, W. Hope, expectancy, and reactions to the unexpected. *Journal of Personality and Social Psychology,* **2** (1965), pp. 45–52.

Harvey, O. J., Kelley, H., and Shapiro, M. M. Reactions to unfavorable evaluations of the self made by other persons. *Journal of Personality,* **25** (1957), pp. 393–411.

Jones, E. E. *Ingratiation: A social psychological analysis.* New York: Appleton-Century-Crofts, 1964.

Jones, E. E., Gergen, K., and Davis, K. E. Some determinants of reactions to being approved or disapproved as a person. *Psychological Monographs,* **76** (2), (Whole number 521) (1962).

Lott, A. J., and Lott, Bernice E. Group cohesiveness as interpersonal attraction: A review of relationships with antecedent and consequent variables. *Psychological Bulletin,* **64** (1965), pp. 259–309.

Maehr, M., Mensing, J., and Nafzger, S. Concept of self and the reaction of others. *Sociometry,* **25** (1962), pp. 353–357.

Manser, A. Pleasure. *Proceedings of the Aristotelian Society,* **61** (1960–61), pp. 223–238.

Mischel, T. Personal constructs, rules, and the logic of clinical activity. *Psychological Review,* **71** (1964), pp. 180–192.

Ossorio, P. G. *Persons.* Unpublished manuscript, 1965.

Rhees, R. Can there be a private language? *Proceedings of the Aristotelian Society,* Supl. V. 28, 77–99 (1954).

Secord, P., and Backman, C. Personality theory and the problem of stability and change in individual behavior: an interpersonal approach. *Psychological Review,* **68** (1961), pp. 21–32.

Taylor, C. C. W. Pleasure. *Analysis Supplement,* **23** (1963).

Videbeck, R. Self-conception and the reaction of others. *Sociometry,* **23** (1960), pp. 351–359.

Walster, E. The effect of self-esteem on romantic liking. *Journal of Experimental Social Psychology,* **1** (1965), pp. 184–197.

White, A. R. *Attention.* Oxford: Blackwell, 1964.

Chapter 36 Human Motives and the Concept of the Self

ERNEST R. HILGARD

No problems are more fascinating than those of human motivation, and none are more in need of wise solution. To understand the struggles which go on within economic enterprise, to interpret the quarrels of international diplomacy, or to deal with the tensions in the daily interplay between individuals, we must know what it is that people want, how these wants arise and change, and how people will act in the effort to satisfy them.

American psychologists typically believe that adult motivational patterns develop through the socialization of organic drives. Our preference for such an interpretation is understandable because our science is rooted in biology. Man is assuredly a mammal as well as a member of society, and we begin to understand him by studying what he has in common with other animals. When we accept as the biological basis for motivation the drives present at birth or developing by maturation, it is natural to think of the learned social motives as grafted upon these or in some way derived from them. Despite the variations in the detailed lists of primary drives which different ones of us offer, and some alternative conceptions as to the ways in which socialization takes place, we find it easy to agree that adult motives are to be understood through an interaction between biology and culture.

Without reviewing any further the genetic development of motives, I wish to turn to some of the problems arising as we attempt to understand how these motives affect conduct. In our textbooks there is usually some important material left over after we have finished the chapters on physiological drives and social motives. I refer to the problems raised by the so-

SOURCE. Ernest R. Hilgard, "Human Motives and the Concept of the Self," from *The American Psychologist,* 4 (Sept. 1949), pp. 374–382. Copyright 1949, *The American Psychologist.* Reprinted by permission of The American Psychological Association.

called defense mechanisms or mechanisms of adjustment.

THE MECHANISMS OF ADJUSTMENT IN MOTIVATIONAL THEORY

The mechanisms of adjustment were the features of Freudian theory that we earliest domesticated within American academic psychology. They now have a respectable place in our textbooks, regardless of the theoretical biases of our textbook writers.

The mechanisms did not burst all at once upon the psychological scene. Freud had begun to write about them in the '90's, and by the time of his *Interpretation of dreams* (1900) he had named repression, projection, displacement, identification, and condensation. In his *Three contributions to the theory of sex* (1905) he added fixation, regression, and reaction formation. It remained for Ernest Jones to give the name rationalization to that best-known of the mechanisms. He assigned this name in an article in the *Journal of Abnormal Psychology* in 1908. Among the books which brought the mechanisms together and called them to the attention of psychologists none was more popular than Bernard Hart's *Psychology of insanity,* which appeared in 1912 and went through several editions and many reprintings. Hart treated especially the manifestations of identification, projection, and rationalization, and introduced that by now familiar friend, logic-tight compartments.

It remained for Gates to collect the mechanisms into a list in a textbook intended for the general student. The evolution of his chapter on mechanisms is itself instructive by showing how styles change in psychology. In his *Psychology for students of education* (1923), Gates called the chapter "The dynamic role of instincts in habit formation." In the first edition of his *Elementary psychology* (1925) he changed the title to "The dynamic role of the dominant human urges in habit formation."

Then in the next edition (1928) he used the contemporary sounding title: "Motivation and adjustment." The content of the chapter underwent only minor revisions with these changes in title. These widely used books did much to place the mechanisms on the tips of the tongues of psychology students and professors twenty years ago, for by that time the mechanisms were already part of the general equipment of psychology, and not reserved for abnormal psychology or the clinic.

Some of the tendencies found in Gates' early treatment have persisted in more recent discussions of the mechanisms. For one thing, we took over the mechanisms when as a profession we were hostile to other aspects of psychoanalytic teaching. As a consequence, we often gave only halting recognition to their psychoanalytic origins. Nearly all the mechanisms do in fact derive from Freud, Jung, Adler, and their followers. Among the mechanisms in Gates' 1928 list, psychoanalytic writers originated introversion, identification, rationalization, projection, defense mechanisms, and compensation. Yet Gates' only mention of psychoanalysis was in some disparaging remarks about the "alleged adjustment by repression to the unconscious," and explanation of adjustment which he rejected as neither true nor useful.

In subsequent discussions of the mechanisms, textbook writers have seldom felt called upon to take responsibility for serious systematic treatment. In order to avoid a mere listing of mechanisms, many writers have attempted some sort of classificatory simplification but there has been little agreement which mechanisms belong together. Gates, for example, had included four mechanisms under rationalization: projection, sour grapes, sweet lemon, and logic-tight compartments. He gave defense and escape mechanisms separate places, although psychoanalytic practice has been to consider all the mechanisms as forms of defense. Shaffer (19) separated adjustments by defense from adjustments by withdrawing, but he took back much of the distinction by treating withdrawing as a defense. In his recent books concerned with the mechanisms, Symonds (23) (24) provides a rich collection of descriptive material, frankly psychoanalytic in orientation, but he succeeds little better than those who preceded him in giving a unified treatment of the mechanisms in relation to motivation.

The lack of systematic treatment of the mechanisms has had consequences for their development as part of psychological science. When there is no effort to be systematic, problems are not sharply defined. When problems are not sharply defined, anecdotal evidence is used loosely, and sometimes irresponsibly. A consequence is that very little evidence of experimental sort is introduced into the chapters on the mechanisms. This does not mean that evidence does not exist. It means only that problems have to be more carefully formulated before the relevance of existing evidence is seen, and before gaps in knowledge are discovered which evidence can fill.

THE MECHANISMS AND THE SELF

It would take us too far afield to review the individual mechanisms at this time, and to consider evidence in relation to them. Instead, we may examine some of their most general characteristics, as they relate to motivational theory. These characteristics lend support to a thesis which I propose to defend: the thesis that all the mechanisms imply a self-reference, and that the mechanisms are not understandable unless we adopt a concept of the self.

The thesis that the mechanisms imply a self-reference need come as no surprise. Psychoanalysts have thought of the mechanisms as protecting the ego. Anna Freud's book on the subject bears the title: *The ego and the mechanisms of defense* (6). Nonpsychoanalysts have occasionally endorsed a similar thesis. In their recent text, for example, Guthrie and Edwards have given a very straightforward account of the defense mechanisms. Although their text remains within the broad framework of behaviorism, they do not hesitate to relate the mechanisms to the ego. In fact they define defense mechanisms as "the reaction patterns which reestablish the ego" (7, page 137).

Let us examine two of the characteristics of the mechanisms to see how the thesis of self-reference is implied. We may chose to view the mechanisms as defenses against anxiety, or we may see them as self-deceptive.

1. The Mechanisms as Defenses against Anxiety

The natural history of anxiety in relation to learning has been much illuminated by the series of experiments with animal subjects performed by Mowrer, e.g. (13), Miller, e.g. (12), and their collaborators.

A white rat is confined in a rectangular box of one or more compartments. The animal can escape electric shock either by some action within the shock compartment (such as depressing a lever to shut off the current), or by escaping from the dangerous place (as by leaping a barrier). Both Mowrer and Miller find that in situations like this a new drive is acquired, sometimes called anxiety, sometimes called fear. This new drive can motivate learning very much like any other drive. They accept the general position that drive-reduction is reinforcing. Anything which reduces the fear or anxiety will reinforce the behavior leading to this reduction. Thus any sort of activity or ritual which would reduce fear or anxiety might be strengthened. Such activities or rituals might have the characteristics of defense mechanisms.

The natural history of anxiety, according to this view, is somewhat as follows. First, the organism has experiences of pain and punishment—experiences to be avoided. These are followed in turn by *threats* of pain and punishment, which lead to *fear* of the situations in which such threats arise. Other situations are assimilated to these fear-provoking ones, so the added circumstances may lead to apprehension. Fears with these somewhat vaguer object-relations become known as anxiety states. Sometimes as the apprehensive state becomes more and more detached from particular frightening situations, clinicians refer to it as a state of free-floating anxiety. All of these acquired states of fear, apprehension or anxiety are tension-states. Any one of them may serve as an acquired drive and motivate learning. Activities which lessen fear and anxiety are reinforced because tension is reduced. Thus behavior mechanisms become reinforced and learned as ways of reducing anxiety.

The Mowrer-Miller theory of the origin of fear, and of its role as an acquired drive, is acceptable as far as it goes. But it needs to be carried one step further if it is to deal with the kinds of anxiety which are found in the clinic. This step is needed because in man anxiety becomes intermingled with *guilt-feelings*. The Mowrer and Miller experiments with animals carry the natural history of anxiety through the stages of fear and apprehension, but not to the stage of guilt-feelings.

In many cases which come to the clinic, the apprehension includes the fear lest some past offense will be brought to light, or lest some act will be committed which deserves pain and punishment. It is such apprehensions which go by the name of guilt-feelings, because they imply the responsibility of the individual for his past or future misbehavior. To feel guilty is to conceive of the self as an agent capable of good or bad choices. It thus appears that at the point that anxiety becomes infused with guilt-feelings, self-reference enters. If we are to understand a person's defenses against guilt-feelings, we must know something about his image of himself. This is the kind of argument which supports the thesis that if we are to understand the mechanisms we shall have to come to grips with a concept of the self.

2. The Mechanisms as Self-Deceptive

Another way of looking at the mechanisms is to see them as bolstering self-esteem through self-deception. There is a deceptive element in each of the mechanisms. Rationalization is using false or distorted reasons to oneself as well as to the world outside; using reasons known to be false in order to deceive someone else is not rationalization but lying. It is entirely appropriate to consider self-deception as one of the defining characteristics of a mechanism. As another example of what I mean, let us consider when aggression should be thought of as a mechanism. Aggressive behavior which is a form of fighting directly for what you want or as a protest against injustice is not a mechanism at all, even if it is violent and destructive. It is then simply a direct attempt at problem-solving. But displaced aggression has the characteristics of a mechanism, because false accusations are made, and the object of aggression may be related only remotely to the source of the need to express aggression. Displaced aggression thus contains the elements of self-deception, and fits the pattern of the mechanisms.

There are two chief ways in which we deceive ourselves. One is by *denial* of impulses, or of traits, or of memories. The second is through *disguise,* whereby the impulses, traits, or memories are distorted, displaced, or converted, so that we do not recognize them for what they are. Let us see what evidence there is for denial and for disguise.

The clearest evidence for denial comes through amnesia, in which memories are temporarily lost. If such memories can later be recovered without relearning, support is given to an interpretation of forgetting as a consequence of repression. Often in amnesia the memories lost are the personal ones, while impersonal memories remain intact.

The man studied by Beck (2), for example,

had no trouble in carrying on a conversation, in buying railroad tickets, or in many other ways conducting himself like a mature adult with the habits appropriate to one raised in our culture. It is a mistake to say that he lost his memory, for without memory he would have been unable to talk and make change and do the other things which are based upon past experience with arbitrary symbols and meanings. But he did lose *some* of his memories. He could not recall his name, and he could not recall the incidents of his personal biography. The highly selective nature of the memory loss is an important feature of many amnesias. Under treatment, the man referred to recovered most of his memories, except for one important gap. This gap was for a period in his career in which he conducted himself in a manner of which he was thoroughly ashamed.

Disguise, as the second form of self-deception, shows in many ways. The most pertinent evidence from the laboratory comes in the studies of projection defined as the attribution of traits. Undesirable traits of his own of which the person prefers to remain unaware are assigned in exaggerated measure to other people (Sears, 18). In some cases, the deception goes so far as to become what Frenkel-Brunswik calls "conversion to the opposite." In one of her studies (4) it was found that a person who said, "Above all else I am kind," was one likely to be rated unkind by his acquaintances. In the studies of anti-Semitism which she later carried on collaboratively with the California group she presents evidence that anti-Semitism is sometimes a disguise for deep-seated attitudes of hostility and insecurity having to do with home and childhood, and nothing to do directly with experience with Jews (5).

If self-deception either by denial or by disguise is accepted as characteristic of a mechanism, the problem still remains as to the source of or reasons for the self-deception. The obvious interpretation is that the need for self-deception arises because of a more fundamental need to maintain or to restore self-esteem. Anything belittling to the self is to be avoided. That is why the memories lost in amnesia are usually those with a self-reference, concealing episodes which are anxiety or guilt-producing. What is feared is loss of status, loss of security of the self. That is why aspects of the self which are disapproved are disguised.

In this discussion of the mechanisms I have tried to point out that they may be integrated with other aspects of motivation and learning provided their self-reference is accepted. Then it can be understood how they provide defenses against anxiety, and why they are self-deceptive through denial and disguise.

THE SELF PRESENT IN AWARENESS

The mechanisms are comprehensible only if we accept a conception of the self. This poses us the problem of the nature of the self-concept that we may find acceptable. Two main approaches lie before us. One approach is to look for the self in awareness, to see if we can find by direct observation the self that is anxious, that feels guilty, that tries various dodges in order to maintain self-respect. The second approach is to infer a self from the data open to an external observer, to construct a self which will give a coherent account of motivated behavior. Let us examine these two possibilities in turn.

We enter upon the task of discovering the self in awareness with the warnings from past failures. Any naive person who started out to develop a psychology of the self would expect to find the task relatively easy because self-awareness seems to be commonplace. Everybody knows that people are proud or vain or bashful because they are self-conscious. But the psychologist knows that this self-evident character of self-awareness is in fact most illusive. You presently find yourself as between the two mirrors of a barber-shop, with each image viewing each other one, so that as the self takes a look at itself taking a look at itself, it soon gets all confused as to the self that is doing the looking and the self which is being looked at. As we review the efforts of Miss Calkins (3) and her students to demonstrate that there was a self discoverable in every act of introspection, and find how little convinced Titchener and his students were, we are well advised not to enter that quarrel with the same old weapons. Introspection was taken seriously in those days and psychologists worked hard at it. There is little likelihood that we can succeed where they failed.

Their difficulty was not due to the insistence upon trained observers. Self-observation of a much freer type by naive subjects is little more satisfactory. Horowitz' study of the localization of the self as reported by children was not very encouraging in this respect (9). Children located their selves in the head or the stomach or the lower jaw or elsewhere, each individual child being reasonably consistent, but the whole picture not being very persuasive as to the fruitfulness of an approach through naive self-observation.

But the reason for rejecting a purely introspective approach to the search for the self is not limited to the historical one that earlier attempts have proved fruitless. It is based also on the recognition that defense mechanisms and self-deception so contaminate self-observation that unaided introspection is bound to yield a distorted view of the self.

Having said all this by way of warning, we may still allow some place for self-awareness in arriving at our concept of the self. Two aspects of the self as seen by the experiencing person appear to be necessary features in understanding self-organization.

The first of these is the continuity of memories as binding the self, as maintaining self-identity. To the external observer, the continuity of the bodily organism is enough to maintain identity, but the person himself needs to have continuous memories, dated in his personal past, if he is to have a sense of personal identity. One of the most terrifying experiences in the clinical literature is the state known as depersonalization, in which experiences are no longer recognized as belonging to the self. Break the continuity of memories and we have dissociation, split personalities, fugue states, and other distortions of the self.

The second feature of self-awareness which cannot be ignored in forming our concept of the self is that of self-evaluation and self-criticism. I earlier pointed out that we need to understand the feelings of guilt which go beyond mere anxiety. Guilt-feelings imply that the self is an active agent, responsible for what it does, and therefore subject to self-reproof. The other side of self-evaluation is that the self must be supported and must be protected from criticism. One component of the self is provided by those vigilant attitudes which are assumed in order to reduce anxiety and guilt. It is this vigilant self-criticism in its harshest form which is implied in Freud's concept of the superego. Evaluative attitudes toward the self, including both positive and negative self-feelings, come prominently to the fore in the interviews recorded by Rogers and his students (16), (17).

Another way of putting this is to state that the self of awareness is an object of value. McDougall referred to the sentiment of self-regard, as in some sense the master sentiment. Murphy, Murphy, and Newcomb put it tersely:

"The self is something we like and from which we expect much." (15, page 210.) Perhaps I might amend the statement to read: "To some people the self is something they dislike and from which they expect little." In any case it is an object about which attitudes of appreciation and depreciation are organized. Snygg and Combs state as the basic human need the preservation and enhancement of the phenomenal self (21, page 58). It would be easy to multiply testimony that one of the fundamental characteristics of self-awareness is an evaluative or judging attitude toward the self, in which the self is regarded as an object of importance and preferably of worth (1), (14), (20).

Despite the difficulties in introspective approaches to the self, we find that our self-concept needs to include some information based on private experience. The continuity of memories maintains personal identity, and the awareness of the self as an object of value organizes many of our attitudes. More is needed, however, to enrich the concept of the self and to make it square with all that we know about human motivation.

THE INFERRED SELF

This points up the need for a more inclusive self-concept, one which will make use of all the data. Such a self-concept I shall call the inferred self. Like any other scientific construct, it will prove to be valid to the extent that it is systematically related to data, and it will be useful to the extent that it simplifies the understanding of events.

I wish to suggest three hypotheses needed in arriving at an inferred self. Each of these, although plausible, is not self-evident, and therefore requires demonstration. In order to be scientifically useful it is important that the inferred self should go beyond the obvious. The inferred self will prove acceptable only if these hypotheses, or closely related ones are supported.

The first hypothesis is that of *the continuity of motivational patterns*. This means that the organization of motives and attitudes that are central to the self is one which persists and remains recognizable as the person grows older. Reactions to present situations will be coherent with reactions to past situations. For those who prefer the habit concepts the inferred self may be thought of as a pattern of persisting habits and attitudes. The organization of structure which is implied is a learned one, and like any habit structure it carries the marks of the past in the present. When new goals are substituted for old ones, there is continuity with the past in the ways in which the goals are selected and in the ways in which gratification is obtained. This is all plausible, but it is by no means self-evident, and it is greatly in need of empirical study. It is a matter for study and demonstration whether or not a continuity can be traced between nursing arrangements, thumb-sucking, nail-biting, cigarette-smoking, and overt sexual behavior. The first hypothesis implies that there is such a continuity, whatever motivational strands are being followed, so that one form of gratification fades imperceptibly into the next. If we but knew enough, we could trace the continuity throughout the life span.

The second hypothesis supporting the inferred self is that of *the genotypical patterning of motives.* This hypothesis suggests that motives unlike in their overt or phenotypical expression may represent an underlying similarity. It will do no good to try to appraise personality by a study confined to its superficial expression. What we know about the mechanisms of denial and disguise tells us that the genotypical pattern will have to be inferred. Unless we move at the level of inference and interpretation, much behavior will be baffling or paradoxical.

The inferred self goes beyond the self of awareness by including for purposes of inference much that is excluded from self-awareness. Awareness includes the not-self as well as the self. In dreams and hallucinations we have products of the self, present in awareness, but products for which the self takes neither credit nor responsibility. It is hard to see the self as giving the stage-directions for the dream, or as selecting the epithets hurled by the hallucinated voices. Yet in making a reconstruction of genotypical motives, these products of the self enter as evidence. Some items, then, remain in awareness, but are not part of self-awareness. Other items are excluded from awareness by inattention or amnesia. Facts such as these necessitate indirection in the reference to motivational organization. A description of overt conduct is not enough to permit an accurate appraisal of motivational patterning.

These assertions may be made with some confidence, but again confidence of assertion does not constitute proof. We need to show by rigorous proof that predictions based on the concept of genotypical patterning of motives will account for behavior either more economically or more accurately than predictions based on phenotypical manifestations of motivated action.

The third hypothesis is that *the important human motives are inter-personal both in origin and in expression.* Despite the fertility of Freud's mind and the penetration of his observations, this is one hypothesis about the self which he never fully grasped. By good fortune he laid his emphasis upon the one organic need—sex—which is inevitably interpersonal in its fullest expression. Even so, he remained within the instinct tradition. Once we reject the self as the unfolding of an inevitable pattern, but see it instead as an individual acquisition, we are impressed by the part which other people play in the shaping of an individual self. Because the parents and others who transmit the culture are themselves a part of the culture, there are some uniformities in socialization, producing pressure in the direction of a modal personality (10). In addition, there are diverse roles which are ready-made for the individual, to which he conforms with greater or less success. There are the roles of man and of woman, of eldest and youngest child, of mother and father and in-law, of employer and employee, of craftsman and white-collar worker. Finally there are the individualizing influences of heredity, of birth accidents, of childhood experiences. There are many details to be filled in, but there is little doubt about the general course of socialization, leading in the end to internalizing much of the culture in the form of personal ideals and standards of conduct.

The self is thus a product of interpersonal influences, but the question remains whether the end-product is also interpersonal in its expression. Does the self have meaning only as it is reflected in behavior involving other people, either actually or symbolically? Is it true that you can describe a self only according to the ways in which other selves react to it? I am inclined to believe that the self, as a social product, has full meaning only when expressed in social interaction. But I do not believe that this is obvious, because I can conceive that it might not be true, or might be true in a limited sense only.

These uncertainties about the truth of the hypotheses regarding the inferred self need not be regarded as signs of weakness in the concept. On the contrary, the concept has greater potential richness of meaning precisely because it goes beyond the self-evident and requires empirical study and justification. If it turns out that in some meaningful sense motivational patterns are continuous, that we can unravel their genotypical organization, and that we can know in what precise way they are interpersonal, then we will have a concept of an inferred self that will be genuinely useful.

What does the inferred self imply as to the unity of personality? It does not necessarily imply unity. Conflict as well as harmony may be perpetuated through genotypical organization. The healthy self, however, will achieve an integrative organization. Note that I say

integrative and not integrated. It is the integrative personality which can handle the complexity of relationships with other persons in a culture like ours, a culture which makes plural demands. An integrated personality soon leads to its own isolation or destruction if it is not also integrative. Lest this seem to be an idle play on words, let me point out that the paranoid psychotic with highly systematized delusions is among the best integrated of personalities. He is integrated but not integrative. The genotypical patterns of motivation which comprise the inferred self may or may not be integrative.

REFERENCES

1. Allport, G. W. The ego in contemporary psychology. *Psychol. Rev.*, 1943, **50**, 451–478.
2. Beck, L. F. Hypnotic identification of an amnesia victim. *Brit. J. med. Psychol.*, 1936, **16**, 36–42.
3. Calkins, M. W. The self in scientific psychology. *Amer. J. Psychol.*, 1915, **26**, 495–524.
4. Frenkel-Brunswik, Else. Mechanisms of self-deception. *J. soc. Psychol.*, 1939, **10**, 409–420.
5. Frenkel-Brunswik, Else. A study of prejudice in children. *Human Relations*, 1948, **1**, 295–306.
6. Freud, Anna. *The ego and the mechanisms of defence.* London: Hogarth Press, 1937.
7. Guthrie, E. R. and Edwards, A. L. *Psychology.* New York: Harper, 1949.
8. Hilgard, Josephine R. Sibling rivalry and pseudo-heredity. *Psychiatry* (To appear).
9. Horowitz, E. L. Spatial localization of the self. *J. Soc. Psychol.*, 1935, **6**, 379–387.
10. Kardiner, A. *The psychological frontiers of society.* New York: Columbia Univ. Press, 1945.
11. MacKinnon, D. W. and Henle, Mary. *Experimental studies in psychodynamics; a laboratory manual.* Cambridge: Harvard Univ. Press, 1948.
12. Miller, N. E. Studies of fear as an acquirable drive: I. Fear as motivation and fear reduction as reinforcement in the learning of new responses. *J. exp. Psychol.*, 1948, **38**, 89–101.
13. Mowrer, O. H. Anxiety-reduction and learning. *J. exp. Psychol.*, 1940, **27**, 497–516.
14. Murphy, G. *Personality: A biosocial approach to origin and structure.* New York: Harper, 1947.
15. Murphy, G., Murphy, Lois B., and Newcomb, T. *Experimental social psychology.* New York: Harper, 1937.
16. Rogers, C. R. Some observations on the organization of personality. *Amer. Psychologist*, 1947, **2**, 358–368.
17. Rogers, C. R., and others. A coordinated research in psychotherapy. *J. consulting Psychol.*, 1949, **13**, 149–220.
18. Sears, R. R. Experimental studies of projection: I. Attribution of traits. *J. soc. Psychol.*, 1936, **7**, 151–163.

19. Shaffer, L. F. *The psychology of adjustment*. Boston: Houghton, Mifflin, 1936.

20. Sherif, M., and Cantril, H. *The psychology of ego-involvements*. New York: Wiley, 1947.

21. Snygg, D. and Combs, A. W. *Individual behavior*. New York: Harper, 1949.

22. Sullivan, H. S. Conceptions of modern psychiatry. *Psychiatry,* 1940, **3**, 1–117.

23. Symonds, P. M. *The dynamics of human adjustment*. New York: Appleton-Century, 1946.

24. Symonds, P. M. *Dynamics psychology*. New York: Appleton-Century, 1949.

25. Tolman, E. C. *Drives toward war*. New York: Appleton-Century, 1942.

Chapter 37 Self-Control and Concerted Action

TAMOTSU SHIBUTANI

It has been noted that concerted action among human beings is not automatic, but highly flexible. Although there is a network of conventional norms in all recurrent contexts, each historical situation is unique. Nothing happens twice in exactly the same manner; even in ritualistic observances accidents occur. Unexpected events take place, but men are versatile and devise ingenious ways of meeting such difficulties. Such flexible coordination is possible because *each participant acts independently,* making adjustments to his associates as they move together toward a common goal. Social structures provide the general framework within which cooperative activities go on, but they do not determine the contribution of any particular person. In each case the man exercises judgment and acts according to his own estimate of the situation.

Each person is capable of violating group norms. It is precisely because such deviations are possible that the fixing of responsibility is such a widespread practice. Unless each person had some choice, there would not be any point in talking about his personal responsibility. The existence of such a notion implies that the offender could have acted differently had he chosen to do so.

But if each person acts separately, how does cooperation occur? It was George Mead's contention that mutual adjustments among independently acting men are greatly facilitated by their ability to form perceptual objects of themselves through role-taking. A portion of the perceptual field of each participant becomes differentiated into what he experiences as himself; each person is able to form a *self-image*. This enables each party to examine whatever he is about to do from the standpoint of the others involved in the situation. In the previously used example of the intercepted pass, each football player is able to see himself in relation to all of the other athletes on the field. If a blocker notes that he is the only man on his team between the ball carrier and two potential tacklers, he must gird himself for a difficult task. He is able to fix his own responsibility because he can imagine how he appears to the others, and it is generally understood that a blocker in such a situation should attempt to immobilize both opponents. Personal responsibility in each situation is fixed, then, by the actor's imagining what the others expect of him. The separate lines of action of the various participants fit together in a reciprocating fashion because each can take the roles of the others, form a self-image from their presumed standpoint, and make adjustments to the intentions and expectations imputed to them.[1]

Contrary to common sense belief men are not always aware of themselves as distinct units; indeed, the extent to which they are self-conscious varies remarkably. There are times when self-consciousness is acute. A person unaccustomed to public speaking who is called upon to address a large group may become so preoccupied with himself that he forgets what he had planned to say. A young man being introduced to a strikingly beautiful woman may be so concerned over the impression that he is making that he stumbles clumsily over the furniture. A person applying for a job may become tongue-tied from paying undue attention to himself. On the other hand, there are circumstances in which self-consciousness disappears almost completely. When one is absorbed in an exciting motion picture or novel, he is unaware of anything but the development of the plot. His vicarious participation is so complete that he becomes aware of himself only when the drama is over or when something unusual happens to disrupt his concentration. Similarly, when relaxing on a beach with

SOURCE. Tamotsu Shibutani, *Society and Personality: An Interactionist Approach to Social Psychology,* Englewood Cliffs, New Jersey: Prentice-Hall, 1961, pp. 87–95. Copyright © 1961. Reprinted by permission of Prentice-Hall, Inc., Englewood Cliffs, New Jersey.

[1] George H. Mead, *The Philosophy of the Present* Arthur E. Murphy, ed., Chicago: Open Court Publishing Co., 1932, pp. 176–95.

his face covered, one can hear the roar of waves and occasional voices of yelling children; his experience is such that he feels as if he blends into the landscape. There is no awareness of oneself as a distinct object, set off from everything else. Some religious mystics have even attempted to cultivate a special capacity for having this kind of experience. Most of the time men range somewhere between these extremes. The extent to which they are conscious of themselves varies from situation to situation, and this suggests that there may be identifiable conditions under which self-images are formed.

The formation of self-images is especially noticeable in those situations in which a person is participating in some kind of joint enterprise in which his own gratifications depend upon the cooperation of others. There are many forms of activity in which success calls for such reciprocation; on a primitive level, reproduction is possible only with the cooperation of some party of the opposite sex, and the survival and well-being of the human infant requires the care of elders. Since organisms are sensitive to anything likely to affect the consummation of an on-going act, any person who must depend upon the cooperation of others becomes responsive to their views. He must be careful to conduct himself in a manner designed not to alienate them. He cannot afford to do anything that would lead others to hesitate, withdraw their support, or oppose his efforts. Whenever men are interdependent, they must concern themselves with the kind of impression they are making upon one another. The formation of self-images, then, is an extension of the adjustive tendencies found in all living creatures. It is well developed in human beings because men always live in association with one another.

Images emerge when there is some kind of interference in activity, and this general principle holds true for self-images. One becomes conscious of himself when there is some strain, opposition, or struggle. A person does not notice his own breathing until his respiration becomes difficult. Self-consciousness is enhanced in situations in which action has been interrupted by some uncertainty concerning the reactions of the other participants. When purchasing a newspaper at the corner stand there is little self-awareness because the exchange is carried out in a routine manner. But where there is the possibility of alternative responses, as in the case of a client who might accept, decline, delay, become insulted, or laugh upon being asked to conclude a transaction, there is much concern over the kind of impression that is being made. Acute self-consciousness occurs in situations in which a person is completely at the mercy of others, as in the case of a man who has belched loudly at a formal dinner party. A man becomes aware of himself as a distinct object, then, in the kind of situations in which he is in some manner dependent upon others, when he is a participant in some joint enterprise in which his success requires the assistance of others and when there is a possibility that such cooperation may not be forthcoming.

It may be objected that people are sometimes self-conscious even when they are all alone. When returning home from a party one may suddenly realize that he had made a stupid blunder, and he may blush in embarrassment while sitting by himself in a street car. He is physically alone, but others are present in his imagination. He imagines what the other people who were present must be thinking and rehearses what he might say upon encountering them on the next day. Thus, he is still performing in a social context.

Mead argued that human beings are able to control themselves because of their capacity to act toward themselves in much the same manner as they act toward other people and as others act toward them. Thus, a person can berate himself, praise himself, make excuses to himself, or indulge himself—just as he can do these things to others. One can become the object of his own activities. Similarly, each can act toward himself just as others act toward him. In well defined situations he can anticipate what others are likely to do and react to himself in the same manner. Anyone who does something that is generally disapproved can expect a scolding, and men often scold themselves for their own misdeeds even before being detected by others. The mistreatment of a helpless old lady is likely to arouse aggressive reactions on the part of witnesses, and a person who even considers such a possibility often feels guilty. As Freud pointed out, guilt feelings may be regarded as a form of self-punishment. Thus, a man becomes conscious of himself as a distinct unit through role-taking; he responds to his own activity as if he were someone else. He responds covertly to his own behavior in the same way in which he expects others to respond overtly. The capacity to form self-images, then, makes self-criticism and self-control possible.

Self-control is impossible without self-images. Unless one can form a perceptual object of himself and visualize what he is about to do, he cannot possibly respond to it. Once a person has formed a self-image there is an imaginative rehearsal in which the possible reactions of others can be evaluated. Because he can appreciate the point of view of the other participants he can anticipate what each of them is likely to do in response to his actions. Such anticipation makes possible the inhibition of some alternatives and the facilitation of others, thus making it more likely to elicit the desired reactions. A blocker attempting to take out an opposing tackler can appreciate the intention of his opponent to break through. If moving to his left gives him his best opportunity, he may deliberately feint to throw his adversary off balance and then hit him from the desired direction. Because a man can respond vicariously to his own forthcoming behavior he can manipulate himself and others to exercise some measure of control over the situation.

Self-consciousness provides protection against impulsive behavior. An infatuated young man may be sorely tempted to seize the girl and to smother her with kisses, but he can readily imagine how repulsive such conduct would appear both to her and to the others who may be present. He can also anticipate her chagrin as well as the dismay of those who rush to her rescue. Since the self-image he forms is displeasing, he recoils from it and redirects his attention elsewhere. Self-consciousness is therefore a way of isolating people from one another and of making their conduct more conventional. With the introduction of deliberate planning activity becomes less spontaneous, but the mutual adjustment of persons with diverse interests proceeds much more smoothly.

Self-control refers to behavior that is redirected in the light of the manner in which it is imagined to appear from the standpoint of other people who are involved in a cooperative task. Once a person defines a situation and locates himself within it in terms of a conventional role, he becomes cognizant of expected patterns of behavior both for himself and for the other participants. Men are continually inhibiting themselves out of consideration for others. People who dislike alcohol become "social drinkers" rather than disappoint a tactless host, and they refrain from speaking sharply lest they inadvertently offend someone. Self-control, then, is a recurrent form of behavior, a complex process whereby a person responds to images of himself and thereby channels his conduct. In this sense, a man's self-image may be regarded as a part of his effective environment, for he responds to himself just as he takes other objects into account.

The capacity for self-control apparently gives man many of his unique attributes. Mead believed that man's ability to form a perceptual object of himself constituted one of the major differences between human beings and other living creatures. Other animals can respond directly to one another; human beings can also do this, but in addition they can respond to what they experience as their own activities. Other animals presumably have a variety of experiences, but probably not self-consciousness. They can hear, see, smell, and feel, but they probably do not have knowledge of themselves as distinct objects. Only man is aware of the fact that it is he himself that has these experiences.

This discussion suggests that social control rests largely upon self-control. Human society is an on-going process in which each participant is continually checking his own behavior in response to real or anticipated reactions of other people. Coordination is possible because each person controls himself from within, and it is self-consciousness that makes such voluntary conduct possible. Concerted action depends upon the voluntary contributions of the individual participants, but since each person forms a self-image from the standpoint of the perspective shared in the group, such self-criticism serves to integrate the contributions of each into an organized social pattern. But there are vast differences in the manner in which conventional roles are enacted. Some make their contributions with considerable reluctance; others, with a sense of duty; others, with sadistic glee. This suggests that some of the people who perform adequately would actually prefer to be doing something else. This leads to the question of the "real" man who stands behind such a "front."

Chapter 38 Some Implications of Self-Esteem for Social Influence*

ARTHUR R. COHEN

Research on the relationship between personality and persuasibility has indicated the general importance of self-esteem as a determinant of the individual's responsiveness to influence from both mass media and social interaction. Evidence presented by Janis and his co-workers indicates that people of high and low self-esteem, as measured by feelings of personal adequacy, differ in their responsiveness to persuasive communications: those with low self-esteem are more persuasible than those of high self-esteem, who are better able to resist influence in mass-communication situations. Also, the author observed (1959) that individuals of different degrees of self-esteem tend to differ in their reactions of the threatening exercise of power over them, these tendencies centering around their vulnerability to an experimental situation. Those with high self-esteem appeared to repudiate the power situation with greater ease and were more self-protective and self-enhancing, whereas those with low self-esteem seemed to be more dependent upon the situation and more vulnerable to its pressures.

The present chapter continues the discussion of self-esteem, focusing on some of the relationships of this personality factor to social influence. An attempt will be made to show how these relationships can be accounted for in terms of some basic personality mechanisms.

A person's self-esteem affects the evaluation he places on his performance in a particular situation and the manner in which he behaves

when in interaction with others. Self-esteem concerns the amount of value an individual attributes to various facets of his person and may be said to be affected by the successes and failures he has experienced in satisfying central needs. It may be viewed as a function of the coincidence between an individual's aspirations and his achievement of these aspirations.

Self-esteem, then, may be defined as the degree of correspondence between an individual's ideal and actual concepts of himself. If a person has set certain ideals for himself, the degree to which he has met these ideals should result in feelings of success or failure. And feelings of success and failure experienced in any given situation should generalize to his entire self-percept. Thus, a discrepancy between ideals and actual attainment points to a state of motivation within the individual in which need satisfaction has not occurred. It is possible to think of ideals and attainments as centering around a range of specific needs and to think of success and failure in terms of these needs. For example, if a person has failed to meet certain of his achievement standards, we may speak of a level of aspiration for achievement which has not been attained and expect resultant feelings of failure. When an individual's needs are aroused, his ideals with regard to these needs become salient, and the degree to which he feels that these ideals can be or have been met should affect his experience of success or failure. If we determine this sequence for a variety of needs operating in a variety of situations, we will have a good indication of the individual's general self-esteem.

Since an individual's experience with a variety of needs in a variety of situations contributes to his over-all level of self-esteem, persons of low self-esteem should suffer characteristic failure experiences whereas those with high self-esteem generally should be more successful in meeting their aspirations. This implies that persons with high self-esteem

SOURCE. Arthur R. Cohen, "Some Implications of Self-Esteem for Social Influence," from Carl I. Hovland and Irving L. Janis, eds., *Personality and Persuasibility,* Volume II, New Haven, Conn.: Yale University Press, 1959, pp. 102-118. Copyright 1959. Reprinted by permission of Yale University Press.

* The studies referred to in this chapter were carried out at the University of Michigan under USPH M–659 and M–701C.

would differ from those who are low in self-esteem in their reactions to an immediate experience relevant to their need satisfaction. Individuals with high self-esteem might be expected to react to new situations with expectations of success since characteristically they have been successful in the past in meeting their needs. Those with low self-esteem, characteristically expecting failure, may be more vulnerable to the effects of failure experiences, thereby reinforcing the general discrepancy between self-ideals and self-percept. Persons of low self-esteem may allow their attitudes about themselves and others to be more affected by what other persons communicate to them concerning their performance and responsibilities.

These considerations generate a number of very broad hypotheses. First of all, we may expect that, since persons of high self-esteem appear to be less susceptible to events in mass-communications and power situations, they may, in general, be less susceptible to interpersonal influence in social interaction. We may also expect persons with high self-esteem to be less susceptible to influence from those of low self-esteem than vice versa. In addition, it may be inferred that persons of high self-esteem may exert more influence attempts than persons of low self-esteem when they interact.

Since people with high self-esteem may protect themselves from negative self-evaluation and may be less vulnerable to the impact of outside events, they may also be expected to be less affected by the communication of failure experiences and more responsive to success experiences than are persons of low self-esteem. Furthermore, they should be less responsive to the expectations for their performance communicated to them by their social group.

These broad hypotheses will be explored in the present chapter. Data from a number of studies which bear on one or another of the hypotheses will be cited. Some of the ways self-esteem and social influence are related will be discussed, and an attempt will be made to provide support for the relationships in some relatively basic personality mechanisms.

THE MEASUREMENT OF SELF-ESTEEM

The instrument for measuring self-esteem (used in all the studies) was designed in accordance with the definition given at the beginning of this chapter. It was modeled after one used by the author (1953), who, in turn,

was stimulated by Shapiro's (1952) use of an ideal-actual discrepancy measure in a study of determinants of friendship choice. The instrument is a modified Q-sort. The items are brief paragraphs, each describing a hypothetical situation in which a person faces a potential frustration of a need. Five representative need areas are included: achievement, autonomy, recognition, affiliation, and cognition. Each of these need areas is placed within three contexts: one of individual behavior and judgment, one concerned with interpersonal relations, and one in a more general group framework. This makes 15 hypothetical stories and permits a representative sampling of needs in situations.

After reading each paragraph, the subject indicates how the person would react by choosing among five behavioral alternatives. He is asked to note his reactions to each situation twice: once in terms of how a person *ideally* should behave and once in terms of how a person *actually* does behave. He is asked also to choose the behavioral items *most* and *least* descriptive of both the ideal and real behavior. The individual's self-esteem score is fixed by the pattern of agreements and disagreements between his choices for most and least on the ideal set and on the real set. On any one item the individual can obtain a score varying from $+2$ to -2. The responses are scored $+1$ for each occasion where the reaction selected as most descriptive of an actual solution is the same as that seen as most descriptive of an ideal reaction; also where the solution viewed as least descriptive of an actual reaction coincides with that regarded as least descriptive of an ideal reaction. A score of -1 is given for the coincidence of the least descriptive actual reaction with the most descriptive ideal reaction, and for the most descriptive actual reaction with the least descriptive ideal one. If no coincidence whatever occurs, no score is given. The person's total score indicating the over-all extent of agreement or discrepancy is obtained by summing algebraically across all items. The size of the discrepancy or agreement between his ideal and real choices of "most" and "least" is assumed to reflect the degree to which his ideals for meeting need satisfaction have been attained. It is thus assumed to provide a measure of self-esteem.[1]

---

[1] The reliability of this instrument has been tested in several samples (Air Force personnel, graduate students, and undergraduates) and in revised form

It should be understood that self-esteem is used in the present chapter as a preselected personality variable. All results dealing with the effects of self-esteem are based upon the measurement and identification of self-esteem groups before the application of any experimental stimuli or manipulations. Such a procedure, of course, allows some ambiguity of interpretation because of the possible correlation of self-esteem with other variables which could be responsible for the obtained results. Therefore any assessment of the present data should be made within this framework.

RESEARCH EVIDENCE

Perceived Social Influence in Social Interaction

Theoretical considerations led to the expectation that persons of high self-esteem would exert more influence attempts than persons of low self-esteem in interactions between the two. Data bearing on this hypothesis were obtained from two experiments on self-esteem and interpersonal relations.

In one experiment, by Thomas and Burdick (1954), 30 members of a graduate course in social psychology were paired with each other according to their self-esteem levels. Those with high self-esteem were paired and those of low self-esteem were paired. Each subject was given general "case history" material, asked to assess it individually and then discuss it with his partner. After this discussion, each subject reassessed the material individually. Predictions were made concerning each subject's perception of the influence attempts exerted by his partner.

The data in Table I show that among the pairs of highs more attempts at influence were perceived than among the lows. On an a priori eight-point rating scale highs rated their partners higher in attempted influence than lows rated their partners ($p < .05$).

In another experiment (Cohen, 1956), 44 undergraduate members of a social fraternity were paired in terms of their defenses against common psychosexual conflicts and asked to

yielded odd-even correlation of .84 and Spearman-Brown reliability coefficient of .91. Homogeneity analysis has shown that all the needs and all the situations were working in a generally similar fashion, and the correlation of this instrument with other measures of self-evaluation (such as the inferiority and ascendancy scales of the GAMIN) indicated reasonable validity. A shorter form also has been developed.

TABLE I

Self-Esteem and Rating of Partner's Attempted Influence within Each Pair ($N = 15$ pairs)

Self-Esteem	Low Influence*	High Influence
High-high pairs	4	5
Low-low pairs	6	0

* The mean of the two influence ratings made by the pair of subjects was taken as the perceived influence score. The data were then broken into the best median split.

interact around some common conflict-arousing "case history" accounts, made individual assessments and interpretations of the case histories, discussed the material with his partner and, finally, he and his partner together made a joint assessment and interpretation of the material. Predictions were made as to the quality of interaction and, specifically for the present purposes, as to the perception of mutual influence. Since the subjects had been measured for self-esteem as well as ego-defense before the conduct of the experiment, it was possible to study the influence which persons of high and low self-esteem perceived themselves to have exerted on the partner.

When the data from this experiment are examined (Table II), it can be seen that persons of high self-esteem perceived that they made more efforts to exert influence than the lows perceived of themselves ($p < .10$). In sum, the data indicate that, both in terms of their own perceptions and in terms of their partners' perceptions, high self-esteem persons are seen to exert more attempts at influence in interaction situations.

Actual Social Influence in Social Interaction

It was further expected that persons of high self-esteem would be more resistant to social

TABLE II

Self-Esteem and Perception of Own Attempted Influence ($N = 44$ individual subjects)

Self-Esteem	Low Influence*	High Influence
High self-esteem	9	18
Low self-esteem	10	7

* Low and high categories were determined by making the best median split.

TABLE III

Self-Esteem and Actual Influence within Each Pair ($N = 15$ pairs)

Self-Esteem Groups	Low Content* Corre- spondence	High Content Corre- spondence
High-high pairs	1	8
Low-low pairs	5	1

* Low and high categories were determined by making the best median split.

influence than persons of low self-esteem when they were paired with one another. They might also reasonably be expected to accomplish more influence than the lows. Data bearing on these hypotheses come from both interaction experiments.

In the experiment in which graduate students were paired with others of the same self-esteem level (Thomas and Burdick, 1954), actual influence accomplished was measured by the correspondence between content elements in the individual stories written after interaction. The data in Table III show that pairs of subjects of high self-esteem exhibited a greater degree of mutual influence than did pairs of persons with low self-esteem ($p < .01$).

The ego-defense and interpersonal-relations experiment (Cohen, 1956) provides further data concerning the amount of influence accomplished by persons of different levels of self-esteem in mutual interaction. Actual influence was measured by comparing the contribution of the person's individual assessment of the material before interaction to the combined assessment he and his partner made after interaction. The data show that the low's interpretations of the task never dominated in the final joint assessment. In all nine pairs combining high and low individuals, the assessment made before interaction by the high contributed more to the final joint assessment than did the assessment by the low.

In these particular data, it is difficult to separate the amount of influence exerted from the amount of influence accepted, or accomplished. Taking the data in Tables I and II into account, it would certainly seem that highs attempt more influence than lows. But it is not clear from the present data whether the greater amount of influence accomplished by the highs is due to their more frequent attempts at influence or to the lows' greater responsiveness to

influence attempts. However, the evidence does seem to support the general hypothesis concerning the differential effects of self-esteem on social influence and attitude change. Compared to persons of low self-esteem, those of high self-esteem appear to exert more influence and to be able to change their partner's viewpoints more readily when the two interact.

The Communication of Group Expectations, Success or Failure, and Self-Evaluation

Theoretical considerations led to the hypothesis that people of high self-esteem would be less affected by failure experiences in their social group, and possibly more affected by success experiences. Data from an experiment performed on 175 male undergraduates are relevant here (Stotland, Thorley, Thomas, Cohen, and Zander, 1957). Through experimental manipulations, members of the subject's group presumably communicated to him that they had either high or low expectations as to the quality of his achievement on individual tasks. The tasks were described as either relevant or nonrelevant to the purposes of the group. Half the subjects within each of the four conditions were allowed to succeed and the other half were told that they had failed. Measures of self-esteem were available for all participants. The dependent variable of interest is the individual's attitude toward his performance on the task (his evaluation of his success or failure), measured by an eight-point a priori rating scale.

The data indicate that although there are no differences between those who succeeded on the task in terms of their final self-evaluation, members who received word that they had failed differed considerably in their self-evaluation according to their level of self-esteem. When all other variables were held constant the mean self-evaluation for the subjects with high self-esteem was 2.55; for the lows it was 1.75 ($p < .05$).

Furthermore, though self-esteem does not appear to serve as a referent when the task is relevant to the purposes of the group, it does appear to have differential effects on self-evaluation when the task is nonrelevant. The data in Table IV indicate that where the group communicates both high and low expectations and the person fails on a task, those with high self-esteem have higher evaluations of their performance than persons with low self-esteem. The difference between the means in the high-

TABLE IV

Mean Evaluation of Success on Task for Nonrelevant Conditions $(N = 86)$

| | When Communications from Group Create: | |
	High Group Expectations	Low Group Expectations
Failure		
Persons with high self-esteem	2.67	2.45
	$p = .05$	$p = .01$
Persons with low self-esteem	1.50	1.20
Success		
Persons with high self-esteem	4.82	5.25
	ns	ns
Persons with low self-esteem	5.11	4.59

expectations condition is significant at the .05 level; in the low-expectations condition it is significant at the .01 level. Where the subjects succeeded there were no significant differences. Thus, under conditions of low task relevance, persons of high self-esteem protect themselves against poor evaluations more than do those of low self-esteem. We may infer from these data that persons of low self-esteem show a greater responsiveness to criticism of their performance and to failure experiences communicated to them by members of their social group: their attitudes toward their performance are more affected than are the attitudes of persons with high self-esteem.

The Communication of Group Expectations, Success or Failure, and Concern with the Group's Expectations

The above data suggest that persons of high self-esteem do not always rate their own performance better than do persons of low self-esteem. What role do the expectations communicated by the group play in this? The following data indicate that persons with high self-esteem, compared with individuals of low self-esteem, are less responsive to the expectations communicated by the group.

In the course of the experiment with undergraduates, ratings were obtained of the subject's concern with the expectations for performance communicated to him by the group. As may be seen in Table V, persons with high self-esteem stated that they had relatively little concern for the group's expectations when they failed and the group's expectations were high, as compared with those of low self-esteem under the same conditions. The means are 2.83 for the highs and 4.63 for the lows; p is beyond the .01 level. In addition, subjects with high self-esteem said that they were most concerned with the group's expectations when they succeeded and the expectations were low. Their mean concern was 4.11 while that of the lows

TABLE V

Mean Concern with Expectations Communicated by the Group for Nonrelevant Conditions $(N = 87)$

| | When Communications from Group Create: | |
	High Group Expectations	Low Group Expectations
Failure		
Persons with high self-esteem	2.83	2.91
	$p < .01$	ns
Persons with low self-esteem	4.63	2.70
Success		
Persons with high self-esteem	3.18	4.11
	ns	$p = .01$
Persons with low self-esteem	3.68	2.94

under the same conditions was 2.94. The difference is significant at the .01 level.

It appears that subjects with high self-esteem reacted to the group's expectations when these expectation levels were easy to reach and in fact had been reached, and were less responsive to the group's expectations when these were difficult to reach and they had failed to perform at the required level. Persons with low self-esteem showed the opposite trend: they became responsive to the group's wishes when these were difficult to achieve and were less concerned when these were easily available and they had succeeded. The results suggest that persons of high self-esteem better protect themselves against unfavorable evaluation by becoming unresponsive to the expectations communicated by their group when an unfavorable comparison with others would be likely.

DISCUSSION

The results of these explorations indicate that differences in self-esteem are associated with considerable differences in individuals' responses to external pressures. Persons of high self-esteem dealt with their experiences in experimental interaction situations in a way that helped them to maintain their high self-esteem. They tended to respond to failure by evaluating themselves more highly than did individuals with low self-esteem. Furthermore, they became responsive to the group's expectations only when favorable self-evaluation was readily possible. Persons with low self-esteem reacted to their experiences in a way that made it difficult for them to improve their self-regard: they reacted strongly to failure and became responsive to the group's expectations when an unfavorable self-evaluation was most likely. Different levels of self-esteem appear to induce different patterns of protective reaction to experiences of failure.

Differential responsiveness to social influence was further indicated by the data on perceived and actual influence in the interaction experiment. Persons of high self-esteem exerted more influence upon those of low self-esteem when the two were in interaction. Subjects with high self-esteem were also seen to exert more influence and perceived themselves as attempting to exert more influence than did the lows.

It would appear that some construct centering around the idea of degree of openness to change and negative self-evaluation would

allow these results to be meaningfully interrelated. Thus people of high self-esteem may be less willing or able to permit their self-picture and views of the social world to be vulnerable to influence from others. There is good evidence for this interpretation in studies dealing with the relationship between characteristic ego-defenses and self-esteem (Cohen, 1954). In these studies, using the Blacky Test (Blum, 1949) and its associated Defense Preference Inquiry (Goldstein, 1952), high self-esteem has been found to be associated with the preference for avoidance defenses against unacceptable impulses, while low self-esteem is associated with the preference for expressive defenses. Avoidance defenses (reaction formation and avoidance) may be said to block the expression of unacceptable impulses and therefore to permit the creation of a self-protective façade. The expressive defenses (projection and regression), on the other hand, permit the unacceptable impulse to gain some sort of outlet. In effect, people of high self-esteem, who appear to be less responsive to outside influence, are also characterized by a preference for ego-defenses which help them to repress, deny, or ignore challenging and conflictful impulses. Individuals with low self-esteem, who are more open to outside influence, show a preference for the more expressive defenses, those which allow them to play out their impulses; being inclined to "act out" they may be more dependent upon situations and events.

The picture of self-esteem which emerges is an exceedingly complex one, but one that can be based upon the notion of the self-system's degree of openness to change. Persons of high self-esteem appear to take on early in life a defensive mode which handles challenging experience by a strong self-protective façade. They repress, deny, ignore, or turn about their potentially disturbing impulses in contrast to persons who express these impulses more directly by projection or regression. There are significant consequences for the person depending upon his use of one or the other of these defensive modes. For one thing, projection and regression are primitive defenses which occur early in psychosexual development. Within the world of everyday adult reality they may cause difficulties. The individual may find it hard to effect some kind of need satisfaction for his strong drives, expressed as they are in a direct fashion. The avoider, on the other hand, uses defenses which are far more socially facilitative and he thus may indirectly experience impulse gratification. The relationships found by Blum (1954) between general psychosexual conflict and the use of projection, on the one hand, and relative lack of conflict and the use of reaction formation, on the other, attest to the plausibility of this line of reasoning. Further support for this interpretation is provided by evidence relating low self-esteem to underlying psychosexual conflict (Cohen, 1954).[2]

Secondly, the use of avoidance defenses permits the individual to organize a cohesive and encapsulated self-picture. After they have been developed as a means of handling inner impulses, avoidance defenses become behavioral modes themselves and determine the social reality to which the person exposes himself. Consequently, persons with avoidance defenses can turn away from experiences which reflect unfavorably on their self-picture. Such

persons may emphasize enhancing experiences, thereby preserving an insulated but positive self-picture. Persons whose defenses are more expressive may not be able to deal so selectively with external stimuli. Perhaps their low self-esteem is even partly a consequence of their failure to live up to generally accepted moral standards concerning the expression of forbidden impulses.

This implies that the different self-esteem groups are differentially able to fulfill the important acquired motive of maintenance of self-esteem at the highest possible level. Through their use of avoidance defenses and their greater expectations of need satisfaction, the highs are able to maintain a high-level equilibrium in the structure of their organized self-picture, whereas the lows are more dependent upon experiential variations. Thus, the highs are much more resistant to change which may disturb their self-picture, as well as to influence in general.

The notion of the structure of the self, self-concept, or self-picture is thought to represent a coordinating construct. By this is meant the general percept the individual has of himself and of his potentiality for success in meeting needs. Defenses may be utilized in the service of a good self-image and may also allow persons to succeed differentially. Furthermore, they may allow the individual to organize his self-structure so that he is less open to new information, new influence, or any other disturbance of his existing view of the relationship between himself and the world.

---

[2] Throughout this chapter it has been assumed that self-esteem is on a continuum. High and low self-esteem are not pure types; for convenience of analysis the self-esteem continuum has been broken into two groups by a median split. Other data (Cohen, 1954) present a more differentiated picture. When a middle group is isolated, its members show a more socially adjusted picture than either the highs or the lows: they have least psychosexual conflict, prefer projection least, and use avoidance defenses most. By definition, the medium self-esteem group took a more moderate approach to their own self-judgment on the self-esteem questionnaire; they selected a differentiated pattern of aspirations and achievements, scoring high on some and low on others.

REFERENCES

G. S. Blum, A study of the psychoanalytic theory of psychosexual development. *Genetic Psychology Monograph,* **39** (1949), pp. 3–99.

G. S. Blum, "Procedure for the Assessment of Conflict and Defense," University of Michigan, Unpublished manuscript (1954).

A. R. Cohen, *The Effects of Individual Self-Esteem and Situational Structure on Threat-oriented Reactions to Power,* University of Michigan, Unpublished Doctoral Dissertation (1953).

A. R. Cohen, "Some Explorations of Self-Esteem," University of Michigan, Unpublished manuscript (1954).

A. R. Cohen, "Experimental Effects of Ego-defense Preference on Interpersonal Relations," *Journal of Abnormal Social Psychology,* **52** (1956), pp. 19–27.

S. Goldstein, *A Projective Study of Psychoanalytic Mechanisms,* University of Michigan, Unpublished Doctoral Dissertation (1952).

D. Shapiro, *Psychological Factors in Friendship Choice and Rejection,* University of Michigan, Unpublished Doctoral Dissertation (1952).

E. Stotland, S. Thorley, E. Thomas, A. R. Cohen, and A. Zander, "The Effects of Group Expectations and Self-Esteem upon Self-Evaluation," *Journal of Abnormal and Social Psychology,* **54** (1957), pp. 55–63.

E. Thomas and H. Burdick, "Self-Esteem and Defense Preference as Related to Social Behavior," University of Michigan, Unpublished manuscript (1954).

Part VI Self-Conception and Psychopathology

In the preceding chapters we have glimpsed the multiple functions that self-conception may serve for the person. We have found that the person's views about himself may largely structure the ways in which he perceives and orients himself within his social environment, and we have seen how self-conception may serve as a primary touchstone for behavioral exchange. With few exceptions, however, such discussions have centered on the healthy or "normally" functioning human being. We have been sensitized to the possibility of breakdown in normal self-processes by Tiryakian's analysis of the ontic mode of existence (Chapter 7), Erikson's description of extreme forms of identity diffusion (Chapter 18), and the discussions of Kardiner and Ovesey (Chapter 24) and Goffman (Chapter 25) on the effects of various forms of social oppressions. We are thus in a good position to focus more sharply on the issue of the self vis-à-vis psychological malfunctioning. What forms of pathology may be intrinsically related to self-conception? What social conditions, both on a societal and interpersonal level, may generate such pathological forms? And what types of behavior, on the part of the person and others, may be important in bringing him into a state of full functioning? The selections in Part VI treat these issues in various ways.

It may be said at the outset that thinking about psychopathology has only recently turned toward the role that self-conceptions may play in mental illness. The Freudian psychodynamic model has dominated the scene for many years, and clearly the most impressive psychological discoveries of the century have been concerned with unconscious determinants of pathology. Such discoveries were perhaps overly compelling, however, in shifting attention away from what the person thought and felt about himself. Combined with the flagellating character of the superego, the overriding sexual energies, and the challenges posed to the ego by an often malevolent environment, little place seemed left for the person's inward turning and his possible queries about who he was, what he was, and what he felt about himself. The Freudian concept of the ego, however, may have provided the escape hatch in this regard. Since the chore of adjusting to or coping with the world was largely relegated to the ego, the door was open to asking about those facts in the world with which the person must cope. One very salient fact demanding the person's concern was found to be himself.

The work of three psychoanalysts, Erich Fromm, Karen Horney, and Harry Stack Sullivan, marked the advent of serious investigation of the relationship between self-conception and pathology. The contributions made by Fromm on the significance of self-love in personal relations (Chapter 32), by Horney on self-alienation (Chapter 40), and by Sullivan on the development of the self-dynamism (Chapter 15) are of cardinal importance in the history of thinking about neurosis. The development of such formidable groundwork prepared the way for theories of personal identity, best represented by Erikson (Chapter 18), and for the existential-phenomenological approach.[1] Recent years have also seen many attempts to re-integrate the concepts of self and personal identity into more traditional psychoanalytic theory. Of course, the contributions of Erikson and Hilgard, Chapters 18 and 36 in this volume, are quite relevant. Schachtel's discussion of the metamorphosis of the self represents a major attempt in this direction.[2] Wheelis has even suggested that the problems faced by contemporary man are not of the traditional psychoanalytic variety, and that current theory must extend itself far beyond this tradition in order to deal at close range with the problem of identity.[3]

Although a number of the chapters in this Part have drawn sustenance from the Freudian tradition, an attempt has been made to include a more wide-ranging sample. In this way, thinkers from several different traditions can be seen converging on the same phenomena, each illuminating a different aspect. The first three papers are all concerned with a topic of wide current interest: alienation. The two initial papers are classics of their kind, and the third represents the fruits of perhaps the most significant research departure in the area. In Chapter 39, Marx incisively argues that alienation in a number of forms is a major by-product of the capitalistic economic system. The reader may want to trace carefully these arguments as well as their application to existing facts. However, the more important aspect of the contribution is that it calls attention to the connection between the social organization of production and the person's relationship to his work, to others, and to himself. Whereas thinking about congenital and familial determinants of pathology has dominated the field, Marx's treatment strongly suggests that the economic structure and the social organization of work deserve equal consideration.

Karen Horney's highly influential work (Chapter 40) is a leading example of the psychological approach to the problem of alienation. Her work has spurred a growing concern among psychoanalysts who find that the types of problems that she pinpointed are widespread in modern societies. The reader who wishes to explore current thinking along these lines should consult the Horney Memorial Issue of the *American Journal of Psychoanalysis*.[4] However, it should be realized that it is misleading to speak of "the" problem of alienation, as if there were a single issue or phenomenon at stake. As we have seen, Marx talks about multiple forms of alienation, Horney centers her discussions on one particular syndrome, and Keniston's way of speaking about alienation will be found quite different in character. Many have attempted to point out common threads in these and other approaches, but one must maintain constant watch for semantic pitfalls.[5]

---

[1] R. May, E. Angel, and H. F. Ellenberger (eds.), *Existence,* New York: Basic Books, 1958.
[2] E. G. Schachtel, "On Alienated Concepts of Identity," *The American Journal of Psychoanalysis* (Nov. 1961).
[3] A. Wheelis, *The Quest for Identity,* New York: W. W. Norton, 1958.
[4] *The American Journal of Psychoanalysis,* **1** (1961).
[5] Cf. M. Seeman, "On the Meaning of Alienation," *American Sociological Review,* **24** (1959), pp. 783–791.

In spite of the widespread interest in alienation, there has been all too little systematic research on the topic. Without the reality checks provided by empirical research, a concept like alienation may be subject to the whims of fashion. Keniston's original paper, published here as Chapter 41, is important not only because it relies on systematic empirical techniques, but also because he centers on aspects of alienation having substantial consequence in educational as well as other organized institutions. The focus on parental behavior as a determining factor also forms an important link with the earlier chapters treating the development of self-conceptions in childhood (Chapters 14, 15, and 16). Keniston's query as to the social value of alienation is additionally provocative.

Although it does not focus specifically on alienation, Laing's (Chapter 42) exploration of ontological insecurity is highly germane. Laing's work can also be seen to derive from the phenomenological tradition represented in Part II of this volume. The pathological experiences which he describes should also be compared with Erikson's description of identity diffusion (Chapter 18). Laing acutely describes the potentially debilitating effects "of being sucked into the whirlpool of another person's way of comprehending oneself." This view stands in marked contrast to the entire thrust of the symbolic interactionist position (cf. Part III). The reader may also find it useful to juxtapose Laing's chapter with Riesman's discussion of personal autonomy in the Epilogue.

The chapters described thus far place slightly more emphasis on the causes and results of mental difficulty than on ways in which anguish may be alleviated. The final two papers in this section are more optimistic in tenor. Jourard (Chapter 43) first discusses the significance for mental well-being of one's disclosing himself to others, and then describes various research endeavors related to his thesis. It is fruitful in this instance to compare the kinds of self-descriptive behavior discussed by Jourard with those emphasized by Gordon (Chapter 11), Gergen (Chapter 30), and Goffman (Chapter 31). While a core self which can be withheld or revealed to others is implied in Jourard's work, these other papers suggest that what a person feels to be core may shift from one relationship to another. From this latter point of view, what is revealing behavior in one situation may not be in another. Yet the experience of self-revelation may continue to be of extreme significance for the individual. The reader may also wish to compare Jourard's discussion with Tiryakian's description of the authentic mode of social interaction.

The final selection (Chapter 44) is an early but very important statement by Carl Rogers of the significance of self-regard in the psychotherapeutic process. In that his theoretical speculations are tied closely to both clinical observation and systematic research, Rogers' work is unique and compelling. The present contribution may also be compared with Fromm's thinking on self-love and love for others (Chapter 32), Cohen's research (Chapter 38) on self-esteem and persuasibility, and the Kardiner and Ovesey (Chapter 24) discussion of oppression and self-esteem. All point to the potentially debilitating effects of low levels of self-evaluation. Subsequent research has also suggested that exceedingly high self-esteem may be accompanied by other forms of malfunctioning. In later works, Rogers has pointed to the significance of unconditional positive regard on the therapist's part in buttressing the patient's self-regard. This position is, of course, quite closely tied to that taken by the symbolic interactionists.

Although the various contributions represented within Part VI demonstrate the utility of the concept of self in understanding certain psychologically dysfunctional states, some feeling may also be obtained of the current limitations of such a perspective. Few important inroads have yet been made in thinking about psychotic forms of behavior. Laing's (Chapter 42) contribution may stand as an exception with regard to schizophrenic disorders. However, manic-depressive, psychopathic, and hysterical syndromes still remain recalcitrant. Data concerning delusional states, paranoia, and split personalities seem rich and highly suggestive as wellsprings for future work in this area.

Chapter 39 On Alienated Labor

KARL MARX

We shall begin from a *contemporary* economic fact. The worker becomes poorer the more wealth he produces and the more his production increases in power and extent. The worker becomes an ever cheaper commodity the more goods he creates. The *devaluation* of the human world increases in direct relation with the *increase in value* of the world of things. Labor does not only create goods; it also produces itself and the worker as a *commodity,* and indeed in the same proportion as it produces goods.

This fact simply implies that the object produced by labor, its product, now stands opposed to it as an *alien being,* as a *power independent* of the producer. The product of labor is labor which has been embodied in an object and turned into a physical thing; this product is an *objectification* of labor. The performance of work is at the same time its objectification. The performance of work appears in the sphere of political economy as a *vitiation* of the worker, objectification as a *loss* and as *servitude to the object,* and appropriation as *alienation.*

So much does the performance of work appear as vitiation that the worker is vitiated to the point of starvation. So much does objectification appear as loss of the object that the worker is deprived of the most essential things not only of life but also of work. Labor itself becomes an object which he can acquire only by the greatest effort and with unpredictable interruptions. So much does the appropriation of the object appear as alienation that the more objects the worker produces the fewer he can

possess and the more he falls under the domination of his product, of capital.

All these consequences follow from the fact that the worker is related to the *product of his labor* as to an *alien* object. For it is clear on this presupposition that the more the worker expends himself in work the more powerful becomes the world of objects which he creates in face of himself, the poorer he becomes in his inner life, and the less he belongs to himself. It is just the same as in religion. The more of himself man attributes to God the less he has left in himself. The worker puts his life into the object, and his life then belongs no longer to himself but to the object. The greater his activity, therefore, the less he possesses. What is embodied in the product of his labor is no longer his own. The greater this product is, therefore, the more he is diminished. The *alienation* of the worker in his product means not only that his labor becomes an object, assumes an *external* existence, but that it exists independently, *outside himself,* and alien to him, and that it stands opposed to him as an autonomous power. The life which he has given to the object sets itself against him as an alien and hostile force.

Let us now examine more closely the phenomenon of *objectification,* the worker's production and the *alienation* and *loss* of the object it produces, which is involved in it. The worker can create nothing without *nature,* without the *sensuous external world.* The latter is the material in which his labor is realized, in which it is active, out of which and through which it produces things.

But just as nature affords the *means of existence* of labor in the sense that labor cannot *live* without objects upon which it can be exercised, so also it provides the *means of existence* in a narrower sense; namely the means of physical existence for the *worker* himself. Thus, the more the worker *appropriates* the external world of sensuous nature by his labor the more he deprives himself of *means of existence,* in two respects: first, that the sensuous

SOURCE. Karl Marx, "On Alienated Labor" (1848), from Erich Fromm, ed., *Marx's Concept of Man,* T. B. Bottomore, tr., New York: Frederick Ungar Publishing Company, 1961, pp. 95–106. Originally published in T. B. Bottomore, tr. and ed., *Karl Marx: Early Writings,* London: C. A. Watts and New York: McGraw-Hill. Copyright 1963 by T. B. Bottomore. Reprinted by permission of C. A. Watts and Company Ltd., London.

external world becomes progressively less an object belonging to his labor or a means of existence of his labor, and secondly, that it becomes progressively less a means of existence in the direct sense, a means for the physical subsistence of the worker.

In both respects, therefore, the worker becomes a slave of the object; first, in that he receives an *object of work,* i.e., receives *work,* and secondly that he receives *means of subsistence.* Thus the object enables him to exist, first as a *worker* and secondly, as a *physical subject.* The culmination of this enslavement is that he can only maintain himself as a *physical subject* so far as he is a *worker,* and that it is only as a *physical subject* that he is a worker.

*   *   *

Political economy conceals the alienation in the nature of labor insofar as it does not examine the direct relationship between the worker (work) and production. Labor certainly produces marvels for the rich but it produces privation for the worker. It produces palaces, but hovels for the worker. It produces beauty, but deformity for the worker. It replaces labor by machinery, but it casts some of the workers back into a barbarous kind of work and turns the others into machines. It produces intelligence, but also stupidity and cretinism for the workers.

The direct relationship of labor to its products is the relationship of the worker to the objects of his production. The relationship of property owners to the objects of production and to production itself is merely a *consequence* of this first relationship and confirms it. We shall consider this second aspect later.

Thus, when we ask what is the important relationship of labor, we are concerned with the relationship of the *worker* to production.

So far we have considered the alienation of the worker only from one aspect; namely, *his relationship with the products of his labor.* However, alienation appears not only in the result, but also in the *process,* of *production,* within *productive activity itself.* How could the worker stand in an alien relationship to the product of his activity if he did not alienate himself in the act of production itself? The product is indeed only the *résumé* of activity, of production. Consequently, if the product of labor is alienation, production itself must be active alienation—the alienation of activity and the activity of alienation. The alienation of

the object of labor merely summarizes the alienation in the work activity itself.

What constitutes the alienation of labor? First, that the work is *external* to the worker, that it is not part of his nature; and that, consequently, he does not fulfill himself in his work but denies himself, has a feeling of misery rather than well being, does not develop freely his mental and physical energies but is physically exhausted and mentally debased. The worker therefore feels himself at home only during his leisure time, whereas at work he feels homeless. His work is not voluntary but imposed, *forced labor.* It is not the satisfaction of a need, but only a *means* for satisfying other needs. Its alien character is clearly shown by the fact that as soon as there is no physical or other compulsion it is avoided like the plague. External labor, labor in which man alienates himself, is a labor of self-sacrifice, of mortification. Finally, the external character of work for the worker is shown by the fact that it is not his own work but work for someone else, that in work he does not belong to himself but to another person.

Just as in religion the spontaneous activity of human fantasy, of the human brain and heart, reacts independently as an alien activity of gods or devils upon the individual, so the activity of the worker is not his own spontaneous activity. It is another's activity and a loss of his own spontaneity.

We arrive at the result that man (the worker) feels himself to be freely active only in his animal functions—eating, drinking and procreating, or at most also in his dwelling and in personal adornment—while in his human functions he is reduced to an animal. The animal becomes human and the human becomes animal.

Eating, drinking and procreating are of course also genuine human functions. But abstractly considered, apart from the environment of other human activities, and turned into final and sole ends, they are animal functions.

We have now considered the act of alienation of practical human activity, labor, from two aspects: (1) the relationship of the worker to the *product of labor* as an alien object which dominates him. This relationship is at the same time the relationship to the sensuous external world, to natural objects, as an alien and hostile world; (2) the relationship of labor to the *act of production* within *labor.* This is the relationship of the worker to his own activity as something alien and not belonging to him, activity as suffering (passivity), strength as powerlessness, creation as emasculation, the *personal* physical and mental energy of the worker, his personal life (for what is life but activity?) as an activity which is directed against himself, independent of him and not belonging to him. This is *self-alienation* as against the above-mentioned alienation of the *thing*.

We have now to infer a third characteristic of *alienated labor* from the two we have considered.

Man is a species-being[1] not only in the sense that he make the community (his own as well as those of other things) his object both practically and theoretically, but also (and this is simply another expression for the same thing) in the sense that he treats himself as the present, living species, as a *universal* and consequently free being.

Species-life, for man as for animals, has its physical basis in the fact that man (like animals) lives from inorganic nature, and since man is more universal than an animal so the range of inorganic nature from which he lives is more universal. Plants, animals, minerals, air, light, etc. constitute, from the theoretical aspect, a part of human consciousness as objects of natural science and art; they are man's spiritual inorganic nature, his intellectual means of life, which he must first prepare for enjoyment and perpetuation. So also, from the practical aspect they form a part of human life and activity. In practice man lives only from these natural products, whether in the form of food, heating, clothing, housing, etc. The universality of man appears in practice in the universality which makes the whole of nature into his inorganic body: (1) as a direct means of life; and equally (2) as the material object and instrument of his life activity. Nature is the *inorganic body* of man; that is to say, nature excluding the human body itself. To say that man *lives* from nature means that nature is his *body* with which he must remain in a continuous interchange in order not to die. The statement that the physical and mental life of man, and nature, are interdependent

means simply that nature is interdependent with itself, for man is a part of nature.

Since alienated labor: (1) alienates nature from man; and (2) alienates man from himself, from his own active function, his life activity; so it alienates him from the species. It makes *species-life* into a means of individual life. In the first place it alienates species-life and individual life, and secondly, it turns the latter, as an abstraction, into the purpose of the former, also in its abstract and alienated form.

For labor, *life activity, productive life,* now appear to man only as *means* for the satisfaction of a need, the need to maintain his physical existence. Productive life is, however, species-life. It is life creating life. In the type of life activity resides the whole character of a species, its species-character; and free, conscious activity is the species-character of human beings. Life itself appears only as a *means of life*.

The animal is one with its life activity. It does not distinguish the activity from itself. It is *its activity*. But man makes his life activity itself an object of his will and consciousness. He has a conscious life activity. It is not a determination with which he is completely identified. Conscious life activity distinguishes man from the life activity of animals. Only for this reason is he a species-being. Or rather, he is only a self-conscious being, i.e. his own life is an object for him, because he is a species-being. Only for this reason is his activity free activity. Alienated labor reverses the relationship, in that man because he is a self-conscious being makes his life activity, his *being,* only a means for his *existence*.

The practical construction of an *objective world*, the *manipulation* of inorganic nature, is the confirmation of man as a conscious species-being, i.e. a being who treats the species as his own being or himself as a species-being. Of course, animals also produce. They construct nests, dwellings, as in the case of bees, beavers, ants, etc. But they only produce what is strictly necessary for themselves or their young. They produce only in a single direction, while man produces universally. They produce only under the compulsion of direct physical need, while man produces when he is free from physical need and only truly produces in freedom from such need. Animals produce only themselves, while man reproduces the whole of nature. The products of animal production belong directly to their physical bodies, while man is free in face of his product. Animals

[1] The term "species-being" is taken from Feuerbach's *Das Wesen des Christentums* (The Essence of Christianity). Feuerbach used the notion in making a distinction between consciousness in man and in animals. Man is conscious not merely of himself as an individual but of the human species or "human essence."—*Tr. Note*

construct only in accordance with the standards and needs of the species to which they belong, while man knows how to produce in accordance with the standards of every species and knows how to apply the appropriate standard to the object. Thus man constructs also in accordance with the laws of beauty.

It is just in his work upon the objective world that man really proves himself as a *species-being*. This production is his active species life. By means of it nature appears as *his* work and his reality. The object of labor is, therefore, the *objectification of man's species life*; for he no longer reproduces himself merely intellectually, as in consciousness, but actively and in a real sense, and he sees his own reflection in a world which he has constructed. While, therefore, alienated labor takes away the object of production from man, it also takes away his *species life,* his real objectivity as a species-being, and changes his advantage over animals into a disadvantage in so far as his inorganic body, nature, is taken from him.

Just as alienated labor transforms free and self-directed activity into a means, so it transforms the species life of man into a means of physical existence.

Consciousness, which man has from his species, is transformed through alienation so that species life becomes only a means for him.

(3) Thus alienated labor turns the *species life of man,* and also nature as his mental species-property, into an *alien* being and into a *means* for his *individual existence*. It alienates from man his own body, external nature, his mental life and his *human* life.

(4) A direct consequence of the alienation of man from the product of his labor, from his life activity and from his species life is that *man* is *alienated* from other *men*. When man confronts himself he also confronts *other* men. What is true of man's relationship to his work, to the product of his work and to himself, is also true of his relationship to other men, to their labor and to the objects of their labor.

In general, the statement that man is alienated from his species life means that each man is alienated from others, and that each of the others is likewise alienated from human life.

Human alienation, and above all the relation of man to himself, is first realized and expressed in the relationship between each man and other men. Thus in the relationship of alienated labor every man regards other men

according to the standards and relationships in which he finds himself placed as a worker.

We began with an economic fact, the alienation of the worker and his production. We have expressed this fact in conceptual terms as *alienated labor,* and in analyzing the concept we have merely analyzed an economic fact.

Let us now examine further how this concept of alienated labor must express and reveal itself in reality. If the product of labor is alien to me and confronts me as an alien power, to whom does it belong? If my own activity does not belong to me but is an alien, forced activtity, to whom does it belong? To a being *other* than myself. And who is this being? The *gods*? It is apparent in the earliest stages of advanced production, e.g., temple building, etc. in Egypt, India, Mexico, and in the service rendered to gods, that the product belonged to the gods. But the gods alone were never the lords of labor. And no more was *nature*. What a contradiction it would be if the more man subjugates nature by his labor, and the more the marvels of the gods are rendered superfluous by the marvels of industry, he should abstain from his joy in producing and his enjoyment of the product for love of these powers.

The *alien* being to whom labor and the product of labor belong, to whose service labor is devoted, and to whose enjoyment the product of labor goes, can only be *man* himself. If the product of labor does not belong to the worker, but confronts him as an alien power, this can only be because it belongs to *a man other than the worker*. If his activity is a torment to him it must be a source of enjoyment and pleasure to another. Not the gods, nor nature, but only man himself can be this alien power over men.

Consider the earlier statement that the relation of man to himself is first realized, objectified, through his relation to other men. If therefore he is related to the product of his labor, his objectified labor, as to an *alien*, hostile, powerful and independent object, he is related in such a way that another alien, hostile, powerful and independent man is the lord of this object. If he is related to his own activity as to unfree activity, then he is related to it as activity in the service, and under the domination, coercion and yoke of another man.

Every self-alienation of man, from himself and from nature, appears in the relation which he postulates between other men and himself and nature. Thus religious self-alienation is necessarily exemplified in the relation between laity and priest, or, since it is here a question of the spiritual world, between the laity and a mediator. In the real world of practice this self-alienation can only be expressed in the real, practical relation of man to his fellowmen. The medium through which alienation occurs is itself a practical one. Through alienated labor, therefore, man not only produces his relation to the object and to the process of production as to alien and hostile men; he also produces the relation of other men to his production and his product, and the relation between himself and other men. Just as he creates his own production as a vitiation, a punishment, and his own product as a loss, as a product which does not belong to him, so he creates the domination of the non-producer over production and its product. As he alienates his own activity, so he bestows upon the stranger an activity which is not his own.

*   *   *

Thus, through alienated labor the worker creates the relation of another man, who does not work and is outside the work process, to this labor. The relation of the worker to work also produces the relation of the capitalist (or whatever one likes to call the lord of labor) to work. *Private property* is therefore the product, the necessary result, of *alienated labor,* of the external relation of the worker to nature and to himself.

Chapter 40 The Struggle Toward Self-Realization

KAREN HORNEY

In terms of the devil's pact, the abandoning of self corresponds to the selling of one's soul. In psychiatric terms we call it the "alienation from self." This latter term is applied chiefly to those extreme conditions in which people lose their feeling of identity, as in amnesias and depersonalizations, etc. These conditions have always aroused general curiosity. It is strange and even startling that a person who is not asleep and has no organic brain disease does not know who he is, where he is, or what he does or has been doing.

These are, however, less bewildering if we do not regard them as isolated occurrences but see their relation to less conspicuous forms of alienation from self. In these forms there is no gross loss of identity and orientation, but the general capacity for conscious experience is impaired. There are for instance many neurotics who live as if they were in a fog. Nothing is clear to them. Not only their own thoughts and feelings but also other people, and the implications of a situation, are hazy. Also related, in still less drastic terms, are conditions in which the dimming out is restricted to intrapsychic processes. I am thinking of people who can be rather astute observers of others, who can lucidly size up a situation or a trend of thought; yet experiences of all kinds (in relation to others, nature, etc.) do not penetrate to their feelings, and their inner experiences do not penetrate to awareness. And these states of mind in turn are not unrelated to those of apparently healthy people who suffer from occasional partial blackouts or from blind spots concerning certain areas of inner or outer experience.

These are only a few variations of what we could properly call an alienation from the ac-

tual self. All of what a person actually is or has, including even his connection of his present life with his past, the feeling for this continuity of his life, may be blotted out or dimmed out. Some of this process is intrinsic in every neurosis. Sometimes patients may be aware of disturbances on this score, as in the case of one patient who described himself as a lamppost with a brain on top. More often they are unaware of it, although it may be fairly extensive; and it may gradually unfold only in analysis.

At the core of this alienation from the actual self is a phenomenon that is less tangible although more crucial. It is the remoteness of the neurotic from his own feelings, wishes, beliefs, and energies. It is the loss of the feeling of being an active determining force in his own life. It is the loss of feeling himself as an organic whole. These in turn indicate an alienation from that most alive center of ourselves which I have suggested calling the *real self*. To present more fully its propensities in the terms of William James: it provides the "palpitating inward life"; it engenders the spontaneity of feelings, whether these be joy, yearning, love, anger, fear, despair. It also is the source of spontaneous interest and energies, "the source of effort and attention from which emanate the fiats of will"; the capacity to wish and to will; it is the part of ourselves that wants to expand and grow and to fulfill itself. It produces the "reactions of spontaneity" to our feelings or thoughts, "welcoming or opposing, appropriating or disowning, striving with or against, saying yes or no." All this indicates that our real self, when strong and active, enables us to make decisions and assume responsibility for them. It therefore leads to genuine integration and a sound sense of wholeness, oneness. Not merely are body and mind, deed and thought or feeling, consonant and harmonious, but they function without serious inner conflict. In contrast to those artificial means of holding ourselves together, which gain in importance as the real self is weakened, there is little or no attendant strain.

SOURCE. Karen Horney, *Neurosis and Human Growth: The Struggle toward Self-Realization,* New York: W. W. Norton and Co., 1950, pp. 155–167 and 173–174. Reprinted from *Neurosis and Human Growth* by Karen Horney, M. D. By permission of W. W. Norton and Company, Inc. Copyright 1950 by W. W. Norton and Company, Inc.

The loss of self, says Kierkegaard, is "sickness unto death"; it is despair—despair at not being conscious of having a self, or despair at not being willing to be ourselves. But it is a despair (still following Kierkegaard) which does not clamor or scream. People go on living as if they were still in immediate contact with this alive center. Any other loss—that of a job, say, or a leg—arouses far more concern. This statement of Kierkegaard's coincides with clinical observation. Apart from the pronounced pathologic conditions mentioned before, its loss does not strike the eye directly and forcefully. Patients coming for consultation complain about headaches, sexual disturbances, inhibitions in work, or other symptoms; as a rule, they do not complain about having lost touch with the core of their psychic existence.

Let us now, without going into detail, obtain a comprehensive picture of the forces responsible for the alienation from self. It is in part the consequences of the whole neurotic development, especially of *all that is compulsive in neurosis*. Of all that implies "I am driven instead of being the driver." It does not matter in this context what the particular compulsive factors are—whether they operate in relation to others (compliance, vindictiveness, detachment, etc.) or in the relation to self, as in self-idealization. The very compulsive character of these drives inevitably deprives the person of his full autonomy and spontaneity. As soon as, for instance, his need to be liked by everybody becomes compulsive, the genuineness of his feelings diminishes; so does his power to discriminate. As soon as he is driven to do a piece of work for the sake of glory, his spontaneous interest in the work itself decreases. Conflicting compulsive drives, in addition, impair his integration, his faculty to decide and give direction. Last but not least, the neurotic pseudo-solutions, though representing attempts at integration, also deprive him of autonomy because they become a compulsive way of living.

Secondly, the alienation is furthered through processes, likewise compulsive, which can be described as *active moves away from* the real self. The whole drive for glory is such a move, particularly through the neurotic's determination to mold himself into something he is not. He feels what he *should* feel, wishes what he *should* wish, likes what he *should* like. In other words, the tyranny of the should drives him frantically to be something different from what he is or could be. And in his imagination he *is* different—so different, indeed, that his real self fades and pales still more. Neurotic claims, in terms of self, mean the abandoning of the reservoir of spontaneous energies. Instead of making his own efforts, for instance, with regard to human relations, the neurotic insists that others should adjust to him. Instead of putting himself into his work, he feels entitled to having it done for him. Instead of making his own decisions, he insists that others should be responsible for him. Therefore his constructive energies lie fallow, and he actually *is* less and less a determining factor in his own life.

Neurotic pride removes him a step further from himself. Since he now becomes ashamed of what he actually is—of his feelings, resources, activities—he actively withdraws his interest from himself. The whole process of externalization is another active moving away from his self, actual and real. It is astonishing, by the way, how closely this process coincides with Kierkegaard's "despair of not wanting to be oneself."

Finally, there are *active moves against* the real self, as expressed in self-hates. With the real self in exile, so to speak, one becomes a condemned convict, despised and threatened with destruction. The idea of being oneself even becomes loathsome and terrifying. The terror sometimes appears undisguised, as one patient felt it when thinking: "This is me." This appeared at a time when the neat distinction she had made between "me" and "my neurosis" started to crumble. As a protection against this terror the neurotic "makes himself disappear." He has an unconscious interest in not having a clear perception of himself—in making himself, as it were, deaf, dumb, and blind. Not only does he blur the truth about himself but he has a vested interest in doing so—a process which blunts his sensitiveness to what is true and what is false not only inside but also outside himself. He has an interest in maintaining his haziness, although he may consciously suffer under it. One patient, for instance, in his associations often used the monsters of the Beowulf legend, who emerged at night from the lake, to symbolize his self-hate. And once he said: "If there is a fog, the monsters can't see me."

The result of all these moves is an alienation from self. When we use this term we must be aware that it focuses on only one aspect of the phenomenon. What it expresses accurately is the subjective feeling of the neurotic of being removed from himself. He may realize in analysis that all the intelligent things he has said about himself were in reality disconnected from him and his life, that they concerned some fellow with whom he had little if anything to do and the findings about whom were interesting but did not apply to his life.

In fact, this analytic experience leads us straight into the core of the problem. For we must keep in mind that the patient does not talk about weather or television: he talks about his most intimate personal life experiences. Yet they have lost their personal meaning. And, just as he may talk about himself without "being in it," so he may work, be with friends, take a walk, or sleep with a woman without being in it. His *relation to himself has become impersonal;* so has his relation to his whole life. If the word "depersonalization" did not already have a specific psychiatric meaning, it would be a good term for what alienation from self essentially is: it is a depersonalizing, and therefore a devitalizing, process.

I have already said that the alienation from self does not show as directly and blatantly as its significance would suggest, except (speaking of neuroses only) in the state of depersonalization, feelings of unreality, or amnesia. While these conditions are temporary, they can occur only in people who are estranged from themselves anyhow. The factors precipitating the feelings of unreality are usually severe injuries to pride together with an acute increase of self-contempt, exceeding what is tolerable for the particular person. Conversely, when—with or without therapy—these acute conditions subside, his alienation from self is not thereby essentially changed. It is merely again restrained within such limits that he can function without conspicuous disorientation. Otherwise the trained observer would be able to perceive certain general symptoms pointing to an existing alienation from self, such as deadness of the eyes, an aura of impersonality, an automatonlike behavior. Writers like Camus, Marquand, and Sartre have described such symptoms excellently. For the analyst it is a source of never-ending astonishment how comparatively well a person can function with the core of himself not participating.

The *availability of energies* in neurosis varies in all gradations from a pervasive inertia through sporadic unsustained efforts to consistent, even exaggerated, outputs of energy. We cannot say that neurosis per se makes a neurotic person more or less energetic than a healthy one. But this inclusiveness obtains only as long as we think of energies in a merely quantitative way, separate from motivations and aims. One of the main characteristics of neurosis, as we have stated in general and elucidated in particular is the shift of energies from developing the given potentials of the real self to developing the fictitious potentials of the idealized self. The fuller the grasp we have of the meaning of this process, the less are we puzzled by seeing incongruities in the output of energies. I shall mention here but two implications.

The more energies absorbed in the services of the pride system, the fewer are those available for the constructive drive toward self-realization. To illustrate this with a common example: the ambition-ridden person can display an astounding energy in order to attain eminence, power, and glamor, yet on the other hand have no time, interest, or energy for his personal life and his development as a human being. Actually it is not only a question of "having no energies left" for his personal life and its growth. Even if he had energies left he would unconsciously refuse to use them in behalf of his real self. To do so would run contrary to the intent of his self-hate, which is to keep his real self down.

The other implication is the fact that the neurotic does not *own* his energies (feel his energies as his own). He has the feeling of not being a moving force in his own life. In different kinds of neurotic personalities different factors may contribute to this deficiency. When a person for instance feels that he must do everything that is expected of him, he is actually set in motion by the pushes and pulls of others, or what he interprets as such—and he may stand still like a car with a run-down battery when left to his own resources. Or, if somebody has become scared of his own pride and has set a taboo on ambition, he must deny—to himself—his active share in his doings. Even if he has made a place for himself in the world, he does not feel that he has done it. What prevails is the feeling of "it happened." But, quite apart from such contributing factors, the feeling of not being the moving force in his own life is in a deeper sense true to facts. For he is indeed not moved primarily by his own wishes and aspirations but by the needs evolving from his pride system.

* * *

The role of the real self comes into clearer relief when we compare it with Freud's concept of the "ego." Though starting from entirely different premises and going along entirely different roads, I seemingly arrive at the same result as Freud, with his postulate of the weakness of the "ego." True enough, there are obvious differences in theory. For Freud the "ego" is like an employee who has functions but no initiative and no executive powers. For me the real self is the spring of emotional forces, of constructive energies, of directive and judiciary powers. But, granted that the real self has all these potentials and that they actually operate in the healthy person, what great difference is there between my position and Freud's as far as neuroses are concerned? Is it not the same for all practical purposes whether on the one hand the self is weakened, or paralyzed, or "driven from sight" by the neurotic process or on the other hand *inherently* is not a constructive force?

When looking at the beginning phases of most analyses we would have to answer this question in the affirmative. At that time very little of the real self is visibly operating. We see the possibility of certain feelings or beliefs being authentic. We can surmise that the patient's drive to develop himself contains genuine elements besides the more obvious grandiose ones; that, over and beyond his need for intellectual mastery, he is also interested in the truth about himself; and so on and so forth—but this is still surmise.

During the analytic process, however, this picture changes radically. As the pride system is undermined, the patient, instead of automatically being on the defensive, does become interested in the truth about himself. He does start to assume responsibility for himself in the sense described: to make decisions, to feel his feelings, and to develop his own beliefs. All the functions which, as we have seen, have been taken over by the pride system gradually regain spontaneity with the return to power of the real self. A redistribution of factors takes place. And in this process the real self, with its constructive forces, proves to be the stronger party.

Chapter 41 The Psychology of Alienated Students*

KENNETH KENISTON

The term "alienation" has become a fashionable catch word for the varied problems and malaises of our age. The term's meanings are extremely diverse: "alienation" has been used to describe such diverse conditions as the separation of spirit from nature (Hegel, 1931), man's loss of relationship to his work (Marx, 1844), the individual's estrangement from some deep and productive part of himself (Horney, 1945; Fromm, 1955), his loss of his own sanity (Kaplan, 1964), disillusionment with politics and politicians (Levin, 1960), the violational behavioral norms (Cloward and Ohlin, 1960), and a variety of other conditions. Many writers have attempted to disentangle the meanings of "alienation"; this will not be my topic here (but see Josephson and Josephson, 1962; Feuer, 1961; Seeman, 1959; Keniston, 1965). My point is rather that the term "alienation" is today so ill-defined that anyone who sets out to study the psychology of "alienated" individuals must begin by defining carefully what it is he is studying.

Especially since the beginning of the industrial revolution, historians and social commentators have noted that intellectuals, artists, writers and students have often rejected the major value assumptions of bourgeois, industrial, capitalist or technological society. Indeed, one of the most salient characteristics of "the intellectual" in modern society is his skeptical, critical, or repudiative attitude toward much of his culture. Such men and women are often said to be "alienated"; and it is in this sense of the term that I will use the word in this report. Alienation will mean "an explicit rejection of what are seen as the dominant values of the surrounding society."

Given this definition of alienation, it be-

comes possible to develop empirical measures (questionnaires, ratings, tests) that will give us some rough index of the degree to which any individual is alienated. And once such measures have been developed, it is then possible to study the distinctive characteristics of those who are highly alienated, contrasting them with those who are less alienated, or extremely *non*-alienated. For it follows from this definition of alienation that not all men and women are equally alienated from their society; on the contrary, in modern American society, explicit and vehement rejection of the surrounding culture is the exception rather than the rule. Thus, we can reasonably ask why some individuals are alienated from their society while others are not. The study to be summarized here is an effort to answer that question for a group of highly talented male American college students.

Many of the details of this study have been or will be reported elsewhere (Keniston, 1965; forthcoming). In essence, the study consisted of three parts. First, empirical measures of alienation were developed and the correlates of alienation were studied systematically in personality tests, in background factors, in fantasy, and in interpersonal behavior. Second, a group of extremely alienated students were identified and chosen for intensive psychological study. And finally, the understanding of individual alienation required a more speculative inquiry into the social and historical factors which cooperate with psychological factors to produce alienation in some, but not all, young Americans. In this essay, I will be primarily concerned with the second part of the research, that is, with the psychology of a small group of intensively studied and extremely alienated students.

THE ALIENATION SYNDROME

In order to study alienated individuals, we must first have some reliable way of identifying

SOURCE. Kenneth Keniston, "The Psychology of Alienated Students," will also appear in Henry A. Murray, *Aspects of Personality*, forthcoming.

* The research reported here was supported in part by NIMH grants M-1287 and M-8508.

them. Over a period of several years, my colleagues and I developed a series of highly intercorrelated questionnaire scales that enabled us to identify extremely alienated students. In the course of this study, we were able to define thirteen related alienated outlooks. If a student held one of these outlooks, he was extremely likely to hold the rest as well; if he disagreed with one, he was likely to disagree with the rest. These attitudes constitute a kind of empirical cluster or "alienation syndrome."

Amplifying the earlier work of Henry Murray and Anthony Davids (1955), we eventually ended with the following thirteen alienation scales: (1) Distrust ("Expect the worst of others and you will avoid disappointment"); (2) Pessimism ("There is little chance of ever finding real happiness"); (3) Resentment ("At times, some people make you feel like killing them"); (4) Egocentricity ("You will certainly be left behind if you stop too often or too long to give a helping hand to other people"); (5) Anxiety ("Whether he admits it or not, every modern man is a helpless victim of one of the worst ailments of our time—neurotic anxiety"); (6) Interpersonal alienation ("Emotional commitments to others are usually the prelude to disillusion and disappointment"); (7) Social alienation ("Trying to cooperate with other people brings mainly strains, rivalry, and inefficiency; consequently I much prefer to work by myself"); (8) Cultural alienation ("The idea of trying to adjust to society as it is now constituted fills me with horror"); (9) Self contempt ("Any man who has really known himself has had good cause to be horrified"); (10) Vacillation ("I make few commitments without some inner reservation or doubt about the wisdom of undertaking the responsibility or task"); (11) Subspection ("First impressions cannot be relied upon; what lies beneath the surface is often utterly different"); (12) Outsider ("I feel strongly how different I am from most people, even my close friends"); (13) Unstructured universe ("The notion that man and nature are governed by regular laws is an illusion based on our insatiable desire for certainty"). Together these scales constitute the empirical definition of the "alienation syndrome." The average scale-to-scale correlation is +.47, and the average correlation of Distrust with all other scales is +.58.

These scales enabled us to select a small group of subjects for intensive clinical study. From a large group of volunteers, 83 male Harvard College sophomores with satisfactory academic standing were chosen for testing and were given these alienation scales and other questionnaires. On the basis of their scores, three groups were selected for intensive clinical study: (1) A highly alienated group, (2) A highly non-alienated group, and (3) A third "comparison" group of students with medium scores on alienation. Including students drawn from this group and earlier groups, 11 alienated undergraduates, 10 non-alienated undergraduates, and a comparison group of a dozen students were studied. The modal alienated student was in the most alienated 8% of the college population; the typical non-alienated student was in the least alienated 8%; and the members of the comparison group stood very near the middle.

All of these undergraduates took part in at least one year of the research study and most of them were studied throughout the last three years of their college careers. During this time, they gave approximately two hours a week to the research, for which they were paid. The research ranged over a wide variety of topics. All students wrote a length autobiography and a detailed statement of their basic values and beliefs. All were repeatedly interviewed about matters autobiographical, ideological, vocational, ethical, and experimental. All took the Thematic Apperception Test (T.A.T.), a test of fantasy in which students make up imaginative stories to twenty ambiguous pictures. In addition, all of the research subjects took part in a great variety of other specific psychological experiments. By the end of the three year period, large amounts of information had been collected about almost every aspect of the individual's life.

The clinical study of alienation focused on the following questions.

1. What is the ideology of alienation as seen in these students? Written statements of basic values, interview material, and added questionnaire material helped answer this question.

2. What common characteristics of behavior and life style do these alienated students possess? Systematic studies of behavior in experimental groups, interview materials, and informal observations of the students in college helped answer this question.

3. What features of past life (infancy, family characteristics, childhood, adolescence) do these alienated students share? Written auto-

biographies and interviews provided most of the data here.

4. What are the central features of the fantasy life of alienated students? The T.A.T., reports of fantasies and dreams, and imaginative productions like poems, short stories, plays, and drawings were the basis for efforts to answer this question.

5. What hypotheses can be advanced that might explain the psychological basis of alienation? Here, I sought for interpretations and hypotheses that might enable me to construct a coherent explanation of how alienation develops within the individual.

In an attempt to answer these questions, the case records of each student were first studied independently. Then, alienated students were systematically contrasted with the non-alienated, and with the comparison group. In certain respects, of course, all three groups were similar: for example, all students in all three groups were intelligent and academically oriented, and most were from relatively privileged social backgrounds. But in the account to follow, I will emphasize only those characteristics of the alienated students which were not found to the same degree among the non-alienated or the comparison group.

THE IDEOLOGY OF ALIENATION

Statistical studies had suggested that distrust was a primary variable in the alienation syndrome. Clinical investigations confirmed this finding. For alienated students, distrust extends far beyond a low view of human nature; they also believe that intimacy ends in disillusion, that attachment to a group entails the loss of individuality, and that all appearances are untrustworthy. Nor can American culture be trusted: it is mechanical, boring, trashy, cheap, conformist and dull. Any kind of positive commitment is viewed negatively: life is such that the alienated can never be sure of anything; every choice precludes equally desirable alternatives.

In addition, most alienated students are native existentialists. Few of them, when they began the research study, had read existentialist philosophers; yet they had often spontaneously arrived at a view of the world close to that of the most pessimistic existentialists like Sartre. And when later in their college careers they read such writers, it was usually with a sense of *déja vu*. From middle adolescence on, alienated students had become increasingly aware of

the darkness, isolation and meaninglessness of life. The human condition as they had come to see it provides the basis for universal anxiety. The universe itself is dead, lacking in structure, inherently unpredictable and random. Individual life, too, is devoid of purpose and preordained form. Consequently, any meaning or truth that an individual finds is inevitably subjective and solipsistic. The "truth" that one man creates is not necessarily that of his fellows; and in writing about their "philosophies of life," the alienated stress that these are merely expressions of subjective and arbitrary belief. Morality, too, is seen as inevitably egocentric, arbitrary and individualistic. Given the unpredictability of the future, long-range ethical idealism is impossible; the present becomes overwhelmingly important. Alienated students are usually moral "realists" who see immediate feeling, mood and pleasure as the only possible guide lines for action.

Alienated undergraduates do not react stoically to this view of the world. On the contrary, their response is scorn, bitterness and anger. Love and hate, they insist, are inseparable. Their own hostilities and resentments are close to awareness, and their scorn is especially intense when they confront those who are not alienated. They do not suffer fools gladly, and they consider most of their fellows fools. Indeed, their anger is so corrosive that it extends even to themselves. True to the logic of their position, they maintain that the consequences of self-knowledge are self-contempt, and are quick to admit their own self-revulsion. Similarly, their resentment is expressed in their conviction that all men inevitably use each other for their own purposes, whatever their altruistic rationalizations.

Much of the explicit philosophy of these students is negative. They are, like Nietzsche (one of their favorite writers), philosophers with hammers, whose favorite intellectual sport is exposing the hypocrisy of others. They distrust all Positive Thinking and therefore find it almost impossible to agree with any questionnaire statement that clearly expresses an affirmative view. But despite the negative cast of their explicit views, the alienated share an implicit positive search in a common direction. Their philosophies emphasize the value of passion and feeling, the search for awareness, the cultivation of responsiveness, the importance of solitude and the need somehow to express their experience of life. Their main values are therefore "expressive" or esthetic, in that their main focus is the present, their main source is the self, and their main aim is the development of awareness, responsiveness, expressiveness and sentience. Rejecting the traditional American values of success, self-control and achievement, they maintain that passion, feeling and awareness are the truest forces at man's disposal. For most of them, the primary objective in life is to attain and maintain openness to experience, contact with the world and spontaneity of feeling. Anything that might fetter or restrain their responsiveness and openness is opposed: the goal, as one student puts it, is "circumscribing my life as little as possible." And the same student goes on to say that he will some day be able to "express all or part of what I feel about life."

These alienated outlooks contrast sharply with "traditional" American views about the self, life, others, society and the universe. Indeed, each alienated view is a rejection of the conventional wisdom of our society. Thus, the unifying theme of the ideology of alienation is the rejection of what are seen as dominant American values, an unwillingness to accept the trusting, optimistic, sociocentric, affiliative, interpersonally oriented, and culturally accepting values which were, in less troubled times, the foundations of the American world view.

ALIENATION AS A STYLE OF LIFE

When we turn from alienated views of the world to the everyday life of alienated students, we find much less surface distinctiveness. Formal socio-economic and demographic variables do not distinguish these students from their classmates, nor does a casual search through college records, high school records or even police records. The alienated do not look different from their classmates, and the overt pattern of their daily activities shows relatively little that is distinctive. But if we examine not what they do, but *how* they do it, we soon discover that the alienated have a characteristic life style that reflects and complements their alienation.

One crucial feature of this style of life is intellectual passion. In their approach to intellectual matters, these students are distinguished by their passionate concentration on a few topics of intense personal concern. They pursue their intellectual interests with such single-minded dedication that they almost completely disregard the conventional distinction between "work" and "goofing off" made by most of their classmates. Their capacity for intense

intellectual concentration stands them in good stead during the last days before examinations, when they are capable of accomplishing extraordinary amounts of work. Moreover, when they are challenged in their work, and above all when their assignments strike some deep personal chord, they can become totally absorbed in intellectual work. Thus, despite erratic performances before examinations, the overall averages of these students are about what was predicted for them on arrival in college.

Alienated students, when they become involved in extra-curricular activities, are specifically drawn to those that allow them to express their artistic and "esthetic" interests. But in whatever they do, the style of their participation is alienated: it characteristically involves a preference for the role of the observer. Thus, as a group, they avoid positions of responsibility or, when accorded them, repudiate them immediately. One student, elected to an important national position, confounded everyone from his parents to his classmates by dropping out of college on the eve of assuming his new office. Since the alienated see all groups as destructive of individuality, they distrusted even the beatnik group which, during the years they were studied, flourished around the college: they found beatniks conformists and "not serious."

Their favored stance as detached observers led these students into semi-systematic wanderings. Whenever they were confronted with a problem or conflict, they were likely to "take off," sometimes for a long walk at night, sometimes for a few years out of college. In all of these wanderings, they seem to be searching not so much for escape, as to immerse themselves in intense experience. Sometimes they found such experience. In their interviews and autobiographies, there are occasional mentions of epiphanies, mystical experiences, and revelations of Everything in the garish pennants of a filling station, in the way the light of the setting sun falls through an archway or in the smell of burning leaves.

Only on rare occasions did the alienated become active participants. In intellectual discussions in small groups, however, they are active, dominant, negative and hostile, interrupting and correcting their fellows, impressing others with their scorn and contempt. But in stressful two-person situations, when confronted with an experienced and skilled antagonist, they find it difficult to express their anger at the time, but later lapse into enduring resentment.

Thus, direct expression of hostility to another person is not easy for these students; they find it most comfortable to channel their annoyance into intellectual discussions.

But despite their outward appearance of detachment from others, alienated undergraduates are highly though ambivalently involved with them. They are often simultaneously attracted to and somewhat fearful of an admired person—tempted to emulate him, but afraid that emulation might mean the sacrifice of their inner integrity. Given this ambivalence, it is understandable that these students tend to ruminate, often obsessively, about all close personal relationships. No friendship escapes detailed analysis from every point of view; every relationship becomes a matter of the preservation of identity. This ambivalent examination of relationships is especially pronounced with girls. Almost invariably, alienated students choose girls who are either profoundly dissatisfying to them or else strongly rejected by some crucial portion of their background. Thus, when they do become close to a girl, it is either to one who is described as passive, dependent and subservient, or to one who is so totally unacceptable to their parents as to precipitate a complete break between the student and his family. In these relationships with girls, as in most of their relationships with other people, they combine an agonizing desire for closeness with a great fear of it.

In interviews as in questionnaires, alienated students are quick to admit their confusions, angers, anxieties and problems. Given a list of neurotic symptoms, they check them all, describing themselves as confused, depressed, angry, neurotic, hostile and impulsive. Yet the inference that these students are grossly disturbed can only be made with reservations. For one, they reject the value assumptions upon which most questionnaire measures of "maturity," "ego strength," and "good mental health" are based. Furthermore, they make a great effort to undermine any "defenses" that might protect them from unpleasant feelings. For most of these students, openness to their own problems and failings is a cardinal virtue; and they make a further point of loudly proclaiming their own inadequacies. Their drive to be totally honest with themselves and others makes them consistently put their worst foot forward.

But even when we make due allowance for the tendency of alienated students to exaggerate their own failings, many of these students are in fact confused, disoriented and depressed. In interviews, their public face of contempt often gives way to private admissions of unhappiness and apprehension. Secretly, some harbor doubts that this unhappiness may be of their own making, rather than merely a consequence of the human condition. Thus, many alienated students can be aptly described in Erikson's terms (1959) as in a state of more or less intense identity diffusion. Their sense of themselves seems precarious and disunified, they often doubt their own continuing capacity to cope; they have little positive sense of relatedness to other people; the boundaries of their own egos are diffuse and porous. Strong in opposition, these students are weak in affirmation; unable to articulate what they stand for, they have little sense of self to stand on. As a group, then, alienated students are not characterized by happiness, optimism, tranquility or calm; they are more notable for the intensity of their convictions, the vehemence of their scorn, the passion behind their search for meaning.

ALIENATION AND THE PERSONAL PAST

A careful examination of what alienated students tell us about their families and their earlier lives shows a remarkable consistency in their views. When discussing their mothers, for example, they frequently emphasize the renunciations and sacrifices their mothers have made. To their sons, these women appear to have been talented, artistic, intense and intelligent girls who gave up promise and fulfillment for marriage. They also seem to their sons vivid, sensuous and magnetic; and alienated students often wonder aloud "whether marriage was worth it" to their mothers. Throughout, these students express their special sympathy for and identification with their mothers and their sadness at their mothers' lack of fulfillment.

But the mothers of alienated sons have another set of common characteristics—dominance, possessiveness, excessive involvement with their sons, over-solicitude. The typical alienated student tells of his mother's intrusiveness, of her attempts to limit, supervise and restrict his independence and initiative. And although few of the alienated admit that their mothers have been successful in controlling *them,* they do on the whole believe that their mothers have succeeded in controlling their fathers. Thus, it was Mother who paid Dad's way through college, it was Mother who made

Dad's mind up to marry her, it is Mother who somehow decides how things are done in the family. Seen through her son's eyes, she emerges as a woman who has turned her considerable energies to the domination of her family.

About their fathers, alienated students volunteer less information than do most undergraduates. We already know that fathers are usually seen as dominated by mothers. Fathers are also described as men who, despite public success, are "failures in their own eyes," "apostates," disappointed, frustrated and disillusioned men. But often, in addition, their college age sons portray them as having once had youthful dreams which they were unable to fulfill, as idealists whose idealism has been destroyed by life. The precise agent of this destruction varies: sometimes it was Mother; sometimes it was the father's own weakness, particularly his inability to stand up against social pressures. So despite their frequent scorn for their dominated fathers, alienated students retain much sympathy for the same fathers as they might have been—a covert identification with the fantasy of a youthful idealistic father.

In characterizing their fathers at present, however, the alienated again and again emphasize qualities like detachment, reserve, inability to express affection, loneliness and withdrawal from the center of the family. Contrasted with the expressive, emotional, controlling and dynamic mother, the father appears weak, inactive, detached and uninterested. The greater portion of these students' current sympathies goes to their mothers, whose frustrations are seen as imposed from without, while their fathers are more often directly blamed for their failure to live up to their youthful dreams.

In their earliest memories, alienated students make unusually frequent references to "oral" themes, that is, to issues of consuming, being nurtured and cared for, to food aversions, feeding problems and in one student, to the assumption that his voracious nursing produced breast cancer in his mother. In these memories, women are always present; men are striking by their absence. Although these subjects' fathers were usually present during their early childhood, it was the mother or other women who appeared to have mattered. Especially striking are idyllic recollections of happy times alone with mother on vacations, or family expeditions when father was away from home. All of these memories suggest an unusually intense attachment between mother and son in early life.

In primary and secondary school, alienated students, like most undergraduates at Harvard College, were capable intellectually and interested in their schoolwork. But they differ from many of their classmates in that they seem consistently to have preferred imagination, thought and staying at home to outgoing activities with others; they speak less than most students of group activities and "running with the gang"; they usually describe themselves as quiet, homebound, unrebellious and obedient children.

But during adolescence, alienated students seem to have undergone even greater turmoil than most of their classmates. The symptoms of their turmoil are extremely varied: intense asceticism, tentative delinquency, vociferous rebellion, speeding, drinking and, in one case, a half-hearted suicide attempt. From other evidence, it seems that the arrival of adult sexuality was unusually disturbing to these young men. In discussing their sexual fantasies as college students, they emphasize to an unusual degree their desire for passivity, oblivion and tranquility, and often mention difficulties about being initiating and "aggressive" with women. Only a few alienated students have found sexual relationships fully satisfying, and many mention enduring feelings of anxiety, discomfort or apprehension connected with sex. All of this suggests that one of the major problems in adolescence was especially great anxiety about assuming the traditional male sex role.

There is no mention of overt alienation in the life histories of these students until mid-adolescence—about the age of sixteen. At this age, we hear accounts of growing feelings of cynicism, distance, estrangement and scorn—initially for school classmates, later for parents and teachers, finally for all of society. In most cases, these feelings appeared spontaneously, though sometimes they were precipitated by the views of a friend, a trip abroad, or some other specific event. This growing sense of alienation usually contrasted sharply with continuing academic and social success; and the contrast between inner alienation and outer success led to increasing feelings of estrangement from all those who accepted them merely at face value. Their alienation developed more or less in isolation and more or less spontaneously; it was usually only after they became alienated that these students sought out books and people who would confirm and support them in their alienation. Among the students studied, alienation could not be explained as the result of identification with an alienated parent; on the contrary, it always seemed to involve a sharp repudiation of perceived parental values.

ALIENATION IN FANTASY

The fantasies of alienated students, as seen on the T.A.T., are different from the fantasies of other students both in style and in content. Stylistically, alienated fantasies are rich, vivid, imaginative, antisocial, unconventional, and sometimes bizarre. The typical alienated fantasy involves an inferior or unusually sensitive hero who becomes involved in a difficult relationship with another person. The relationship goes from bad to worse, leading to great resentment and hurt, especially on the hero's side. Efforts to repair the relationship invariably fail, and the hero is profoundly and adversely affected. This plot format contrasts sharply with the typical stories of non-alienated students, whose competent and superior heroes enter into positive and enduring relationships from which all concerned profit and grow.

Within this general plot format, the alienated characteristically tells stories reflecting one or both of two major themes. The first of these is the loss of Eden. Alienated fantasies are distinctively concerned with the loss of supplies, with starvation, with forcible estrangement and a yearning to return to bliss. Sometimes these fantasies involve isolated heroes who die of starvation; more often, they entail a hero who seeks to regain his union with a lost loved one, usually a woman. Alienated fantasies are a catalogue of yearnings for the past: undertakers enamored of their female subjects, ghoulish grave-robbers, heroes obsessed with the recovery of the lost Gods, grief-stricken husbands who crawl into their wives' graves, detectives searching for missing persons, lovers mourning the dead, husbands who kill themselves on their wives' coffins.

The same theme of reunion with a lost love is reflected in other stories where the hero loses himself in some warm, fluid or embracing maternal medium. Some heroes are lured to their deaths by warm and friendly voices speaking from the sea or calling from the air. Other fantasies involve heroes who dive to the bottom of the ocean, never to return. Developmentally, these often archaic and weird stories seem to refer to an unconscious obsession with the lost early relationship with the mother. The fantasy

of fusion with the lost maternal presence—a fantasy which exists somewhere in the hearts of all men—constitutes an obsessional theme for these college students.

A second important motif in alienated fantasy is the theme of a pyrrhic Oedipal victory. Most college students, when given the Thematic Apperception Test, are at some pains to avoid stories which involve competitive rivalrous triangles: rivalry between men is usually minimized, and struggles between two men for the love of a woman are especially rare. The alienated, in contrast, take rivalrous triangles for granted, often importing them into stories where the picture in no way suggests this theme. Even more striking is the peculiar form and outcome of such fantasies. Again and again, it is the younger man who defeats the older man, but only to be overcome himself by some extraneous force. Attacks on fathers and father figures are almost inevitably successful: the father dies, the Minister of Interior Affairs is assassinated, the boss who has propositioned the hero's wife is killed. Or, in the many stories of political revolution told by these apolitical students, the established regime is seen as weak, corrupt and easily overthrown. Traditional male authority topples at the first push.

Yet these stories of rebellion, rivalry and revolution are, paradoxically, cautionary tales. The revolution succeeds, but it is followed by a disaster: the revolutionary murderer is assassinated by his own men; the revolutionary regime turns into a despotism worse than that which it overthrew, the avenged cuckold is killed in an automobile accident. These fantasies suggest that although traditional male authority is weak, its destruction leads to a new and worse tyranny.

These fantasies are consistent with the hypotheses that the rebellious son believes that he indeed succeeded in deposing his father, but that this deposition was followed by a new maternal tyranny. The victor was neither father nor son, but mother, who now dominates them both. Supporting this hypothesis is the fact that most alienated fantasies portray adult women as active, controlling and possessive. In particular they restrain men's sexuality, aggressiveness and nonconformity: they try to keep their sons from going out with girls; they keep men from fighting; they try to make their husbands settle down and conform—and almost invariably, they succeed.

The dominant theme of relations between the sexes, then, is not love and intimacy, but the control of men by women. When intimacy begins to seem possible, the story usually ends disastrously. Furthermore, women are not only seen as controlling and possessive, but, on occasion, as murderous and destructive: as lizard goddesses who eat their victims, apparently loveable ladies who murder their husbands, as emasculating and destructive figures. Fathers and older men, in contrast, are almost always portrayed as weak, corruptible, absent or damaged. Men are controlled by women, and even men who initially appear strong eventually turn out to be fraudulent and weak.

HYPOTHESES ABOUT THE PSYCHOLOGICAL SOURCES OF ALIENATION

The themes of ideology, life style, past history and fantasy summarized here are of course open to many different interpretations. In some respects, the psychological origins of alienation are different for each alienated individual, and no composite account can hope to do justice to the uniqueness of each person. Nonetheless, the existence of many shared strands of belief, present feeling, past experience and imagination suggests that, insofar as we can take these students' accounts as an adequate basis for an explanation, general hypotheses about the psychological origins of alienation are possible.

One of the most striking findings of this study is the great similarity in the families of alienated students. Both parents seem to have been frustrated and dissatisfied. The mother's talents and emotionality found little expression within her marriage; the father's idealism and youthful dreams were crushed by the realities of his adult life. The mothers of alienated students seem to have turned their drive and perhaps their own frustrated needs for love onto their sons. Often, these mothers explicitly deprecated or disparaged their husbands. And confronted with this deprecation, the fathers of alienated students seem to have withdrawn from the family, becoming detached, embittered, and distant. Forced to choose between their families and their work, they almost to a man turned their energies outside of the family, leaving mother and son locked in a special alliance of mutual understanding and maternal control.

This basic family constellation is reflected and elaborated in fantasy. Unconsciously, alienated students seem to believe that they defeated their fathers, who are therefore seen as weak and inadequate models of male adulthood. Probably like most small boys, they attempted a "revolution" within the family in order to overthrow the tyrannical father and gain the exclusive love of the mother. But unlike most, these boys believe that their revolution succeeded in destroying male authority. Yet paradoxically, their apparent victory did not win them maternal love but maternal control, possessiveness, and over-solicitude. Furthermore, by displacing their fathers, they lost the right of every boy to a father he can admire. The son thus gained something very different from what he had wanted. At least in fantasy, he found himself saddled with the possessive and intrusive mother, and he lost the youthful idealistic father he could respect.

If these hypotheses are correct, they may help us explain some of the other characteristics of these alienated students. For such a childhood experience would clearly leave a boy or even a college student with the unconscious assumption that apparently admirable men were really weak and impotent; and that apparently nurturing and loving women were really controlling, possessive and even emasculating. Conventional adulthood as epitomized by the father —that is, the dominant value assumptions about adulthood in American society—would also seem unattractive and have to be rejected. Adult closeness with women would be frightening, as it would evoke fears of being dominated, controlled and emasculated. Similarly, competition and rivalry would be avoided in everyday behavior, not out of the fear of failure, but from a fear of another phyrric victory. Furthermore, the inability of our subjects' mothers to love them as sons, coupled with the apparently sudden change in the sons' image of the mother from that of a nurturer to an emasculator might help explain the persistence into early adulthood of recurrent fantasies about fusion with the maternal presence, the dominance of the theme of loss of Eden.

The psychological factors that predisposed these students toward alienation are thus complex and interrelated. The sense and the stance of alienation are partially reflections of the unconscious conviction of these subjects that they are outcasts from a lost Eden, alienated forever from their mothers' early love. Then, too, the repudiation of conventional adulthood, of the dominant values of American society, is closely related to their unconscious determination not to let what happened to their fathers happen to them, and to covert identification with the fantasy of a youthful, idealistic father before he was "broken" by life. Similarly, the centrality of distrust in the emotional lives and ideologies of aliented students is probably in part a reflection of an early family situation in which neither parent turned out to be what he or she had seemed to be. In a variety of ways, then, these students were prepared by their past experience and by the fantasies through which they interpreted this experience to be alienated from American culture.

NON-PSYCHOLOGICAL FACTORS IN ALIENATION

An account of the psychological factors that predispose certain individuals to be alienated is by no means a complete or adequate account. For one, such an account will have, to many readers, an implicitly "reductive" quality: it may seem to suggest that alienation is "nothing but" a reflection of a particular kind of family constellation and childhood experience. It is far from my intention to "reduce" alienation to childhood history here; on the contrary, while the links between early experience and later alienation are clear, these links in no way entail that alienation is "nothing but" a reflection of unfortunate childhood. On the contrary, the childhood events and fantasies I have discussed here could be viewed as the fortunate and enabling factors that permitted these students to be aware of the very real deficiencies in their society to which their less alienated fellows remain obdurately blind.

Furthermore, this psychological account is, even in its own terms, far from complete. It is probable that the family factors I have outlined will dispose a young man to *some* kind of hesitancy about or repudiation of conventional adulthood. But these family factors alone do not suffice to explain why this hesitancy took the particular form of cultural alienation. For further explanations, we would need to consider the early propensity of these students to solve problems with their imaginations rather than their fists, their generally privileged social backgrounds, their very high talent, intelligence and imaginativeness, and their very great sensitivity to the evils in themselves and in the world around them. We would have to consider the impact of talented and often artistic mothers on their eldest or only sons, and we would have to prepare a more adequate catalogue not only of the major psychological themes of alienation, but of the specific strengths and weaknesses of alienated students.

Another dimension omitted from this psychological account of alienation is even more important—it is the social and historical context and traditions within which these students live. Alienation of the sort here described is by no means an exclusively contemporary phenomenon; especially during the past two centuries in the Western world, many of the most creative men and women have been highly alienated from their own cultures. Furthermore, the precise forms, manifestations and content of alienation are always given by the surrounding society; for example, during the years these students were studied, the late 1950's and early 1960's, there were a few available student movements of social change and reform into which alienation might have been channeled. At least a few of these alienated students, had they been in college six years later, might have found a channel for the constructive expression of their alienation in the civil rights movement or the peace movement.

Finally, this account of alienation is incomplete in the most fundamental way of all. Although alienated students are especially sensitized and predisposed toward alienation by their pasts, their alienation itself is a reaction *to* and *against* the society in which they live. In other words, alienation is a transaction between an individual and his society, and we can understand it adequately by examining not only the individual and his psychology, but the characteristics of the wider society as they impinge upon students like him. To attempt to characterize the major trends and pressures of American society is far beyond my topic here. But it should be said that the pressures and demands of modern American society seem to me profoundly alienating in many respects. Thus, we could with full justice ask of the *non*-alienated why their individual psychology so blinds them to these "alienating" aspects of our society which the alienated perceive so sharply.

Alienation, then, as studied in this small group of talented college students, is the product of a complex interaction of psychological, sociological, cultural and historical factors within the experience of each individual. It is not enough to attribute alienation solely to the characteristics of modern technological society—such an explanation makes it impossible for us to account for the majority of Americans who are not alienated. But it would be equally misleading to see alienation purely as an expression of individual psychology. Like most outlooks, alienation is the product of the inner world and the outer world as they came together in the developing individual's experience.

REFERENCES

Cloward, R. A., and Ohlin, L. E. *Delinquency and Opportunity.*
    Glencoe, Ill.: Free Press, 1960.
Erikson, E. "The problem of ego identity," in "Identity and the life cycle,"
    Psychological Issues, I (1) (1959).
Feuer, L. "What is alienation? The career of a concept," *New Politics*
    1–19 (1961).
Fromm, E. *The Sane Society.* New York: Holt, Rinehart and Winston, 1955.
Hegel, G. W. F. *The Phenomenology of Mind.* New York:
    Humanities Press, 1931.
Horney, K. *Our Neurotic Conflicts.* New York: Norton, 1945.
Josephson, E., and Josephson, M., eds., *Man Alone: Alienation in Modern
    Society.* New York: Dell, 1962.
Kaplan, B. *The Inner World of Mental Illness.* New York: Harper and
    Row, 1964.
Keniston, K. *The Uncommitted: Alienated Youth in American Society.*
    New York: Harcourt, Brace and World, 1965.
Keniston, K. *The Alienated Student.* Forthcoming.
Levin, M. *The Alienated Voter.* New York: Holt, Rinehart and
    Winston, 1960.
Marx, K. *Economic and Philosphic Manuscripts of 1844.* Moscow: Foreign
    Languages Publishing, 1959.
Murray, H. A., and Davids, A. "Preliminary appraisal of an auditory projective
    technique for studying personality and cognition," *American Journal
    of Ortho-Psychiatry,* **25** (1955), pp. 543–544.
Seeman, M. "On the meaning of alienation," *American Sociological Review,*
    24 (1959), pp. 783–791.

Chapter 42 Ontological Insecurity

R. D. LAING

We can now state more precisely the nature of our clinical inquiry. A man may have a sense of his presence in the world as a real, alive, whole, and, in a temporal sense, continuous person. As such, he can live out into the world and meet others: a world and others experienced as equally real, alive, whole, and continuous.

Such a basically *ontologically*[1] secure person will encounter all the hazards of life, social, ethical, spiritual, biological, from a centrally firm sense of his own and other people's reality and identity. It is often difficult for a person with such a sense of his integral selfhood and personal identity, of the permanency of things, of the reliability of natural processes, of the substantiality of natural processes, of the substantiality of others, to transpose himself into the world of an individual whose experiences may be utterly lacking in any unquestionable self-validating certainties.

This study is concerned with the issues involved where there is the partial or almost complete absence of the assurances derived from an existential position of what I shall call *primary ontological security*: with anxieties and dangers that I shall suggest arise *only* in terms of *primary ontological insecurity*; and with the consequent attempts to deal with such anxieties and dangers.

The literary critic, Lionel Trilling (1955), points up the contrast that I wish to make between a *basic existential position of ontological security* and one of *ontological insecurity* very clearly in comparing the worlds of Shakespeare and Keats on the one hand, and of Kafka on the other:

. . . for Keats the awareness of evil exists side by side with a very strong sense of personal identity and is for that reason the less immediately apparent. To some contemporary readers, it will seem for the same reason the less intense. In the same way it may seem to a contemporary reader that, if we compare Shakespeare and Kafka, leaving aside the degree of genius each has, and considering both only as expositors of man's suffering and cosmic alienation, it is Kafka who makes the more intense and complete exposition. And, indeed, the judgment may be correct, exactly because for Kafka the sense of evil is not contradicted by the sense of personal identity. Shakespeare's world, quite as much as Kafka's, is that prison cell which Pascal says the world is, from which daily the inmates are led forth to die; Shakespeare no less than Kafka forces upon us the cruel irrationality of the conditions of human life, the tale told by an idiot, the puerile gods who torture us not for punishment but for sport; and no less than Kafka, Shakespeare is revolted by the fetor of the prison of this world, nothing is more characteristic of him than his imagery of disgust. But in Shakespeare's cell the company is so much better than in Kafka's, the captains and kings and lovers and clowns of Shakespeare are alive and complete before they die. In Kafka, long before the sentence is executed, even long before the malign legal process is even instituted, something terrible has been done to the accused. We all know what this is—he has been stripped of all that is becoming to a man except his abstract humanity, which, like his skeleton, never is quite becoming to a man. He is without parents, home, wife, child, commitment, or appetite; he has no connection with power, beauty, love, wit, courage, loyalty, or fame, and the pride that may be taken in these. So that we may say that Kafka's knowledge of evil exists without the contradictory knowledge of the self in its health and validity, that Shakespeare's knowledge of evil exists with that contradiction in its fullest possible force (pp. 38–9).

We find, as Trilling points out, that Shakespeare does depict characters who evidently experience themselves as real and alive and

SOURCE. R. D. Laing, *The Divided Self,* London: Tavistock Publications, 1960, pp. 40–51 and 54–56. Copyright 1960 Tavistock Publications Ltd. Reprinted by permission of Tavistock Publications Ltd. and Quadrangle Books, Chicago.

[1] Despite the philosophical use of "ontology" (by Heidegger, Sartre, Tillich, especially), I have used the term in its present empirical sense because it appears to be the best adverbial or adjectival derivative of "being."

complete however riddled by doubts or torn by conflicts they may be. With Kafka this is not so. Indeed, the effort to communicate what being alive is like in the absence of such assurances seems to characterize the work of a number of writers and artists of our time. Life, without feeling alive.

With Samuel Beckett, for instance, one enters a world in which there is no contradictory sense of the self in its "health and validity" to mitigate the despair, terror, and boredom of existence. In such a way, the two tramps who wait for Godot are condemned to live:

ESTRAGON: We always find something, eh, Didi, to give us the impression that we exist?

VLADIMIR (impatiently): Yes, yes, we're magicians. But let us persevere in what we have resolved, before we forget.

In painting, Francis Bacon, among others, seems to be dealing with similar issues. Generally, it is evident that what we shall discuss here clinically is but a small sample of something in which human nature is deeply implicated and to which we can contribute only a very partial understanding.

To begin at the beginning:

Biological birth is a definitive act whereby the infant organism is precipitated into the world. There it is, a new baby, a new biological entity, already with its own ways, real and alive, from *our* point of view. But what of the baby's point of view? Under usual circumstances, the physical birth of a new living organism into the world inaugurates rapidly ongoing processes whereby within an amazingly short time the infant *feels* real and alive and has a *sense* of being an entity, with continuity in time and a location in space. In short, physical birth and biological aliveness are followed by the baby becoming existentially born as real and alive. Usually this development is taken for granted and affords the certainty upon which all other certainties depend. This is to say, not only do adults see children to be real biologically visible entities but they experience themselves as whole persons who are real and alive, and conjunctively experience other human beings as real and alive. These are self-validating data of experience.

The individual, then, may experience his own being as real, alive, whole; as differentiated from the rest of the world in ordinary circumstances so clearly that his identity and autonomy are never in question; as a continuum in time; as having an inner consistency, substantiality, genuineness, and worth; as spatially coextensive with the body; and, usually, as having begun in or around birth and liable to extinction with death. He thus has a firm core of ontological security.

This, however, may not be the case. The individual in the ordinary circumstances of living may feel more unreal than real; in a literal sense, more dead than alive; precariously differentiated from the rest of the world, so that his identity and autonomy are always in question. He may lack the experience of his own temporal continuity. He may not possess an over-riding sense of personal consistency or cohesiveness. He may feel more insubstantial than substantial, and unable to assume that the stuff he is made of is genuine, good, valuable. And he may feel his self as partially divorced from his body.

It is, of course, inevitable that an individual whose experience of himself is of this order can no more live in a "secure" world than he can be secure "in himself." The whole "physiognomy" of his world will be correspondingly different from that of the individual whose sense of self is securely established in its health and validity. Relatedness to other persons will be seen to have a radically different significance and function. To anticipate, we can say that in the individual whose own being is secure in this primary experiential sense, relatedness with others is potentially gratifying; whereas the ontologically insecure person is preoccupied with preserving rather than gratifying himself: the ordinary circumstances of living threaten his *low threshold* of security.[2]

If a position of primary ontological security has been reached, the ordinary circumstances of life do not afford a perpetual threat to one's own existence. If such a basis for living has not been reached, the ordinary circumstances of everyday life constitute a continual and deadly threat.

Only if this is realized is it possible to understand how certain psychoses can develop.

If the individual cannot take the realness, aliveness, autonomy, and identity of himself and others for granted, then he has to become absorbed in contriving ways of trying to be real, of keeping himself or others alive, of

---

[2] This formulation is very similar to those of H. S. Sullivan, Hill, F. Fromm-Reichmann, and Arieti in particular. Federn, although expressing himself very differently, seems to have advanced a closely allied view.

preserving his identity, in efforts, as he will often put it, to prevent himself losing his self. What are to most people everyday happenings, which are hardly noticed because they have no special significance, may become deeply significant in so far as they either contribute to the sustenance of the individual's being or threaten him with non-being. Such an individual, for whom the elements of the world are coming to have, or have come to have, a different hierarchy of significance from that of the ordinary person, is beginning, as we say, to "live in a world of his own," or has already come to do so. It is not true to say, however, without careful qualification that he is losing "contact with" reality, and withdrawing into himself. External events no longer affect him in the same way as they do others: it is not that they affect him less; on the contrary, frequently they affect him more. It is frequently not the case that he is becoming "indifferent" and "withdrawn." It may, however, be that the world of his experience comes to be one he can no longer share with other people.

But before these developments are explored, it will be valuable to characterize under three headings three forms of anxiety encountered by the ontologically insecure person: engulfment, implosion, petrification.

1. ENGULFMENT

An argument occurred between two patients in the course of a session in an analytic group. Suddenly, one of the protagonists broke off the argument to say, "I can't go on. You are arguing in order to have the pleasure of triumphing over me. At best you win an argument. At worst you lose an argument. *I am arguing in order to preserve my existence.*"

This patient was a young man who I would say was sane, but, as he stated, his activity in the argument, as in the rest of his life, was not designed to gain gratification but to "preserve his existence." Now, one might say that if he did, in fact, really imagine that the loss of an argument would jeopardize his existence, then he was "grossly out of touch with reality" and was virtually psychotic. But this is simply to beg the question without making any contribution towards understanding the patient. It is, however, important to know that if you were to subject this patient to a type of psychiatric interrogation recommended in many psychiatric textbooks, within ten minutes his behaviour and speech would be revealing "signs" of psychosis. It is quite easy to evoke

such 'signs' from such a person whose threshold of basic security is so low that practically any relationhip with another person, however tenuous or however apparently "harmless," threatens to overwhelm him.

A firm sense of one's own autonomous identity is required in order that one may be related as one human being to another. Otherwise, any and every relationship threatens the individual with loss of identity. One form this takes can be called engulfment. In this the individual dreads relatedness as such, with anyone or anything or, indeed, even with himself, because his uncertainty about the stability of his autonomy lays him open to the dread lest in any relationship he will lose his autonomy and identity. Engulfment is not simply envisaged as something that is liable to happen willy-nilly despite the individual's most active efforts to avoid it. The individual experiences himself as a man who is only saving himself from drowning by the most constant, strenuous, desperate activity. Engulfment is felt as a risk in being understood (thus grasped, comprehended), in being loved, or even simply in being seen. To be hated may be feared for other reasons, but to be hated as such is often less disturbing than to be destroyed, as it is felt, through being engulfed by love.

The main maneuvre used to preserve identity under pressure from the dread of engulfment is isolation. Thus, instead of the polarities of separateness and relatedness based on individual autonomy, there is the antithesis between complete loss of being by absorption into the other person (engulfment), and complete aloneness (isolation). There is no safe third possibility of a dialectical relationship between two persons, both sure of their own ground and, on this very basis, able to "lose themselves" in each other. Such merging of being can occur in an "authentic" way only when the individuals are sure of themselves. If a man hates himself, he may wish to lose himself in the other: then being engulfed by the other is an escape from himself. In the present case it is an ever-present possibility to be dreaded. It will be shown later, however, that what at one "moment" is most dreaded and strenuously avoided can change to what is most sought.

This anxiety accounts for one form of a so-called "negative therapeutic reaction" to apparently correct interpretation in psychotherapy. To be understood correctly is to be engulfed, to be enclosed, swallowed up, drowned, eaten up, smothered, stifled in or by another person's supposed all-embracing comprehension. It is lonely and painful to be always misunderstood, but there is at least from this point of view a measure of safety in isolation.

The other's love, is therefore, feared more than his hatred, or rather all love is sensed as a version of hatred. By being loved one is placed under an unsolicited obligation. In therapy with such a person, the last thing there is any point in is to pretend to more "love" or "concern" than one has. The more the therapist's own necessarily very complex motives for trying to "help" a person of this kind genuinely converge on a concern for him which is prepared to "let him be" and is not *in fact* engulfing or merely indifference, the more hope there will be in the horizon.

There are many images used to describe related ways in which identity is threatened, which may be mentioned here, as closely related to the dread of engulfment, e.g., being buried, being drowned, being caught and dragged down into quicksand. The image of fire recurs repeatedly. Fire may be the uncertain flickering of the individual's own inner aliveness. It may be a destructive alien power which will devastate him. Some psychotics say in the acute phase that they are on fire, that their bodies are being burned up. A patient describes himself as cold and dry. Yet he dreads any warmth or wet. He will be engulfed by the fire or the water, and either way be destroyed.

2.   IMPLOSION

This is the strongest word I can find for the extreme form of what Winnicott terms the *impingement* of reality. Impingement does not convey, however, the full terror of the experience of the world as liable at any moment to crash in and obliterate all identity, as a gas will rush in and obliterate a vacuum. The individual feels that, like the vacuum, he is empty. But this emptiness is him. Although in other ways he longs for the emptiness to be filled, he dreads the possibility of this happening because he has come to feel that all he can be is the awful nothingness of just this very vacuum. Any "contact" with reality is then in itself experienced as a dreadful threat because reality, as experienced from this position, is necessarily *implosive* and thus, as was relatedness in engulfment, *in itself* a threat to what identity the individual is able to suppose himself to have.

Reality, as such, threatening engulfment or implosion, is the persecutor.

In fact, we are all only two or three degrees Fahrenheit from experiences of this order. Even a slight fever, and the whole world can begin to take on a persecutory, impinging aspect.

3.   PETRIFICATION AND DEPERSONALIZATION

In using the term "petrification," one can exploit a number of the meanings embedded in this word:

1. A particular form of terror, whereby one is petrified, i.e. turned to stone.
2. The dread of this happening: the dread, that is, of the possibility of turning, or being turned, from a live person into a dead thing, into a stone, into a robot, an automaton, without personal autonomy of action, an *it* without subjectivity.
3. The "magical" act whereby one may attempt to turn someone else into stone, by "petrifying" him; and, by extension, the act whereby one negates the other person's autonomy, ignores his feelings, regards him as a thing, kills the life in him. In this sense one may perhaps better say that one depersonalizes him, or reifies him. One treats him not as a person, as a free agent, but as an it.

Depersonalization is a technique that is universally used as a means of dealing with the other when he becomes too tiresome or disturbing. One no longer allows oneself to be responsive to his feelings and may be prepared to regard him and treat him as though he had no feelings. The people in focus here both tend to feel themselves as more or less depersonalized and tend to depersonalize others; they are constantly afraid of being depersonalized by others. The act of turning him into a thing is, *for him,* actually petrifying. In the face of being treated as an "it," his own subjectivity drains away from him like blood from the face. Basically he requires constant confirmation from others of his own existence as a person.

A partial depersonalization of others is extensively practised in everyday life and is regarded as normal if not highly desirable. Most relationships are based on some partial depersonalizing tendency in so far as one treats the other not in terms of any awareness of who or what he might be in himself but as virtually an android robot playing a role or part in a large machine in which one too may be acting yet another part.

It is usual to cherish if not the reality, at least the illusion that there is a limited sphere of living free from this dehumanization. Yet it may be in just this sphere that the greater risk is felt, and the ontologically insecure person experiences this risk in highly potentiated form.

The risk consists in this: if one experiences the other as a free agent, one is open to the possibility of experiencing oneself as an *object* of his experience and thereby of feeling one's own subjectivity drained away. One is threatened with the possibility of becoming no more than a thing in the world of the other, without any life for oneself, without any being for oneself. In terms of such anxiety, the very act of experiencing the other as a person is felt as virtually suicidal. Sartre discusses this experience brilliantly in Part 3 of *Being and nothingness*.

The issue is in principle straightforward. One may find oneself enlivened and the sense of one's own being enhanced by the other, or one may experience the other as deadening and impoverishing. A person may have come to anticipate that any possible relationship with another will have the latter consequences. Any other is then a threat to his "self" (his capacity to act autonomously) not by reason of anything he or she may do or not do specifically, but by reason of his or her very existence.

Some of the above points are illustrated in the life of James, a chemist, aged twenty-eight.

The complaint he made all along was that he could not become a "person." He had "no self." "I am only a response to other people, I have no identity of my own." . . . He felt he was becoming more and more "a mythical person." He felt he had no weight, no substance of his own. "I am only a cork floating on the ocean."

This man was very concerned about not having become a person: he reproached his mother for this failure. "I was merely her emblem. She never recognized my identity." In contrast to his own belittlement of and uncertainty about himself, he was always on the brink of being overawed and crushed by the formidable reality that other people contained. In contrast to his own light weight, uncertainty, and insubstantiality, *they* were solid, decisive, emphatic, and substantial. He felt that in every way that mattered others were more "large scale" than he was.

At the same time, in practice he was not easily overawed. He used two chief maneuvres to preserve security. One was an outward compliance with the other. The second was an inner intellectual Medusa's head he turned on the other. Both maneuvres taken together safeguarded his own subjectivity which he had never to betray openly and which thus could never find direct and immediate expression for itself. Being secret, it was safe. Both techniques together were designed to avoid the dangers of being engulfed or depersonalized.

With his outer behaviour he forestalled the danger to which he was perpetually subject, namely that of becoming someone else's *thing*, by pretending to be no more than a cork. (After all, what safer thing to be in an ocean?) At the same time, however, he turned the other person into a thing in his own eyes, thus magically nullifying any danger to himself by secretly totally disarming the enemy. By destroying, in his own eyes, the other person as a person, he robbed the other of his power to crush him. By depleting him of his personal aliveness, that is, by seeing him as a piece of machinery rather than as a human being, he undercut the risk to himself of this aliveness either swamping him, imploding into his own emptiness, or turning him into a mere appendage.

This man was married to a very lively and vivacious woman, highly spirited, with a forceful personality and a mind of her own. He maintained a paradoxical relationship with her in which, in one sense, he was entirely alone and isolated and, in another sense, he was almost a parasite. He dreamt, for instance, that he was a clam stuck to his wife's body.

Just because he could dream thus, he had the more need to keep her at bay by contriving to see her as no more than a machine. He described her laughter, her anger, her sadness, with "clinical" precision, even going so far as to refer to her as "it," a practice that was rather chilling in effect. "It then started to laugh." She was an "it" because everything she did was a predictable, determined response. He would, for instance, tell her (it) an ordinary funny joke and when she (it) laughed this indicated her (its) entirely "conditioned," robot-like nature, which he saw indeed in much the same terms as certain psychiatric theories would use to account for all human actions.

I was at first agreeably surprised by his apparent ability to reject and disagree with what I said as well as to agree with me. This seemed to indicate that he had more of a mind of his own than he perhaps realized and that he was not too frightened to display some measure of autonomy. However, it became evident that his apparent capacity to act as an autonomous person with me was due to his secret maneuvre of regarding me not as a live human being, a person in my own right with my own selfhood, but as a sort of robot interpreting device to which he fed input and which after a quick commutation came out with a verbal message to him. With this secret outlook on me as a thing he could appear to be a "person." What he could not sustain was a person-to-person relationship, experienced as such.

*   *   *

It seems to be a general law that at some point those very dangers most dreaded can themselves be encompassed to forestall their actual occurrence. Thus, to forgo one's autonomy becomes the means of secretly safeguarding it; to play possum, to feign death, becomes a means of preserving one's aliveness (see Oberndorf, 1950). To turn oneself into a stone becomes a way of not being turned into a stone by someone else. "Be thou hard," exhorts Nietzsche. In a sense that Nietzsche did not, I believe, himself intend, to be stony hard and thus far dead forestalls the danger of being turned into a dead thing by another person. Thoroughly to understand oneself (engulf oneself) is a defence against the risk involved in being sucked into the whirlpool of another person's way of comprehending oneself. To consume oneself by one's own love prevents the possibility of being consumed by another.

It seems also that the preferred method of attack on the other is based on the same principle as the attack felt to be implicit in the other's relationship to oneself. Thus, the man who is frightened of his own subjectivity being swamped, impinged upon, or congealed by the other is frequently to be found attempting to swamp, to impinge upon, or to kill the other person's subjectivity. The process involves a vicious circle. The more one attempts to preserve one's autonomy and identity by nullifying the specific human individuality of the other, the more it is felt to be necessary to continue to do so, because with each denial of the other person's ontological status, one's own ontological security is decreased, the threat to the self from the other is potentiated and hence has to be even more desperately negated.

In this lesion in the sense of personal autonomy there is both a failure to sustain the sense of oneself as a person with the other, and a failure to sustain it alone. There is a failure to sustain a sense of one's own being without the presence of other people. It is a failure *to be* by oneself, a failure to exist alone. As James put it, "Other people supply me with my existence." This appears to be in direct contradiction to the aforementioned dread that other people will deprive him of his existence. But contradictory or absurd as it may be, these two attitudes existed in him side by side, and are indeed entirely characteristic of this type of person.

The capacity to experience oneself as autonomous means that one has really come to realize that one is a separate person from everyone else. No matter how deeply I am committed in joy or suffering to someone else, he is not me, and I am not him. However lonely or sad one may be, one can exist alone. The fact that the other person in his own actuality is not me, is set against the equally real fact that my attachment to him is a part of me. If he dies or goes away, he has gone, but my attachment to him persists. But in the last resort I cannot die another person's death for him, nor can he die my death. For that matter, as Sartre comments on this thought of Heidegger's, he cannot love for me or make my decisions, and I likewise cannot do this for him. In short, he cannot be me, and I cannot be him.

If the individual does not feel himself to be autonomous this means that he can experience neither his separateness from, nor his relatedness to, the other in the usual way. A lack of sense of autonomy implies that one feels one's being to be bound up in the other, or that the other is bound up in oneself, in a sense that transgresses the actual possibilities within the structure of human relatedness. It means that a feeling that one is in a position of ontological dependency on the other (i.e. dependent on the other for one's very being), is substituted for a sense of relatedness and attachment to him based on genuine mutuality. Utter detachment and isolation are regarded as the only alternative to a clam- or vampire-like attachment in which the other person's life-blood is necessary for one's own survival, and yet is a threat to one's survival. Therefore, the polarity is between separateness and relatedness. The individual oscillates perpetually, between the two extremes, each equally unfeasible. He comes to live rather like those mechanical toys which have a positive tropism that impels them towards a stimulus until they reach a specific point, whereupon a built-in negative tropism directs them away until the positive tropism takes over again, this oscillation being repeated *ad infinitum.*

REFERENCES

Oberndorf, C. P., "The Role of Anxiety in Depersonalization," *International Journal of Psycho-Analysis,* **31** (1950), p. 1.

Trilling, Lionel, *The Opposing Self,* London: Secker and Warburg, 1955.

Chapter 43 Healthy Personality and Self-Disclosure

SIDNEY JOURARD

For a long time, health and well-being have been taken for granted as "givens," and disease has been viewed as the problem for man to solve. Today, however, increasing numbers of scientists have begun to adopt a reverse point of view: disease and trouble are coming to be viewed as the givens, and specification of positive health and its conditions as the important goal. Physical, mental, and social health are values representing restrictions on the total variance of being. The scientific problem here consists in arriving at a definition of health, determining its relevant dimensions, and then identifying the independent variables of which these are a function.

Scientists, however, are supposed to be hardboiled, and they insist that phenomena, in order to be counted "real," must be public. Hence, many behavioral scientists ignore man's self, or soul, since it is essentially a private phenomenon. Others, however, are not so quick to allocate man's self to the limbo of the unimportant, and they insist that we cannot understand man and his lot until we take his self into account.

I probably fall into the camp of these investigators who want to explore health as a positive problem in its own right and who, further, take man's self seriously—as a reality to be explained and as a variable which produces consequences for weal or woe. In this chapter, I

SOURCES. This chapter is composed of a number of selections from the works of Sidney Jourard: "Healthy Personality and Self-Disclosure," (1958), in *Mental Hygiene*, Volume 43 (1959), pp. 499–507. Copyright 1959, *Mental Hygiene*. Reprinted by permission of *Mental Hygiene*: Transition note added by the author. "Some Findings in the Study of Self-Disclosure," in Sidney Jourard, *The Transparent Self* (Insight, #17), Princeton, New Jersey: Van Nostrand Company, 1964, pp. 176–184 and 185–187. Copyright 1964. Reprinted by Courtesy of D. Van Nostrand Company, Inc. Transition note added by the author. "Some Findings in the Study of Self Disclosure," *ibid.*, p. 187.

would like more fully to explore the connection between positive health and the disclosure of self. Let me commence with some sociological truisms.

Social systems require their members to play certain roles. Unless the roles are adequately played, the social systems will not produce the results for which they have been organized. This flat statement applies to social systems as simple as one developed by an engaged couple and to those as complex as a total nation among nations.

Societies have socialization "factories" and "mills"—families and schools—which serve the function of training people to play the age, sex, and occupational roles which they shall be obliged to play throughout their life in the social system. Broadly speaking, if a person plays his roles suitably, he can be regarded as a more or less normal personality. *Normal personalities, however, are not necessarily healthy personalities* (Jourard, 1958, pp. 16–18).

Healthy personalities are people who play their roles satisfactorily and at the same time derive personal satisfaction from role enactment; more, they keep growing and they maintain high-level physical wellness (Dunn, 1959[a,b]). It is probably enough, speaking from the standpoint of a stable social system, for people to be normal personalities. But it is possible to be a normal personality and be absolutely miserable. We would count such a normal personality unhealthy. In fact, normality in some social systems—successful acculturation to them—reliably produces ulcers, piles, paranoia, or compulsiveness. We also have to regard as unhealthy those people who have never been able to enact the roles that legitimately can be expected from them.

Counselors, guidance workers, and psychotherapists are obliged to treat with both patterns of unhealthy personality—those people who have been unable to learn their roles and those

423

who play their roles quite well, but suffer the agonies of boredom, frustration, anxiety, or stultification. If our clients are to be helped, they must change, and change in *valued* directions. A change in a valued direction may arbitrarily be called growth. We have yet to give explicit statement to these valued directions for growth, though a beginning has been made (Fromm, 1947; Jahoda, 1958; Jourard, 1958; Maslow, 1954; Rogers, 1954). We who are professionally concerned with the happiness, growth, and well-being of our clients may be regarded as professional lovers, not unlike the Cyprian sisterhood. It would be fascinating to pursue this parallel further, but for the moment let us ask instead what this has to do with self-disclosure.

To answer this question, let's tune in on an imaginary interview between a client and his counselor. The client says, "I have never told this to a soul, doctor, but I can't stand my wife, my mother is a nag, my father is a bore, and my boss is an absolutely hateful and despicable tyrant. I have been carrying on an affair for the past ten years with the lady next door, and at the same time I am a deacon in the church." The counselor says, showing great understanding and empathy, "Mm-humm!"

If we listened for a long enough period of time, we would find that the client talks and talks about himself to this highly sympathetic and empathic listener. At some later time, the client may eventually say, "Gosh, you have helped me a lot. I see what I must do and I will go ahead and do it."

Now this talking about oneself to another person is what I call self-disclosure. It would appear, without assuming anything, that self-disclosure is a factor in the process of effective counseling or psychotherapy. Would it be too arbitrary an assumption to propose that people become clients *because they have not disclosed themselves in some optimum degree to the people in their life?*

An historical digression: Toward the end of the 19th century, Joseph Breuer, a Viennese physician, discovered (probably accidentally) that when his hysterical patients talked about themselves, disclosing not only the verbal content of their memories, but also the feelings that they had suppressed at the time of assorted "traumatic" experiences, their hysterical symptoms disappeared. Somewhere along the line, Breuer withdrew from a situation which would have made him Freud's peer in history's hall of fame. When Breuer permitted his patients

"to be," it scared him, one gathers, because some of his female patients disclosed themselves to be quite sexy, and what was probably worse, they felt quite sexy toward him. Freud, however, did not flinch. He made the momentous discovery that the neurotic people of his time were struggling like mad to avoid "being," to avoid being known, and in Allport's (1955) terms, to avoid "becoming." He learned that his patients, when they were given the opportunity to "be"—which free association on a couch is nicely designed to do—would disclose that they had all manner of horrendous thoughts and feelings which they did not even dare disclose to themselves, much less express in the presence of another person. Freud learned to permit his patients to be, through permitting them to disclose themselves utterly to another human. He evidently did not trust anyone enough to be willing to disclose himself *vis à vis,* so he disclosed himself to himself on paper (Freud, 1955) and learned the extent to which he was himself self-alienated. Roles for people in Victorian days were even more restrictive than today, and Freud discovered that when people struggled to avoid being and knowing themselves, they got sick. They could only become well and stay relatively well when they came to know themselves through self-disclosure to another person. This makes me think of Georg Groddeck's magnificent *Book of the It* (*Id*) in which, in the guise of letters to a naïve young woman, Groddeck shows the contrast between the *public self*—pretentious role-playing—and the warded off but highly dynamic *id*—which I here very loosely translate as "real self."

Let me at this point draw a distinction between role relationships and interpersonal relationships—a distinction which is often overlooked in the current spate of literature that has to do with human relations. Roles are inescapable. They must be played or else the social system will not work. A role by definition is a repertoire of behavior patterns which must be rattled off in appropriate contexts, and all behavior which is irrelevant to the role must be suppressed. But what we often forget is the fact that it is a *person* who is playing the role. This person has a self, or I should say he *is* a self. All too often the roles that a person plays do not do justice to all of his self. In fact, there may be nowhere that he may just *be* himself. Even more, the person may not *know* his self. He may, in Horney's (1950) terms, be self-alienated. This fascinating term "self-alienation" means that an individual is estranged from his real self. His real self becomes a stranger, a feared and distrusted stranger. Estrangement, alienation from one's real self, is at the root of the "neurotic personality of our time" so eloquently described by Horney (1936). Fromm (1956) referred to the same phenomenon as a socially patterned defect. Self-alienation is a sickness which is so widely shared that no one recognizes it. We may take it for granted that all the clients whom we encounter are self-alienated to a greater or lesser extent. If you ask anyone to answer the question, "Who are you?" the answer will generally be "I am a psychologist," "a businessman," a "teacher," or what have you. The respondent will probably tell you the name of the role with which he feels most closely identified. As a matter of fact, the respondent spends a great part of his life trying to discover who he is, and once he has made some such discovery, he spends the rest of his life trying to play the part. Of course, some of the roles—age, sex, family, or occupational roles—may be so restrictive that they fit a person in a manner not too different from the girdle of a 200-pound lady who is struggling to look like Brigitte Bardot. There is Faustian drama all about us in this world of role-playing. Everywhere we see people who have sold their soul, or their real self, if you wish, in order to be a psychologist, a businessman, a nurse, a physician, a this or a that.

Now, I have suggested that no social system can exist unless the members play their roles and play them with precision and elegance. But here is an odd observation, and yet one which you can all corroborate just by thinking back over your own experience. It is possible to be involved in a social group such as a family or a work setting for years and years, playing one's roles nicely with the other members—and never getting to know the *persons* who are playing the other roles. Roles can be played personally and impersonally, as we are beginning to discover. A husband can be married to his wife for fifteen years and never come to know her. He knows her as "the wife." This is the paradox of the *"lonely crowd"* (Riesman, 1950). It is the loneliness which people try to counter with "togetherness." But much of today's "togetherness" is like the "parallel play" of two-year-old children, or like the professors in Stringfellow Barr's (1958) novel who, when together socially, lecture *past* one another alternately and sometimes simultaneously. There is no real self-to-self or person-to-person meet-

ing in such transactions. Now what does it mean to know a person, or, more accurately, a person's self? I don't mean anything mysterious by "self." All I mean is the person's subjective side—what he thinks, feels, believes, wants, worries about—the kind of thing which one could never know unless one were told. *We get to know the other person's self when he discloses it to us.*

Self-disclosure, letting another person know what you think, feel, or want is the most direct means (though not the only means) by which an individual can make himself known to another person. Personality hygienists place great emphasis upon the importance for mental health of what they call "real-self being," "self-realization," "discovering oneself," and so on. An operational analysis of what goes on in counseling and therapy shows that the patients and clients discover themselves through self-disclosure to the counselor. They talk and, to their shock and amazement, the counselor listens.

I venture to say that there is probably no experience more horrifying and terrifying than that of self-disclosure to "significant others" whose probable reactions are assumed, but not known. Hence the phenomenon of "resistance." This is what makes psychotherapy so difficult to take, and so difficult to administer. If there is any skill to be learned in the art of counseling and psychotherapy, it is the art of coping with the terrors which attend self-disclosure, and the art of decoding the language, verbal and non-verbal, in which a person speaks about his inner experience.

Now what is the connection between self-disclosure and healthy personality? Self-disclosure, or should I say "real"-self-disclosure, is both a symptom of personality health (Jourard, 1958, pp. 218–221) and at the same time a means of ultimately achieving healthy personality. The discloser of self is an animated "real-self be-er." This, of course, takes courage —the "courage to be." I have known people who would rather die than become known. In fact, some did die when it appeared that the chances were great that they would become known. When I say that self-disclosure is a symptom of personality health, what I mean really is that a person who displays many of the other characteristics that betoken healthy personality (Jourard, 1958; Maslow, 1954) *will also display the ability to make himself fully known to at least one other significant human being.* When I say that self-disclosure is a means by which one achieves personality health, I mean something like the following: it is not until I *am* my real self and I act my real self that my real self is in a position to grow. One's self grows from the *consequence of being.* People's selves stop growing when they repress them. This growth-arrest in the self is what helps to account for the surprising paradox of finding an infant inside the skin of someone who is playing the role of an adult. In a fascinating analysis of mental disease, Jurgen Ruesch (1957) describes assorted neurotics, psychotics, and psychosomatic patients as persons with selective atrophy and over-specialization in various aspects of the process of communication. This culminates in a foul-up of the processes of knowing others and of becoming known to others. Neurotic and psychotic symptoms might be viewed as smoke screens interposed between the patient's real self and the gaze of the onlooker. We might call the symptoms "devices to avoid becoming known." A new theory of schizophrenia has been proposed by a former patient (Anonymous, 1958) who "was there," and he makes such a point.

Alienation from one's self not only arrests one's growth as a person; it also tends to make a farce out of one's relationships with people. As the ex-patient mentioned above observed, the crucial "break" in schizophrenia is with *sincerity,* not reality (Anonymous, 1958). A self-alienated person—one who does not disclose himself truthfully and fully—can never love another person nor can he be loved by the other person. Effective loving calls for knowledge of the object (Fromm, 1956; Jourard, 1958). How can I love a person whom I do not know? How can the other person love me if he does not know me?

Hans Selye (1950) proposed and documented the hypothesis that illness as we know it arises in consequence of stress applied to the organism. Now I rather think that unhealthy *personality* has a similar root cause, and one which is related to Selye's concept of stress. It is this. Every maladjusted person is a person who has not made himself known to another human being and in consequence does not know himself. Nor can he be himself. More than that, *he struggles actively to avoid becoming known by another human being.* He *works* at it ceaselessly, 24 hours daily, and it is work! The fact that resisting becoming known is *work* offers us a research opening, inciden-

tally (cf. Dittes, 1957; Davis and Malmo, 1951). I believe that in the effort to avoid becoming known, a person provides for himself a cancerous kind of stress which is subtle and unrecognized but none the less effective in producing, not only the assorted patterns of unhealthy personality which psychiatry talks about, but also the wide array of physical ills that have come to be recognized as the stock in trade of psychosomatic medicine. Stated another way, I believe that *other people come to be stressors to an individual in direct proportion to his degree of self-alienation.*

If I am struggling to avoid becoming known by other persons then, of course, I must construct a false public self (Jourard, 1958, pp. 301–302). The greater the discrepancy between my unexpurgated real self and the version of myself that I present to others, then the more dangerous will other people be for me. If becoming known by another person is threatening, then the very presence of another person can serve as a stimulus to evoke anxiety, heightened muscle tension, and all the assorted visceral changes which occur when a person is under stress. A beginning already has been made, demonstrating the tension-evoking powers of the other person, through the use of such instruments as are employed in the lie detector, through the measurement of muscle tensions with electromyographic apparatus, and so on (Davis and Malmo, 1951; Dittes, 1957).

Students of psychosomatic medicine have been intimating something of what I have just finished saying explicitly. They say (cf. Alexander, 1950) the ulcer patients, asthmatic patients, patients suffering from colitis, migraine, and the like, are chronic *repressors* of certain needs and emotions, especially hostility and dependency. Now when you repress something, you are not only withholding awareness of this something from yourself, you are also withholding it from the scrutiny of the other person. In fact, the means by which repressions are overcome in the therapeutic situation is through relentless disclosure of self to the therapist. When a patient is finally able to follow the fundamental rule in psychoanalysis and disclose everything which passes through his mind, he is generally shocked and dismayed to observe the breadth, depth, range, and diversity of thoughts, memories, and emotions which pass out of his "unconscious" into overt disclosure. Incidentally, by the time a person is that free to disclose in the presence of another human being, he has doubtless completed much of his therapeutic sequence.

Self-disclosure, then, appears to be one of the means by which a person engages in that elegant activity which we call real-self-being. But is real-self-being synonomous with healthy personality? Not in and of itself. I would say that real-self-being is a necessary but not a sufficient condition for healthy personality. Indeed, an authentic person may not be very "nice." In fact, he may seem much "nicer" socially and appear more mature and healthy when he is *not* being his real self than when he is his real self. But an individual's "obnoxious" but authentic self can never grow in the direction of greater maturity until the person has become acquainted with it and begins to *be* it. Real-self-being produces consequences which, in accordance with well known principles of behavior (cf. Skinner, 1953), produce changes in the real self. Thus, there can be no real growth of the self without real-self-being. Full disclosure of the self to at least one other significant human being appears to be one means by which a person discovers not only the breadth and depth of his needs and feelings, but also the nature of his own self-affirmed values. There is no necessary conflict, incidentally, between real-self-being and being an ethical or nice person, because for the average member of our society, self-owned ethics are generally acquired during the process of growing up. All too often, however, the self-owned ethics are buried under authoritarian morals (Fromm, 1947).

If self-disclosure is one of the means by which healthy personality is both achieved and maintained, we can also note that such activities as loving, psychotherapy, counseling, teaching, and nursing, all are impossible of achievement without the disclosure of the client. It is through self-disclosure that an individual reveals to himself and to the other party just exactly who, what, and where he is. Just as thermometers and sphygmomanometers disclose information about the real state of the body, self-disclosure reveals the real nature of the soul, or self. Such information is vital in order to conduct intelligent evaluations. All I mean by evaluation is comparing how a person is with some concept of optimum. You never really discover how truly sick your psychotherapy patient is until he discloses himself utterly to you. You cannot help your client in vocational guidance until he has disclosed to you something of the impasse in which he finds himself. You cannot love your spouse or your child or your friend unless those persons have permitted you to know them and to know what they need in order to move toward greater health and well-being. Nurses cannot nurse patients in any meaningful way unless they have permitted the patients to disclose their needs, wants, worries, anxieties and doubts, and so forth. Teachers cannot be very helpful to their students until they have permitted the students to disclose how utterly ignorant and misinformed they presently are. Teachers cannot even provide helpful information to the students until they have permitted the students to disclose exactly what they are interested in.

*   *   *

I think there is a very general way of stating the relationship between self-disclosure and assorted values such as healthy personality, physical health, group effectiveness, successful marriage, effective teaching, and effective nursing. It is this. A person's self is known to be the immediate determiner of his overt behavior. This is a paraphrase of the phenomenological point of view in psychology (Combs and Snygg, 1959). Now if we want to understand anything, explain it, control it, or predict it, it is helpful if we have available as much pertinent information as we possibly can. Self-disclosure provides a source of information which is relevant. This information has often been overlooked. Where it has not been overlooked, it has often been misinterpreted by observers and practitioners through such devices as projection or attribution. *It seems to be difficult for people to accept the fact that they do not know the very person whom they are confronting at any given moment.* We all seem to assume that we are expert psychologists and that we know the other person, when in fact we have only constructed a more or less autistic concept of him in our mind. If we are to learn more about man's self, then we must learn more about self-disclosure—its conditions, dimensions, and consequences. Beginning evidence (cf. Rogers, 1958) shows that actively accepting, empathic, loving, non-punitive response—in short, love—provides the optimum conditions under which man will disclose, or expose, his naked, quivering self to our gaze. It follows that if we would be helpful (or should I say *human*) we must grow to loving stature and learn, in Buber's terms, to confirm our fellow man in his very being. Probably, this presumes that we must *first* confirm our *own* being.

*   *   *

SOME FINDINGS IN THE STUDY OF SELF-DISCLOSURE

While the above convictions have largely grown out of my own experiences, both within and outside of the clinic, systematic research on self-disclosure has been a continuing necessity. Our approach has largely centered around work with a questionnaire on which the person indicates the degree to which he has given varying types of information about himself to others. In each of six areas (attitudes and opinions, tastes and interests, work, money, personality, and body) the person is asked the extent to which he has made certain things known about himself to various target persons selected by the investigator (cf. Jourard and Lasakow, 1958 for a more complete account).

. . . Whenever one constructs a measuring tool, one wonders whether it is reliable and whether it actually measures what it is supposed to measure. We have been able to demonstrate that our questionnaires (of lengths that include 15, 25, 35, 45, and 60 items) have satisfactory reliability (odd-even coefficients for larger subtotals run in the 80's and 90's), and results until now show this method has some validity. It should not be overlooked, however, that there are always fundamental flaws in any personality measure that is based on self-report. With this precaution in mind, let me proceed to narrate some of our findings.

SUBJECT-MATTER DIFFERENCES

We found that certain categories of personal data are consistently disclosed more fully by our subjects to various target-persons than to others. For example, information bearing upon one's work, one's tastes, hobbies, and interests, one's attitudes toward religion, politics, and the like are evidently more disclosable than the details about one's sex life, one's financial status, and one's feelings and problems in relation to one's body and to one's own personality (Jourard and Lasakow, 1958). There are evidently strong social norms at work here, norms that even extend across the Atlantic, for we found (Jourard, 1961*c*) that female college students in England show patterns of disclosure and concealment of subject matter that are almost identical with those found among American coeds. Melikian (1962), at Beirut, Lebanon, has shown similarly consistent patterns in Near Eastern samples. Male and female Puerto Rican college students likewise resemble Americans in their differential disclosure of subject matter (Jourard, 1963).

Anyone who has conducted psychotherapy knows that patients will more readily disclose some kinds of personal data and will block, or show resistance, with respect to others. Such resistance has been demonstrated with polygraphic measures taken on patients during therapeutic interviews—for example, Davis and Malmo's (1951) work with electromyograms and Dittes' with the GSR (1957). I have shown, by means of what I called my "wiggle-chair" (a stratolounger chair equipped with a movement transducer) that subjects will show increases in their base-rate of movement when they are asked to disclose some kinds of personal data by a given interviewer; and different interviewers elicit different outputs of wiggle, no matter what the subject matter. Of course, there are interactions among interviewee, subject matter and interviewer operative here. Our questionnaire measures also yielded significant interaction between subject matter and target-persons, which signifies only that it makes a difference to whom one discloses what.

TARGET-DIFFERENCES

All our questionnaire studies have shown significant differences in the total amount of personal data that *S*s have disclosed to the various target-persons that we included for consideration, viz.: parents, closest friends, and spouse. As you might expect, the spouse is typically the one to whom most is disclosed. Indeed, the amount of mutual disclosure spouses engage in exceeds the amount that unmarried people disclose to *anyone,* whether parent, relative, or friend (cf. Jourard and Lasakow, 1958). This confirms the view that marriage is the "closest" relationship one can enter, and it may help us the better to understand why some people avoid it like the plague. Anyone who is reluctant to be known by another person and to know another person— sexually and cognitively—will find the prospective intimacy of marriage somewhat terrifying.

Among unmarried subjects, we find a complex pattern of target-preferences that is related to the age of the subjects. Female college students in their late teens indicate that they disclose in about comparable degree to their mothers and closest girl-friends, while they keep their fathers and their present boy-friends somewhat more in the dark. Male college students of similar age keep their parents about equally informed about their subjective being, and in lesser degree, than do females. The person who knows these boys best is their closest male friend. Their female friend is typically disclosed less authentic and varied personal information than is their chum. I must mention the consistency with which we found that the father is disclosed to in the least degree by our subjects. Father is evidently kept more in the dark about the subjective side of his children than are other people. He is the last to know what is going on. This is a finding of interest to sociologists and psychiatrists alike! We may conclude from findings like these that the role of the target-person *vis-à-vis* the self is an important determiner of disclosing oneself to him.

When we focused more directly upon a given target-person in a fixed social role, such as parent, or friend, we found some further correlates of the amount of disclosure. The degree of liking for a target-person was found to correlate substantially with the amount disclosed to him—but, interestingly enough, more strikingly among women than among men. We found that women show this correlation between liking and disclosure to mother, father, and work-associates (Jourard and Lasakow, 1958); Jourard, 1959); among men, the comparable correlations were markedly lower (Jourard and Landsman, 1960). This finding strongly suggests that women are more responsive to their own feelings—that is, they vary their interpersonal behavior in accord with their feelings more so than men do. Both sexes show a correlation between the degree to which they *know* a given target-person and their disclosure to him. Men, evidently, trust their brains, their cognition of the other person more than their feelings, as a condition for self-disclosure.

Related to degree of knowing is another interesting, and I think fundamentally important, datum: for males and females alike, a very strong correlate of disclosure output to a given target-person was the amount of disclosure *input* from that person. I called this input-output correlation the *dyadic effect* (Jourard, 1959; Jourard and Landsman, 1960), and I have proven in my own practice that it extends to the realm of psychotherapy. I have suggested further that the capacity to disclose

authentically, *in response* that is appropriate to the setting, to the authentic disclosure of the other person in a dyad is probably one of the best indicants of healthy personality. It betokens, to use Buber's (1957) terms, the capacity to enter into and sustain dialogue. I think that overly-technical psychotherapists as well as novices probably fall down on the ability to give an authentic, self-revealing response to the disclosures of their patients, and block, thereby, the ongoing process of the therapeutic dialogue. In Buber's terms, they have the capacity for "distance," but not for "entering into relation." Probably, they are still painfully self-conscious about their techniques, and the therapeutic dyad for them is a secret triad—the supervisor is psychically more present to the novice than is the patient. Likely, too, they have little faith or trust either in the healing powers of their own real selves or in the good will of their parents who would come to know them.

GROUP-DIFFERENCES

In this context, I will report some of the over-all differences between groups that we found with our questionnaire measures. You must keep in mind that we were measuring the amount disclosed by an individual to four target-persons. Since there was always interaction between group and target-person, the possibility exists that total disclosure scores based on the sum for all four target-persons may not be different, and yet there could be significant differences between groups in the amount disclosed to a *given* target-person. The findings I wish to report now were ones in which the difference in disclosure output was general—that is, it extended across target-persons.

The most consistent difference we found was between the sexes, with women indicating that they disclosed more about themselves than men (cf. Jourard and Lasakow, 1958; Jourard and Landsman, 1960). I must qualify this finding by saying that it has not been without exception in my studies, and at least two investigators in the northeast failed to find a sex difference at all. Thus, Rickers-Ovsiankina and Kusmin (1958) at Connecticut and Zief (1962), at Harvard did not find the women to be higher disclosers than the men. In fact, Rickers-Ovsiankina found her college male subjects to be slightly more "socially accessible" than women. It is tempting to suggest that in the southeast, where I collected the bulk of my data, the men are men and the women are women; whereas Harvard males and Radcliffe females, whom Zief tested, for example, may not be so different from one another. More generally, the magnitude of the sex-difference in disclosure-output between different groups may be an illuminating phenomenon to study in its own right. I have some data which show that the size of the sex-difference varies in a non-chance way among groups who differed in their performance on the Minnesota Multiphasic Personality Inventory, for example.

In the realm of national differences, we found (Jourard, 1961c) that English co-eds were consistently lower disclosers to the significant people in their lives than comparable American females. Melikian (1962) did not find differences between nine different Far Eastern samples in *total* disclosure output, but did find a significant group by target interaction. He did not report his target means, a serious oversight, so we do not know on which target persons his various populations differed in disclosure output. However, I compared the mean total disclosure scores he reported with scores obtained by male college students tested with a questionnaire identical with his, and the American mean totals were substantially higher. No test for the significance of the difference was possible.

I have some recent data (Jourard, 1963) showing comparisons between N's of 25 male and 25 female Puerto Rican college students with the same N's of American college students, matched for age, religion (mostly Catholic), and fathers' occupational level. The Puerto Ricans had significantly lower total disclosure scores than the Americans. Among the males, the differences extended across all four target persons. In the female sample, the Americans disclosed more to Father, opposite-sex friend, and same-sex friend, but less to Mother than did the Puerto Rican girls. It may well be true that Americans talk more about themselves to others than just about any other cultural group.

A study of interdenominational differences showed that Catholic, Methodist, and Baptist college males did not differ significantly from one another in disclosure output, but they all disclosed less, on the average, than Jewish male college students. Among the females, these denominations did not differ among one another, suggesting that their sex-role was a stronger determiner of their self-disclosing behavior than their religious affiliation (Jourard, 1961b). One wonders at the greater openness of the Jewish males in comparison with their non-Jewish fellow students. Perhaps it betokens a greater need or capacity for intimate personal relationships than is typical for the American culture at large.

I collected data (unpublished) which showed that applicants for clinical services at the campus psychological counseling center were lower disclosers than matched groups of students who had not sought such services. The main trend approached significance, but it tended to be obscured by the fact that some of the applicants for counseling obtained unusually *high* disclosure scores, especially to their parents, in comparison with controls. This suggests that excessive disclosure may be as incompatible with optimum adjustment in the college milieu as unduly low disclosure. Parenthetically, I may add that in one study I cited above (Jourard, 1959), the two women least liked by their colleagues were, respectively, the highest and lowest disclosers of self in their work setting.

Here is a finding that may interest those who are concerned with gerontology. We found (Jourard, 1961a) that, as people get older, the amount they disclose to other people in their lives, especially parents and same sex friend, gradually diminishes. Disclosure to opposite-sex friend, or spouse, increase from the age of 17 up to about the fifties and then drops off. It is possible that, with increased age, the communicative intimacy of relationships with others diminishes, possibly an illustration of the disengagement phenomenon that Henry and Cumming (1959) have written about.

Another group difference that warrants mention has to do with rated interpersonal competence. We tested nursing students with a disclosure questionnaire (Jourard, 1962). A year later, at the end of their period of clinical practice, they were rated for ability to establish and maintain a communicative relationship with patients. The students who received the highest ratings were significantly higher disclosers on the test they had taken the year before than the students receiving the lower ratings. It would appear that those who were most accustomed to making their own subjective being accessible to others learned the most readily to elicit the subjective being of others.

Again with nursing students, we found substantial correlations between scores for disclosure to mother and to girl-friend (obtained while the girls were sophomores) and accumulated grade-point average in *nursing* courses at time of graduation. The students were graded, in nursing courses, not only for knowing correct answers on objective quizzes, but also for ability to convey to their instructors the meaning of their experience at working with patients, reading assorted books and papers, etc., in so-called reaction papers and on essay examinations. Evidently those students least able to be open with female target-persons were least able to behave in the open way with the nursing faculty, the way which seemed to facilitate learning and performance of the valued sort. Two years later, I repeated this study, with a different self-disclosure questionnaire, and got comparable results, though the correlations were not so high.

Here is a group difference which is of a different sort, but one fraught with implications, I believe. Powell (1962) tested a group of underachieving college students at the University of Florida with a self-disclosure questionnaire and with a test of personal security. We anticipated that the underachievers would be lower disclosers and more insecure people than a matched group of adequately achieving students. There were no differences between these groups in mean disclosure to any target-person, and there was some slight evidence that achieving males (but not females) were more independently secure than underachieving subjects. Then, we turned up a nice nugget. Among the achieving males and females, significant correlations were found between closeness to peers and personal security; the comparable r's among underachievers were not significant. Among underachievers, significant r's were found between disclosure to each parent and personal security. Such was not the case among the achievers. We interpreted these findings to mean that underachieving students were less mature, in the sense of being less emancipated from parents, than were achieving students. In other words, security among the underachievers was a function of the intimacy of the relationship with the parents, while security in the achieving groups was more independent of the vicissitudes of the parent-child relationship. Some further evidence that the correlation between self-disclosure scores and measures of intraindividual traits betoken dependency is provided by some data obtained by Terence Cooke (1962), who did a doctoral dissertation with me. He devised a measure of "manifest religious behavior" for Protestants. This questionnaire gets at the intensity of religious involvement by asking Ss to indicate the

frequency with which they attend church, the amount of donation, frequency of prayer, etc. Cooke found insignificant r's between measures of disclosure to parents and strength of manifest religious behavior in a sample of 111 male college students between the ages of 17 and 22. I re-analyzed his data, this time computing separate correlations between disclosure to mother and father and religious behavior for 17–18 year-olds, 19 year-olds, 20 year-olds, and 21–22 years-olds. I found that there were significant r's for the first two age levels, but not for the latter two. This finding indicates that religiosity is related to the degree of closeness to parents among late teen-agers, but becomes more independent of the parent-child relationship as the child becomes older. The utilization of the correlation between an interpersonal measure (self-disclosure scores) and an intrapersonal measure as an indicator of an underlying construct has intriguing methodological implications, it seems to me. It may, for example, point to a dimension of interpersonal "influencability" that is present in one group but not in another. The construct might then be approached more directly by other measurement procedures.

Let me now direct some final remarks about connections I see between self-disclosure as a mode of being with others and psychotherapy.

*   *   *

SELF-DISCLOSURE AND PSYCHOTHERAPY

Increasing numbers of psychiatrists and psychologists are coming to see psychotherapy, not as something which one does to or for a patient, a treatment that calls for careful techniques of verbal responding, but rather as an exploration of the possibilities for dialogue between these two people. The patient may be viewed as one who is terrified of his spontaneous being and is initially unable to reveal himself freely in the therapeutic transaction. The therapist, in turn, may be afraid for many reasons to let himself respond in honesty to the patient. As time proceeds, the pair become increasingly able to carry out unself-conscious dialogue, so that the patient has no doubts in his mind concerning the subjective being of his therapist when the two are together; and the therapist likewise is clearly informed of the patient's experiencing as it unfolds. By this time, many of the symptoms will have vanished.

This concept of therapy is not congenial to

many workers, who see it as a dangerous occasion for therapists to "act out" in ways that do no one any good. The technique-oriented therapist seems to expect his patient to be transparent to him, while he remains an enigma and a mystery, hiding his true experiencing behind a professional façade or couchside demeanor. In another context, I have commented at length upon withholding of authentic disclosure in therapists, and I used the term "resistance in the therapist" to describe such a phenomenon. I think such chronic suppression of being in the therapist makes him sick!

The unduly technique-oriented psychotherapist may be proven to be least effective at helping his patients overcome impasses in their existence, for several related reasons. First of all, the behavior of a technical therapist is easily predicted by his patients, which, in turn, permits them to pick and choose their utterances and expression for some intended effect. Second, we know from research that people will disclose themselves most freely and fully to listeners who are *perceived* as being of authentic good will and as being honestly themselves rather than playing some contrived role. If a therapist is authentically *not* of good will, if he is faking his interest or feelings (instead, he is actually interested in proving his theories, or in making money, etc.), then in time he will be found out by his patient. Finally, the authentic responding of a therapist who has integrated his techniques with the rest of his person provides the patient with some social reality not usually accessible to him from more obviously technical therapists. This exposure to one's impact on another is very educational, to say the least. It maximally exposes one to the possibilities of social reinforcement, as one researcher at Duke (Gergen, 1962) has shown. He coined the term "reflective reinforcement" to describe the fact that honest responses from an interviewer reflect the interviewer's subjective being, and such responses can be effective at modifying a patient's self-concept. Gerald Goodman (1962), a researcher from Chicago, provided some further evidence of the therapeutic power of authenticity; he showed that, with experienced therapists, emotional self-disclosure of the patient and of the therapist increased as therapy progressed—a sort of dyadic effect.

*   *   *

. . . Powell (1962) confirmed the "dyadic effect" hypothesis most strikingly in an experiment employing the operant conditioning paradigm. He conducted interviews, asking Ss to disclose positive and negative features of their own personality. One group of Ss was "reinforced" with approving, supportive response from the interviewer, another group with "reflecting-re-stating" responses, and the third with self-disclosures from the interviewer. Powell found that the approving-supporting statements had no significant reinforcing value, reflection-re-statement increased the output of negative, but not positive self-disclosure from the Ss; and disclosure from the interviewer resulted in significant increases in the disclosure of both positive and negative aspects of the Ss' selves. Powell's study offers strong experimental support for the assertion that interviewers of any sort, who wish to be confided in, must be ready to disclose themselves to their interviewees as fully as they expect the latter to do.

*   *   *

We may conclude from all these data, and my tentative inferences from them, that self-disclosure is a measurable facet of man's being and his behavior, and that understanding of its conditions and correlates will enrich our understanding of man in wellness and in disease.

REFERENCES

Alexander, F. *Psychosomatic Medicine*. New York: Norton, 1950.

Allport, G., *Becoming*. New Haven: Yale Univ. Press, 1955.

Anonymous, A new theory of schizophrenia. *J. abn. soc. Psychol.*, 1958, **57**, 226–236.

Barr, S., *Purely Academic*. New York: Simon and Schuster, 1958.

Buber, M., Elements of the interhuman. William Alanson White Memorial Lectures. *Psychiatry*, 1957, **20**, 95–129.

Combs, A., and Snygg, D., *Individual Behavior* (2nd ed.), New York: Harper, 1959.

Cooke, T. F. Interpersonal correlates of religious behavior. Unpublished Doctor's Dissertation, University of Florida, 1962.

Davis, F. H., and Malmo, R. B. Electromyographic recording during interview. *Amer. J. Psychiat.,* 1951, **107**, 908–916.

Dittes, J. E. Extinction during psychotherapy of GSR accompanying "embarrassing" statements. *J. abn. soc. Psychol.,* 1957, **54**, 187–191.

Dunn, H., What high level wellness means. *Can. J. Public Health,* 1959(a), **50**, 447–457.

Dunn, H. L. High-level wellness for man and society. *Amer. J. Pub. Health,* 1959(b), **49**, 786–792.

Freud, S. *The Interpretation of Dreams.* New York: Basic Books, 1955.

Fromm, E. *Man for Himself.* New York: Rinehart, 1947.

Fromm, E. *The Art of Loving.* New York: Harper, 1956.

Gergen, K., Social reinforcement of self-presentation behavior. Unpublished Ph.D. Dissertation, Duke Univ., 1962.

Goodman, G. E., Emotional self-disclosure in psychotherapy. Unpublished Ph.D. Dissertation, Univ. of Chicago, 1962.

Henry, W. E., and Cumming, Elaine, Personality development in adulthood and old age. *J. proj. Tech.,* 1959, **23**, 383–390.

Horney, K. *The Neurotic Personality of Our Time.* New York: Norton, 1936.

Horney, K., *Neurosis and Human Growth.* New York: Norton, 1950.

Jahoda, Marie. *Current Concepts of Positive Mental Health.* New York: Basic Books, 1958.

Jourard, S. M., *Personality Adjustment. An approach through the study of healthy personality.* New York: Macmillan, 1958 (2nd ed., 1963).

Jourard, S. M., Self-disclosure and other cathexis. *J. abn. soc. Psychol.,* 1959, **59**, 428–431.

Jourard, S. M., Age and self-disclosure. *Merrill-Palmer Quart. Beh. Dev.,* 1961(a), **7**, 191–197.

Jourard, S. M., Religious denomination and self-disclosure. *Psychol. Rep.,* 1961(b), **8**, 446.

Jourard, S. M., Self-disclosure patterns in British and American college females, *J. soc. Psychol.,* 1961(c), **54**, 315–320.

Jourard, S. M., Self-disclosure and grades in nursing college. *J. appl. Psychol.,* 1962.

Jourard, S. M., Self-disclosure in the United States and Puerto Rico. (Unpublished data, 1963.)

Jourard, S. M., and Landsman, M. J., Cognition, cathexis, and the "dyadic effect" in men's self-disclosing behavior. *Merrill-Palmer Quart. Beh. Dev.,* 1960, **6**, 178–186.

Jourard, S. M., and Lasakow, P., Some factors in self-disclosure. *J. abn. soc. Psychol.,* 1958, **56**, 91–98.

Maslow, A. H., *Motivation and Personality.* New York: Harper, 1954.

Melikian, L. Self-disclosure among university students in the middle east. *J. soc. Psychol.,* 1962, **57**, 259–263.

Powell, W. J. Personal adjustment and academic achievement of college students. Unpublished Master's Thesis, Univ. of Florida, 1962.

Rickers-Ovsiankina, Maria, and Kusmin, A. A. Individual differences in social accessibility. *Psychol. Rep.,* 1958, **4**, 391–406.

Riesman, D. *The Lonely Crowd.* New Haven: Yale Univ. Press, 1950.

Rogers, C. R. The concept of the fully functioning person (1954). In Rogers, C. R., *On Becoming a Person.* Boston: Houghton Mifflin, 1961.

Rogers, C. R. The characteristics of a helping relationship. *Pers. Guid. J.,* 1958, **37**, 6–16.

Ruesch, J. *Disturbed Communication.* New York: Norton, 1957.

Selye, H. *The Physiology and Pathology of Exposure to Stress.* Montreal: Acta, 1950.

Skinner, B. F. *Science and Human Behavior.* New York: Macmillan, 1953.

Zief, R. M. Values and self-disclosure. Unpublished Honors Thesis, Harvard Univ., 1962.

Chapter 44 The Significance of the Self-Regarding Attitudes and Perceptions*

CARL R. ROGERS

One of the elements which was noted from the first in clinical experience in client-centered psychotherapy was that attitudes of the client toward himself, often heavily laden with affect, not only were prominent in all phases of therapy, but seemed to undergo marked fluctuations and changes. Whether this was a secondary and insignificant phenomenon or an evidence of a basic personality process was uncertain. As a variety of research studies in therapy have been added to a growing body of clinical experience, we have pursued this question. It has led us to recognize that not only are feelings about the self involved in therapy, but the way the self is perceived. We have also begun to study the ways in which these self-regarding attitudes and self-perceptions are related to behavior and personality. Out of this complex study there have begun to develop certain theoretical formulations regarding the

SOURCE. Carl R. Rogers, "The Significance of the Self-Regarding Attitudes and Perceptions," from Martin L. Reymert, ed., *Feeling and Emotion: The Mooseheart Symposium,* New York: McGraw-Hill, 1950, pp. 374–382. Copyright © 1950. Reprinted by permission of the McGraw-Hill Book Company.

* Though this paper was written in 1948, I find it still expresses quite well the basic evidence and theory regarding the changes in the concept of self which occur during psychotherapy and the correlated changes in attitudes and behavior. Further research has by and large tended to confirm rather than disconfirm these early findings. A somewhat more precise statement of my theories regarding the development of the self concept and the conditions under which it changes is contained in S. Koch, ed., *Psychology: A Study of a Science,* Volume III, McGraw-Hill, 1959. The paper published here, however, is a good statement of my early thinking along these lines. Its tentative quality is due in part to the scattered nature of evidence and in part to the fact that "the self" was at that time a somewhat despised construct. For this reason, it was with some fear and trembling that I advanced the facts and theories contained in this paper.

self and its function in personality. It is the purpose of this paper to give a broad overview of the evidence accumulated regarding the self-regarding attitudes and perceptions, and to suggest a conceptual framework into which this evidence may fit.

Inasmuch as some of the studies upon which this paper is primarily based are as yet unpublished,[1] a word is in order in regard to them. They are all studies based upon small numbers of cases. In several instances the analysis has been made of the hundreds of responses in but one electrically recorded series of interviews. In all instances the reliability of the objective procedures used in analyzing the material has been determined, and while these reliability measures are sufficient to warrant considerable confidence in the results, they are not so high as might be desired. In general the studies bear the marks of their pioneering nature, being more satisfactorily objective than previous investigations in this field, but being still less rigorously objective than is desirable. It has been our experience in opening up the area of psychotherapy to objective scrutiny that fully satisfactory scientific methodology must develop with experience.

It is hoped that these remarks will indicate that the evidence summarized in this paper should be approached with skepticism. It is tentative and suggestive, certainly not definitive or final. It is presented because its coherence and relatedness appear to give it some weight.

THE EMOTIONALIZED ATTITUDES TOWARD THE SELF IN THERAPY

There is now considerable evidence from various studies regarding the emotionalized attitudes and feelings directed toward the self during the course of therapy, as these attitudes

[1] The complete list is included in the bibliography. Any of the unpublished studies may be obtained or borrowed from the Counseling Center, University of Chicago, Chicago 37, Ill.

and feelings are determinable from the verbal material of the interviews. We may summarize the main trend of this evidence quite simply. In cases where there is any indication that change took place or that therapy was to some degree "successful" (whether the criterion is client judgment, counselor judgment, or rating by a judge), the following statements would be true.

There is a trend toward an increasing number and proportion of positively toned self-references and self-regarding attitudes as therapy progresses (12, 20, 26, 28, 30, 31).

There is a trend toward a decreasing number and proportion of self-references and self-regarding attitudes which are negative in emotional tone (12, 20, 26, 28, 30, 31).

Attitudes of ambivalence toward the self, in which positive and negative feelings are expressed together, tend to increase slightly until somewhat beyond the midpoint of therapy, and then to decrease slightly. At no period are ambivalent attitudes a frequent expression (1, 20, 26).

At the conclusion of therapy there are more positively toned self-references than negative (1, 12, 20, 26, 28, 30, 31).

These trends are not found, or are found in lesser degree, in cases regarded as unsuccessful (20, 29).

There are certain other findings, less general in their nature, which tend to qualify these statements.

The sharpest and clearest measure of the above trends is in terms of positive and negative feelings toward the self which are expressed as being currently held. The elimination of past attitudes from consideration heightens the slope of both curves (26).

In the individual case, though the general trends are as described, there may be wide fluctuations from interview to interview in the self-regarding attitudes. After a slow rise in positive attitudes, negative attitudes may become sharply predominant for a time, etc. (10, 20).

Within the general trends described there is more variability in self-regarding attitudes in the later stages of therapy than in the early stages (26).

There is often an initial decrease in the positively toned self-regarding attitudes, before the general upward trend becomes evident (20, 26).

The "unsuccessful" case may remain consistently high in negative feelings about the self or consistently high in positive self-attitudes (20, 29).

One feels tempted to launch at once into possible clinical explanations of these findings. I would prefer, however, to focus our attention solely on the objective facts for the moment— the evidence of change in feelings about the self, the evidence of a general trend which includes wide fluctuations, and the evidence that positive self-references alone do not seem to spell whatever is included in the vague concept of "successful therapy."

THE CHANGING PERCEPTION OF SELF IN THERAPY

In addition to the studies of feelings about the self, there is more scattered evidence regarding the changes in the perception of the self during therapy. The individual comes to perceive himself differently, to form different conceptualizations about himself, and these alterations in perception appear to be concomitant with the alteration in emotionalized attitudes already described. Though more studies are needed in this area, investigating other aspects of the perceptual change and utilizing larger numbers of cases, it may be useful to summarize the evidence now available. Again our knowledge is largely limited to those cases in which, by common sense, general criteria, some "success" or change appears to have occurred. Again the studies are based upon electrically recorded and transcribed cases.

There is a tendency for the "acceptance of self," operationally defined, to increase during therapy. Acceptance of self, according to the definition used, means that the client tends:

To perceive himself as a person of worth, worthy of respect rather than condemnation.

To perceive his standards as being based upon his own experience, rather than upon the attitudes or desires of others.

To perceive his own feelings, motives, social and personal experiences, without distortion of the basic sensory data (27).

The study upon which these statements are based is confirmed by others, most of them less rigorous in nature. From these other studies it would appear that the individual in "successful" therapy tends:

To perceive his abilities and characteristics with more objectivity and with greater comfort (24).

To perceive all aspects of self and self-in-relationship with less emotion and more objectivity (30).

To perceive himself as more independent and more able to cope with life problems (18, 24).

To perceive himself as more able to be spontaneous and genuine (18).

To perceive himself as the evaluator of experience, rather than regarding himself as existing in a world where the values are inherent in and attached to the objects of his perception (17).

To perceive himself as more integrated, less divided (18, 24).

How may we summarize these changes in self-perception? The essential elements would appear to be that the individual changes in three general ways. He perceives himself as a more adequate person, with more worth and more possibility of meeting life. He permits more experiential data to enter awareness, and thus achieves a more realistic appraisal of himself, his relationships, and his environment. He tends to place the basis of standards within himself, recognizing that the "goodness" or "badness" of any experience of perceptual object is not something inherent in that object, but is a value placed on it by himself.

Thus far, then, we may say, on the basis of the evidence, that the feelings and emotions regarding the self tend to change in therapy, and likewise the ways in which the self is perceived. These changes are not random, but appear to have commonality of trend. There is a definite and marked correlation between the degree of positive feelings about the self and the degree to which the self is perceived as adequate, as related realistically to experience, and as capable of evaluating experience (21). These statements are based primarily upon studies of cases in which some progress took place, and experience suggests that they require modification in "unsuccessful" cases.

But thus far these changes are all within the phenomenal field of the client. He feels differently about himself, he sees himself differently, but in the inelegant vernacular, "So what?" There has been a strong tendency in psychology to regard these self-feelings and self-perceptions as notoriously inaccurate, and as an inadequate basis for scientific thinking. Even if these changes occur, does this mean any essential alteration in the behavior or personality of the client? Are these self-attitudes significant of change that is externally observable, or are they merely introspective fluff which must be brushed off before we can see the hard facts underneath? Let us turn to this point.

ATTITUDINAL, PHYSIOLOGICAL, AND BEHAVIORAL CORRELATES

Our objective knowledge regarding the correlates of these changes in the attitudes toward and perceptions of the self is very meager, considering the practical and theoretical importance of the issue. Yet some evidence exists, and it is generally consistent in nature. We may at the present time say that in client-centered therapy the trends which have been described in self-regarding feelings and self-perceptions are correlated with certain other findings bearing upon the attitudes, physiological reactions, and behavior of the individual. The described changes in self-attitudes and self-perceptions are positively correlated with:

A decrease in psychological tension as verbally expressed (2, 15, 25, 33).

A decrease in objectively measured physiological tensions in a frustrating situations. This may be termed heightened frustration-tolerance (32).

A decrease in current defensive behavior, operationally defined and objectively measured in the interview (11, 13).

A decrease in negatively toned attitudes toward others (21, 26, 30).

An increase in attitudes of acceptance of and respect for others (27).

An increase in the maturity of reported behavior (12).

Improvement in adjustment on the job and in job training, as rated by impartial observers (4).

Alteration in personality structure as measured by projective and objective tests, this change being in the direction of lessened anxiety, greater personal integration, greater emotional stability and control, increased adaptability, lessened neurotic and introvertive tendencies, increased sociability and self-confidence (6, 9, 14, 19, 22).

There are two other directions in which there is some evidence. There is scattered and inconclusive evidence that increased functional intelligence and functional learning are correlated with the described changes in self-attitudes and self-perceptions (3, 5, 7, 8). There is also evidence that social adjustment in the community over a two-year period is correlated significantly with the degree of objectivity and realism of perception of self and self-in-relationship-to-environment (23). The research on which this statement is based is a study of self-appraisal in a group of delinquents and is not a study of therapy. It is therefore somewhat different in kind from the other researches cited. The inference is of this order: there is evidence to show that the experience of client-centered therapy is associated with an increase in objectivity of self-appraisal; there is evidence to show that objectivity of self-appraisal is associated, in delinquents, with a prognosis of more satisfactory family, school, and community adujstment; there appears to be a possibility that the experience of therapy may be associated with a prognosis of improved social adjustment. Obviously, until a satisfactory follow-up study of social adjustment in therapy is completed, the evidence is inconclusive.

Pulling together the threads from the three lines of inquiry we have followed, it may be said that within the limitations set by the fairly large probable error of the studies thus far completed, there is some evidence for the following statement. Characteristic changes occur in the emotionalized self-regarding attitudes during client-centered psychotherapy; these changes are correlated with characteristic alterations in the perceptions of self; both of these trends appear to be correlated with changes in physiological tensions, psychological discomfort, social attitudes, defensive behavior, maturity of behavior, personality structure, and social adjustment.

SOME THEORETICAL FORMULATIONS REGARDING THE SELF

It is a consideration of such evidence which has led us to attempt to formulate a theory to include these facts, a theory which involves the use of the theoretical construct, the self. Some of the propositions of that theory will be briefly presented in this paper without the amplification which they perhaps deserve. The aim is not to present a complete and closed theory, but to indicate some lines of thought which may appear profitable in the building of theory.

The central construct of our theory would be concept of self, or the self as a perceived object in the phenomenal field. Drawing upon the evidence and upon clinical experience, it would appear that the most useful definition of the self-concept, or self-structure, would be along these lines. The self-structure is an organized configuration of perceptions of the self which are admissible to awareness. It is composed of such elements as the perceptions of one's characteristics and abilities; the percepts and concepts of the self in relation to others and to environment; the value qualities which are perceived as associated with experiences and objects; and the goals and ideals which are perceived as having positive or negative valence. It is, then, the organized picture, existing in awareness either as figure or ground, of the self and the self-in-relationship, together with the positive or negative values which are associated with those qualities and relationships, as they are perceived as existing in the past, present, or future.

There is no necessary close relationship between the elements of the structure of self and the elements of sensory experience. Thus an individual of average appearance may perceive himself as ugly, distorting the evidence of his senses. He may have the sensory experience of anger at his wife, and perceive himself as feeling only an unruffled affection, denying to awareness his visceral reactions. These phenomena of distortion and denial of sensory experience appear to come about because of his perception of certain attitudes of others toward him. As the structure of self becomes thus formed in part upon a distortion or denial of the relevant sensory evidence, it also becomes selective in its perception, perceiving insofar as possible only those elements consistent with the pattern of self already formed.

The structure of self appears to change primarily under conditions which permit a greater differentiation of the phenomenal or perceptual field. When the self is not under threat, and feels securely accepted, then the organization of self is not perceived as final. Denied sensory and visceral experience may not only be admitted to awareness, but incorporated into the structure of self. Experience which has been distorted may be reperceived and the basic sensory data more adequately differentiated and assimilated into the concept of self. These processes tend to occur since less tension is experienced when the pattern of self is constructed out of the undistorted totality of sensory experience. The changes which occur in portions of the self-structure in the ways just mentioned tend to alter in some degree the whole organizational *Gestalt* of the self.

The self is related to behavior in a significant way, in that all behavior which is perceived as being in the realm of conscious control is consistent with the concept of self. If there are exceptions, they are accompanied by marked distress. Consequently when the concept of self is changed, alteration in behavior is a predictable concomitant. The new behavior will be consistent with the new structure of self.

How would a conceptual framework of this sort contain the research evidence which we have reviewed concerning the emotionalized self-regarding attitudes? They would appear to have a definite relationship to the structure of the self as we have defined it. A positive emotional tone toward the self seems to exist when the self-structure is firmly organized, and a negative feeling about the self exists when the organization of self is threatened by experiences which are vaguely or clearly seen as inconsistent with that structure. Thus, both the integrated individual and the person who is well organized on what might be termed a defensive basis, who completely shuts certain experiences out of awareness, will tend to have positive self-regarding attitudes. The emotionalized attitudes toward the self may be significant primarily of the state of organization of the self, firmness and consistency of organization being associated with positive self-feelings, whereas to the degree that the self is experienced as threatened or lacking in structural firmness, negative self-attitudes exist. In therapy we tend to get the individual who feels threatened, who vaguely senses inconsistencies, and who, after a process of partial disorganization of the self, rebuilds a self-structure more congruent with his basic experience and thus increases in positive self-feeling. Thus our theoretical formulation would hold that feelings about the self tend to be more a measure of the quality of self-organization than a measure of basic adjustment.

Our theory would also relate to the ways in which the self is perceived, some of these self-perceptions seeming to have a relationship to basic integration. When the self is seen as being able to permit all experience to enter awareness, then self-integration and self-confidence develop on the foundation of a fluid and adaptable self-organization. One client puts this realization thus: "You must even let your own experience tell you its own meaning; the minute *you* tell it what it means . . . you are at war with yourself." It is this permissiveness of the self toward all experiences and impulses, accepting them without denial or distortion, which appears to be the measure of sound personality integration.

Perhaps these preceding paragraphs begin to suggest the ways in which a theory developed out of concepts regarding the self might bring together into a coherent system the varied sorts of research evidence summarized in this paper. It would make comprehensible the wide fluctuations in self-regarding attitudes which occur in therapy as denied and distorted experiences are admitted to awareness, disturbing the organization of self. It would provide a rationale for the fact that the individual at the conclusion of therapy feels more comfortable, that he is more nearly his "real self," that he experiences himself as more unified, as all sensory and visceral experiences are perceived more nearly in their own terms. It would enable us to conceptualize the fact that behavior and attitudes other than self-attitudes change with the organization of self. In thus endeavoring to provide a meaningful theory of therapeutic change, it is believed that a significant contribution would be made to general theory regarding personality. It would also be a theory which could be stated in terms of operational definitions and thus put to experimental test. This could play a useful part in forwarding the science of personality study.

REFERENCES

1. Aidman, T. Changes in self perception as related to changes in perception of one's environment. Master's thesis, Univ. Chicago, 1947. Digest presented to American Psychological Association, Boston, 1948.
2. Assum, A. L., and Levy, S. J. Analysis of a nondirective case with followup interview. *J. abnorm. soc. Psychol.*, 1948, **43**, 78–89.
3. Axline, V. M. Nondirective therapy for poor readers. *J. consult. Psychol.*, 1947, **11**, 61–69.
4. Bartlett, M., and staff. Data on the Personal Adjustment Counseling Program for Veterans. Report of the Personal Adjustment Counseling

Division, Advisement and Guidance Service, Office of Vocational Rehabilitation and Education, Veterans Administration, 1948.

5. Bills, R. E. An investigation of the effects of individual and group play therapy on the reading level of retarded readers. Presented to American Psychological Association, Boston, 1948.

6. Carr, A. C. An evaluation of nine nondirective psychotherapy cases by means of the Rorschach. *J. consult. Psychol.,* 1949, **13**, 196–205.

7. Combs, A. W. Case of Edith Moore. In W. U. Snyder (Ed.), *Casebook of nondirective counseling.* Boston: Houghton, 1947. Pp. 268–311.

8. Combs, A. Follow-up of a counseling case treated by the nondirective method. *J. clin. Psychol.,* 1945, **1**, 145–154.

9. Cowen, E. L. A qualitative and quantitative follow-up study of thirty-two cases counselled by nondirective methods. Unpublished master's thesis, Syracuse Univ., 1948.

10. Curran, A. *Personality factors in counseling.* New York: Grune and Stratton, 1945.

11. Haigh, G. Defensive behavior in client-centered therapy. *J. consult. Psychol.,* 1949, **13**, 181–189.

12. Hoffman, A. E. A study of reported behavior changes in counseling. *J. consult. Psychol.,* 1949, **13**, 190–195.

13. Hogan, R. The development of a measure of client defensiveness in a counseling relationship. Doctor's dissertation, Univ. of Chicago, 1948.

14. Kasin, E. S. An exploratory comparison of personality descriptions obtained from nondirective interviews and the Thematic Apperception Test. Master's thesis, Univ. of Chicago, 1948.

15. Kauffman, P. E. An investigation of the relationship of two methods of measuring changes in verbatim protocols of counseling interviews. Unpublished master's thesis, Ohio State Univ., 1948.

16. Kauffmann, P., and Raimy, V. C. Two methods of assessing therapeutic progress. *J. abnorm. soc. Psychol.,* 1949, **44**, 379–385.

17. Kessler, C. Semantics and non-directive counseling. Master's thesis, Univ. of Chicago, 1947.

18. Lipkin, S. The client evaluates nondirective psychotherapy. *J. consult. Psychol.,* 1948, **12**, 137–146.

19. Muench, G. A. An evaluation of nondirective psychotherapy by means of the Rorschach and other tests. *Appl. Psychol. Monogr.,* No. 13, Stanford Univ. Press, 1947.

20. Raimy, V. C. The self-concept as a factor in counseling and personality organization. Doctor's dissertation, Ohio State Univ., 1943. Digest published in *J. consult. Psychol.,* 1948, **12**, 153–163.

21. Raskin, N. J. An analysis of six parallel studies of therapeutic process. *J. consult. Psychol.,* 1949, **13**, 206–220.

22. Reader, N. An investigation of some personality changes occurring in individuals undergoing client-centered therapy. Unpublished doctoral dissertation, Univ. of Chicago, 1948.

23. Rogers, C. R., Kell, B., and McNeil, H. The role of self-understanding in the prediction of behavior. *J. consult. Psychol.,* 1948, **12**, 174–186.

24. Rogers, N. Changes in self concept in the case of Mrs. Ett. *Personal Counselor,* 1947, **2**, 278–291.

25. Rogers, N. Measuring psychological tensions in non-directive counseling. *Personal Counselor,* 1948, **3**, 237–264.

26. Seeman, J. A study of the process of nondirective therapy. *J. consult. Psychol.,* 1949, **13**, 157–168.

27. Sheerer, E. T. An analysis of the relationship between acceptance of and respect for self and acceptance of and respect for others in ten counseling cases. *J. consult. Psychol.,* 1949, **13**, 169–175.

28. Snyder, W. U. An investigation of the nature of nondirective psychotherapy. *J. gen. Psychol.,* 1945, **33**, 193–223.
29. Snyder, W. U. A comparison of one unsuccessful with four successful nondirectively counseled cases. *J. consult. Psychol.,* 1947, **11**, 38–42.
30. Stock, D. An investigation into the interrelations between the self-concept and feelings directed toward other persons and groups. *J. consult. Psychol.,* 1949, **13**, 176–180.
31. Strom, K. A re-study of William U. Snyder's "An investigation of the nature of non-directive psychotherapy." Master's thesis in progress, Univ. of Chicago, 1948.
23. Thetford, W. N. The measurement of physiological responses to frustration before and after nondirective psychotherapy. Paper presented to American Psychological Association, Boston, 1948.
33. Zimmerman, J. Modification of the discomfort-relief quotient as a measure of progress in counseling. Master's thesis in progress, Univ. of Chicago, 1948.

Part *VII* *Epilogue*

On Autonomy

DAVID RIESMAN

PREFACE

When my colleagues Chad Gordon and Kenneth J. Gergen invited me
to contribute a discussion of autonomy as an epilogue for this volume,
drawn from what had been written on this subject in *The Lonely
Crowd,* my first reaction was one almost of embarrassment. For this
material had been published in very inconclusive and fragmentary
form, with the thought in mind that it would be possible later to return
to the area in a less unsystematic and unsatisfactory fashion. Thereafter, in attempting to delineate the potentialities for autonomy in the
profiles of *Faces in the Crowd,* these initial difficulties were illustrated
rather than overcome, for without either depth-psychological material
or observation over a stretch of time, we found it impossible to do
more than adumbrate what autonomy might mean for individual lives.
However, in the last fifteen years my interests have shifted, and I
have not pursued the problem of autonomy, either in the form sketched
in *The Lonely Crowd* or in alternative versions of similar ideas such as
Erich Fromm's "productive orientation," or Robert W. White's concept
of competence, or Abraham Maslow's "self-actualizing person," or
many other comparable terms. All I can do in these introductory
remarks is to remind the reader of some of the things that are missing
in what follows, and some of the things to look for.

The theme of *The Lonely Crowd* which appears to have made the
deepest impression is the hypothesis of a historical shift in recent years
from a dominant middle-class character structure primarily inner-
directed to one primarily other-directed. This characterological shift
was linked to changes in the mode of production and consumption and
these in turn were tied to demographic changes in the direction of a
stabilized population—changes which no longer appear irreversible in
the light of the baby boom after World War II. In any case, demographic changes appear less significant for character structure than
technological changes, although of course these two are related. Many
perhaps somewhat careless readers took it for granted that the person
primarily governed by other-direction was less autonomous than the
person primarily governed by inner-direction, despite our own contention that in either case the direction came from outside: in the first
case, from peers and the mass media, and in the second case, from
parents and their adult counterparts.

The concept of autonomy was, in fact, reserved for a separate non-

---

SOURCE. The Preface to the reprinted selections from the 1961 edition of
The Lonely Crowd was prepared for this volume in July 1966 by David
Riesman. David Riesman, with Nathan Glazer and Reul Denny, *The Lonely
Crowd* (1950), New Haven: Yale University Press edition, 1961, pp. xv–xvi,
xvii–xviii, xxi–xxv, xxvi–xxix, xliii–xliv, xlvii–xlviii, 240–243, 245–252,
253–257, and 259–260. Reprinted by permission of Yale University Press.

historical dimension of character which we termed modes of adaptation: these modes are autonomy, adjustment, and anomie. Such modes, we assumed, could be found in any given culture, although cultures would differ in the degree to which they provided leeway beyond the norm of adjustment. We did not regard "adjustment" as necessarily benign; rather, we defined it as a sort of psychological fit or comfort (or the appropriately valued discomfort) specific to a particular social role, while by "anomie" we meant psychological maladaptation whatever the behavioral consequences, and this in turn would not imply a negative verdict on nonconformity in a life-destroying culture. Moreover, we defined "autonomy" in terms of inner attitudes rather than outer behavior, arguing that a person could preserve his autonomy even while complying with the restrictive demands of a far from Utopian society. Later reflection has raised questions about this way of putting it, the more so as many people have come to define life as a game from which all real commitment is withdrawn; one's actions can be cynically geared to what is apparently demanded or to simply getting by, while one's independence is demonstrated privately to oneself and one's intimate circle. The conditions in a particular society may be so terrible that we cannot ask for more than this without asking for martyrs and saints. But in our own society, acting as if that society is unredeemable is often an alibi for irresponsibility and contempt, and for the kind of grandiosity and even paranoia readily built on these qualities. Thus we have come to feel that autonomy cannot be so readily separated from how one acts in society.

For one thing, for individuals to develop their full potentialities, they need to have an opportunity to extend themselves and to act toward others in such a way that these others will evoke qualities of a differentiated sort in them.[1] In other words, if autonomy is only practiced before a mirror, it is in danger of succumbing to narcissism. Indeed, in the first few of the following pages taken from the preface of the 1960 paperback edition, I comment on the way in which an egocentric individualism is apt to parade as autonomy, ignoring those issues of relatedness to others and commitment to keep intact the precarious structure of civilization, which we Americans are often too apt to take for granted.

It is that structure, with its minimum of obvious constraints and its many and increasing options for conduct, which offers individuals their opportunities for self-development in the direction of autonomy. To be sure, those very opportunities surround many Americans with a baffling plethora of choices: one perhaps paradoxical reason for the common nostalgia for an earlier epoch of firmer restrictions and perhaps fewer anxieties about the roads not taken. In any complex modern society such as our own, there is not a single culture to which individuals must adapt in their character structure, but a whole set of subcultures with quite disparate demands, resulting in many people living on a margin between subcultures and sometimes able to exploit these disparities or sometimes succumbing to them.

The concept of self-development implies that there is a self which is not entirely the legacy of earlier social interactions. That self begins at birth with a specific genetic endowment which in turn evoked differential response from other people. I state here what many would regard

---

[1] Cf. David Riesman, "The Search for Challenge," reprinted in *Abundance for What?*, Garden City, N. Y.: Doubleday, 1964, pp. 349–368.

as a truism because an increasing current in social psychology tends to empty the self of such idiosyncratic and inherited elements, emphasizing with George Herbert Mead the self as refracting the expectations of others in what can become an endless circularity. To become autonomous today means in some measure to be lucky at birth in one's endowment of a certain modicum of intelligence, energy, and perhaps attractiveness. Our definition of autonomy does not require that the individual be creative in any absolute sense (although some of the examples given in the pages that follow might suggest this), but rather that the individual have enough experience of mastery not to be completely the creature of circumstance.

In this connection, I should add that many people seek to bend themselves to circumstance but (to the credit of their unconscious selves) fail in the attempt. There is the story of a German anti-Nazi who, shortly after Hitler's coming to power, had taken a job as stenographer to an SS committee. Everything went well for a while; his convictions remained unshaken and he continued old Socialist associations. But then one day he had a paralysis of his right arm; he could not move it at all. He went to a psychiatrist, who discovered the source of the paralysis in the stenographer's unconscious inability to perform the constant "Heil Hitler" salutes.[2] We may contrast this anecdote with many other instances where an individual may consciously not wish to conform, and yet where his body, as it were, conforms on his behalf.

When *The Lonely Crowd* was composed in 1948–1949, this issue of conformity was not nearly so salient as it has become in subsequent years. Today it has become a cliché to attack conformity, standardized designs for living, mass society, and bureaucracy. Often these attacks suggest that the attacker simply wishes that the planet would become less crowded so that he could have more room and less need for interdependence. Often also, the interdependence that is rejected is of a very specific sort. For example, a few years ago, during the crisis over the integration of the University of Mississippi, I received an agonized letter from several Ole Miss students who informed me that, in fighting the juggernaut of the Federal Government, which wanted to bring the Negro James Meredith to their campus, they were exhibiting their individuality and autonomy. (I responded that with the Mississippi mob in back of them, all together shouting the egocentric slogans of states' rights and individualism, their nonconformity did not impress me as particularly autonomous or courageous.) Although in many respects radicals of the Right and Left do not resemble each other, for example, having very different attitudes toward compassion or toward the powerless, one often hears the rhetoric of a defiant individualism in both groups. And to the outsider it often appears that nonconformity is flaunted by such devices as rude behavior or wearing a beard. Even so, there remain circles in the United States where one must practice autonomy in ways that may appear childish, for the effort to become autonomous is an unending process rather than a concrete result or a product.

If, as I believe, the Southerners just mentioned misunderstood *The Lonely Crowd,* I also believe that the book permits a leeway of mis-

---

[2] I have borrowed this illustration from my essay, "Some Observations on the Limits of Totalitarian Power," in *Individualism Reconsidered,* New York: Free Press, 1954, pp. 424–425.

interpretation by its failure to give a concrete content to the discussion of autonomy in the era of other-direction. David Richards, a senior at Harvard College, calls attention to this in a term paper where he asks whether some Napoleon, claiming transcendence, would be called autonomous because he is spontaneously realizing his creative gifts as a leader of men. And he raises the question as well as to whether *The Lonely Crowd* does not place a premium on spontaneity and creativity as morally valuable *per se,* and as endowing the possessors of these qualities with an almost Nietzschean superiority.[3] Such considerations make plain how complicated can be the linkages between morality and autonomy. Autonomy can have moral value in itself insofar as it expresses and reveals the extent of human possibility. This can be balanced and overbalanced by the evil consequences such expressions can often have. It is also possible to be autonomous in ways that are on balance morally neutral. The great creators of modern art and literature include many men (Eliot, Yeats, Dostoevski, Pound) whose social outlook is regressive, and many others whose personal conduct is hardly a model for mankind as a whole. Human beings are seldom all of a piece, and we may be autonomous in some respects and anomic in other respects. To be sure, one could say that from the perspective of the Deity or of a saint, every single human being has independent and perhaps equivalent moral value. But from the perspective of most of us in our merely planetary existence, life is unfair and distributes its bounties quite unevenly; hence some individuals may have moral endowments which are quite superior, just as they may also have superior sensibility or intellect or financial endowment. In this view of things, I would not today contend that spontaneity or creativity are morally valuable per se; this depends on the context, on the total moral setting. And I have already stressed the solipsistic possibilities inherent in the concept of autonomy when it becomes divorced from human solidarity and interdependence. In recent years, we have seen many young people of comfortable background and unusual talent who insist that they should have no special privileges, whether in deferment from the draft or because their skins are white or their parents well-off. Programs of voluntary service, such as the Peace Corps or VISTA or Civil Rights activities North and South, allow these young people to express, not so much their creativity and individualism, as their feelings about sharing a common humanity and fate. Of course in practice they may express this humanity in spontaneous and often extremely inventive ways.

With these caveats in mind, I hope readers of the pages that follow will regard them as an invitation for further observation, reflection, and perhaps research of their own. The concept of autonomy (like the concepts of adjustment or of anomie) is of course an abstraction, only approximated in individual instances. As a description of character structure, it is only a beginning. These terms—and I hold no brief for any particular ones—can be regarded as signs pointing in the direction of a problem which would seem to be universal, for a society is inconceivable to me which would not confront individuals with some choices—that is, with the dilemmas of being human.

---

[3] See Richards, "On Shame and Related Moral Feelings: An Alternative Approach," term paper for Social Sciences 136, Harvard College, 1966, page 72.

The Lonely Crowd, emphasizing as it does the role of the peer group and the school in adolescence in the formation of character, perhaps itself underestimates the possibility of change as the result of the experiences of adulthood. And while the book as a whole emphasizes specific historical developments from tradition-direction to inner-direction and other-direction, there is nevertheless adumbrated in Part III a more psychological and less historical or cultural sketch of modes of adaptation—there termed "autonomy," "adjustment," and "anomie"—that might in principle be found in any society.[4] Unfortunately, many readers have tended to collapse the historical and the universal dimensions and, as we shall see more fully in a moment, to regard autonomy and inner-direction as equivalent—and conformity, which is found in all societies, as if it were characteristic of other-direction alone. No doubt our focus on conformity—in other words, adaptation and adjustment—and on deviance or anomie, reflects some of the problems of a large-scale differentiated society such as our own. More generally, whereas the explicitly psychoanalytic typologies (such as Abram Kardiner's) move "outwards" from individuals towards society, *The Lonely Crowd* proceeded the other way around: we started with industrial society and with particular historical developments within American society. We concerned ourselves, moreover, with the upper social strata, particularly with what has been called the "new middle class" of salaried professionals and managers. We assumed that there would be consequences for individual character in the loss or attenuation of the older social functions on the frontiers of production and exploration, and the discovery of other frontiers in the realm of consumption and personal relations. We did not assume that an individual would be the replica of his social role, but rather that there might be great tension between an individual's search for fulfillment and the demands of the institutions in which he had a part, or from which he felt alienated. . . .

Because readers of *The Lonely Crowd* have tended to equate inner-direction with autonomy, only a very small minority, sometimes

people brought up in a puritanical milieu, have responded warmly to the values of other-direction, to its openness and lack of inhibition, its interest in the others, and its readiness to change. Quite possibly *The Lonely Crowd* did not sufficiently stress these values; at any rate, the great majority of readers in the last ten years have decided that it was better to be an inner-directed cowboy than an other-directed advertising man, for they were not on the whole being faced with the problems of the cowboy, but rather those of the advertising man.[5] Everybody from the free enterpriser to the socialist has come out against conformity, so much so that when Elaine Graham's study turned up a fervent apostle of other-direction, the student in question was no naive defender of togetherness but a believer in the values of the Israeli kibbutz who hoped to emigrate and take up residence there.

* * *

The concepts of inner-direction and other-direction, loosely used to refer at once to social setting and to social character, helped us organize into clusters a number of possibly related historical developments. However, in the course of history various social and psychological configurations which have seemed permanent splinter and give way to new alignments—much as politcal parties in this country have served at once to divide some interests and to bring others together. Likewise, some of the behavioral items we linked with inner-direction or other-direction can no longer be classified in the same way. For example, many upper middle-class people who, in the 1940's, were proponents of "life adjustment" in school, would today, after Korea and Sputnik, be found in the ranks of those demanding discipline and "hardness." So, too, a current investigation of a California suburb indicates that the language of popularity and group-adjustment is favored by the lower middle class and eschewed by the upper middle class.

The concept of social character, as employed

---

[4] This typology is indebted both for concrete suggestion and in its mode of approach to Robert K. Merton's essay, "Social Structure and Anomie," in his *Social Theory and Social Structure,* rev. ed. Glencoe, Illinois: Free Press, 1957.

[5] See, for an interesting example, Michael S. Olmsted, "Character and Social Role," *American Journal of Sociology,* **63** (1957), 49–57, describing a small study where a group of Smith College students were asked to say whether they considered themselves more inner-directed or other-directed than their parents, their friends of both sexes, and the "average" girl at Smith. Most considered themselves more "inner-directed" than other students.

in *The Lonely Crowd,* involved a tentative decision as to what was important for salient groups in contemporary society. It was thus a different concept from national or modal character, which is usually a more aggregative statement about personality dispositions in a group or nation; we were only interested in certain aspects of character in very imprecisely specified parts of the population, and even there primarily in what was changing. But we did not differentiate carefully enough between character, behavior, values, and a style or ethos of particular institutions—the sorting out that this involves is a still uncompleted task for research. When we were working on *The Lonely Crowd,* we were convinced that the older social sciences—history, political science, economics—gave far too little weight to the understanding of social change that might be gleaned from a better grasp of psychoanalytic psychology; even so, we sought in the book to emphasize both the social character and the major institutions of the modern world and not to assume that the institutions were merely the frozen shapes given to their childhood dreams by rigidly imprisoned adults. And yet all our experience of the world since the book was written has led us to believe that modern industrial society can press into service a great variety of social character types. Thus we see in Japan contemporary institutions which have been powerful enough to incorporate people without waiting twenty or thirty years for a new generation to be created. What the Japanese do and what they say has changed more radically than their social character.[6]

Any sufficiently large society will throw up a slate of psychological types varied enough to suggest possibilities in many different directions; if America is not fascist, for example, it is not for want of sadists or authoritarians. There are plenty of these to staff the more benighted jails and mental hospitals, or to compete for the post of sheriff in many Southern communities; it is the institutional and judicial forms—and their own limitations—that make it difficult for these men to coalesce into a political movement. To be sure, these protections for liberty would collapse in the absence of men of appropriate character to run them; but our point is that, within wide limits, in a

large society institutions evoke within individuals the appropriate character. Or, more precisely, given the range of responses of which men are capable, institutions may select certain of these for reinforcement (while other, more rebellious, impulses are channeled off through a variety of "escapes"); and once the institutions are there—created as Kenneth Boulding points out in *The Organizational Revolution* by the achievements of the full-time organizer—enough facets of enough people prove adaptable to the going concern. Karl Marx saw the factories of the industrial revolution as a massive power, wrung from the labor of the workers and now confronting them with that labor in "alienated" form so that they in turn were alienated. Max Weber saw the bureaucracies of a later stage of capitalism and socialism as an "iron cage" within which man was caught and to which he could only resign himself with stoicism, his historical perspective garnishing his sense of duty.

It is in line with this view that many social scientists have concluded that individual and social character may become of decreasing importance as "factors of production" in the modern world; that indeed to interpret society one need not inquire into the motives of men, but rather notice that the situations they face are much alike, that the power of modern technology and science, modern economic organization, modern ideological and party organization is such that a single style of society becomes possible everywhere: a society based on efficient bureaucracies and the production of great quantities of goods, which may be used either to advance national prestige or power or to improve the material circumstances of life. Many Americans, including the authors of *The Lonely Crowd,* have been reluctant to accept these versions of determinism and have thought it possible to moderate the intractabilities of institutions, believing particularly that it made an enormous difference whether these institutions were created and controlled by a central elite for definite objectives, as in totalitarian countries, or were developed with less central guidance, growing up in more vegetable fashion, as in democratic countries.

On reconsideration, we still resist simplistic answers to the question as to the relative weight of social character and social institutions even in a world unsettled by the drastic message written in the sky above all countries: "You, too, can be modern and industrial."

[6] Compare the illuminating discussion of social and psychological change in Communist China by Robert J. Lifton, *Thought Reform and the Psychology of Totalism,* New York: Norton, 1961.

Despite the residual plasticity of most adults which renders them employable under a variety of social systems, there are limits. The American Indians made poor slaves, the Africans good ones—and this is not only because (as Stanley Elkins points out in *Slavery*) the slave ships broke the spirit and destroyed the cultural cohesion of the latter; some African tribes were better for plantation work, others for household work. For empirical reasons of experience, not on ideological grounds, the Spaniards found themselves eliminating native West Indians and replacing them with more adaptable imports, whose social character made survival under harsh conditions possible. Under our tutelage, the Pueblo Indians have proved less friable than other Indian tribes, more resistant if not more resilient. So, too, the history of immigration in this country is dramatically full of instances of differential response to apparently similar conditions: second-generation Japanese-Americans sought education, while third-generation Chinese were still running laundries and restaurants—and so on throughout the list of entrants, who only begin to approach each other in the third and later generations. Quite apart from the importance of individuals in history, and of their idiosyncratic character, the role of social character independent of institutions can at times be decisive. Moreover, as pointed out in *The Lonely Crowd,* while different kinds of social character can be used for the same kind of work within a society or institution, we believe that there will eventually be consequences of the fact that character types who fit badly pay a high price in anomie, in contrast to the release of energy provided by congruence of character and task.

This is not to say that those leaders of the "developing" peoples are correct who believe that they can retain their unique cultural or racial tradition while also going "modern"; as many are poignantly aware, the effective means they employ tend to become their own ends, so that one can foresee eventual supersession of the regionally distinct religions and cultures which once were created and carried, if not unequivocally cherished, by people of very different social character. Against these means and against the hope of power and plenty (and at times as revenge against those who had previously monopolized these), traditional values fight everywhere a rearguard action, buttressed by decaying institutions and the ineffectively recalcitrant social character of the older generation. If this were the end of the human story, one could invent a new "plastic man," as many writers of science fiction and behavioristic psychology have already done, to take the place of nineteenth-century economic man, and to get rid of the "problem of man" in the social sciences.

We may indeed be coming to the end of the human story. But if man does survive this period, we think we shall see that plastic man was but one of the stages of historical development, intermediate between the widely variegated *social* character types of an un-unified world and the even more widely divergent *individual* character of a unified but less oppressive world.

*   *   *

It is our surmise at present, however, that this change, with a loosening of the sense of personal destiny, is in part a consequence of those forbiddingly powerful and efficient institutions that inner-directed men conceived, organized, and rendered transportable. One of these institutions was the free market which, in late capitalism, affects not only the market for money and goods but the self-salesmanship of individuals (as Erich Fromm's term in *Man for Himself,* "the marketing orientation," makes clear). The term "*other*-direction" may emphasize too much the role of specific others (or their surrogates in the mass media) and insufficiently the role of such institutions as the personality market, for whose often implicit directions the "others" are mere agents.[7]

Men of conviction have not disappeared; they matter very much at present, precisely because they are relatively rare. And they seem to be most rare among young adults. As we went through our interview materials to select examples for *Faces in the Crowd,* there were very few respondents under thirty who could not have been put, with qualifications, under the heading "Varieties of Other-direction"; whatever else might be true of them, they had enough plasticity for that. An analysis of interviews with nearly two hundred college seniors, though far less intensive, later gave an even

---

[7] Cf. Talcott Parsons and Winston White, "The Link between Character and Society," in Lipset and Lowenthal, eds., *Sociology of Culture.* Parsons and White draw a clarifying distinction between goals (the direction toward which) and the agents (those who give directions).

stronger picture of malleability and acquiescence.

Does it follow that the specific American upper middle-class social character we termed other-directed is also the social character of the young in general elsewhere in the world—of those who have what Daniel Lerner refers to (in *The Passing of Traditional Society*) as the "mobile sensibility"? Despite the very great differences of culture which persist, from observations and studies done in many countries it seems that students everywhere now begin to resemble each other in basic outlook as well as superficial fads, so that, despite many cleavages, these students are more like each other than any one of them is like his father or mother. They are alike, as we have been suggesting, in their plasticity, their dependence on situation and circumstance and institutions. Indeed, their alikeness has struck many observers who speak of the whole world as becoming "Americanized."

But the similarity must not be overstated. For better as well as for worse, the specific types of resonance, anxiety, and sensibility characteristic of many well-educated Americans are seldom to be found in countries which have still to eliminate caste barriers and to suffer the pangs of affluence. The current preoccupation in this country with national purpose is not to be found in the countries whose goal is to share (or overthrow) our prowess. And of course there are many other differences, where local color and character affect the impact of the transcultural institutions, so that a Japanese factory preserves certain traditional values that an American or a Russian factory disrupt.

These differences, however, are all under pressure of the discovery—as important as Darwinism in changing the face of the world, and in part reflecting Darwinism—that cultures and religions hold no absolute truth, authority, self-evidentness. Fixed social characters could be maintained by fixed beliefs. Inner-direction wedded fixed social character to flexible behavior, but not to relativistic values. Inner-directed men were able, for a relatively brief historical period, to act as if the Chinese, Indians, Malayans, Africans they encountered were radically different from themselves (and from each other); they could act this way because they were obviously so much superior in power and hence, in many encounters, in poise as well. If they were missionaries they might ask of the others, even in the heart of

darkness, that they learn to act like white men; and—astonishingly, as it now seems to us—millions sought to do so and were converted, impressed by the rectitude as well as the power of their captors and models. It has now become difficult for thoughtful Western men, not encapsulated by prejudice and ignorance, to take their own cultures and practices as absolutes; they cannot, by merely willing it, take them with deadly seriousness—in fact, the current wave of talk about the American Way of Life is a propagandist's vain defensiveness against this very discovery.

Another way of looking at this development is to see that, beneath all or virtually all cultural absolutes, has lain a basic human ambivalence. Anthropologists understandably regret the disintegration of most nonliterate cultures with the coming of the white man (or, today, the white-influenced man of any color); and we, too, feel that many of these cultures have created values our own society lacks. But a great number of nonliterates, not subject to physical coercion or dispersal, have plainly concluded that their once seemingly given culture lacked something; they have gone off, singly or in groups, to join the Big Parade—often meeting the more disenchanted Westerners going the other way. To repeat: the most important passion left in the world is not for distinctive practices, cultures, and beliefs, but for certain achievements—the technology and organization of the West—whose immediate consequence is the dissolution of all distinctive practices, cultures, and beliefs. If this is so, then it is possible that the cast of national characters is finished: men have too many to choose from to be committed to one, and as their circumstances become more similar, so will many attributes held in common, as against those unique to particular countries. Increasingly, the differences among men will operate across and within national boundaries, so that already we can see, in studies of occupational values in industrial societies, that the group character of managers or doctors—or artists—becomes more salient than the group character of Russians or Americans or Japanese, or indeed the conscious ideologies held in these societies.

It would of course be premature to say that nations are no longer important, when they have the power of life and death over us all; and when, since social and national character is a legacy of history, there will remain for a long time differences in national character just as great as differences arising from occupation, sex, and style of life. So, too, relics of parochialism can persist—although as soon as a group or tribe seeks to protect its unique historical legacy by a nativist or revivalist movement, this very effort (as suggested in *Faces in the Crowd*) betokens the end of unselfconscious, taken-for-granted rituals, and hence paradoxically speeds initiation into the modern world where tradition itself becomes an ideology, an aspect of deracination. Modernization thus appears to proceed with an almost irreversible impact, and no tribe or nation has found a place to hide.

In an age when many educated Americans are preoccupied with the nature of their own identities and values, many non-professional readers have come to *The Lonely Crowd* for clues as to what they were like and how they might live. Indeed, many have read it as a test of their character, in the old-fashioned and non-technical sense of the word "character." We did not anticipate such an audience, not only when the book was first published by a university press, but later when it was one of the first "quality paperbacks," for we and the publishers alike thought it might sell a few thousand copies as a reading in social science courses. While the professional academic reader would easily locate the book in the tradition of work in culture and personality, the untrained reader often tended to give us too much credit, or to assume that we spoke with the authentic univocal accent of sociology.

*   *   *

Perhaps one of the most extensive reactions to the concept of autonomy as developed in *The Lonely Crowd* appeared in Meier and Banfield's review. They asked:

> What kind of a person is the autonomous man in a predominately other-directed society likely to be in the future? This is a question which the authors treat fleetingly. We suggest that—if our children and our students are any criteria—the new autonomous type will be very much affected by the tremendous quantities of information that are open to him, and by the comprehensive quick-acting, and relatively unbiased institutions which he can use. His relationship to the machine will be that of designer or diagnostician, but not slave. His logic will be multi-valued, often with concrete statistical formulations. When probabilities are equal for all alternatives, he will choose spontaneously. His loyalties will not be intense; how-

ever, internationalism as an ideal will appeal to him. Play of the imagination will be more varied, but plans for the future will be more prominent (the present vogue of science fiction may be symptomatic of this). His moral outlook will be inquisitive and pragmatic: unfortunate circumstances lead to antisocial actions. Sin, therefore, will have been explained away when its causes are understood. But antisocial action will remain the one thing these otherwise independent personalities will have to avoid. What the consensus establishes as the social good will still be sacred.[8]

The attitude of these reviewers is markedly different from that of most reviewers and, so far as we can tell from correspondence and discussion, most articulate readers of *The Lonely Crowd,* who, as already stated, tended to regard inner-direction and autonomy as much the same thing, and who would regard with horror the fluid and perhaps overloaded sensibilities hopefully viewed by Messrs. Meier and Banfield. Partly, I suppose, the confusion between autonomy and inner-direction that many readers fell into reflects our own inability to make the idea of autonomy a more vivid and less formal one—to give it content, as inner-direction gained content because the concept called to mind many historical exemplars available to everyone's experience. Beyond that, a strand of nostalgic thinking has always been strong in America despite the waves of boosterism and progress-oriented optimism that have often been more dominant.

Indeed, in the 1950's, as we have said, it sometimes appeared that many educated young people saw only two possible roles for themselves: that of the well-heeled organization man (other-directed), and that of the well-shod cowboy (inner-directed); it was in this period that "togetherness" joined "do-gooder" as a term of contempt. In this shrinkage of alternatives, little gestures of personal assertion—or a solipsistic lack of concern for others—have often masqueraded as autonomy. The degeneration of individuality into egocentrism and eccentricity is an old American story.

*   *   *

In discussing social character, we agreed that the world is getting more homogeneous, and that enclaves, whether national or regional, are bound to disappear, providing the existing enclaves do not make us all disappear. Contrary, however, to what many nostalgic people

---

[8] In *Ethics,* January 1952.

believe, the loss of older fixed boundaries of class, caste, and nation does not inevitably mean a growing sameness in the world in terms of the development of personal styles of life. Disappearance of the more exotic differences will only discomfit tourists, provided that the differences that once arose among men due to their geographic location can be replaced by differences arising from the still unexplored potentialities of human temperament, interest, and curiosity. The current preoccupation with identity in this country (notable in the great impact of Erik H. Erikson's work) reflects the liberation of men from the realm of characterological necessity. The power of individuals to shape their own character by their selection among models and experiences was suggested by our concept of autonomy; when this occurs, men may limit the provinciality of being born to a particular family in a particular place. To some, this offers a prospect only of rootless men and galloping anomie. To more hopeful prophets, ties based on conscious relatedness may some day replace those of blood and soil.[9]

* * *

I. THE ADJUSTED, THE ANOMIC, THE AUTONOMOUS

How, one may well ask, is it possible that a large group of influential people in a society should develop a character structure more constricted than the society's institutions require? One answer is to look at history and to see that earlier institutional inevitabilities tend to perpetuate themselves in ideology and character, operating through all the subtle mechanisms of character formation discussed in the early chapters of *The Lonely Crowd*. By the same token, disparities between social character and adult social role can be among the important leverages of social change. It is too simple to say that character structure lags behind social structure: as any element in society changes, all other elements must also change in form or function or both. But in a large society such as the American there is room for disparities, and hence for individuals to choose different modes of reconciliation. In the upper-income strata in America, many of the pressures which individuals feel spring from their shared interpretations of what is necessary to get along. As soon

as one or two in a group emancipate themselves from these interpretations, without their work or their world coming to an end, others, too, may find the courage to do so. In that case, character will change in consonance with the altered interpretations of conditions.

In asking where the one or two innovators may come from, we must remember that social character is not all of character. The individual is capable of more than his society usually asks of him, though it is not at all easy to determine this, since potentialities may be hidden not only from others but from the individual himself.

Of course, social structures differ very much in the degree to which they evoke a social character that in the process of socialization fills up, crushes, or buries individuality. We may take, as extreme cases, the primitive societies of Dobu or Alor. People there seem to be so crushed from infancy on by institutionalized practices that, while they manage to do what their culture asks of them in the emotional tone which the culture fosters, they cannot do much more. The Rorschach tests taken of the Alorese, for instance, indicate that there is a good deal of characterological uniformity among individuals and that few reserves of depth or breadth exist beyond the cultural norm or what Kardiner calls the basic personality type. Such a society might die out as a result of its apathy and misery, especially when further disorganized by white contact, but it is hard to conceive of an internal rejuvenation led by the more autonomous members of the group. Caught between social character and rigid social institutions, the individual and his potentialities have little scope. Nevertheless, even in such a society there will be deviants; as Ruth Benedict has pointed out, we know of no cultures without them. However, before turning to see whether the extent of deviation may be related to population phase, it is necessary to understand more precisely what is meant by deviation.

The "adjusted" are those whom for the most part we have been describing. They are the typical tradition-directed, inner-directed, or other-directed people—those who respond in their character structure to the demands of their society or social class at its particular stage on the curve of population. Such people fit the culture as though they were made for it, as in fact they are. There is, characterologically speaking, an effortless quality about their adjustment, although as we have seen the mode of adjustment may itself impose heavy strains

---

[9] Erich Fromm, *The Sane Society,* New York: Rinehart, 1955, p. 362.

on the so-called "normal" people. That is, the adjusted are those who reflect their society, or their class within the society, with the least distortion.

In each society those who do not conform to the characterological pattern of the adjusted may be either anomic or autonomous. Anomie is English coinage from Durkheim's *anomique* (adjective of *anomie*) meaning ruleless, ungoverned. My use of anomic, however, covers a wider range than Durkheim's metaphor: it is virtually synonymous with maladjusted, a term I refrain from using because of its negative connotations; for there are some cultures where I would place a higher value on the maladjusted or anomic than on the adjusted. The "autonomous" are those who on the whole are capable of conforming to the behavioral norms of their society—a capacity the anomics usually lack— but are free to choose whether to conform or not.

In determining adjustment, the test is not whether an individual's overt behavior obeys social norms but whether his character structure does. A person who has the appropriate character for his time and place is "adjusted" even when he makes mistakes and does things which deviate sharply from what is expected of him—to be sure, the consequences of such mistakes may eventually produce maladjustment in character. (Much in the same way, a culture may be a going concern even if it behaves "irrationally" vis-à-vis its neighbors or material environment.) Conversely, just as nonconformity in behavior does not necessarily mean nonconformity in character structure, so utter conformity in behavior may be purchased by the individual at so high a price as to lead to a character neurosis and anomie: the anomic person tends to sabotage either himself or his society, probably both.[10] Thus, "adjustment," as the term is used here, means socio-psychological fit, not adequacy in any evaluative sense; to determine adequacy either of behavior or character we must study not only the individual but the gear box which, with various slips and reversals, ties behavior in with institutional forms. The person here defined as autonomous may or may not conform outwardly, but whatever his choice, he pays less of a price, and he has a choice: he can meet both the culture's definitions of adequacy and those which (to a still culturally determined

degree) slightly transcend the norm for the adjusted.

These three universal types (the adjusted, the anomic, the autonomous), like our three historical types (tradition-directed, inner-directed, and other-directed) are, in Max Weber's sense, "ideal types," that is, constructions necessary for analytical work. Every human being will be one of these types to some degree; but no one could be completely characterized by any one of these terms. To put it in the extreme, even an insane person is not anomic in every sphere of life; nor could an autonomous person be completely autonomous, that is, not irrationally tied in some part of his character to the cultural requirements of his existence. Nevertheless, we can characterize an individual by the way in which one mode of adaptation predominates, and, when we study individuals, analysis by such a method provides certain helpful dimensions for descriptive and comparative purposes. We can also characterize a society by examining the relative frequency with which the three modes of adaptation occur in it, and the relative importance of the three types in the social structure.

*   *   *

Although much can be and has been said about the anomic person, we know much less about those whom I call autonomous. Many will even deny that there are such people, people capable of transcending their culture at any time or in any respect. Those who become autonomous in our own society, for instance, seem to arise in a family background and class or regional setting that have had quite different consequences for others. In fact, autonomous, adjusted, and anomic types can be brothers and sisters within the same family, associates on the same job, residents in the same housing project or suburb. When someone fails to become autonomous, we can very often see what blockages have stood in his way, but when someone succeeds in the same overt setting in which others have failed, I myself have no ready explanation of this, and am sometimes tempted to fall back on constitutional or genetic factors—what people of an earlier era called the divine spark. Certainly, if one observes week-old infants in a hospital crèche, one is struck with the varieties in responsiveness and aliveness before there has been much chance for culture to take hold. But, since this is a book about culture and

---

[10] See Robert K. Merton, *op. cit.* [in n. 4].

character, I must leave such speculations to others.

It seems reasonable to assume that a decisive step in the road toward autonomy is connected with the social shifts I have linked to the curve of population. To put this in the negative, it is difficult, almost impossible, in a society of high population growth potential, for a person to become aware of the possibility that he might change, that there are many roles open to him, roles other people have taken in history or in his milieu. As the philosopher G. H. Mead saw, this taking the role of the other leads to becoming aware of actual differences and potential similarities between the other and the self. That is why culture contact alone does not lead people to change when their interpretations of the contact spring out of a tradition-directed mode of life. High population growth potential, tradition-direction, and the inability of the individual to change roles—to think of himself as an individual capable of such change—these, as we saw, go together.

For centuries the peasant farmers of Lebanon suffered from invasions by Arab horsemen. After each invasion the peasants began all over again to cultivate the soil, though they might do so only to pay tribute to the next marauder. The process went on until eventually the fertile valleys become virtual deserts, in which neither peasants nor nomads could hope for much. The peasants obviously never dreamed that they too might become cultivators of the soil. This epic has the quality not of human history but of animal life. The herbivores are unable to stop eating grass though they eat only to be devoured by the carnivores. And the carnivores cannot eat grass when they have thinned out the herbivores. In these societies dependent on tradition-direction there is scarcely a notion that one might change character or role.

*   *   *

The more advanced the technology, on the whole, the more possible it is for a considerable number of human beings to imagine being somebody else. In the first place, the technology spurs the division of labor, which, in turn, creates the possibility for a greater variety of experience and of social character. In the second place, the improvement in technology permits sufficient leisure to contemplate change—a kind of capital reserve in men's self-adaptation to nature—not on the part of a ruling few but on the part of many. In the third place, the combination of technology and leisure helps

to acquaint people with other historical solutions—to provide them, that is, not only with more goods and more experiences but also with an increased variety of personal and social models.

How powerful such an influence can be the Renaissance indicates. Then, a richer picture of the past made it possible to live toward a more open future. Italians, newly rich and self-conscious, tried to imitate Greeks; and northern peoples, such as the Elizabethan English, tried to imitate Italians. The inner-directed character type emerged as the dominant type from the new possibilities created at this period; he built both those possibilities and the limits he put on them into his character. From the masses of the tradition-directed there arose many mobile ones who decided that they could be "horsemen" and no longer had to be "cultivators"; and the new technology and new lands beyond the sea gave them the necessary physical and intellectual store for the shift, while at the same time making it possible for the cultivators to support more noncultivators. Ever since, in the countries of transitional population growth, men have robbed the earth of its fruits and the farmer of his progeny in order to build the industrial civilization (and the lowered birth rate) of today. In this process the farmer's progeny had to learn how to become something other than cultivators.

Today again, in the countries of incipient population decline, men stand on the threshold of new possibilities of being and becoming—though history provides a less ready, perhaps only a misleading, guide. They no longer need limit their choices by gyroscopic adaptation but can respond to a far wider range of signals than any that could possibly be internalized in childhood. However, with the still further advance of technology and the change of frontiers from production to consumption, the new possibilities do not present themselves in the same dramatic form of passing from one class to another, of joining one or another side—the exploiting or the exploited—in the factory and at the barricades. In fact, those, namely the the Communists, who try to structure matters according to these older images of power, have become perhaps the most reactionary and most menacing force in world politics.

In a society of abundance that has reached the population phase of incipient decline, the class struggle alters as the middle class expands until it may number more than half of the whole population in occupational terms, with an even larger proportion, measured in terms of income, leisure, and values. The new possibilities opening up for the individual are possibilities not so much for entering a new class but rather for changing one's style of life and character within the middle class.

Under these conditions autonomy will not be related to class. In the era dependent on inner-direction, when character was largely formed for work and at work, it made a great deal of difference whether one owned means of production or not. Today, however, the psychological advantages of ownership are very much reduced in importance; character is increasingly formed for leisure and during leisure —and both leisure and means of consumption are widely distributed. Thus, adjusted, autonomous, and anomic outcomes are often the result of very impalpable variations in the way people are treated by and react to their education, their consumer training, and, generally, their encounters with people—all within the broad status band of the middle class.

To be sure, there may be correlations, as yet unnoticed, between autonomy and occupation. Work is far from having lost its relevance for character even today. And occupational status affects leisure status. Those who are potentially autonomous may select some occupations in preference to others; beyond that, the day-by-day work experiences of members of different occupational groups will shape character. On the whole, however, it seems likely that the differences that will divide societies in the phase of incipient population decline will no longer be those between back-breaking work on the one hand and *rentier* status on the other, between misery and luxury, between long life and short life—those differences that dominated the thinking of men as varied as Charles Kingsley, Bellamy, Marx, and Veblen during the era of transitional population growth. Most people in America today—the "overprivileged" two thirds, let us say, as against the underprivileged third—can afford to attend to, and allow their characters to be shaped by, situational differences of a subtler nature than those arising from bare economic necessity and their relations to the means of production.

II. THE AUTONOMOUS AMONG THE INNER DIRECTED

The autonomous person, living like everyone else in a given cultural setting, employs the reserves of his character and station to move away from the adjusted mean of the same setting. Thus, we cannot properly speak of an "autonomous other-directed man" (nor of an "anomic other-directed man") but only of an autonomous man emerging from an era or group depending on other-direction (or of an anomic man who has become anomic through his conflict with other-directed or inner-directed patterns or some combination of them). For autonomy, like anomie, is a deviation from the adjusted patterns, though a deviation controlled in its range and meaning by the existence of those patterns.

The autonomous person in a society depending on inner-direction, like the adjusted person of the same society, possessed clear-cut, internalized goals and was disciplined for stern encounters with a changing world. But whereas the adjusted person was driven toward his goals by a gyroscope over whose speed and direction he had hardly a modicum of control and of the existence of which he was sometimes unaware, his autonomous contemporary was capable of choosing his goals and modulating his pace. The goals, and the drive toward them, were rational, nonauthoritarian and noncompulsive for the autonomous; for the adjusted, they were merely given.

Obviously, however, as long as tight despotic or theocratic controls of conduct existed, it was difficult to "choose oneself" either in work or play. For, while it is possible to be autonomous no matter how tight the supervision of behavior as long as thought is free—and thought as such is not invaded effectively until modern totalitarianism—in practice most men need the opportunity for some freedom of behavior if they are to develop and confirm their autonomy of character. Sartre, I believe, is mistaken in his notion that men—other than a few heroic individuals—can "choose themselves" under conditions of extreme despotism.

The autonomous are not to be equated with the heroes. Heroism may or may not bespeak autonomy; the definition of the autonomous refers to those who are in their character capable of freedom, whether or not they are able to, or care to, take risks of overt deviation. The case of Galileo illustrates both points. In order to accomplish his work, Galileo needed *some* freedom, such as the freedom to exchange astronomical texts and instruments, to write down results, and so on. Yet he chose a nonheroic course. In the Soviet Union and its satellites today he could not make this choice, since the choice between martyrdom or secrecy is not available under the grisly regime of the NKVD.

The four centuries since the Renaissance have seen the rise and fall of many periods when theocratic, royal, or other authoritative controls were not as tight as in Soviet Russia today; periods also when economic life for many was raised above mere subsistence, thus providing opportunities for autonomy. And there were loopholes for autonomy even in the earlier despotic periods, since the despots were inefficient, corrupt, and limited in their aims. Modern totalitarianism is also more inefficient and corrupt than it is often given credit for being, but its aims are unlimited and for this reason it must wage total war on autonomy— with what ultimate effectiveness we do not yet know. For the autonomous person's acceptance of social and political authority is always conditional: he can cooperate with others in action while maintaining the right of private judgment. There can be no recognition whatever of such a right under totalitarianism—one reason why in the Soviet Union artistic works and scientific theories are so relentlessly scrutinized for "deviationism," lest they conceal the seeds even of unconscious privacy and independence of perception.

Fortunately for us, the enemies of autonomy in the modern democracies are less total and relentless. However, as Erich Fromm has insisted in *Escape from Freedom,* the diffuse and anonymous authority of the modern democracies is less favorable to autonomy than one might assume. One reason, perhaps the chief reason, is that the other-directed person is trained to respond not so much to overt authority as to subtle but nonetheless constricting interpersonal expectations. Indeed, autonomy in an era depending on inner-direction looks easier to achieve than autonomy today. Autonomy in an inner-directed mode is, however, no longer feasible for most people. To understand why this is so requires a glance at the powerful bulwarks or defenses for autonomy that an era dependent on inner-direction provided and that are no longer so powerful today. These include, in the Protestant lands, certain attitudes toward conscience, and everywhere, the bulwarks of work, property, class, and occupation as well as the comforting possibilities of escape to the frontier.

In the first place, a Protestant or secular-

Protestant society of adjusted inner-directed types expects people to conform, not by looking to others but by obedience to their internal gyroscopes or consciences. This affords privacy, for while society may punish people more or less for what they *do,* it lacks the interest and psychological capacity to find out what they see. People are like the yachts in a Bermuda race, attentive not to each other but to the goal in view and the favoring winds.

In the second place, there was always available a line of defense in the existence of frontiers of settlement and the right of asylum. The power to move around the globe in the days before passports placed limits on the tyrants' reach and gave reality to the concept of inalienable rights.[11] Roger Williams lighting out for himself; Voltaire shuttling back and forth over Europe; Karl Marx finding refuge in the British Museum; Carl Schurz fleeing to America —these are scenes from an almost vanished past.

In the third place, the autonomous in the era dependent on inner-direction had available to them the defenses provided by work itself, in a period when the adjusted people also were mainly work-oriented. Though it was hard to admit that one found joy in one's work in the puritan countries, it was permissible to regard it as an end in itself, as well as a means to other ends. The "hardness of the material" attracted the autonomous, indeed—again, like their less autonomous fellows—often hardened them to all other considerations.

*   *   *

In the fourth place, property and class were substantial defenses for those who strove for autonomy. They protected not only the crazy millionaire's conspicuous consumption but the irreverence of the secluded Bentham and the integrated double life of that fine horseman and industrialist of Manchester, Friedrich Engels. People were protected, too, not only by their work and their property but by their position, be it elevated or humble. If people could manage to fulfill their occupational role, what they did in their off hours was more or less up to them. Charles Lamb as a petty official could write in his spare time. Hawthorne, and many other nineteenth-century American

---

11 For fuller discussion of this now dormant freedom, see my article, "Legislative Restrictions on Foreign Enlistment and Travel," *Columbia Law Review,* **40** (1940), 793–835.

writers, held posts that did not require them to give much of themselves—certainly not the self-exploitation on and off the job asked of far better paid writers who hold hack jobs today. The hierarchical chain of occupations, once one achieved a position in it, held people in place with some degree of security, while permitting sufficient tether for the autonomous. Within certain given limits of property and place, one could move without arousing shocked antagonism, traumatic either in terms of one's feelings or one's worldly fate.

Many of these same defenses, however, operated far more frequently as barriers to autonomy than as defenses for it. A society organized in terms of class, private property, and occupation resisted autonomy with all the weapons of family, wealth, religion, and political power: the complaints and protests of political and religious reformers, artists, and artisans against this type of largely bourgeois social organization, now vanishing, were true and just enough. But we must never forget that these barriers could frequently be organized as defenses of the individual; once their flanks were turned by energy and talent, they provided the freedom in which autonomy as well as *rentier* complacency could flourish.

In biographies and memoirs of the last several hundred years, we can reconstruct, as it were, the way in which individuals begin their struggle for autonomy within the despotic walls of the patriarchal family. The family operated, much more than the state, as the "executive committee" of the inner-directed bourgeois class, training the social character both of future members of that class and of future servants to it. Print, however, as we have seen, might succor a child in his lonely battle with parents, teachers, and other adult authorities—though a book might also disorient him and increase the pressure on him. But with good luck a book, like a sympathetic teacher or relative, might break the solid front of authority in the home.

Not until adolescence were other children likely to be of much help, though then, especially when adolescent youth groups later took institutional form, they might assist the break from home. Adolescence, in fact, was usually the period of crisis for the boy or girl who sought autonomy. While even the adjusted had to make the passage from home, they moved thence into a social system that still held them fast, finding such authoritative parent surrogates as were necessary to calibrate their al-

ready internalized parental signals. However, the would-be autonomous youth, in breaking with parents, were breaking with authority as such, internalized as well as external. One can trace this process in all its poignancy in the development of John Stuart Mill, who got out from under his father only when well along in life, or of Franz Kafka, who never did.

Once out in the world, the person struggling for autonomy faced directly the barriers of property—if he was without it; of hierarchy—if he sought to climb or oppose it; of religion—if he contravened its controls on expression. In strongly Protestant communities in particular, one's discreet overt behavior could not assure to oneself the freedom Erasmus or Galileo had made use of. The result was that between the oversteered and the understeered there was little room for autonomy. The struggle to turn these obstacles into defenses was often too tough, and the individual was scarred for life, as were Marx, Balzac, Nietzsche, Melville, E. A. Robinson, and many other great men of the era dependent on inner-direction. Still others, however—John Dewey, wiry Vermonter, was a magnificent example and so, in a very different way, is Bertrand Russell—more favored by fortune, could live lives of personal and intellectual collision and adventure with little inner conflict.

III. THE AUTONOMOUS AMONG THE OTHER-DIRECTED

Lawyers and lawmakers have a technique called "incorporation by reference;" by means of it they can refer in one statute or document to another without full quotation. In the same way I would like to incorporate by reference here the writings of Mill which deal with individuality: the *Autobiography,* the essays *On Liberty* and *On Social Freedom,* and *The Subjection of Women.* These writings represent an extraordinary foreshadowing of the problems of the autonomous individual when, with the decline of the older barriers to freedom, the newer and far more subtle barriers of public opinion in a democracy arise. Indeed, in reading modern writers, such as Sartre, Simone de Beauvoir, Erich Fromm, José Ortega y Gasset, and Bertrand Russell, who deal with similar themes, one is struck by the degree to which, underneath differences in idiom, their philosophic outlook resembles Mill's in many important respects.

Mill wrote: "In this age the mere example

of nonconformity, the mere refusal to bend the knee to custom, is itself a service." But his interest was more in the individual than in the service. He observed two tendencies that have grown much more powerful since he wrote. He saw, as many others did, that people no longer took their cues "from dignitaries in Church or State, from ostensible leaders, or from books" but rather from each other—from the peer-group and its mass-media organs, as we would say. He saw, as few others did, that this occurred not only in public matters but also in private ones, in the pursuit of pleasure and in the development of a whole style of life. All that has changed, perhaps, since he and Tocqueville wrote, is that the actions they saw as based on the fear of what people might say—on conscious opportunism, that is—are today the more automatic outcome of a character structure governed, not only from the first but throughout life, by signals from outside. In consequence, a major difference between the problems of Mill's day and ours is that someone who today refuses "to bend the knee to custom" is tempted to ask himself: "Is this what I really want? Perhaps I only want it because . . . ."

This comparison may overstate historical changes; the autonomous at all times have been questioners. The autonomous among the inner-directed, however, were partially shaped by a milieu in which people took many psychological events for granted, while the autonomous among the other-directed live in a milieu in which people systematically question themselves in anticipation of the questions of others. More important, in the upper socioeconomic levels in the western democracies today—these being the levels, except for the very highest, most strongly permeated by other-direction— the coercions upon those seeking autonomy are not the visible and palpable barriers of family and authority that typically restricted people in the past.

This is one reason why it is difficult, as an empirical matter, to decide who is autonomous when we are looking at the seemingly easy and permissive life of a social class in which there are no "problems" left, except for persons striving for autonomy. These latter, in turn, are incapable of defining the "enemy" with the relative ease of the autonomous person facing an inner-directed environment. Is the inside-dopester an enemy, with his sympathetic tolerance, but veiled disinterest, and his inability

to understand savage emotions? Are they enemies, those friends who stand by, not to block but to be amused, to understand and pardon everything? An autonomous person of today must work constantly to detach himself from shadowy entanglements with this top level of other-direction—so difficult to break with because its demands appear so reasonable, even trivial.

One reason for this is that the autonomous person of today is the beneficiary of the greater sensitivity brought into our society, at great personal cost, by his autonomous predecessors of the era of inner-direction. The latter, in rejecting the Philistine norm, were frequently very much preoccupied with taste, with what they liked; in their sensuous openness to experience, their awareness of personal nuance, many of the Romantic poets and other artists of the nineteenth century were strikingly "modern." What they put into their poems and other works, in refinement and subjectivity, is part of their legacy to the emotional vocabularies of our own day. These precursors, moreover, had no doubt as to who their enemies were: they were the adjusted middle-class people who aggressively knew what they wanted, and demanded conformity to it—people for whom life was not something to be tasted but something to be hacked away at. Such people of course still exist in great numbers but, in the better educated strata of the larger cities, they are on the defensive; and opposition to them is no longer enough to make a person stand out as autonomous.

Autonomy, I think, must always to some degree be relative to the prevailing modes of conformity in a given society; it is never an all-or-nothing affair, but the result of a sometimes dramatic, sometimes imperceptible struggle with those modes. Modern industrial society has driven great numbers of people into anomie, and produced a wan conformity in others, but the very developments which have done this have also opened up hitherto undreamed-of possibilities for autonomy. As we come to understand our society better, and the alternatives it holds available to us, I think we shall be able to create many more alternatives, hence still more room for autonomy.

A heightened self-consciousness, above all else, constitutes the insignia of the autonomous in an era dependent on other-direction. For, as the inner-directed man is more self-conscious than his tradition-directed predecessor and as the other-directed man is more self-conscious still, the autonomous man growing up under conditions that encourage self-consciousness can disentangle himself from the adjusted others only by a further move toward even greater self-consciousness. His autonomy depends not upon the ease with which he may deny or disguise his emotions but, on the contrary, upon the success of his effort to recognize and respect his own feelings, his own potentialities, his own limitations. This is not a quantitative matter, but in part an awareness of the problem of self-consciousness itself, an achievement of a higher order of abstraction.

As we know all too well, such an achievement is a difficult thing; many of those who attain it cannot manage to mold it into the structure of an autonomous life but succumb to anomie. Yet perhaps the anomie of such processes is preferable to the less self-conscious, though socially supported, anxiety of the adjusted who refuse to distort or reinterpret their culture and end by distorting themselves.

Author Index

Murphey, L., 332
Murphy, A. E., 379
Murphy, G., 339, 342, 346, 375, 377
Murphy, Lois B., 375, 377
Murphy, W., 280
Murray, H. A., 82, 196, 414
Murtagh, J. M., 270, 272

Naegele, K. D., 23, 126
Naeve, L., 272
Nafzger, S., 363, 366, 369
Natanson, M., 35
Nebergall, N. S., 153
Nelson, E. A., 194, 196
Neugarten, Bernice L., 240
Newcomb, T., 349, 354, 375, 377
Nietzsche, F., 128, 331, 420
Norris, Sara, 269

Odbert, H. E., 148, 152, 340, 346
O'Dowd, D. D., 292, 296
Ogawa, N., 194, 196
Ogilvie, D. M., 124
Ohlin, L. E., 405, 414
Olds, J., 23, 194, 196
Olmsted, M. S., 449
Omwake, K. T., 153
Osgood, C. E., 118
Ossorio, P. G., 283, 355-368
Ovesey, L., 8, 35, 158, 259-266, 283, 391, 393

Park, R. E., 93, 94
Parsons, T., 7, 9, 11-23, 36, 38, 71, 76, 82, 126, 127, 129, 156, 240, 241, 451
Pascal, R., 329
Paul, K., 115
Peak, Helen, 146, 153
Peirce, J. R., 290, 296
Pepitone, A., 39, 283, 347-354
Perls, F., 280
Petersen, P. G., 247, 249
Petrullo, L., 76
Pfuetze, P. E., 86
Phillips, E. L., 146, 153
Piaget, J., 20, 23, 220
Piers, G., 189, 190, 196, 220, 226
Pillsbury, W. B., 185, 188
Pitts, J. R., 23, 126
Pizzorno, A., 82
Portmann, A., 255
Powell, W. J., 431, 432, 433
Pratt, K. C., 188
Preiss, J. J., 8, 156, 157, 207-218, 208, 281
Preston, Anne, 193, 195
Proust, M., 225

Quinn, R. D., 153

Rabson, Alice, 193, 195
Raimy, V. C., 145, 153, 440
Rainer, D., 272

Rank, O., 253, 279
Rapoport, R. N., 190, 196
Raskin, N. J., 440
Reader, N., 207, 440
Reeder, L. G., 118
Reichard, Suzanne, 247, 249
Reymert, M. L., 196
Rhees, R., 357, 369
Rice, S. A., 94
Rickers-Ousiankina, Maria, 429, 433
Riecken, H. W., 243, 249
Riesman, D., 8, 189, 196, 248, 249, 284, 393, 425, 433, 445-461
Rioch, D., 251
Ripley, H. S., 153
Robeson, Anna, 334
Robinson, D., 302
Rogers, C. R., 6, 8, 34, 39, 75, 116, 118, 122, 145, 146, 152, 153, 158, 276, 280, 282, 284, 300, 301, 375, 377, 393, 424, 427, 433, 434, 435-441
Rogers, N., 440
Rohde, S., 302
Roheim, G., 108
Rosen, B., 192, 196
Rosenberg, B. G., 118, 145, 153
Rosenberg, H., 224
Rosenberg, M., 122, 282, 339-346
Rosow, I., 235
Ross, Dorothea, 191, 195
Ross, Sheila, 191, 195, 196
Rotter, J. B., 147, 153
Royce, J., 25, 161
Ruesch, J., 426, 434

Sandrold, K. D., 302
Sarbin, T. R., 118, 145, 153, 156, 179-187, 188
Sartre, J. P., 80, 82, 225, 348, 403, 419, 420
Schachtel, E., 220, 332, 392
Schachter, S., 350, 354
Scheler, M., 76, 224
Schilder, P., 8, 28, 37, 107-114, 158, 198, 205, 220, 332
Schutz, A., 34, 35, 37, 61-73, 115, 117, 120, 282
Schwartz, M., 273
Sears, P., 354
Sears, R. A., 193, 195, 196, 374, 377
Secord, P. F., 6, 83, 156, 281, 283, 289-296, 363, 368, 369
Seeman, J., 440
Seeman, M., 392, 414
Selye, H., 426, 434
Sewell, W. H., 228, 240
Shaffer, L. F., 372, 378
Shakespeare, W., 89, 225, 415
Shanas, E., 249
Shapiro, M. M., 363, 369, 384, 389
Sheerer, E. T., 440
Sheffield, F. D., 345, 346
Sherif, C. W., 345, 346
Sherif, M., 240, 345, 346, 378

Subject Index